MANAGEMENT I
MR. MOBLEY
10:10 - 11:10
T Th F
ROOM 105S

Perceptive Management and Supervision

PERCEPTIVE

HARRY W. HEPNER

Professor Emeritus
Syracuse University
Management Consultant

FREDERICK B. PETTENGILL

Human Relations Program Director
Syracuse University

MANAGEMENT AND SUPERVISION

Social

Responsibilities

and

Challenges

PRENTICE-HALL, INC., Englewood Cliffs, New Jersey

Second Edition

PERCEPTIVE MANAGEMENT AND SUPERVISION
Social Responsibilities and Challenges

HARRY W. HEPNER and FREDERICK B. PETTENGILL

C-13-656991-9

Library of Congress Catalog Card No.: 75–147056

Current printing (last digit): 10 9 8 7 6 5 4 3 2 1

Printed in the United States of America

PRENTICE-HALL, INTERNATIONAL, INC., *London*
PRENTICE-HALL OF AUSTRALIA, PTY. LTD., *Sydney*
PRENTICE-HALL OF CANADA, LTD., *Toronto*
PRENTICE-HALL OF INDIA PRIVATE LIMITED, *New Delhi*
PRENTICE-HALL OF JAPAN, INC., *Tokyo*

Dedicated

with warm appreciation to the following companies, their executives, and employees with whom I had the privilege of working either as a fellow employee or, in most cases, as a consultant during the past three decades. Of course this statement of appreciation does not imply that the managements of these companies, either now or at the time I was with them, agree with everything stated in this book. Each, however, contributed to my development of whatever insights I offer the reader.

H. W. H.

The Air Preheater Corporation,
New York and Wellsville, N.Y.

The Bank for Savings,
New York.

Batten, Barton, Durstine & Osborn, Inc.,
New York and Syracuse, N.Y.

The Carborundum Company,
Niagara Falls, N.Y.

Commercial Solvents Corporation,
New York: Terre Haute, Ind.;
Peoria, Ill.; Sterlington, La.

The Crosley Corporation,
Cincinnati, Ohio.

Crouse-Hinds, Company,
Syracuse, N.Y.

First National Bank,
Palm Beach, Florida

Goodyear Tire & Rubber Co.,
Akron, Ohio

The Herald Company,
Syracuse, N.Y.

Kaufmann's Department Store
Pittsburgh, Pa.

Merchants National Bank and Trust Co.,
Syracuse, N.Y.

Northwest Nitro-Chemicals Ltd.,
Medicine Hat, Alberta, Canada

Onondaga Savings Bank,
Syracuse, N.Y.

Paterson Savings & Trust Co.,
Paterson, N.J.

Philadelphia Co. & Affiliated Corporations,
Pittsburgh, Pa.

Syracuse Lighting Company,
Syracuse, N.Y.

Union Carbide & Carbon Corporation,
Sault Ste. Marie, Mich.

Preface

The intelligent student of today realizes that he has certain needs for enlightenment beyond those encountered by members of previous generations. He becomes more acutely aware of his needs whenever he watches a televised news program or reads a newspaper article that dramatizes new evidences of the turmoil of our time. He becomes even more disquieted when he sees some of his peers assert their antagonisms through bizarre attire or even destructiveness against institutions designed to be of service to them and other good people.

Intellectually, he seeks more than quick and simple answers—he wants to learn about basic influences that are bringing about our changing social order. What psychological patterns, for example, seem to characterize those dissidents who are so unhappy that they strike out blindly in various directions? Most important to him, how can he as an individual, through his future work and other activities, make constructive contributions to the developing social order?

The revision of this book has been written in terms of the following assumptions about you and your interests as a student:

1. That you want to become acquainted with significant findings from behavioral science studies that will offer ideas for the developing of your own points of view, which in turn, may lead you to discover guidelines regarding your social responsibilities as an educated person and as a responsible member of a career group, most likely of the business world. And you prefer to think of the problems of our social order as offering challenge and opportunity—not as cause for dismay.

Chapter 2 provides helpful information on the above predominant needs of the student in these times. All the other chapters treat the leadership and perceptivity aspects of human relations in business as stated in the three paragraphs that follow.

2. That you think of yourself as a person who intends to advance to greater responsibilities involving people. Regardless of whether you are a student, a trainee, a supervisor, or a technical specialist you intend to move ahead to further growth through your work situations. You want to be able to learn from and to think with progressive management men as a member of a work group. You especially want to know significant findings from behavioral science researches that apply to human relations in work situations.

3. That you expect to supervise the work of others and to deal with management either as an executive or as a specialist in business-related functions. You recognize the importance of insight and skill in human relations in supervisory effectiveness. You want to sharpen your perceptiveness in everyday human relations situations.

You want to learn about fundamental principles underlying "how to" procedures of daily practices.

To help fulfill these expectations, most chapters in this book include condensations of pertinent reports of systematic investigations. End-of-chapter references, questions, and problems have been organized into three groups to fit the desires of readers who have introductory or practical needs as well as those with advanced scientific interests.

We have benefited from the help of many individuals. Authors of published research reports and their publications have been acknowledged in standard form. Our indebtedness to them is very great, indeed. Certain business leaders have added to our own growth in dealing with people by giving assignments as a management consultant. Faculty colleagues have stimulated us to improve our thinking. It is difficult to name specific individuals who have been of special aid in writing this revision. However, two must be mentioned for reading and improving certain chapters: they are Delmont K. Pfeffer and Forrest E. Ferguson. Gladys K. Kennedy not only typed and edited the manuscript but also made numerous inspections to insure accuracy. Our acquaintance with members of industry was especially helpful in obtaining information.

Harry W. Hepner
Frederick B. Pettengill

Contents

INTRODUCTION

PART **I**

Business is People

SITUATIONS YOU ARE LIKELY TO MEET

How would you meet each of these situations:

    a. *Before* you have read the chapter? What would you say to yourself or to the individual?

    b. *After* you have read the chapter? How have your answers changed?

1. An ambitious friend has so strong a determination to succeed in business that he wants nothing to hinder him in attaining his goals. He says to you: "I am going to concentrate my energies on making the company profitable. I shall feel responsible only to those who directly or indirectly help me to contribute to doing a good job for the customers. When business concerns make profits, the governmental, welfare, church, and related organizations can also receive more money and function better."

2. Your ambitious friend assumes that some day he will be the president of a large company and have specialists in his company to deal with the problems of human relations. Therefore, human relations functions will be under the management of an executive who will relieve the president and the other executives of their problems with people, thus allowing the president and his staff to concentrate their efforts on other bigger problems.

3. Let us assume that one of your fellow students says to you: "As long as I am in college, I shall not make an extra effort to develop skills in my relations with peo-

ple—I'll just enjoy college. After I leave college, then I can learn how to handle human relations in business by watching how real managers do it in real life situations."

Basically, business is people who voluntarily cooperate to produce and distribute goods. A business enterprise produces and offers a product or service which people buy for what it will do for them.

Perhaps you think that this definition puts too much emphasis on the human side of producing goods or services, at the expense of the material and logical aspects. If so, an old truism in transportation suggests an acceptable modification: "An airline is 5 percent metal and 95 percent men."

For our purposes, we can define human relations in business and industry as the development of greater appreciation for the psychological and social relationships between

management and the employee,
the employee and management,
the employee and fellow employees,
company and customers, and
the larger social contexts in which management, employee, customer, and citizen all function.

Perceptive management implies a search for better understanding, finer skills, and livelier sensitivities in dealing with people. We all know that a tremendously important part of the job of a businessman, regardless of the industry or the level of his position, is getting along with people. The people with whom he deals include not only employees and customers but also stockholders, creditors, union officials and members, politicians, fellow businessmen, and the public. In some cases, the list even includes those who hate business and would like to destroy it.

Many executives realize that the richest assets as well as the most difficult problems of a company are its people. People provide business with its greatest strengths and, at the same time, require management to do its best creative thinking.

4

Fundamentally, the main difference between one business firm and another operating in the same field is people. Every company has access to the same sources of raw materials and to the purchase of the same equipment. The main body of technological information is largely a matter of common knowledge. Capital is available to all who qualify. The same markets are available to all companies who can serve customers under competitive conditions. As has often been said: "All these means are open to everyone and, generally speaking, on equal terms. The main difference is people."

Certainly, our greatest wealth as a nation is not in our physical resources—our acres of fertile land, tons of ore, board feet of timber, barrels of oil, or acre-feet of water. Our wealth exists, rather, in our people—the men and women who have built America and the boys and girls who hold the future of America in their hands. And of all the resources we have, it is our human resources that are least efficiently used. It is here, also, that we have the greatest opportunity for improved economic performance in the future if we can release the full potential of people in their work.

A generation ago, our scientific research was such that we boasted of living in an electronic age. Currently, we are living in an atomic age that is moving into an interplanetary age. But we still have to learn how to live in a human age.

The miracles of physical science are not enough to solve the problems of our day. Modern scientific developments require that the knowledge of the human mind and the understanding of man's relationship to his fellow men keep pace with the effects of technological advances. It is only through such dual progress that we can hope to cope with and enjoy our rapidly changing world. Our greatest asset is not usually listed on a corporation report, however. And yet, Andrew Carnegie recognized the value of this unlisted asset when he declared that if he were stripped of all his material wealth but retained the people in his organization his business could be rebuilt in four years. He realized that the greatest asset of any concern lies in the potential of the people who operate it.

Business executives of the current generation are keenly aware of the importance of people, people as individuals as well as the unidentified human beings who contribute to the profit or loss of the business enterprise. This awareness was indicated when *Dun's Review and Modern Industry* magazine asked the 111 company members of their Presidents' Panel about their most difficult decisions. Two out of every three respondents said that the hardest decisions they have to make are those involving people.[1]

Similarly, when the American Management Association asked 335

[1]Kenneth Henry, "When Presidents Decide," *Dun's Review and Modern Industry*, November 1957, p. 34. Copyright © 1957 by Dun & Bradstreet Publications Corporation. See related article in *Personnel*, Vol. 41, No. 5, pp. 51–54.

company presidents who were enrolled in AMA training programs about their three biggest problems, human relations problems loomed very large in their answers. Here are a few replies which bear out this point, in answer to the question: "What is your most pressing personal problem in your day-to-day business relationships?"

> "Development and training of executives."
>
> "Good men to make sound, responsible decisions."
>
> "Developing an effective management team."
>
> "Fully to develop the human resources of our management group so that the company may avail itself of a striking challenge which requires product and [personnel] development at almost superhuman rate."
>
> "Development and/or acquisition of competent young executive personnel."
>
> "Spending enough time with each man responsible to me in reviewing and criticizing his work."

The company presidents expressed an awareness of the problem of developing able successors. This was particularly true of the older men whose retirement was a prospect in the foreseeable future. The younger presidents complained of pressure from the old hands who kept them from acting as quickly or as often as they would like while the older men said that they were having difficulty developing a successor and getting the younger men to accept responsibility.

One question was, "Can you give an example of a human relations problem in your work recently and how it was solved?" Only a few examples from the presidents' replies can be quoted here:

> When I have a difficult problem with my key executives I turn over to them the investigation and recommendations; then it becomes their idea and they study the merits from their point of view.
>
> In a dispute between two executives of equal rank they were required to have an objective discussion with me; it developed that their differences were not so great after all and that an intelligent approach could solve what seemed to be a serious problem.
>
> One of my key executives became disturbed over pressures exerted on him recently; felt he should take less responsibility with the company; I solved it by intensive listening and a few suggestions.
>
> Problem—salary administration; solution—series of meetings with supervisors explaining our policy and setting up a program for regular organized review of salaries by each supervisor and his imme-

diate supervisor with a check on such reviews by the personnel manager.

Failure of outstanding staff executive to be effective because of intolerance and impatience; corrected by placing him in line responsibility for a year where he soaked up the understanding of frustrations and emotions affecting people and the job of getting things done.

Problem—getting old timer VP to move over and make way for younger men; solution—finding top-flight back-up man acceptable to the old timer and employing outside management counselor to help sell need for change.

I believe the root of nearly all human relations problems is misunderstanding, either self-misunderstanding or misunderstanding of the motives of other people; a frank, open discussion with all the people concerned has always effected a solution.

The overriding importance of an ability to get things done through people, to understand people, to communicate effectively with them, to draw out the best in them and to maximize their creativity not only as individuals but as a team is evident not only from the high rating given human relations, but by the presidents' estimate of the most important single benefit which they got from college.[2]

As one president noted, an executive's work in the final analysis "is almost nothing but solving human relations problems."

Lawrence A. Appley, former president of the American Management Association and a confidant of many company presidents, described it in a somewhat different way when he called management "the art of getting things done through people."

A related survey made by Heidrick and Struggles, Inc., of the presidents of 471 of America's largest companies found that among the areas demanding most attention planning ranked first, 21.3 percent. Marketing was second, 15.9 percent, but motivating people was third, 11.8 percent, and personnel, 11.4 percent, was fourth. If these last two are combined, the areas of dealing with people become highest, 23.2 percent.[3]

Of course the many areas of management that demand a president's attention cannot be compartmentalized; even the seemingly impersonal problems of engineering do involve consideration of the people of the

[2]"Top Managers' Three Biggest Problems," *Nation's Business* (Chamber of Commerce of the United States), September 1957, Vol. XLV, No. 9. Original Source: "The Man in the Front Office: An Unretouched Portrait of the Company President Today," *The Management Review*, American Management Association, Inc., September 1957.

[3]"Profile of a President," Heidrick and Struggles, Inc., 245 Park Ave., New York, N. Y. 10017. Copyright 1967.

department—some engineers, for example, are more introverted and non-communicative than others.

Even though surveys of top management men indicate that people give the executive many of his most bothersome troubles, we do not assume that management men have no concern about the problems and functions of business operations such as accounting, finance, marketing, and production. Management men are men of action. Their action plans have the objectives of producing and selling goods and services at a profit. Sometimes they are preoccupied with technology, production, and the mechanics of business. Fundamentally, however, they realize that the goal of work is the satisfaction of human needs. Even though they are members of management, they are human too. They know that employees need understanding as well as security and that human dignity as well as fair wages is important to the individual. Admittedly these concepts of sound human relations in business have not become an integral part of the daily practices of all businessmen but they are accepted as objectives by the leaders.

Alfred North Whitehead, the philosopher, once defined a great society as one in which men of business "think greatly about their functions." The challenge to leaders of business today is not only to think about meeting the growing material demands of people but to become concerned about all the problems of society. Work and productivity are not just ends in themselves but the means whereby we can improve the quality of our society and our individual lives. Progress means change. It also means, in one form or another, colleagueship in directing the change toward more creative and satisfying living.

Stages in the development of human relations in business

It would be interesting to chronicle the recognizable stages in the concepts and objectives that have characterized the history of human relations in industry. An examination of the record in this and other countries of the world would, however, carry us too far afield for our purposes. Our purpose is not to note the historical development but to sense the current problems and to develop ourselves for intelligent participation in the present and the future. In earlier stages of industry's growth toward modern technology, the power of the employer was often all-controlling. Employees were looked upon as servants. They were expected to be obedient and grateful for whatever the master cared to grant them.

Gradually the master-servant framework of thinking changed to an employer-employee concept in which the employee was recognized as having certain rights as a free man. The employee could seek work wherever he thought it would be advantageous for him to do so. Employers found it profitable to attract industrious cooperative workers. Later, some workers also protected their rights and increased their bargaining power through membership in trade unions. The pay envelope became the favorite motivational device of most employers. The economic incentive was and still is considered by certain employers to be the only incentive that appeals to the individual worker.

The modern employee is caught in a web of industrial forces which he neither controls nor knows how to utilize. He lives and works in a world he does not fully understand. Because of his confusion, he often demands more protection and fringe benefits, in the hope that more will allay his fears. The employer too in his confusion imagines that giving more economic benefits will bring about the harmonious relations that he seeks. Managements are like the bewildered parent who realizes that his children are drifting away from him. In his ignorance of their needs, he gives them gifts in the hope that gratitude will bring about the desired happier relationships.

We are, however, now entering the *era of creative mutual growth* in which we recognize the need for advancement on the part of employer, employee, and other members of society who have not as yet been able to adjust to the effects of a rapidly changing technology. Management leaders realize that company and employee can hope to move ahead better when all participate in bringing about improved ways of life for all members of society.

The basic attitude of enlightened managements is that of colleagueship, not that of mere kindness or looking after inferiors. Every man wants to be treated as an individual who respects himself as a person. Any man who is not treated as a worthy colleague, whatever his abilities or limitations may be, is not likely to develop respect for his own accomplishments or for the society in which he lives.

Management men and employees are gradually discovering that their relationships, including those of the disadvantaged, are so closely interrelated and reciprocal that each contributes to or hinders the well-being of the other. All are learning that "no man is an island." The day when we could read about the inability of others to participate in the life that modern technology can produce and feel uninvolved has gone. Whether we like it or not, all have become members of an interdependent society, psychologically as well as economically.

Our perceptual paradox

One of the great paradoxes of our time is the fact that despite the universal recognition of the importance of the human being in industry, management men and employees are still unable to fulfill the spiritual as well as the economic needs in their relationship. The men in responsible positions want to carry out the best in human relations. Employees too want to have satisfying, even enriching work relations with their employers. Each of the two parties would like to know how to live and work in a world of understanding, mutual respect, and devotion to common goals.

But each person who finds that he is a participant in a human relations difficulty tends to think that he is sensible and fair. It's the other fellow who is stupid and unfair. In the case of a strike, for example, the labor union leaders often claim that they do not want the strike and blame the stubborn employer for causing it. The employer too claims that he does not want a strike and blames the irrational power-seeking union leaders for causing the strike. Both the labor union leader and the employer claim that the other hates him without just cause. Rumors and suspicions abound. The misunderstandings and the erroneous perceptions flare into slowdowns, work stoppages, and the full-fledged strike. But each party to the typical conflict perceives himself as being intelligent and fair. Why the lack of agreement in perceptions?

To some extent, the typical situation in human relations in industry is similar to that of two awkward teen-agers, a boy and a girl who want to get better acquainted although neither knows how to go about it. The boy likes the girl and she senses that he likes her. She likes the boy and he senses that she likes him. Each, however, waits for the other to prove his interest by acceptable action. Eventually one or the other resolves the dilemma by overtly showing his desire for friendship. Once this step has been taken, the relationship can develop normally and may lead to courtship.

The awkward teen-agers exemplify an important principle for the student of human relations in business. This principle is that individuals or groups who do not know and understand each other need the experience of getting acquainted. In our example of the teen-agers, it would be a mistake for some sophisticated adult to step into their situation, tell them what to do, and make overtures on their behalf. Much time and emotional wear and tear might be saved by the aid of such a do-gooder, but the teen-agers would miss the development that comes from the normal search for growth. The same principle applies to our human relations in industry. We cannot solve the human relations problems *for* people. We as individuals can, however, learn how to participate more intelligently in the human relationships that we ourselves experience. We can increase our understanding of ourselves and of others. We can seek development through the everyday situations that necessitate sensitivity to the perceptions and needs of others.

Contrary to accepted opinion, most people get along rather well with each other. Most employers like and respect their employees. Most employees like and respect their employers. The most extensive survey of employee opinions on this question obtained the reaction of a half-million workers of 850 companies. It showed that 86 percent were proud of their firms and 81 percent felt their jobs were important.[4]

The same kind of favorable reactions would also be obtained from customers in regard to the products they buy and the firms from which they buy them. Most families like their neighbors. Most children like their parents. Most students like their fellow students and most students like their teachers. We should keep these positive reactions in mind when we discuss human relations of any kind, particularly those involved in business. This positive perspective becomes especially important when we deal with problems and problem persons. Basically, our chief interest is not in the variations from the average or normal situation; these are of secondary importance. We are concerned primarily in learning how people now manage to work and to live satisfactorily with each other. We want to understand and extend the favorable daily human relationships in business. We want to see how people now carry on their human relations so that we can accentuate the positive and seek possible answers for the points of friction and misunderstanding.

Learning human relations through participation in business activities

Some facts can most easily be learned from books, scientific journals, and laboratory experiments. Others can best be learned from experience. Human relations as a subject of study lends itself especially well to a combination of several major approaches to learning. Principles can be learned from the reports of scientific investigations such as the Western Electric Company's famous experiment at its Hawthorne plant (see Chapter 3); the studies conducted by the Institute for Social Research, University of Michigan (see pages 96 and 106); and other reports from investigators who have analyzed interpersonal relations systematically.

In addition to the studies conducted by trained scientists, many keen observers and leaders of business and industry have reported significant findings from their observations and personal experiences.

If the student in human relations in management develops the habit of observing people and how they react in different situations, he can enrich his social knowledge and improve his skills in dealing with people with whom he studies and works. He should, in fact, practice the development of alertness to human relations while he studies business and management.

[4]From *Changing Times*, The Kiplinger Magazine, October 1954. The results referred to are from surveys in many companies. The questionnaire form used is the SRA Employee Inventory, published and serviced by Science Research Associates, 259 East Erie, Chicago, Ill. Further information may be had by writing to SRA's Management and Personnel Research Division.

To become effective in human relations it is necessary to practice insight and social skills wherever one may be.

The chances are that when you enter industry to perform some function as a worker no one will have pointed out the human relationships involved in the work. You will have to learn to sense them yourself, either while you are still in school or on the job. In this book, we shall offer principles and points of view that will stimulate your awareness of the human relations involved in subjects that you study in school or practice on the job, particularly those of management and supervision.

Objectives in our study of human relations

Many human relations programs have doubtful values. A few mistakenly assume the main purpose to be largely one or more of the following:

1. To be kind to people.
2. To make everyone happy.
3. To make the worker feel important.
4. To let the worker do as he pleases.
5. To readjust the maladjusted people in business and thus help them attain a high level of psychological maturity.
6. To manipulate other people to your own ends, to get the worker to conform with what you want him to do in a calculated manner on your part. This may even include undue invasions of his privacy or an amoral concern about his emotional life.
7. To manage the lives of other people on the assumption that your intentions are good and that the other person is not managing his life in a way that is satisfactory to you.
8. To motivate people, either by some special manipulative technique or by offering extra rewards. This has been dubbed the carrot-and-stick theory.
9. To study human relations for the personal satisfaction it gives you as a study. Some writers on the subject have been accused of this because they seldom put themselves into a work situation that requires special skills in the use of their own behavior with others. They suffer from ivory tower detachment. These individuals typically overemphasize a particular method of study to the extent that the method becomes an end in itself.
10. To be able to recognize the problem persons, the psychopaths, and other deviants who cannot respond to our most intelligent efforts however well-meant they may be. When we recognize deviants, we can avoid them, but the more intelligent attitude is to try to function with so much understanding on our part that

we can accept their characteristics and at the same time, seek ways to develop an effective colleague relationship.

Whenever we set up objectives for a course of study that applies to industry, we should remind ourselves that in America we have an evolving way of life. Our business way of life should assume that each person seeks the fulfillment of certain values for himself and others. Typical of these values are the following:

1. To do work.
2. To work productively: to improve our methods of work and to produce more today than yesterday in order that our standard of living may rise.
3. To cooperate intelligently with the people who are involved in the work. Each business is a social as well as an economic institution.

The objective in our study of human relations can be stated as, "To learn how to work as intelligently as we possibly can with the people who are involved, directly or indirectly, in the work we do." If we pursue this objective, we shall become equipped to play our part in the evolution of our way of life.

The man or woman who wishes to become effective in his human relations in business must first of all be a competent person in the particular job or operation for which he is responsible. If he does not as yet know it thoroughly, he should be growing in his knowledge of it. If he has little or no desire for competence in some phase of business such as production, sales, finance, or some other function but thinks of himself primarily as an "expert" in human relations, he's probably a politician rather than a businessman. Skill in dealing with people is an important part of working effectively in this age, but it is not the only part.

In the main, this book treats human relations in terms of the established organizational structures and common situations in business and industry. Typical problems with people are discussed or mentioned to help the reader develop his perspective and insights. Some readers may even find the problems at the ends of chapters more interesting than the textual treatments.

The several chapters on the contributions of behavioral science studies in Part 2 precede the chapters that deal with management, supervision, and the management and department functions. This arrangement has been made because findings from these studies concerning the psychodynamic and social influences in business have value for all managerial and supervisory functions, regardless of the level of responsibility or the specific department. The several terminal chapters of the book are devoted to certain principles that may be useful to you in your own advancement in business through the development of your social skills and your relations with the people of your work environment.

An author, at best, can only provide an organizational plan and some informative materials for the student, although he hopes to allow for vision as well as guidance. Only the student can do the learning. And the student will learn best when he himself acquires and contributes new ideas to the material presented. The study of human relations offers the student splendid opportunities to add to the learning of his colleagues as well as his own. What you take with you when you leave college will greatly be influenced by what you have given of yourself while in college. You as a student can contribute by being observant and analytical of your own experiences and by sharing with your fellow students what you learn.

QUESTIONS ON THE CHAPTER

1. What do we mean when we say, "Business is people"?
2. What is the greatest wealth in our nation, and how well do you think we are using it?
3. What did the AMA survey indicate were the major problems of executives? In what ways are these executives working toward the solutions of these problems?
4. Describe the status of the employee in the early stages of industry's growth. What era are we now approaching?
5. In what ways do employees and management often react to the confusions of the industrial world?
6. What principle can the student of human relations in business learn by recognizing the possible approaches to a problem of the awkward teen-ager?
7. In most situations in life, do people usually get along with each other? How does your answer apply to the business world?
8. Differentiate between the old objectives in studying human relations and the newer approaches presented in this text.
9. How should a study of human relations increase our ability to deal with problem persons?
10. Name three typical values that the individual seeks to fulfill in his work life.
11. What did human relations mean to you before you read the chapter? How did your reading of the chapter modify the former meanings?

12. Skill in dealing with people is an important part of working effectively, but it is not the only part. What else should the student seek to attain in his preparation for life and work?

PROBLEMS AND PROJECTS

For All Students

1. No single textbook can possibly supply all the information now published in this field. As an aid to your study, examine and compare the tables of contents and the prefaces of available textbooks. Compare the objectives of different authors.
2. Even though you may have had only limited experience in business, you have probably had some human relations problems with people in business situations. Describe any experiences that stimulated you to study this field.

For Advanced Students

3. Visit your library and list some of the available periodicals that should be of value to you in this field of study. Read and condense several articles that interest you. Explain how or why they stimulated your interest.
4. Now that you have had some academic training, what challenges have aroused your interest in the field of human relations? Consider one challenge as a possible career for yourself. What additional training would you need?

For Men in Business

5. To what extent are good human relations now practiced in the company where you work? What improvements might be made? List your recommendations for changes but modify them from time to time as you read the text.
6. Give an example from your experience to illustrate the need for the principle: "Human relations means working *with* people, not doing things *to* them."

COLLATERAL READINGS

For All Students

Massie, Joseph L., *Essentials of Management* (2nd ed.) Englewood Cliffs, N.J.: Prentice-Hall, Inc., 1970. Provides the reader with a synthesis of the traditional and newer quantitative and behavioral science approaches to the subject of management.

Newman, William H., Charles E. Summer, and E. Kirby Warren, *The Process* of

Management (2nd ed.). Englewood Cliffs, N.J.: Prentice-Hall, Inc., 1967. Chapter 2 treats the eruption of thought about management, the enlarging concept about management, and the behavioral approach.

For Advanced Students

Bennett, Edward, James Degan, and Joseph Spiegel, *Human Factors in Technology*. New York: McGraw-Hill Book Company, 1963. Presents some of the current research in human factors as reported by fifty-four prominent scientists and engineers.

Twenty Years of Management Development: A Conference. Reprint Series No. 144. Ithaca, N.Y.: New York State School of Industrial & Labor Relations, 1963. Proceedings of a one-day conference conducted in New York City on March 23, 1963 by the N.Y. State School of Industrial & Labor Relations.

For Men in Business

Koontz, Harold, and Cyril O'Donnell, *Principles of Management: An Analysis of Management Functions*. New York: McGraw-Hill Book Company, 1964.

Morell, R. W., *Management: Ends and Means*. San Francisco: Chandler Publishing Co., 1969. Emphasizes the ends-and-means approach as more appropriate than a functional one for students of management.

The New Dimension of Management: Our Changing Social Order– Challenges and Opportunities

SITUATIONS YOU ARE LIKELY TO MEET

How would you meet each of these situations:
   a. *Before* you have read the chapter? What would you say to yourself or to the individual?
   b. *After* you have read the chapter? How have your answers changed?

1. A politically oriented friend discusses some of the crucial social problems of our time and says: "If government would appropriate more billions of dollars to aid education, welfare, and housing, our social unrest would soon disappear."
2. Another friend says: "If all the laws we now have on the books were really enforced by the police and by those who are in positions of responsibility, the disrupters would become law-abiding and we could all live together peacefully."
3. A student who plans to major in history states: "The social sciences do not advance as rapidly as the physical sciences and technology. Therefore, we should halt all research in the physical sciences and the related technologies for a number of years until the social sciences can be brought into coordinated relationships with the physical sciences."
4. An executive from a foreign country visits America and says: "In America it is easier for a young man to advance into effective managerial leadership than it was for young men of previous generations—we now have so much research available in the managerial

fields that any studious young man should be able to become an able member of top management."

Gone are the days when a young man could train himself for responsible adulthood without considering the larger social context in which he would live and pursue his career. Gone also are the days when a top-level executive could function successfully as a leader by thinking in terms of his employees and the company's customers without giving a thought to the company's social responsibilities.

Some of the outward manifestations that have demanded the attention of business leaders as well as that of individuals in training for leadership are the protests by minority groups, resentful dissidents, and riotous militants. The usual explanations for these outbursts of dissent and disorder have attributed them to various factors: race issues, police actions, military service, poverty, and to specific area injustices. In some cases such explanation are pertinent, but inadequate.

Riotous hostilities and social ferment have been worldwide

Explanations of disorders that fit one time and place may not be applicable to others. Among the countries that have had significant disorders (that is, the police or military were used to restore order) are East Germany, West Germany, Spain, Japan, Canada, Mexico, England, China, France, Lebanon, Sweden, India, South Africa, South Korea, Turkey, U.S.S.R., and the United States.

Characteristics common to most, if not quite all, of the uprisings were the following:

1. Their targets were symbols of authoritarian power, such as universities, political institutions, or corporations.
2. They appeared independently of the political ideology of the country involved, but all were a revolt against established authority.
3. The main focus of the dissatisfaction on the part of the dissidents was their hostility toward "The Establishment." (This term usually refers to those persons who through the use of authority, keep the social, economic, or controlling system going in the same forms as in the past.)[1]

The man who wishes to train himself for intelligent leadership wants to know causal influences, the common denominators that underlie outbursts of hostility as they occur in different areas especially those that apply to the United States. We cannot at this time identify all the interrelated influences that will eventually be recognized, but we can note some underlying factors that are clearly at work. Recognition of these underlying factors should enable us to develop constructive approaches and alert us to the development of basic attitudes and to the use of those policies that offer promise for the future.

FOUR MAJOR CAUSAL FACTORS

Causal factors often mentioned are:

1. *The rapid rates of growth in knowledge of the physical sciences versus the lower rates of the social sciences.* This is usually mentioned by researchers as the one basic causal factor that leads to social disorders. Until this century began, knowledge was, according to the best estimates, doubling on itself approximately every two thousand years. This rate has increased dramatically. Unfortunately, however, knowledge does not increase at the same rates in all fields:

> Knowledge in the physical sciences is said to be doubling every 15 years, while growth in the social and management sciences is doubling every 50 years.[2] This may explain why we are less adept in

[1] For a more comprehensive treatment, see "The Children of Change," *Kaiser Aluminum News*, Vol. 27, No. 1, Kaiser Aluminum and Chemical Corporation, 1969.

[2] Ellis A. Johnson, "Crisis in Science and Technology," *Operations Research*, Vol. 6, No. 1 (1958), 11–34.

handling the social or "people" problems which do not have a numerical or logical basis. These are the kinds of problems which not
only take up the larger portion of the manager's time and energies but
which, in fact, are behind most of the fundamental issues of the day.[3]

This means that one outstanding factor in our social ferment is that the
individual lives in a world produced by the facilities of great scientific and
technological advancements. However, the knowledge and facilities for
dealing with his social and psychological problems lag far behind. Disjointed rates of growth in the different segments of modern life accentuate
his difficulties in making happy and easy adjustments to his problems in
living.

The researchers in the physical sciences will continue to make their
advancements regardless of the inability of social scientists to know how to
direct human beings to fit their behavior into the culture that technology
helped create. It would be contrary to the very nature of the universe and
to human progress to insist that advancements in certain fields should be
held back in order to coordinate them with advancements in all other
fields. Change and progress must continue to take place in disjointed ways
in order to have the benefits of advancements in knowledge as soon as possible. Certainly, no one would want to hold back researches that lead to
increased life expectancy:

> Many of the modern miracles of medical care have been made
> possible by hundreds of new drugs discovered since 1940.
>
> Consider just the drop in death rates since that date. From tuber-
> culosis, a drop from 45.9 per thousand—to four. From whooping
> cough, diphtheria, and scarlet fever—to almost zero. Also, the death
> rate for infants under one year has dropped 56 percent; for children
> 1 to 4, 69 percent; and for children 5 to 14, 60 percent. As a matter
> of fact, even the most common causes of death among young people
> have changed. From pneumonia and infant diarrhea, it has changed
> to accidents.
>
> Ten years have been added to life expectancy since the 1930s.
> Literally, 5 million people living today would have been dead if the
> drugs that exist today hadn't been discovered.

[3]Norman J. Ream in a panel discussion, "The State of Information Retrieval
and Data Processing in the year 2000 and its Implication for Management," *Manage-
ment 2000.* The American Foundation for Management Research, founded by the
American Management Association. Mr. Ream spoke at the dedication of the AFMR
Manager Learning Center and Donald W. Mitchell Memorial Library, Hamilton, N.Y.,
August, 1967. Copyright 1968 by the American Foundation for Management Research,
Inc. See p. 61.

Another spectacular change has occurred in the field of mental health. The trend of increased admissions to mental hospitals was reversed in 1956 when psycho-pharmaceuticals were first used extensively; today there are 117 thousand fewer patients in these hospitals than in 1955.

New drugs, preventive medication and immunization are credited for having helped bring about these changes.[4]

To appreciate some of the difficulties before us, we must recognize that knowledge is much more than descriptions of facts and reports of experiments stored in libraries. Knowledge leads to action, particularly when it is applied to the production of goods. It results in changes in men's daily work, in their daily living habits, as well as in their views of themselves and their universe. Some changes that occurred in the nineteenth and twentieth centuries that resulted from advances in technology took the following form:

Agriculture moved toward industrialization; that is, toward large farms with tractors, combines, and other machinery.

Rural and small-town life gradually shifted to an urban or a kind of urbanized rural society.

We moved from an economy of scarcity to one of abundance.

We changed from a localized society to a more mobile one.

We moved away from a decidedly work-oriented to a more leisure-oriented use of time. And yet, the points of view and mental habits of many people changed relatively little in some areas during these periods. Static thinking dominated the lives of numerous individuals who were involved in these economic and social changes. A simple example that is still too evident today is the assumption on the part of many a young person that if he learns a trade or a profession he can continue to practice it all the years of his work life without making appropriate improvements in his knowledge and skills. A current example of such effects often occurs in regard to the computer and its effects on the work life of individuals, directly and indirectly involved in its use.

2. *Computers.*   These devices enable businessmen and researchers to do mathematical computations in a few hours that a dozen statisticians a few years ago could not have done in their combined lifetimes.

The benefits of computers, great as they are, also bring special problems for some people. Introduction of the first computer by a company usually means that some employees are displaced from their jobs. But a

[4]From "The Problem of Drug Abuse," Pharmaceutical Manufacturers Association, 1155 Fifteenth Street, N.W., Washington, D.C., 1969, p. 3.

more serious effect on many young people is the realization that they cannot qualify for the new technology. They do not happen to be mathematically inclined. As in similar instances in the past, a fast-developing technology is likely to have severe impact on the people of minority groups who may be divided into those who can meet the new training standards and those who cannot.

3. *Television.*   This mass medium is believed to be one of the strongest thought-provoking inventions of all time. Surveys indicate that the most intensive listening-viewing age is the five-to-six year bracket. By the time the average American youth graduates from high school he has seen 500 movies and viewed television 22,000 hours. He has seen not only comedy and mystery, but also bloodshed, starvation, and rioting set against backgrounds of places in all parts of the world. As a result, much of his social thinking may be described as *one-worldness.*[5] He has seen many examples of the use of violence as a means of redress for wrongs of almost any kind, unbearable and trivial.

> Thomas P. F. Hoving, retiring chairman of the National Citizens Committee for Broadcasting, an organization formed to end the threat to our children's values, tastes, and sensitivity posed by prevailing television patterns, states flatly that 95 percent of all prime time regularly scheduled programming undermines, rather than reinforces, those values that any normal parents would wish to impart to their children as responsible members of society. At the present time, says Mr. Hoving, $52 billion in public funds is being spent annually on public education. He adds: "Yet the 22,000 hours of television that an average American child will watch before the age of eighteen will undo at night all that we have done with our tax dollars during the day." Mr. Hoving says that, while the child is "receiving 50 percent more of his basic education and initial impressions in front of a television set than he will in the classroom, he will be witnessing five acts of violence for every viewing hour."[6]

The effects of television on today's youth is evident in the appearance of the dissident young—they have chosen the costumes, the long hair, cowboy boots, headbands, bare feet, fringe and leather jackets of the Western cowpoke as seen in current Indian horse operas of the Old West.

---

[5]See Dewitt C. Riddick, director of School of Communications, University of Texas, *Proceedings of Governor's Committee on Aging.* Texas Agricultural Extension Service, Austin, 1967.

[6]Richard L. Tobin, "Five Acts of Violence Per Hour," *Saturday Review,* March 14, 1970, p. 103.

Some young people who see the use of violence, have also experienced a loosening of ties of family, neighborhood, and religion, those influences that have helped to mold and steady the lives of members of previous generations. This has been especially evident among young people of the tradition-bound rural areas who moved to the urban centers where a stranger is likely to find himself alone and uninvolved in the life of the community. He naturally feels that he should belong to a group of young people who are determined to improve the world. In this way he tries to achieve a more worthy identity though unaware of what he is seeking for himself.

These lonely people see television and view movies where they note how other privileged members of our society enjoy exciting associations while the transplanted, rootless, lonely individuals remain lonely and unappreciated. They do not have simple emotional ties that are equivalent to those a farm boy might have who has raised a colt to adulthood. Small wonder that many transplanted-to-the-city young people feel that somehow the conditions of life there are unjust and that something drastic should be done about them. Any change—whatever its nature or its form might be—seems to offer hope to the lonely for more self-fulfillment.

The TV tube has also made the dissident young impatient with orderly procedures in getting things done.

> The child who is raised with the television tube experiences events instantaneously. He wonders why, then, it takes so long to get anything done in this society. His impatience with slow and orderly processes grows out of experience with the miraculous and instantaneous. Remember his inputs. Conceptually most of them came from movies and television, some from comic books, a precious little from formal, conventional schooling, and perhaps a little from his family. Most of his knowledge of the real world he picked up in the street, and mostly from other children in his own approximate age group.[7]

4. *Modern Technology Has Led to a Life of Affluence for Many Young People.* The productive effects of modern technology affect the incomes of many homes as exemplified by the increasing number of parents whose incomes are so high that they can afford to give their children ample funds for spending. Relatively few young people from managerial and professional homes have learned to support themselves wholly or even in part before they leave school or college. If they have desires for food, clothing, shelter, or luxuries, they "expect them to be there." As a result many young people are not especially conscious of the need for personal effort and planning in order to enjoy any kind of good life they visualize for themselves or for

[7]From "The Children of Change," *op. cit.*, p. 8.

others. The fact that many a young person has had most of the material things he ever wanted when he wanted them, has led him to take them for granted. He put forth too little effort to realize how much planning and effort are really required on the part of the gainfully employed to overcome hunger, to provide transportation, to receive medical care, or to support and raise a family.

REACTION PATTERNS TO CAUSAL FACTORS

Every person develops characteristic adjustment patterns in his behavior, patterns that enable him to adjust to, or as we usually say, deal with his problems in living. Adjustment patterns are universal. The same patterns appear in persons of every generation and every culture. Some patterns enable an individual to deal happily and effectively with his problems of living; other patterns handicap him. Those individuals whose dominant patterns handicap them severely are called neurotic, maladjusted, or some other term used by psychologists. The layman is likely to say they are "sick."

The preceding part of this chapter presents four kinds of problems to which a person of this age must adjust. Most persons have developed patterns that enable them to adjust their thinking and living to these problems or conditions of our time. Other persons, a minority of young people, have been unable to adjust satisfactorily to these changes which are occurring. A few have developed patterns, such as those of the activists, and demand quick and easy solutions for themselves. Some of these have become "unrelenting stylists" (see page 28) who cannot redirect their motivations into constructive action programs. Fortunately, most young people are open-minded and willing to cooperate in finding constructive approaches to the problems of our social evolution.

If you wish to be able to recognize patterns of adjustment that characterize some dissidents, you can learn to do so but the purpose of your insight should not be therapy. Rather, the developmental purposes, in some instances, should be:

1. When one can recognize patterns that are evident in a person's behavior, he usually can imagine how an important pattern came about. If he thinks that he understands the individual sufficiently, he can take the next step with those persons who cooperate.

2. The individual's unsatisfactory pattern can be discussed in terms of how it may have come about and what it really means to him in regard to his motivations.

3. That discussion, perhaps, will lead to gaining the individual's

cooperation in bringing about his involvement in constructive rather than destructive programs.

Some dissidents do review their psychological tendencies by discussing them with themselves (introspectively) and with friends whom they trust. In some cases the insightful friend or associate can be helpful. To be helpful, the discussion should be a two-way procedure in which both discussants benefit. If either merely states what the other should think or do, little insight or growth takes place. The person who learns how to discuss with others his patterns of behavior gains not only insights into his own behavior but he also learns psychological skills that will be of decided benefit later when he holds a supervisory or other position of leadership.

As an aid to the student who finds himself in discussions with friendly dissidents, several questions are suggested on pages 41–50 for possible use in regard to the patterns described. These questions are not presented as a standard list for such purposes but as aids in stimulating the interested student in developing appropriate questions of his own.

Five patterns of adjustment found among dissidents

1. *Boredom.*   Destructive acts such as riots do not always arise from any deepseated forms of psychological malajustment. They may develop from simple boredom. Certainly, some riotous demonstrations were headline-grabbing incidents by young people who sought excitement.

Young people who have little or no responsibility for what they consume and enjoy have led some social theorists to believe the following:

> Today's youth are not rebelling because of a deep-rooted moral commitment to better their society. They are rebelling because they are bored.
>
> They are bored because our society has sought to tranquilize them by dangling in front of them a collection of prizes to be won for good, cooperative social behavior.
>
> They are bored to death with a society that has tried its best to eliminate risk, danger, and adventure from their lives.
>
> Every healthy youth is driven by a primeval need to validate his self-esteem by demonstrating to himself and others his ability to endure, take stress, and surmount obstacles.
>
> Since they cannot satisfy this need through socially acceptable means, young people are doing it by rebelling against the social system.
>
> To win them back we must reopen our society to individual

risks and excitement, allow youth to try itself. . . . We must spurn
the counsel of those who would attempt to deny to man his right to
struggle, to achieve, not only in the private recesses of his consciousness, but in the public light of recognition.[8]

Certainly, when young people are denied the privilege of struggle and
responsibility, some become bored. This is normal for healthy young people. Unfortunately, certain unhappy individuals who have not learned to
live with confidence in their own mental powers become members of
groups in search for excitement. These are likely to resort to periods of
destructive violence, punctuated by other periods of retreat into states
of drug "trips" that offer temporary ecstasies or hallucinations of terror.
They lack the inner strengths of individuals who are engrossed in the pur-
suit of satisfying constructive activities. Those who are constructively engrossed have no need to resort to drug addiction for excitement.

2. *Alienation.*   A frequently mentioned explanation of young rebels is that
these people do not fit into society because they have been mistreated or
at least misunderstood. The reasons given for the misunderstandings may
be the child's inability to meet his own expectations or the expectations of
adults in regard to his schoolwork. He therefore defines himself as a failure
and so becomes aggressively hostile. Or his failures may be attributed to
neglect by parents or to too much attention from parents. Both have been
used to explain the generation gap. The generation gap is a convenient
explanation but it probably is not as wide as often assumed:

> A couple of social scientists from the University of Southern
> California attacked some myths concerning American society when
> they appeared before the Senate Subcommittee on Aging. Dr. James
> E. Birren and Dr. Vern L. Bengtson presented their data in a paper
> which they wrote on the subject of how young and old react to one
> another.

Myth number *one*, the generation gap:

> "It has been found in preliminary research," these two experts
> declare, "that almost four-fifths of a student group surveyed reported
> they felt their parents understand them most or all of the time. Eighty-
> three percent thought there was generally good or perfect communica-
> tion between themselves and their parents. Seventy-eight percent
> reported they felt somewhat close or very close to their parents. Only
> three percent checked the very distant category."

Myth number *two*, the value of rebellion:

---

[8]This Theory is presented in the 1969 edition of the *Intercollegiate Review* by
Donald Zoll, associate professor of philosophy and political science at the University
of Saskatchewan. From *Modern Maturity* (October-November, 1969), p. 17.

"Research on student activists at other universities has consistently shown that they are just as much like their parents—perhaps more so—than the non-demonstrators."

All of which means that the age groups are not as alienated as we are sometimes led to believe. Mutual understanding is possible and real.[9]

3. *Projection.*   Of all the forms of adjustment to problems by human beings, projection is one of the most common. The individual, for example, realizes that he has done some wrong or has failed to meet his expectations of himself. For him to admit guilt or failure to himself is painful. He therefore reduces his self-criticisms or feelings of inadequacy by pointing to the "greater" faults of some other person or institution. As an example, consider the many instances of students who cheat in an examination and then relieve their own feelings of guilt by pointing to the father's cheating on his income tax. Or the alcoholic husband who blames his wife for his downfall. Or the man who borrowed money from a bank, is unable to pay the loan, and then "discovers" that the bank loaned money to a foreign nation that the loan defaulter does not like. If one emphasizes the other person's fault enough, he can convince himself that the faulted person or the things he represents should be destroyed. If the whole world seems to be at fault, why not destroy the world as it is and the people who are enjoying it?

4. *End-of-the-World Syndrome.*   As one would expect, unhappy young people of today use the same old mental dodges regarding their responsibilities that human beings have been using for centuries. As an example, certain ones justify whatever they do by saying: "Oh well, the bomb will kill us anyway!" This is called evasion by means of the "end-of-the-world syndrome."

Historically, when some individuals in times of peace as well as in war, have found it very difficult to cope with change, they gave up all hope of achieving peace with their world or peace within themselves. Some of those in deep despair looked toward an ending of their world as they knew it. Sometimes those who reached these depths of despair would even forecast the end of the world on a specific date. Others expected an impending doom to destroy them but did not date it.

These are very old forms of adjustment to all kinds of adversity. Many religious sects, cultists, and pseudotheorists of every age have sought answers by this stance. If you want to estimate how often movements of this kind have occurred over the centuries, start with the Apocalypse and list recorded dogmas and movements that had as a theme of their belief or

[9]From *Retirement Planning Newsletter,* published by *Harvest Years* (November-December 1968), p. 2.

creed a designated way in which their world would end. Then think of the millions of people of today who still believe in an eventual "judgment day."

Consider also, the numerous reports of sociologists and others who have found students who claim that they take it for granted they will not survive the next ten years.[10]

True, the destruction of large areas of the earth's surface and great numbers of people could take place, but the individual who dies under such conditions, the dimensions of the area destroyed, and the number of persons killed with him are of little importance to him—death by means of a bomb, or any other means is death for him. Indeed, most of us, if a choice were possible, would prefer to die quickly rather than be hacked to pieces as often occurred in wars during the pretechnological ages. Psychologically, the claimed expectation of imminent death is a sign of mental immaturity, not evidence of objective thinking.

The protestor groups who emphasize destruction as a phase of their inability to think in constructive terms differ markedly from those leaders who seek to improve their own abilities in order to deal with social problems by effective means. The objective thinker first tries to improve himself as an individual. He knows that when a man tries to improve himself as a man, he will rise to the best within himself, faith and hope will still persist, and whatever the temporary chaos in the world without, he will face his problems intelligently.

5. *The Unrelenting Stylist.*   Of course, the kinds of psychological adjustment patterns found among dissidents are so numerous and varied that many trained clinicians will have to do more research to describe them. However, one outstanding pattern has been described by Seymour Halleck, professor of psychiatry and director of Student Health Psychiatry at the University of Wisconsin:

> There is a type of patient who might best be thought of as an unrelenting stylist—an individual whose life is dominated by the values of immediacy, relevance, social maneuverability, psychological mindedness and dissent.
>
> The stylist is a young person, usually intelligent, who comes to the therapist with complaints of boredom and meaninglessness; he wants to get over his "hang-ups." He is a drop-out or is simply going through the motions at school.

Dr. Seymour Halleck points out that when therapy goes past a few hours, the patient and the therapist have difficulties in communicating with each other.

[10]See Paul Goodman, "The New Reformation," *New York Times Magazine* (September 14, 1969), p. 33.

At least one explanation of this difficulty is that the patient's commitment to life in the present does not give him sufficient experience to deal in depth with any problem, including his own. He has completely rejected the kind of planning or search for mastery that makes it possible to define and deal with issues. The patient cannot focus in depth because he has learned to rely on social techniques that allow him to react comfortably and stereotypically to a wide variety of situations.

It often appears that the communication gap is related to the patient's poverty of thoughts and experiences; the stylist lives one day at a time and while he wishes to experience everything that can be experienced, he experiences nothing in depth. One week he is "into poetry," the next week "into Marcuse," the third week "into painting." The poem or painting is never completed; the books are never read beyond the first chapter.[11]

Of course, the attainment of a benign social order will require the efforts of many intelligent men and women. It will not develop from aimless jabs by stylists or those who can point out what is wrong. It will come through those individuals who strengthen themselves by persistent constructive efforts to improve themselves as individuals. Some protestors make mild efforts to do this as indicated by a frequently asked question on the part of those dissidents who say during their interviews with psychiatric counselors: "Am I crazy, Doc?" and "Tell me that I'm not crazy!"

Revolution vs Evolution.   The term, "revolution," has many meanings. Usually, it refers to an insurrection that casts off subjugation to rulers or authorities. Others use the term loosely as applied to any development that disturbs an established order and moves in new and presumably better directions.

Some people imagine that every true revolution enables people to do away with despotism. And yet, students of revolution have found, as one writer stated: "Every revolution in history that was started by those determined to pull down the city always ended in despotism and ironhanded power wielders, as brutal as had been experienced before, and sometimes more so." This same writer also pointed out that, contrary to what many Americans imagine, the American Revolution was not a revolution in terms of the usual acceptance of the word.[12]

[11]Seymour Halleck, "You Can Go to Hell with Style," *Psychology Today,* (November, 1969), p. 16. See also Margaret Horton and Romualdas Krianciunas, "Minnesota Multiphasic Personality Inventory Differences between Terminators and Continuers in Youth Counseling," *Journal of Counseling Psychology,* March 1970, pp. 98-101. From this study it was concluded that poor adolescent prospects for counseling are those characterized by marked rebellion toward authority.

[12]From Jack Valenti, "Revolution: Is it Idealistic . . . or Just Destructive," *Washington Post Service,* May 9, 1970.

The American Revolution was started and directed by those who had the most to lose, not by the downtrodden or those who rebelled against their society. The leaders liked the society they had. They were not interested in tearing down their social order, but they were determined to have their own kind of government, one free from arbitrary decrees by a distant government that intruded on the lives of the Colonists, particularly on the businessmen.

CHALLENGES AND OPPORTUNITIES

The disturbed social order of today should neither overwhelm nor confuse us. Instead, the situations before us should challenge us to search for better answers to the many problems which we are only beginning to perceive and to treat in terms of their causal influences. Dissidents, militant activists, as well as peaceful protestors will continue to appear in the future.[13] Social disorder will not disappear in the foreseeable future—the causes are still with us:

Physical and social sciences will continue to develop in disjointed relationships.

Computers and other new technologically produced equipment will, from time to time, displace workers who cannot or do not wish to adjust to changed requirements for employment.

Television and other mass news media will continue to overemphasize the negative news.

Wealth and its resultant affluence, except for periods of business recessions, will continue to increase, and some parents will continue to give money too liberally to their children—relatively fewer children will gain a sense of responsibility for what they consume.

Tourism and facilities for travel will continue to increase the individual's mobility and the number of persons who feel rootless.

Some human beings will adjust to their personal worlds by feelings of boredom, alienation, projection, end-of-the-world syndromes, unrelenting life styles, plus numerous other forms of adjustment and maladjustment. The fact that the old and some new forces of conflict will appear in the years ahead should not dismay us. The members of the dissident minority, those whose strongest motivations are unrelenting hatreds, will continue to destroy good works as well as bad, great institutions as well as obsolete ones. These deviants have made their presence known in every civilization.

Social progress has usually taken place, not through those who claimed to hate the bad so much that they had to destroy evil by randomized de-

---

[13]This is on the assumption that the United States will not have an authoritarian form of government such as a dictatorship.

structiveness, but through those who respected the good they felt within themselves. They worked quietly and constructively to improve themselves and the good around them.

A basic challenge to the young man of today is whether he wants to give vent to hatreds within himself by destroying what he does not like (things that symbolize evil to him) or whether he wants to improve himself and the world by working with those who want to work constructively to bring about the good that builds a better future gradually and surely. In short, does he align himself with the destroyers or the builders, the destructive-oriented or the constructive-minded?

This decision can be made by asking himself the question, "How strong is my motivation for improving myself through systematic training until I meet the usual requirements for having the kind of career I want?" The activists who intend to improve the social order through destruction can get the thrills of a certain kind of quick success without training—a moron can throw stones, set fires to buildings, and plant bombs. Such feelings of false achievement do not lead to the development of one's potentials.

This contrasts sharply with the training requirements that must be fulfilled by the individual who wants to improve the social order through rebuilding what has been destroyed or has become obsolete. He must also strengthen his positive perspectives to the extent that he enjoys the attaining of successes that involve long periods of time. To attain the constructive goals he sets for himself, he needs the friendship of other like-minded men who hold to their constructive objectives in spite of inevitable setbacks in their efforts to bring about social progress. *Colleagueship is our most hopeful answer.*

The constructive-minded man who trains himself for business management develops a spirit of colleagueship. He knows that neither he nor business managements can alone correct all the wrongs and shortcomings in our changing social order. Nor can government. Nor can the dissidents. Nor can the educators. Nor can the parents in the home. Eventually, the answers must come through the combined efforts of many intelligent, socially aware men and women who live and work as colleagues in achieving the kind of social advancements that our science, technology, and goodwill make possible, indeed necessary. This will not come instantly through an explosive revolution, but gradually through progress brought about by those people who search quietly for constructive answers.

Constructive social relations efforts of companies

Managements vary in their interpretations regarding their social responsibilities. Many executives believe that their greatest contributions to human progress are in the products they make and the services they render to customers. Generally, managements have considerable pride in what they sell and the ways their products help to raise standards of living in this and in foreign countries. They believe that what their products do for people is more important than any speeches they can make about their helpfulness to underprivileged people.

However, a new trend developed in recent years. Now managements recognize more and more that they should seek to be not only good managers of employee and stockholder relations but also good members of their community and of society.

Some provide job training for those who have few or no skills to offer. Even former criminals may be sought and trained. Trainees are paid while learning and jobs are offered when the skills are passably adequate.

Those managements with experience in this field not only offer training and jobs but they also realize that certain kinds of underdeveloped individuals have never learned normal work habits such as coming to work on time or getting to work at all. The company appoints sponsoring employees to encourage these employees to develop normal work habits. Their training program may include systematic efforts to raise the self-respect and self-confidence of this type of employee.

Hundreds of companies have developed special urban affairs departments. The managements in many cases were anxious to prove their sense of social responsibility and planned rather extensive programs. Hopes were high. After the programs of 247 corporations had been in operation for several years, a systematic survey was made. Part of the report stated:

> The complex tasks of planning and managing urban affairs programs require more thought and skill than many of their sponsors realized at the start. One chief executive officer said: "I don't think any of us really knew what we were getting into. We saw action was needed, and we moved fast, maybe too fast. The task turned out to be Herculean." Many others, likewise chastened by experience, are reluctant to set their hopes too high for future achievement, and some are despondent about how little they have been able to accomplish to date.[14]

The survey findings indicate that many managements will have to study the benefits of their past programs and develop new approaches to our social disorders. We shall be able to read reports of studies in this field as published in business journals from time to time, but the young men

[14]Jules Cohn, "Is Business Meeting the Challenge of Urban Affairs?" *Harvard Business Review* (March-April 1970), p. 79.

currently in training for management will want to know how their training can be enriched to enable them as individuals to help overcome problems of our social order.

Opportunities for those in training
for management

The members of managements of the future will have the same basic functional responsibilities as in the present such as planning, organizing, staffing, supervising, and coordinating, in accordance with company objectives and policies. Managerial contributions to our social evolution will be in directions such as the following:

1. *More consideration of effects of decisions on the community*, on people who have only *indirect relations* with the company. Managements will have to consider the hiring, training, and promoting of employees in relation to the various groups of the community, particularly opportunities for the underutilized people. Questions of possible pollution of the environment will be more important when new products, production methods, and locations of plants are being considered.

2. *Direct supervisory relations* with employees will improve in regard to what management itself expects to do about the meaning of the job to the employee. In times past, most management men thought that when the company offered a job to an applicant, the man hired should feel grateful and work hard simply because he had been given the opportunity to make a living. Future executives will be expected to do far more—interpret the job in terms of its creative contributions to society and particularly to the worker as a person. Work challenges will be more necessary than in the past. Participative management and job enrichment techniques will receive more emphases, not only in a young man's plans for training himself but also in the daily thinking of the managerial and supervisory staff members. Knowledge of the behavioral sciences and humanistic concepts will be considered essential to an executive's qualifications for carrying out the company's social responsibilities.

3. *Managers of the future must have the ability to learn more rapidly* than ever before. As previously stated, knowledge in some of the technological fields will double every decade or two. Knowledge in the social sciences and management will double more slowly but the "knowledge explosion" will require more than a willingness on the part of executives to attend institutes of a semisocial nature—concentrated study will be essential. Reading skills and acquaintance with information sources will be given increased attention by young executives of the future.

4. *The companies that have organized departments to deal with urban*

affairs will offer opportunities to those men who wish to specialize in the field of corporate relations and the social order. The survey of the 247 companies that had had urban affairs programs presented interesting findings for the man who thinks of a career in urban affairs.

> Typically, the urban affairs man is in his early thirties. He has served in other functions before moving into his current job, and he plans to move on to another, bigger job, in the company eventually.
>
> Several company presidents indicated that urban affairs is a job for young executives, not older, seasoned, or highly trained people. "Young people understand urban problems better than middle-aged line officers," said the chief executive of a San Francisco company known for its active work in urban affairs. "I think it's good training for junior executives."
>
> While I found no fiery-eyed evangelists among corporate urban affairs officers, roughly half of the men interviewed expressed enthusiasm, even excitement, about their assignment.
>
> Some saw it as an opportunity to make the corporate structure more responsive to human needs. . . .
>
> Most of the other younger people saw their jobs as a career opportunity—a place to get "exposure" and to make contacts, both within the company and on the outside. The older man seemed to see it as a good berth, after years of work in higher pressure jobs. Only seven urban affairs men planned to make their careers in this area. "If the action were in some other area, I'd be there," said a 30-year-old vice-president of personnel, "and, when it moves, I'll hand urban problems over to someone else." The youngest officers, in this group frequently expressed the opportunistic-cum-idealistic view that a stint in urban affairs is like a tour of duty in the Peace Corps: two years off to do some good.[15]

Generally, the opportunities in management for young men who have a sense of social responsibility will not be as numerous in specialties such as urban affairs as in the day-to-day supervisory and executive functions. The opportunities in these latter areas will utilize the findings and principles developed not only by the behavioral scientists but by the many insightful men who have been dealing with employees for many years. The chapters in this text emphasize these points of view. They are integral aspects of the fifth way a man in business can express his sense of social responsibility. See page 35.

[15]*Ibid.*, p. 79.

HOW CAN A YOUNG MAN IN BUSINESS
EXPRESS A SENSE
OF SOCIAL RESPONSIBILITY?

He can do it in five general ways:

1. He can work in a company that is making or marketing products or services that benefit people. The products or services may help people to become healthy, to travel more safely, to overcome problems of pollution, or provide other benefits. See pages 36–41.

2. He can work in a company that is a good neighbor in its community by conducting programs such as training unemployables for jobs, modernizing slum buildings, tutoring children, investing funds in health research or education, and the like. Some companies have community health relations departments headed by men who are trained for their work. These departments may be called "urban affairs" departments. Pages 42–44.

3. He can, as an individual, volunteer to help others who need encouragement, friendship, legal protection, or financial counseling. Thousands of persons are not at all interested in using violence as a means of bringing about social change, but they give their time and skills without pay as a way of expressing their concern for the well-being of their fellow human beings. And they do it sincerely. They outnumber by many millions those who have gotten extensive publicity for their rioting or other forms of violent dissent. Page 45.

4. Certain men of outstanding initiative note a human need that stimulates their imagination, and they tackle the problem without thought as to whether they are using one of the above forms of expressing their social responsibility. They use an approach that fits the problem. Men who express their social responsibility in this way arouse the admiration of observers who are likely to say to themselves: "Young men like that sure give us hope for the future of the human race." Pages 46–48.

5. He can, as a perceptive member of the business world, constantly seek to develop his own understanding, his sensitivities, and his skills in dealing with people. The most frequent, and in many cases, the most important expressions of a sense of social responsibility take place in the many everyday informal relationships with people, those relationships where one man is intelligently and sincerely considerate of the other man or men with whom he is dealing.

All the succeeding chapters of this book implement or involve this fifth possible approach.

THE FASTEST WAY TO CHANGE THE WORLD IS TO WORK IN A BUSINESS THAT DOES.

You're about to decide what you're going to do with your life. Teaching. Social work. Government. Peace Corps. The professions. Or business.

Wait a minute. Don't write off business so fast.

You can do more about poverty, slums, ignorance, unemployment, starvation and backward nations in business than in any other field.

Maybe you don't know how deeply business is involved in these problems.

Young men from 18 companies (Avco to Xerox) are running Job Corps Centers for the Office of Economic Opportunity. With the help of teachers and the labor unions, these men are outfitting school dropouts with the skills they need for a new life.

A 24-year-old Esso man is growing thriving forests in the Libyan desert.

Sixty men at General Electric are creating plans to build new 100,000-population cities from the sidewalk up. (We have to build twice as many dwelling units in the next 30 years as exist today.)

A project manager at U.S. Gypsum is rebuilding tenements in East Harlem at half the cost of public housing.

A Philco-Ford man is introducing computer instruction systems in four Philadelphia schools.

A team from two U.S. chemical companies just helped set up a model agribusiness complex in India that will help feed 10 million people.

The list is almost endless.

These men have a strong sense of accomplishment, because it is the nature of business to get things done. Looking at other fields, businessman David Lilienthal says, "I am dismayed by the number of people who specialize in making studies, yet would be scared to death of carrying them out."

If you want to do something about the mess you inherited, think about a business career. The facilities are here. The financing is here. The managerial skills are here. The technology is here. And the action is here.

Now all we need here is you.

Courtesy of the Advertising Council, Inc., 825 Third Avenue, New York, N. Y.

Beneath this soft and warm exterior, there lies a heart of plastic.

So far, it's only a valve. Eight-year-old Janet Hernandez has one.

It may not be long before a whole working heart will be made out of plastic.

Men in plastics research at Union Carbide are working on the almost impossible job of designing plastics compatible with the body.

Their most crucial job is making an ultra-thin polypropylene fabric for lining the inside of the heart. A fabric coated with parylene that will allow human tissue to grow into and around it to keep blood from clotting.

A plastic heart isn't the only part of the body we're working on. Maybe someday there will be a little plastic in all of us.

Right now, we've got you surrounded by our plastics. We were in plastics before most people knew the word. We make more plastics than anyone else. We haven't scratched the surface yet.

Why is a great big company like Union Carbide so concerned about a little bit of plastic for the body?

Because.

Beneath our corporate exterior, there beats a heart.

UNION CARBIDE   THE DISCOVERY COMPANY

If we could get our mitts on those engines, you couldn't hear them a block away

The average person only sees a turbine engine when it's moving a jet airplane—like the 250-ton XB-70 above.

But this marvelously efficient engine is showing up in the most unlikely places. A turbine-engine car came within a hairbreadth of winning the Indianapolis Race this year. Gas turbines will power the 160-mph train being planned for the New York-Washington run. But the fastest-growing use is for electric power generation—everything from a monster 10-engine cluster in Cincinnati, to a 125-lb. 10 kilowatt unit that can be lifted by two men.

The thing about gas turbines is that some of them are noisy.

And noise has been plaguing man ever since 50 B.C. when Caesar banned chariots from the streets at night so his fellow Romans could sleep.

One expert estimates that the sound level in cities is growing by one decibel per year. He thinks that in 30 years the noise could be literally lethal.

Koppers is on top of this problem. When it's equipped with a Koppers silencer, you can run a turbine engine in the middle of town and nobody even knows it's there. The armed forces use Koppers silencers to ground-test F4G Phantom jet engines without splitting everybody's eardrums. Koppers silencers will

be on that 160-mph train, too. So far, we can't quiet in-flight aircraft noise because present Koppers silencers are so big and heavy they'd never get the plane off the ground.

Noise abatement is only one of the problems being solved by Koppers Environmental Control specialists. We're helping to clean the air with industrial precipitators and "clean rooms" for precision work. We're helping to clean the nation's water supply with a wide range of sewage treatment devices.

Man seems determined to foul his own nest. Koppers is determined to clean it.

Koppers Company, Inc., Pittsburgh, Pa. 15219.

KOPPERS

Environmental Systems · Chemicals and Coatings · Plastics · Architectural and Construction Materials · Engineered Products · Engineering and Construction

Beauty treatment for 87 acres of trash.

In this age of affluence, we have more of everything. Including more trash.

Each of us produces about five pounds a day. For the country as a whole, that's a yearly problem weighing 182,000,000 tons.

Where does it all go?

If we burn it, the smoke and fly ash drifts down on our cities and towns. And on us. If we dump it, we provide breeding grounds for insects and vermin. And disease.

Waste is growing faster than population. By 1980, we'll be faced with 280,000,000 tons each year.

What's the answer?

For many cities, the answer is to bury the problem. It's cheaper, cleaner, more efficient and healthier.

Waste burial, or sanitary landfill, is also an economic method of transforming low value land into a community asset. For example, Los Angeles County, California, reclaimed an abandoned strip mine in Torrance by compacting refuse and burying it in layers.

The result is the lush, 87-acre South Coast Botanical Garden.

At present, the county is reclaiming another 133 acres this same way.

But changing an eyesore into a place of beauty or usefulness takes planning. You can start by writing for the free booklet, "What can you do with refuse?" to Dept. 718T, Caterpillar Tractor Co., 100 N.E. Adams St., Peoria, Illinois 61602.

Your local Caterpillar Dealer can help your town get started.

You have a lot to gain. Like clean air, for example.

We can make the world a better place to grow up in. Caterpillar machines will help.

Caterpillar, Cat and CE are Trademarks of Caterpillar Tractor Co.

NI SOMBRA DE LO QUE FUE!

2 MESES DESPUES

Si, en sólo dos meses este niño mal alimentado y débil de la izquierda se transformó en el niño fuerte, robusto y alentado de la derecha. (INCAP CASO PC-65)
Una alimentación a base de INCAPARINA hizo posible esta maravillosa transformación.

A CUAL DE ESTOS NIÑOS LE GUSTARIA QUE SE PAREZCA SU HIJO?
Usted dirá y con razón: "al niño sano y sonriente". Está muy bien. Siga este consejo:
En todas las comidas dé a su niño: INCAPARINA
el alimento que tiene:
• Proteínas como la carne y la leche.
• Fósforo como el pescado.
• Calcio como la leche.

INCAPARINA
ES MUCHO ALIMENTO Y CUESTA MENOS!

A war is being fought in Latin America, and on at least one battleground—in Columbia—The Quaker Oats Company is leading the attack. This is no ordinary war, for the common enemy is malnutrition. And Quaker's weapon is a remarkable product called Incaparina.

Incaparina is the result of years of research by the Institute of Nutrition of Central America and Panama, commonly known as INCAP.

In 1961, Quaker was granted an exclusive license to manufacture and market Incaparina in Columbia and several other Latin American countries. The company developed special advertising campaigns and hired professional nutritionists to make the rounds of public health clinics to explain the benefits of Incaparina. One of the major difficulties was to promote a product whose visible results took time to be apparent even though the cost, in comparison with other protein foods, was very low.

Source: The Quaker, February, 1968.

Concern

How do you define a beautiful environment?

When you're concerned with improving environments it's natural to first think of what is clean and spacious and harmonious and safe. That's where you have to begin.

But even when you have these things, you haven't solved everything. The best environment happens when you know who you are and can exult in using all the talent that is in you. Surely, we want our children to have that part of a beautiful environment, too.

The free enterprise system has developed many successful programs to help young people develop confidence in themselves.

We of the Investor-Owned Electric Light and Power Companies are very much involved in youth conferences, scholarship programs, training programs and youth associations. And we are going to do more.

We made up our minds a long time ago to give the communities we serve the world's best electric service at the most reasonable price. But we also made up our minds that our responsibilities to people don't end there.

Our concern for the communities we serve goes far beyond the supplying of electricity.

The people at your Investor-Owned Electric Light and Power Companies*

American business adds a

new department—*neighborhoods*

I N troubled Watts, Los Angeles, Aerojet-General Corporation bought a building and hired 45 Negro men and women to make tents — a product with a high labor content. Today 450 have good jobs there.

United States Gypsum Company in New York, Chicago and Cleveland, buys slum apartments — rebuilds and modernizes them for local non-profit groups, which rent them to lowest-income families at bargains.

Also in Cleveland, Warner & Swasey has organized the Negro-managed Hough Manufacturing Company and is training unemployed "unemployables" to make needed products such as machined parts. We'll supply working capital and technical assistance until the concern is self-sufficient, and then let the workers buy it if they wish.

In Philadelphia, Smith Kline & French helped a housing authority cooperate with a private developer to buy old run-down houses, make modern apartments of them, and rent them at low rents to poor families. (It's worth recording that these tenants are taking pride in keeping up their sparkling-clean homes, and Warner & Swasey is having the same experience in the slum apartment we rebuilt).

None of all this is easy, and it is costly indeed in money and especially in time and effort. But we for one are finding a vast satisfaction in getting involved in this business of being a good neighbor, in community preservation.

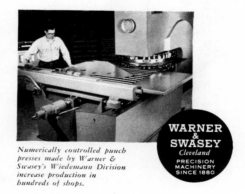

Numerically controlled punch presses made by Warner & Swasey's Wiedemann Division increase production in hundreds of shops.

WARNER & SWASEY
Cleveland
PRECISION MACHINERY SINCE 1880

When banks, business and churches join hands

something good is bound to happen

WARNER & SWASEY, 5 banks, three churches of various faiths are buying property in just about the worst block in the poorest slum in Cleveland. We will modernize the apartments, rebuild the big-old-once-fine houses for large families, tear down the hopeless buildings and eventually build single-family homes on the sites. And we'll do it with our money, not wait for government.

Warner & Swasey will manage the rehabilitation, the banks and we will put up the money, the churches will then run the operation. *That,* we think, is a good working partnership. We know it can be done — Warner & Swasey has had experience in rehabilitating three old apartment houses, one completed months ago and now successfully operating and providing clean modern living for self-respecting families.

This is an invitation to other cities to come and watch this latest venture — an adventure in decent living.

Turret Lathe using cut-off tool made by Manchester Tools, a Division of Warner & Swasey.

WARNER & SWASEY
Cleveland
PRECISION MACHINERY SINCE 1880

YOU CAN PRODUCE IT BETTER, FASTER, FOR LESS WITH WARNER & SWASEY MACHINE TOOLS, TEXTILE MACHINERY, CONSTRUCTION EQUIPMENT

When you invest a billion dollars to help the cities, you learn some things.

Like hope.

Troubled minds: Back some 18 months ago, there were a lot of troubled minds all over this country. Including many in our business. The life insurance business. And what troubled everyone was the cities. There was poverty and frustration and decay and much ugliness all the way around.

In that atmosphere, when there was precious little hope anyplace, a lot of companies from our business got together to do something about it. To give it a try. You can't ride out the ups and downs of business without a certain inherent strain of optimism.

The life insurance business decided to invest a billion dollars worth of loan funds in the city core areas. Money that would create more jobs. More housing. Hopefully, more hope. And we made a public pledge of this investment.

You may say, this was just business as usual.

Because historically, life insurance companies invest in housing and in enterprise that makes jobs.

But this was different.

This was a new and special case of investment.

It went to an area—the inner cities—where capital was not readily available on reasonable terms, because of risk and location. Our business felt this special commitment was essential.

After all, our business is totally bound up with the health and safety of people. And people live in the cities. You could say people are the cities.

If those cities crumble, people are going to crumble, and business—ours, yours, anyone's—is apt to crumble right along with them.

In a businesslike way, our business was investing in its own future.

Due to the nature of the problem, the life insurance companies would need the closest cooperation of government and responsible leaders of the community. And they're getting it. With the result that the billion is now almost completely committed.

What we learned, was people.

By our very involvement in the core areas, we of the life insurance business found ourselves getting a lot closer to where people live.

We found that despite all the talk of

backlash and Blacklash, there's an even greater drive to work together. A drive to create, not to hate.

We confirmed a deep feeling. That the problem of the cities needs people —people in government, business, and labor, working together—to help solve it. And we discovered we weren't trying alone; other businesses were making special efforts.

The life insurance companies are re-learning a basic truth. Let everyone do what he does best. We ourselves know investment in housing and enterprise. Local planners, developers, and agencies know their communities and know their needs.

Our business has learned that its hope was justified.

Sure, minds are still troubled today. The situation won't "just go away." But...

The life insurance business has so much hope that it's taking another step.

A second billion.

A second billion devoted to the same aims.

While knowing that it doesn't nearly fill the whole need, the life insurance business regards this, like the first billion, as an investment in its own future.

Isn't it your future, too?

If you would like some suggestions on what you can do, write for the booklet "The cities...your challenge, too." Dept. L

Institute of Life Insurance
On behalf of the life insurance companies in America
277 Park Avenue
New York, N.Y. 10017

A social services center grows in Bedford-Stuyvesant, being built with mortgage money provided by the life insurance investment. One of hundreds of projects in 227 cities.

This job is too big for Uncle Sam.

It needs you.

You must know how sick your town is. You see it in the headlines. You hear it over the radio and on TV. Problems with the kids. Discipline. Education. Drugs. Crime.

Washington can't provide the cure all by itself. It's too far away. With too many other big things on its mind. Besides, it's nearly always faster and better to solve local problems locally. And a lot cheaper.

You can help. You *must* help, if you want the job to get done.

What can you do? Start helping the folks that are already doing a job.

The volunteers who man the member agencies of the United Way. The people who go out into the streets and alleys and deal first hand with the problems of youth. Who visit the sick, the old, the aged.

Pick up the phone today. Call an agency that appeals to you. Make a date to watch it in action. You don't need special training. Just two hands, your head. And your heart.

You gave money the United Way? Fine. That's a great first step. But it isn't enough. **Give more than money . . . give you.**

Volunteerism. Few college students realize that each year more than 55 million Americans volunteer to work for nonprofit agencies and that the number increases each year. Young people who are not especially aware of these volunteers can, on second thought, recall housewives who rang the doorbell to solicit dimes or dollars for medical research. There are more than a half million volunteers giving their services in our hospitals. Our national health agencies alone have more than 30 million volunteer workers annually.

The typical student rarely knows of the many busy executives and professional people who spend weekend and evening hours in planning campaigns or meeting with those who can use their services. Employees of certain corporations donate thousands of hours in volunteer work each year.

Some employee groups specialize in getting jobs for unemployables, conducting sports programs for delinquent boys, making friends with problem children, or reconditioning and rebuilding rundown homes of the perennial poor. Students, as one would expect, tend to do tutoring. One estimate placed at 250,000 the number of students who work as volunteers in activities other than tutoring. Anyone who is interested in volunteerism can consult a local United Fund, Council of Social Agencies, Chamber of Commerce, or similar service organization. If he does not want to affiliate himself with a formal organization, he can find plenty of people and problems of his community that need his friendship.

Social problems cannot be overcome by spending more money to improve physical environments. The personal influence of thousands of sincere volunteers is necessary. For further information on this topic, see John A. Hamilton, "Will 'Work' Work?," *Saturday Review,* May 23, 1970.

He has time to kill

Caught up in an aimless existence which offers few chances for fun, many boys turn to a life of crime. Your United Way gift can help steer them right, by providing counseling service, recreational opportunities and a sense of purpose. Please give them time to grow instead of to kill.
Your fair share gift works many wonders ✓ THE UNITED WAY

She's being punished... She has to go out and play

Many children in our cities have nowhere to play but filthy alleys and littered streets. Your United Way gift helps support organizations that provide recreation and guidance for thousands of deprived children. Please help make playtime fun for them, not punishment. Please give.
Your fair share gift works many wonders ✓ THE UNITED WAY

Bronson Gentry headed campaign to build this new Detroit school. Now he enrolls these students to help keep it new and sparkling.

Borg-Warner benefits from good work of its employee citizens

Like most companies, Borg-Warner tries to be a good "corporate citizen." But while corporations can give money to support worthy projects, it is people who must supply the talent and energy that make these projects work. Borg-Warner is proud of the contributions of many of its employees to many good causes.

An outstanding example is Bronson Gentry. In 1969 he received from George Romney, Secretary of Housing and Urban Development, a $5000 award from the Lane Bryant Foundation for service to the Detroit community. Projects he has initiated have significantly reduced crime and vandalism. In part as a result of his leadership, his neighborhood has better recreation areas, a pool and fieldhouse, and the new school shown above. He has developed good rapport with neighborhood youth. Also in 1969 Mr. Gentry, an employee of Borg & Beck Division, won from the Detroit

Police Department its "Good Citizen" Award for outstanding community service.

Although hardly typical, Mr. Gentry is one of many hundreds of employees of Borg-Warner, from hourly employees through top management, who take more than a passing interest in the work to be done by individual citizens in welfare, health, community relations and government. Many serve as volunteer workers or trustees of hospitals; as fund raisers of united funds, colleges and other cooperative endeavors. Borg-Warner's Chairman serves as a regional leader for the National Alliance of Businessmen, along with other unpaid jobs for the community.

The role of the Corporation is primarily to encourage such activities as part of its role in society. Happily, there is a bonus not only in the resulting community improvements, but in the personal development of the employees themselves.

Bronson Gentry is a janitor in a Detroit factory who voluntarily has organized and led campaigns against dilapidated housing, for the construction of neighborhood athletic fields and the distribution of Thanksgiving baskets to the needy, as well as having paroled in his custody boys involved in vandalism and petty theft. The parolees in his custody must spend a few weeks working with saws and lathes in Gentry's basement. Youngsters rarely want to leave when the "sentence" has been completed.

Glen McDermed and some members of his first class. Now these men are able to teach others.

"The State of Arizona, like any state, has a lot of computer programs to write. Sometimes, more work than their people can handle," relates Glen McDermed, IBM Marketing Representative of Phoenix, Arizona.

"In 1967, I had an idea. Why not teach prison inmates how to write them? It would provide a programming pool for the State, and the men would learn something useful for the future.

"I explained the idea to my people in Phoenix and to the Arizona State Prison authorities. They all told me to give it a try.

"To our surprise, forty inmates turned out for the project—even some who were serving life sentences! Eleven prisoners made up the first class.

"IBM supplied all the training manuals. My management also suggested that some of us take time off from our jobs to teach classes. We taught the first class in October, a month after the idea was proposed.

"The men worked hard. They gave up going to the movies to study the manuals. They took homework to their cells. And they caught on fast.

"In June of '68, they got their first real program to write. It came from the Arizona Department of Public Safety. Then a request came from the State Finance Department. Another from the Arizona Highway Department. A couple of colleges asked for programs.

"Today the men are writing 56 computer programs, from seven separate sources. Two of the men who have left the prison now have jobs as programmers.

"The project has given these inmates a sense of accomplishment, and encouragement for their own futures. And the State of Arizona is getting some welcome help from an unexpected source."

IBM

QUESTIONS ON THE CHAPTER

1. What is a purpose of trying to recognize the underlying factors that are at work in our social ferment?
2. State the one most basic factor at work in social change and unrest.
3. Name several ways in which television is a factor in social unrest.
4. What is meant by "rootlessness" in our society?
5. To what extent do you agree and disagree with the effects of affluence described in the chapter?
6. Do you agree or disagree with the findings of James E. Birren and Vern L. Sengtson concerning the generation gap?

QUESTIONS SUGGESTED FOR DISCUSSIONS ON ADJUSTMENT PATTERNS

Boredom

1. If you have observed children who complained about their boredom, how did their behavior differ from that of other children who never had that complaint? If you have associated with adults who suffered from boredom, did they, at times, seem to make a nuisance of themselves to overcome boredom?
2. If and when you have children of your own, how do you intend to help them develop interests that will prevent their being bored as they grow older? To do this, should their life be made easy for them or do you want to challenge them by giving them problems appropriate to their capacities?
3. Is every adult who suffers from boredom, whatever the real or the imagined cause, really responsible for his boredom or does he have a right to blame others for it?

Alienation

1. When teenagers have told you that they do not get along well with their parents, to what aspects of their parental relationships did they refer?
2. When some parents recognize that their teenage son or daughter "hates" them, they offer gifts and extra privileges in their hope that the relationship will improve. If you were a parent faced with this kind of problem, what would you do?
3. If you have talked with an appreciable number of young people who said that they did not get along with their parents, you may have noted that some of them turned to nearby adults for friendship. Others adjusted to their situation by avoiding all adults—all adults symbolized or aroused the antagonisms they felt for their parents. Can you suggest any constructive approaches to the solutions of such problems?

(Questions continued on page 50.)

Projection

1. If you were going to organize a group of young people to have lively discussions, which would be the easier: to organize a group where the members discussed their own faults or to organize a group that discussed the faults or shortcomings of others?

2. Which is the easier for an individual:

(a) To recognize his own shortcomings and feelings of guilt about things he wishes he had done or not done, to accept the blame, and then try to correct what he can or

(b) Ignore his own shortcomings but call attention to and criticise others for their faults? Why?

3. Which kind of behavior, (a) or (b), is the more fruitful and gives the greater longterm satisfactions? What undesirable consequences may ensue when either (a) or (b) is carried to an extreme degree?

End-of-the-World Syndrome

1. To what extent has the possibility of being killed in an automobile accident depressed you or made you pessimistic about the future? (More than 150 lives are lost each day on U.S. highways)

2. If a person does not worry about being killed in an automobile accident, why should he worry about the atom bomb? Are these two possibilities comparable in the sense that they are both equally undesirable? Has either possibility modified your personal philosophy or attitude toward our civilization?

3. In addition to the atom bomb as a threat to the people of large areas, what other means of total annihilation can be made and used by any nation that happens to have advanced technical resources available?

PROBLEMS AND PROJECTS

For All Students

1. Collect and summarize some of the published information available to you on the title of this chapter. If this field interests you, make a set of folders for use in filing new information that comes to your attention from time to time.

2. Prepare a list of benefits that have come to people as a result of advancements in the sciences. Examples might be antibiotics that cure ailments which were incurable a generation ago. Discuss with several older adults whether they want only the benefits of technology but none of the problems that come with the benefits. State your findings.

For Advanced Students

3. Make a study of volunteerism, particularly programs or actions that might be taken by students to help others. Get a copy of James Tanck, *College Volunteers* (produced with the support of VISTA) by National Program for Voluntary Action, 451 Seventh St., S.W., Washington, D. C., or similar publications that you may find in your libraries.

4. Examine some of the books on training for management that are available to you. Read the preface and the table of contents of each. To what extent do they seem to duplicate or differ from the aims set forth in this chapter?

For Men in Business

5. You probably know companies or individuals who have been directly affected by dissidents who disturbed the social order. Report their comments about claimed causes and effects.

6. Now that you have had some academic training and business experience, what challenges appeal to you in the field of human relations? Choose one challenge as a possible career for yourself. What additional training would you need?

COLLATERAL READINGS

For All Students

Brandon, Henry, "A Talk with Walter Lippmann, at 80, About This Minor Dark Age," *The New York Times Magazine*, Sept. 14, 1969.

Cohn, Jules, "Is Business Meeting the Challenge of Urban Affairs?" *Harvard Business Review*, March-April, 1970.

For Advanced Students

Banfield, Edward C., *The Unheavenly City*. New York: Little, Brown and Company, 1970.

Hepner, Harry W., *Psychology Applied to Life and Work*. Englewood Cliffs, N. J.; Prentice-Hall, Inc., 1966. Chapters 2 to 6 on adjustment patterns.

For Men in Business

The Chamber of Commerce of the United States presents updated versions of *Where the Action Is*, descriptions of programs that involve businessmen and associations that have dealt with or are dealing with major urban problems. Case problems are available. State your specific interest in the problems you wish to study in your community. Address The Chamber Clearinghouse, 1615 H St., N.W., Washington, D.C. 20006.

Bradley, Gene E., "What Businessmen Need to Know about the Student Left,"

Harvard Business Review, September–October 1968. Corporate involvement in society's problems is no longer just a "nice" thing to do; we have reached a question of survival. Business will have to develop "an instinct" for survival in a political world.

Michael, Donald N., *The Unprepared Society: Planning for a Precarious Future.* New York: Basic Books, Inc., Publishers, 1968. The author urges radical changes in our educational philosophy and institutions to develop the kind of leadership we shall need if we are to survive in the planless and disrupted world of the future.

BASIC FACTORS: INSIGHTS FROM BEHAVIORAL STUDIES

PART

Perception–
The Hawthorne Studies
and Their Meaning for Us

SITUATIONS YOU ARE LIKELY TO MEET

How would you meet each of these situations:
   a. *Before* you have read the chapter? What would
      you say to yourself or to the individual?
   b. *After* you have read the chapter? How have
      your answers changed?

1. A young friend in college has high ideals about improving the lot of factory and office workers. He has
   never worked in industry or in any other field. He
   thinks he will go into production, become a top-level
   executive in a year or two, and then improve the
   work life of workers. He does not intend to do it
   through slow evolutionary methods but simply by
   posting a few bulletins which will do away with
   monotonous tasks and let everyone enjoy his job. He
   tells you about his goals and plans.
2. Assume that upon leaving college you take a job as
   a trainee for production management. You are being
   oriented in the company by working under the supervision of several foremen—some are progressive and
   some are not. A foreman tells you that some of the
   workmen are disciplining their fellow workers for rate
   busting by "binging" each rate-buster. What would
   you say or do to an employee when you see a worker
   do this?
3. As a trainee for production management you associate with other trainees in the company. One of
   your fellow trainees has never studied job enrich-

ment programs of leading companies. He is unhappy because too much of his work is repetitive. He is thinking of quitting and getting a job as a salesman because he sees no interesting future for himself in production. If he asks for your thoughts as to whether the boredom of repetitive work can ever be removed, how will you try to answer him?

When the typical industrial excutive finds that some of his employees do not cooperate in the attainment of management's objectives, he feels hurt and rebuffed, like a well-meaning father who discovers that his son prefers to assert himself as a man rather than be an obedient son. Just as a father and a son do not always see eye to eye, so management and the industrial worker often see their responsibilities in different ways.

Of course, we all know that two different individuals may perceive any situation in different ways. We have common expressions for this idea, such as "If you want to understand the other fellow, put yourself in his shoes." Numerous social science studies have emphasized the importance for the industrial executive of recognizing differences in perception.

This and the succeeding chapters of Part II present some of the findings of important behavioral studies that are significant for the executive and the supervisor. These studies do not reveal the existence of wholly new or unsuspected mental processes such as perception or communication. The processes as such have been known to man ever since he became aware of the processes in his mental life. The studies do however point up for us certain very valuable *emphases* for our current thinking in human relations. We shall begin our presentation of these emphases by reviewing briefly the famous Hawthorne studies for their historical background and for their significance in studying modern problems in human relations. The special emphases of these studies show not only the need for development of our perceptiveness when we study human relations in industry but also the resulting colleagueship through job enlargement.

When workers control their output

One of the most common ways for industrial workers to show that their perceptions of the job differ from those of management is through the restriction of their production. Workers rather than management often control their output, particularly in manufacturing. Sometimes they restrict their production to an unnecessarily low level.

Usually, however, the members of a work group keep the output level at a point they consider fair to the company as well as to themselves. Most men do not want to loaf on the job. But they do want to feel that they, rather than management, control their ouput. They resent pressure from above, particularly pressure that they themselves have not accepted as a regular part of the work situation.

Workers generally have an informal agreement among themselves as to how many units of work they will produce. A new worker is told by the older workers what is expected of him. If he fails to produce the established output, they remind him of his obligation. If he produces considerably more than the quota they have set, they will ostracize him, hide his tools, or annoy him until he conforms. In many cases the "rate-buster" becomes a source of friction to everyone, even the foreman. The foreman, of course, wants high production but he does not want it at the expense of disrupted morale in his group.

One investigator made a study of production in twelve companies operating in several industries. The plants employed three hundred to twenty-five hundred workers. His findings showed that the average worker was not producing at a level even approaching his potential. According to the systematic observations made, the average employee could easily have done a fair day's work that would have increased the volume of his production by 25 percent, in some cases as much as 100 percent.[1] This kind of situation has been known to exist in most industrial plants for many years. As a result, numerous methods of stimulating employees to produce in accordance with their capacity have been developed by production analysts, experts, and consultants. If you take a course in production, you will learn about many of the incentive systems developed by production experts.

THE FAMOUS HAWTHORNE STUDIES

Historically, one of the first scientific studies which caused production engineers to become especially interested in human relations was made in the Hawthorne plant of the Western Electric Company. These early

[1]See H. Edward Wrape, "Tightening Work Standards," *Harvard Business Review*, July–August 1952, p. 64.

studies are classics that have had a broad influence on human relations in industry. Every executive and student of industrial relations should be acquainted with them. The researchers began in 1927, with the stated aim of finding "the relation between conditions of work and the incidence of fatigue and monotony among employees."[2]

Relay assembly-room experiments

In a special test room designed for the experiment, five girls assembled telephone relays at a work bench. Trays containing parts for assembly were opposite them. A sixth girl procured necessary parts for the assemblers and performed other routine duties. A male supervisor and one or two assistants sat facing the assemblers. The supervisor in charge obtained and kept numerous records relating to quantity and quality of output, reasons for temporary stops, length of time spent in bed by each girl every night, periodical medical reports of their physical condition, and other factors. Room temperatures and relative humidities were recorded hourly. The supervisor and his assistants made extensive daily notes of conversations and of the relations that developed among the workers. The workers were also occasionally interviewed in a separate room by an experienced interviewer. Furthermore, an automatic device recorded, to a fraction of a second, the instant at which each girl completed each assembled relay. Hence, a minute-to-minute record of output with supplementary information was available for each girl over a five-year period.

The five girls selected for the test room were told to work at a comfortable pace; conversation was allowed. The kinds of records that had been approved by the girls were kept, and the records they did not want were not kept. The working atmosphere was quite permissive, and management's interest in the girls was certainly much greater than in the usual worker.

Different experimental conditions of work, such as changes in the number and duration of rest pauses and in the length of the working day and week, were introduced in this relay assembly test room. For example, the investigators first introduced two five-minute rests, one in the morning and one in the afternoon. Then they increased the length of these rest periods. Later they introduced the rest periods at different times of the day. Also, during one experiment period, the operators were served an especially prepared lunch. In later periods, the length of the working day was decreased by one-half hour and then by one hour. For a while, operators were given Saturday morning off. In the course of one two-year period, thirteen changes in working conditions were introduced.

[2]F. J. Roethlisberger and W. J. Dickson, *Management and the Worker* (Cambridge, Mass.: Harvard University Press, 1939), p. 5.

In the first stages of the investigation, both the investigators and the operators were pleased because as conditions of work improved the output rate rose steadily. The early findings offered strong evidence in favor of the engineers' preconceived hypothesis that fatigue was the major factor limiting output. One investigator, however, suggested that the original conditions of work should be restored, that is, the five girls should go back to a full forty-eight-hour week without rest periods, lunches, or other aids to overcome fatigue. Instead of decreasing as expected, output strangely maintained its high level.[3]

Analysis and interpretation of the unexpected results opened a wholly new line of thought. The best interpretation was that "the responses of workers to what was happening about them were dependent upon the significance these events had for them." It became clear that the efficiency of a worker on a job is the result not only of the physical conditions of his work or the level of his wage but of how he feels about his job, what he thinks of his associates, and his relations with his supervisor and with the officials above him. The Hawthorne relay assembly experiment showed that the workers were "cooperating with the experiment" and kept on doing so even after the poorer original conditions of work were restored.

How certain social relationships were analyzed

Several provocative aspects of these experiments have been described by Whitehead[4] and are here summarized because of their significance in explaining certain aspects of production.

During the five-year period there was a general increase of output. The increase, however, was not steady. Definite fluctuations took place from week to week in the quantity each girl produced.

When the production of each worker was charted in graphic form, it was found that wavelike irregularities were exhibited by each graph. Some of the waves lasted for months; others only a week or two. The output figures also showed that similar irregularities occurred with durations of as little as a minute or two.

At first it was supposed that these variations in working speed might be related to the experimental changes deliberately introduced or possibly to other changes in physical circumstance, such as temperature or the

[3]F. J. Roethlisberger, *Management and Morale* (Cambridge, Mass.: Harvard University Press, 1941), pp. 12, 13. Copyright © 1941 by the President and Fellows of Harvard College.

[4]"Social Relationships in a Factory: a Study of an Industrial Group." This title was used by T. N. Whitehead for a paper read before Section J (Psychology) of a British Association meeting in Norwich, England, September 1935, and later published in *The Human Factor* (National Institute of Industrial Psychology, London), Vol. IX, No. 11.

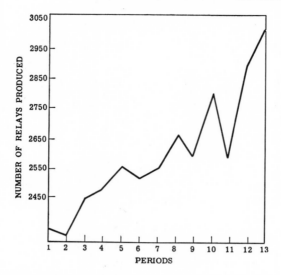

Average weekly output of five workers assembling telephone relays, who received much individual consideration under a variety of work conditions. The following summary describes the various "periods" of work:

Period	Duration in Weeks	Description
1	2	In regular department
2	5	Introduction to test room
3	8	Special "gang" rate
4	5	2 5-minute rest periods
5	4	2 10-minutes rest periods
6	4	6 5-minute rest periods
7	11	15 minute morning rest with lunch
8	7	Same as 7, but with 4:30 stop
9	4	Same as 7, but with 4:00 stop
10	12	Same as 7
11	9	Same as 7, but 5-day week
12	12	Same as 3 (no lunch or rest)
13	36	Same as, 7, but operators furnish own lunch

In this study extending for more than two years, a group of workers were placed with usual equipment in a separate room, shown friendly individual consideration, and repeatedly interviewed regarding their opinions of various incentive conditions that were being investigated. The noteworthy thing is that regardless of the incentive or the work conditions introduced, output continued to increase! As an outgrowth of this study, the company has since instituted a plan of widespread interviewing of individual workers. Data from Elton Mayo, "Supervision and Morale," *Human Factor*, Vol. 5 (1931), pp. 248–260. Chart and comment on Mayo's data taken from Sidney L. Pressey, J. Elliott Janney, and Raymond G. Kuhlen, *Life: A Psychological Survey* (New York: Harper & Row, Publishers, 1939), pp. 542–543.

worker's physical state. However, careful analysis of the data showed that irregularity in output failed to correlate with any known changes of physical circumstance.

The researchers next considered changes in the girls' social relationships. Study along these lines produced positive results. It was found that individual output varied markedly with changes in the sentiments entertained by the workers toward each other, toward their supervisors, and toward the group. The social history of the test room offered an explanation for the seemingly irregular fluctuations found in the graphs.

The seating arrangements of the girls at work were especially significant as indicative of the leadership and friendship structure within the group. The girl in seat No. 1 was of Polish origin, a placid follower and close friend of No. 2, of Italian origin, and the natural leader of the group. Nos. 3 and 4 were both of Polish origin and were good friends, though they had little in common besides their Polish ancestry and their proximity during most of the working time. No. 5, a Norwegian by birth, had little in common with the other girls since she was older, was the only one married, and spoke very broken English.

Analysis of relationships in output of the individuals showed marked similarities after the girls had been working closely for fifteen months. They had developed strong loyalties and common interests.

Three months later, however, a collapse of the integrated structure took place. No. 5 left the employ of the company and was replaced by 5a, selected on the recommendation of 2, a close friend. Although 5a had more in common with the other four girls than with 5, she was unused to the group activity; and this unintegrated new member also caused a breakdown of the mutual influences in production.

Three months later, however, an even higher level of integration— the highest attained in the five-year period of study—had been achieved.

Six months later this high integration had broken down as a result of: (1) a change in seating position (the girls were arranged in a 4, 2, 5, 3, 1 order); (2) the replacement of 5a by the rehired 5. This latter action was strongly opposed by the group, and the dislike was directed to No. 5 herself. She was completely isolated. No. 2, though seated next to 5, seldom spoke to her except to snub her. The extent of 5's isolation is indicated by the fact that whenever a girl of the group had a birthday, the others gave her a present of chocolates, but No. 5 neither gave presents to nor received them from the others after her reappearance in the group.

Three months later, the group showed evidence of reintegration.

Seven months later, the output figures reflected the collapse of the developing structure after the restoration of the original seating arrangement: 1, 2, 3, 4, 5. Also by this time, a real antipathy had developed between No. 2 and No. 5, resulting in a very significant negative correlation—

that is, when one increased her production, output for the other decreased.

Ten months later, in January 1932, at the deepening of the depression when hope had been displaced by resignation, integration was low.

The curves in production were not learning curves because all the workers had had several years' experience in the work before they came into the test room. The plateaus and spurts in output were decidedly suggestive, and analysis showed that:

> It was the organization of human relations, rather than the organization of techniques, which accompanied spurts in these cases. This illustrates the futility of attending exclusively to the economic motivation of workers, or to their physical conditions of work. These things are of high importance; but no group of workers can be expected to remain satisfied, or co-operative, unless their social organization and sentiments are also protected at the working level.[5]

As the experiment progressed, the girls developed common interests and loyalties. The girls took their discipline out of the hands of the supervisor and supervised themselves. For example, when a girl wished to have a half-day's leave she had to obtain permission from the supervisor. The girls themselves developed a custom whereby no girl would ask for such leave unless the group approved the request.

In general, the output of individual workers was directly related to their sentiments toward each other. The feelings of *approval, antagonism*, and *indifference* toward each other influenced their individual variations in output. One of Whitehead's final generalizations was the following:

> Perhaps the main conclusion to be chosen from this type of analysis is the vital importance of human relationship as a factor in the motivation of an industrial group, and in its ultimate stability. The logical motive in economic activity is financial; and endless ingenuity has been expended in devising schemes of payment, designed to secure a maximum of employee satisfaction and efficiency. But, in the last analysis, buying power is largely a means for satisfying social sentiments; and money incentives will never secure a full measure of activity and contentment until firms are organized with greater regard for the social stability of their own working groups, *at the working level*.[6]

---

[5]Whitehead, "Social Relationships in a Factory," *loc. cit.*

[6]*Ibid*. The author's summary of this outstanding experiment in worker efficiency has of necessity omitted many important aspects. The reader may want to read the more complete reports listed in Roethlisberger and Dickson, *Management and the Worker.*

Bank-wiring room: fifteen male workers

Another experiment conducted in the Western Electric Company involved fifteen young men who did wiring, soldering, and inspecting of electrical apparatus. This study added several important findings to those obtained in the experiment with the women workers.

Nine wiremen were organized in three groups of three men. Each group of three wiremen had one solderman. Two inspectors judged the work of these twelve men, and one supervisor was in charge of the fourteen employees. All fifteen men worked together in a room separated from the other workers of the plant. Within the group, the supervisor had the highest official status, the inspectors ranked second, the nine wiremen third, and the three soldermen lowest. However, a more elaborate social organization soon developed. The group split into two cliques. These cliques were not divided according to social status levels but cut across one of the wiring groups and across the various occupations. Each clique or subgroup had its own leader. The members of one subgroup considered themselves superior to the members of the other clique. Each member's status within his subgroup was important to him, and he would not jeopardize his status by conduct unacceptable to the other members. Interpersonal relations such as playing games, trading jobs, eating lunch with others, quarrels about opening and closing windows, and horseplay were carried on mainly with the members of the same subgroup.

The custom that developed within the group related to the organization and performance of the work. Output and performance of the work were controlled through the customs that the men, rather than management, developed.

The men decided on certain levels of output from each individual. These levels were maintained through forced breakdowns, interruptions, and other behavior that wasted time. If any worker indicated that he was exceeding his allowance of work, he was "disciplined" by the others. If a man turned out too much work, he was called a "rate-buster." If he turned out too little, a "chiseler." If he told a supervisor anything that would harm an associate, a "squealer." In addition to sarcasm and ridicule as a means of control, they also applied "binging," a hard blow on the muscles of the upper arm. The supervisor, too, was more or less forced to accede to the workers' control.

The wage incentive system did not function as management had planned. Output was controlled by the workers. Their control was exercised for the purpose of protecting the group from managerial interference. They jealously guarded what they believed to be their rights and privileges as workers. In a sense, the workers were protecting themselves not only against economic injustice but also against social ignorance on the part of management.

One important lesson revealed by the experiment with the fifteen men is that the administrator should appear to the workers as one who is guarding and developing *their* ways of life and the emotional character of *their* group, rather than representing only the economic policies and wishes of the management. The men resisted outside threats to the integrity of *their* group.

The contrasting results in production during the experiments with the two groups of workers of the same company, the five girls versus the fifteen men, cannot be attributed to a sex difference but rather to the fact that in the girls' group, ways and sentiments were integrated to a much greater extent with the economic purposes of the management. The girls' perceptions of their work situation differed from those of the men.

The reports of these experiments caused later investigators to pay more attention to the attitudes of workers, to the role of the subgroups within the work group, and to the social organizations within the work situations. The experiments showed that the strength of the work group can be greater than the rules and disciplines established by management. The group often operated quickly and effectively to protect itself from violations within the group as well as from the outside.

When reports of these researchers were published, managements' thinking about methods of improving industrial production gradually changed. Changes in productivity were no longer assumed to be solely an effect of changes in pay, hours of work, illumination, or physical fatigue. Human relations between worker and worker as well as between manager and worker became recognized as important factors in output. The findings suggest that an executive not only should promote the efficiency of his employees but also should guard and develop their social sentiments toward each other.[7]

Obviously, incisive perception was one of the basic factors in these researches. Accurate and unbiased perception is always so important in all human relations observations that the highly descriptive adjective, "perceptive," has come into great favor when applied to the reactions of individuals in their human relations. When we wish to compliment a person in this respect, we say "He is a very perceptive man."

Effectiveness in human relations in industry requires keen perceptiveness on the part of the supervisory executive, but that ability in itself is not sufficient—it must be supplemented with creative thinking. Alert management must discover ways to improve relations with the employees. The creative thinking done after the research reports have been analyzed determines the extent of the improved productivity. Creative managements have made many improvements in productivity of employees and, at the same time, improved relations with employees. One of the newer approaches that has proven mutually beneficial in some plants is "job enlargement."

[7]See Whitehead, "Social Relationships in a Factory."

JOB ENLARGEMENT—JOB ENRICHMENT

The term *job enlargement* is gradually being replaced by the term *job enrichment*. The two terms in many cases are used interchangeably, but the distinction often made is that job enlargement involves adding to a job horizontally. Tasks are added to a task already being performed. The newer concept, job enrichment, loads the job vertically, primarily by giving the worker more authority and discretionary power. Generally, a larger job content accompanies the granting of more power.

Managers recognize today that job enrichment is one possible method of increasing the job satisfaction and fulfillment of the psychological needs of employees. Not all workers will accept or be happy with job enrichment. The perceptive manager must have a practical understanding of how people differ in abilities, experiential backgrounds, needs, and goals. Individuals change and grow at different rates. The feasibility of a job enrichment program assumes that many or most people have work goals and gain satisfaction in working toward an understood and accepted goal. The employee must perceive the goal as realistic and practical. This newer concept of management eschews the old "carrot-and-stick" negative motivation for the employee for one where he no longer waits for the supervisor's orders but takes responsibility for his own production.

One successful implementation of these tenets has taken place at the Advanced Dynamics Center of the Northern Electric Company, a subsidiary of the Bell Telephone Company of Canada. The center is structured to emphasize team effort—membership in a team rather than employment—with a major consideration being creative work output rated more important than hours on the job. Managers guide and assist instead of order. Members constitute a process team with a process leader (foreman). Each individual has a chance, within limits and interests, to participate in every decision affecting him. Weekly meetings at which each team is represented are held to discuss grievances, set production goals, resolve problems, and check progress toward goals. The meeting is chaired by a discussion leader instead of a supervisor or manager.

Key personnel men have titles to recognize systems values and eliminate departmental barriers; examples are resources environment manager, chairman of systems operating council (general manager), manufacturing resources manager (production manager), human resources manager (personnel manager) and accounting resources manager (financial controller). Office doors are ordinarily open to welcome a member to talk it over. The almost universal parking problem is solved by first come, first served.

Experiments in job enrichment by Dr. Robert N. Ford of the Bell Telephone System were so successful that the project was extended throughout the American Telephone and Telegraph Company. He inaugurated a job enrichment program called the "work itself", a term that has become part of the job enrichment lexicon. In the first trial at making the "work itself" important, supervisors in the treasury department were asked to change the jobs of 120 girls by asking the girls, 70 percent of whom were college educated, to do the research needed and to compose, as well as sign, their own letters to stockholders without having their letters checked by supervisors. Turnover of personnel in the group dropped 27 percent, and 24 girls did the work that 36 had done previously. Savings were estimated at $448,000 over a period of eighteen months. Eventually, similar trials were made with more than 1,000 employees of AT&T Co.[8]

Expansion of the program throughout the corporation was not by command. The personnel director of manpower utilization explained the program in sessions of supervisors. In the beginning, a group would volunteer to experiment. Managers who wanted to "wait and see" would serve as a control group. Eventually, no one chose to be in a control group.[9]

Job enrichment experiments at American Telephone and Telegraph Company are also proving that the old craftsman concept is not dead. One of these experiments, initiated at the Northeastern Area plants of the Long Lines Department, is resulting in reduced errors, absence, and overtime work.

The framemen at the plant were previously split into two groups, testing and doing cross-connection work performance. Under the old system, the cross-connection employees were performing isolated functions without the satisfaction of seeing the job through to the completion and testing of the telephone hookup. Supervisors spent too much time assigning and coordinating work with the various crews and consequently had less time for planning.

Now, the two groups are combined in work teams of two or three men who handle both the work and the testing. Supervisors have more time for planning and methods improvement since team leaders make many of the procedural decisions.

According to Robert N. Ford, AT&T's personnel director—manpower utilization, "We are not implying that we should stop automating jobs. We must automate as much as possible, especially if we can go all the way and get rid of boring jobs. If unavoidable vestiges remain, however, we should strive to attach them to larger tasks where motivational rewards remain.[10]

The results of the well-known experience of the Maytag Company in

[8]See Robert N. Ford, *Motivation through Work Itself* (New York: American Management Association, Inc., 1969).

[9]Ralph M. Barnes, *Motion and Time Study: Design and Measurement of Work*, 6th ed. (New York: John Wiley & Sons, Inc., 1968), p. 678.

[10]*The Manager's Letter*, American Management Association, Inc., November 18, 1968, p. 4.

twenty-five job enlargement projects over a six-year period have been summarized as follows:[11]

1. Quality has improved.
2. Labor costs are lower.
3. A large majority of operators came to prefer job enlargement in a relatively short time.
4. Problems inherent in paced groups have been largely eliminated. For example, realignment of each operator's job content is no longer necessary whenever production levels change, resulting in less training, higher productivity, fewer changes in production standards, reduction in grievances, etc.
5. Equipment and installation costs have been recovered by tangible savings in an average of about two years.
6. Space requirements for enlarged jobs of the type described here are comparable to that required for powered conveyor-line assembly.

In job enrichment tasks are increased in number and variety, the individual sets his own pace, determines his own working method, and is responsible for quality control. Fewer rejects and other production cost savings can be expected in addition to increased employee motivation, morale, and job satisfaction. An especially important result of job enrichment has been an increasing emphasis by foremen and workers alike on training. Furthermore, employees who have learned to work under this policy are not fearful that they will produce so much that they will work themselves out of a job. They develop the kind of pride in craftsmanship that is found among skilled workers who feel secure in industry.

If you work in or study production

Presumably you will continue to study and work in some business field. Even though your major interest is not in production, you should be alert to note evidences of better understanding of the people in production. Enlightened leadership will be evident in factors such as improved wage payment plans, skilled supervision, and job enrichment. These better relations with production people will have impact for the members of management and the public.

Most employees and union officials seem to agree that the responsibility for the development, maintenance, and administration of a human

[11]See David M. Francis, "Business," *Christian Science Monitor* (Boston). Seven articles on job enrichment beginning April 23, 1968.

relations program should rest with the company. This means that the young people who plan to enter or attain leadership in business must become acquainted with and skilled in the use of techniques that elicit the full cooperation of the employees who produce products and services.

Industry will continue its drive for technological improvements that reduce requirements for high-effort work and manpower. The coming of the new technology with its growth of automation will affect almost every production worker. It will require him to do a complete job or larger segment of the job. He will have to learn how to maintain and control machines that do the repetitive routine work for him. This means that he will need especially good instruction and supervision to perform effectively under job enrichment and related programs. Scientific and skilled managements will be more essential than in the past. This emerging kind of business leadership will have to come from the students who are now in college or from the alert young men in business.

QUESTIONS ON THE CHAPTER

1. The author uses the term *emphases* for pointing up the significance of findings from the social science studies reported in the Part II chapters. Why?

2. Discuss briefly the aim, design, and results of the famous Hawthorne study. What benefits did the study contribute to our beliefs about important factors in worker productivity?

3. Explain the main findings from the wage incentive system among the wiremen in the Western Electric Company study. To what factors did the researchers attribute the differences found in the experiments with the men versus the women?

4. Summarize the main generalizations of the Hawthorne study.

5. Objective perception is essential for effective human relations in industry but that alone is not sufficient. What must be added? Give an example.

6. What benefits were obtained from the job enrichment plans by AT&T and by Maytag?

7. To what type of plant operation do you think the application of job enrichment might be advisable? Not advisable?

8. Of all the ideas presented in this chapter, which ones are of special interest to you in regard to their probable influence on your behavior in business?

9. What do you think the chapter contributes to your future relations with (a) the men who supervise your work, (b) the employees whom you may supervise?

PROBLEMS AND PROJECTS

For All Students

1. Conduct a friendly interview with a factory worker or employee who does semiskilled or skilled work. Establish rapport. Have him discuss the pay rates and the extent to which workers restrict production.

2. Conduct a similar interview with some employees of an office, bank, or store. How do their attitudes toward management, the work, and their fellow workers differ from those found among factory workers whom you know?

For Advanced Students

3. Make a systematic study of business journals that publish articles on human relations aspects of production. What are the subjects treated, the emphases, and the writing styles?

4. List organizations and sources of information, other than journals, that deal with human relations in production. Examples are the American Management Association and the Federal Small Business Administration in Washington.

For Men in Business

5. One of the major purposes of this chapter is to emphasize the differences in the perceptions of workers and members of management. Think of some of the supervisors under whom you have worked: how did their perceptions of you and your fellow workers differ from those of the supervisors?

6. Apply the idea of job enrichment to the production practices where you now work or have worked. To what extent would it be feasible? Do some of the supervisors where you work now practice job enlargement? How?

COLLATERAL READINGS

For All Students

Davis, Louis E., "The Design of Jobs," *Industrial Relations*, October 1966. This analysis reviews several job enrichment projects and makes an excellent case for reconsideration by the industrial engineer of the human element in his job designs.

Herzberg, Frederick, "One More Time: How Do You Motivate Employees?" *Harvard Business Review*, January—February, 1968. This is one of the clearest descriptions of the theoretical principles that underlie much of the current work in job enrichment. It is a helpful introduction to these concepts.

For Advanced Students

Landsberger, Henry A., *Hawthorne Revisited*. Ithaca, N.Y.: New York State School of Industrial and Labor Relations, Cornell University, 1958. Presents a description of the methods and principal results of the Western Electric studies.

Mayo, Elton, *The Human Problems of an Industrial Civilization* and *The Social Problems of an Industrial Civilization*. Boston: Division of Research, Graduate School of Business Administration, Harvard University, 1946 and 1945. Two classics that are as enjoyable and significant today as when they were written.

For Men in Business

Foulkes, Fred, *Creation of More Meaningful Work*. New York: American Management Association, Inc., 1969. This work presents case studies of six company experiences with job enrichment.

Lesieur, Frederick G., *The Scanlon Plan*. New York: The Technology Press and John Wiley & Sons, Inc., 1959. A collection of articles that evaluate and explain an unusual program for encouraging production workers and giving them participation. Available in a later printing, New York: The Viking Press, 1960.

Enhancing Participation
by Employees

SITUATIONS YOU ARE LIKELY TO MEET

How would you meet each of these situations:
   a. *Before* you have read the chapter? What would
      you say to yourself or to the individual?
   b. *After* you have read the chapter? How have
      your answers changed?

1. You are conducting a supervisory training group of
   foremen. Two of the foremen take opposing points of
   view on the effectiveness of participative versus authoritarian supervision. The believer in the participative methods says that he will be willing to have the
   employees of each department elect their foreman.
   The authoritarian foreman argues that it will not
   work and uses an analogy from the field of professional athletics. He quotes from a newspaper col-
   umnist in regard to what happens when the owner
   of a professional team lets the men elect their own
   coach and tell the coach what to do: "He is worse
   than a bad businessman. He is simply walking around
   with a deep-seated death wish. It simply doesn't
   work."
2. Assume that you are a senior in college and that one
   of your friends says that the next time he applies for
   a job, he will look for a company where the boss is
   boss. He prefers to deal with an executive who tells
   him what to do and how to do it. Period. Another
   friend says that he prefers to deal with an executive
   who wants the ideas of all employees involved in the

work to be done and he asks for them. Each of these two friends invites you to go with him when the next company recruiter comes to interview applicants. Which of the two friends would you join? Why?

3. You meet an executive who tells you that his management tried to get suggestions from employees by means of suggestion boxes, but so few employees turned in suggestions that the boxes were removed. He also says: "We found that employees only want more pay for less work—they really do not want to participate in helping to solve the company's problems or to become involved in doing anything other than what is required by the job."

In the past, managements usually assumed that employee morale could be achieved by having the company do kindnesses *for the employees* or by solving their problems for them. Many executives did not realize that morale is highest when employees also do things *for the company.*

When employees feel that they are not worthy participants in the action, they are less satisfied and become more demanding of satisfactions not closely related to the work. They demand more fringe benefits, bigger swimming pools, longer vacations, fancier rest rooms, earlier retirement, and other privileges of secondary importance. Conversely, when they feel that they are participating as colleagues with management in overcoming the problems of the company and in attaining management's objectives, the fringe benefits and other secondary privileges become less important.

When managements began to see relationships between greater involvement and decreased demands, they began to admit to themselves that waste in human resources in industry stems not so much from employees' unwillingness as from management's ineptness. As a result, progressive executives developed new attitudes and procedures toward enabling employees to feel that they are respected participants in attaining management's goals.

Executives learned that employees do not want to decide the big problems of the business or run the company, but they want to feel that management thinks of them as worthy participants.

Psychologically, employees would like to feel that they are colleagues with management in achieving the objectives of the company. *Colleagueship* expresses a warmer, closer relationship between management and men than the usual term, *participation*. However, participation is the more widely used word, and we shall use it here because it is more commonly used in the literature. Also, in many companies managements think that they grant employees the privilege of sharing in the action. Eventually, more executives will feel that employees are constituent members with members of management in attaining the organization's objectives.

Participation may be defined as a management practice that encourages employees to have mental and emotional involvement in their work situations. It is sought by pursuing the practice of enabling the employee to share responsibility for choosing goals (solutions to business problems) and contributing to their attainment. The term usually applies to the members of the organization below the managerial levels.

The idea of participation has developed in America as a phase of our cultural emphasis on the use of democratic rather than authoritarian principles. Legally, we believe that all men are equal before the law. We believe in respect for the individual regardless of his social or economic status. We assume that his ideas as well as those of his supervisory superiors should be given consideration. We believe in the right of appeal in regard to any important treatment that involves justice. Our managements as well as our courts are, to some extent, controlled by the belief in the right of the individual to participate in attaining decisions, plans, and actions.

In former generations, executives, particularly owners of businesses followed the practice of choosing business goals and determining plans without very much regard for the wishes of the employees. Employees were expected to do as they were told. This kind of authoritarian philosophy does not fit our contemporary culture very well. We now are in a process of social evolution in employee relations, and we shall therefore evaluate some of the newer participative procedures, their benefits, and their limitations.

Many employees of today have a level of ability that in an earlier time would have enabled them to become owners. Self-employment is not impossible today, but conditions have changed so that a larger proportion of members of our population are employees rather than owners. This shift in outlets for men of ability has intensified the pressure for the use of democratic processes in business management. As Lawrence A. Appley, former president of the American Management Association, has well stated:

We talk today about the shift from the autocratic, one-man type of operation to the democratic, consultative type of supervision. What we are talking about is the person who exercises judgment versus the person who gets others to exercise judgment. We talk about centralization versus decentralization. What we are referring to is having all the decisions made in one place versus having them made at many places by people in much better positions to make them.[1]

Managements have learned that the effective supervisor tries to organize his work and relations with workers so that they will perform their jobs as productively as possible by contributing their know-how and ideas as well as those of the supervisor. An effective supervisor cannot hope to tell each employee exactly what to do, when, and how. The employee must be encouraged to contribute the special knowledge and judgment that he possesses as the one person who performs the task. Every employee has some knowledge or skill that he can contribute to do the job more quickly, more easily, or with less cost and effort than the boss.

Anyone who becomes acquainted with employees' after-hours activities will discover that some carry on do-it-yourself hobbies or other recreational projects that require imagination and high intelligence. The supervisor of such an employee wonders why he does not demonstrate the same level of ingenuity on the job. In most cases, the answer is that the supervisor has failed to give the employee a sense of real participation in the job.

Pseudo-participation

As in many techniques that involve a social evolution, the philosophy of participation is, at times, practiced in a nongenuine manner. A few management men imagine that they practice participation with employees when they are merely putting on an act. When, for example, a meeting is held by such men, it is held in a manner that indicates that management has already made the decision. If the employees vote in a contrary manner, this type of management man uses persuasion to bring about a vote in line with the previously made decision. Sometimes management just disregards the opinion of the majority, does as it had planned, and gives no explanations. Naturally, workers are not fooled by a pseudoparticipative procedure. They are just as smart as this kind of management.

Participative techniques are more difficult to put into effect than many people realize. When a typical executive of today finds that some important improvement must be made, he has an intellectual recognition of the need for participation on the part of the employees involved in bringing about the desired change. He usually invites the department heads and key

[1]Lawrence A. Appley, "It's More Difficult," *Management News*, American Management Association, Inc., February 1959.

employees to a meeting where he explains the need for the desired improvement, asks for their suggestions for bringing about the change, and gets each to commit himself as to the actions he will take. Later, he presses the department heads and reminds them of their commitments. He keeps the heat on. Progress meetings are held. Between meetings, the pressure is maintained by means of office memos in order that assurances given will be kept.

In spite of all the pressure and effort, the results obtained are seldom completely satisfying to the manager. Frictions develop. Anxieties are accentuated. Wasted efforts are evident. All these and other disappointments occur in spite of the management man's assumption that he practiced participative procedures with his subordinates.

Modern managements are under constant pressure for the development of procedures that are better than their conventional ones because they frequently hear expressions that indicate the need for participation. Examples are:

"I don't like changes which I don't understand and that's why I'm not going along with this one."

"Some of the fellows say there is a gimmick in it. We'll have to work harder and then the brass will eliminate a lot of the jobs."

"These changes you want to make were dreamt up by a bunch of whiz kids in engineering. Our foreman doesn't even know what it's all about."

The effective practice of participation involves more than holding meetings or tacking up some suggestion boxes, good as they may be. It requires a basic theme of thinking. It becomes a kind of operating philosophy. The management men who have not as yet learned this theme require courage to depart from traditional procedures to search for newer better managerial practices. Skill and imagination are needed to draw from employees on routine jobs their best suggestions and their assistance in making a profit for the company. Managements usually find it difficult, at first, to give employees a genuine sense of participation. Of course, to be genuine, "participation" must be consistent with what is feasible and sensible. Workers should not be asked to "decide" questions that are beyond their experience or interest unless the decision and the putting into effect of the decision is part of their work.

Comparative studies in participative leadership

The most frequently quoted experiment in this field is one conducted at the Harwood Manufacturing Company, Marion, Virginia, under the direction of Alfred J. Marrow, former president. The experiment concerned work groups in a clothing factory.

One of the big problems faced by the company (it manufactured ladies' undergarments and pajamas) was the reluctance of employees to adapt themselves to new methods in production. Changes in style constantly plague the ladies' garment industry. This means frequent overhauling of the production process. Workers have to relearn their operations and this "relearning" is costly. A girl operator may take three to six months to reach a level of output that will net a profit on the product. Marrow noted that even the most experienced operators often took longer to learn a new stitch or fold than the newcomers. Accordingly he hired social scientists to aid in tackling the problems: (1) why do workers resist change and (2) how to get the employees to relearn faster.

A real-life action experiment was designed to study the problems. Three experimental groups and one control group of transfer employees were set up.

1. The *control group* went through the usual factory routine. The production department modified the job, and a new piece rate was set. A group meeting was then held in which the control group was told that the change was necessary because of competitive conditions, and that a new piece rate had been set. This rate was thoroughly explained by the time-study man, questions were answered, and the meeting dismissed.

2. In *Experimental Group 1*, the change was made differently. Before any changes took place, a group meeting was held with all the operators. The need for the change was presented as dramatically as possible. The employees were shown two identical garments. One sold for 100 percent more than the other. The group was asked to identify the cheaper garment. It couldn't. This made the group aware of the problem of cost reduction. Management then asked for suggestions on how these economies could be made. The management then presented a plan to set the new job and piece rate. This plan was essentially the same as the usual one except for one important modification—a few representatives of the group were elected to help the management to work out the new method and the new rate. These few participated not only in developing the new pay rate and the new method but also in training their co-workers in the new method.

3. *Experimental Groups 2* and *3* went through much the same kind of change meetings. However, since the groups were smaller, all operators were chosen as "special" operators; that is, they were all to participate directly in the designing of the new jobs, were all

to be studied by the time-study man. These employees made so many suggestions in the meetings that the stenographer had difficulty in recording them.[2]

The figure below shows what happened.

The results of the experiment were fairly clear. The control group dropped in production immediately upon change, and by the end of the experiment showed no appreciable amount of recovery. Resistance developed almost immediately. There were marked instances of aggression against management, deliberate restriction of production, lack of cooperation with the supervisor. Nine per cent quit during the first 15 days after the change. Grievances were filed about the piece-rate which, upon checking, was found to be even a little "loose."

The recoveries for Groups 2 and 3 were dramatic. Both groups recovered to their pre-change level of production the second day after change, and by the end of the experiment they had actually surpassed their pre-change level by about 14 percent. They worked cooperatively with their supervisors, there was no indication of aggression, and there were no quits during the 15-day period.

Group 1 required more time to recover (possibly because of an unavoidable operational problem), but reached the pre-change level by the 14th day after change, and by the end of the experiment had exceeded its pre-change level. Here, too, no quits were recorded. One act of aggression was observed which was neither prolonged nor serious. . . .

The success of the experiment seemed to be attributable largely to the fact that experimental transfers were given the opportunity to participate in planning the change, in planning their own work future. Thus, where such external motivating forces as monetary rewards, management pressure, and other means had failed, group involvement and decision developed internalized motivation for the accomplishment of a goal mutually desirable to management and worker.[3]

Later, Harwood purchased a clothing company whose management style was authoritarian and which was operating at a loss. Technical com-

[2]See Stanley E. Seashore, "Administrative Leadership and Leadership and Organizational Effectiveness," in Rensis Likert and Samuel P. Hayes, Jr., eds., *Some Applications of Behavioural Research* (New York, Paris: UNESCO, 1957), Chap. 2, pp. 51, 52. For complete and exact wording of this material, see L. Coch and J. R. P. French, Jr., "Overcoming Resistance to Change," *Human Relations*, 1948, pp. 512–32.

[3]Alfred J. Marrow, "Human Factors in Production," *Personnel*, American Management Association, Inc., March 1949, pp. 343–44.

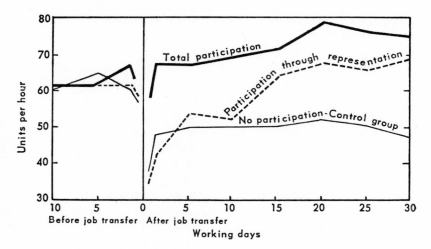

Employee participation in decisions about a job change eliminated the usual drop in productivity.

L. Coch and J. R. P. French, Jr., "Overcoming Resistance to Change," *Human Relations* (1948). This chart was adapted for *Some Applications of Behavioral Research,* edited by Rensis Likert and Samuel P. Hayes, Jr. (UNESCO, 1957), p. 53.

petence was present in the second company, but little attention had been given to the human organization and infrastructure. Behavioral scientists and the Survey Research Center of the University of Michigan's Institute for Social Research were contacted to work with Harwood personnel to install a new management system which would be participative. Recognition was given to the importance of modern general systems theory whereby managers, engineers, finance personnel, and others worked with the behavioral scientists to implement change. Recognition of the sociotechnical system demonstrated the interdependence of a system's parts—one part cannot be changed without affecting the others. A new adaptation must take place.

The company was profitable within two years. Turnover of new employees had been 90 percent but was reduced to about 50 percent within four months. Absences of production workers, which had run as high as 12 percent, were cut to 3 percent, the same rate as at the main Harwood plant —a rate considered normal.

The study indicated that positive changes cannot be expected immediately. Attitudes and work patterns established over a long period of time change slowly. Also, sudden and fast introduction of change without first bringing about employees' understanding and acceptance can lead to a personnel problem such as excessive labor turnover. In a Puerto Rican Harwood plant a sharp upturn in turnover took place when employees were asked to participate in problem-solving meetings. The workers thought that management was incapable! Cultural patterns of Puerto Ricans were different from those of employees in other Harwood plants, and the interpretations of participative techniques differed markedly with certain patterns. Self-management is created when the employee participates in decision making and in problem solving to the extent that he assumes responsibility for success.[4]

Several investigations show that many workers feel deprived of an opportunity to apply their skill and knowledge in full measure to their jobs. A series of interviews conducted by the Survey Research Center of the University of Michigan among nearly six hundred employees in a typical company revealed that over 75 percent of them wanted more opportunity to help decide things. Of the remaining 25 percent, half were already making decisions and felt they had responsibility enough; only 11 percent, all told, made no decisions at all and were content not to do so.

The findings by Harwood and others are substantiated by a whole series of studies made by the Institute for Social Research, University of Michigan, as found in a systematic investigation about participation in one company:

1. In work groups where morale was highest, a high percentage of employees felt that the company took considerable interest in their ideas and suggestions. Very few in low-morale groups felt this way.
2. In high-morale groups, most employees felt that group discussions with their supervisors were worth while. Not so in low-morale groups.
3. Both supervisors and employees felt that group meetings resulted in increased job interest and the group's working together more as a team.
4. Supervisors who held meetings with employees which employees felt were worth while in general looked on their supervisor as being good at handling people. If the supervisors held meetings, but employees didn't think them worth while, they generally felt their supervisor wasn't good at handling people.
5. In work groups having low absence rates, employees felt relatively free to discuss job and personal problems with their supervisor. In low-absence groups, the employees thought their work group had high group pride and good team spirit.
6. Supervisors who are given quite a good deal of "say" in spending

[4]See Alfred J. Marrow, David G. Bowers, and Stanley E. Seashore, *Management by Participation* (New York: Harper & Row, Publishers, 1967), p. 70.

money budgeted to them are more cost-conscious than those who don't have much "say."

7. Supervisors who were appraised by their supervisors as doing a good job, and who were considered best qualified for promotion, met frequently with their employees and, in turn, participated frequently in decisions with their superiors.[5]

These findings are similar to those obtained in other studies on the nature and value of participation.

Involvement rather than facts convinces people

When John R. P. French, Jr., psychologist, was director of research for the Harwood Manufacturing Company, he wanted to convince staff members that women over thirty possess the kind of skill required in this factory. At a number of staff meetings he cited scientific proof. The staff listened attentively, but its attitude remained unaffected. More talks and more evidence were supplied, but this bias against employing women over thirty withstood every assault of reason and logic.

French finally recognized that offering more data would contribute little to changing this attitude and that it was necessary for the members of the staff to unlearn their mistaken beliefs.

Accordingly, the psychologist set up a plan that would involve the top staff members in a research project on their own. The project suggested was that if older workers were inefficient, it would be advisable to determine how much money the company was losing by continuing the employment of older women already in the plant.

The staff members analyzed the production records very carefully. Gradually, they discovered that older women not only equaled but surpassed younger women in work performance. The data also showed that the older workers learned new skills more rapidly. Comparisons of absenteeism and turnover data were in favor of the older workers.

When the staff members were faced with a conflict between prejudice and facts analyzed by themselves, they trusted the facts they themselves had developed.[6] This illustrates the old principle that the typical employee has most confidence in verdicts when he himself exercises his judgment. He believes that he knows how he arrives at his opinion; he does not know how the other person, even though he is an expert, arrives at his opinion. This reaction on the part of employees is especially evident in organizations that

[5]Rensis Likert, "Motivation: The Core of Management," *Personnel Series*, No. 155, American Management Association, Inc., 1953, p. 37.

[6]See Alfred J. Marrow, *Making Management Human* (New York: McGraw-Hill Book Company, 1957), pp. 92, 93.

It is easy to say "Everyone who works in a company is a worthy participant," but can the statement be implemented so that it contributes to the company's success?

Some companies are doing it very effectively, as demonstrated by the Ex-Cell-O Corporation, Detroit, Michigan. Called "Operation Customer," the program teaches the worker that in some respects his real boss is the customer. The sources of the convincing instruction are the sales and service reports, customer correspondence, and a committee in each department. Letters and other items are posted on a bulletin board. Then a flashing yellow light, labeled "Customer Grievances," along with a red lens reading "Orders Lost," signals the bad news to the employees. There is also a green light labeled "Orders Received." Employees hustle to read both the bad and the good news.

In this way every employee from janitor to president is placed across the desk from individual customers where he can learn what is required of his company if it is to prosper and provide job security.

The program also enhances the company's reputation as a company that is customer-oriented. Customers realize that every employee develops a personal commitment to meet the demands of the marketplace.

Operation Customer is not purely a "shop oriented" program. Here, sales and office personnel stop to read about orders lost, customer grievances, and orders received during a two-week period.

"Operation Customer" is a copyrighted program developed by Ex-Cell-O Corporation, P. O. Box 386, Detroit, Michigan 48232. Full permission to use all aspects of the program without charge is granted on request. Descriptive literature that includes a step-by-step list of the seven fundamentals for executing the program is available.

are highly computerized. In such companies, one is likely to hear an employee say: "This decision posted by management is probably correct. At least, the computer says it is. But I didn't have any part in reaching the decision. So, even though it may be right, I'm not happy about it."

The effects of nonparticipation also appear in the reactions to a kindhearted employer's good intentions. It is most evident when the benign management decides to do something "nice" for the employees. Management may, for example, decide to pipe music into the office, cafeteria, or shop. To management's surprise the main reaction from the employees is one of faultfinding. They do not like the programs, the hours the music is played, or some other aspect. Why should they? They were not consulted. They were simply informed that a broadcast system was being installed and that music would be played at certain intervals throughout the workday.

When management has an employee relations problem such as having too many employees of the plant washing up too soon, the responsible executive often calls a meeting and "lays down the law." Everyone present immediately becomes defensive. Some feel that they have been unfairly accused. Without true participation, they merely carry out a new regulation for a short time. If they have no real involvement in selecting the plan, they do not feel responsible for its implementation. If, on the other hand, the executive does not state a criticism but simply describes the problem and asks for solutions, he is likely to get cooperation. Some of the employees will develop corrective plans and will feel responsible for putting them into effect. They will also encourage the rebels to follow the practice of the majority.

Multiple management

McCormick and Company, the famous spice house of Baltimore, has been using a multiple management plan which enables employees of all levels to participate in decision-making roles. The plan has been in operation since 1932 when "junior boards" discussed the company's problems and passed their ideas to the actual corporate, or senior, board. A major purpose is to have employees interested in the company and to have them understand that their best economic interests and the company's are the same. An important benefit of the plan is its training for increased responsibility.

Each major division of the company has its own board of management employees. The recommendations of the various miniboards are coordinated so that a constant flow of proposals reaches top management. In the course of one five-year period, 2,109 proposals were sent up to top management and all but 6 of the proposals were adopted.[7]

[7]See "Miniboards Give Spice Maker Zest," *Business Week*, May 10, 1969, p. 174.

The program of Texas Instruments Incorporated

The Texas Instruments program evolved over a period of several years. The manager of corporate personnel administration has described the program, in part, as follows:

> Employee dissatisfaction on the job may derive from either poor maintenance or poor motivation factors, but the outward manifestations of the dissatisfaction may be very similar—negativism, complaints, deterioration of performance, and so forth. But the improvement of the lighting or cafeteria or level of pay won't do much good if the origin of the dissatisfaction is in the absence of a meaningful assignment. By the same token, if an employee is dissatisfied with what he thinks is inequitable pay, the introduction of additional challenge in his work may only make matters worse.
>
> This point seems almost too obvious to mention, but it seems to be frequently missed. One of the reasons is that sometimes poor motivational conditions result in faultfinding behavior. It is easy for an employee to express frustrations in complaints about pay, benefits, lunch rooms, and the like, but most people can't readily articulate resentment in terms of abstract concepts such as personal growth, responsibility, and achievement.

Seminars in motivation were organized for managers at all levels. Purposes were to enable supervisors to decrease employee dissatisfaction and to maximize employee motivation. Eventually, more than two thousand supervisors at all levels took training in motivating employees. Small peer groups of five to ten participants met in six two-hour sessions over a period of several weeks.

Significant factors in employee morale and motivation were listed and classified into categories of logical relationships. Surveys of employee attitudes and reactions were made at regular intervals. Each of the sixty-two departments of the plant were given comprehensive reports of category results. Project teams were then organized in each department to identify trouble spots and plan corrective actions. Overall survey results, plus actions taken and planned, are fed back to all employees on a continuing basis.

A basic conclusion of the author of the TI plan was stated as follows: "The prevalent problem in industry today is not a lack of individual employee motivation, but a failure of management to comprehend its nature and to use compatible management techniques."[8]

[8]Warren J. Bowles, "The Management of Motivation: A Company-wide Program," *Personnel Magazine*, July/August, 1966. Copyright by the American Management Association, Inc., 135 West 50th St., New York, N. Y. 10020.

Limitations of the participative approach

We must not assume, however, that all studies of leadership demonstrate the superiority of participative over authoritarian techniques. The literature on the subject shows that the benefits of participative leadership did not always take place as expected.

In one study, for example, the company faced a competitive situation which, in the judgment of its top officials, required it to undertake a program of substantial cost reduction. Inasmuch as the management was encouraging the use of participative methods in meeting its problems, it was decided to employ these methods to reduce costs. The management held a series of committee meetings, extending over a period of months. Managerial and supervisory staff members attended. At these meetings, the conditions that made cost reduction imperative were explained, current costs were analyzed, and many suggestions for reducing costs were discussed. As a result, some improvement in cost reduction was made, but not as much as was anticipated nor as much as the situation required.

The situation was overcome, however, by an official who used the older, more authoritarian, methods. He conducted committee meetings, forcefully explained the need for cost reduction, and gave personal and specific instructions to individuals on how and where they should cut costs.

The supervisory and managerial staff members were put under pressure. His methods achieved the desired purpose but they also aroused much antagonism, anxiety, and resentment. Definite disruptive effects were produced throughout the organization.

This case was discussed by a seminar group of experts who themselves favored the participative approach. They considered the crisis aspect of the situation, the conditions under which participative methods are likely to prove effective, their inherent advantages and their limitations.

They concluded that this company's experience did not demonstrate that authoritarian methods are necessarily more effective than participative methods, even in a crisis, but they agreed that to make participative leadership work, certain principles must be followed:

1. Before an effective group decision or action can be reached, the group must accept the necessity of reaching a decision or taking appropriate action. In addition, there must be group recognition and acceptance of the hard, objective realities which establish the problems to be solved and the limits of freedom of decision by the group. In the case of this company, the requirements of the situation were a cost reduction of a given magnitude to be achieved within a specified time; these had to be met in any solution which could be regarded as acceptable.

2. It is the responsibility of individual leaders to see that the re-

quirements of the situation, including the need for action, are made clear to subordinate groups. It is not inconsistent with participative leadership that objectives and limiting conditions should be set by higher authority.

3. Discussion alone is not enough, although formal meetings and informal discussions are an essential part of the participative leadership process. Discussion is useful only if it leads to agreement, decision and action.

4. Decisions reached by means of participative leadership will not lead to effective action or change unless there is understanding of the goals sought and unless members commit themselves to specified action.

5. The effectiveness of participative leadership practices depends on who is allowed to participate. The process of participation and group decision should ordinarily extend throughout the organization and include all those who will be affected by a decision and whose understanding and help are needed.

6. The responsibility of a group engaged in participative leadership does not end with agreement or decision, but includes deciding upon responsibility for follow-up, review, and appraisal of progress toward the agreed-on goals.

Did the company's programme for cost reduction through participative leadership methods include these essential features? It was not possible during the seminar period and with the information at hand to make an appraisal of this particular company's use of participative leadership practices. However, it appeared to the group that the company's programme, even though conducted with evident sincerity and considerable expenditure of time and energy, may have been deficient in several important respects. . . .

A final—and critical—observation of the seminar participants was that committee meetings were carried down to the foreman level, but not to the workers' level. Yet the co-operation of the workers with whatever programmes were developed to meet the crisis was plainly essential. It was they who would have to take some of the action for reducing costs. They were sure to be affected by many of the cost-reduction measures likely to be adopted—for example, lay-offs and work re-assignment. Their understanding and acceptance of such measures and their active co-operation were certainly important.[9]

[9]Stanley E. Seashore, "Administrative Leadership and Organizational Effectiveness," in Rensis Likert and Samuel P. Hayes, Jr., eds., *Some Applications of Behavioural Research* (Paris and New York: UNESCO, 1957), Chap. 2.

The seminar members agreed that the participative approach has its limitations. It will not accomplish miracles. Considerable skill is required to make it work effectively. In some situations, participative methods are inappropriate.

The extent of employees' readiness to accept and expect participative leadership methods influences its effectiveness. The degree of effectiveness may depend upon the history of the organization. Many organizations are moving gradually toward greater reliance on participation.

Principles and purposes in the use of participation

Participation in regard to problems must be made reciprocal—employees can easily give numerous problems to management. If management merely solves the problem, no participative action takes place. If, on the other hand, management asks for suggested solutions to the problems dumped into management's lap, participation is likely to develop.

Participation varies in degree.

1. It is low when the employee is merely informed about policies that directly affect him.
2. It is increased when information regarding the reasons for action or a policy are added.
3. It increases even more when the employee is invited to make suggestions on handling a problem situation.
4. It becomes dynamic when the employee is involved in the action plan to the extent that he feels responsible for the outcome.

Many problems are beyond the scope of the average worker. He cannot participate in dealing with major financial, managerial problems. Those who are moving too rapidly toward large-scale employee participation may find that their employees are not yet ready to take on the unexpected responsibilities.

Participative methods require greater leadership skills on the part of management than do other more conventional kinds of leadership.

A great many executives simply do not want to bother with a participative procedure. It takes too much time. Other executives are not psychologically capable of sharing problems and accepting recommendations made by subordinates. This was one of the major difficulties found by Robert N. McMurry, senior partner of McMurry, Hamstra and Co., personnel consultants. After he had participated in a study of nearly one thousand top-level and middle-management executives, he concluded that the hard-driving men at the top have had to keep the power in their own hands to rise. These top-level men do not want the system.[10]

Clearly, management men, supervisors, and employees need time and practice to learn these more complex skills and to develop the climate in an organization essential for the effective functioning of participative methods.

The time stages needed in one company have been reported by the president of the company, in part, as follows:

> As our first experiment, we created what we called "forums," in order to develop "communication from the bottom up." These were conducted by top management or staff men, and we talked about company matters. We explained programs, invited comments and questions, and dealt with some controversial shop questions.
>
> However, while we were helping the men and women in the shop, we were putting great *pressure* on the foremen and management.
>
> Our next step was to take a much keener look at the predicament of supervision, of the foremen and staff running the plant. We realized more than we had what a difficult position the foreman is in. His task of trying to bring together in some kind of effective way the interest and needs of the men and women in the shop with the objectives of management is considerable.
>
> We saw for one thing that to install a "participation system" and to insist that people participate—when there may be built-in factors that make participation contrived—can be manipulative, and not even as straightforward as autocratic methods.
>
> When we recognized our bottoms-up effort for what it was, we drew back from the unnatural interference of top management's going directly to the bottom of the organization. Instead, we tried to provide a freer, less controlling situation for supervision. We attempted to put as much of the decision-making, policy-making and actual operation responsibility as we possibly could into the hands of the foremen and staff group. . . .
>
> The positive effects of this were remarkable and richly rewarding. The foremen and staff men changed from passive, dependent, and acquiescent men to men who were effective, self-starting, responsible, and deeply involved. In the course of time, this development among our plant supervisory group became extremely mature. . . .
>
> We decided that a manager should have the prime responsi-

---

[10]See Robert N. McMurry, "Case for Benevolent Autocracy," *Harvard Business Review*, January–February 1958,

bility for the over-all vitality and health of the organization, and should be rewarded accordingly. We felt that the traditionally prime function of motivating, goading, and controlling might become a secondary function, and might conceivably, in a free organization, even disappear. This might then free him to be creative *with* the organization rather than *for* it.

Over a number of years, there gradually developed throughout the management the capacity for group processes based on a sense of informality and open exchange. . . .

The positive results have clearly been to relieve men of a coglike feeling and a sense of dependency. The relevant point to me, is that this is not a system. It is a *process* of direct, living relationships which cannot be synthesized but must be grown.[11]

At its best, the modern management practice of having employees function as participants in the business has purposes more important than those of building up the egos of employees by asking them to express their opinions. The greater purposes are those of enabling them to function psychologically as colleagues. As colleagues, they can discover that they too are responsible members of our evolving socioeconomic order and that they can help improve it through their creative ideas, judgment, and sense of responsibility for their workmanship which only they, because of their close contact with the work, can give the company.

QUESTIONS ON THE CHAPTER

1. Define participation. To whom does the term participation usually apply? How does the term *colleagueship* differ from participation?
2. Why is America a logical place for the idea of participation to develop?
3. Why are suggestion boxes not a fully effective practice of participation?
4. In the Harwood Manufacturing Company study, what explanation is given for the difference in production rates between the control group and the experimental groups?
5. What are some outward manifestations of employee dissatisfaction?
6. What does faultfinding behavior on the part of employees really mean?

[11]James E. Richard, "A President's Experience with Democratic Management," Chicago: Industrial Relations Center, The University of Chicago, 1960. Also see M. Patchen, "Labor-Management Consultation at TVA—Its Impact on Employees," *Administrative Science Quarterly*, Vol. X, 1965, for a brief report on the benefits and factors in the success of a TVA participative program.

7. When employees are not convinced by facts presented to them, what should management do?

8. How do high-morale and low-morale groups differ in their attitudes toward employee-supervisor group discussions?

9. What should an executive do instead of "laying down the law" in a problem situation?

10. How does multiple management, the junior board of executives, type of plan function?

11. Discuss some of the limitations of the participative approach as reported by Stanley E. Seashore and others.

12. What are three principles that should be followed in order to make participative leadership work?

13. Of the ideas presented in the chapter, which ones are of special interest or value to you?

14. What did the chapter contribute to your future relations with (a) the men who supervise your work, (b) the employees whom you may supervise?

PROBLEMS AND PROJECTS

For All Students

1. What differences can you note between the use of participation on the part of students in the classroom and by employees of a business? Should the teacher ask students what they wish to study? Does management ask employees what products they wish to make? What are some of the advantages and disadvantages of having students participate frequently in classroom discussions?

2. Describe the ways in which you intend to use participative procedures in your family life. At what age do you think that children can benefit from participation in making decisions that involve the family? An example might be the decision as to where the family will spend a vacation or the determination of the kind of automobile that is to be purchased.

For Advanced Students

3. Utilize the resources of your library in examining the benefits and limitations of "brainstorming" as a method of encouraging employees to contribute their suggestions for dealing with specific business problems.

4. Utilize the resources of your library to find out which labor unions do and which do not practice participation in regard to union affairs. Which unions appear to be the stronger? Which ones contribute more to the development of the member as a person in industry?

For Men in Business

5. One important factor in the effectiveness of participation by employees is their readiness to accept participative leadership methods. Evaluate the readiness for such methods on the part of executives and employees of a company where you know both the executives and the employees.

6. Consider several individual executives whom you know. Which ones would be able to use participative methods effectively? How do they differ from the others? Which type of executive would you rather have supervise your work? Why?

COLLATERAL READINGS

For All Students

Likert, Rensis, *New Patterns of Management*. New York: McGraw-Hill Book Company, 1961. This volume summarizes the principles and practices used by today's most productive managers and proposes a management system based on these principles.

Tannenbaum, Arnold S., *Social Psychology of the Work Organization*. Belmont, Calif.: Wadsworth Publishing Co., 1966. Topics of interest are the relationship of man to the organization in which he works: his sense of satisfaction, involvement, feelings of identification of loyalty, conflicts, and tensions, as well as his effort in support of, or in opposition to, the formally defined goals of organization.

For Advanced Students

Davis, Keith, "The Case for Participative Management," in *Human Relations in Management* (2nd ed.), eds. I. L. Huneryager and S. G. Heckmann (Cincinnati: South-Western Publishing Co., 1967).

Newman, Summer, and Warren, *The Process of Management*. Englewood Cliffs, N.J.: Prentice-Hall, Inc., 1967. Chapter 22 discusses degrees of participation and recognizing when participation is feasible.

For Men in Business

Gellerman, Saul, *Motivation and Productivity*. New York: American Management Association, Inc., 1963. See pages 20–22, 41–42, 70–71, 90–91, 219–21, 261, 264, and 272.

Marrow, Alfred J., David G. Bowers, and Stanley E. Seashore, *Management by Participation*. New York: Harper & Row, Publishers, 1967. This volume reports an extraordinarily successful improvement of a failing organization through the introduction of a new management system. An unprofitable enterprise was made profitable and a better place to work in the short span of two years. Many managers and students of management will want to know how this was done.

Group Dynamics
and
Teamwork

SITUATIONS YOU ARE LIKELY TO MEET

How would you meet each of these situations:
  a. *Before* you have read the chapter? What would you say to yourself or to the individual?
  b. *After* you have read the chapter? How have your answers changed?

1. If you were supervisor of a large group of construction workers consisting of carpenters, plumbers, electricians, and plasterers, all of whom work on building houses, you might find that some of the men like certain members of the group more than others. If some of the members of the different crafts asked to be assigned to a group that has many individuals whom they like personally, would you grant or refuse their request? Why?
2. As a supervisor you may find that your group of men has one or more factional leaders. How would you treat each factional leader—as a person to be kept in line with the other men or as an undesignated "assistant" of yours?
3. One of your friends asks: "When workers stick together and are members of a cohesive group, do they invariably become more productive?" How would you answer him?

The spirit of an organization can be gauged, to some extent, by the percentage of employees who habitually refer to the company as "we" instead of "they." If the pronoun commonly used is "they," the employee implies that members of management, not he or his associates, are responsible for the company's products, policies, profits, losses, and so on. If he says "we," he identifies with the organization and implies that he too is partially responsible for the company's success and failures. He of course also uses these pronouns when he refers to subgroups within the total company group.

The term *group dynamics* refers to the forces operating in groups: factors that give rise to them, conditions that modify them, and ways in which they may be directed by leaders who are aware of these influences.

The systematic study of group dynamics has come about, in part, because experience in business has frequently shown that the important contacts and interpersonal influences in a company do not follow the pattern called for in the organization chart. The formal structure does not usually indicate the informal lines of communication or the ways in which decision making takes place or the ways in which work gets done. People just simply do not follow in their entirety the relationships visualized by the chart makers.

Anyone who works in the business world soon senses that the members of some groups "hang together" very tightly; members of other groups seem to function as isolated individuals. Leaders are aware of these differences.

A group may be cohesive or disruptive in influence on its members. A method of determining the interrelations that operate in any group was developed by Dr. J. L. Moreno, a psychiatrist and the founder of "sociometry."

The method he originated is still widely used in research studies of group relations. When used in industry, it consists of questioning each member as to his attitude toward the other members in his work group: *Whom does he like and whom does he dislike? With whom does he prefer to work, to eat, to live beside, to take his troubles to, and whom does he prefer to avoid?* By means of this kind of information, the researcher can construct a simple diagram called a "sociogram" which shows how members of the group feel about one another. The patterns of likes, dislikes, and indifferences indicate the interconnections in the influences at work in the group. It is easy to see which group members are popular, which ones are unpopular, who is the most powerful as a leader, and which persons are "isolates." In large groups, cliques are easily recognized.

Experience in watching how groups function indicates that the isolates and peripheral members are likely to get less satisfaction from their jobs than those who are liked. Isolates feel that they do not belong and are likely to quit their jobs sooner than those who feel that they do belong. The isolates tend to leave the group under pressure and are disruptive.

Moreno's sociograms are useful in predicting group behavior. He made sociograms of the interpersonal relations in a reformatory for girls at Hudson, New York. He found that fourteen girls who ran away within a few weeks were members of a network. Apparently each girl in the same network prodded and emulated the other members of her group. The reformatory had an epidemic of attempted escapes. On the other hand, girls who were "isolates" and ran away did not stimulate others to follow their example.[1]

An instance has been reported of a corporation president who discovered, after dealing for two years with the same group of research engineers, that he could predict their individual votes on alternative decision problems with such high accuracy that he was tempted to dissolve the group. It could tell him nothing he could not find out without consulting it.

Of course people often act differently in different groups and when playing different roles. Their relations with different groups or with different individuals within a group changes from group to group. In some companies, a high percentage of the members of one group do not like the members of another group. This is more or less frequent in the attitudes of members of the engineering department toward the members of the shop. To overcome the antagonism, some managements appoint a tactful old shop man of good technical training to act as liaison between engineering and the shop. Similarly, in newspaper offices, the clerical workers are likely to think of the members of the editorial room as a bunch of lazy reporters who come and go as they please while the accounting department employees work. Publishers try to overcome the disruptive influence by appointing members of both groups to committees that require the two to work together.

The greater the degree of psychological integration of work teams, the higher the level of job satisfaction. This is especially evident in studies of

[1]See Alfred J. Marrow, *Making Management Human* (New York: McGraw-Hill Book Company, 1957), pp. 60–62.

railroaders and miners where the nature of the work requires much inter-action of group members. However, in assembly operations like meat pack-ing and automobile manufacturing, the technological structure is such that the majority of the workers perform their operations individually. The man on an assembly line can talk only to the man in front of, behind, and across from him. Therefore, few stable work groups develop. Worker satisfaction in such an industry will probably be less than in railroading, mining, or steel making where social integration is likely to be an essential to the performance of the work.[2]

These attitudinal relationships in business are so important that when a new employee is to be hired or an old employee is to be transferred, three questions are likely to be asked: (1) "Can he do the work?" (2) "How well would he get along with the people where he would work?" and (3) "How well would he get along with the other groups whose work is related to that of his group?" Some managers do not say so publicly but they follow a policy of hiring new employees from all available religious and racial affiliations. They believe that "mixtures" help to overcome the development of cliques and increase cooperation.

Why people belong to groups

Obviously, there are many reasons why the individual belongs to groups. He could hardly function effectively in our kind of civilization as a hermit or an isolate. In addition to the need from the functioning stand-point, the normal individual gains feelings of security and belongingness from his membership in a school club, neighborhood gang, church, political party, union, or business organization. He feels more complete when he knows that he is accepted as a person by members of groups whom he likes. Alfred J. Marrow reported an incident in an English oil refinery where the workers wanted an increase in pay because the plant was being automated. They referred to the desired extra pay as "lonely money," a compensation for their losing the companionship of workmates.

It is also probable that when a workman can gain little satisfaction as a craftsman because of the growth of large scale industry with its auto-mated operations, he feels more dependent upon his fellow workers. He needs extra emotional satisfactions to compensate for loss of ego maximation that he might have had through craftsmanship. To the worker on an assem-bly line system, the sense of worthwhileness must come as a group member, not as an independent individual.

[2]See Robert Blauner, *Work Satisfaction and Industrial Trends in Modern So-ciety*, Institute of Industrial Relations (Berkeley, Calif.: University of California, 1960).

Shared beliefs often cause groups. A collection of people develop group feelings from shared views about work, politics, or other interests. The sharing of ideas and beliefs is called "social closeness" in contrast to physical closeness.

As in physical space, there is also social space. When we are members of a group of people who talk about topics of no interest or when they express opinions distasteful to us, we are socially distant. We do not enjoy full group membership. Social space affects behavior and is a force affecting the feeling of group membership.

When group dynamism is destroyed

One of the best examples of the destruction of group dynamics occurred during the Korean War. Although the experiments of the Chinese Communists in this field met with little success, their assumptions about group dynamics are valuable in helping us understand it more fully.

To many United States soldiers the reasons behind the Korean War were obscure, and the Chinese found it easy to exploit the soldiers' doubts about the goals of the war. One of the Chinese Communists' most effective weapons in breaking down the morale of their prisoners was to systematically destroy all formal and informal group structure. The officers were separated from the enlisted men; thus each group was composed solely of equals and was left virtually leaderless. The loss of their leaders who had described the soldiers' goals and channeled their energies left the men unable to act as an effective unit, and being deprived of a sense of unity, the individual was unsure of his position and duties. The Chinese further destroyed the prisoners' feelings of comradeship by encouraging mutual criticism discussion groups in which the soldiers sat and verbally assaulted each other. One of the most powerful influences on the prisoners' morale was the presence of turncoats and informers. When an officer or an enlisted man whom they had respected collaborated with the Chinese, the doubts of the prisoners as to the validity of their beliefs were greatly increased.

The absence of a leader, the idea of mutual criticism, the lack of strong beliefs in their way of life, and the defection of their comrades deprived the prisoners of a feeling of unity, of the sense of being on a team.[3]

Numerous studies are being conducted concerning group behavior. Some of the early studies have dealt with easily measured factors such as the optimum size of a group to give each member full in-groupness feeling. For purposes such as discussion, five is the optimal number. Factions begin to appear when the group becomes larger than twelve.

[3]See Edgar H. Schein, "Some Observations on Chinese Methods of Handling Prisoners of War," *Public Opinion Quarterly* 20 (1956), 321–27.

Outstanding research in the field of group dynamics is being conducted by the Institute for Social Research of the University of Michigan.[4]

Van Zelst's use of sociometric procedures with construction workers

The building trades are especially well adapted to the use of sociometric procedures because they are not subject to the same limitations that are typical of mass industry where a regrouping of workers means that each worker must learn an entirely new job. The subjects of this study by Raymond H. Van Zelst were four total work groups: a carpenter group of twenty members, another carpenter group of eighteen members and two separate groups of bricklayers, each having sixteen members. These men were working on the same housing project but were split into two separate groups by a highway running through the middle of the site. In housing construction the foreman normally assigns men arbitrarily to work crews, but in Van Zelst's study he asked the men to indicate their first, second, and third choices as to preference for teammates. The foreman assigned workers into these new groups, respecting each man's choices as far as possible.

The following graphs show the results in terms of costs. The savings in both materials and labor are quite evident. Furthermore, the men liked the new system much better than the old. The experiment showed that the use of sociometric procedures resulted in increased satisfaction for the workers and greater financial returns for management. The company's chief construction engineer in his report to management revealed that the savings due to this psychological procedure exceeded those of any previous work-saving device that had been tried by the management. The financial benefits were such that the company could construct every twenty-ninth building entirely from savings in labor and material costs.[5]

[4]The Institute for Social Research is comprised of four basic research centers. The Survey Research Center is primarily concerned with the study of large populations, organizations, and special segments of society and generally utilizes interview surveys.

The Research Center for Group Dynamics is concerned with the development of basic science of behavior in groups and seeks to explain the nature of the social forces that cause group behavior, the relations among members, and the activities of the group as a whole.

The Center for Research on Utilization of Scientific Knowledge studies the processes required for the full use of research findings and new knowledge. A fourth center for the study of political behavior has also been organized.

The Institute publishes many research reports and papers. A complete list of publications may be obtained without charge upon request. Publications Division, Institute for Social Research, The University of Michigan, 426 Thompson St., Ann Arbor, Mich. 48106.

[5]See Raymond H. Van Zelst, "Validation of a Sociometric Regrouping Procedure," *Supplement to the Journal of Abnormal and Social Psychology*, April 1952.

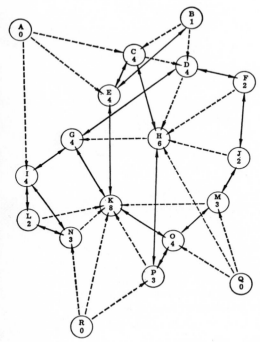

This sociogram shows a work group of eighteen carpenters, from data collected by Raymond H. Van Zelst. Each circle represents one man. Each member of the group was requested to nominate the three men with whom he would most like to work. Arrows indicate the direction of choice; broken lines indicate one-way preferences; solid lines indicate mutual choices. Total number of votes for each individual is shown in the circle. "R" chose "N," "K," and "P." "R" is an isolate because no one chose him.

Source: Raymond H. Van Zelst, "An Interpersonal Relations Technique for Industry," *Personnel* (American Management Association, July 1952), pp. 68–77.

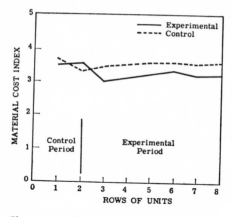

Fluctuations between experimental and control groups on materials costs compared for entire three-month period

Fluctuations between experimental and control groups on labor costs compared for entire three-month period

These figures show cost differences in the work done by an experimental group on which sociometric procedures were used and a control group where these procedures were not used. Both groups worked on the same housing project during the same time. They were separated from each other by a highway. Note that the cost indexes for both materials and labor were lower in the experimental group—the one that received the benefit of sociometric techniques.

Source: Raymond H. Van Zelst, "An Interpersonal Relations Technique for Industry," *Personnel* (American Management Association, July 1952). See also "Validation of a Sociometric Regrouping Procedure," from *Supplement to the Journal of Abnormal and Social Psychology* (April 1952).

Walker's study of thirty men and a machine

Production executives of today are keenly interested in the reactions of employees to automation. Automation is one of the most significant trends of our time, but few serious studies have been made of the actual impact on workers and work groups of a major technological innovation. A notable new contribution to the literature has been made by Charles R. Walker.[6] He reported a three-year study of the mechanical, social, and human difficulties encountered in "getting the bugs out" of a new semi-automatic plant of the United States Steel Corporation.

One of the most striking findings that emerged from this report of "a three-year battle between 30 men and a machine" is that many of the human relations troubles arose from management's tendency to view the

[6]Charles R. Walker, *Toward the Automatic Factory, A Case Study of Men and Machines* (New Haven: Yale University Press, 1957).

workers in the new mill as a collection of individuals rather than as members of a team. Thus when, after seventeen months, an incentive plan was finally announced, it was indignantly rejected because it eliminated two men from each of the three crews and covered only the crew operators. After management offered to retrain and find new jobs for the six men and broadened the plan to include indirect labor, production rose sharply, only to slump again when the old mill shut down and several crew members in the new mill were "bumped" out of their jobs. Almost three years were needed to achieve a state of high productivity and good morale. As Mr. Walker pointed out, a better understanding of the plant as a work community and a social system might have avoided much of the conflict and confusion along the way.

Much grief might have been avoided by giving employees a more extended technical and psychological preparation for the change. In the early critical months, the men did not believe that the mill would reach estimated capacity or that it would ever earn, for them, as much as they had made in the old type of mill. They felt that their job security was only temporary and that either all or some of them would soon be out of work. Even though events proved that all these fears were unfounded, the worry about security persisted. Even at the end of the study period, the men were not sure in their own minds that the new mill represented progress *for them*.

While the workers welcomed the relief from their former physical drudgery, they were concerned about the fact that an operating crew in the new mill consisted of nine men, instead of the twenty or thirty who had been needed in the old mill. In the event of a depression, they reasoned, they might lose three days' work out of four because the new mill turned out four times as much as the old. There were fewer job classes, and hence fewer opportunities for promotion. None of them had any hope of rising in the mill hierarchy—the better jobs, they felt, would henceforth go to "college boys." In general, there was a feeling that the company was getting much more out of increased production than the men were sharing.

The study points up the kinds of difficulties that will be encountered increasingly as automation gathers momentum. The adoption of automation puts a burden on management and labor leaders alike to prove that technological progress really means progress for everyone—or, in Mr. Walker's words, "to make it so, if it isn't."[7]

Workers' restriction of production

Perhaps the most poignant interest in group dynamics on the part of management men has arisen as a result of workers' restriction of production.

[7]See *Personnel*, American Management Association, Inc., January–February 1958, pp. 5, 6.

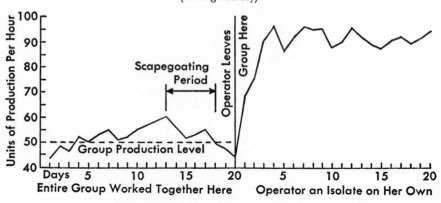

EFFECT OF GROUP EXPECTATIONS
(Sewing Factory)

GROUP RESTRICTION OF PRODUCTION

Obviously, the attitude of the individual worker toward the amount of work he should produce is often influenced by the members of the group with whom he works. Performance of the individual worker is often controlled by what the group members believe to be fair. The effect of such social influence on the worker is illustrated by the above figure. In this case, the output of a girl increased greatly when group pressure was removed. As stated by Lippitt from the study by Coch and French at the Harwood Manufacturing company:

> We see the day-by-day production curve of a girl belonging to a work group with a group production level of 50 units per hour represented by the dotted line. On the 11th and 12th days her production began to rise noticeably above the group standard and when she on the 13th day, hit standard production of 60 (a psychologically very important deviation for the other members) she became a scapegoat of the group with a great deal of social aggression directed toward her. Under this pressure her production decreased toward the level of the other group members. After 20 days the work group had to be broken up and the members transferred to various other units. The scapegoated operator remained on the same job, alone. As can be seen, her production shot up from about 45 to 96 units per hour in a period of 4 days. Her production stabilized at a level of about 92 and stayed there for the remainder of the 20 days. Clearly the induced forces on behavior from a strong subgroup may be more powerful than those induced by a progressive friendly management, and by personal needs for economic reward.

Evidence that the group influence often restricts the production of the individual members is available in almost every factory, but we should not assume that the group influence is restrictive only. Sometimes it aids productivity very decidedly. This has been proved by several laboratory experiments where group members participated wholeheartedly in the solution of complex problems such as code problems. Group effort was found to be more productive than solitary effort. The benefits of group participation are pronounced when problems require originality, insight, and rejection of incorrect ideas.

Source: Lester Coch and J. R. P. French, Jr., "Overcoming Resistance to Change," *Human Relations*, Vol. I, No. 4 (1948), after Ronald Lippitt, *Current Trends in Social Psychology* (University of Pittsburgh, reprinted 1951).

Anyone who examines records of production by factory workers is likely to find that their output does not fluctuate from day to day. One would expect that each worker would have some good days and some bad days. Instead, their output remains fixed for months. Those on piece work usually turn out an exact number of units every day. This means that the workers have established a level that they can attain on poor days. This level is in line with what management expects or what in-plant custom has determined. (See pages 57–64.)

Workers on a piece rate or other incentive system often limit their own wages by restricting production. Many would like to earn more money but they seek satisfactions which are more important than money. Each prefers to maintain his status as an accepted member of the group. When the group members have an informal agreement among themselves on a fair day's output, most members will conform to that standard. If an overzealous "eager beaver" tries to violate the code, the others will subject him to ridicule, threats of physical harm, and perhaps actual harm.

In our social system, the urge to conform generally wins out over the urge to excel, especially among wage earners. A worker might like to get more money for producing more, but he normally holds back if his co-workers take a dim view of superior accomplishment on the job. He usually decides that the extra pay is not worth the extra effort or, perhaps, the extra risk.

This group influence is not wholly bad. Group solidarity also provides important benefits to the individual worker. The group often protects its weakest members. If the weakest cannot do as well as the best, the best may voluntarily restrict their production so that the differences in earnings cannot be used as a reason for discharging or transferring the weakest. This is especially likely to occur when the weakest are socially popular. Any supervisor who has wanted to identify the employee who has made a serious error knows how difficult it is to be sure of the way the error occurred and who was responsible. The employees protect each other by giving the supervisor dubious information.

The group as a whole may work slowly to create the impression that the piece rate is too low. This is likely to occur whenever the union is asking for a higher rate. Management, of course, usually knows what the workers are doing, but the power of the group is often greater than that of management.

Responsiveness to group pressures differs among individuals

The evident influences of group dynamics in industry should not cause us to imagine that every member of the group is equally susceptible to group pressures.[8] In any industrial group, certain employees will invariably go along with majority opinion; others tend to identify and side with management insofar as they can without antagonizing their colleagues. Some few will even choose management's points of view at the risk of losing the friendship of their colleagues.

In factory production, every large employee group also contains a few isolates who are so individualistic that they do not care for the goodwill of the group. Many of these men are "experts" who achieve status through unique skills. Mechanics of this category typically demonstrate their superiority by handling intricate assignments with ease. They do not enter into group affairs. They do not compete for informal leadership. They satisfy their limited needs for group acceptance through job skills which other employees cannot or do not care to attain. Smart supervisors recognize the contributions of these isolates and give them special places to work, privileges to use certain restricted kinds of instruments, and recognitions that are not accorded to other workers. The other workers classify these isolates as "special" members who are not required to conform to all their group practices. Needless to say, these special workers lead a more lonely work life than the others.

Informal groups and factional leaders

Employees normally develop certain interpersonal work relations which management has not specifically planned. They borrow tools from each other, give to or withhold information from certain associates, counsel certain fellow workers, and associate with some employees and ignore others during the nonwork hours and days. They are attracted to some and repelled by other employees of the job environment. As a result of these and other influences, factions develop. As one writer has well stated in regard to the social satisfactions of the clique:

> Belonging to a clique affords certain social satisfactions and a sense of status. The office boys matching pennies in the stock room feel a kinship based upon mutual distaste for their betters in other departments who order them around. The executive secretaries find special satisfaction in being identified with their bosses who are deferred to by others in important positions. The typists can enjoy a sense of superiority over the file clerks, and they in turn are keenly aware of the social distance separating them from the messengers or office boys.

[8]Solomon E. Asch, "Opinions and Social Pressure," *Scientific American*, November 1955, pp. 31–35, presents an excellent report on studies of differences in reaction to social pressure on the part of college students.

These cliques have considerable influence over their members—sometimes more than the formal organization has; and they can invoke disciplinary measures.[9]

Some managements who discover the presence of strong cliques try to overcome their influence by transferring clique members to other departments. Others accept them and try to align them toward company goals.

An oft-mentioned example of informal leadership is the situation that arose when a new social worker came to work with juveniles of a settlement house. The social worker was conducting a recreational program in the building the first evening on the job. He could handle the juveniles in the building, but his efforts were repeatedly thwarted by a few boys on the outside who purposely made noise and disturbed the indoor program. The social worker came out several times and appealed to the individual boys to let up because they were disturbing the others inside. The boys persisted in making a disturbance. Finally, a local old-timer in the settlement house decided to put a stop to the nuisance. He came out to the boys, quickly recognized the leader of the group, and gave him responsibility for controlling the other boys of the group. The disturbance ended immediately. Factional leaders can be utilized to accomplish ends of benefit to the group and to related larger groups. Generally, most managements accept the fact that cliques exist and cannot be ordered to disband even though they may be gradually weakened.

In nonunion plants, the cliques are watched to see whether a clique is becoming the nucleus of a formal union that will spearhead group hostility to management. If such cliques are developing, it usually means that management has failed in its communication responsibilities. The employees have not been given a participative relationship with management. Progressive managements therefore avoid making abrupt changes that affect the social organizations of the employees. Changes are planned to enlist the support of the cliques. Management also considers the physical facilities such as office space and telephones in regard to their significance to employees. These status symbols often have important bearings on the feelings of clique members.

The factional leader is looked to as the informal leader. To some extent he functions as a "big brother" in a family setting. He is expected to get action or follow through with the supervisor on problems or wishes of the group. He is an unofficial spokesman. Giving him special status symbols will add to his position as the informal leader.

Most managements expect each supervisor to know the cliques in his

[9]George S. Odiorne, "The Clique—A Frontier in Personnel Management," *Personnel*, American Management Association, Inc., September–October 1957, pp. 38–44.

group. He should know his people well enough to identify each clique and its leaders.

The foreman who is socially alert realizes that he must get spontaneity of cooperation through the informal groups and their leaders. If he ignores their existence because they are not mentioned on the organization charts, he will become the victim of extra resistance. If he introduces technical changes or new methods of work without any attention to their effects on group relations, he will find that his employees are likely to develop mannerisms and attitudes that indicate that they harbor the feeling that they are being "pushed around." Those who have the feeling invariably discover ways of pushing in the opposite direction to that desired by management. They can slow down the production rate, lose tools, damage equipment, or "forget" to perform tasks that they would ordinarily perform.

According to the findings of Zaleznik's study of group behavior in a factory, work groups tend to provide themselves with stable social structures. To Zaleznik, it looked as if in the "work group" as in the "body" there is a "wisdom" greater than that which resides in any one of its parts.

In the particular group he observed, for example, the intricate social patterns of behavior that had evolved and that seemed to be helping to resolve the potential sources of conflict that were present, seemed to him to have in them a wisdom far greater than anything management could have "cooked up."

This hypothesis has, of course, tremendous implications for management and administration. From it one could conclude that those managements who are overly concerned with what *they* can do to improve the productivity and satisfaction of work groups are not taking full advantage of what the groups, if not interfered with too much, can do better and more wisely themselves.

But let us not jump to this conclusion too quickly. Although it contains a half truth—and even perhaps a little more than half—it still does not quite entirely state the whole story . . . it is astonishing how most work groups accommodate themselves to the reality in which they have to survive and live. But this very adjustment may be also from the point of view of *adaptation* a failure in growth and development. Thus work groups that are "adjusted" at one level may also be "frozen" at another.[10]

[10]From F. J. Roethlisberger's Foreword in A. Zaleznik, *Worker Satisfaction and Development* (Boston: Harvard University Press, 1956), Division of Research, Graduate School of Business Administration.

This suggests that to overcome the dangers of a static social organization it is necessary for leadership to introduce challenges into the group. Furthermore, new members who come into the group, new equipment, and new supervisors as well as new work objectives are essential to overcoming "frozenness."

Group cohesiveness

Groups differ greatly in their "cohesiveness," the attraction they have for their members. Some are loosely bound. Members drift in and out. The group may even disintegrate and vanish. Other groups are strong and command the active support of most members.

In a "high-cohesive" group, one strongly attractive to its members, the pressure to conform will be much greater than in a "low-cohesive" group.

Anyone who walks through a plant may observe that in one department the men are hostile to one another. They quarrel frequently. When an employee needs help, no one offers to assist him. If he asks for help, he gets the answer: "Yes, it's tough for you. You worry about it."

In contrast, the employees of a nearby department work together cheerfully. They help each other. They consult about ways to do the work. The employees obviously are enjoying the day's activities. They like each other. They are members of a cohesive or closely knit group.

Some groups are more closely knit than others. Formerly, it was assumed that a highly cohesive or closely knit group was likely to be more productive than a loosely knit group.

The Institute for Social Research, University of Michigan, has made outstanding research investigations which have thrown new light on this assumption. One approach has been to study the characteristics and performances of high-producing and low-producing work groups. In one series of researches the degrees of cohesiveness of different work groups were studied by asking each employee questions like: "Would you rather remain in this work group than move to another one even if you can get the same pay and do the same kind of work?"

Strangely, one of the findings from the study of cohesiveness was that the productivity of the cohesive work groups was only slightly higher than that of the groups that were not cohesive. Some of the closely knit groups showed both very high and very low extremes of productivity.

Subsequent analysis showed that attitude toward their company was a key factor in understanding the exceptions to the teamwork rule. When highly cohesive work groups were convinced that the company really had their interests at heart, that they could rely on what they were told, and that achieving the company's goals would help them, they showed exceptional productivity.

Just the opposite happened when a cohesive working team felt insecure about its company. Robert L. Kahn, director of the Center's Organizational Behavior Program, amplifies this point: "We now recognize that a highly cohesive group can motivate its members to work toward whatever the group has defined as its goal. If the group has accepted high productivity as its goal, then its members will be high producers. But if the group is hostile to management, then its cohesiveness will be a most effective means of reducing and restricting productivity of its members."[11]

Every teacher who has taught many classes of students has recognized that some groups are much easier to teach than others. The members of the groups that are easy to teach usually have pleasant feelings toward each other and the institution. Team spirit, of course, is less strong in college than in business groups. It is most evident in industrial and military groups. When a supervisor has good teamwork, the group produces well and has good morale. Leadership is a pleasure.

Supervisory practices that have been found effective in developing teamwork in plants are insisting that foremen listen patiently to individual workers, having employees participate in deciding which day each individual may have as his day "off," making sure that each employee is content with his work, not transferring or lending employees to other departments, letting employees control their own rest-pause system, consulting and discussing the work with the employees, and giving them a sense of mutual responsibility and teamwork.[12]

The wise supervisor lets his men feel that they are important in getting the work done. He lets them feel that they are responsible for getting the work done. When possible he gives credit to the entire team. When errors occur, he does not pin the blame on any one person but lets the group know that he expects the men to help each other in preventing errors. If output of individuals can be measured, he encourages each individual to outstrip his own best performance rather than that of a teammate.

One deterrent to teamwork is evident when individual employees engage in "petty politics" for the purpose of getting ahead. An executive dislikes the idea of people "buttering him up" because he knows that when em-

[11]See *Modern Management* (The Bureau of National Affairs, Inc., Washington, D.C.), August 15, 1955, p. 2. The most comprehensive report of the program's work in this area is Stanley Seashore, *Group Cohesiveness in the Industrial Work Group*, Monograph Series #14, Survey Research Center, The University of Michigan, December 1955.

[12]See Elton Mayo and George F. F. Lombard, *Teamwork and Labor Turnover in the Aircraft Industry of Southern California* (Boston: Bureau of Business Research, Harvard University Graduate School of Business Administration). Copyright © 1944 by the President and Fellows of Harvard College.

ployees are willing to sabotage each other in order to get ahead, team spirit has declined.

Developing company group feelings

Some subgroups within a company have strong group spirit but relatively little identification with or group feeling toward the company. Most managements like to have strong company-group as well as subgroup feelings. They prefer to have employees feel that they belong to the company and gain a sense of security and satisfaction from membership in the total organization.

Generally, company-group feeling is not likely to be strong if members of subgroups have closed ranks against other subgroups such as departments. A company group cannot successfully compete with subgroups for the loyalty of their members. Management can, however, encourage cooperation among the subgroups. Company-group feeling will be weak if the subgroups are in conflict. This means that management cannot build a strong company group by attacking or attempting to undermine an employee group such as the union. If management uses this kind of strategy, the employee groups will close ranks in opposition and the company-group feeling will be further weakened.

Company-group feeling will not be developed if management believes that its objective is to do something *to* or *for* employees. Instead, management must give employees a sense of participation in dealing with company problems and of working toward the achievements that benefit everyone.

Disaster is an important influence in developing positive company-group feelings. When a chemical company, for example, has an explosion that wrecks the plant, the workers respond willingly above and beyond the requirements of their regular jobs. Some of our finest demonstrations of loyalty and helpfulness occur when a company suffers a disaster.

Production employees should be encouraged to work happily with other vitally important groups such as junior executives, salesmen, engineers, office workers, and supervisors.

Companies that have strong company-group feelings among employees usually have executives and department heads who like each other. Routine problems have a way of solving themselves at the lower levels of the organization when the department heads enjoy working with each other.

In unionized plants, the management cannot usually blame the union when company-group feeling is poor. Company loyalty varies among nonunion as well as among union plants. Management and employee groups are hostile to each other in unorganized as well as in organized plants. The results are equally costly. True, employees who are hostile often unionize before a strike. But low productivity, high labor turnover, and other products of dissatisfaction with the company probably cost American industry more than strikes.

The management that wants to instill the "we" feeling, if it does not exist, cannot follow any simple formula. It develops naturally when the conditions are favorable. First of all, the members of top management must genuinely feel that they want the help of every person in the organization, that they are concerned about helping each employee achieve his purposes. When management provides that kind of leadership, the workers will very quickly feel that they and their work are important. They will work together to solve company problems and will identify their own happiness and welfare with the prosperity of the organization. They will trust and believe in the management that believes and trusts in them. The "we" spirit is a by-product.

Criticisms of the group emphasis

Certain leaders in industrial relations have criticized personnel programs and policies in industry today that are heavily group oriented. They fear that the need for individual recognition has almost disappeared from corporate thinking. They would like to have team spirit without losing individual identity.

Some sociologists have voiced fears that our society has gone overboard in its reliance upon the group. They see in it the seeds of a new totalitarianism.

In actual practice, most American business managements are still emphasizing the individual in their personnel relations. They have increased fringe benefits such as group insurance and union relations, but the individual has not been forgotten. After all, the executive still selects a specific employee rather than a group for promotion. Of the two approaches for the improvement of employee relations, the group and the individual, the factors in effective group behavior have been neglected far more than those that treat the employee as an individual.

You can sharpen your perceptiveness of group dynamics

As previously stated, one of the main objectives in your study of human relations is the acquiring of an increased sensitivity to the forces in the behavior of others. This increased sensitivity is just as essential in regard to the dynamics in group as in individual behavior. If you have this objective in mind as you study people in business, you will see many examples of group dynamics and thereby enrich the ways in which you function with others.

As stated in the early part of the chapter, people do not follow in entirety the relationship visualized by the chart makers, but this does not mean that organizational charts have no value. The better view is that good organizational structure is basic to effective functioning but you should be alert to the ways in which group dynamics function in accordance with the charts and the situations when they do not. Reports of many helpful studies of the subject appear in our journals from time to time.

QUESTIONS ON THE CHAPTER

1. Define the term group dynamics. Name influences that caused study of the subject to come about.
2. What are sociograms and how are they useful in interpreting group behavior studies? Who was the founder of "sociometry"?
3. List some reasons why people belong to groups.
4. Describe the functions of the Research Center for Group Dynamics, University of Michigan.
5. In the Walker study of the steel plant, what factor was found to be one of the main reasons for worker dissatisfaction with the introduction of automation?
6. What are the functions of the factional leader of a group?
7. How do workers limit production when they wish to do so?
8. What is meant by group cohesiveness? In what ways do high-cohesive and low-cohesive groups differ in production performance?
9. In what ways should a company encourage or discourage the formation and behavior of subgroups among the employees?
10. According to some sociologists, what is a danger of overemphasis on the group in our present society?
11. Name some of the supervisory practices that have been found effective in developing teamwork.
12. Of all the ideas presented in the chapter, which ones are of special interest or value to you?
13. What did the chapter contribute to your future relations with (a) the men who supervise your work, (b) the employees whom you may supervise?

PROBLEMS AND PROJECTS

For All Students

1. Make a study of the psychological relationships that exist between the mem-

bers of some group that you know well. Use the sociometric technique. If you were to supervise these members, how would your knowledge be of value to you?

2. Think of the students whom you know. Which ones are factional leaders? How do they exert their informal leaderships? Contrast them with some isolates.

For Advanced Students

3. Search the available literature for additional studies of group dynamics. Look particularly for reports by the Research Center for Group Dynamics, University of Michigan. Scan the tables of contents of business journals for recent articles.

4. The National Training Laboratories has been developing its unique approach to leadership growth. Reports of their conferences are published periodically. You may also wish to write to them at the National Education Association, 1201 16th St., N.W., Washington, D.C. 20036, for available booklets and bibliographies.

For Men in Business

5. It is easy for an alert employee in industry to recognize the groups in his company. Here is a list of questions supplied by one writer:

   (a) How many groups and subgroups can you think of in your own business organization?

(1) The entire company	(11) The natives of the community
(2) Top management	(12) The old-timers
(3) The office staff	(13) The female factory employees
(4) The office girls	(14) The men who bowl together
(5) The salesmen	(15) The members of the same church
(6) Junior executives	(16) The shop stewards
(7) Foremen	(17) The ex-GI's
(8) Union members	(18) Others?
(9) Members of factions within the union	
(10) Employees in each department (welders, cutters, etc.)	

   (b) How many groups and subgroups can you think of to which you belong, inside the plant and out?

   (c) How would you rate each of these groups, so far as each concerns you personally?

      (1) "Belonging" is essential to me. Can't think of anything that would drive me out.

(2) "Belonging" is very important. It would take something really big to drive me out.

(3) I want very much to "belong," but I can think of some possibilities that would make me willing to get out.

(4) "Belonging" is a good idea.

(5) Don't care much one way or the other.

(6) I'm not sure I really "belong" there anyway.

COLLATERAL READINGS

For All Students

Cartwright, Dorwin, and Alvin Zander, eds., *Group Dynamics: Research and Theory* (3rd ed.) New York: Harper & Row, Publishers, 1968. An authoritative summary of group dynamics theory and research is presented in this volume.

Mann, F. C., and L. R. Hoffman, *Automation and the Worker: A Study of Social Change in Power Plants.* New York: Holt, Rinehart & Winston, Inc., 1960. Describes conditions favorable to positive results when extensive changes are contemplated.

For Advanced Students

Athos, Anthony G., and Robert E. Coffey, *Behavior in Organizations: A Multidimensional Approach.* Englewood Cliffs, N.J.: Prentice-Hall, Inc., 1968. Chapter 11 treats intergroup behavior and discusses intergroup problems and conflicts and approaches to minimizing conflicts.

Zaleznik, Abraham, *Human Dilemmas of Leadership.* New York: Harper & Row, Publishers, 1966. By means of a variety of concrete examples, the book illustrates the different personality conflicts of leaders and subordinates and how they react to each other.

For Men in Business

Sayles, Leonard R., *Behavior of Industrial Work Groups: Prediction and Control.* New York: John Wiley & Sons, Inc., 1958. A field study of three hundred work groups shows why some groups are "always troublesome" while others are cooperative and suggests ways management can predetermine worker reaction to supervision.

Stanley, J. D., "How to Live with Worker Cliques," *Personnel Journal,* June 1958. Informal groups are constantly exerting substantial influence upon the performance of personnel functions. Describes countermeasures that may be used.

Identification and Status Symbols

SITUATIONS YOU ARE LIKELY TO MEET

How would you meet each of these situations:

- a. *Before* you have read the chapter? What would you say to yourself or to the individual?
- b. *After* you have read the chapter? How have your answers changed?

1. If an employment interviewer were to ask you to describe the kind of furnishings you expect to have in your office where you work thirty years hence, what furnishings and other status symbols would you describe? After reading the "Exec-chart," to what extent did your list change?
2. Assume that you are head of a large department in a company. One of your best men, you think, deserves a raise in pay. When you discuss the desired raise with your superior, he tells you that the man is already receiving the highest rate allowed in his classification. In view of that fact, your superior asks whether you favor giving a raise in title instead of a money increase? How would you answer him?
3. Assume that a friend tells you that he expects to get a job in a company where he can become president about ten years after he leaves college. He also tells you that when he expressed this expectation to an older executive, the older man said to him: "You might know enough to get by in the job, but you

would not be a good leader of men simply because in that time you would not have suffered enough to stimulate employees to identify with you or the company." What would you say to your young friend about the older man's answer?

To understand group dynamics more fully, we should appreciate the influences of identification and status symbols. Whenever you as a stranger come into a new group of people such as factory or office workers, the people there are likely to react to you by saying to themselves, "Is he one of us?" And when you come into a new clubroom, religious congregation, or student body, the people there have the same kind of question as part of their feelings toward you.

If they were able to verbalize their feelings more fully, they would say, "What are his identifications—do his feelings really make him one of us?"

Identification means that the individual feels that he is part of another person, situation, or institution. In some cases, he feels that he is part of the purpose of the institution, activity, or person. The process is one of feeling rather than of intellect.

When you attend a football game, you not only cheer for your favorite team but you also "play" the game—you "become" the player who is carrying the ball. You do the things the team is trying to do.

When you are in the theater, you identify yourself with the hero, fight his battles, endure his hardships, conquer the villain, and finally marry the heroine. You are, for the time being, more than a mere observer or onlooker —you are the admired character in the picture or the play, psychologically speaking. If instruments were attached to your body to measure your bodily reactions, they would show that you make many incipient movements that give reality to your imaginary acting.

Every person in business, particularly the leader, should be conscious of the psychodynamic influences of identification. It is essential to certain needs of the individual such as the sense of belongingness and achievement by membership in a group or on a team. Every sports fan knows that the successful team is the one in which the members identify themselves with the team as a whole. Each player does not play an individual game but integrates his playing with that of the entire team. Even though business is not a game, the team spirit and the ability of individual members of the team to identify with the team are important. Employees then use the pronouns "we" and "our" rather than "they" and "their" when they refer to the company.

Through the achievements of other persons, groups of persons, and institutions, the individual may reduce tensions arising from his own inadequacies. Identification may be made with social and political organizations or reform movements. An individual may also identify himself with his material possessions, as exemplified by the housewife who cleans and protects her home so well that it becomes uncomfortable to others. Possessions such as the house, clothing, automobile, office desk, or factory machine may be used to gain many subconscious satisfactions as well as obvious prestige values.

Positive identification is one of the human being's most valuable means for enjoyment. It is a recognizable theme in the development of every well-balanced happy person; it is absent from the mental lives of certain patients in hospitals for the mentally ill. In other patients, the identifications appear in an extreme form as in those who identify themselves so fully with heroes or villains that they become "Napoleons," "Messiahs," "Hitlers," or "Jesse Jameses." The well-adjusted person is one who has learned the art of identifying himself intelligently with the people and the tasks of his daily contacts. The factors that involve growth in his mental life are integrated into an effective working unit. He feels at home with his associates, his supervisors, his community, his family. Unlike the cynic, he finds the world in which he lives reasonably admirable because he has identified himself with its admirable aspects.

Identification is fundamental to a happy marriage and married life. Ideally and typically, two people marry not mainly for sexual gratification but for more complete identification of their emotional and spiritual selves. In the course of evolution mankind has developed many institutions to enable its members to identify themselves with satisfying personalities. In addition to marriage, we have the church, which aims to have the individual identify himself with the cosmic mind.

The good citizen identifies himself with his community and his nation. The well-adjusted student identifies himself with his college, his fellow students, and his teachers. In business, the happy effective employee identifies with his fellow workers, his supervisor, the management, the customers, and the company as a whole.

Intelligent business executives try to assist their employees in identifying themselves not only with the company but also with the community in which they live, the institutions of which they are a part, and the social groups in which they are nurtured and have received their racial heritage. The true business leader of men not only directs employees' work efforts but also helps them to appreciate their place in the scheme of things. He does this by pointing out the trends in the business, changes in methods, and the problems of today that challenge them to excel in their development of new and better products. He enables them to realize that the benefits of the mechanisms and activities of business enlarge their perspectives and enrich their lives through service to customers. People live more happily as a result of ego involvement in the products or services they help to produce and sell.

How identifications are acquired

Numerous and complex influences enter into the development of a person's identifications and no one can explain every phase in their development. When we want to help a person develop positive identifications with a company or a person, we can contribute toward that end by means of the following procedures:

1. We must provide goals for the individual that are worthwhile to him. When management talks about the things that interest management—higher profits, lower costs, and better competitive position—the employee is not impressed. Such goals are not especially worthwhile to him as an employee. To make the goals worthwhile, they should be stated in terms such as the greater number of people, usually customers, who are benefited by the bigger production and lower costs.
2. The people who benefit should be the kind whom the worker likes or respects, usually people who are similar to himself—workers rather than stockholders. This principle has proven its value time and again in advertising. Housewives who view television commercials identify readily with other housewives of refinement but not with society matrons, crude comic characters, or sexy models. Children lose interest in programs when there is an emphasis on adults. Instead, they like to hear children's voices and to see children of their own age participating in children's activities.

   The parent who tells stories to a child knows that the boy or girl wants to hear about children of the same age. The child wants to identify himself with someone not older, nor markedly younger, but a person like himself.

   Similarly, television commercials that sell men's products should portray masculine men rather than "eggheads." If the viewer or reader can identify himself with the users of the product, if he can see himself in the situation portrayed in the advertising, then his feelings become involved and the process works toward believability and acceptance. It is identification that makes it "for me."

3. Identification is developed through shared experiences. Its strongest forms are often brought about through personal sacrifice as in the case of soldiers who have been together in combat or in rigorous training as exemplified in our Marine Corps. Their shared hardships cause them to identify grimly with members of their group. In like manner, children who are reared in families where all members of the family share to the point of personal sacrifice for the family life often have deeper family loyalty than children of families where the parents do all the sacrificing. In business, the executive who inspires employees to sacrifice their own comfort in order to make a contribution to the business develops far stronger identification of the employees with the company than the executive who thinks mainly in terms of what he or the company can do for the employees. The identifications of most persons are intensified when they learn how to "give of themselves" to ideals, persons, and institutions outside themselves. Employees who buy stock in the employing company usually improve the strength of their identification.

This means that management must give the employee ego involvement on the part of the employee toward the products and services of the company. One method is to challenge the employee to make or help make the best pies, or television receivers, or whatever the company makes that have ever been made. Most workers want to be good craftsmen and worthwhile members of society. We fail them when we do not supervise them in that spirit. Business and profits must be thought of in this manner by management.

Of course this means that managements have to learn how to give the worker a feeling of colleagueship in the business, not as an "expense" that can be eliminated. The inability of managements to give the employee emotional as well as economic identification with the company has been a strong influence in causing employees to form associations of their own and, through those associations, compelling employers to bargain with them.

When an employee identifies with his company, he learns to realize that the management is similar to the head of a family—the head must withhold some desired rewards and earnings in order to distribute the available income where it is needed most. The head of a family cannot afford to give each child everything he wants, nor can a management give each employee everything he wants.

4. Constant communication and participation are essential to the development of strong identification with a company. That is one reason why managements give attention to such programs. The frequent exchange of information between the company and the employee are necessary for strengthened identification.

5. Symbols of identification are helpful. Think of all the badges, diplomas, and titles which are sought and treasured by the people in business. This topic is so large and varied in its implications that special attention will be given to it in this chapter. We should, however, also recognize some of the dangers in the misuse or overemphasis of identification before we treat the topic of symbols in business.

Limitations and dangers in identification

The able executive who has insight into the processes of identification among his employees is careful to see that they clearly differentiate between interest in him and interest in their work. The executive who enables employees to identify themselves with his personality should also help them to transfer their identifications to other tasks, persons, and institutions. He may direct them so well that they wish to become a boss "like him." Later, the employees may find they are really interested not in the intrinsic values of their tasks but in the person who happened to supervise them. Each worker should be led to find the intrinsic values of his work and to feel that his work makes him a worthwhile member of the organization to which he belongs.

Those workers who identify too blindly with a superior and fail to develop themselves in relation to the work are likely to be among the first laid off in a recession. Generally, the weaker men in a department are the ones laid off first, but their weakness as employees may be the result of overidentification. Such men cater to the department head as a person. They coast in their work because they feel secure in their relationship with the chief. In contrast, the man who consistently does very good work is likely to find that he is needed regardless of recessions and organizational changes that may occur. Catering to the boss as a person and coasting in regard to the work seldom provide as much security as doing good work.

When men are chosen for supervisory positions, consideration is given to the directions of their strongest identifications in employee-management relations. Anyone who observes the degrees of identification between an executive and his foreman will notice that some foremen identify strongly with their boss but keep their subordinates at a distance. They tend to be critical of the workers and feel that the workers are not trying to do a good job. Such a foreman is not interested in his employees as individuals. They, in turn, sense that he is aloof and disinterested in them. When they are in his office or associate socially with him, they feel uncomfortable. They notice that he seeks contacts with his superiors when on company premises as well as at outside community social affairs. Sociologists often use the term "social distance" to describe these relationships between the executive, the foreman, and the employees. Ideally, of course, all three identify with each other—the social distances between them can be minimal.

When a college senior is interviewed as an applicant for a management-training program, the directions of the applicant's identifications are considered. If the senior identifies only with workers or those whom he considers underprivileged, there is little value in hiring him as a management trainee. On the other hand, if he identifies with management so strongly that he lacks any genuine interest in workers, he might develop into a good controller but a poor supervisor or personnel manager. The direction of a person's identifications help to shape his career and should be recognized early by the individual who wants to enjoy his life in business.

How can a person recognize his identifications? The answer is "The same ways in which a skilled employment interviewer recognizes them in an applicant." He knows from answers to questions such as the following: "With whom or with what people have you associated in the past?" "What kinds of people do you like to work with on the job?" "Where would you like to live?" "To what organizations do you now belong and which ones do you intend to join?" "What kind of job do you expect to hold ten years hence? Twenty years from now?" "What diplomas, badges, or symbols of achievement do you hope to earn in the years ahead?"

SYMBOLS

A man's identifications are often revealed by the symbols he desires. Symbols play a far greater role in the mental life than most persons appreciate. Actually, people think and react in terms of symbols rather than logical ideas. Ideas stated in the abstract are meaningful to only the select few who have trained themselves to analyze and evaluate abstractions in the field to which the abstractions apply. The "select few" are exemplified by the researcher who has specialized in a specific science. Ability to think in the abstract is limited to the area in which the thinker has specialized. That is one reason why a trained scientist can, for example, think well in the field of physics, but in the field of politics he may react with little regard for facts and base his thinking mostly on symbols and his own unconscious motivations.

Symbols are also necessary for logical thinking, as in mathematics. The educated and the noneducated need them. If we hear or see the words

"United States," we visualize the term as a map or a flag. *Peace* is often symbolized by a dove, *innocence* by a happy child, and *silence* by a forest scene. A flag is a dyed piece of cloth and an engagement ring is a metal band on a girl's left hand, but we attach deep emotions to them because of what they symbolize. Each person acquires his own unique set of symbols, but certain symbols are so common and significant in human relations in business that we should become aware of them.

The symbols of executive status in most business concerns are the following:

1. An organization chart that bears his name
2. Name listed in company telephone directory
3. A private office
4. Stenographic help
5. Access to rooms for holding meetings and private conversations with subordinates
6. No requirement to punch a time clock
7. Invitations to meet with other management members at conferences, dinners, social events, etc.
8. Opportunities to attend convention, visit other plants, etc., to enlarge knowledge and grasp of his job
9. Introduction to plant visitors
10. Facilities comparable to those of other management members with respect to parking, dining, and washrooms.

In a lighter vein, "A Ready Guide for Evaluating Executives," by K. B. Bernhardt, director of personnel, Monsanto Chemical Company, is shown on page 120. Among the outward and visible signs of achievement at different organizational levels listed in this "guide" are briefcases, office desks, office tables, carpeting, plant stands, vacuum water bottles, library, shoe-shine service, parking spaces, and luncheon menus. No mention is made of salary, titles, or clothes. Lists of this kind are, for the most part, not intended to be taken seriously, but the importance of such signs of status is well recognized—the very fact that they are ridiculed testifies to this. Even though the individuals in an organization often ridicule them, they are evident and highly valued within most organizations.

Salary is an outstanding indicator of status in the organization. According to a Dartnell Corporation survey of executive compensation, when the president's salary is used as a base of 100 percent, salary of the top marketing executive is 60 percent; the top financial executive, about 54 percent; the top production executive gets around 54 percent; and the industrial relations executive receives, on the average, 37 percent of the salary paid his company's president.[1]

[1]*Executive Compensation*, The Dartnell Corporation, Chicago, 1961.

A READY GUIDE FOR EVALUATING EXECUTIVES

EXEC-CHART

Visible Appurtenances	Top Dogs	V.I.P.'s	Brass	No. 2s	Eager Beavers	Hoi Polloi
Briefcases	None—they ask the questions	Use backs of envelopes	Someone goes along to carry theirs	Carry their own—empty	Daily, carry their own filled with work	Too poor to own one
Desks, Office	Custom Made (to order)	Executive Style (to order)	Type A "Director"	Type B "Manager"	Cast-offs from No. 2s	Yellow Oak—or cast-offs from Eager Beavers
Tables, Office	Coffee tables	End tables or decorative wall tables	Matching tables Type A	Matching tables Type B	Plain work table	None—lucky to have own desk
Carpeting	Nylon—1-inch pile	Nylon—1 inch pile	Wool-Twist (with pad)	Wool Twist (without pad)	Used wool pieces—sewed	Asphalt tile
Plant Stands	Several—Kept filled with strange exotic plants		Two—Repotted whenever they take a trip	One medium-sized Repotted annually during vacation	Small Repotted when plant dies	May have one in the department or bring their own from home
Vacuum Water Bottles	Silver	Silver	Chromium	Plain painted	Coke machine	Water fountains
Library	Private collection	Autographed or complimentary books and reports	Selected references	Impressive titles on covers	Books everywhere	Dictionary
Shoe Shine Service	Every morning at 10:00	Every morning at 10:15	Every day at 9:00 or 11:00	Every other day	Once a week	Shine their own
Parking Space	Private in front of office	In plant garage	In company garage—if enough seniority	In company properties—somewhere	On the parking lot	Anywhere they can find a space—if they can afford a car
Luncheon Menu	Cream Cheese on Whole Wheat Buttermilk and Indigestion Tablets	Cream of Celery Soup Chicken Sandwich (White Meat) Milk	Fruit Cup—Spinach Lamb Chop—Peas Ice Cream—Tea	Orange Juice Minute Steak French Fries—Salad Fruit Cup—Coffee	Tomato Juice Chicken Croquettes Mashed Potatoes Peas—Bread Chocolate Cream Pie Coffee	Clam Chowder Frankfurter & Beans Rolls and Butter Raisin Pie à la Mode Two Cups of Coffee

Titles are important in giving a person appropriate recognition in regard to his job. Each company has its unique method of determining job titles, but in most companies the use of *general* before another title, as exemplified in *general manager*, indicates superior status. *Director* is often applied to a staff rather than a line position and is in some cases analogous in status to *general*.

Titles are often established to satisfy the ego needs of specific department heads. If the head of a department believes that other people in the company downgrade his department in their thinking, he is apt to ask management to change the name of his department and to give him a high-sounding title. Every large organization is likely to experience special requests of this kind. Some department heads will request a change in title for a subordinate in order that he may be granted a salary increase. Others give the subordinate a better title *instead* of a pay increase. Many executives, too, prefer to have a title such as vice-president rather than receive a substantial raise with no title change. Using status symbols in this respect often creates problems, however, as evidenced by the reorganization that one large company made in its newly decentralized areas. In order to bolster the feeling of individual responsibility, they renamed the heads of the areas and their functional subordinates divisional presidents and vice-presidents, respectively. In time, the "presidents" became more and more independent in their work, and serious interdivisional problems arose. Top management hesitated to enforce the authority it had more or less abdicated because of its possible demoralizing effect on the status-conscious divisional presidents. As a result, the company suffered great losses before a new chief executive regained proper control of the subordinate units.

Certainly, many titles are not indicative of the true ability or status of the holder. The only safe procedure for a newcomer to a company is to inquire about the functions of individuals who hold various titles. Even then, the inconsistencies are likely to be more pronounced than the consistencies. Most difficult of all, some top managements avoid the use of any titles as much as possible.

White-collar versus blue-collar

Office and shop employees are easily distinguished on the streets as well as on the company premises. When we walk on a street of a northern city, we note that the responsible office and professional worker tends to wear heavy shoes, padded coat, white shirt, drab-colored suit, and constricting necktie. These clues to his status indicate that he thinks of himself as a person of responsibility. In contrast, the worker who wears slacks and other clothing suitable for the factory rather than the office is assumed to be a wage earner rather than a salaried employee. Clothes indicate the general occupational level with which the wearer identifies himself.

White-collar people are expected to dress somewhat somberly; their working attire is not a uniform, nor is it different from clothing generally suitable for street wear. Management men often "dress down" for those occasions when their attire might cause others to think of them as snobs. This occurs at company picnics and mixed social affairs. Also when a labor union contract is signed, the newspaper pictures of the signing often show the union representatives dressed in somber "Sunday best" suits, white shirts, and ties, but the company men are seen without their coats and with their sleeves rolled up. Apparently, the union representatives try to establish their equality by dressing as they think their management counterparts do. The management representatives, on the other hand, "dress down" for the occasion to avoid giving any impression that they think of themselves as superior to the workers.

The new employee soon senses the kind of clothes appropriate for him to wear. He realizes that he may remain an outsider if, unknowingly, he violates the group norm. Very few managements have ever attempted to encourage or enforce the wearing of any specific clothing except for safety purposes—executives realize that each employee will adopt the group norm. If he deviates markedly from the norm, he indicates that he identifies himself with those classes whose symbols he chooses.

Payroll classifications often indicate status. Generally, executives, staff specialists, office workers, foremen, and supervisors are on a salary basis. In some companies, executives are paid once a month; office workers twice a month; and factory workers once a week. Those who are on the monthly payroll need not punch a time clock. Some differentiation may also be made as to whether the salaried employee is on the home office or on the local plant payroll. Those on the home office payroll usually have the more important positions and greater job security. A beginner in the company may progress from an hourly payroll to a weekly, to a semimonthly, to a monthly at the local plant, and finally to a monthly payroll of the home or main office. Complaints about pay and requests for higher rates often indicate a desire for greater recognition as to the payroll classification—higher status —rather than a need for more money.

Tools and tool boxes of factory workers indicate status. Zaleznik in his study of workers in an instrument factory found that job title and pay rate were not the only symbols of difference in job status among the men. In the machinist trade, the tradition for expressing job status differences through the kind of tool box the machinist owns is evident. A first-rate experienced machinist owns a tool box filled with various hand tools and instruments. It is usually located conveniently near his most frequent work position. The machinist's work coat or apron may also indicate status.[2]

2See A. Zaleznik, *Worker Satisfaction and Development* (Boston: Harvard Business School, Division of Research, 1956), pp. 20, 21.

Authority symbols and fear of authority

Many a worker fears every individual who symbolizes authority. Logically, there is no need for the fear; psychologically there is. The fearful worker does not fear the general manager as a person but what the general manager represents. He is a symbol of authority. As a symbol, he represents the power of giving and withholding privileges, even imposing punishment.

The desire to please others and to avoid punishment is learned by children long before they become employees. The child is rewarded, admonished, and punished by parents and other adults through thousands of instances that eventually condition him against all symbols of authority. The child soon learns that he must please authority to get what he wants. Eventually this idea becomes an integral and a partially unconscious influence in his character. It carries over into adult life. Even though the boss is a genial, easygoing person, this kind of employee feels that he must please the boss to get a promotion and obtain desired privileges such as a trip to an industry convention.

The influences of authority symbols and fears of authority are often discussed in relation to political life. In World War II, these predisposing influences were analyzed and reported in journals and newspapers. German Nazis and anti-Nazis were studied by psychiatrists. One study, for example, found that anti-Nazis oftener than not grew up in families where the maternal influence was stronger than the paternal. An Army psychiatrist who had made extensive studies in postwar Germany conducted three- to four-hour, or sometimes longer, interviews with 150 German men, 90 of whom were presumptive anti-Nazis, 40 confessed Nazis, and the remainder borderline cases. He investigated family and other influences that make men either total conformists ready to accept authoritarian leadership or individuals capable of forming their own judgments and acting accordingly.

According to this psychiatrist, the average German father is a *"respektsperson"*—a term that was frequently used by Nazis in describing their own fathers. As one Nazi said: "With one look in his eye he made us children obey him." Corporal punishment, administered almost as a ritual by the father, was the rule rather than the exception in the German home at that time.[3]

Obviously, home influences such as these are likely to have some bearing on a person's reactions to authority and authority symbols.

"Status anxiety"

Certain individuals on all levels in industry are constantly in a state

[3]See Dorothy Dunbar Bromley, "Maternal Influence Seen Factor in Creating German Anti-Nazis," *New York Herald Tribune*, April 28, 1946.

of emotional disturbance over their status. They compare their position relative to others. An inadequately adjusted, worrisome person of this kind notes whether a colleague gets more recognition from the boss than he does. He expects others to recognize his proper status, to use his correct title whenever possible, and to confer with him about every problem that is even remotely related to his functions. This kind of tense individual is likely to be an ambitious person who has failed to achieve the level he thinks he deserves. As a frustrated person, he is apt to exhibit various nervous disorders such as insomnia and feelings of persecution.

Of course the effects of these anxieties become evident to others. Executives tend to withhold additional responsibilities from such persons. Indeed, one of the most common questions asked about an individual who is under consideration for advancement to additional responsibility is, "Can he take it in stride or would the extra responsibility increase his anxieties too greatly?"

Top executives note the ways in which junior executives react to and use the titles they have earned in the past.

Jim Bright, for example, is proud of the fact that he has been given the title of assistant traffic manager of his company. If someone asks him, in the presence of his boss, what his job is, he will be expected to say, "Oh, I help Mr. Bye in purchasing." Jim's direct mention of his own title would indicate too much anxiety about its importance.

Many top executives grant titles to subordinates, but assume that the titles will be taken seriously only by the holder's wife! Franklin J. Lunding, Jewel Tea Co. chairman, has been reported as once remarking that if he found a manager in the organization markedly interested in his own title, "then he doesn't work here any more."

The junior executive should play down his own title, but he may, under certain circumstances, play up the titles and prerogatives of others, particularly those persons who suffer from status anxiety. Most mature, well-adjusted executives are unconcerned about their own titles; when titles are emphasized, they are annoyed rather than pleased.

The smart junior executive who functions for his boss at such times as vacation periods is always careful to make known that he is only acting for the boss temporarily. He keeps himself in the background and the boss in the foreground. After all, the boss, not the temporary fill-in, is responsible for whatever goes wrong as well as for what happens during his absence.

Prestige symbols of the public

Symbols of success or failure are highly personal, vary with the individual, and change from one generation to the next. In former generations, the presence of a maid in the home was a status symbol; later, it was the

EVOLUTION OF AN AD MAN
(1955 To 19??)

1955 ...the publication's fault about the key address.

> Sincerely,
>
> SMITH, JONES, INC.
>
> *J. P. Shmart*
>
> J. P. Shmart, Copy Dept.

1963 ...due to the inexperience of a cub copywriter.

> Very truly yours,
>
> SMITH, JONES, INC.
>
> *Joseph P. Shmart*
>
> Joseph P. Shmart, Chief Copywriter

1970 ...and will get the copy chief on the ball.

> Cordially yours,
>
> SMITH, JONES, INC.
>
> *J. Purloine Shmart*
>
> J. Purloine Shmart, Acc't. Executive

1974 ...to assure you a new man on the account.

> Cordially,
>
> SMITH, JONES, SHMART, INC.
>
> *Jos. P. Shmart*
>
> Jos. P. Shmart, Vice-President

LAST ...agree that we need new faces on the board.

> Best Regards to Your Wife,
>
> SHMART, SMITH, JONES, INC.
>
> *Jos. P. Shmart* by E.L.
>
> Jos. P. Shmart, President

Source: by Hunter, *Printers' Ink* (December 11, 1953), p. 39.

ownership of a piano. Then the automobile became the number-one status symbol. However, a car is no longer the prestige item it was years ago. When eleven hundred advertising executives were asked whether the automobile is losing its role as a status symbol, slightly more than half (51 percent) said yes, but 40 percent insisted that a car is still number one among status symbols. The remaining 9 percent believed that the automobile is still a status symbol but in another form—the prestige comes in owning a sports car, a foreign car, or in being a two-car family. Ownership of a smart-looking late-model car is the rule rather than the exception in America. Hence, consumers are turning to other products or services for status symbols such as beautiful suburban homes, power boats, hi-fi sets, expensive furs, and travel.

These prestige symbols are mostly possessions or privileges of a material nature. In addition, the public also recognizes prestige symbols of a nonmaterial nature, such as achievements in the professions and the fine arts. These are rated higher than those dependent upon income.

Can businessmen minimize the importance of minor-value prestige symbols?

Many executives realize that the public and employees overemphasize the value of prestige symbols. They would prefer that recognition be given to true achievement rather than symbols of achievement. After all, certain symbols are often acquired more or less accidentally and without demonstration of great merit. This is a very common situation in the universities—certain possessors of degrees have fulfilled the formal requirements for the degree but have failed to get an education.

A few business leaders try to overcome the spurious values of status symbols by ignoring the prestige privileges they have earned. One corporation president, for example, each morning pilots his car into the least desirable spot in the company's parking lot—a place reserved for him at his own request.

The chairman of a giant midwestern company guides his conspicuously old low-priced car past the rows of gleaming new models, owned by his subordinates, to his regular space.

These and other top executives are trying to downgrade that much maligned but omnipresent appurtenance of corporate power—the status symbol. They are fighting a losing battle.

Most members of the public and employees have deep-seated psychological needs for status symbols. Many corporate leaders also defend them as an aid to discipline and operating efficiency. Status symbols in business underscore the lines of authority and indicate to employees where power and responsibility are centered. In addition, status privileges provide "fringe benefits" for executives and employees, benefits that may be more attractive than taxable increases in pay.

Even though symbols have significance only in accordance with the meanings that the seekers and holders give them, they are essential to the emotional well-being of most members of the human race. It is necessary, therefore, for the supervisor to become perceptive in regard to what specific symbols mean to the individuals with whom he works.

QUESTIONS ON THE CHAPTER

1. Name ways in which identification may affect the behavior of the individual.
2. Discuss the relationship between shared experiences and identification in connection with business.
3. Why do management interviewers consider an applicant's identifications when he is being considered for hiring?
4. Comment on some dangers of overidentification.
5. Is it possible for an individual to know his identifications? If so, how?
6. Why are titles in companies not always indicative of true ability or status?
7. In what respects do payroll classifications indicate status?
8. Why do some adults fear individuals who symbolize authority?
9. Describe some characteristics of an individual suffering from "status anxiety."
10. How should a junior executive react to the use of his own title?
11. Explain the two classifications of prestige symbols.
12. Why are prestige and status symbols essential to most individuals?
13. Of the ideas presented in the chapter, which ones are of special interest or value to you?
14. What did the chapter contribute to your future relations with (a) the men who supervise your work, (b) the employees whom you may supervise?

PROBLEMS AND PROJECTS

For All Students

1. Identification involves feelings that are deeper than admiration or respect. A mother identifies with her son even though she may not admire his behavior. She usually remains loyal to her identification. Can you apply this idea to a business concern or institution that has some personal meanings for you?
2. Discuss status symbols sought by students of your institution. Are the students who seek the status symbols more loyal to the institution than those who do not seek them? What are some of the disadvantages of status symbols?

For Advanced Students

3. Make a study of status symbols found in authoritarian *versus* those in democratic forms of government. Do status symbols seem to enable the

holders to flaunt power? Do your findings offer suggestions for business managements?

4. Some studies of people who live in suburban communities indicate that they are especially active in community organizations. Many of the members work for large companies and are moved about frequently. As a result they lack roots. Activity in the local organizations gives them roots. Make a study of this thesis.

For Men in Business

5. Which departments or employees of a specific company you know are downgraded in the thinking of some executives and employees? What factors brought it about? Do these downgraded departments have any outstanding executives with whom employees can identify themselves? How might the situation be improved?

6. The supervisor who lacks identification with his management is likely to show it when he explains to an employee that management denied his request such as the desire for a title or increased pay. He blames the top management. Give an example from your experiences with supervisors to describe the difference between the supervisor who does identify with management and the one who does not.

COLLATERAL READINGS

For All Students

Gellerman, Saul, *Motivation and Productivity*. New York: American Management Association, Inc., 1963. Chapters 13 and 16 present information regarding prestige and the concept of the self. The individual throughout life is partly motivated to behave in a manner consistent with the symbolic role he has accepted as himself.

Newman, Summer, and Warren, *The Process of Management*. Englewood Cliffs, N.J.: Prentice-Hall, Inc., 1967. Chapter 11 discusses authority, power, influence, and status of key men in the company.

For Advanced Students

Aronson, Elliott, and Judson Mills, "The Effect of Severity of Initiation on Liking for a Group," *Journal of Abnormal and Social Psychology*, September 1959. Presents findings that indicate that persons who go through a severe initiation find the group more attractive than do persons who become members without going through a severe initiation.

SYMBOLOGY: *The Use of Symbols in Visual Communication*, ed. Elwood Whitney. New York: Hastings House Publishers, Inc., 1960. This book seeks to answer such questions as how symbols work on us, the implications of symbols for industry, and whether or not visual communication contributes its full share in forming and changing opinions.

For Men in Business

Haynes, W. Warren, and Joseph L. Massie, *Management: Analysis, Concepts and Cases.* Englewood Cliffs, N.J.: Prentice-Hall, Inc., 1969. Presents a framework for integrating research findings regarding the extent that individuals identify with the group to which they belong.

Levinson, Harry, *The Exceptional Executive.* Cambridge, Mass.: Harvard University Press, 1968. Chapters 8–12 discuss identification: process, uses in childhood, transference, and need for fulfillment.

Communication
with Employees

SITUATIONS YOU ARE LIKELY TO MEET

How would you meet each of these situations:
   a. *Before* you have read the chapter? What would
      you say to yourself or to the individual?
   b. *After* you have read the chapter? How have
      your answers changed?

1. You are manager of production in a plant that has
   ten foremen. A salesman for a closed-circuit television
   service makes a sales pitch to you, using the argument that some of your foremen are not communicating management's plans, particularly in regard to
   facts involved in debunking rumors. Assuming that
   the company can afford the purchase, what will you
   decide? Why?

2. A top management executive of a company tells you
   that he has published certain important financial
   facts about the company in several publications, but
   employees do not believe them. He says that there
   just simply isn't any other way to try to get the facts
   across to them. What would you say?

3. A person who attends many committee meetings is
   likely to have met the perennial critic who always
   finds a flaw in any conclusion reached by others. (Incidentally, when you read many business journals,
   you will also find certain writers who concentrate on
   exposing the flaws in the writings of others in their
   field.) Some committee members believe that the in-

dividuals who like to impress others by their criticism should be kept from expressing their faultfinding views. Assume that you will be the chairman at a forthcoming meeting and a friend recommends shutting out a certain perennial critic who will attend, what will you say?

Communication is more than talking with or writing to people—it is the exchange of meanings. It uses many media and methods: face-to-face conversations, telephone calls, memoranda, publications, speeches, group conferences, newspapers, radio, television, and posters, among others. The extent to which it takes place depends upon factors such as the psychological climate, mental sets of individuals, face-to-face relationships, semantics, and the channels for transmitting the message.

Nonverbal communication

People communicate with each other not only by means of words but by facial expression, gesture, and their actions as well as through symbolic and practical objects. In everyday life a large part of social interaction is not verbalized. Visual observation is essential for the full comprehension of communicative behavior. Every time you meet anyone, he not only hears your words but also observes and reacts to nonverbal cues. He notes your approximate age, body structure, glasses, wristwatch, necktie, clothes, car, facial expression, body posture, tone of voice, muscular tension, and other signs and symbols of what you are and do. He looks for cues to feelings as well as statements. All human beings spontaneously look for and react to these nonverbal cues to identify the person and to sense his underlying motives. These may be more revealing than his words.

Listening is more than hearing words. It includes the hearer's estimate as to whether the speaker is sincere or merely trying to put something over to his advantage. The employee who is listening to his boss speak about the company looks for meanings in what is not said as well as in what is said.

Does the boss imagine that he is clever or is he honestly trying to explain the subject in a sincere way? Does he himself really believe what he says? Is he speaking in terms of his own biases only or is he objective? Sometimes silence is more eloquent than words.

Both the sender and the receiver must be active participants in the communication process. The receiver may appear to be a passive participant. Actually, communication is a dynamic process in which both parties participate. The best example of good communication is that of a man-to-man discussion in which both parties alternately speak and listen, answer questions, correct misconceptions, agree on the extent to which they agree or disagree, and plan an appropriate course of action.

Communication in itself is not an end or a goal. Rather, it is a tool for conveying meaning and, in the business world, a basic factor in inducing action. Without it, management could not coordinate the various elements that make a business enterprise out of men, materials, and money. Management must give instructions so that employees and other people understand and act on them. In industry, the channels of communication are of three kinds: up-line, down-line, and cross-line, depending on the direction from the source to the ultimate recipient of the message.

COMMUNICATION WITH EMPLOYEES

The supervisor as an agent in communication

Communication with employees has been of increasing concern to management. If it is to be a mutual process in which the employees are active participants, organized ways must be provided to enable them to express their ideas in their everyday relations with management. Furthermore, they must be confident that management is listening.

Surveys of employee opinion indicate that management does not always know the employees' attitudes toward their work, the job, and the company. Management tends to assume that they are, or should be, the same as management's.

Management wants employees to have respect for the company and the men at the top. Certainly the old policy whereby management thought it could win the employees' respect by being the victor in a last-ditch fight between labor and management is no longer sensible.

Most companies rely upon the foremen to be the active communicators of management's policies and objectives to the employees. The foremen are in close relation with the workers and should be able to pass on management's directives, answer their questions, and provide explanations. Unfortunately, many foremen are not as articulate as management wishes. To overcome the problem, the more alert managements seek additional avenues for keeping employees informed. In some cases, the personnel department is assigned the responsibility for communications, not only those of the routine variety such as posting changes in rules or policies on the bulletin boards but also those of the educational type that require the organizing of special meetings and the writing of instruction booklets.

"ACCENTUATE THE POSITIVE."

By reshuffling a few phrases and rephrasing a few words, a safety man in a railway yard cut accidents in half. He simply took the usual safety slogans and translated them into more personal and positive terms. Here are his revisions:

"Remove your gloves when operating this machine" was changed to: "Save your fingers—and your income—by removing your gloves."

"Danger! High voltage" was given this addition: "Even 240 volts can kill; there are 660 volts here."

"Wear goggles at this grinder" was revised to read: "Eyes aren't replaceable; goggles are. Please use both at this machine."

"No smoking" was expanded to: "Lighted cigarettes cause fires, damage and death. Please—don't light up."

"Pick up those tools" was changed to a less bossy and more informal: "Scattered tools cause accidents. Pick up your tools and save your conscience."

Over the wrench stand he put the sign: "There's the right wrench— and the wrong one. Use the right one first."

On doors he cautioned: "Careful now: Danger may be on the other side of this door."

Most signs outlive their usefulness after a while. They become part of the walls they are stuck on and are no longer noticed. This is the fate of all danger signs, no matter how startling their message. Frequent change of position, design and phrasing is a good method for keeping signs effective.

Source: *The Foreman's Letter*, March 22, 1950.

The foreman, in spite of his limitations, remains the key agent in bringing about communication in both directions, up and down. Some supervisors make it easy for employees to bring their complaints, suggestions, and even their personal problems to them. Management must, however, select and train foremen to perform effectively in two-way communication.

If their interest in the problem is only casual or occasional, the effectiveness of communication is uncertain and intermittent. One of the most common indicators of a supervisor's failure to communicate effectively takes place when a supervisor loses a good employee and says: "Why didn't he come in and talk to me before he quit—we could have straightened out the problem!" The fact that a supervisor associates or even fraternizes with his employees does not mean that employees will fully communicate with him. They may know him so well that they realize he does not want to hear about certain problems or discuss them. They usually know what topics are "off limits" in his thinking.

To be a good communicator, management must provide special training for the supervisor. He must be stimulated to act on management's messages. The supervisor must be led to appreciate that without a sound communications system, a top executive operates partially in the dark. The supervisor should realize that he communicates the top manager's ideas, feelings, purposes, and goals, indeed his whole personality.

BARRIERS TO COMMUNICATION

Almost all people are "touchy" about certain topics. Think of all the people with whom you would not start a discussion on religion, politics, race, family ancestry, higher education, etiquette, and a host of other topics about which a specific individual may be especially, though often unnecessarily, sensitive.

Certain persons in a company are touchy subjects—the kind that people discuss only with those whom they trust. Perhaps the most common example is the unique personality of a key executive. He may be a man of considerable ability, highly respected, and competent, but his idiosyncrasies are irritating or bothersome to some associates and subordinates. Remarks about him are likely to be answered by, "He's just that kind of a guy and there's nothing anyone can do about him—so let's not talk about him."

Certain subjects, too, are avoided because a member of management has fixed ideas about them. The plant manager, for example, who spends several years in developing a bonus system for the shop may be so loyal to his brainchild that no one has the courage to suggest changes in the bonus system.

Executives recognize that employees are overly sensitive about certain topics. They maintain "zones of silence" as indicated by these typical comments: (a) "If we speak up, our message will be called propaganda," (b) "The union wouldn't like it," (c) "Let sleeping dogs alone—discussion is too risky. Employees will ask questions we can't answer the way they want them answered," and (d) "That's a topic that always gets the person into trouble when he talks about it. 'Never wrestle with a pig, you'll both get dirty.' "[1]

Generally, the management that wants to inform employees about its policies and plans can do so. And the management that is tight-lipped cannot be helped by setting up a formal plan or by hiring a communications expert.

On the assumption that people who engage in communication may have some insights, The National Industrial Conference Board asked this question of more than 750 company members whose general level of responsibility places them in the management category: "What are the barriers to communication within a company?"

The barriers cited by these management representatives were found to fall into three major groups:

> Barriers arising from the fact that individuals are involved in communication—and individuals differ. These might be called pre-existing barriers to communication, which a company inherits because they are common to society.
>
> Barriers arising from the company's "climate," or atmosphere, which tend to stultify communication.
>
> Barriers that are largely mechanical in the sense that they stem from lack of proper facilities or means of communication.[2]

Status relationships as a barrier to communication are in the first category. People who are in subordinate or superior positions tend to slow down the free interchange of information. The typical subordinate likes to tell his boss only what the latter is interested in hearing. He prefers to cover up mistakes, failures, and bad news. He modifies or withholds information going up. He wants to anticipate what the boss wants to know or what he may want to know later. He tries to present things in such a way that his boss will feel that the situation is not too bad. He prefers to give good news.

The superior, in turn, cannot always describe his problem to his subordinate. Some information such as the names of persons selected for promotion and details about new products and organizational plans must be withheld until the time is propitious. As a result, the subordinate interprets and misinterprets actions and attitudes of his superior.

Of course, distortion and filtering of information both up and down the line is lessened when there is an atmosphere of permissiveness and where

---

[1]See C. J. Dover, "Silence—An Employee Relations Pitfall," *Advanced Management*, September 1957.

[2]"Barriers to Communication," *Management Record*, National Industrial Conference Board, January 1958.

the team spirit is so strong that criticism can be given and taken without rancor.

Mental sets of men of management and unions

"Mental set" is often defined as "a readiness to think or respond in a predetermined way." We all note a person's mental set at any given time by his posture, tone of voice, muscular tension, and facial expression. Even though he says no words, we note whether he is resistant or receptive to an idea. A mental set often becomes a hindrance to change. A set may be so fixed that it does not permit the possibility of change. Many people have developed so rigid a pattern of thinking and living that we can predict their reactions to specific situations.

Experiments indicate that a single adjective may reorganize the whole view of a person described, its effect going far beyond the simple, logical relevancy of the word and, in addition, such a reorganization modifies other aspects of the observer's behavior toward the subject.

Mason Haire, for example, has reported an experiment in which the subjects were 76 members of a Central Labor Council and 108 representatives of management—industrial relations or personnel men from plants or employers' organizations. All members of both groups lived and worked in the San Francisco Bay area. Many members of these two groups (though not necessarily all) had bargained with one another.

> The test materials consisted of two pictures and four descriptions. The pictures were chosen in an attempt to represent "ordinary people"; they were middle-aged, moderately dressed men, with no particular expression on their faces. The four descriptions were made up in the following manner: all four descriptions contained the information that (1) the person was almost 46, (2) was healthy, (3) had been married for a long time and had a family, (4) had held several jobs, all successfully, (5) had few hobbies or interests outside of family and work, and (6) read newspapers and fixed things around the house. In half the cases these items were arranged in different order so that it did not sound like the identical man, though in fact the same items were present. Further, in half the cases the man pictured was described as "local manager of a small plant which is a branch of a large manufacturing concern," and in the other half as "Secretary-Treasurer of his Union." . . .
>
> The subjects were told that this was part of a research project to see how well people could analyze personality on the basis of a few facts. They were given one minute to study the picture and description, then were told to turn the page where they found a list of 290

adjectives relating to personality. At the head were the following instructions:

Directions: A number of common adjectives are listed below. Please read them over quickly and check all those you would consider to apply to the man in the photograph. Don't worry about duplications, contradictions, etc. Work quickly and do not spend much time on any one adjective. Check your first impression of each adjective. You may check as many or as few as you like.[3]

The most striking result is as follows: when a member of either group (management or labor) describes a person, the description varies markedly depending on the role of the person described, although the facts and the pictures are identical. Thus, 74 percent of the subjects in the managerial group chose the word "honest" as descriptive of Mr. A, *when he was identified as manager*. The same managerial subjects, however, chose the word "honest" to describe Mr. A only 50 percent of the time when he was identified as a representative of the union.

The experiment showed, in this particular instance, that a single person looks very different depending on whether he is seen as a manager or a union secretary. Moreover, the nature of this difference depends on whether he is thus seen *by* a manager or a union man.

In summary, from looking at these data, we can say:

(1) The general impression of a person is radically different when he is seen as a member of management than when he is seen as a representative of labor.

(2) Further, the change effected by membership is different when it is seen by members of management and labor. The kind of effect of such a characteristic or group membership is influenced by the group membership of the perceiver himself.

(3) Management and labor each sees the other as less dependable than himself.

(4) Management and labor each sees the other as less appreciative of the other's position than he himself is.

(5) Management and labor each sees the other as deficient in thinking, emotional characteristics, and interpersonal relations in comparison with himself. . . .

On the basis of these data it seems clear that labor and management are not talking to the same people when they confer with one another. Labor sees itself and management so differently and man-

[3] Mason Haire, "Role-Perceptions in Labor-Management Relations: An Experimental Approach," *Industrial and Labor Relations Review*, January 1955.

agement sees itself and labor so differently that, although they are [the] only two people in the room, four people seem to be involved in the conversation. Consider, for example, the meaning of a statement like "we are anxious to work with you." Let us suppose it is made by Mr. B., a labor representative. He is seen by labor to be honest, dependable, and efficient. However, by management he is seen as persistent, opinionated, argumentative, and outspoken. He is seen by labor to have high thinking ability, to be dependable, and to see the other's side of the problem. He is seen by management to be a less clear thinker than management is, to be relatively undependable, and to fail to see management's side of the problem. Under these circumstances, it seems hardly possible that the statement can mean the same thing to both parties. Though only one man speaks, the masks through which the statement comes are so different that it is hardly the same thing any longer.[4]

Research studies of this kind confirm what we know from daily experience with people in business—mental set causes members of management and of labor to perceive each other in terms of their own characteristic reactions. It is also involved in the way a subordinate perceives his superior and the superior perceives his subordinate. All persons have mental sets that color their perceptions of others in the family and in school as well as in business life.

The number of barriers to communication is so great that extended study is necessary to appreciate them. One phase of communication, the grapevine, is often treated as a barrier. Actually, it is a symptom of inadequate communication.

The grapevine

Every company has one or more "rumor mills" or centers from which rumors are passed on to employees by means of a communications procedure, ordinarily called the grapevine. Its information is often distorted, at best, incomplete.

If management ignores the grapevine and it is allowed to operate unchecked, it may cause discord, layoffs, or even strikes. At its worst, it may unjustly damage the reputations of innocent individuals. Some managements ignore the grapevine, particularly during a strike period. In a period of labor tension the union involved will usually distribute, openly or by grapevine, information favorable to the union while management remains silent.

Some companies are grapevine riddled, year in and year out. Common

[4]*Ibid.*

rumors are that the plant is going to be closed down and its operations merged with another factory, that pay scales will be raised, that pay will be cut, that the president is going to resign, and so on and on. The origin of such rumors may be in the misinterpretation of an overheard telephone conversation or someone's overactive imagination.

One source of rumors is the personnel who operate duplicating equipment in an office. Some of the operators cannot understand or interpret simple information when they read it. The duplicating machine operator who sees the first copy giving news of a management decision may tip off his or her friends days before copies of the release are distributed to others. Even though he is given instructions to maintain secrecy, the mimeograph operator may be unable to control his urge to tell "inside dope" that will excite others.

A few managements have duplicating equipment installed in the executive office suite and train a reliable secretary to operate it, so that confidential matters may be kept confidential until the time of official release. Dictating records and transcriptions also require extra control. All those who take part in processing information as well as the sender and the receiver are participants. Those who should not receive the message are also participants in a sense. In modern business, a very important party to many routine transmissions of memos and letters is the person who should receive a carbon copy.

Several executives have advocated using the grapevine for spreading plant information. They think of the "grapevine" as a medium of communication. Actually, as more experienced writers have pointed out, the "grapevine is only a measure of the vacuum that exists in a communication system." When anyone attempts to use it as a channel for sending information to employees, he will find that he has no control over the content of the message once the "leak" is made and when made, no assurance that the message will go to the right people.

Management should not, however, use the public address system to debunk a rumor because this method seems to make the rumor better remembered than the refutation.

A rumor should be interpreted as a psychiatrist would a symptom: "What anxiety or attitude does this rumor reflect?" The cause of the anxiety, rather than the rumor per se, should be corrected.

Whenever a company finds itself in competition with a "rumor factory" going full blast among its plant employees, it means that normal communication channels are not open and available. Rumors flourish most in the absence of reliable information.

Supervisors can be taught to be attentive to the questions and complaints of their employees and to relay distortions of fact that might create trouble later. The management that keeps its employees informed at regular and frequent intervals about its plans and problems is likely to have little trouble with its grapevine.

Few rumors arise when each worker feels secure, regards himself as a member of a team, and knows facts and plans that involve him. Rumors arise and are spread when employees do not know the facts.

Participation is the most effective form of communication

For the employee to believe in his employer, he needs more than words, kindness, or managerial integrity. This has been discovered by certain corporation executives who assumed that the publishing of an annual financial report on the business, including the percentage of profit on the sales dollar, would convince employees that the employer was fair in the amount of the income shared with the employees.

Surveys made after financial reports had been published showed that employees read the financial reports but still said: "The company makes too much money!" So a few executives decided they could convince the employees of the company's fair dealings by asking each employee by means of an unsigned questionnaire how much profit he would expect on each sales dollar if he were to invest ten thousand dollars of his money in a business. Their answers mostly were to the effect that they would, in their own business, expect to make at least twenty-five cents on the sales dollar. Quite logically the employer said: "You say that you would want a profit of 25 percent if you were in business for yourself. Look at the company's financial statement. We make a profit of only 4 percent. Don't you think that we are generous to you, the employee, when we make much less profit than you yourself would expect if you were the employer?"

The reaction of employees to this kind of explanation about corporate profits was a loud and emphatic: "The company makes too much money!"

Upon getting the same old answer from the employees, most of these employers threw up their hands and said: "What the hell! If employees can't be convinced after all the proofs and logical explanations we have given them, they just can't be convinced. We'll do the best we can and quit trying to convince them about the fairness of our treatment of them."

Fortunately, a few employers did not quit trying. They analyzed the situation further and came up with the rediscovery of a very old psychological principle, namely: *People believe in the extent to which they participate.*[5]

Certain managements do convince their employees of the company's fairness by giving them a sense of participation in the business. This has been done by explaining the company's plans and problems to the em-

[5]See Ross G. Walker, "The Misinformed Employee," *Harvard Business Review,* May 1948.

ployees and by getting them to help solve the small and the ordinary everyday problems. Employees are given more than information—they are asked as colleagues to help by doing their own work more easily and profitably. Most of this has been done successfully without benefit of either a formal suggestion or a profit-sharing system. The supervisors have learned to practice this philosophy because the executives above them believe in and practice it. The vital factor has been the application of the American philosophy of thinking of employees as colleagues rather than as subordinates.

When the employees are taken behind the scenes in the management of the company and are sincerely given participation in those problems within the range of their abilities, the doubts and misgivings about the employer's fairness in management disappear. The employees come to believe in the employer and the business when they understand, through participation, management's problems. In a sense, they feel that they sit in the president's office every day.

The best communication technique is usually direct face-to-face oral communication between people. The use of this technique is even possible in a large modern company where management is genuinely anxious to communicate with its employees.

Harry D. Kolb, manager of the Employee Communication Division, Esso Standard Oil Company, has described how it can be done. He defines communication in industry not as a device to sell, convert, or attack but rather as a process of exchanging ideas, feelings, and information. Further, a good communications system should stem from the belief that the employees have a right to hear and be heard.

As an example, Kolb cited the work of one of his plants of seventeen hundred. In contrast to an old attitude of keeping business secrets for a chosen few, they began with the attitude that, as one of their own executives put it, "We have no business secrets that we need to keep from our people." Their first step was to hold a forum-type meeting of supervisors and employees. Nineteen groups met and discussed past records, present situations, and future plans. As a result, four thousand questions were presented, which the top men then attempted to fully answer.

They did not stop there. Instead, following this, there were a large number of face-to-face group discussions between and within all levels. For example, weekly staff meetings were held not only by the top management but also by the lower echelon groups. In the line of printed communications, biweekly bulletins were circulated among the supervisors. In addition, a four-page tabloid, edited by a trained man, was distributed throughout the plant.

The meetings not only demonstrated the leader's interest in his men but also stimulated positive reactions and a feeling of participation on the part of the employees. In addition, groups accomplished more when they had looked into their goals and problems and attempted to tackle them together. Thus, it was found that only frank and open communication can minimize suspicions, correct misunderstandings, and build the teamwork essential to the continuing success of a company.

Kolb emphasized that all this and more was done to maintain a steady and timely flow of information. Of course, each company must adopt the best methods for its own situation. When properly organized and carried out, a good communications system builds a sense of colleagueship among employees in all strata. Each individual then realizes that he does play an important and active part in the daily operations of business.[6]

This suggests that everyone in business should be concerned about his media commonly used for distributing information to employees. The media usually utilized for this purpose are employee magazines, bulletin boards, moving pictures, and meetings. Helpful suggestions are offered in numerous books and articles published on the subject. In the remainder of this chapter we shall give attention to those communication procedures of special interest to the student of human relations who expects to work in management circles.

Meetings for communicating with executives and with other staff members of the organization are so much a part of American business that it is important to give some attention to them.

COMMUNICATION IN MANAGERIAL AND STAFF CIRCLES

Meetings

The terms *conference, committee meeting,* and *meeting* are often used interchangeably. Generally, a *conference* in business is called by one or more executives to get information in order that the executives may make a decision or develop a plan. A *committee* is usually charged with responsibility for making a recommendation or carrying out an action plan. The individuals chosen for a committee are also likely to be chosen with more care than the members of a conference. A *conference* is, by definition, "a formal consultation . . . an interchange of ideas." A *meeting* may be distinguished from a conference as being less formal.

Many American executives feel harassed by the practice of holding meetings. When an executive is told that a conference is to be held to discuss a problem, his answer is likely to be something like this:

[6]See Harry D. Kolb, "Creating the Organizational 'Atmosphere' for Improved Communication," *Personnel,* American Management Association, Inc., May 1954, pp. 482–87.

"Oh, no! Not another meeting. I've had to attend fifteen meetings in less than a week. As a result, I've had to stay late every evening this week to get my work done."

Many meetings are unproductive and wasteful of time. In spite of their unpopularity, they continue to be used. When rightly planned and conducted, they can be very productive. To be productive, the meeting should have a purpose of interest to all who attend.

A meeting that does not keep to its purpose becomes dull and unproductive. Without control, irrelevant matters are brought up, and a few people take up the time of the others discussing a subject of interest only to them. Matters are brought up that frequently can't be settled. Or someone wants to talk about a subject that must be discussed later because someone concerned is not present at the meeting.

In business a meeting is usually run by the man who calls it. A time limit should be set in advance. The shorter the time, the better. A meeting lasting up to ninety minutes is likely to be productive. After that, the time-work ratio declines. For some chairmen, participation is their main problem. Their usual procedure is to make a statement and say:

"Anybody have any questions?"

Generally, only silence follows, and the meeting ends without discussion. But some of the people who remained silent *had* questions. They were reluctant to ask them. Perhaps the man who presided gave the impression that he really did not want questions. If the chairman genuinely desires questions, he asks in an inquiring tone. He turns to someone and asks: "What do you think about it?" or "How can we handle this problem?"

Group members who do not ask questions or express opinions in some cases may exclaim to another member afterwards, "It's no use talking to him—he knows it all," or "He doesn't really want our ideas. Did you notice that he looked down his nose at us at the same time that he was asking the questions?"

Sometimes the chairman gets plenty of questions and opinions of the argumentative variety. As the chairman he would like to develop enlightening discussion without useless argument. Carl R. Rogers, a psychologist, suggested an effective technique for avoiding the kinds of arguments that change no one's opinion and for bringing about, instead, a real listening and understanding when conflict prevails. The technique recommended is that the leader of the meeting stop the heated debate and get everyone to agree that no one will speak until he has first restated the ideas and feelings of the person who has last spoken. He must do this accurately and to that person's reasonable satisfaction. The meeting does not go on until this is done.

This rule is often difficult to put into effect, but it does require each speaker, before presenting his own opinion, to listen receptively enough to "get" the previous speaker's opinion and the thinking behind it. It means that each speaker must clearly comprehend and state what the other has said. It usually reduces emotional tensions; "The heat goes out of the argument," as Rogers put it. Of course the speaker whose ideas have been paraphrased may also modify his original statement. The main point is that effective communication requires a conscious effort on the part of every member to get at the meaning of the other person's feelings.

Committees

For many persons in responsible positions, attending committee meetings is one of their most time-consuming activities. Department heads, for example, spend as much as 20 percent of their time in committee. The amount of time spent in committees seems to be increasing. Some managements are so addicted to this kind of communication that almost every problem of importance is treated by a committee before a decision is made. In some companies, as one humorist stated, "The president himself usually attends and he sits as a majority of one!" Fortunately, most presidents who attend committee meetings have a warm sensitivity to human values, listen well, and are tolerant of the opinions of others.

A survey by *Harvard Business Review* showed that regular or standing committees are found in more than 80 percent of the twelve hundred companies polled. Top executives are involved in more committees than executives who are further down the management ladder. The average executive spends nearly three and one-half hours a week in committees; he serves on three committees. He usually has seven other members sitting on the committee with him, but he thinks that four would be better. In addition to attending these formal committee meetings, the executive spends the equivalent of one working day a week in informal conferences and consultation with fellow executives. Interestingly, the respondents to this poll did not criticize committees as such—the issue of the worthwhileness of the committee idea lies with the quality of the membership and the ways the committees are run. The key to the solution, most executives believe, is the committee chairman.[7]

The fact that several men of sound judgment come into an office for a conference does not mean that they combine their thinking and develop more sound judgment than anyone alone would do. A group may cause each one to rely on the opinions of the others and to exert less individual care himself. The greater the confidence in his colleagues, the stronger this tendency. Sometimes a group of competent executives will make mistakes that no one of them would commit alone.

When responsibility is spread across a committee, no one person feels

[7]See Rollie Tillman, Jr., "Problems in Review—Committees on Trial," *Harvard Business Review*, May–June 1960, pp. 5f.

responsible for a decision. Committees not only avoid responsibility by making a decision an action of a committee but a committee can also be a whipping boy that enables the individual members to escape chastisement for bad action.

Certainly, many good ideas get lost in committees. As the late Charles F. Kettering stated when he was General Motors' research chief: "The surest way to kill a valuable new proposal is to lay it before the average committee." A. Whitney Griswold, president of Yale from 1950 to 1963, was quoted as having asked: "Could Hamlet have been written by a committee? Or the Mona Lisa painted by a club?"

One reason for the failure of a committee to function well is in the psychological peculiarities of some members. Every committee is likely to have at least one member who knows nothing about the subject presented to the committee. This individual is apt to feel that he ought to justify his membership by comment on the proposal. It is easier to call attention to dangers in the proposal than to comment on it constructively. He therefore criticizes and helps to kill what may be a good idea.

The astute chairman wants those present to participate, but he knows there are several kinds of participators. There is the kind of involvement with others present that makes a member of the group feel important. Such a person is more conscious of his own needs than of the problem under discussion. The satisfaction of his need for prestige or self-regard is his main objective. This kind of participation is called *ego-involvement*.

Some persons present wish to be participants but are unable to express themselves in regard to the major topic or to contribute to the exchange of ideas. They go through the verbal motions of participating but are obviously unable to do more than repeat words. This kind of participation is called *verbal-involvement*. The wise chairman seeks responses that show that the members of the group are thinking about the problem rather than their own psychological needs.

After studying hundreds of committees in operation, several researchers have set seven members as the top limit for efficiency. Beyond that point, "low participators" tend to stop talking to each other. Certain "top men" do most of the talking; and when low participators do talk, it is likely to be to the top men only.

On being a good participant in a meeting

The main requirement for intelligent participation in any meeting is a genuine interest in the problem under discussion. At the same time that one presents his ideas and learns those of other members of the group, he must also recognize the human relations situations involved in the people present. Almost every conference group has at least one defensive member, the kind

of individual who has an urge to impress others. Or there may be the perennial critic who always finds a flaw in the conclusion reached by the others.
Such a person cannot be cured—he can only be held in check by the chairman and endured by the others. Intelligent, mature persons who attend
meetings rise above the annoyances imposed upon them by the emotionally
immature members of the group.

The young ambitious employee who is invited to attend an important
conference of executives is likely to feel somewhat self-conscious and betray
it by either talking too much or not at all. He can overcome such tendencies
on his part by means of the following principles:

1. Be prepared. When executives invite a bright young man to sit in
   on a conference, they are giving him an opportunity to get acquainted with the organization and its problems but they also hope
   that he will contribute tactfully to the discussion. He can find out
   the topic for discussion and prepare his ideas in advance. He can
   ask his associates for their ideas, get facts and figures, and plan
   his presentation.
2. Be on time. The executive who invites the bright young man expects him to be sufficiently respectful of his responsibilities to be
   on time. The old college classroom habit of wandering in when
   the spirit moves is not tolerated by most executives.
3. Be courteous toward other members of the group. This means
   staying awake, looking interested, and asking sensible questions.
   Listen respectfully to the ideas of others, but do not try to flatter
   anyone or give compliments. Mature men do not need them from
   a youngster. Anyone who uses the conference table to make a
   testimonial speech to flatter the boss is not likely to get much
   respect from the boss and none from the others. The nearest to
   giving a compliment that is possible for the young man is to nod
   his head in approval of what someone says.
4. Avoid showing up anyone even if he is wrong. No one likes to be
   made to appear stupid or ridiculous even if the evidence might
   prove it. No one in a conference should be forced to lose face.
5. Skip all the clever jokes or funny stories that come to mind during
   the meeting. Do not tell them unless they are very brief and
   pointed to the problem under discussion. Executives do not like
   to waste their time listening to long stories. Only the presiding
   member is expected to use humor to liven the meeting.
6. Respect the confidences of other members of the group. Matters
   of a semi-secret nature are often mentioned in conferences. One
   mark of the responsible business executive is the ability to keep

quiet when he is unable to answer a question without revealing confidential information.[8]

QUESTIONS ON THE CHAPTER

1. What is communication? How does nonverbal communication take place?
2. What is the function of communication in the business world?
3. Who is the key agent in bringing about communication in industry, both up and down?
4. What are three groups of communication barriers within a company, according to a National Industrial Conference Board survey?
5. What method is often used to ascertain the mental set of a person? Describe the findings of Mason Haire in his study of the perceptions of labor union leaders and of representatives of management.
6. In what ways may the grapevine be considered a barrier and an aid to communication?
7. Explain the situations in which rumors are most likely to arise.
8. What is the best communication technique and how has Harry Kolb described a way that it can be carried out?
9. Differentiate between a conference, a committee meeting, and a meeting.
10. How much time do department heads spend in committee meetings?
11. What two types of participators should a committee leader be able to recognize?
12. In what respects is preparation important to committee work?
13. Name four principles that would be advantageous for a young employee to follow in executive committee meetings.
14. Of the ideas presented in the chapter, which ones are of special interest or value to you?
15. What did the chapter contribute to your future relations with (a) the men who supervise your work, (b) the employees whom you may supervise?

PROBLEMS AND PROJECTS

For All Students

1. Articles on the subject of communications appear from time to time in many

[8]Adapted from Frank M. Kleiler, "Etiquette for Business Bull Sessions," *The Office Economist*, June 1957. Copyright © 1957, Art Metal Construction Company, Jamestown, N.Y.

business and scientific journals. Examine available copies, particularly *Business Week* and *Dun's Review and Modern Industry*. State some of the new ideas you learned that are not covered in the text.

2. Attend a meeting as an observer. Evaluate the chairman's leadership and the participation by members. Describe what happened. Were there any examples of the subject covered in this chapter? What specific suggestions did you get for yourself for your acting as chairman in the future?

For Advanced Students

3. Examine some of the behavioral science textbooks available to you—your own and those of fellow students. What information do they contain about communication?

4. Some companies give employees a great deal of economic information that shows how well off they are in comparison with workers of the Soviet State. Would you present information of this kind in the company's publication for employees? Give reasons for and against its use with employees.

For Men in Business

5. Obtain copies of various company publications for employees. Study their contents and the themes of the articles by management. How do they differ from publications put out by unions?

6. Some companies subscribe to a poster or bulletin service for employees. These services usually admonish the employees in regard to safety, thrift, and other virtues. How do you evaluate such services?

COLLATERAL READINGS

For All Students

Massie, Joseph L., *Essentials of Management*. Englewood Cliffs, N.J.: Prentice-Hall, Inc., 1964. Chapter 7 treats communicating as a link among all other functions of the managerial process.

Newman, Summer, and Warren, *The Process of Management*. Englewood Cliffs, N.J.: Prentice-Hall, Inc., 1967. Chapter 25 treats two-way personal communication, transmission of feelings, and empathetic listening.

For Advanced Students

King, Donald C., "A Multiplant Factor Analysis of Employees' Attitudes Toward Their Company," *Journal of Applied Psychology*, August 1960.

Pemberton, W. H., "Talk Patterns of People in Crises," *Personnel Administration*, March–April 1969. Studies of talk patterns of conversational exchanges in crises fall into three styles: sullen silence, attack, and deception.

For Men in Business

Following Up Attitude Survey Findings, Studies in Personnel Policy, No. 181, National Industrial Conference Board, Inc., 1961. This study presents a description of the Champion plan plus comprehensive and helpful reports for the benefit of other users of attitude surveys.

Vardaman, George T., and Carroll C. Halterman, *Managerial Control through Communication*. New York: John Wiley & Sons, Inc., 1968. Introduces a new model of managerial activity based directly on the manager, communication, and control.

The Corporate Image
and
Public Relations

SITUATIONS YOU ARE LIKELY TO MEET

How would you meet each of these situations:
   a. *Before* you have read the chapter? What would you say to yourself or to the individual?
   b. *After* you have read the chapter? How have your answers changed?

1. Shortly after you take a job with a company, the president says to you: "This company has a poor image in the community—people do not realize how much we are doing that is for the benefit of the people and, to some extent, for social advancement. You went to college. You know how to talk to people. As an assignment, I'd like you to make a survey of our company's public image. Before making the survey, tell me how you intend to go about it."

2. A senior vice-president has been with his company for many years. He has followed the ups and downs of the company's reputation in the community. He tells you that his experience shows very definitely that some people hate the company because they hate or at least do not believe anything good about any business. The attitudes of these people cannot be changed by means of surveys or public relations programs. How would you answer him?

3. You are an executive in a company. A teen-ager has been brought to you because he stole valuable company property. When you talk with him, he tells you

that he meant no harm—he stole from the company, not from a person. How would you answer him?

A company is more than an office, a production or service building, and some machines. It is a personality. Its product (or service) has a personality.

The "corporate image" is what people see in their mind's eye when the name of the company is seen or heard. It varies with individuals and their relations to the company: employees, customers, suppliers, dealers, stockholders, and nonusers of the company's product.

An image can be defined as all the ideas and visual symbols that are associated with or suggested by mention of a company, product, or brand. These ideas and visual symbols arouse and carry characteristic meanings whenever a company or its product is mentioned or seen. Visual symbols communicate much faster than word descriptions because they involve less mental effort than thinking in terms of words. Images simplify our existence.

Alert managements are keenly interested in their corporate and product or brand images. Research firms are conducting costly "image building" programs with continuous surveys of their image problems. These companies have discovered that the impression that employees and customers have of them is not always what management thinks it is. One manufacturer of household appliances, for example, found that most people had an image of the company as that of a solid, unexciting, heavy goods producer of electrical equipment. The image of the company's principal and financially more successful competitor, in contrast, was that of an alert, progressive company that creates products of advanced design.

Brand images are stronger and more durable than corporate images because the customer knows more about the brand than about the company, but the corporate image, when known, is merged with that of the brand.

The more favorable the image, the more active people are in recommending a company's products to friends. This is shown by a study made of twelve companies that market consumer goods. When the customers of these firms were grouped according to their image of the companies, the proportion of each group that had recommended the companies' products in the

151

A corporate image reflects the character of a corporation. And when that corporate image is an especially good one, it not only sells merchandise, it can help do a lot of other things. For example . . .

A corporate image tends to make the busiest of men find time to see you when you call.

A corporate image creates confidence in any product that bears your company's name.

A corporate image helps assure you of acceptance for a new product, in advance.

A corporate image gives your company an edge in attracting good talent.

A corporate image helps keep the people at your company feeling it's a good place to work.

A corporate image helps attract capital to your company at favorable terms.

A corporate image causes a stockholder to seek out your stock and select it over another.

A corporate image gives your company an edge with dependable sources of supply . . . helps you secure efficient, profitable distribution.

A corporate image can be the difference between a lawmaker's "yes" and "no."

A corporate image helps a community understand a company, accept it as a good neighbor.

Source: From a house advertisement by Time Inc., publishers of *Life, Time, Fortune, Sports Illustrated, International Editions* of *Time* and *Life*; published in *Time*, June 9, 1958. Quoted by special permission.

last year increased as the favorableness of the corporate image rose. The results of the study[1] can be summarized as follows:

Least favorable image 13%

More favorable 21%

More favorable 35%

More favorable 46%

Most favorable image 54%

Corporate images tend to be self-propagating through word of mouth and become part of the people's tradition. The old monopoly charge against

[1]*Executive Control of the Corporate Image*, The Public Opinion Index for Industry (Opinion Research Corporation, Princeton, N.J.), July 1958, p. 5.

Standard Oil, and Ford's five-dollar-a-day wage, still influence public thinking. Hence the need to create favorable images and continually reinforce them through a flow of fresh experience and exciting information.

How company images are estimated

Research firms that specialize in the study of company and brand images use several techniques in their surveys. Some techniques involve skilled depth interviewing. The techniques more commonly used are likely to involve the following:

1. A simple question may be asked such as "What does the name (company or brand) suggest to you?" Anything that is answered is considered as part of the image.
2. The respondent may be given an incomplete sentence and asked to complete it: "Mr. A works for Company X. He probably works there because he ———."
3. The respondent may be given a cartoon that has a partly empty balloon emanating from the mouth of a figure. The incomplete statement in the balloon may have the words: "I ought to work for Company X if I ———."
4. Pictures of various kinds may be used; the respondent is asked to invent certain kinds of stories appropriate to the picture. Of course, many persons are unable to fill in anything simply because they have no imagery associated with the company or its products. This too is significant—it means that the management has failed to build any image whatsoever.

The questions can be framed to elicit ideas as to the kinds of persons who would be most likely to work for a company: alert, intelligent, unambitious, or dull people. Also, the kinds of people who would be most likely to use the company's products might be found to be professionals, executives, manual workers, old folks, sickly customers, alert young men, or others.

The use of these and more incisive techniques requires some special training in the social sciences. Our major attempt here is not to describe these techniques but to cause those who enter or work in business to become aware of the importance of mental images in business, to seek to know more about the images associated with a given company, and to contribute toward the development of desirable corporate and brand images. Every executive, employee, salesman, friend, enemy, and acquaintance of a company helps to build its image.

What kinds of images do managements seek to develop?

Dun's Review and Modern Industry asked the presidents of 162 companies, three-fourths of them among the 500 largest in this country, about the kind of company impression they want to make on their various publics —employees, customers, stockholders, and others. In most answers, these company presidents said the image they try to create in the public mind is that of a company making and selling a reliable product at a fair price.

The consensus was that company prestige begins with the product itself—its quality, reliability, and constant improvement.

Some presidents, however, seek to develop recognition for certain additional qualities for which they want their companies to be known. These are personality characteristics such as competence, leadership, integrity, friendliness, vigor, forthrightness, warmth, reliability, progressiveness, and so on.

Only 4 percent of the presidents think their companies are doing an "excellent" job of achieving a positive public identity. At the other extreme, 4 percent admitted that they are doing a "poor" job. But three-fourths of the companies believed they are doing a "good," "fair," or "satisfactory" job.[2]

The need for building more accurate imagery

The fact that top management men want their company to be known as producing good products and conducting their business in a spirit of responsible service does not mean that most people think of them in that manner. When, for example, Gilbert Research Company conducted a survey of 1,923 teen-agers of forty-two cities, the attitude of many could be summed up in the statement: "Big businesses run everything in America— they have all the money."

Asked to express whatever came into their minds when they heard the phrase "big business," 31 percent responded by picturing a sort of giant monopoly spread across all America. Many feared that in the future all free enterprise would be swallowed up in one or two gigantic trusts.

One-third of the young people believed that electric and telephone companies make between twenty-five and forty-nine cents on every dollar of income; one-tenth thought they make fifty cents or more. Only 29 percent of

---

[2]See Kenneth Henry, "Creating and Selling Your Corporate Image," *Dun's Review and Modern Industry*, July 1958; copyright © 1958 by Dun & Bradstreet Publications Corporation.

the teen-agers could even vaguely define common stock or had any idea of the number of stockholders in large companies.[3]

Even though capitalism is an important part of our business way of life, many adults think of it in negative terms only. Douglas Williams reported this example:

> We once tested a film for a company, fortunately while it was still in unfinished form. The intent of the film was to demonstrate to the employes that the company stock was widely held by people in all walks of life—not restricted to a few secluded, wealthy people.
>
> Our procedure was to show this film to employes, then ask them what they thought of it. Almost universally, the first response was a question: "What's the purpose of this film?"
>
> That pretty well sums up how far the film had missed its target.
>
> I remember one girl who said she did learn some things from seeing the film. She said she now realized that a newspaper boy, an elderly couple, the corner grocer, and similar people owned stock in the company. So they could, she supposed, be thought of as capitalists. Nevertheless, she said: "I don't want anybody ever to call me a capitalist."
>
> It was a dirty name in her mind.
>
> If management had appreciated her image of capitalism, it would have used a different approach.[4]

Source: by Al Kaufman, *The Management Review* (January 1958), pp. 32–33. Courtesy American Management Association, Inc.

[3]Reported in *Industrial Relations News* (230 West 41 St., New York, N.Y.), October 20, 1956. See also *The Management Review*, American Management Association, Inc., March 1957, p. 35.

[4]Douglas Williams was interviewed in "Six Policies Increase Will to Work," *Nation's Business*, November 1958. Copyright © 1958 by *Nation's Business—the Chamber of Commerce of the United States.*

When the United States Chamber of Commerce analyzed returns from a questionnaire submitted to 1,443 high school students in thirteen schools in a typical industrial county, organized labor was rated by 56 percent of the students as having done most to improve living standards; business management, by 16 percent; government, by 14 percent; and 14 percent had no opinion.

The average score on questions about basic facts of the American economic system was 47.1 out of a possible 100. The following examples point up some typical "blind spots":

Only 11 percent knew that the average profit on sales was between 3 percent and 6 percent; most thought it was over 10 percent. Though one-third of all corporations show no net income every year, fully 77 percent of the students thought few companies operated at a loss. More than half felt that of each dollar divided between company and employees, the larger share went to the owners.

More students (49 percent) thought a strong and able union afforded better protection for job security than the employer's ability to meet competition (31 percent). Productivity as a factor in raising living standards was rated low by 71 percent of the students, who answered no to the question: "Should the worker produce all he can?" Asked what was the "most practical way for workers to increase their living standards," 66 percent of the respondents said, "Get more of the company's money"; only 34 percent said, "Produce more."[5]

Interestingly, many people, old as well as young, visualize big business as an ogre even though they, at the same time, admire certain big companies. Some companies are perceived as progressive minded, efficient, and modern. They are felt to be warm and friendly. The managements are described as fair, considerate, and public spirited.

An examination of the purposes of the image-building programs indicates that they vary from an emphasis on leadership in atomic development to getting along well with labor unions.

The Metropolitan Life Insurance Company is a big company, but it has built a favorable image. Management started with the definite objective of equating itself with leadership in health rather than in leadership in death. At the time, this was contrary to the common practice. The company really sells death insurance, not life insurance, and in England it is still called death insurance. However, the company has put forth extra effort to promote all kinds of measures that cut down the death rate.

General Electric has given the public fascinating "progress reports." The company spends time and money to publish and broadcast information

[5]*Industrial Relations News* (230 West 41 St., New York, N. Y.), February 26, 1955. See also *The Management Review*, American Management Association, Inc., May 1955, p. 342.

about bridges and radar equipment that no individual consumer buys personally. This, however, causes members of the public to feel favorably disposed toward the company and indirectly causes many buyers of smaller appliances and items to choose the GE brand.

One automotive manufacturer for years has sought to spread a prestige aura over the entire product family.

Another manufacturer tries to picture his firm as the one company that makes the housewife's life easier.

A manufacturer of farm products builds his image as one of helpfulness to the farmer.

One reason for building a strong corporate image is to attract potential investors. Of course, when that is a major purpose, financial and investment publications get a large part of the advertising.

The merged company and its image

Many large companies have to define who they are and what they make because mergers, acquisitions, and interchanges of divisions have left the public confused as to the products made. In the case of mergers, management must find what comes first with a customer—his confidence in the product or his confidence in the company behind the product. The good reputation of one can support the other.

One important decision for the management of a merged corporation involves the question as to which company—the parent or the subsidiary —should be featured in the image-building program. When a company with a reputation for precision engineering acquires several subsidiaries doing less exacting, price-competitive work, should all the companies be lumped together? Should the parent company continue to maintain the identity of a subsidiary? Instead of using an all-embracing, identifying family name for all products, should they follow a policy of individual product identity and promotion for each company?

If the company name already has strong association or imagery woven around it—of fashion, mechanical precision, or homey wholesomeness— that image-rich name can be used to promote the products of a new and dissimilar subdivision.

The broadcast personality

In recent years, the person used in television and radio advertising has often become symbolical of a company and its products. Examples can be seen on the television screen every day.

The well-chosen broadcast personality delivers the commercials with a straightforward sales pitch that tells more than words. These individuals perform not only salesmanship functions but also provide public relations values. The television announcer becomes the personification of the corporate personality. For most people he is the personal contact personality for the company. Television announcers are among the best known personalities of our time. A hundred million people will see a company's announcer in the course of a year. His personality adds believability to the sales message. Some corporations think that he should be considered a member of the corporate executive staff and be accorded the same treatment as a top management executive.

The broadcast personality has, to some extent, displaced the old testimonial writer. Testimonials are still, however, effective in much advertising because we want to copy those whom we deem superior in taste, knowledge, or experience. We respect those whom we consider authorities or admirable even though they talk about a prosaic product.

Advertising men, copy writers, and artists not only plan the advertising to maintain continuity of character by means of specific styling but also guide the design of the product and the package in accordance with the essential character desired for the brand. This character is as fully developed and recorded as a character in a play. In a play, the concept of the character guides the director, the costume designer, and the actor. Each interprets the character under varying conditions. In like manner, successful managements strive to create individual characters for their products in the eyes of the consumers whom they wish to reach.

The airline that inaugurated "executive flights" gave facts about its transportation but added atmosphere: cigars, filet mignon, no women allowed on the flight, and a red carpet as the passengers leave the plane.

When the Marlboro cigarette had become known as a high-style cigarette for women, it was decided to change the brand image to make the cigarette attractive to men. The strategy used was:

1. No women were featured in the magazine illustrations or television commercials—only men.
2. All the models were nonprofessionals of the virile type: cowboys, mechanics, outdoor workers, etc.
3. Each man had a plainly visible tattoo on his hand. The tattoo was one of the standard U.S. Navy tattoos. The personalities portrayed in the art work were symbols of meanings that could not be expressed in words. And yet, the men were of the masculine types that appeal to women—he-men, virile, and self-confident.

Just as the rugged tattooed man in the Marlboro cigarette advertisements symbolized the cigarette's new brand personality more effectively than words, so images often speak volumes for companies and their products.

PUBLIC RELATIONS

New emphases in the field of public relations have developed recently. *Harvard Business Review* issued a study of the more thoughtful books on public relations that were published after 1963. Three major ideas emerged:

1. It is argued that U. S. business has become urgently aware of its social responsibilities, and that it sees PR as playing a key role in deciding and executing those actions of the corporation most appropriate to the "public interest."
2. It is claimed that the corporate PR manager of the future must be a trained behavioral scientist.
3. It is predicted that effective PR programs will be increasingly based on and judged by responsible, continuous research on the attitudes of the many publics that ultimately grant the corporation its permit of social survival.[6]

The social responsibilities of corporations are emphasized by numerous writers as exemplified by the following:

Wise managers of large corporations have long realized that to earn any profit at all one must gain public acceptance by acting in the public interest.

Business cannot function, let alone make a profit, in a period of instability. Therefore it is obviously in the interest of business to help to remove the causes of riot and to work toward developing domestic and foreign tranquility, for without both, the chance of profitable operation becomes slim. . . . The very fact that American capitalism has been able to survive proves its ability to adjust to a changing society. . . .

When James M. Roche, chairman of the board of General Motors, reported that his company had hired more than 21,700 hard-core unemployed in eight months, he made some additional important points. "The disadvantaged must have incentives to contribute their own best efforts. These incentives to the deprived include employment opportunities, education and training, proper housing and proper guidance, to enable them to become productive members of our society." Business is finding that to be involved with one aspect of the problem simply means becoming involved in a whole related complex of others.[7]

[6]Kenneth Henry, "Perspective on Public Relations," *Harvard Business Review*, July–August 1967, p. 14.
[7]L. L. L. Golden, "Public Relations—The Difficult Years," *Saturday Review*, February 8, 1969, p. 63.

Fundamentally, public relations is not a program, but a philosophy. It is not a kind of "lotion" that can be applied when needed. It is a point of view or an attitude that permeates all of a corporation's activities. It is a way of business life that demonstrates a continuing sense of responsibility toward every institution and person who is directly or indirectly related to the company. It seeks to earn and maintain the confidence and respect of people. Respect and confidence must be deserved—not acquired by a program of publicity. Modern management realizes that it must have a full awareness of the public judgments which will be passed on actions when they are known.

The man responsible for public relations in any company is the president. As executive officer, he has the responsibility of chief decision maker. All members of the public relations department must be really helpful to the president and other executives who give their leadership to the company and the community.

Many people imagine that public opinion can be purchased. A common delusion is that if a company has enough money to pay for printing, advertising, and "propaganda," people's minds can be changed. This is not so as Earl Newsom, a leader in the field, pointed out in the following statement:

You may remember the effort made some years ago to make Cincinnati "United Nations conscious." During a six-month campaign almost 13,000 people were reached directly through the PTA; every school child took home literature on the UN programs; 10,000 in the Catholic PTA were exhorted by the Archbishop to support the UN; club women sent 1,000 letters and 1,350 telegrams to the American delegation; local radio stations averaged more than 150 spots a week. There were newspaper features, club speakers, and car cards. In all, more than 59,000 pieces of literature were distributed.

At the end of the six months, only half as many people considered the United Nations a means of preventing war as thought so at the beginning. There was almost no change in the number of those who thought the UN should take an active part in world affairs. At the beginning, 76 percent of Cincinnatians were in favor of the United States joining a movement for an international police force; at the close 73 percent. Fewer people favored UN control of atomic bombs. There was no change in the number of those feeling the U.S. should trade more with other countries. There was no improvement in those knowing what the UN is and how it works. Criticism of the record of the UN actually increased during the campaign.

Why did people respond in this way? Perhaps because most of us tend to resist when somebody tries to *sell* us something that is going to change our views. But I suspect that the people in Cincinnati during that six months got their chief impressions of the United Nations, not from the campaign but from their observations of what was happening at the UN during that particular time. Corporate managements are fast learning that their public behavior in times of crisis and trial does far more to create public attitudes toward them than most of the "literature" they develop to "educate the public" in between times.[8]

Purposes of public relations programs

Certain managements assume that a company's publics should be "educated" to understand and go along with the company in attaining its objectives. The management thinks mainly in terms of interpreting the company to the public through education. Such programs often fail. Companies that seek to educate their publics so that they will be more sympathetic toward the company are likely to be disappointed. Educational programs can perform some important functions as in giving information about matters that affect the public directly such as airline flight schedules, safety precautions, and services available, but deep-seated convictions and attitudes are not often changed merely by giving information.

This was strongly indicated in studies by McMurry, Hamstra and Company, management consultants. They theorized that much of the public attitude toward a company is determined by factors other than what a company does. According to their belief, attitudes toward individual companies are affected by class ideologies toward business in general and big business in particular. The personality type may be important as exemplified by the dependent type of person who favors big companies.

To test these hypotheses, the consultants made a pilot study of 250 respondents for Standard Oil of Indiana. Their tests revealed that the responses showed a high correlation of attitudes toward the company with attitudes toward big business in general and with personality types of the individual respondents.

Robert McMurry interpreted the findings to mean that 75 percent of public attitudes toward companies are immutable because they are so deeply ingrained. This kind of finding suggests that public relations programs should include researches to find the open areas where people can be reached and new messages can be gotten across to them. Accurate data on public attitudes and problems in changing or accepting them are essential.[9]

[8]"A Philosophy of Corporate Public Relations," a report of an interview conducted by editors John H. Smith, Jr. and Edwin C. Kepler in Mr. Newsom's office in New York on March 1. pr (*Quarterly Review of Public Relations*, 1010 Vermont Ave., N.W., Washington, D.C.), April 1957, pp. 7–14.
[9]See *Management Review*, American Management Association, Inc., August 1958, p. 54. Condensed from *Printers' Ink*, May 2, 1958. Copyright by Printers' Ink Publishing Company, Inc., 1958.

Employees who lack what the company considers to be a fair attitude toward the company's goals and profits will not have their attitude changed by a formal information program. They need a changed management framework of thinking from that of the old master-servant relationship to one of participation.

Realistic-minded managements do not seek to change basic attitudes of employees or members of the general public such as voters. Instead, their public relations programs have more feasible purposes, such as seeing to it that the company is a good member of the community where a plant is located, that it carries out the company's responsibilities as a "citizen," and that it works with every one of its publics to their mutual advantage. A sound public relations program is a "two-way street" and includes as a major purpose interpreting the public to the management.

Some managements claim that they have no public relations program. In actuality, every company has public relations whether or not it wants to. It deals with people. The value of a "formal program" is that people become conscious that an effort is being made, and they give credit accordingly. Many managements are doing some things quite well, but they are not getting credit for them from their people. They have not formalized their efforts, clarified them, and made people conscious of them.

Every employee of a company is, in a sense, a member of the public relations department.

A large oil company in the Midwest made a survey several years ago in the communities where its plants were located in order to find out what people in the community thought of the company. The most interesting finding was that 77 percent of the people who held favorable opinions of the company had received their good impressions from talking with one or more satisfied employees. Conversely, 56 percent of those who held unfavorable opinions about the company had talked with one or more dissatisfied employees.

The study provided startling proof of the importance of satisfied employees to any public relations program. On the basis of this and similar studies it seems plain that while good employee relations may be possible without good public relations, it is not possible to have good public relations without having good employee relations.[10]

Big business

Most companies, particularly big corporations, need more friends. This was indicated in a report made by Erwin O. Smigel, sociology professor at Indiana University. He found that a person forced by unusual circum-

---

[10]*Public Relations Journal*, Vol. VIII, No. 9. See also *The Management Review*, American Management Association, Inc., January, 1953, p. 11.

stances to steal from an organization would probably pick a big business as his victim. More than 60 percent of those questioned would pick on big business ahead of small business and government. The reason most commonly given: Big corporations "can afford it best." The study also showed that while most disapprove of stealing in any form, they feel strongly opposed to cheating small businesses.[11]

The well-known attitude of hostility toward bigness has caused corporations to utilize advertising. This kind of advertising has the purpose of building in the minds of millions of readers a mental image of the company as a friendly group of people who are good neighbors, good citizens, and good customers. Managements of big companies realize that they must do more than make good products at reasonable prices and build industrial plants that are necessary in national defense—they also have to make themselves liked as a company and be looked upon as a friend.[12]

Community leaders

One of the most effective points of entry into a community is through the persons of top levels of status and authority. Every community has certain informal leaders who have influence in manipulating rumor and opinion. Company managements supply the leadership to many progressive communities.

Sometimes we can appreciate this most easily when we see its evidence in the negative form—the lack of real leadership. A business magazine, for example, described the situation in one large midwestern city in these terms:

> Lagging economically behind competing cities, its efforts to keep pace are hampered by lack of dynamic leaders, business hesitancy in a labor-run town, caution of capital.
>
> Downtown's decline has been hastened by the failure of the city to attract outside risk capital, by the conservatism of its own third and fourth generation wealth, and by the slowness of its public improvements. . . .
>
> . . . But this year, when the Civic Progress group hoped to replace the 1914 city charter with one that would weaken the ward politicians and strengthen the mayor, they failed. . . .
>
> "It may be," a sociologist says, "that our businessmen are afraid to stick their necks out in a labor-run town."

Other reasons, too—other influences, quite likely, also are at work:

11See *Business Week*, January 19, 1957, p. 174.
12See G. D. Crain, Jr., "Big Business Needs Friends," *Advertising Age*, February 4, 1957, p. 72.

By scattering to several suburbs, businessmen may have broken the links that held them together.

Increasingly, as firms sell out or merge, [this particular city] is becoming a city of absentee-controlled companies. A man who yesterday ran his own firm today is only a vice-president of a larger one from out of town. His [local] stature is downgraded.[13]

Participation in community affairs by management involves some obvious dangers. When a company takes sides in a controversial issue, some enemies are made. The company is also accused of running the town. As a result, some companies discourage their local managers from becoming active in civic affairs. They are not allowed to contribute personal leadership, time, or money to local causes. The home office management may also fear that when their local manager becomes involved in the community, he will not be a good manager because he will let his feelings toward the community interfere with his business judgment. Eventually such a policy brings more problems than solutions—the company is looked upon as an exploiting force rather than a friendly neighbor. In spite of the dangers of misinterpretation of management's good intentions, progressive companies want the management and the employees to become integral parts of the community. Management men can participate in civic affairs, give financial support, and offer leadership without being accused of running the town or imposing political domination for the company's financial benefit.

The people of most communities today take an intense interest in the affairs of business concerns that affect them, their friends, and their neighbors. This development can be attributed, at least in part, to the fact that as corporate businesses grow, more and more people, as employees, suppliers, customers, investors, and as neighbors, are directly and indirectly affected by what the corporation does and how it does it. Sensible managements recognize this mutuality of relationships. When a survey of public opinion was made in a midwestern industrial city, opinions toward seven corporations were evaluated. The findings showed that the company that paid the highest wages was not considered the best place to work. Instead, the most respected and best-liked companies were those that had transmitted to their neighbors the feeling that they were something more than profit-making machines. Over the years, they had convinced the residents of the community that management wanted to help create better lives for those who worked and lived there.[14]

One of the most striking developments in modern business is the concern of top executives with plant-community relations. The ex-

[13]*Business Week*, August 24, 1957, pp. 56–68.
[14]See *The Management Review*, American Management Association, Inc., June 1957, pp. 44, 45.

planation for this concern is not quite so simple as critics sometimes make it out to be. Critics may think it lies solely in the profit motive, but when executives are questioned about it, they often reveal that they are interested in a good plant-community relations program not simply because it is "good business" but also because they think it is "right"—a fitting and proper aspect of the activities of a responsible business.[15]

The "good neighbor" policy of any company in its community relations is best implemented not by a formal program of economic arguments but by a sensitivity to the feelings of the people in the community. Here is an example:

> The Texas and Pacific Railway has lines only in Texas, Louisiana and New Mexico. W. G. Vollmer has been T & P's president since 1945. Since then the old T & P has become very human indeed. One day—for instance—the Dallas office got a heartbroken letter from a little girl along the railroad's line: "Your big train killed my black cat named Cinder. He had one white whisker and I loved him very much. Marlene W——." T & P folks spent a lot of time locating another black cat with one white whisker and a lot more time patiently negotiating with a little boy and persuading him to swap the cat for a puppy. But one morning the same "big train" that had run over Cinder I stopped at Marlene's home. The engineer climbed down and put Cinder II in her arms. There wasn't a dry eye on the train.[16]

Plant tours for employees

One way of increasing a community's knowledge about the activities of a local business is through a program of tours of a company's plants and grounds. These may be either for the employees or for members of the community. Plant tours for employees are highly beneficial in companies of almost every size. The employees in a company of only fifty people may be just as remote from management as those in companies having thousands of employees.

Plant tours for employees are easily conducted. Usually, a director of the tours is appointed from the personnel department. He asks each department head to select one employee for the next tour. The director invites those chosen to spend an hour as a group with him. He briefs the employees on where they will go, what they should try to see, and whom they will

15Adapted from editorial comments about the work of Hazel C. Benjamin, *Harvard Business Review*, September–October 1956, p. 22.

16"The Human Side—Working for the T & P," *Sales Management*, September 1, 1953, p. 8.

meet. He tells them that the group will meet the president (or other top-level executive) in his office for an hour or two at which time he will try to discuss topics of interest to them.

In advance of the tour and while still in the group meeting for briefing, each member of the group writes out a question that he would like the president to answer. The suggested questions are discussed openly, and the group decides which questions are to be submitted to the president. The chosen questions in written form are given to the president before the tour begins. He mentally prepares himself for his session with the tour members.

A time and place for the start of the tour are agreed upon. As the tour group visits each department, a member of the tour group who works in that department acts as a guide to the group. He takes care of questions about the department and makes the introductions essential to a friendly visit. When all departments have been visited, the tour group enters the president's office. The president then becomes the host, discusses the questions submitted in advance, and explains his current goals for the business.

The costs of these tours are negligible, but the results obtained from this simple procedure have been markedly successful. The plan can be adapted to and used by any company. Employees like it because they get a chance to ask questions, to visit departments they would like to see in order to note how the work of other employees ties in with their own, and they get a chance to sit in the president's office while he talks to them about the business.

Plant tours for community members

Members of the public learn and accept new ideas slowly and—even more important—what they learn is often by interaction of neighbor on neighbor without a formal program. On the basis of the flow of ideas, the American public can be stratified into three categories: idea starters, idea spreaders, and the very large group of inert citizens, the idea users.

The idea spreaders are mostly easily recognized. As an example, barbers are community opinion spreaders. A few companies pay special attention to them by holding an annual "Barbers' Day" at the plant. Every barber in the area is invited to a plant tour. Color movies and discussions with top brass are on the agenda.

Plant tours and open house days for other idea-spreader groups are arranged by many companies. Certain occupational groups may be especially invited such as teachers, ministers, newspaper editors, engineers, civic officials, and key customers. An open house program should have a theme. The theme should be dramatized. One company that had just constructed a new building chose accessibility to the city as its theme. This was dramatized by having several clients arrive simultaneously by different means: one group came by cruiser, another by helicopter, others by car and plane. Newspapers played up the story with three-column headlines: "Visitors Arrive by Land, Sea, Air."

By tradition, top management men stay in the background at an open house. They are available and usually constitute a receiving line. If the number of guests is large, however, the company officials show by special signs that their offices are open to any visitors. Tour guides may introduce them in the course of the tour.

Relations with the press

Newspaper reporters are always on the alert for stories of news value. The reporter who has heard about a layoff, a labor dispute, or a proposed management reorganization assumes that he has a right to know all about it. Unfortunately, too many reporters are more anxious to present in screaming headlines something that is wrong than to explain calmly the things that are right. Even though all the facts are given a reporter, the emphasis in his write-up is more likely to be faultfinding than strictly factual. Hence, top management should appoint a contact man to the press. The contact man will learn how to get along with the local newsmen and give them what they want with a minimum of danger to the company's good relations with the public.

The contact man will learn that he cannot threaten, scold, or pressure newsmen. Newsmen do not want to think that personal friendship influences their evaluation of a story's news interest. They also think that being an advertiser should have no bearing on whether a story is published or how it is written. If the news is bad, they want to present it as they wish.

Generally, most smart contact men know how to handle publicity of an unpleasant nature—they face up to it. They present to the press all the bad news in a complete package and deliver it to the papers immediately. Under no circumstances do they permit unfavorable news to be withheld and reported at a later day. The policy of airlines, railroads and industry in general is "get the bad news off the front page the first day."

Most companies that want to hire public relations men expect the candidates to be able to write and to establish good relations with the press. This is indicated by the findings when records were checked of a public relations personnel placement agency in New York. The records showed that 94 percent of the placed applicants had demonstrated writing ability and 77 percent had worked for wire services, trade magazines, or newspapers.[17]

[17]Study by Paul Burton, *Corporate Public Relations* (New York: Reinhold Publishing Corp., 1966). See also Kenneth Henry, "Perspective on Public Relations," *Harvard Business Review*, July–August 1967, p. 15.

Top management, not the specialists,
must control the corporate image

Most college students who are considering public relations as a career assume that a company's public relations should be controlled by the public relations director and his department. This is an erroneous assumption. A company's public relations should always be under the control of the top management. The specialist in public relations suggests objectives and programs and puts the approved ones into effect *after* they have been approved by top management. The chief executive must synthesize the public relations into a consistent image of the whole company. The public relations specialist is a staff man, not a line executive. His thinking must be integrated with that of management. As someone has said: "Public relations, like war, is much too important to leave to the specialists."

QUESTIONS ON THE CHAPTER

1. What is meant by the term "corporate image"? What benefits may a favorable image give a company?
2. Differentiate between brand image and corporate image.
3. In the survey of company presidents, where did the majority feel that company prestige began?
4. What methods are used for estimating corporate images?
5. Mention some of the persons and factors that build a company's corporate image.
6. Why should public relations be considered a philosophy and not a program?
7. What may be learned from the results of the movement to make Cincinnati "United Nations conscious"?
8. What is meant by the statement that 75 percent of public attitudes toward companies are immutable?
9. Why do progressive companies want both management and employees to participate actively in civic affairs?
10. Why are plant tours valuable for companies of all sizes?
11. What principle lies behind an occasion such as "Barbers' Day"?
12. Who should control a company's public relations? Why?
13. Of all the ideas presented in the chapter, which ones are of special interest or value to you?
14. What did the chapter contribute to your future relations with (a) the men who supervise your work, (b) the employees whom you may supervise?

PROBLEMS AND PROJECTS

For All Students

1. Collect several advertisements that were designed to help build a corporate image for the company. Ask several friends to state the image that they think each of the advertisers is trying to build. Compare the answers for each company.

2. Assume that you have been placed in charge of public relations for the institution you are attending. State the problems and your objectives. Do you wish to overcome the negative or build the positive? To whom are you directing your program?

For Advanced Students

3. Many students look forward to a career in public relations but have only vague ideas about it. Examine the available literature in order to clarify the purposes and techniques of modern community or public relations. You might begin your study by reading *Saturday Review*, August 9, 1969, p. 49. Describe the work from the standpoint of its possible effects on our evolving social order.

4. Some persons think that absentee-owned companies take less interest in the community than locally owned companies and that when executives of a company are moved from plant to plant they have less interest in the community. Make a study of these two questions. You might find that a lot of the best community leadership in many communities comes from the large corporations that have plants in different areas.

For Men in Business

5. Describe the corporate image of a company that you know well. Does the company have a formal or planned program? If it does, describe it. If it does not, suggest suitable objectives and procedures for building a worthy image.

6. Interview several employees and ask each to describe the image of the company for which he works. Ask each to assume that a friend is thinking of applying to the company for a job. How would he describe the company to the friend?

COLLATERAL READINGS

For All Students

Henry, Kenneth, "Perspective on Public Relations," *Harvard Business Review*, July–August 1967. Treats concepts, methodology, and practice. The experts believe that important changes are developing.

Miller, Robert W., *Profitable Community Relations for Small Business,* Small Business Administration, Superintendent of Documents, Washington, D.C. 20025.

For Advanced Students

The Advertising Council, Inc., 825 Third Ave., New York, N.Y. 10022. Its primary purpose is "to provide the means of marshaling the forces of advertising for the common good." Study copies of their latest reports.

The Public Relations Society of America, Inc., 845 Third Ave., New York, N.Y. 10022. A professional organization of qualified men and women actively engaged in public relations work. The monthly *Public Relations Journal* is the official society publication.

For Men in Business

Gellerman, Saul W., "The Company Employment Image: Attracting People of the Caliber You Want," *The Management Review,* American Management Association, Inc., March 1960. Discusses employment images as an aspect of corporate planning.

National Better Business Bureau, Inc., 230 Park Ave., New York, N.Y. Promotes truthful advertising and selling practices to help business and the public obtain satisfaction in their everyday relations. Study their latest available published reports.

The Psychological Climate in a Company

SITUATIONS YOU ARE LIKELY TO MEET

How would you meet each of these situations:
   a. *Before* you have read the chapter? What would you say to yourself or to the individual?
   b. *After* you have read the chapter? How have your answers changed?

1. Several fellow students are talking about the kind of company they want to work for. A says that he wants to get a job with a manufacturing company that is expansion minded, brings out many new products, tries new methods, and buys up other companies. B says that he wants to lead a more secure, less hectic work life and live in a small town. He intends to go with a public utility and enjoy his family. What comments would you make to each of your friends?
2. You are discussing with a near-retirement executive his thoughts about management of our rapidly changing social order. He has been a member of a very aggressive company in a highly competitive field. He thinks that the trend in the development of industries will be in the direction toward more small, more highly competitive companies, not toward large firms working closely together but still competing with each other. What questions would you ask him?
3. Assume that an employment interviewer asks you to mention some of the ways in which you think that you could contribute to the development of a good psychological climate of a company where you might work. How would you answer him?

Whenever you visit several homes or educational institutions, you will, if you are alert, note that each has a distinctive psychological atmosphere. Every company, too, has a climate of its own. Each department or work group may have a unique climate. The atmosphere of one, for example, is tense because of the presence of an authoritarian boss and a lot of neurotic employees. In another place, the pervading atmosphere is cheerful and friendly because the boss is an emotionally mature leader and the employees are relaxed and cooperative. The people, not the buildings or the furnishings, determine the atmosphere of a place.

The psychological climate in industry is so important that every student and supervisor should be aware of its influences. He should be sensitive to it whenever he enters an office or a factory. He should observe it, not merely to evaluate it, but for ways in which he can contribute to a positive psychological climate wherever he goes. No one has ever found a perfect climate, geographically speaking, and no one will ever find a company that always has a perfect psychological climate. We can, however, note factors that add to or detract from its beneficent aspects and intelligently play our own role in its sunlight or its shadow.

Many of the factors that are influential in producing the climate within a company have been discussed in the preceding chapters. In this chapter we want to increase our awareness of various kinds of psychological climates and sharpen our abilities to distinguish them. The alert member of industry who visits or works in different companies soon learns to sense the climate of each firm. Here are several examples:

A very large public utility operates under close government regulation and entrenched labor union influence. The employee setup is highly mechanized. The personnel department is rigidly limited in making its decisions. Even the hiring is automatic when the formal specifications are fulfilled by the applicant. The employees who work in this atmosphere merely need to know and follow the rules. Individual initiative is quite circumscribed. Only those who seek life-long security and are willing to conform to the operational climate tend to remain with the company. Few have any strong desire to grow. Their motto, "Nobody here ever sticks his neck out," is not hung in a frame on the wall of each office—it's so evident that it need not be put into words.

In contrast with this public utility, a large retail clothing company is fast paced—decisions on style selection are proved right or wrong in a few weeks. Executives tend to hire employees who also are fast paced. Here the members of the personnel have to function far more rapidly than in the public utility where decisions must wait months for approval from regulatory agencies.

In a certain company of another industry, the dominant climate is cold and logical. Engineering knowledge is essential to corporate effectiveness. Everyone seems to think or try to think in a mathematically precise manner. Logic rather than feeling is dominant. Management men have come from the engineering staff.

A metal manufacturing concern is still under the control of a fatherly founder who runs the place in a paternalistic manner. Executives and employees have to be careful not to disagree with or hurt the feelings of "The Old Man."

Obviously, the personalities of controlling executives will always have considerable influence on a company's climate. In addition, the larger environmental settings in which the company operates also have some important influences on the climate.

SEVEN QUESTIONS TO EVALUATE
A COMPANY'S CLIMATE

1. What extracompany environmental influences should be noted?

Social scientists who study "climatic" influences from outside the company are especially interested in cultures. *Culture* may be defined as a "body of learned behavior," a collection of beliefs, habits, practices, and traditions shared by a group of people (a society) and successively learned by new members who enter the society. Cultures are found in nations, communities, and companies. The older the institution, the more certain the likelihood of finding such a body of learned behavior. A culture is more than a collection of loose, disconnected ideas. Rather, it is a somewhat unified whole, no element of which can be disturbed without repercussions on a wide scale. If, for example, an American agricultural specialist is assigned to improve the economic well-being of the people of a foreign undeveloped area, his natural tendency is to attempt to organize the land areas in fields sufficiently large for the use of agricultural machinery. To accomplish this, he may have to take account of graves, shrines, dowries, and sex habits as well as rights of way, inheritances, and property laws. Failure to recognize these cultural influences is likely to bring about firm resistance. People who believe in their own cultural heritages will sabotage a program even though it would undoubtedly bring about economic benefits for them.

Employees adapt to what they believe is expected of them by their superiors or, on the other hand, they may develop negative attitudes if the job climate seems to allow and encourage it. It is here that informal organization plays a role: cliques develop, coffee breaks breed and spread attitudes and false perceptions. The supervisor who ignores job climate does so at his own risk. Climate affects the employee's receptivity and mental set in supervisory and interview situations.

Employees from different backgrounds and life histories have various behavior patterns. Note the difficulties of communicating with the hardcore unemployed and protest groups. Communication blocks are almost inevitable because of individual background, experience, and attitude differences.

Cultural differences in regions of this country are often influential. Many supervisors believe that persons reared in rural areas are likely to have somewhat different attitudes toward work than those reared in the city. Rural-reared employees are more willing to accept and attempt to fulfill management's work expectations. Generally, morale surveys of industrial firms indicate that the attitudes of employees toward management are relatively better in the South than in the older industrial centers of the East.

The mores of the people of one geographical location often differ from those of another region. Studies have shown, for example, that the Tennessee Valley Authority had certain supervisory problems because southern workers were not accustomed to the rough-and-ready language of those foremen whose previous work experience had been in the North.[1]

2. What is the dominant orientation of the management?

One of the most easily noted orientations of a management is in the relative importance of production in comparison with that of sales. In a production-oriented company, the management is especially concerned with the manufacturing equipment, the shop employees, and the engineering staff. Quality control is a popular topic in management meetings. And a frequently stated criticism is that the sales department makes too many ridiculous promises to customers in regard to delivery dates. Executives are likely to be pessimistic about what the product will do. To make the production

---

[1]See Milton M. Mandell, "The Effect of Organizational Environment on Personnel Selection," *Personnel*, American Management Association, Inc., July 1953, p. 14.

easier and technically more correct, this kind of management likes to get large, long-term contracts with the big merchandising firms such as the Chicago mail-order houses. That kind of arrangement makes it easy to put production on a stable, efficient basis.

In contrast, management in a sales-minded firm usually prefers small contracts with many customers. Selling, not production, is fun. The popular topics in management meetings are marketing and advertising. Executives try to find out what the customers want by means of expensive market researches. They are apt to assure the customer who buys that the product will do or be just what he wants. And they are optimistic about the quality of the product.

In some companies, the significance of the sales volume to the top management men is especially important. Sales volume may be sought to build high salary-paying practices and retirement benefits for the major executives, to earn profits for important stockholders, or to satisfy status needs. Fortunately, most professional management men have a desire to develop a bigger and stronger company because of the challenge and not for the sake of special benefits to any one interest group.

In small companies, wholly or largely owned by one man, the basic orientation may be toward the building up of an estate for the benefit of heirs. Few profits are spent for research or further growth. Instead, the policy is usually described in such words as "The old man is milking the company in order to take care of his incompetent heirs." The owner of such a company may have one or two competent assistants, but most employees are chosen because they can do a passable job and are willing to work for below-average pay. No one is selected for employment because he has excellent potentials for growth or because he eventually will become a first-rate aggressive executive. If, by chance, a young man of drive and high aspiration is employed in such a company, he soon leaves for a better job in a growth company where the psychological climate is more favorable.

3. Is the management expansion minded?

The average industrial employee is likely to prefer to work in a climate of stability, a place where few changes take place. The ambitious young man, in contrast, usually prefers to work in a less stabilized place, one where the growth of the company is more important than piling up cash. Relatively few managements like to pile up profits into cash reserves. They prefer to invest profits in expansion programs. Historically, the contrasts between cash-rich and expansion-minded managements are often studied by comparing the earlier development of Montgomery Ward under Sewell Avery and of Sears, Roebuck and Company under General Woods. Avery followed a policy of piling up cash. Woods used cash for expansion. Later,

Montgomery Ward management recognized that profits are most productive when put to work.

Most American executives subconsciously think of expansion first and profits second. Business boom and growth are more thrilling to the aggressive executive than money in the bank. Many have sought expansion for the sake of expansion with little regard for profit. Certain managements find this necessary, at times, for competitive reasons. Short-term return on money invested in expansion may be less important than ultimate survival. The history of automobile manufacturing offers examples of this kind of need for disinterest in profits in one year for the sake of later corporate health.

An important need for survival expansion arises when the company's main product is declining in sales simply because it is approaching the end of its life cycle. New products are like people—they are born, grow slowly, reach the vigor of maturity, decline, and eventually die. Alert managements therefore seek to retain their corporate vigor by expanding their activities toward the acquisition of other products and companies, often through mergers.

A company may have any of several reasons for seeking to bring another firm into its own organization: to strengthen product lines, to join forces with another firm that deals in the same product, to build a vertically integrated unit as exemplified by the textile maker who buys a clothing manufacturing company, to diversify its products, and to bring about operating savings. In some cases, the competitive position may be improved through the acquisition of a larger sales force or a better geographical distribution of sales offices.

A common reason for mergers is the need for high-grade management. Perhaps the management of the acquiring company consists of old men, while that of the acquired company has a crop of capable young executives.

One of the benefits for the small companies is that they may have a chance to grow under the umbrella of a large organization.

Fundamentally, however, expansion is a part of our business way of life. If growth through further enlargement of the company's current activities is no longer feasible, expansion must be made into unrelated lines. The company diversifies. Some of these diversifications may be organized in a manner that brings about integration—others merely bring about a polyglot collection of companies.

Many merged companies suffer severe varieties of "indigestion" before the added segments become profitably integrated with the parent company. Some never seem to reach stable profits and growth. This suggests that the growth-minded man who chooses a company for its expansion mindedness should also try to note whether the executives are as able and versatile as the expansion program requires.

On the human relations side, personality clashes and conflicts of interest often arise between members of the acquiring and the acquired managements. The controlling company's management may make decisions that the acquired company's executives know to be wrong. Or the latter may give only lip service to the central management's programs while running the operations in a manner that produces only mediocre results. Members of a central management and those of a subordinate management need years of experience with each other to develop mutual confidence and wholehearted cooperation. Until such time as they have gone through tribulations together, they lack identification with each other and remain a polyglot collection in spirit as well as in structure. The psychological climates of merged companies often remain varied and uncertain until their members have experienced suffering and success with each other.

4. Is decision making centralized or decentralized?

Every large company, whether resulting from a merger or not, can be viewed as a grouping of smaller business units. Decision making may be so highly centralized that no subordinate can act on his own until he has got a signal from someone up the line. Initiative on the part of middle management men is stalled. Personal growth is difficult because of hampering red tape.

Emphasis on decentralized decision making has increased and is a direct result of the desire to improve human relations in the large organization. The current policy in some large companies is to create a small business atmosphere by dividing the company into a number of smaller units, each headed by a man who has broad responsibilities. The concept, as the late Harlow H. Curtice of General Motors expressed it, is:

> . . . to divide the business into as many parts as consistently as [sic] can be done, place in charge of each part the most capable executive that can be found, and develop a system of coordination so that each part may strengthen and support each other part; thus not only welding all parts together in the common interests of a joint enterprise, but importantly developing ability and initiative through the instrumentalities of responsibility and ambition—developing men and giving them an opportunity to exercise their talents, both in their own interests as well as in that of the business.[2]

[2]Harlow H. Curtice, *The Development and Growth of General Motors*, Statement before Subcommittee on Antitrust and Monopoly of the U.S. Senate Committee on the Judiciary, December 2, 1955. From Alan C. Filley, "Human Relations in the Growing Company," *Personnel*, American Management Association, Inc., September–October 1957.

One of the best ways to utilize human relations for business success is through the delegation of the decision-making power, as Curtice pointed out. Henry Ford almost lost his business as a result of failure in this realm.

Anyone who has risen to top levels in management, whether as the owner-manager or as a driving member of a large organization, is likely to feel that the success of the business is due to his efforts. It is difficult for him to let others make important decisions because he learned to depend upon himself rather than others. To develop his subordinates, however, he must learn how to allow them to make mistakes. Generally, executives who really want their subordinates to grow do so by choosing the goals but letting them decide how the goals will be attained. For the ambitious young man, the extent to which he will have the privilege of decision making in regard to operational procedures is one of the most important aspects of a company's psychological climate.

5. Who are the controlling personalities in the company?

The formal head is not necessarily the most influential leader in a company. The man in the president's chair may in reality be a figurehead—some other executive may be setting up the goals, pushing the sales, and directing the organization. He, rather than the formal head, may also be looked to as the leader by the customers.

In some companies, the financial powers may be the controlling influences. These may be represented by very intelligent, forward-looking men who know how to select and inspire the company's leaders. Or they may be conservative old fuddy-duddies who try to hang on to a traditional dividend rate.

The fact that a company is under the financial control of a banking group or a foundation does not mean that the management provides a good or a poor climate, one that is favorable or unfavorable for the young man who wants to grow. If he knows, however, who the controlling personalities are, he can evaluate their influence more accurately.

If the founder of the business has, in his old age, turned the company over to a charitable foundation for control, the climate is likely to be one of conservatism, and a conservatism that leads to the decline and eventual death of the company. Continuity of family control is often safeguarded by the placing of large blocks of stock in the hands of a trust which retains them for the benefit of the original owners' children and grandchildren.

If an heir remains at the helm, the management may be competent or incompetent, probably competent because the founder usually trains able assistants who can guide the heir. In many cases, too, the founder puts the heir through years of strenuous training for later responsibilities. If the heir does not achieve an acceptable level of ability, the board of directors quietly arranges for his departure from the company. The members of the board and other executives are likely to have so great an investment in time and money in the company that they will not allow a weak scion to jeopardize their investment through poor management. In American business, dynastic succession is less prevalent than popular fancy imagines. A survey of public opinion on the subject, made by The Psychological Corporation, indicated that almost one-third of the public believes that most of industry is run by a few wealthy families like the Rockefellers, du Ponts, and Fords. Yet careful analysis of the top command echelons of the five hundred largest publicly owned corporations of the United States revealed only a 14 percent incidence of dynastic relationships, much of it at secondary levels. Relatively few managements take a fixed stand on the question of nepotism—the showing of too much favor by one in power to his relatives. Informally, many companies do not employ relatives. Even though they have no established policy, they feel that hiring relatives tends to mean trouble. Also, many able young men refuse to work in their fathers' companies because they want to earn their titles and responsible positions. Besides, some sons know the father too well!

Many heirs are sons of forceful fathers. Such fathers are apt to be exceedingly demanding and intensely critical of their sons' performances. Many fathers are still at the height of their own powers when their sons reach adulthood. "In the very best of circumstances, sonship in dynastic industrial families is no bed of roses. The pressure can be intense, and an heir's opportunity to spread his wings may be long delayed."[3]

6. What are the ages of the top management men?

Boards of directors usually want the management to have some young men rather than a management group of old men only. The perpetuation of the company is a basic responsibility of a board. They like to be able to refer to the management as "young and aggressive." Of course a company that has only young men may be as weak as one that has only old men.

Age is a poor criterion of managerial ability. Many of our most competent top executives are in their fifties and sixties. Some are even older. Generally, top management men need judicial wisdom that has developed from years of experience. Their greatest contribution is in guiding the younger, more aggressive members of middle management. "Judgment ripens as the hair whitens." The fact that a management can be described as "young and aggressive" does not necessarily mean that it is efficient and successful.

[3]See "Heirs at the Helm," *Forbes*, November 15, 1957, pp. 63–72.

The full development of a personality often takes place in the later years of life. Maturity means that the emotional roadblocks of youth have been overcome so that energies are fully released for constructive activities. Of course when senility is evident, its ability to influence management should be, and usually is, reduced.

Actually, the continuation of executives in jobs that they are no longer able to fulfill is not management's most serious problem in regard to age. Instead a greater difficulty centers in the presence of old men on all levels who have become embittered through the years. Their unhappiness tends to permeate the department or division to such an extent that they create a psychological climate of pessimism, frustration, and criticism. Top management is usually aware of their negative influence on the younger employees but does not want to be so unkind as to remove them. It is up to the younger person, therefore, to evaluate objectively the pessimism of the disgruntled old employees and plan his career without letting their soured outlook affect him.

7. Do the personalities at the top mesh together?

Management spirit is a tremendously important factor in corporate growth. When individual executives have a strong drive to achieve and are dynamic in their thinking, they are bound to develop some frictions with their colleagues.

Many young people in business imagine that the ideal company climate is one where no frictions can be found—only sweetness and light. This kind of thinking should be avoided. A complete absence of friction among executives means that the members of the organization are not thinking aggressively, not stimulating each other to do better work. Such an atmosphere is not found in growth companies, those noted for their growth in financial or technological development. Growth company management men have strong achievement motivations. They like to accomplish things. They like to take the lead in making improvements. They are imaginative in their thinking. As a result they tend to develop some frictions with their colleagues. But their frictions usually occur in regard to objectives and the means of attaining them, not in regard to petty or personal differences. Their conflicts have corporate purposes and usually result in a meshing of personalities.

When a smart management man realizes that his own personality limitations are a handicap to his associates and subordinates, he selects a colleague who provides for the gaps in his own personality pattern. One well-known American corporation is headed by a man of driving ambition and pride. He is meticulous in attire and in speech but mercurial in temper and abrupt with people. He has become so aware of his negative characteristics with people that he has delegated most human-relations responsibilities to a fellow executive who is of great ability but the opposite of himself in attire, manner, and speech.

PEOPLE WANT TO WORK FOR A COMPANY THEY CAN RESPECT

They want to be proud of their organization—its reputation, its product or service, its worth-whileness in the community. If they are asked where they work, they want to be able to reply with the name of an outfit with a good standing.

If a company departs from ethical standards in any of its dealings—not only with employees, but with customers, suppliers, stockholders, neighbors in the community, and so on—low employe morale results. This extends to matters such as a company not keeping up its equipment, or letting the appearance of its buildings go downhill.

I can think of a plant which was starting to allow poor quality goods to get out into the market. This seriously affected employe attitudes there. Conditions of pay, working conditions, work required, all stayed the same —and by this I mean in a favorable sense—but the defection on quality hurt employe spirit.

I know of another company, about the same size, making a similar product. The president could be described as just plain tough. Fair, but really tough. And employes griped about the work that was returned to them because Quality Control set such high standards.

But their morale was higher than in the other plant. They were able to take pride in their company's product. And tough though he was, they respected the president. He was able, and he was on the level.

Source: Douglas Williams as interviewed in "Six Policies Increase Will to Work," *Nation's Business*, November 1958. Copyright © 1958 by *Nation's Business—the Chamber of Commerce of the United States.*

How companies acquire good climates

Very few managements can hope to acquire a favorable climate by issuing directives or by hiring outside experts to produce it. If, for example, the president is upward oriented in the direction of spending most of his time and thinking to gain the goodwill of financial interests while he neglects his associates and subordinates, the climate is not likely to change until he takes a sincere interest in the members of the organization. In time, when he has solved the company's financial problems, he or his successor can modify the climate by concentrating on giving the employees greater psychic income. He will organize programs and direct his colleagues in ways that will provide for the employees' emotional participation in the business.

He will treat all members of the organization as colleagues whom he likes. He will conduct himself in accordance with high ethical standards, and he will hold employees to high work standards. The systems he installs will be backed up by his continuing efforts to work with his people. As someone has stated: "Today's weather is tomorrow's climate."

A superior top management not only sends its junior executives to special institutes to take management courses but also realizes that courses will not change a company's climate. Further, alert managements realize that subordinates cannot put into effect any new practices they learn that contradict those of their superiors. The middle-level man who learns sound principles in a course knows that it is unwise for him to do his work in a manner that is markedly different from what his superior expects. Wise managements know that middle-level leadership of, say, the participative variety cannot function with top-level leadership of another variety, such as the authoritarian. The climate of an organization will not be changed by a few injections of some new philosophy of leadership.

A good climate is more likely to develop when there is a normal growth pattern of structural changes in the organization. Rapid changes disrupt the climate. An organization may be rather loose knit by design. After all, the structural organization is less important than its spirit. Frequent reorganizations tend to destroy the spirit. Structural changes, when made, should be minor and should evolve slowly over the years. They should bend to the requirements of growth, not be imposed suddenly. Climate is likely to be favorable when the company has a record of steady growth and a low percentage of personnel turnover.

Climate is developed when employees know that management is sincerely interested in their welfare. Every executive should spend a large part of his time in close individual contact with employees in regard to their work. Each employee should feel that the boss is interested in helping him to do his work, not merely in inspecting him or his work. The functions of a supervisor are to evaluate the job the employee is doing and to help him do a better job.

One clue to the extent that a management is vitally interested in employees as human beings is the company's effort or lack of effort in finding jobs for capable employees in other organizations if management cannot, in its own company, provide opportunities that will use the employee to the full. Few employers follow this policy, and yet this policy not only attracts superior men but also causes many of those who have left to come back with experience and loyalty that could not be obtained otherwise. Some managements also assist laid-off employees in locating positions elsewhere. They do more than offer good wishes—they make vigorous effort to help them find new positions.

Another clue to the climate encouraged by a management is indicated by the way members of the organization preface explanations of new ideas. If they present them in an extremely apologetic manner as "Now I know this sounds silly" or "This is just off the top of my head," the climate within the organization probably does not stimulate growth through individual initiative. An employee should voice respect for his colleagues, but he should not have to apologize for an idea that he believes might be helpful. If executives have indoctrinated subordinates with the dictum, "Don't open your mouth until you are sure of what you are saying," they are promoting second-guessing rather than original thinking. The test of an idea is to see it in action. The employee who presents only sure-fire ideas is not a creator—only a describer of old ideas.

The company that has a good psychological climate is likely to have many executives who are always accessible to the employees. Employees can easily identify themselves with them because they are true leaders who practice participative methods. Men of great character and goodwill usually enjoy and contribute to the positive psychological climates wherever they go.

The supervisor's influence on the climate

Even though many members of an organization contribute to its climate the supervisor is in a key position of influence. If he is lacking in emotional control, he is likely to have many employees who feel that they are working under intense pressures. A tense atmosphere prevails. The typical tense supervisor is demanding in his directives. Emergencies seem to take place every few minutes. Urgently needed materials have not arrived. A machine breakdown is slowing production. Defective products have been returned by a customer, and so on.

Some work groups have many tense members. Sometimes the cause for their presence may be found in a selection bias practiced by the personnel manager—he just happens to like people whom he designates as the "ulcer type." In a tense group, whatever the causes of the continuing strain, the supervisor usually looks tired. The typical harried supervisor says that he cannot trust anyone to do anything right. He claims that he cannot hire good men these days. Either they do not know their jobs or they do not do an honest day's work for their pay, and so on ad infinitum.

The emotionally mature supervisor has few of these problems or convictions. Instead, he likes his employees and speaks well of them. He has few crises because his employees help him to plan ahead and to anticipate problems. He stimulates productivity because he has developed a climate where people are genuinely interested in the work problems and in doing good work. They know that the boss likes them and respects them and their abilities. Good work climates do not develop by chance. Instead, they are produced by leaders of goodwill and competence.

Workers judge an executive by what they *think* his motives are. If they sense that he is for them, they will put a good construction on what he says. If they sense that he is basically disinterested in them, they will read negative meanings into his words and efforts even though what he says and does would appear to be favorable to them otherwise. Employees sense the psychological climate from daily personal contacts rather than from formal media of communication.

The employees will recognize whether management is concerned about them as human beings as well as in their production. A company may, for example, recognize that certain employees have to work over a chemical bath that gives off unpleasant fumes. When an exhaust system is installed to draw off the fumes, morale goes up or down depending upon whether the workers think that the exhaust system was installed for their benefit or to boost output only. When workers are suspicious of the reasons behind management's moves, the improvement of working conditions will not change morale.

"Of course I want it back today! If I had wanted it tomorrow, I would have called you tomorrow."
Source: by Interlander, *Advertising Agency Magazine* (September 27, 1957).

Formerly management men assumed that when they improved the physical environment of the factory or office, the morale and production would automatically improve. Progressive managements learned years ago that the best morale and highest production come out of an atmosphere of friendliness and personal understanding between management and workers.

The significance of this kind of understanding was shown when General Motors, using seventy-nine of its own plants as a laboratory, conducted an interesting study on the effect of physical environment on productivity. The company has some plants that are the last word in employee comfort as well as other older plants where there is less emphasis on the mechanics of comfort. The survey showed that there was no difference in output between the slick and the staid plants. Workers who are impressed by swank factories and bowling leagues will normally gravitate to such plants, it seemed, while others, who do not care for externals or sports, take jobs with companies that do not go in for showmanship. The study showed that whereas frills and fringes made no dent one way or the other in individual productivity, the degree of understanding between management and men in the department or plant made a tremendous difference in ultimate output.[4]

The behavioral scientists are finding more and more indications that productivity and satisfaction in the work situation are closely related to the psychological climate in the day-to-day relationships between management and fellow workers.

QUESTIONS ON THE CHAPTER

1. What factors are influential in determining the atmosphere of a home, schoolroom, or company?
2. Differentiate between the production-oriented and the sales-oriented company.
3. How do regional differences affect the attitudes of employees?
4. Which is the more important to most American executives, profits or expansion?
5. What are some reasons for company mergers?
6. Discuss possible effects on company climate of the ages of top management men.
7. Explain the current emphasis on decentralized decision making.
8. What is the danger of turning a company over to the control of a charitable foundation?

[4]See Lawrence Stessin, "Good Feeling is Key to Productivity, Survey Suggests," *Forbes*, October 1, 1952.

9. Differentiate between the public belief and the actual percentages in regard to the frequency of dynastic relationships in industry.

10. What are some characteristics of the executive who tends to make a work atmosphere one of tension?

11. Describe ways in which executives may develop a good company climate.

12. Of the ideas presented in the chapter, which ones are of special interest or value to you?

13. What did the chapter contribute toward your future relations with (a) the men who supervise your work, (b) the employees whom you may supervise?

PROBLEMS AND PROJECTS

For All Students

1. Describe some of the psychological climates that you have experienced in living centers or classrooms. What key personalities were influential? Did you try to improve any negative or depressing climates? How?

2. When you enter the business world as a worker, you will note the climate of the new work environment. If you try to contribute to its favorable aspects, what dangers should be recognized? Must a contributor be more tactful than a noncontributor?

For Advanced Students

3. Examine the available literature on growth companies. Note their main characteristics. Begin by studying recent issues of business magazines, particularly *Forbes* and *Fortune*.

4. If you are interested in rating scales for personality traits of individuals, try to develop a rating scale for measuring psychological climates of companies. Little research has been done in this field, but checklists are available.

For Men in Business

5. Describe the climates in some of the departments or companies where you have worked. If the climate changed in the course of time, describe probable causes. Did you change in your reactions to it or did the climate really change?

6. Perhaps you have worked in a company where the advent of a new executive head changed the climate. Describe the before-and-after situations. How did the changes affect you? Were you able to contribute to any improvements of the climate? How?

COLLATERAL READINGS

For All Students

"How to Set a Profitable Work Pace," *Dun's Review*, August 1960. Discusses the
question as to whether permissive approaches to supervision may be less
productive than climates where executives must "face the music."

Stanley, David T., "Federal Executives and the Systems that Produce Them,"
Personnel Administration, May–June 1969. Some aspects of psychological
climates found in governmental employment can be deduced by the reader,
especially if he is interested in entering the civil service.

For Advanced Students

Litwin, George H., and Robert A. Stringer, Jr., *Motivation and Organizational
Climate*. Boston, Mass.: Harvard Business School, 1968. Introduces the concept of organizational climate and explains how the theory can be applied to problems facing managers.

Revolution of Ideals: Critical Issues and Decisions, Series IV, ed. Dee W. Hender-
son. Washington, D.C.: U.S. Dept. of Agriculture Graduate School Press,
1967. Four lecturers discuss what we want as ends in a new technical society
where productive means is no longer the problem.

For Men in Business

"Checklist of Factors Affecting the Business Climate," Economic Research Department, Chamber of Commerce of U.S., 1615 H St., N.W., Washington, D.C.
20006. Designed to aid leaders in identifying factors that affect the climate
and in planning a program of constructive action. Free booklet.

Examine available lists of publications by the Small Business Administration,
Washington, D.C., for booklets on psychological climates: John Perry, "Human Relations in Small Industry," presents examples of good versus poor
climates and discusses influences involved.

MANAGEMENT, SUPERVISION, AND MANAGEMENT FUNCTIONS

PART **III**

Management:
Its Upper Levels

SITUATIONS YOU ARE LIKELY TO MEET

How would you meet each of these situations:
- a. *Before* you have read the chapter? What would you say to yourself or to the individual?
- b. *After* you have read the chapter? How have your answers changed?

1. Some members of management are devoted to the importance of having a well-developed organizational structure that has been charted with the chart prominently displayed. You happen to meet one of these enthusiasts who tells you, "All you need to know about a company in order to understand how the organization functions as an organization is to look at the company's organization chart." What questions would you ask him?

2. Another executive says that he does not pay much attention to organization charts. He believes in working closely with the individual of an organization who is assigned to do a specific task. He therefore personally communicates his instructions directly to employees of echelons below without following the chains of command. What are the dangers of this kind of action?

3. A friend of yours knows the president of a large corporation very well. Your friend likes him but thinks that the president should discuss his business and its problems more often—get closer to his business associates by talking "shop" with his associates. What comments would you offer your friend for his consideration?

If you visit the home office of a corporation and talk with a member of the upper echelon of management, you may find an organization chart hanging on the wall. The executive also probably has a loose-leaf book that describes the company's formal organization: the chain of command, the span of control, and the formal policies. The book will also describe certain specialized functions and define their place in departmental relationships.

The mentally alert person who takes a job in a large company is especially anxious to see the organization charts and any accompanying descriptions of their meanings. The charts will orient him in regard to any subsidiary companies, major divisions, and departments. The charts show how the company is structured as an organization. The chain of command is indicated from the stockholders down through the board of directors, president, vice-presidents, department heads, foremen, and operating personnel.

Managerial practices in regard to charting the organization vary. Some companies have elaborate and detailed organization charts. They may even have an expert who devotes all of his time to the study and planning of new chartings. Other companies may have no charts hanging on the walls and no descriptions filed in executive desk drawers. All companies do, however, have some kind of framework within which their activities are organized. That is why many courses and books on management give so much attention to organizational structure. Of course, the formal organization is of itself without significance except as human beings give it meaning and value. The meanings and values that are expressed by the people who work in the organizational framework are part of the informal organization. In this book, we are devoting most of our thought to the informal organization, but we must also appreciate the need for the formal organization.

The formal structure delineates the duties, obligations, and work rights of each member. It reveals to whom and for whom each member is accountable in the performance of his functions. It provides a base that sets forth the expectations of the members as to the extent that each person may look to or expect designated persons to carry out assigned tasks. Lines of communication and work channels are indicated.

Some experts in company organization believe that organizational structuring should be done on a strictly logical basis. They think of it as essentially an engineered system or framework into which people will fit themselves. There is, of course, need for logic in planning a company's organizational structure. Textbooks and courses in management treat the topic in terms of necessary logical work relations.

The need for a formal organization

In a small business, the head can oversee and direct every operation. He himself can supervise and train his few employees as he works with them in his shop. He may wrap shipments and take them to the post office. He can keep his records, write his checks, and make the bank deposits. He may even write the advertising and put the stamps on the outgoing mail. He can, however, keep sole control of the operations only as long as the business is small. As the business expands, he must delegate more and more responsibility. In time, he must have department heads who supervise the performance of certain designated functions. If the business grows still more, departments become major divisions or subsidiary companies. Eventually so many problems arise that a formal organization must be planned in a logical manner.

A formal organization develops because the setting of objectives, planing, and coordinating of resources, technical and human, can be achieved only when some persons are given authority to direct the work of others. The area of authority usually needs definition. Persons accountable for specific functions and operations must be designated.

The top coordinating authority cedes to subordinates parts of his authority. These in turn yield parts of their authority to lower echelons of management and supervision. Theoretically, the level of ability to manage decreases in the flow of authority from top to bottom. The individual at the top is always responsible for those under his direction regardless of how remote they may be. Even though he has never seen them, he is still their operational superior. The president of a corporation having a hundred thousand employees who live in various countries and cities is their organizational head regardless of the number of managerial levels between him and them. The productiveness of employees on all levels may be helped or hindered by the formal organization, but the informal relations are likely to be even more important. If you know the informal functioning of management, you will find any future study of the formal organizations more fruitful.

The type of product sold, size of the company, method of distribution, and selling policies of the company are all factors that help determine the type of formal organization a company develops. The formal organization is, however, constantly modified by the human beings in the organization. Some executives are more competent and more ambitious to grab additional responsibilities from others. As a result, the formal framework is warped to fit the strong and the weak people in the organization. To appreciate some of these formal and informal relations we shall discuss them in terms of the formal structure as indicated by the usual line of authority from the board of directors downward.

Top management consists of the policy-making executives who are responsible for the overall direction of all company activities. These include the chairman of the board of directors, the president, the vice-presidents in charge of major divisions or functions, the officers of the company, and the more responsible key executives. They develop the broad plans for the organization's future activities. Middle management puts them into effect through procedures that implement the plans. Lower management, often called supervision, puts the procedures into effect on the operational level through personal supervision of line workers.

Boards of directors

A board of directors is an official body of persons who direct the corporation. They have important legal status and certain responsibilities. They give the corporation perpetuity. They function as a balancing influence between the operating management and the stockholders. They have the responsibility of protecting the stockholders' investment. They are expected to direct the company so that investors gain an adequate return on their investment. They may or may not hold positions on the boards of other corporations. Some are paid for their services; others are not paid. The board has the responsibilities of electing the management, borrowing money, approving major capitalization expenditures, acquiring other companies as in mergers, declaring dividends, approving salaries of major management men, overseeing basic corporate affairs, and establishing corporate policies and objectives. They evaluate and approve or disapprove the president's long-range plans and deviations from past policies.

In fiction and drama, directors are often pictured as dopey old men of wealth who somehow fell into membership on the board, usually as a result of inheritance or family connections. Actually, most members of boards are intelligent and conscientious and take their responsibilities seriously. Most are able men whose abilities as business leaders have been proven. Generally, they work with the operating management as advisors, as controls, and as stimulators.

Their personal contacts with members of the organization are mostly with the president and other officials such as the treasurer. They rarely express opinions or give directions to any member of the operating personnel. Minutes of their meetings are circulated among few persons other than themselves, and anyone who sees their minutes is expected to keep in strict confidence any knowledge of their plans and problems.

In theory, they hire and fire the members of top management, particularly the president. In actual practice, the president often selects the men who are to become members of the directorate. In some companies, the president functions under a hand-picked board that looks to him for counsel and instruction in regard to the board's actions. Obviously, the president who has such a board is the key controlling member of the entire company. If he is a man of outstanding ability, the company prospers. If he is of mediocre ability, the company is likely to drag along with passing success until such time as the president retires or dies, or the board decides that the management should be changed.

The effect on a company's vitality of a hand-picked board often depends upon the kinds of persons with whom the president likes to associate in business and in his social relations. If he enjoys friendly social relations with financial men, such as heads of banking firms, he naturally selects financial men for membership on his company's board. A board made up of the president's friends may be, but is not necessarily, a rubber stamp for the president. When a man becomes a member of the board of a large corporation, his sense of responsibility to the company usually takes precedence over personal friendship.

Also, we should recognize that a president may have a hand-picked board because the president himself is a strong character. He is an individualist, knows the business well, and is determined to run the company as he sees fit. He usually chooses men who know some phase of the business that he does not care to deal with himself. He may even choose very able men whom he is trying to develop for future needs of the company. He, too, wants a board that will approve his plans, but he retains the presidency because he is the ablest man in the management. A company under such a president is likely to be successful as long as he remains vigorous. He, however, is likely to hold on to the presidency too long and thus cause the business to decline. Furthermore, he seldom develops men who are as strong as he. He is likely to be so strong a manager himself, and so individualistic, that he is unable to build men who can take his place as soon as his energy and leadership ability begin to decline. Sometimes he is removed from the presidency in a proxy fight, but usually he keeps control of enough stock to enable him to have himself reelected as long as he wishes.

Some boards consist of the company's leading stockholders only. If each member owns stock and the directors are appointed because of their stock holdings, the board members are likely to give the affairs of the company regular attention.

If several financial firms have invested heavily in a company's stock, they naturally wish to be represented on the board. These "bankers on the board," as they are usually called, are likely to know very little about the company's products, how to make or sell them. They do know how to read financial statements. They are likely to be poor leaders of men because they have learned how to develop the respect of other financial men but not the respect of operating executives or employees. Strangely, many of these financial men on boards are not so greatly concerned about whether the company makes money as about their continued membership on the board. Membership on a number of boards gives the prestige-hungry financier about the same kind of satisfaction as that which is enjoyed by the academic man who likes to be a member of many committees of professional organizations.

Fortunately, those financiers who seek membership on as many boards as possible do not usually express a drive for power by imposing their will on executives or employees. After they have helped to select the top executive of a company, they deal with him, and he may manage the company as he wishes—so long as he produces profits or can satisfactorily explain why profits are not being made.

Another type of board consists of major executives of the company. These men are not financiers. Each is an experienced, tested member of top management. Some of our largest and most successful companies have boards of this kind. These are full-time, not part-time, boards. They meet every working day. Some investors prefer to invest their money in companies that have a board made up of executives who own large amounts of stock. The president of such a board is likely to be an able leader who knows how to build and direct a team of able men.

A good board of directors is made up of men of ability—men who look upon their membership as a serious responsibility. They give the company their best in counsel and direction.

The president

Fortunately, most presidents of America's corporations are men of ability. They think of managing as a profession that requires special abilities in the functions of management: organizing, planning, staffing, executing, and appraising. As the chief executive officer, they realize that they are expected to strike equitable balances among the conflicting interests of employees, customers, stockholders, and the general public. They have a deep sense of responsibility for their office.

The typical president associates with other businessmen and attends meetings to keep in touch with trends that affect his business. He may not be especially sociable for the mere purpose of being with people. When he goes to a meeting, he goes to learn rather than to fraternize with associates. He of course identifies himself with other successful leaders in business. He wants their goodwill, but he wants to earn it by their respect for the kind of business he directs.

He reads the financial pages, business journals, and newsletters to give himself the background needed to do his job. He is mentally alert to all matters that affect his company and the industry of which the company is a part. He is informed about national and world affairs. He thinks of his company in terms of its setting in the affairs of business and society. He constantly improves his perspectives. He wants to be able to interpret the courses of events and predict how his company will be affected so that he can take appropriate action.

In many cases, the man chosen for the presidency is the executive vice-president or one of the other vice-presidents. If the members of the board of directors have been foresighted, they have directed the staffing of the company with able management men so that the office of the president can be filled whenever the president retires or leaves.

The usual fictional description of the way men are selected for the presidency is one of intense rivalry between vice-presidents. Each candidate is portrayed as using chicanery to gain ascendance over his rivals. The most ruthless man supposedly wins! This kind of situation does occur, but only rarely. Far more commonly, the board of directors studies the company's needs to increase its chances for future success. If the company's finances have been weak or too limited, the directors may decide that the next president should be a financial man who has the ability to influence other financial men and institutions that can strengthen the company's financial resources.

If the company's greatest need appears to be the reducing of production costs, an able production man may be chosen. If the sales record has been disappointing, an effective sales manager may be the choice. If the research and development of new products has been too slow to meet competition, the man chosen is likely to be an executive who has a successful record in that function, and so on. The company needs that seem to be the greatest are a dominant influence in the kind of man the board members elect. Sometimes the board members choose an "interim president," someone who can build up the company in regard to what is believed to be a short-term need such as establishing more workable relations with labor unions. This type of man is likely to be near retirement age, and the directors tell him about their hopes and expectations so that he can prepare a successor for the long-term needs of the company. Presidents, in short, are chosen in a businesslike manner—not to provide drama that will entertain spectators.

Management technology

Leaders in management technology realize that the best term to describe the unique character of management organization efforts in the United States is the word *pragmatic*. Experimentation and the best available

tools of research are used. H. Bruce Palmer, president of the National Industrial Conference Board, has aptly described certain major aspects:

> Other nations have, in the past few years, begun to emphasize
> the "management gap" that exists between them and the United States.
> It is management technology, they stress, and not breakthroughs in
> research and development alone, that has made the United States pre-
> eminent in the economic world.
>
> Management technology, or the management process, as prac-
> ticed by U. S. companies encompasses many diverse but related parts.
> Of these, planning, communication, and control are major elements.
> But organizing—and United States methods of organizing—to manage
> a complex, diverse, and ever-changing business has been a key-input
> in the management process.[1]

Some of our modern companies have become so large that the president's responsibilities have become exceedingly complex and numerous. As
chief executive officer the president must make the final decisions. He needs
assistants or associates who can share the decision making to get his job
done. Hence, the proliferation on organization charts of titles such as "special assistant to the president," "executive assistant," and numerous senior
vice-presidents who function in designated fields. In most companies, the
executive committees are likely to be prominent.

In some foreign countries as in England and Holland, a very large
company may have a *collegium* of as many as a dozen managing directors
(presidents) who share certain powers equally. Most American companies,
however, cling to the use of the one-man-at-the-top concept, but managements are of necessity searching for a new multiperson type of headship or
some other means of relieving the harried president.[2]

Modern technology is gradually coming to the aid of some of the
larger companies. Formerly, it was assumed that a president could handle a
top limit of only six executives reporting to him. With closed circuit television and other instant communications devices, plus the aid of computers,
an appropriately equipped president can keep in touch with more men than
the old standard six.[3]

Presidents must somehow keep in touch with their subordinates and

[1]H. Bruce Palmer, *Corporate Organization Structures*, Studies in Personnel
Policy No. 210, p. 1. Copyright 1968 by National Industrial Conference Board, Inc.,
845 Third Ave., New York, N. Y. 10022.

[2]See John Berry, "More Room at the Top?" *Dun's Review*, March 1967, p. 29.
Also "The Palace Revolt," *Dun's Review*, September 1968, p. 42.

[3]See Edward J. Crane, "The Management Man of the Future," *Advertising &
Sales Promotion*, July 1969, p. 19.

their main problems. As one stated: "It's important to keep up with things, because the most dangerous situation is where one of our men has a problem and either tries to save you trouble, or lets his pride get involved. In either case, he tries to lick the problem himself. You can't just be 'available'. You've got to probe to find out if he needs help."[4] This kind of responsibility caused one man, H. A. Hopf, to offer the significant definition: "Leadership may be defined as the art of being able to get people to express more ability in action than they are aware of having in reserve."

The excitement factor

One approach to the arousing of unrealized reserves on the part of employees is the use of the *excitement factor*. One president stated it as follows: "Let's face it. If a company doesn't continue to do new and exciting things, its management dies. So does the company. You just have to keep growing. Stagnation in management makes you just as vulnerable as stagnation in the market."[5]

The productive power of the excitement factor has been dramatically demonstrated by new presidents who have come into companies that were on the brink of disaster because of extremely burdensome indebtedness as well as by presidents of growth companies such as International Business Machines, Polaroid Corporation, and Texas Instruments.

Decisions in such companies tend to be made against tighter deadlines, often without the benefit of fully completed staff work and individual failure is less tolerable than in the average company. Yet executives in these companies do not seem to be consciously responding to pressure from above. Instead they seem to be engaged in a kind of self-generated speedup, exhilarated by a challenging management environment.

In these growth companies, of course, this excitement is in part attributable to the constant pressures of technological change. New processes, new materials, new end uses and new products all have their effects on the responsibilities of the individual executive. No heart palpitations result in such companies when a packet of responsibilities is taken from one executive and given to another; such reshuffling happens too often to be unusual.

Excitement within an executive group probably cannot be generated solely by pressure from the top. But the critical spark that generates the excitement factor in a growth company must be pro-

[4]See *Business Week*, June 18, 1966, p. 116.
[5]"Without Excitement, a Management Dies," *Forbes*, November 1, 1968, p. 51.

vided by a leadership that sets demanding goals and somehow secures a common belief in them.[6]

Behavioral scientists who study trends in astutely managed corporations believe that top management men will increasingly seek to develop their techniques in bringing about challenges to the individual, regardless of his level of responsibility. Distinctions between the worker and lower and middle managements will become less clear-cut. Job enrichment programs will develop rapidly in some companies, particularly those that utilize science and technology in operations having well-educated employees.

According to Saul W. Gellerman, a management consultant with behavioralist orientation, "The most important thing management can do is deliberately maintain the necessity to learn." He sees enforced job change and added responsibility as ways of challenging both the manager and the employee.[7]

Human relations problems of presidents

Presidents recognize their own human relations problems. They discuss them with other presidents and consultants. The kinds of problems that concern them were indicated in one of the American Management Association's "Presidents' Round Tables."

These meetings are a strictly off-the-record affair, attended by a score of chief executives of companies with sales ranging from a few million dollars a year to hundreds of millions annually. Each chief executive has an opportunity to share his confidential problems and innermost thoughts with others of equal rank and to get their joint comments, advice, and suggestions.

One of the chief headaches discussed in a recent meeting was the problem of *judging the performance of a company's management personnel.* The presidents wanted to know how best to size up the results of their executives' actions, how to appraise the individual executive, and what measuring sticks to use.

Another and related problem which the participants were eager to hear about was how their colleagues get measurements of their own personal performance as president.

As one would expect, a question that struck sparks was *"How can I*

[6]Gordon L. Lippitt and Warren H. Schmidt, "The Dangerous Stages of Corporate Growth," *Harvard Business Review*, November–December 1967. Copyright by the President and Fellows of Harvard College. See also *Management Review*, American Management Association, Inc., January 1968.

[7]See *Business Week*, July 13, 1968, p. 74; and Saul W. Gellerman, *Motivation and Productivity* (New York: American Management Association, Inc., 1963).

know what's really going on in my company? What system of review can I set up that will warn me of trouble before it gets too serious?"

A group of problems that interested these men revolved around *the art and science of delegation.* The round table participants wanted the other presidents' advice on where to draw the line between too much and too little delegation, which matters a president can delegate to others and which he cannot, how he can tell when he is delegating properly, and how he can delegate and still participate in company operations as much as he thinks he should.

Other high-interest topics included ways of improving communications between departments; getting the most out of research and development; building the right kind of board of directors; and developing broad, constructive, and creative thinking about the company on the part of all its management men. Along with these came other human relations questions:

Whom do you put in charge when the company's chief executive is away?

Is the failure to designate someone a sign of poor organization?

Should you let people in the company know whether you have chosen your successor—and who he is?

When should an executive retire?

What, if any, are the advantages of filling top management jobs from outside the company as against promotion from within?

How can you get the feeling of management as a professional activity to pervade your organization?

When a man is being considered for a position, how much weight, if any, should be given to the kind of wife he has?[8]

These and related daily problems of presidents as well as those of other members of management have resulted in the common definition of management as "the art of getting things done through people."

Assistants to the president

The pressures on a president are numerous and the responsibilities varied. Quite often, he realizes that he should be in two or more places at the same time. Also, he may have some work that he does not want to entrust to a female secretary. One solution for his needs is to appoint one or more staff assistants who are given the title of "assistant to the president," "executive assistant," or "administrative assistant." Generally, the assistant has staff rather than line responsibility. If he has line responsibility, he is

[8]For full details of this report, see Harwood F. Merrill, "The Listening Post," *Management News*, September 1957, p. 6.

called "assistant" rather than "assistant to." The "assistant to" is not held accountable for operating results. His functions are limited to furnishing services of a specialized nature.

One of the arguments for the appointment of assistants to the president is that the job gives the appointees training and development for greater responsibility. The position enables the incumbents to share the boss's problems and to gain top management perspective. Many an executive needs one or more assistants who are trained in his way of doing things, men whose loyalty can be depended upon. Certain presidents could not function effectively without such assistants.

Other presidents believe that the position of "assistant to" should not exist. If a man is to be trained for line or other major responsibility he should hold a line job and be an assistant who can be held directly responsible for operating results. The way to learn to manage is to manage. A man must direct employees and have employees look to him for direction, not to someone above him, if he is to be developed for management. He must be on his own rather than have his thinking dominated by that of a chief whom he serves so closely that only the chief's thinking appears to be right.

The trend in management practices is to have the president or other manager appoint a subordinate manager, a next-in-command man, rather than install an assistant to himself. If a top executive needs a subordinate to take over during his absence, the next-in-command type of executive assumes the full role of the executive whose position he fills temporarily.

Vice-presidents

Men who have important responsibilities near the top management level and do an especially good job may be given the title of vice-president. They have major responsibilities such as heading production or sales. Generally, the title is earned rather than acquired as the result of nepotism. In many companies the executive vice-president is chosen from the vice-presidential group. This is a highly sought position not only because of its extra responsibility but also because it suggests the possibility that the executive vice-president is in line for the presidency.

In some industries, particularly in communications and banking, the title of vice-president may not involve executive responsibilities. The title may merely mean that the holder is a customer contact man who needs the title in order to deal more effectively with clients or customers.

Span of control

In some companies, the president may have as many as twenty subordinates reporting to him; in others, only the executive vice-president is directly accountable to him. Most companies have a span of control for executives of eight or less. Generally, the concept of span of control is applied to the highest operating officer of a company or the head of a major division.

Most top executives try to limit their span of control to six or eight subordinates. The directing executive wants to be able to keep in close touch with each subordinate executive's operations and accomplishments. He must, however, do more than keep himself informed in a factual manner. He must also give each executive personal attention on a continuing basis. He must enable each subordinate to feel that he is important as a person and that his superior is so keenly interested in his work that the work is constantly checked regarding its current progress and how management may help him do his job as expected.

"He simply refuses to delegate authority!"
Source: by Dale McFeatters, courtesy Publishers Syndicate (30 North LaSalle, Chicago).

STYLES OF LEADERSHIP

Every executive has developed a style of leadership that is likely to be more obvious to others than to him. He can, if he is sufficiently determined, improve his leadership by analysis and counsel, but there is no quick-and-easy solution to the development of a new style. However, a knowledge of leadership management theory can help him to improve his practices. Certainly, appreciation of good theory plus practice in managerial experiences can result in marked advancement in the development of his managerial style.

One of the best known concepts is that of Douglas McGregor's "Theory X and Theory Y." Theory X is the older style military chain-of-command type of supervision. Labor is considered as a commodity, and the employee in relationship to management is thought of as a servant analogous to the old master-slave relationship. In Theory Y, individuals are self-actualizing—they are willing to work and find it satisfying to participate.

A related theory is Robert Blake's "Managerial Grid Scale" where concerns for people and production are evaluated on a scale from one to nine. The extremes of the scale indicate concern for production versus concern for people. In most cases reported, the people-oriented supervisors achieved higher levels than the work-oriented supervisors.[9]

Another oft-mentioned description of leadership or managerial styles is based at one extreme on authoritarian principles and at the other extreme on the degree of participation—Rensis Likert's Systems 1, 2, 3, and 4. System 1 is "exploitative, coercive, authoritative"; System 2 is "benevolent authoritative"; System 3 is "consultative"; and System 4 is a "participative," group-based organizational system. Modern managements aim at operating as much as possible under System 4. Managerial theories are too numerous and complex to treat all of them, but the Likert system is briefly described as follows:

System 1.

This management system assumes that labor is largely a market commodity, with time freely sold and purchased. It conceives of the manager's job as consisting of decision, direction, and surveillance, relies primarily upon coercion as a motivating force, and makes little or no provisions for the effects of human emotion and interdependence. As a result, communication in this system is sluggish, largely downward in direction, and frequently distorted. Goals are established and decisions are made by top management only, based upon fragmentary, often inaccurate and inadequate information. This produces disparity between the desires and interests of the members and the goals of the organization. For these reasons, only high levels of the organization feel any real responsibility for the attainment of established objectives. Their reliance upon coercion as a motivating force

---

[9]See R. R. Blake and Jane S. Mouton, *The Managerial Grid* (Houston, Tex.: Gulf Publishing Co., 1964).

leads to an almost total absence of cooperative teamwork and mutual influence and to a quite low true ability of superiors to exercise control in the work situation. Dissatisfaction is prevalent, with subservient attitudes toward superiors, hostility toward peers, and contempt for subordinates. Performance is usually mediocre, with high costs, excessive absence, and substantial manpower turnover. Quality is maintained only by extensive surveillance and a great deal of rework.

System 2.

This management system assumes that labor is a market commodity, but an imperfect one: Once purchased, it is susceptible to periodic emotional and interpersonal "interferences." Consequently, to decision, direction, and surveillance it adds a fourth managerial duty: expurgating the annoying affect of subordinate members. This fact permits some small amount of upward and lateral communication, although most is downward, and sizable distortion usually exists. Policies are established and basic decisions are made by upper management, sometimes with opportunity for comment from subordinate supervisory levels. Some minor implementation decisions may be made at lower levels, but only within the carefully prescribed limits set by the top echelon. Managerial personnel, therefore, usually feel responsibility for attaining the assigned objectives, whereas rank-and-file members usually feel little or none. Very little cooperative teamwork exists, and superiors at lower echelons are able to exercise only moderate true control in the work situation. Attitudes toward superiors are subservient, and hostility is prevalent toward peers, but the absence of open contempt toward subordinates makes dissatisfaction less intense. Performance may be fair to good, although high costs, absence, and manpower turnover frequently occur.

System 3.

This management system does not assume labor to be a market commodity. It still reserves to the manager the tasks of decision and direction but removes surveillance as a major function. Little recourse to coercion occurs. In their places recognition of the frequently disruptive effects of human emotion is expanded to include employee involvement through consultation. This practice encourages a moderate amount of valid upward communication, although lateral communication is limited by the prevalence of man-to-man, rather than group, decision making. Communication is, therefore, usually accurate and only occasionally distorted. In line with this broad policy, decisions are made at the top, but specific objectives to implement these policies are entrusted to lower managers for consultative decision making. For all these reasons, a substantial proportion of the members of the organization feel responsible for attaining established objectives, and the system makes use of most positive motivational forces, except those that would otherwise arise from group processes. Some dissatisfaction may exist, but normally satisfaction is moderately high, with only some degree of hostility expressed toward peers, some condescension toward subordinates. Performance is ordinarily good; costs, absence, and turnover moderate; and quality problems no cause for major concern.

System 4.

This management system assumes that employees are essential parts of an organizational structure that has been built at great cost and necessarily maintained with the same attention and care given more tangible assets. It conceives of decision making as a process rather than as a prerogative, with the manager's responsibility consisting, not of himself deciding, but of making sure that the best possible decisions result. In this light, he focuses his efforts upon building an overlapping structure of cohesive, highly motivated, participative groups, coordinated by multiple memberships. Within this highly coordinated and motivated system, characterized by high mutual confidence and trust, communication is adequate, rapid, and accurate. Because goals are established and decisions are made with the participation of all those affected, objectives are comparatively closely aligned with the needs and interests of all members, and all motivational forces push in the direction of obtaining the established objectives. The closely knit system permits superiors and subordinates alike to exercise great control over the work situation. Employees at all levels are highly satisfied, but without complacency, and feel great reciprocal respect and trust. Performance is very good; costs, absence, and turnover are low; and high quality is the natural concern of all.[10]

Of course there is no one style of leadership that fits all types of organizations. An emergency situation might be dealt with more effectively by some form of autocratic leadership than by a usually recommended nondirective democratic type. The trend today, especially in these days of our changing social order, is toward the participative styles, those that develop a sense of colleagueship on the part of the members of the group.

[10]See Alfred J. Marrow, David G. Bowers, and Stanley E. Seashore, *Management by Participation* (New York: Harper & Row, Publishers, 1967), pp. 216–18. See Rensis Likert, *New Patterns of Management* (New York: McGraw-Hill Book Company, 1961). Rensis Likert, *The Human Organization: Its Management and Values* (New York: McGraw-Hill Book Company, 1967).

The informal organization

Many students who study management structure are inclined to think of authority and responsibility as if they were physical entities. This, of course, is not true. Organizational structures should be thought of in terms of the individual perceptions and mutual expectations of the members of an organization. If these do not agree with the lines on the organization chart and its corresponding manual, the chart and the manual are mostly window dressing. Only the human relations as they really are give the organizational structure its true meaning.

As stated by a leader in management studies: "It is not difficult to find managers who nod approval of advanced management theories and practices that have been fostered by our changing environment. However, it is very difficult to find managers who not only approve of these theories and practices but employ them in the management of their concerns."[11]

Anyone who works in the business world knows that almost every employee interacts with other employees and executives who have no charted relationship with them. The coordination of work activities requires it. These interaction relationships are not so vague or surreptitious that they cannot be recognized. Instead, the newcomer to an organization who has studied the formal organizational structure learns, if he is smart, to look for the informal relationships. These can be identified by the alert observer.

The person who wants to be an intelligent participant in business will seek to learn about the logical planning of organizational structures, but he will find his study of a company more interesting when he asks questions such as, "Is the official (usually the president) shown at the top of the chart really the controlling personality or a secondary influence?"

"Is a given corporate framework a kind of straitjacket that restrains initiative, spontaneity, and imagination, or is it one that stimulates individual and company growth?"

"Is the organizational structure master or servant?"

"Does the structuring unify the activities of the people who are now in the organization and make them more effective in their work? Or is the structure designed for theoretically ideal people rather than real ones?"

"Is the framework so designed that it enables a dominant personality such as an owner-manager to continue to dominate the organization by keeping control in his hands? Or is it designed to give many subordinates a chance to grow?"

An organization chart is not a substitute for competent men of goodwill who get together and work at the jobs to be done. Nor does it protect

[11]Norman J. Ream, *Management 2000*, The American Foundation for Management Research, founded by the American Management Association, Inc., 1967, p. 60.

the company against stupidity at the top, in the middle, or at the bottom of the organization. It does, however, aid in attaining objectives, and every executive should recognize it by communicating his instructions to the echelon members directly below him. When he does not follow the chain of command, the sense of responsibility deteriorates on the part of those who are ignored. Some top management men commit this error because they like to deal personally with individuals whom they know. This error, however it may be justified by the errant superior, reduces the effectiveness of his subordinates.

Appraising a management

Managements of companies are frequently appraised by members of the company, by financial analysts, by consultants, and by others. There is, however, no generally accepted method.

Of course, financial men examine thousands of management records to note whether a specific corporation is making or losing money, how much, and for how long. Their opinions, as the result of their findings, are expressed to some extent in the price they are willing to pay for the company's stock. Many appraisals of both incorporated and nonincorporated companies are made by bankers, especially when the company seeks to borrow money.

A determining factor in the appraisal of a company's financial worth is the management. Prospective investors especially want to know the quality of the management. One financial writer expressed the investor's interest by the question, "Is your money riding with a top management team?" Another used a similar question, "Is it a 'pace-setter' or an 'also-ran' type of management?"

Of the total of some three hundred thousand industrial firms in the United States approximately 10 percent are believed to have management of high quality. Even though the quality of management cannot always be measured statistically, the best judgment indicates that these thirty thousand firms are members of a very select group.

In some of the remaining two hundred seventy thousand firms, the quality of management is so obviously poor that astute judgments are not necessary. Lack of quality can be recognized by failure to hold a proper share of the market, by the slowdown or decline in growth, and by lack of drive among executives in the top management levels.

Weakness or excellence of management is likely to be in direct proportion to the amount of deadwood at the top. When deadwood executives hold the best positions, able young men of ambition do not wait until they can take over more responsibility—they move to other companies.

Generally, graybeards must give way to crew cuts, but a company may also have too high a proportion of crew cuts. The management evaluator wants to know whether the crew cuts are merely young and riding high on the momentum given the company by the old men or whether the young men have acquired the lusty risk-taking powers of the old heads that built the business. The mere presence of young men in management is not enough to impress the seasoned evaluator of managements. He wants to know whether the intrinsic strengths of the old pioneers have been transmitted to the younger generation of executives. Years are of less significance than the degree of strength of the dynamic leadership attained by the successors.

Family-run enterprises are suspect as to the quality of management. Most families want to have increasingly higher dividends. They do not want to give up dividends in order to pay for new equipment or high salaries of able staff members. As a result, they often have outmoded equipment, go-as-you-please production methods, sketchy accounting, skimpy advertising budgets, inadequately paid salesmen, and high-cost uncoordinated operations. Nor are they likely to hire outside consultants who might put them on a sound basis. They just continue to coast along until dividends decline to the point where the family members decide they had better sell out and take whatever they can get before bankruptcy.

Islands of autonomy exist in many large organizations. Clusters of executives and employees who "grew up together" understand each other and they function well, but they are apt to function with a certain disregard for the other divisions of the organization. This kind of situation is especially likely to occur when one large company buys another company and transfers the personnel from the purchased to the purchasing company. The transferees naturally know and trust each other to a greater extent than they do members of the company that has absorbed them.

Some islands of autonomy also develop because the head of a division is unusually able. He hires men who admire him and they become more loyal to him than to the organization as a whole. When a number of these islands develop in a company, division heads whose offices are on the same floor may not confer with other heads in regard to mutual problems. They may even compete with each other to the extent of buying supplies outside the company rather than from divisions of their own firm. Tie-in sales that might be made are given to outsiders. In one chemical company, for example, the division heads of one office rarely conferred with related heads who happened to have offices in another building only two blocks away. As a result, these two blocks were called the "longest distance in the chemical business."[12]

Depth of management is a criterion applied to large companies. A

[12]See *Business Week*, June 1, 1957, p. 71.

management may have able men in each top job but few or no replacements. Or the replacements that are available may be of a decidedly lower grade than the members of the top echelon. Hence, the death or retirement of a few men may weaken the organization to a dangerous extent. To overcome this danger, some leaders in management teach their subordinates that the test of a good executive is that he is not afraid to have a second man who is a real challenge to him. To be strong, a management must be built in depth. The men directly under the top men should be as good as, if not better than, the top men.

Top executives function in a "lonely" manner

Napoleon is supposed to have stated: "There's something awful in the loneliness of supreme command." One of the loneliest of men in a large corporation is the president. Even though he is by nature a friendly person, his position insulates him from others. He is not one of them in the fullest sense. His social life is largely limited to persons of similar station in life.

If the business is very large, the information that comes to him is likely to be prepared for him. People who come to see him plan their approach. He cannot learn how other people really feel and think through ordinary everyday contacts where everyone is natural. He spends most of his time in talking to people, but he cannot talk about his own personal problems. And yet he must win the loyalties and respect of those who depend on him for leadership.

The top level executive cannot discuss some of his own thoughts and plans with his subordinates. He cannot, for example, "think out loud" as to which of several men he ought to promote to an important vacancy. If he mentions their names to someone else, his mention is likely to be construed and reported as though he had made a final choice.

He cannot discuss financial problems, new product plans, negotiations for purchase of plant sites, and a host of other topics until his own thinking has reached an appropriate stage. He must even consider the effects on others when he goes to lunch with subordinates. "Lunch with the boss" may imply significance in regard to an impending promotion to an existing vacancy and arouse apprehension on the part of those not invited.

The higher the executive in the hierarchy of management, the more insulated and lonely his position makes him. As a result, he may turn to consultants for counsel and business companionship.

Management men often hire a consultant in order to check their own evaluation of their business situation. As one executive stated: "I hire a consultant's services on a regular basis because if he can tell me something I haven't already known, I have been asleep!"

Consultants feel at home in the top echelons of management. They customarily associate with men of ability. Top management executives know that the consultant has management's perspectives. The consultant is free from the ties that executives of the company have toward each other when they have worked side by side for many years. Men who work together cannot be entirely frank with each other because each knows the other man's blind spots, idiosyncrasies, and emotional needs. The consultant is a newcomer to these personal ties. He can be more objective than personal friendship may permit.

The ways in which a corporation president or top executive must function suggest that he should not usually be treated with awe. Instead, a friendly manner resulting from appreciation of his psychological situation is likely to be more appropriate.

QUESTIONS ON THE CHAPTER

1. Differentiate between formal and informal organizations.
2. Why is a formal organization necessary?
3. What are the functions of the three main levels of management?
4. Describe the general duties of a board of directors.
5. What is meant by "rubber-stamp board of directors?"
6. Define management technology.
7. How are presidents often described fictionally?
8. What are the arguments for and against having "assistants to the president"?
9. To whom does the concept of span of control generally apply, and what is the average span in most companies?
10. What is a determining factor in the appraisal of a company's financial worth?
11. What is meant by the statement that "to be strong, a management must be built in depth"?
12. Of all the ideas presented in the chapter, which ones were of special interest to you?
13. What did the chapter contribute toward your future relations with (a) the men who supervise your work, (b) the employees whom you may supervise?

PROBLEMS AND PROJECTS

For All Students

1. Numerous articles in business journals are published each year on the duties and problems of corporation presidents. Examine the journals available to

you and summarize some of the main findings. Compare your findings with those presented in this text on this topic.

2. Would you like to become a member of a board of directors? How can a person become a member? For reference, see E. Everett Smith, "The Neglected Board of Directors," *Harvard Business Review*, May–June 1958 or other sources.

For Advanced Students

3. Examine the available literature regarding psychological factors involved in management's actions. An example might be Melville Dalton, *Men Who Manage: Fusions of Feeling and Theory in Administration*. New York: John & Sons, Inc., 1959.

4. Consultants and outside specialists can disrupt an organization. Make a study of some of the likely hazards in their use. Consult W. L. K. Schwartz, "What to Do Till the Doctor Comes," *The Management Review*, August 1958.

For Men in Business

5. When out-of-town members of top management visit a plant, it is cleaned and spruced up before they arrive. This is a poor concept of top management. How can such visitors be given more positive meanings for the employees?

6. Some executives who retire go into consulting work. Does consulting demand skills that differ from those of the typical executive? Describe your own experiences with consultants, particularly those of the retired executive variety.

COLLATERAL READINGS

For All Students

Gutenberg, Arthur W., and Eugene Richman, *Dynamics of Management*. Scranton, Pa.: International Textbook Co., 1968. Part III deals with organizational patterns, human limitations, and organizational behavior found in certain companies.

Likert, Rensis, *The Human Organization: Its Management and Value*. New York: McGraw-Hill Book Company, 1967. Describes more fully the system of management presented in the author's *New Patterns of Management*. The nature of science-based management is discussed.

For Advanced Students

Bennis, Warren, "The Climate for Opportunity," and Jane Templeton, "The Changing Challenge," in *Sales Management*, September 10, 1969, present a basic concept for management: "As corporate employees increasingly seek satisfaction in their work, management must create a climate that will channel these concerns into greater productivity."

Wingo, Walter, *Patterns for Success*. Garden City, N.Y.: Doubleday & Company, Inc., 1967. Presents strategies and techniques of managing a corporation at the top level as outlined in the nation's leading executive development course.

For Men in Business

Haynes, W. Warren, and Joseph L. Massie, *Management: Analysis, Concepts and Cases*. Englewood Cliffs, N.J.: Prentice-Hall, Inc., 1969. Chapters 27 and 28 deal with management in different nations and societies.

Uris, Auren, *The Management Makers*. New York: The Macmillan Company, 1962. Described as a behind-the-scenes view of management; how management is made and unmade by the people who act as management makers.

Middle Management
and the Effects on People
of Changes in Management

SITUATIONS YOU ARE LIKELY TO MEET

How would you meet each of these situations:
    a. *Before* you have read the chapter? What would you say to yourself or to the individual?
    b. *After* you have read the chapter? How have your answers changed?

1. A friend, Mr. A, decides that when he graduates from college, he will go to graduate school for a year or two and then take a staff job. He enjoys making statistical analyses and writing technical reports. Another friend, Mr. B, has decided to go directly into industry and work in a line department. He considers himself an "action man" who likes to supervise men. The two men discuss the likelihood of their advancing into a position of major responsibility via the route each has chosen. They ask your opinion. What would you say to them?

2. A young man tells you that he does not want to become the president of a company or a major executive. Instead, he prefers to advance to middle management and to enjoy life on that level. What questions would you ask him as to the problems that he may meet and whether he can meet them emotionally?

3. Assume that you have been called an "eager beaver" by some of your friends. You do want to get ahead, to gain power in any organization where you work. By what policies do you intend to gain the

power? Assuming that you want to have lots of friends and few enemies from the side effects of your climb to power, how can you do that?

Of all the dynamic influences that bring about changes in an organization, one of the strongest is that of the upward pressures exerted by the ambitious members of the *middle management group.* The executives who function on levels of responsibility between the top policy makers and the plant foremen or office supervisors constitute middle management. Examples are heads of the larger departments, managers of small plants, the chief accountant, the chief product development engineer, and the regional sales manager. Many of these men are so important to management that they, as well as the members of top management, are given annual bonuses.

Members of top management of the more progressive companies take an active interest in the morale and development of the men in the middle management group. As the men mature, the most able move up the line into the top management positions. The training and experience of these men represent a heavy investment. Many perform key operations in the business. Some have important direct personal contacts with customers. Top managements try to avoid loss of members of middle management. If several leave for better jobs elsewhere, their going is of deep concern and top executives try to correct the causes that bring about their departure. They are difficult to replace.

Their importance as a source of top management positions is indicated by the likelihood that about one-half of the top-level executives in the course of a decade leave because of retirement, disability, or death. Generally, companies prefer to find replacements from the middle management group. Their development is of vital importance to the continued vitality of the enterprise. To move to the top, these men must become acquainted with the company's overall situation. They must learn through daily job experience how to delegate authority to get results from their subordinate supervisors.

The attainment of middle management positions is fairly easy for the intelligent, ambitious individual. Most college graduates can do it if they wish. They need not acquire many new personality patterns or do they have to learn how to assume responsibilities that are markedly beyond those found in many jobs on the lower levels. However, only a relatively few middle management men have the drive needed for advancement to the top levels where executives set general policies, develop broad plans, and establish business contacts with other top level men. Many middle management people prefer to remain where they are. They know that they have important positions and that their work translates top management's general policies and broad plans into practicable procedures. They have the satisfaction of knowing that they put plans into effect. Some are content because they prefer to enjoy life without the pressures and extra responsibilities inherent in the top management jobs within their view.

The more able middle management men are, in their thinking, oriented both upward and downward. They are oriented *downward* in the sense that they are concerned about operations, particularly with getting production out through the line workers. They are oriented *upward* in the sense that they keep upper levels of management informed about production: reasons for inability to ship a customer's order on schedule, need for new equipment, serious causes of dissatisfaction on the part of the workmen, and so on. One of the signs of the lower levels of management is in their lack of orientation beyond the department.

Many members of middle management, though ambitious to advance, have much difficulty in reorienting their thinking beyond the department level. The skills, habits, and perspectives that enabled them to rise to middle management are not sufficient for top management functions. Some find it hard to understand why promotions and salary increases no longer come their way. The ability and energy that carried them to the midway stage in business are not sufficient to go to the top. Middle management men, to become effective members of top management, need special training to help them shift their thinking upward.

The need for training managers

The Research Institute of America made an eighteen-month survey of seven hundred company presidents regarding the question: "What distinguishes the successful manager from the also-ran?" Certain major qualities were repeatedly identified and ranked in the following order of importance:

Ability to manage. This means both the ability to get things done through other people and to manage one's own personal efforts. The typical company president feels that half his middle managers are deficient in general management skills. . . .

The top executive believes that the most common problem is the middle manager's tendency to get so involved in putting out fires that he fails to step aside from that job long enough to plan for what his department must do.

Fiscal responsibility. One president complains, "Not 10% of my managers really know how to read our financial reports and make sense out of them. Even more important, they do not know how to read a competitor's statement."

Another company president, asked if he wanted his managers to treat the company's money as if it were their own, replied, "Good grief, no! Our managers are altogether too conservative with their own funds. We want them to understand the principle of risking capital in order to make profit." . . .

Involvement in the future. Presidents feel that too many managers are preoccupied with today's business, leaving the future to top management. Yet, an alert middle manager is in a position to spot an important change in the business environment before it comes to the attention of top management.

Professional competence. Many company presidents are worried about their most successful department head on this score. The reason they give is: They're not doing anything to prepare for the future, not keeping up with the latest thinking in their specialty. One president cited the fact that the "half life" of a chemical engineer today is seven years. By that time half of what he has learned in school will be outdated unless he works to reeducate himself. . . .

This means improving and perfecting your own personal skills—communications, delegation, problem-solving and decision making. It also means knowing about and being able to use a range of old and new managerial tools like value analysis, operations, research, critical path scheduling and, of course, our friend the computer.[1]

The computer has become so important in many management operations of today that some enthusiasts believe that it will eliminate most middle management positions. Others believe the opposite. The National Industrial Conference Board study of the situation offers a more evolutionary conclusion regarding the effects of EDP on corporate organization structures:

Electronic data processing—the computer—offers management a range of possibilities as a management tool. Its impact on the management process, company experience attests, depends largely on the uses to which the computer is put. To some companies, it is the biggest, best, and fastest adding machine so far invented. And it is used that way. To other companies, the computer is looked at as a kind of

---

[1]Edward J. Crane, "The Management Man of the Future: What Will He Need to Know?" *Advertising & Sales Promotion*, July 1969, pp. 19f. Copyright 1969, Crain Communications, 740 Rush St., Chicago, Ill. 60611.

Rorschach test: its possible application is limited only by the imagination (and the ability to develop the accompanying soft ware). In some companies, it has brought about a whole new concept of planning and control and made possible a technique increasingly referred to as systems management.

Its impact on organization structure has varied depending upon how it has been applied. On the most mundane level, there are companies that state that EDP has made possible a thinning of their middle-management ranks. The computer displaced numerous employees and thus the number of supervisors could be cut. But organization planners often argue that the middle-management ranks thus thinned weren't really middle management or didn't represent a real management level in the first place.

On a different plane, it has been argued that the vast new information technology made possible by EDP has also made possible greater centralization of decision-making. And there are many companies that can enumerate areas of inventory control, production planning, purchasing, shipping—the many logistical features of the business—that are now handled centrally. The effect has been to strip certain discretionary elements from the job of middle- and lower-level managers.

But the total effect of EDP, or more appropriately of the new information technology, on organization structure is still far from conclusive. And whether it promotes greater centralization or decentralization is still a moot point. For economic reasons, the equipment, the hardware, and all data-processing services may be centered at one location. But a central location does not necessarily mean centralized decision-making. A point often made is that the computer can develop information that can quickly be fed to the lower levels—making even greater decentralization possible. The safest thing that can be said—and organization planners are saying it—is that EDP increases the options available to management in determining the locus of decision-making authority.[2]

DECISION MAKING—BUSINESS GAMES

A business simulation or game may be defined as a sequential decision-making exercise structured around a model of a business operation in which

[2]*Corporate Organization Structures*, Studies in Personnel Policy No. 210, p. 4. Copyright 1968 by National Industrial Conference Board, Inc., 845 Third Ave., New York, N. Y. 10022.

participants assume the role of managing the simulated operation. Business games are training techniques for teaching decision making.

As in the real business world, a game is a continuing process in the sense that the earlier decisions made in the game affect the later decisions. The purposes of the game are to teach men to make decisions at *top management* levels.

Games can be simple or so complex that the use of electronic computers is necessary. In a sense, the players learn by telescoping years of experience into short time periods, thus reducing the learning period essential in learning the effects of decisions made over longer periods which in actual practice usually involve many years.[3]

Business game playing has developed rapidly in recent years as a result of the knowledge explosion that has taken place in the last few decades. These play-and-learn techniques are being adopted more and more each year simply because they reduce the learning time involved in training men for the most responsible positions in business. Numerous business associations schedule and publish the dates when their simulation sessions are available to members of the industry.

In some sessions several teams of executives are organized into "companies" that battle for two days for a common market. Their simulated work is divided into imaginary quarters and spans an imaginary ten- to twenty-year period. Each "company" makes decisions for the next three months on pricing, marketing, production, research, development, and the like. Each team strives to increase its assets, but the real objective is to learn the techniques of figuring out why certain decisions produced gains and others losses. Another objective is to show the interrelationship of decisions among management functions—for instance, the effect of a pricing decision on production or of a financial decision on research and development.

With the aid of an IBM computer, complex details become organized results after each quarter; and at the end, the winner—the team representing the company that has amassed the most assets—is announced. No individual loses, however, no matter what decisions his team made during the game. Instead, it has been found that each participant gains in knowledge and insight that he not only uses himself in the future but also shares with members of his company. The benefits of a situation like this are immeasurable, for there is much hashing among the members of the teams for long hours after the decisions are made and the results are in.

This method of teaching as applied to business is organized and designed to give practices in analysis, decision making, human relations de-

[3]See Samuel Eilon, *"Management Games," Operational Research Quarterly,* June 1963; Adair Smith, Thomas H. Scobel, and Ronald J. LeFrois, "General Motors Institute Experiences with Business Gaming," *Training Directors,* April 1961; and John R. Carson, "Business Games: A Technique for Teaching Decision Making," *Management Accounting,* October 1967.

velopment, and broadening the points of view of the executives who are in training by this technique. In some uses of the game, the conclusions reached in the "student's" thinking are manually tabulated.

The game approach in business, by using quick answer calculators, tries to create the environment of time pressure for those who make the decisions. Educators of academic institutions, however, believe that their allowance for greater time and analysis with emphasis on background knowledge is more realistic for learning. Most educators believe that the pauses allowed between "plays" in conventional college teaching permit the "players" to discuss and digest issues at hand and thus acquire "assimilated" knowledge in the process of learning.

In 1951 Mr. Cordiner, president of General Electric Company, instituted a research program into the factors involved in the development of management people. The project cost something over a million dollars. Participants were a dozen General Electric men and such consultants as Peter Drucker, Zip Reilley of McKinsey and Company, three men from the Harvard Business School, and others. Some of the basic principles that emerged from more than a decade of research were that:

> *Development is an individual matter.* The uniqueness of the individual, said Albert Einstein just before he died, was one of the few things he felt sure about. . . . It follows that we cannot run a successful development program by means of canned, assembly-line methods. Because what is good for one man may not be good for another. Not one but many development plans are needed, each one tailored to the particular strengths and needs of a particular man and aimed at helping him grow in the direction that is best for him.

> *All development is self-development.* Development is not something you do "to" a man. In fact, a manipulative approach is seldom successful. The motivation, the effort, the obligation, and the responsibility for development lie within the man himself.

> All over the country, young men are now entering the business world, proclaiming, as it were, "Here I am. Develop me." . . . What the newcomer ought to be told is something like this: "We'll give you a real opportunity to grow and plenty of educational activities. But please do not come in here unless you want to work hard and earn your pay and develop *yourself.* Don't come to us unless you recognize that the responsibility for your development is primarily yours. . . .

> *Day-to-day work is the chief source of development.* Exploring this subject, a group of outside interviewers talked with 300 GE managers, men who had developed to the point where they had been given positions of managerial responsibility. The interviewers asked these men, "What do you consider the most important factor in your de-

velopment?" . . . And nine-tenths of them said, "I developed the most when I was working for so-and-so and in such-and-such a place. . . ." By far, the outstanding factors in the development of this group had been the manner in which they were managed in their daily work, the climate in which they worked, and their work relationships, particularly with their immediate supervisors.[4]

The problem of developing executives is one of the most pressing problems facing top management today. The first logical step in the actual process of guiding the development of the individual to become a manager is guided experience, or coaching on the job. The best way for a man to learn how to manage a big job is to let him get the experience of managing a lesser job. He cannot read a book or look over someone else's shoulder only. He must learn by doing under the guidance of a manager who can stimulate, praise, and reprimand him. Generally, one of the best measures of a manager is his ability to develop managers. The factors that make for success or failure in a management job are more an art than a science. A management that finds it necessary always to go outside the company to get its managers is not likely to be a strong management. Some outside blood may help the "body economic," but too little growth from within indicates a basic weakness.

Of course, the training of middle managers and other members of the personnel have great impact on the organizational structure and operations of a company. Training accentuates the "upward thrust" of the ambitious people in a company. In addition, several other influences such as mergers and reorganizations also have pronounced effects on employees.

Reasons other than mergers, for changes in the organization

When the organizational structure of a company is changed, many employees are emotionally disturbed before, during, and after the change. The changes are disturbing because they often require the employee to modify his work habits, to accept a new executive as his supervisor, and to wonder whether he can meet the expectations of those who work with him. Many employees prefer an organization to remain static. This, of course, is not possible for many reasons, some of which are the following:

1. A company must grow or perish. New products and new services must be developed to fit the changes in the market.
2. Some members of management die or move to other companies.

[4]Moorhead Wright, "Individual Growth: The Basic Principles," *Personnel*, American Management Association, Inc., September–October 1960, pp. 8f.

Their replacements change the organizational set-up because they believe that they can work more productively in a structure that they like.

3. The ambitious young people who come into an organization want new outlets for their energies and ideas. The men above them do not retire, die, or leave as fast as the ambitious young men prefer. They are ready to handle bigger jobs and top management recognizes that they are ready. One way to capitalize on their potentials is for management to buy a new company, add some new products, or set up corporate objectives that challenge the able men who want to get ahead. Companies grow from the upward surge of young executives.

4. Some corporate structures must be reorganized because too many executives and other members of the personnel have grown antiquated in their thinking and are slow-moving and incapable of meeting competition. The old executives need not be fired—they can be given fancy new titles that sound well but prevent them from functioning in the old ways that retarded growth.

5. Conversely, when certain aggressive members of the organization try to outrun the company as a whole, they ignore teamwork in order to increase their individual power. "Empire building" takes place. These empire builders set up goals of their own. They are often efficient and productive. Top management may allow them to continue their empire building for a time. Eventually these aggressive power seekers go too far and top management reorganizes the company structure to keep them under control.

6. Companies that are family controlled are likely to collect so many barnacles in the form of incompetent staff members that a reorganization with new executive heads may be necessary to displace the deadwood at the top.

Generally, reorganizations are made in order to enable a company to move faster, to meet competitive threats, to produce new and better products, or to take advantage of an opportunity to merge with another company. The influences that cause reorganizations to be made are numerous and varied. The causal factors are of less interest to us than the effects of the changes on the people who are involved. The impacts on people are so great and so easily recognized that the board of directors of one of America's largest corporations has an unwritten policy of selecting a new president who is not more than fifty-five years of age. Their reasoning is that the first five years of a new president's term of office are needed to enable the other executives to learn to accept him and to work with him. Thus, if he retires at age sixty-five, he has only five years of effective cooperation to do his job well.

One of the most important effects of a change in structure that results from placing a new man at the head of a company or business is the displacement of the old "favorites of the court." In royalty, every king has his favorite counselors and friends. Even though a corporation president thinks that he rules impartially, the members of the management circle know who his favorites are. When a new managerial "king" comes to the throne, the favorites of the old one are usually replaced by a new set. The typical American top executive would probably deny that he has any special favorites in the company—all, he claims, are treated impartially. All may be treated impartially in regard to privileges and perquisites, but he speaks in a more friendly tone to some than to others. His face lights up more when he meets certain individuals. He asks their opinions more often. He gives them special assignments that involve extra confidences. He does all these and other things that reveal his deeper liking for them. The nonfavorite members of his staff soon learn to identify the boss's favorites and accept without complaint their own places in the circle. Those who find themselves on the outer fringes of the select few and resent their positions are usually glad to see a new head appointed—maybe things will be different for them.

Most employees know whether their own supervisor rates high, low, or medium with top management. (In very large companies having several plants, "top management" often means the plant manager.) The employees sense his status by the number of times their own chief attends top-level conferences, by the ability levels of the men with whom he associates, and by the way he acts when he returns to his office after visits to the superior's office. If his manner is cheerful or depressed on his return, the employees notice it and gradually develop a pretty good estimate as to whether he is in the center or on the fringe of those who count at the top.

Besides, the chief has a secretary—she probably tells her best friends in the washroom about certain incidents which indicate how her boss feels and acts. At any rate, the acceptance status and the pronounced emotional ups and downs of a department head are often sensed and known by his subordinates.

Possible effects of changing the department head

When a department head is changed, the employees expect the new boss to make changes in the operations and the personnel. Some employees look forward to the changes they hope he will make, others fear the effects. Much depends upon how keenly they are interested in their work and on how well they know and like the new head. Normally, they assume that the new head will try to give the functions and the operations some new emphases. They try to forecast his probable emphases by noting his experience background.

A good example of the effects of a change in department heads as influenced by the experience of each head occurred in a well-known company that has a marketing department which employs more than a dozen college graduates. The man who developed the department was an executive whose experience had been in the marketing of Product A. He was succeeded by a man who had a background of experience in marketing Product B. These two department heads, 1 and 2, not only differed in their experience backgrounds but also in their emphases in the work of the department.

Department head 1 placed the offices of the men who were most important in his thinking near his own office. When he left, the new department head, 2, in the course of one month, moved the offices of the men most important in his thinking near his own office. He also discharged several Product A men and hired more Product B men. (See floor diagrams

FIRST LAYOUT

DEPT. HEAD #1 Product Background (A)	MARKETING MAN Product (A)	MARKETING MAN Product (A)	MARKETING MAN Product (A)	MARKETING MAN Product (A)	MARKETING MAN Product (A)
MARKETING MAN Product (A)	MARKETING MAN Product (A)	MARKETING MAN Product (A)	OFFICE MACHINE ROOM	STATISTICIANS	
MARKETING MAN Product [B]	MARKETING MAN Product [B]	MARKETING MAN Product [B]	MARKETING MAN Product [B]	MARKETING MAN Product [B]	

SECOND LAYOUT (one month later)

DEPT. HEAD #2 Product Background [B]	MARKETING MAN Product [B]	MARKETING MAN Product [B]	MARKETING MAN Product [B]	MARKETING MAN Product [B]	MARKETING MAN Product [B]
MARKETING MAN Product [B]	MARKETING MAN Product [B]	MARKETING MAN Product [B]	OFFICE MACHINE ROOM	STATISTICIANS	
MARKETING MAN Product (A)	MARKETING MAN Product (A)	MARKETING MAN Product (A)	MARKETING MAN Product (A)	MARKETING MAN Product (A)	

Note that department head #1 had an A product background and that he placed A men in offices near his own. Contrast this floor layout with that of a month later when department head #2, B background, placed B men in offices near the corner office. The B men were moved near the controlling center of the department.

above.) Naturally, the discharged Product A men resented the sudden change in their status.

An objective evaluation of the effects on the personnel by the changed emphases in the department was that the weaker men in the department were the ones who were discharged. These men had catered to department head 1 as a person. They also had coasted in their work because they felt secure in their relationship with the chief.

What the discharged men had failed to appreciate can be stated in terms of two basic principles:

1. Anyone who studies business intelligently soon learns that the dynamic influences at work in business compel us to expect and prepare ourselves for changed emphases in the growth of a business.
2. The man who consistently does very good work is likely to find that he is needed regardless of organizational changes that may occur. Catering to the boss as a person and coasting seldom provide as much security as doing good work.

Systematic studies of the effects of turnover in top management indicate that such changes do not necessarily disrupt efficiency. Professor Donald B. Trow's tests of the performance of small groups subjected to successive job rotations of their supervisors indicated that irregular changes seemed to produce confusion but that employees can adapt themselves to just about any rate of succession provided the rate is steady and the successors are of adequate ability.[5]

Dynamics in the line-staff relations

One of the organizational points of friction in human relations often occurs in the changes made in the evolving line-staff working relations. We can appreciate the likelihood of such frictions arising when we understand the functional connections between line and staff.

Certain departments in any large company are responsible for making and distributing its products or services. They are usually considered to have line organization functions. Production and sales are examples. Other departments and individuals of the company such as accounting have no direct responsibility for making or distributing the company's product and are called staff divisions of the organization. A department of the line organization may have staff divisions to offer advice and give assistance in the performance of line responsibilities. The sales department, for example, may have need for the benefits of market research, usually considered a staff

[5]See "How to Prevent Changes at the Top from Upsetting an Organization," *Business Week*, November 19, 1960, p. 146.

function. Staff departments are often shown on a formal organization chart by placing their names on the side of the direct flow of authority from top to bottom.

A staff man helps top executives and line personnel to carry out their operating responsibilities. He supplements but does not displace the line men.

Staff specialists give procedural, legal, and financial counsel. They coordinate sales with production schedules. They audit records. They inspect the product. They do research and have departments of their own such as employment, insurance, research, and accounting.

The functions of the staff are often described as providing the line with counsel, control, and service. Staff members collect and present information, determine the degrees to which policies and plans are carried out, and perform other services that enable line people to perform their functions more quickly and productively. This indicates that staff specialists are subordinate to the line. Many staff men are intellectually inclined and technically well trained, but they can only make recommendations—they do no actually have responsibility for putting recommendations into effect. At the same time, they are often blamed for failures when line men say that they did what the staff recommended. Perhaps the counsel given was good but the line's execution was weak or faulty?

Small wonder that heated discussions take place between line and staff. Conflicts between the two are so common that top managements have to realign the organizational relationships from time to time.

Theoretically, staff people cannot tell line people what to do. Actually, line executives often give specialists instruction to carry out certain policies. Also, staff people interpret policies, measure results, and make reports to management of their findings in regard to the line's achievements or lack of achievement.

Obviously, confusion and disputes arise as to boundaries of function and authority. If a staff or a line man has empire-building tendencies, conflicts are especially likely to arise.

The line man is, according to the staff specialist, supposed to accept and adapt himself to the recommendations made by the staff. The line man may believe that certain recommendations are unrealistic—theoretically good but practically worthless. The staff man, in turn, may think that the line man is too stupid or too unconcerned to put the suggested program into effect. Line men are wont to say that staff men should mind their own business and not stick their noses into operating decisions or supervision of their personnel.

The kinds of situations that give rise to conflict are exemplified by these three instances:

1. While walking through the plant, the safety engineer of a manufacturing company noticed a machine guard out of place. He went over, adjusted the safety device correctly, and criticized the careless worker. The foreman immediately came up and said angrily, "Who are you to be pushing my men around? This damn safety business gives me a pain in the neck, anyway. No wonder we never get anything done around here!"

2. A department superintendent gave the personnel officer the names of two men he wanted for a particular job. They did not measure up to specified job requirements, so the personnel officer turned them both down and sent two other candidates instead. The supervisor angrily burst in, asking "Who's running my department, anyway? The hell with the your fancy tests—I guess I know what kind of men I want to hire for my shop, and I've been around here long enough to know a good worker when I see one."

3. The design engineer who created and developed a new product kept moving in on the production line after the item had been turned over for manufacture. He talked to his old associates who had been transferred to production, made adjustments, criticized quality, and gave instructions to employees. The supervisor soon found that the employees were turning to the engineer for their orders.[6]

As American business managements hire more and more specialists, frictions tend to increase. Even though the functions of line and staff men are supposedly well defined, problems continue to develop. Interactions between the two are necessary and continuous. They are bound to continue because staff men often have greater technical knowledge and are likely to be more ambitious. Some are also forceful. A few are more skilled in supervising people than the typical line supervisor. When the specialist proposes the making of changes, the line man may feel threatened—perhaps top management has more confidence in the specialist than in the line supervisor.

Staff people must be generous in giving credit for improvements to the line. If, for example, a methods engineer develops an improvement in operations, credit for the improvement cannot be given to the methods man alone. Credit must be shared with the line foreman even though he played a relatively small part or even exerted an inhibiting influence in effecting the change.

Management cannot turn back the clock of progress and eliminate the

[6]*Acme Reporter* (Association of Consulting Management Engineers, Inc.) No. 2, 1957. See also "Line and Staff—Conflict or Cooperation?" *The Management Review*, American Management Association, Inc., September 1957, p. 26.

staff specialists. Rather, their numbers are likely to increase; statistically they are on the rise in relation to line jobs. New production techniques and new machines of the automation variety call for an ever-increasing number of engineering and staff specialists. They must work with and for line personnel. Line and staff complement each other.

Admittedly, these are "nice" recommendations which are more easily made on paper than put into effect in real life. Staff versus line arguments are never ending. They seem to be as much a part of business as frictions in a happy marriage. Also, frictions frequently arise between line and line as exemplified by the criticisms of the production department when the sales department makes promises that production cannot possibly meet. All these frictions, whatever their cause, cannot be eliminated as long as human beings remain as they are, but we as individuals can seek to learn to recognize and to deal with them intelligently whenever and wherever possible.

The tendency to overemphasize power politics as a factor in change

Politics exists in all organized societies; perhaps even when authority is accepted as hereditary, politics is more intense than ever. It is found in religious groups, schools, hospitals, and in trade unions as well as in the civil service. Almost everyone becomes acquainted with power seeking as practiced by some of history's political leaders. He also hears about power seekers in politics and in business. After he gets a job in a business organization, he notes the machinations of certain ambitious employees who are referred to as "empire builders," "eager beavers," or "crown princes, self-appointed." These men function at first as factional leaders. They are likely to move into any group situation where the group lacks leadership or where a power vacuum exists. Power politics in the work situation exists in many companies, and the new employee must become sensitive to the effects. If he becomes a party to the influence in its worst forms, he is likely to develop certain crafty qualities which may at first appear to give him advantage over his associates.

As one writer has stated, there are several different types of power seekers. Some operate only in a relatively small group. They use various methods. A few, but not all, are ruthless. The empire builder may acquire his empire by any one of several beneficial procedures:

    (a) by skillful maneuver when others fail or retire or both, or
    (b) by sheer ability and applied imagination, being two or three jumps ahead of his colleagues, or

(c) by being multi-functional in his work. The more departments he controls the greater his effectiveness.[7]

Generally, these procedures benefit the company and the employees. If they are likely to have more harmful than good effects, top management controls the power seeker.

We must not imagine that only ruthless power seekers advance in business. Those are likely to be more conspicuous than the more representative men who advance in business through unselfish service. There are, in every large company, certain good sound men whose aggressiveness is objective and sensible. They are able men who are usually well adjusted as personalities. They have not sought power—it has come to them because they learned to seek *power with* rather than *power over* others. They have vision. They have ability. They help others get ahead. But the dominating center of their thinking is the work, the job to be done. They do not perceive themselves as ends in the attainment of self-centered power but as agents in getting things done well. Finally, every member of an organization should realize that change, even painful change, is as necessary for the growth of a company as for the development and progress of a human being. This means that the individual employee in industry should perceive the changes taking place, adapt himself to them, and view them with pleasure, not fear.

QUESTIONS ON THE CHAPTER

1. Which executives are classified in the middle management group?
2. Describe the upward and downward orientations of middle management men.
3. What did the General Electric Company study conclude about the development of managers?
4. How can a management find out whether a man is capable of managing a big job?
5. In what ways do the attitudes of business men and educators differ concerning the game approach?
6. What is empire building and how can it be controlled?
7. Who are the "favorites of the court" and how are they affected by change?
8. What did the NICB study indicate about the likely effects of EDP on the numbers of middle management men in the future?

[7]See John Marsh, "Power Politics and Power Politicians," *Personnel Administration*, July–August 1957.

9 Differentiate between line and staff divisions of an organization. How can staff men gain the cooperation of line men?

10. What are the characteristics of the men who seek power *with* rather than *power over* others?

11. Of all the ideas presented in the chapter, which ones were of special interest or value to you?

12. What did the chapter contribute toward your future relations with (a) the men who supervise your work, (b) the employees whom you may supervise?

PROBLEMS AND PROJECTS

For All Students

1. Interview an executive whom you know. Ask him to describe his developmental history, and his formal and informal training. Also ask him to tell of the persons who were especially influential in his advancement to major executive responsibilities.

2. Interview several employees in regard to the effects on employees of having middle management men move up to top management. Who benefited and who lost in the change? Did some employees leave because of the change?

For Advanced Students

3. Read a biography or an autobiography of a successful businessman. Note the developmental influences in his life history. Did the writer have insight into his development? What suggestions did you gain for yourself from the reading?

4. Examine available current literature on the use of simulation (business games) for management training. Publications of the American Management Association should be especially helpful. Compare findings with those of this text.

For Men in Business

5. Think of several middle management executives whom you know. Why are certain ones obviously moving toward top management levels while others seem to prefer to remain in middle management? Is it lack of drive or intelligence?

6. If you have had several years' experience in business, you may have seen how the job importance of certain employees has risen or fallen with changes in management. Describe one of the transitions. What kinds of employees gained? What kinds lost? What did you learn for yourself from the occasion?

COLLATERAL READINGS

For All Students

Burlingame, John F., "Information Technology and Decentralization," *Harvard Business Review*, November–December 1961. "Are the middle manager and the decentralized organization doomed to extinction or destined to take an even greater role in business?"

Dearden, John, "Can Management Information Be Automated?" *Harvard Business Review*, March–April 1964. The author thinks that one reason for the confusion about management's use of computers is the failure to segregate management's functions.

For Advanced Students

Colburn, Robert, "In Our Opinion," *Science and Technology*, April 1964. Points out a danger that since computers deal with the "expectable," their output may reduce creativity.

Porter, L. W., "Differential Self-Perceptions of Management Personnel and Line Workers," *Journal of Applied Psychology*, April 1958. Management men tend to describe themselves in terms of leadership traits; line workers in cooperative follower terms.

For Men in Business

Dyer, Frederick C., *Executive's Guide to Handling People*. Englewood Cliffs, N.J.: Prentice-Hall, Inc., 1958. Written for the executive at or near the top. Practical advice on developing a positive "executive style" and having effective human relations.

Weiner, Jack B., "Cutback in Middle Management," *Dun's Review*, July 1964. Presents effects on middle managements when the profit picture of certain companies changed.

The Executive

SITUATIONS YOU ARE LIKELY TO MEET

How would you meet each of these situations:
   a. *Before* you have read the chapter? What would you say to yourself or to the individual?
   b. *After* you have read the chapter? How have your answers changed?

1. One of your individualistic friends says: "I am not going to become an organization man in any company by giving up the use of my creative potentials in order to become an executive who advances by being dutifully complacent." What would you say to him?

2. An attractive young woman tells you: "I am not going to marry a young man who plans to become a business executive and then find that he is under so much stress that I'll have an unhappy worried semi-invalid on my hands. No sir, I am going to settle for an easygoing fellow who has no ambitions—just wants to spend all the time he can with his wife and children." Well, go ahead and answer her!

3. "The young man who becomes an executive must always be somewhat conscious of himself as an example setter to others. In that respect, he might as well be a preacher's son" is a statement of a friend.

   Ask a preacher's son about this comment before you read the chapter. After reading it, confer with the same preacher's son and note changes, if any, in your thinking.

What is an executive? One humorist defined him as "someone who can hand a letter back to a redheaded secretary for a third retyping." The president of The American Arbitration Association described the boss as "a fellow who has worked his way up to where most of the headaches are." Another described him as "a person who goes out to find work, finds someone willing to pay for having it done, and then hires somebody to do it." A more acceptable definition is "Any person who is charged with administrative work or the management of a business function." Generally, *manager* is more likely to be used than *executive* when the function or operation is specified, for example, *sales manager* contrasted to *executive vice-president*. The terms manager and executive are, however, often used interchangeably. In this chapter we shall think of an executive as a person who has developed the abilities to be responsible for certain operations of a business. He has earned the assignment to those responsibilities as a result of his self-development, not merely because he said to himself: "I think I'd like to be an executive."

The *public image* of the business executive is shaped, to some extent, by the fiction writers. In "business novels," the executive characters rarely do any specific work. Many appear to spend most of their time trying to defeat each other in some underhanded manner in a race for promotion. If, as happens occasionally, they are depicted as strong characters, they are pictured as resisting pressure to conform to some unethical corporate requirement. The details of their jobs are nebulous, but their sexual frustrations are likely to be elaborated in detail. If any heroes are presented in the play, they are government officials or heads of charitable foundations. The typical executive is portrayed in fiction as a rascal, rogue, or weakling. Very few executives could recognize themselves or their colleagues in terms of these dramatic portrayals, written by authors who wish to entertain rather than inform.

Systematic studies of executive characteristics

Fortunately, some serious studies have been made of real rather than fictional executives and the factors that seem to make them successful. The studies indicate that no one or two characteristics determine an individual's chances for success as an executive, but significant patterns of characteristics are evident. One of the studies used the case-history approach. The "whole" executive, past and present, was studied systematically in relation to his work situation. The investigators used interviews, questionnaires, and psychological tests. A total of thirty-three executives from twenty-nine organizations completed the diagnostic materials of the study.

These findings apply to the typical top-level executive in terms of where he came from, the nature of his psychological equipment, and, in general, how he has developed.

1. Some of the general conclusions that are supported by the findings of this investigation are the following:

Important

(1) The educational level completed by the typical executive is far above the average of the general population.

(2) He takes full advantage of varied educational opportunities.

(3) He is an active participant in and leader of social organizations during childhood and throughout his career as a worker.

(4) He is interested in religion as a force toward developing high moral and ethical standards.

(5) He has experienced and continues to experience good health.

(6) He is interested in people—particularly in selling them on the idea of fundamental cooperation. He is interested in the written and spoken word as a means of communicating his ideas. He is not preoccupied with the technical phases of his work, but rather with promoting harmonious human relationships.

(7) He possesses very superior mental and analytical ability.

(8) He is serious and conscientious in his approach to work. He is willing to take risks only after full consideration of the available facts.

(9) He is forceful and intense, actively seeking new work to be done and new methods of doing it.

(10) He is objective in facing his personal problems, frank and straightforward in his dealings with people, and spontaneous in his interpersonal relationships.

(11) He is ambitious and able to identify his ambitions with those of his company to an outstanding degree. . . .

If there is one broad implication to be drawn from this study, it is that an executive to be successful must feel himself an integral part of his organization and be vitally interested in the people around him. The executives studied were found to have recognized the importance of the human element and to have identified themselves with their

Brown's Job

Brown is gone, and many men in the trade are wondering who is going to get Brown's job.

There has been considerable speculation about this. Brown's job was reputed to be a good job. Brown's former employers, wise, gray-eyed men, have had to sit still and repress amazement, as they listened to bright, ambitious young men and dignified old ones seriously apply for Brown's job.

Brown had a big chair and a wide, flat-topped desk covered with a sheet of glass. Under the glass was a map of the United States. Brown had a salary of thirty thousand dollars a year. And twice a year Brown made a "trip to the coast" and called on every one of the firm's distributors.

He never tried to sell anything. Brown wasn't exactly in the sales department. He visited with the distributors, called on a few dealers, once in a while made a little talk to a bunch of salesmen. Back at the office he answered most of the important complaints, although Brown's job wasn't to handle complaints.

Brown wasn't in the credit department either, but vital questions of credit usually got to Brown, somehow or other, and Brown would smoke and talk and tell a joke, and untwist his telephone cord and tell the credit manager what to do.

Whenever Mr. Wythe, the impulsive little president, working like a beaver, would pick up a bunch of papers and peer into a particularly troublesome and messy subject, he had a way of saying, "What does Brown say? What does Brown say? What the hell does Brown say? —Well, why don't you do it, then?"

And that was disposed.

Or when there was a difficulty that required quick action and lots of it, together with tact and lots of that, Mr. Wythe would say, "Brown, you handle that."

And then one day, the directors met unofficially and decided to fire the superintendent of No. 2 Mill. Brown didn't hear of this until the day after the letter had gone. "What do you think of it, Brown?" asked Mr. Wythe. Brown said, "That's all right. The letter won't be delivered until tomorrow morning, and I'll get him on the wire and have him start East tonight. Then I'll have his stenographer send the letter back here and I'll destroy it before he sees it."

The others agreed, "That's the thing to do."

Brown knew the business he was in. He knew the men he worked with. He had a whole lot of sense, which he apparently used without consciously summoning his judgment to his assistance. He seemed to think good sense.

Brown is gone, and men are now applying for Brown's job. Others are asking who is going to get Brown's job—bright, ambitious young men, dignified older men.

Men who are not the son of Brown's mother, nor the husband of Brown's wife, nor the product of Brown's childhood—men who never suffered Brown's sorrows nor felt his joys, men who never loved the things that Brown loved nor feared the things he feared—are asking for Brown's job.

Don't they know that Brown's chair and his desk, with the map under the glass top, and his pay envelope, are not Brown's job? Don't they know that they might as well apply to the Methodist Church for John Wesley's job?

Brown's former employers know it. Brown's job is where Brown is.

Batten, Barton, Durstine & Osborn
Incorporated

ADVERTISING
383 Madison Avenue, New York

Source: *The Wedge* with special permission of Batten, Barton, Durstine & Osborn, Inc., 383 Madison Avenue, New York 17, N. Y.

various activities at every turn of the road—from early life on. Hence, the man who can identify himself with his company to the degree that his greatest motivation and satisfaction stem from increased business development, and who has appropriate qualifications otherwise, will be a good bet for executive training.[1]

2. *Dun's Review and Modern Industry* queried in confidence a panel of 110 presidents of key companies in regard to themselves and their jobs. One part of the study dealt with the problems they worry about when not at work. Regardless of the time, at work or at home, they worry most often, three times out of ten, about people—the people they have and the people they need. One man's answer: To get young people to have the same enthusiasm and to work as hard as he did years ago so that they too may qualify for advancement and the taking over of key positions. The selection, development, and stimulation of people was frequently mentioned as a problem.[2]

Of course the presidents who head the 110 Panel companies of this study are aware of many of their own flaws. Four out of ten men think they are too impatient, intolerant, or reluctant to delegate responsibility.

Eighteen of the presidents called impatience their main weakness— "Impatience with mediocrity," impatience "with slow motion in others," and impatience "with those supposed to be competent." In contrast, another five presidents consider themselves overpatient, too lenient, or too "softhearted." Eight men feel they are intolerant or overcritical of others, and one said his chief personal difficulty is "unconsciously setting a pace which may be difficult for my associates to follow." Next to impatience, the most frequently mentioned personal shortcoming was the "desire to do things myself and failure to delegate properly."[3]

The student who hopes to become an executive can, from these and other studies, gain much insight into the personal qualities that are needed to attain such responsibility. He will have some difficulty, however, in evaluating his characteristics in comparison with those of the patterns reported. One approach to the evaluation of himself in regard to his characteristics as a possible future executive is to note the personal profile of the typical executive in terms of work factors such as vacation, after-hours work, plans for the future, and how he feels about his job. A study of this kind by the American Management Association obtained answers from 335 presidents.

[1] Robert M. Wald and Roy A. Doty, "The Top Executive—a Firsthand Profile," *Harvard Business Review*, July–August 1954, p. 53.
[2] Kenneth Henry, "110 Leaders of Industry Look at Their Jobs—and the Future," *Dun's Review and Modern Industry*, July 1957, p. 32. Copyright © 1957 by Dun & Bradstreet Publications Corporation.
[3] *Ibid.*

Work patterns of executives

As to *vacations*, the vast majority take two weeks or more but business is likely to intrude. Many take their vacations by traveling or touring because of their constant concern about the business. Two men out of five conduct some business while away on vacation. Some of this is briefcase and dictaphone work, but more is convention going and customer visiting.[4]

About one-half take less than the total amount of vacation time allocated to them. Some take no vacation at all.

In regard to the *work week*, a high percentage of executives take work home from the office. This practice, however, varies with the industry. Of one thing we can be certain—executives are not members of a leisure class. Manual workers of today have far more leisure than any occupational group such as executives. Men who are in the highest managerial status groups usually have the least amount of leisure time.

One of the major conclusions from one survey of management executives was that for a top executive, overtime does not mean overwork. When asked why they worked overtime, many respondents gave answers such as "Lots to do—and interesting," and "I like to accomplish what I feel is necessary." Most had a gratifying sense of responsibility. The largest single portion of a typical executive's time goes into planning and thinking for his company.

Company meetings take up a large portion of the working time. Generally, the more meetings an executive attends, the longer the hours he is likely to work. The one respondent who attended the largest number of meetings per week stated that the greatest single waste of his time is "listening to people take an hour to say what could be said in ten minutes."

Of internal meetings and conferences two-thirds or more are conducted partly or wholly for the purpose of decision making. Half the executives feel that some of these decisions could have been reached as effectively by a single individual. But the gospel of group thinking has taken so strong a hold that few have an inclination to pass the decision making back to the individual. Group participation on many decisions is believed to be necessary for purposes of cooperation, communication, and morale. One company president sums it up: "I believe in the management team concept and practice group discussion even though very often an individual could or in effect does make the decision."

In addition to spending a large portion of his time in planning and decision making, the typical executive is future-action-minded. He is not interested in analysis as a mental exercise or in pinning blame for wrongs committed. Rather, he thinks in terms of action for the future. The effec-

[4]See Lydia Strong, "The Man in the Front Office," *The Management Review*, American Management Association, Inc., September 1957.

TABLE 12–1

How Much of Their Total Time Do Executives Devote to
Their Jobs and to Other Selected Activities?
(Average Hours per Week)

Activity	Time
At their jobs	
At office or other place of business	42.7 hours
At home	
Doing paper work, business reading, etc.	6.8
Doing "business entertainment"	2.6
Traveling between home and office	5.3
At combination business-social functions outside the home	2.8
Business travel	6.6*
In other activities	
Civic and political activities	2.4
Literary and cultural activities (including good reading)	5.2
Hobbies, sports, TV, movies, visiting friends, relaxing, etc.	21.8
Study to further career	3.5
Church activities	2.1*

*Based only on subsample; may overlap other figures slightly.

The above findings were presented and interpreted by two men who were engaged in a broad study of leisure by The Twentieth Century Fund which cooperated with *Harvard Business Review* in this study at the executive level. The foreword in the HBR article included the statement:

> From the 5000-plus responses and a score of depth interviews, an interesting pattern emerged. Executives do work hard and long. They do yearn for more leisure. But their leisure chasing is like a dog chasing a car . . . they're not sure what to do with it after they get it. See "Executive Leisure," *Harvard Business Review*, July–August, 1959.

tive executive does not merely react to situations; rather he acts to make things happen. Top managements that are most successful in using job challenge as a primary motivation for their executives and supervisors obtain a high degree of productivity from the top and middle management executives. The job challenge motivation is more significant than the kind of activity that results from fear of discipline such as the withholding of promotion for failure.

The desire for high status and earnings is not a strong motivating influence in the lives of great executives. Opportunities for creative thinking, solving problems, making decisions, and a liking for new and varied experiences are more likely to characterize the great executive than the desire for money or title. Money and title when they are attained, are attained as by-products rather than as ends in themselves. Central to the work of creativity, people play an important role in their satisfactions.

Effective executives enjoy their jobs because of, not in spite of, people.

They like and identify with the people and the organization of people which they direct. The closer a man is to the top of the organization, the more likely he is to identify himself with the company organization, all the people in the company. The further he is from the top of the organization, the more likely one is to find that he makes statements such as "I don't own the joint. I just work here."

Nonfinancial compensations

Very few business executives work for salary alone. Many go from a well-paying position in one company to a job in another company that pays less but offers more opportunity. Opportunity usually means that the executive expects to have more voice in the management of the new employing company. In many cases he expects to have more independence of action in discharging his responsibilities.

A true executive wants to be treated as an executive: he wants responsibility for getting work done, competent men to direct in doing the work, a voice in determining policies, privilege of making decisions, and a chance to set up goals for the company.

Even though the salary with a new employer may be higher, the increase is more likely to be a token of appreciation than extra take-home pay. Some managements expect each executive to be a substantial shareholder so that he will find a part of his recompense in helping to increase the value of the company's stock and its yield through the higher profits that he helps to bring about.

Money alone does not enable corporations to hire and keep executive talent. The tax bite taken out of high-bracket incomes is now so great that a raise in salary is virtually meaningless. Many companies therefore offer the hope for more reward by means of the stock option plan.[5] These offers usually go to members of top-level management.

Most top managements think of the executive as a human resource. They want him to be as well paid as he would be in a similar job in another company. They realize that salary alone will not enable him to be efficient and comfortable. They therefore supply extra satisfactions in the form of attractive offices. The offices are often decorated by a professional interior decorator or by companies that specialize in office designs. Many of the new offices resemble a living room more than a conventional office. The less formal decor is especially likely to be the design for an executive who spends most of his time in conferring and reading. For him, conversation areas with armchairs and coffee tables are more appropriate.

Expense accounts are a symbol of status in the business world:

[5]Under a stock option plan, company stock is sold to the executive at a special price, usually 95 percent of the market value of the stock at the time the option is granted.

most employees have no expense account privileges, some have specific allowances or reimbursement privileges, and certain others have liberal allowances, the degree of liberality depending upon the policies of top management. Some top managements are generous, others stingy in regard to expenditures such as trips to annual industry conventions, visits to foreign branches, and entertainment for customers. Relatively few have use of a company limousine or plane!

The most popular way to handle the executive's expenses is by direct reimbursement for expenditures made on the company's behalf. Executive expenses are under the control of some official even though policies are liberal. Managements recognize that spending habits of the men at the top set an example for the entire organization. They are expected to have the same consideration for the company's money as other employees.

Executives generally have highly developed consciences about the company's money. The idea of claiming reimbursement for money they did not actually spend is repugnant to an overwhelming majority. The psychological effect of a discretionary accounting procedure sets their already proven honesty on a still firmer foundation: "If the company takes our word for it and trusts us to use our own good judgment, how can we take advantage of that trust and turn it to personal gain?"[6]

The executive's relations with upper management

The individual executive, depending somewhat on his rank, is likely to have close associations with the management men above him. Of those relations to which he must give special thought, the getting of approval for his plans is probably most important. He must defend ideas and plans in which he believes, but he must also accept good suggestions from others. Ever present in his mind is the realization that his management is responsible for making a profit and that he must develop plans for contributing to the profit making.

In addition to preparing major plans for future action, he also carries out certain practices that help to improve his relations with management. These usually are:

1. Keeps members of management informed about accomplishments and failures in his area of responsibility. He lets his colleagues and superiors know what is going on in his department

[6]See "Executive Expense Accounts: A Survey of Company Practices," *American Business*, January 1957 for a report of a survey on executives and their use of expense accounts. See also Edward E. Furash, "Expense Accounts," *Harvard Business Review*, March–April 1960, pp. 6f.

and why he has adopted policies and practices that involve other executives.

2. Provides *a well-organized budget message* including (a) results of the current year's program, (b) analysis of next year's objectives, (c) specific goals for the future, (d) an explanation as to the methods for achieving the goals, (e) the reasoning behind the method, and (f) a listing of the estimated costs for the recommended program.

3. Gives his superiors *a carefully planned presentation* of his budget, including, in some companies, (a) the use of visual illustrations and (b) a reading aloud of the budget message in the presence of management.[7]

Psychological roles of the executive

Almost every executive must work with other people and get them to work with him. This means that he must have their respect and confidence. His personal habits as well as his ability bear importantly upon how well he is able to establish effective work relationships.

To the employees whom he directs, he is far more than an assigner of tasks. He also fulfills certain vital roles of an unconscious nature. As he acquires years of experience in dealing with people, he realizes that to certain individual employees he is an *authority figure, impartial judge, target of affection, target for hostility, confidant, catalyst,* or *tone-setter*. He must meet or help to fulfill the deeper psychological needs of people, needs of which they themselves are not aware. His most important functions are likely to be in the symbolic meanings that he represents for each of his employees. In some cases, failure of a given executive can be directly traced to his inability to fill successfully the role expected by the employee. He is sensitive to the deeper psychological needs of people (see Chapter 24), and he is likely to increase his skills in becoming the kind of role symbol that makes his leadership effective.

The executive who has developed an acute sensitivity to the feelings of others toward him realizes that he communicates and receives feelings as well as ideas. What he says in words is often less significant than the feelings that he transmits and receives. When, for example, he feels that a subordinate is not very important, he realizes that his feelings are transmitted to the subordinate even though his verbal behavior does not state the message.

He knows that covert hostility is expressed toward him by subordinates through behavior such as excessive absenteeism, tardiness, resistance

---

[7]See Raymond P. Wiggers, "How to Work Better with Other Departments of Your Company," *Industrial Marketing*, December 1956.

to his suggestions, and subtle blocking of his program. These and other forms of opposition often stem from difficulties that have their origins in symbolical as well as in unexpressed difficulties that remain covert. Some executives who sense these covert influences in interpersonal relationships believe that the best way to overcome them is to bring them out into the open. Sometimes a frank exchange of feelings, even though somewhat bitter, may clear the air and improve the situation.[8]

One of the factors that often develops or is involved in covert resistance is the difference in social rank between the executive and the subordinate. If either the subordinate or the executive is conscious of a difference, adjustment for the employee may be difficult. Fortunately for most executives, many a shop employee has just as much respect for his craftsmanship and the importance of his job as for the executive and his ability. When the executive-employee relations are in line with basic American democracy, neither the boss nor the subordinate is awed by the other "partner" in the work situation. One of the gratifying experiences in business is to see the kind of relationship between executive and employee where each has a genuine liking and respect for the other. Relatively few modern executives think of employees as subordinates—they are colleagues who occupy a different position in the organization structure. In terms of feelings, the high-grade executive does not think of the employee's position as an inferior one. Each of the two has certain functions to perform, appropriate to the individual's abilities, and each is worthy of the other's respect.

The executive as an exemplar

The top executive has certain responsibilities in regard to his daily human relations. He is under close observation by those with whom he works: superiors, subordinates, associates, and the public. One of the main parts of his job is example setting. He is aware of the effects of his own conduct in relation to what he asks of his employees. If, for example, his superiors issue instructions to curtail annual leave during a heavy work period, he realizes that he himself cannot take his vacation while his employees are denied theirs.

Many everyday decisions involve basic ethical principles. Even though the situations are casual, he cannot overlook the moral judgment required. If he does, he will encourage a cynical attitude on the part of employees, customers, and the public. Now and then he must decide big questions of an ethical nature as in these two examples:

[8]For a more comprehensive treatment of these covert interpersonal relations, see William C. Schutz, "The Interpersonal Underworld," *Harvard Business Review*, July–August 1958.

1. If he is the president, threatened with a proxy fight by financial interests who seek personal gain rather than the giving of long-term economic leadership, should he attack the insurgents on a personal basis?
2. If a labor union head promises labor peace in exchange for under-the-table payments, should he go along with the offer so that his employees may go back to work much sooner than they could if he were to hold to his principles?[9]

The man who is basically honest, however, does not acquire a reputation for integrity as a result of a few big decisions. That comes from little daily decisions as to how employees and customers shall be treated. Nor does he turn his principles off and on as situations arise—he lives within a basic ethical framework that is part of himself.

Each executive attracts some people and repels others

Many students of management assume that every executive should have, or try to acquire, a standard personality pattern or at least a standard pattern of behavior in dealing with people. The inexperienced person imagines that the human relations techniques used by executives are or should be as standardized as the techniques of a surgeon. This kind of developmental objective for the student is impracticable. Managing men is an art that is an integral part of the personality of the individual manager. He cannot conform or try to conform to a specific pattern—he must be himself. Of course he can improve his techniques. He can learn from others and from his own errors and successes, but he must still function as a genuine person, not as an imitator or as one who seeks to conform to a pattern that is unnatural for him.

This means that his personality and his techniques in dealing with people will attract some persons and repel others. Those who are attracted will tend to remain with him. Those who are repelled will tend to leave his department or company.

An alert observer who visits a department or company headed by a specific executive can often see a relationship between the chief and the employees under his direction. This does not mean that the employees are near-duplicates of the chief's personality. Instead, the executive in charge unconsciously symbolizes answers to basic needs on their part. If he is a

[9]See Wayne G. Broehl, Jr., "Ethics and the Executive: The Small Decisions that Count," *Dun's Review and Modern Industry*, May 1957. Copyright © 1957 by Dun & Bradstreet Publications Corporation.

domineering person, he is likely to have many employees who feel more secure when they work for an autocrat. If he is the teacher type of executive, he is likely to have many employees who like to be treated as intelligent colleagues.

We must not assume however that all employees at any one time are there because the personality of the boss and the employee complement each other. Certain employees, those of superior psychological qualities, may remain for several years under the direction of a repellent personality because of interest in the work itself. These stronger persons usually have definite career objectives, and they will "put up with" or ignore the characteristics of an executive who repels them. These exceptional individuals usually remain only as long as necessary to gain a desired amount of experience or other objective that fits their specific needs. Then they move on.

The health of executives

Surveys indicate that many executives take short or inadequate vacations, that they usually take too much of their work home with them at night, and that at lunch they do more shoptalking than eating. If an executive achieves success for his company, it is often believed that he does so at considerable personal cost.

When an ambitious young man hears adverse comments and reads reports about the hazards in executive responsibility, he may conclude: "Success as an executive is too hazardous—I'd rather settle for less and live longer."

Certainly, the ambitious young man who is considering a career as an executive should know the findings of the best researches available on health probabilities.

The best available research indicates that tension comes from within a man, not primarily from his job. Tension is not inherent in an executive's job. When a businessman feels that he is under constant pressure, it is more likely to be the fault of his own personality development or of problems outside business than of the job itself. This conclusion was reached by the Life Extension Foundation, Inc., after compiling answers given anonymously by 6,013 businessmen in 179 companies. The foundation is part of Life Extension Examiners, the medical organization that each year handles physical examinations for some 15,000 executives.

The study also showed that the majority of the businessmen, 78.5 percent, are happy in their work and that they think they are not working too hard. However, one out of seven reported that he felt under constant tension.

The men who felt under tension while at work were also the ones who most frequently had personal problems, had trouble living on their incomes, worried about their health (although their report of their own health was not substantially different from that of the non-tense management men). The members of this tense minority typically drink more cocktails, smoke more cigarettes, take less exercise, and use sleeping pills and tranquilizers much more than the non-tense majority. This adds up, the report concluded, to the fact that it is a man's attitude toward his life and his work that makes him feel the pressure, not "age, occupation, or job demands."[10] As stated by Dr. Walter D. Woodward, full-time psychiatrist for the American Cyanamid Company: "The incidence of emotional illness is just about the same in every walk of human endeavor."

Further researches may vindicate the belief from experimental studies that every person has his own natural stress level at which his mind and body function without ill effects. When deviations are forced beyond the individual's natural base line, ill effects follow. If this is true, it may be just as bad to restrain a naturally energetic person from functioning at his intense pace as it is to force a slow-paced individual to perform at an unnaturally rapid rate.[11]

This point of view would seem to be confirmed by a six-year, 1956 through 1961, study of 86,750 du Pont Company executives and subordinates. The researchers found the annual heart attack rate among vice-presidents, plant managers, assistant plant managers, district sales managers, laboratory directors, division managers, and departmental general managers was only 2.2 per 1,000 employees. By contrast, the highest risk group, which included foremen, clerical supervisors, and other lower-level management personnel, had a rate of 4 per 1,000.

Skilled, semiskilled, and unskilled wage workers as a group had an intermediate rate of 3.2 per 1,000. The middle-management workers just below the executive level had a rate only slightly higher than executives: 2.5 per 1,000. The rate among the lowest-level salaried workers, mostly clerical workers, was 3.7 per 1,000. All statistics were adjusted for average age differences.

In attempting to explain the low rate among executives, the researchers offered:

> Stress cannot be measured or described by the external circumstances with which a person must contend, but rather by his reaction to these circumstances. One man's stress may be another man's pleasure.
>
> Thus the demands of a top-management job may be no more

10See *Business Week*, March 15, 1958, p. 21.
11See *Management Review*, American Management Association, Inc., December 1963, p. 55.

stressful than situations commonly encountered by persons in lower job levels, at work and at home. Secondly, men chosen for advancement may be those whose personal qualities are characteristic of both executive talent and resistance to coronary disease.

It is conceivable for example, that in selecting persons to assume greater responsibilities, supervisors and managers, knowingly or unknowingly, may tend to choose the better adjusted individuals, who by virtue of their personality and psychic state are better able to cope with life's stresses in general.[12]

One of the major implications for the prospective young executive from these and related studies is that the man who wants to become an executive may strive for mere extrinsic values in life, particularly status and money. If he strives for these, he is likely to be a tense person with many worries. He will worry about his security in the job, about what a rival associate hints concerning his faults, about whether he will get a hoped-for increase in salary, about whether he will or will not be promoted, about what intrigues are going on behind his back, about how his wife impresses the boss, about hidden meanings in apparently simple statements, and about a host of other incidental daily experiences.

If, on the other hand, he disregards the usual achievement goals of status and money but seeks instead to attain goals of intrinsic value such as making a good product or providing employment, he will probably have few erosive tensions and, in the end, enjoy greater success. The man who seeks intrinsic values is deeply interested in the work as work, in solid achievement, and sincerely thinks "to hell with the title and the pay—those will come of their own accord when I do a really good job."

Some young men start their careers with high ideals but fail to hold to their original intrinsic goals. They shift their thinking because of a disconcerting experience or two such as finding that a less able rival has successfully played politics to achieve his ends. When this happens, the impressionable or hasty young man may decide that "If that is what the business world wants, I'll play it smart and forget about my fine ideals of doing good work and letting my work speak for itself."

If such a disillusioned young man resorts to chicanery or even cleverness, he will probably fail to advance himself, especially if his basic life style is one of integrity rather than one of misdirected cleverness. The eventual reward for uncompromising integrity is confidence, the confidence of associates, of subordinates, and of persons outside the company. When a man's word is as good as his bond and his motives are above suspicion,

---

[12]Sidney Pell and C. Anthony D'Alonzo, "Acute Myocardial Infarction in a Large Industrial Population—Report of a Six-Year Study," *Journal of the American Medical Association*, September 14, 1963, pp. 831–38. Also correspondence with authors dated September 18, 1964.

SIGNPOSTS ON THE ROAD TO EXECUTIVE DECLINE

How do you tell when an executive is slipping? The retired president of a large steel company thinks these are the tell-tale signs that a manager has passed his peak of usefulness:

1. When he talks more about what he did in the past than what he plans to do in the future.

2. When he blames his failures on new competition, the weather, or "conditions."

3. When he begins to lose interest in statistics that pinpoint opportunities for improving company operations.

4. When he begins to think the company can't get along without him.

5. When he becomes adept at thinking of reasons why a new idea or method won't work.

6. When he begins to feel sorry for himself and tells friends that his boss does not appreciate the years he has "given" to the business.

7. When he begins to feel that his position rates a bigger office or or a larger staff.

8. When he arrives at work later, lunches longer, and leaves the office earlier.

9. When he tries to convince people that the excessive time he spends on the golf course is good for the business.

10. When he loses the knack of talking *with* people and begins to talk *at* them.

Source: Courtesy of *American Business*, July 1957.

people conduct their relations with confidence. Confidence is so valuable an asset in business relations that it easily outweighs any temporary advantage that may be gained by sharp practice. Integrity and sincerity are closely related. They provide more powerful strength and influence than titles or wealth. Instead of succumbing to the temptation of using the questionable tactics of others, the young man ought to review his career objectives and techniques for attaining them. This is the time when he will benefit from a frank heart-to-heart talk with some wise old-timer who himself has a record of solid achievement.

"The Organization Man"

William H. Whyte, Jr. has pointed out the dangers of having members of the young executive group become too organization minded.[13] Presumably, as the young managerial men grow prosperous in the large corporation,

[13]See his book, *The Organization Man* (New York: Simon and Schuster, Inc., 1956).

they become content. They are assumed to lose their initiative and individuality. As a consequence, they are described as also losing their vigor and as relapsing into an uncreative way of life. Incidentally, Whyte conceives of this sapped vitality as possibly permeating other institutions: the medical clinic, the scientific laboratory, and the "law factory."

This kind of fear in regard to the effects of the institution is very old. Rousseau, the individualist, expressed the same kind of danger in prerevolutionary France:

> So long as government and law provide for the security and well-being of men, . . . they stifle in men's breasts that sense of original liberty, for which they seem to have been born; and cause them to love their own slavery.[14]

Several writers have analyzed Whyte's contention in detail. Inasmuch as the term "Organization Man" has become a synonym for dutiful complacency in business, we should examine some of the reasons why the dangers are not as great as imagined.

First, we must admit that some young executives do succumb to the pattern of acquiescence encouraged by the bureaucratic organization. Those who become apathetic conformists are not, however, the executives who rise to the top in today's dynamic organizations. Few businesses could grow if their spirit were of this variety. Growth requires men who have a drive to get ahead of the crowd, to compete, to do better this year than last, to reduce costs, to sell more, and to increase profit.

Second, one effect of success on superior men who have made some advancement is to seek more advancement. We see this occur in politics and labor unions as well as in business—those who achieve some power often want more power.

Third, modern corporations hire many men who have assignments that require creativeness: researchers, designers, inventors, methods men, advertising experts, specialists in sales promotion, consultants, and others.

Fourth, the rugged individualism in the business world of a century ago has not degenerated into nothingness in the big corporations of our time. Instead, it has been tempered by greater skill in a leadership that stimulates employees to cooperate in attaining new goals as stated in the objectives set up by management. Teamwork, not mechanical compliance, is sought. Leaders of today have profound respect for the individual—even the janitor is asked, not ordered. Certainly the young man of today should emulate the leaders rather than the conformists.

As General Lucius D. Clay stated: "In point of fact, the decentraliza-

---

[14]J. J. Rousseau, *A Discourse on the Arts and Sciences*, tr. by G. D. H. Cole, (New York: Everyman's Library, E. P. Dutton & Co., Inc., 1950), p. 147.

ion of responsibility which is the mark of modern management gives greater play to individuality than ever before, and the young man of today carries responsibilities that would have been considered far beyond his years a decade ago."

QUESTIONS ON THE CHAPTER

1. The two chapters that precede this one also treat the executive. How does the treatment in this chapter differ from the others?
2. What have researchers found relative to the effects of stress on executives?
3. Compare the leisure time available to manual laborers and executives.
4. What is the most successful primary motivation that top managements use for their executives and supervisors and how does this affect middle management?
5. What factors are especially important in causing the effective executives to enjoy their jobs?
6. List four signs that indicate that a manager is on the road to executive decline.
7. Why is it impracticable to assume that every executive should acquire a standard pattern of behavior in dealing with people?
8. How does an executive who strives for goals with extrinsic values differ from the executive who seeks to attain goals with intrinsic values?
9. What is the eventual reward for the man whose basic life style is one of uncompromising integrity?
10. What factors seem to lessen the danger that Whyte describes in *The Organization Man?*
11. List some of the factors that the effective executive considers or uses in his relations with higher management.
12. Describe some of the roles of an unconscious nature that the executive represents to other people.
13. Of the various ideas presented in the chapter, which ones are of special interest or value to you?
14. What did the chapter contribute toward your future relations with (a) the men who supervise your work, (b) the employees whom you may supervise?

PROBLEMS AND PROJECTS

For All Students

1. Look over some of the available literature, particularly the business journals, for articles on the executive, his personality, methods, etc. Write a summary of your main findings. Compare with the content of this text.

2. Interview several executives whom you know. Describe your image of each. How do your descriptions differ from those often portrayed by fiction writers? Are the men you interviewed hard workers?

For Advanced Students

3. Students as well as experienced executives may wish to apply for employment in executive training positions in companies that administer psychological tests. A knowledge of the kinds of tests given and their significance is often helpful. Read articles such as J. R. Hinrichs, "Comparison of 'Real Life' Assessments of Management Potential with Situational Exercises, Paper-and-Pencil Ability Tests, and Personality Inventories," *Journal of Applied Psychology,* October 1969. Perhaps the most important findings are the significance of upward mobility—occupational level, ascendancy, risk taking, self-assurance, or supervisory qualities.

4. You may find helpful Stuart M. Klein, "Two Systems of Management: A Comparison that Produced Organizational Change," *Proceedings of the Sixteenth Annual Meeting,* Industrial Relations Research Association, December 1963. This kind of article will indicate for you the influences of the executive in bringing about organizational change.

For Men in Business

5. To become better acquainted with the actual methods used in selecting executives by companies recognized as successful in American industry read Edith Sands, *How to Select Executive Personnel.* New York: Reinhold Publishing Corp., 1963.

6. Consider the individual executives whom you know. Describe one or more in terms of his (a) work habits and (b) psychological characteristics. How do you and other employees have to adapt yourselves to his strong and weak characteristics? To what extent do you identify yourself with each?

COLLATERAL READINGS

For All Students

Mackenzie, R. Alec, "The Management Process in 3-D," *Harvard Business Review,* November–December 1969. Presents a diagram showing the activities, functions, and basic elements of the executive's job.

Warner, W. Lloyd, and James Abegglen, *Big Business Leaders in America.* New York: Harper & Brothers, 1955. A report of a research study of the characteristics of eight thousand business leaders. Summarizes qualities correlated with leadership.

For Advanced Students

Brady, Joseph V., "Ulcers in 'Executive' Monkeys," *Scientific American,* October

1958. A research study in which monkeys subjected to psychological stress develop gastrointestinal lesions. May have suggestions for overcoming executive stress.

Levinson, Harry, *The Exceptional Executive*. Cambridge, Mass.: Harvard University Press, 1968. Specifically directed to executives. Treats the dominant motives of individuals.

For Men in Business

Cady, E. L., *Developing Executive Capacity*. Englewood Cliffs, N.J.: Prentice-Hall, Inc., 1958. A how-to book for self-development. Presented in an easy-reading style, it offers suggestions for executive growth and action.

Federal Executive Institute, U.S. Civil Service Commission, Route 29 North, Charlottesville, Va. 22903, is an advance study center for senior executives of the civil service. Ask for latest reports of their educational program.

The Supervisor:
Man in the Front Lines
of Management

SITUATIONS YOU ARE LIKELY TO MEET

How would you meet each of these situations:
- a. *Before* you have read the chapter? What would you say to yourself or to the individual?
- b. *After* you have read the chapter? How have your answers changed?

1. A college student of business management says: "I want to learn how to handle men, and I am going to get a job in a factory where the foreman of a group of men is the *one* boss—none of these fancy-pants staff men from the office is going to boss my men—I'll be the one and only boss. If I let staff men butt into my production responsibilities to do my work for me, I'll never become a good manager of men." That's an easy target to bat down in theory, but how are you going to answer this able young man who has a dominant personality and an excellent record as quarterback and leader of the football team?

2. The above-mentioned athletic leader also says to you, "When I become a foreman, I shall not only act like a foreman but I shall also ignore my old friends in the shop—no more playing cards or fraternizing with the machine tenders and operators. I'll associate with other foremen and management men."
What would you advise him to bear in mind?

3. One of the axioms of skilled supervision is that the supervisor should not only give clear instructions to

an employee as to what he is to do but also tell him why it is important that it be done. Describe an occasion when you did this in a simple everyday situation and another occasion when you failed to do this. This might have occurred, for example, when you directed preparations for a college social affair.

Many ambitious students aspire to become executives but few look forward to becoming foremen in a factory or supervisors in an office; yet that is the first stage in advancement through human relations skills to top management. As has often been said: "In business you have to show the people above you that you can capably handle the people below you if you want to get ahead of the people beside you."

The supervisory function is more than a stepping-stone upward—it is a key role in human relations in industry. In a sense, the supervisors are management's employee-relations mirrors. Their attitudes reflect what the workers think of the company and its management. Top executives are aware of the important role of supervisors in management and in employee relations.

The supervisor is the immediate contact man with the employees. The solution of technical and methods problems can be delegated to specialists, but the handling of people is an endless function for all supervisory members of the organization. The supervisor is the leader who deals with and directs the efforts of the individual employee. He is the one person who must get the work done by employees, and he must deal with each individual employee who is careless, moody, hot-tempered, lazy, resentful, or anything else, good or bad, that a human being may be or do while at work. He is the front line of management.[1] The foreman of today is expected to be both a production engineer and a human engineer.

Why many foremen are confused about their status

When the responsibilities of the present-day foreman are compared with those of the foreman a generation past, we note that his position today

[1]The general term for a member in this front line of management is *supervisor*. If he functions in the factory, he usually is called a *foreman*. If he functions in an office, he is called a *supervisor* or head of a specific section or group of employees.

We can understand why many foremen of today feel uncertain and confused about their importance in a modern industrial plant. New equipment, equipment that did not exist in their imagination when they started to work in industry, is taking over many of their technical responsibilities.

In the above photograph we see the computerized control room of the float glass line at the Ford Motor Company's Dearborn, Michigan, glass plant. At some of the Glass Division's plants, automobile windshields are being made with a revolutionary new computer-controlled float glass process. Computers control temperature, pressure, and composition of the molten glass from its beginning in the furnace to its formation into a shiny flat sheet of glass one-eighth inch thick and 100 inches wide at the rate of more than eight miles per twenty-four-hour day, seven days a week.

In the float process molten glass is floated on a 175-foot bath of molten tin. As the glass moves over the tin, heat is reduced gradually until the glass hardens and takes on the flatness of the molten tin. The ribbon then floats through a 350-foot annealing furnace, emerges as finished glass, and is cut automatically into desired sizes.

Source: Ford News Department.

calls for a leadership quite different from that of the old-time "driver" who could do as he pleased. In many instances, today's foreman feels frustrated by the policies laid down by staff departments such as personnel, by collective bargaining contracts, and by a cultural setting that requires democratic consideration for the individual worker rather than obedience to arbitrary authority. His duties have increased while his authority has decreased. He must persuade rather than command employees. He thinks of his job as only slightly higher than that of the rank-and-file worker.

He is no longer in complete control of his department. He cannot hire, promote, demote, transfer, punish, or reward as he alone feels inclined. He cannot dominate by means of fear. Many of his disciplinary decisions are or can be overruled by management. Even methods of work and getting out the production are directed by a staff organization. The science of management has cast him in a more subservient role than he occupied in the old days. He is expected to motivate employees, be their friend and counselor. Today's supervisor in industry is expected to get employees to *want* to do their best. He is the responsible front-line leader both to management and to his men.

The traditional role of the formal leader in times past involved an arm's-length relationship with his employees. In our present industrial world, aloofness on the part of the foreman is not effective. In the shift, however, from aloofness to our new form of leadership, the foreman has often become confused—he has thought of democratic leadership as the equivalent of letting people do as they please or as requiring him to be a "good fellow" to everybody.

As one management man stated: "Everywhere we hear that the foreman is a key man whose job must be built up, but we won't build it up if he has a fuzzy picture of his responsibilities that doesn't agree with his superior's picture of them."

The typical foreman's insecurity is complicated by the procedures used in selecting new foremen. Some are chosen from the ranks by reason of proficiency and seniority. Some are made foremen because they have demonstrated leadership ability in elected union positions. Some are assigned to supervision because they are college graduates who are beginning their managerial training. The typical foreman who sees how men are selected for supervision is likely to wonder whether his position is really secure.

Why foremen "take sides"

Contacts with foremen of industry indicate that in too many cases the foreman feels somewhat forgotten. He sees himself as responsible to executives, but he is not always recognized as a full-fledged member of the management team. He is in charge of production workers yet not fully accepted by the employee group. As one foreman stated: "You're really everybody's whipping boy."

The typical supervisor is an active member of two work groups. One group consists of his peers and his superior, the other is made up of his subordinates and himself. This dual role is often difficult to fulfill.

If he plays the role as a representative of his employees only, he loses effectiveness in helping management gain its objectives. If he acts as a representative of management only, he may lose effectiveness with his men. When he tries to integrate the two directions of his responsibilities, difficulties may arise. He therefore tends to take sides as a means of overcoming conflict. Some conflicts are bound to occur, but investigation indicates that those supervisors whom management has regarded as most ready for advancement differ from other supervisors in their ability to deal effectively with employees on both the individual and on the group basis. The employees feel more free to discuss job and personal problems with them. They hold more group meetings where problems can be discussed. They create more opportunities for two-way communication between themselves and the employees under their supervision because they participate more with their superiors in decision making.

The supervisors' conflict as to goals

One of the most important problems facing the business leader of today is choosing between, or balancing, or integrating, two seemingly conflicting approaches to management. One approach emphasizes an immediate work or profit objective: high production and low costs. The other approach emphasizes morale and organizational maintenance as a means for reaching objectives.

The conflict between these emphases is felt at all levels of leadership as well as among supervisors. Top executives must strive for a balance between production and financial goals on the one hand and long-range effectiveness and stability of the organization on the other. The supervisor is torn between the goal of pushing for immediate productivity and that of trying to improve his workers' ability to produce in the future.

The problem of reaching the proper balance can be surmised, in part, from some of the research conducted by the Human Relations Program of the Survey Research Center, University of Michigan. Certain studies there indicate that leaders can be classified as primarily "employee oriented" or as "production oriented." The employee-oriented leader is one who sees his job mainly in terms of maintaining good human relations and a smoothly running organization. The production-oriented leader is primarily concerned with the processes and techniques that contribute to high-level and efficient production.

Generally, the findings from research projects support one another on the principle that a supervisor's style of leadership is likely to be influenced considerably by the demands placed upon him by the organization and by his own superior. The studies fail to show the universal superiority of any one style of leadership. There may be no one style of leadership or set of leadership practices that is ideal for all situations. Just how a particular organization should decide on the proper balance for its needs is still a question for further research.

One conclusion has emerged from several studies, namely, that *first-line foremen, far more than workers themselves, hold the key to both quantity and quality of production.* This conclusion is supported by several researches made by the Survey Research Center, University of Michigan, as well as by others. One investigation, for example, studied section gangs working for the Chesapeake & Ohio Railroad.

In the C. & O. studies, data were gathered from seventy-two section gangs—thirty-six of them rated by company officials as high producers, thirty-six as low producers. Three of the major findings were:

1. Foremen of the highest-producing section gangs considered themselves leaders—not just superior workmen. Their men also perceived the foreman as having good planning ability.

2. Foremen of the high-producing groups were more positive toward their men, and took a more personal approach to them. They tended to be employee-minded rather than job minded. They considered the employee's motivation. They were more "men-oriented."

3. High-production section foremen were found to evaluate their sections more highly than the low producers thought of theirs. They had more pride in their work groups.[2]

The supervisor supplies important supportive relationship

If a worker feels: "My work is generally approved and accepted; others are trying to help me do a good job and satisfy my needs," he is said to view his relationship with his associates as supportive. The supportive relationship aids a person in achieving a sense of accomplishment and a feeling of self-respect. He feels that he has personal influence, recognition and appreciation. He believes his abilities are well-used. All of which makes self-actualization easier. . . .

Central to any consideration of supportive relationships is the

[2]D. Katz, N. Maccoby, G. Gurin, and L. Floor, *Productivity, Supervision and Morale among Railroad Workers* (Ann Arbor: Institute for Social Research, 1951). See also Richard L. Waddell, "Good Supervision: Key to Productivity," *Supervision*, February 1952; and *The Management Review*, American Management Association, Inc., December 1952, p. 785.

concept of perception. Things are not always what they appear, and the manner in which an individual perceives another person in their interrelations is crucial. A supervisor, for example, may indeed respect an employee, accept him, and appreciate him. But if the employee perceives him as distant, critical, or disapproving, the relationship cannot be called supportive. Furthermore, if the employee feels that the supervisor is not truly supportive he is apt to approach his work without much enthusiasm and with a resulting low degree of productivity, according to a large amount of research.

The concept of the supportive relationship is by no means unilateral. Supervisors are supportive of subordinates, but the reverse is true, too. Supportiveness is desired in relationships between one employee and another. It applies equally to the relationship of any individual to a group, and of a group to the individual. Indeed, groups may be viewed as supportive of other groups.

The importance of developing supportive relationships becomes evident when the cumulative nature of these relationships is observed. Just as hostility is cumulative, so is supportiveness. The tendency of an angry man is to "take it out" on somebody else, and for that person, in turn, to "take it out" on another, and so on; supportiveness, too, is cumulative and reinforcing within a group. Research shows that a person who perceives his associates as supportive tends to act supportively toward others in the organization.[3]

Many a supervisor is a father figure to employees. They react to him in accordance with their reactions to their father. Sometimes they may even test him to find out whether they can depend upon him as a father figure. The supervisor who senses his symbolism as a father tries to keep a balanced or optimal psychological distance between himself and the employee, neither so close that he is hampered by emotional ties nor so distant that he loses beneficent contact.[4]

One study of leaders of small groups indicated that the effective leader's social distance from his men is distant only or mainly from the poor co-workers rather than from all of his co-workers.[5]

In addition to his unconscious roles, he also has the responsibility of

[3]Harold M. F. Rush, "The Language of Motivation," *The Conference Board Record*, January 1966, p. 45.

[4]See Frances M. Karp, Bart M. Vitola, and Frank L. McLanathan, "Human Relations Knowledge and Social Distance Set in Supervisors," *Journal of Applied Psychology*, 47, No. 1 (1963), 78.

[5]See E. B. Hutchins and F. E. Fiedler, "Task-Oriented and Quasi-Therapeutic Role Functions of the Leader in Small Military Groups," *Sociometry*, 23 (1960), 393–406.

example setting. He must be aware of the effects of his own conduct in relation to what he asks of his employees. If, for example, his superiors issue instructions to curtail annual leaves during an especially heavy work period, he realizes that he cannot take his vacation when his employees are denied theirs.

Supervisory techniques

Some training programs for supervisors give detailed instructions in the mechanics of supervision: how to say "good morning," how to give work assignments to employees, when to take sides with the employee rather than with management, and so on. Skill in the performance of the mechanics or incidental procedures involved in human relations is not, of course, the basis of effective supervision. The basis is the psychological strength and sensitivity of the supervisor. If he respects employees, genuinely likes them, and is sensitive to their feelings, he handles the daily procedures in ways that are natural for him. Employees learn to accept him as their leader because he is sincere and follows a consistent pattern of behavior which they understand.

Standard patterns of supervision that every foreman should follow are few. A pattern that is appropriate for one foreman may not be appropriate for another. The foreman of a construction gang may be able to cuss his men and they will respect and like him. To them, he is genuine. The same tactics used with a group of accountants in an office would frighten them into resigning their jobs.

Most employees size up the boss rather accurately. If, for example, he recommends employees for promotion or takes sides with them in a conflict with management, his espousal of the employees' interests will affect employee morale in the degree to which the supervisor is believed to be influential with management. If he is known as having considerable autonomy in his relations with management, the employee's satisfaction will be high. Employees usually know whether the foreman occupies a position of high or low influence.

Employees also know whether the foreman is in a position where he must shield certain relatives or friends. They know which members of his group must be "carried." They know his entangling alliances. In many cases, they even know how well he gets along with his wife. Many do not resent his special situations—they may even cooperate in helping him to fulfill his difficult personal obligations.

The wise foreman, in turn, is sensitive to the employees' personal and work situation needs. If irregular overtime work must be done, he announces it as far in advance as possible. He does not tell them on Friday afternoon that they are expected to work the next day because he realizes that such requests disrupt many personal plans and cause resentment. He tries to arrange overtime hours that will be most convenient for each employee. He also allocates overtime assignments so that everyone gets equal opportunity to make extra money.

The socially skilled supervisor recognizes the mood of an employee before he explains a new task. He also emphasizes the value of the task before beginning instruction. If the employee to whom he is talking is tense or very slow in his comments, the supervisor helps him to relax by talking slowly himself.

The alert supervisor knows that variety is important to job satisfaction. He knows which job assignments offer variety and which employees need variety and which ones prefer monotonous tasks. He moves employees around accordingly. He also knows how to explain an assignment so that the worker feels that the task, however monotonous, is really important in its contribution to production.

Anyone who establishes rapport with workers and asks them to describe their supervisor is likely to hear many comments on his supervisory practices and his personality. Here are seven examples:

1. Yes, I like my supervisor. He's on a good basis with the workers —I feel at ease with him but yet he keeps a proper distance. He's always around when he should be and always knows what's going on. He has a lot of interest in us and you always feel free to talk to him any time. He wouldn't spread confidential information. He's very conscientious and pushes himself too much—he's always run ragged. There's nothing I can do to help him—I do my work and I'm harmonious with the others.

2. I like him as a person but he has no backbone—he's afraid of stepping on people's toes. He's very soft spoken and quiet but if he knows you'll take his screaming and yelling, he'll scream at you. If he knows you won't, he's passive. He should have more enthusiasm and work more closely with the management people in the office. I can't help him—it's not my place anyway.

3. Yes, I like her very much. She's understanding, patient, and has a good personality. She's very efficient and undemanding. If my work isn't done, she finishes it herself but I'd rather be made to do it—I do more when she isn't around. She's too sweet, too. You can't trust her—have to take her just on a friendly basis. She also tries to be motherly and that really gets me. She never talks of personal problems though, and that's good.

4. Yes, I like him. He's very understanding and patient. At first, my typing speed was down but he didn't say anything. He never asks me to do anything he can't do. He takes a lot of interest in my

work and always praises me when I come up with a decent piece of work. He jokes around a lot and is real easy to talk to—I always take my problems to him. He's not overly friendly and never gets fresh. Most of the men here are. He's a great guy!

5. Yes, she's wonderful. She trusts me to do things and is patient and very helpful. She can put her foot down and still be nice. She shows confidence in me which makes me feel good. She's a good organizer—everything's always done on time. She's so good herself that I want to do my best.

6. He's all right. He's kind of a mousy little guy. He isn't very pleasant—there's something wrong with his personality. He never kids around—always all business. He's also very moody—sometimes he doesn't talk at all. He's very fussy and exact too—everything has to be letter-perfect. I admire the work he does though, he has ability and does well in his field. He's just too quiet and reserved. I suppose I could try to draw him out more.

7. Yeah, I like him. He's very fair and understands the worker's point of view because he worked his way up. He distributes the work equally so that no one is overburdened. Actually though, he's a bit zany—he's always kidding around and acting nuts. If he would act more mature, he might get more accomplished. He could get more work from the workers if he were more forceful, I think. I take advantage of him myself and don't work up to capacity.

Fortunately, many employees can dislike or feel neutral toward the supervisor but still enjoy their work. Dislike for the supervisor does not always cause the employee to dislike the company or the job. Generally, workers in the lower grade jobs are less likely than others "to obtain satisfactions directly from their work and are therefore more desirous of obtaining satisfactions from close interpersonal relationships with supervisors as well as fellow workers."[6]

Disciplining employees

Many supervisors consider the disciplining of workers as their most difficult recurrent problem. Difficulties with work procedures clear up in time, but problems with workers as persons tend to persist. Obviously, the employee who violates a safety rule or habitually comes to work late must be given some kind of special attention by the supervisor. The higher the

[6]See Howard M. Vollmer and Jack A. Kinney, "Informal Requirements for Supervisory Positions," *Personnel*, American Management Association, Inc., March 1957, p. 439.

level of the supervisor in management, the more he will be willing to initiate disciplinary action. The lower-level supervisors usually identify more with their work groups and therefore hold a less critical attitude toward workers. Besides, they are not sure that top management will back them up in their disciplinary actions.

One of the most important aids in dealing with discipline problems is to revise shop rules to make them fair and reasonable, to change any plant conditions that create violations, and to agree on the enforcement of the rules.

Many companies have some obsolete rules. Rules must be rewritten, to make sure that the things expected of people are reasonable.

The plant areas where trouble is frequently encountered can be studied in order to remove the possible causes.

Instructions should be clear so that each employee knows exactly what is expected of him.

Reasons should be given for required standards of conduct and performance.

Most approaches to problems of discipline can be classified into two groups: the judicial and the educational. In the judicial approach an attempt is made to determine the rightness or wrongness of an employee's actions in a work situation that requires disciplinary attention. If investigation shows that the employee's conduct was wrong, he is reprimanded or punished in accordance with established rules or customs in the plant. In the considerate or educational approach the emphasis is placed on the reeducation of the worker.

The trend in progressive managements is to think of discipline as mainly an effort to correct a worker's attitudes through training. One analogous situation is that when a machine gets out of order, the repairman does not punish the machine. Instead, he tries to find out the cause of the trouble. He then makes the necessary adjustments or repairs. In like man-

"He's a stickler when it comes to coffee breaks!"

Source: American Management Association, Inc., *The Management Review* (December 1958).

ner, the human being who does not respond as expected is given similar constructive attention in an attempt to correct the cause of his trouble.

Some investigations have been made of the effectiveness of role playing in getting supervisors to accept the educational human relations approach. The situation used in role playing usually requires that disciplinary action be taken, as in violation of a no-smoking rule in a plant where flammable gases, if ignited, many cause death. One person plays the part of the supervisor, another the part of the union steward, and a third person identifies himself with the worker who is to be disciplined. The background of the case makes the violation of a no-smoking rule clear-cut so that a three-day layoff is in order. In the role playing the steward intervenes, however, and tries to get the foreman to change his decision.

The results of one study of this kind of situation indicated:

> The human relations approach was more successful than the judicial approach in that (a) satisfaction for foremen, stewards, and workers was greater; (b) the interview was more of a problem-solving type discussion than an argument; (c) the worker was more inclined to be satisfied with the steward; (d) the worker was less inclined to reduce his future production; and (e) the steward was less inclined to file a grievance.[7]

Most managements believe that the supervisor tends to create his own disciplinary problems.

He is responsible for his own disciplinary atmosphere. The working relationships he has established with the more influential senior workers' group, and through his own example, set the tone for his employees' expectations and conduct. If he lets some offenders and offenses go without prompt attention, he encourages continued digressions. If he tries to solve his worst disciplinary cases by transferring or even promoting the offender, he incurs the disdain of all workers. The supervisor's own personal conduct is the most important influence for positive discipline. If he himself is well disciplined, his employees will tend to follow his example.

Fraternizing with subordinates

When a worker is promoted to a supervisory job, he is confronted with the question as to whether he should continue to pal with his old shop companions. If he gains his greatest social satisfaction from the continuance of old companionships, he fails to learn how to associate happily with mem-

---

[7] See Norman R. F. Maier and Lee E. Danielson, "An Evaluation of Two Approaches to Discipline in Industry," *Journal of Applied Psychology*, October 1956.

bers of management. His thinking is likely to remain on the leadman level. Also, he increases his difficulties in maintaining discipline.

On the other hand, he runs the risk of being labeled a snob when he abruptly discontinues pleasant old relationships. Some new supervisors try to solve the problem by explaining the requirements of the job to the old associates and asking for their help. Most employees appreciate the situation and assume that the new foreman will act like a foreman and will want to find satisfying companionship with those of his own or higher rank. They do, however, expect him to be friendly. They especially resent being ignored.

The new supervisor must learn to appreciate that to some employees, the supervisor is a father image, a person to be respected and obeyed. To others, he may be an authoritarian symbol, a person who should be avoided. The supervisor who becomes aware that such symbolisms apply to himself wants to have his employees avoid an unrealistic view of himself. He does not want them to see him as having either a halo or horns. To help them modify their image, he can explain his responsibilities to them in terms of the work. He must keep the requirements of the work situation in the forefront of his conversations with them. Above all, he cannot grant special privileges to some and withhold them from others.

A frequent question in the minds of many employees is, "How am I doing?" or "Where do I stand?" The employees look for answers in the supervisor's manner. They interpret his smiles and frowns in terms of their psychological needs. If he is brusque or unresponsive, they are likely to feel that he dislikes them personally or that he is displeased with their work. Some will develop or accentuate anxieties about their status in the company. They will deduce a fear that the boss wants to get rid of them.

"This will be your desk. We have a two-hour break for lunch: from twelve to one, when we go out, and from one to two, when the boss goes out."
Source: by Al Kaufman, *The Management Review* (December 1957). Courtesy American Management Association, Inc.

No amount of assurance will overcome all these anxieties, but the supervisor can follow the policy of thinking and acting in terms of the work requirements and, at the same time, seek to maintain an atmosphere of approval and respect for each employee as a person.

Coaching by superiors

The most common form of training supervisors is informal coaching by superiors. The disparity between the kind of supervision that executives want and the kind they are actually getting can be estimated from the replies of supervisors to this question in a questionnaire answered by 138 supervisors:

How many times during [the past year] did you and your boss get together to discuss how well you were doing your job or some particular part of it?

The number varied from twelve or more—reported by 26 percent—to none at all—reported by 16 percent. Yet 62 percent of the supervisors said that they would like to have discussions with their superiors once a month, and 88 percent wanted sessions at least quarterly. Generally, supervisors had fewer discussions with their superiors than they feel they needed.

Asked whether they found the discussions helpful, 22 percent of the respondents said, "not at all" or of "very little help." Thirty-nine percent thought that the conferences were of "some help" and 36 percent reported that they had helped "very much" enabling them "to do a much better job." This survey indicated that some management men are less effective than others in talking with their subordinates about improving job performance. Most companies should consider the need for educating top executives in working more closely, more frequently, and more effectively with their managerial subordinates.[8] One effective method of doing this is called the "send-him-upstairs method." This technique is used by the executive when he gives an understudy an occasion to represent him at a meeting of other executives or subordinates, preferably at a conference or meeting where the understudy will get better acquainted with the people and the problems of the company.

Formal training programs for supervisors

Anyone who conducts training programs of this nature soon discovers that there is a big difference between what supervisors know they should do and what they actually do in supervision. Indeed, a member of such a class who mouths the best answers as to how employees should be super-

---

[8]See Erwin K. Taylor, "Management Development Begins at Home," *Personnel*, American Management Association, Inc., January–February 1958, p. 33.

vised may himself be the poorest supervisor in the class. Men do not change their ways of handling people simply by going to a few lectures or conferences; their motivating influences are too deep and strong to be changed easily.

A good example is the insecure foreman who is especially ingratiating toward members of management but exhibits other forms of defensiveness toward employees. They think of him as a domineering, egocentric, feather-my-nest type of person, and they will find many ways to impede the production of his department.

When a management man recognizes the motivations of a specific foreman who fails to develop sound working relations with colleagues and subordinates, he may try to help him overcome the influences of the unconscious motives. He may even tell him directly: "Don't be ingratiating to me—it only makes your men hate you." This may help the offender cease one variety of offensive behavior but adopt another equally offensive to someone else. The deep-seated needs within a man's psychic life are not easily throttled—they are merely redirected, most likely misdirected.

This means that the best way to retrain the inadequately adjusted supervisors and others is to have them become more aware not only of themselves—their motives, prejudices, values, goals, and feelings—but also of how these influence their everyday behavior in the plant and the impacts they have upon their colleagues and subordinates.

Training courses should aim at self-awareness and a new tolerance for one's own makeup. If the individual can be helped to understand and tolerate himself, perhaps he can also achieve greater tolerance of others. This has become especially evident when underprivileged workers are hired. Corporate employment officers cooperate with the local skills banks and with public and private community employment agencies such as "Jobs Now" in Chicago and the "Jobs Clearing House" in Boston, as well as with Urban League and NAACP centers. Coaching pays in holding employees. "Jobs Now" in Chicago reported that 83 percent of youths referred to jobs stayed when they were given counseling support compared with 24 percent where such support did not exist.[9]

The ideal method of training supervisors is not as yet available to most companies or colleges. Its use requires a leader who has a clinical background and unusual skill in enabling members of a group to gain insight into the workings of their minds without inflicting psychological harm. Certainly, the temperament and unconscious motivations of a supervisor are more important in determining his success than his factual knowledge of

[9]See Theodore V. Purcell, "Break Down Your Employment Barriers," *Harvard Business Review*, July–August 1968.

supervisory practices. The need for this kind of specialized knowledge and skill is great. Eventually our behavioral scientists will develop the research and skills needed for removing mental blockings from supervisors who are emotionally incapable of learning new supervisory techniques.

Even though clinically oriented training leaders are not yet available in sufficient numbers, certain other training procedures are available and helpful. The most promising at this time is role playing.

Role playing is a method of training that does not seek to rebuild the trainee psychologically or to remove deep-seated emotional blockings in order that training may be effective. It does, however, contribute to the kind of training that is experienced without words. It does help to educate feelings and provide some benefits for personality growth.

In role playing one trainee takes the part of a problem employee such as the always tardy worker or the incompetent who expects a promotion. Another trainee takes the role of the supervisor. The other trainees observe and make notes. The plays are unrehearsed. No script is used. All the characters act spontaneously. The method does afford some opportunity to see and to experience the emotions of people who deal with difficult situations.

Role playing is to many persons an "unnatural" form of group training where the participants act parts in public. Many are shy. They do not think of themselves as "actors." Some even feel silly. Some fear that their performances may betray to others their personal anxieties. However, when skilled leadership directs the role playing, it often becomes helpful in training men to become more skilled as supervisors.

The "play" gives the problem a "reality" which words alone cannot provide. It is a reality that comes home to the work life of all the members. It provides the training of leaders with a practical tool.

Most training programs for supervisors use conventional procedures: group discussions, round table workshops, case problems, plant tours, visits to customers, lectures, and others. Each method probably has some merit. When the Extension Division, Department of Agriculture, made a study of different methods of getting ideas across, it was found that each method yielded worthwhile results. Two used in combination were better than one, and so on up to combinations of five. After that there was very little improvement with the employment of additional procedures.[10]

The effective supervisor as viewed by practical management and research

When the man of extensive business experience combines his evaluations of supervisors with those of the researcher, the two can usually agree

[10]Harold A. Edgerton, "Some Needs in Training Research," *Personnel Psychology*, 1955, pp. 19–21.

on certain basic characteristics of the typical successful supervisor. These are that the effective supervisor—

1. Takes seriously his job of supervision. He identifies with management and management's objectives but also recognizes the needs of his employees. He seeks to balance organizational objectives and human needs. He views his function as one of leadership. He respects his responsibilities and enjoys an inner pride in his achievements and in himself as a person.
2. Instills pride in the employees as members of a work group. He wants each person in his work group to be proud of the group and its members. Workers who have high group loyalty tend to show more teamwork and to cooperate with each other. The good supervisor finds it easy to say: "I am proud of you and our group." Good work groups have good interpersonal relationships among the members.
3. Gives general rather than close supervision. He tries to have each employee feel responsible for his work, know the company's objectives, and appreciate the results of his efforts as to whether they are good or poor. But he lets the worker do the work in the way that he thinks best.
4. Maintains his own morale at a high level. He realizes that he must feel friendly in order to be friendly. He knows that he must keep an optimistic confident manner in regard to his work standards and his own performance as well as the performance of his workers. He cannot succumb to the influence of the difficulties in the job or of his personal life but must view them in a constructive spirit in order that he may convey a constructive spirit to others.
5. Rises above his own negative motivations or urges toward hostility, self-pity, power, and revenge. Instead, he seeks to be of service to others. One of his most used answers when he senses that someone wants to make a request is, "How can I be of help to you?"

QUESTIONS ON THE CHAPTER

1. Why is it said that supervisors are the employee-relations mirrors for management?
2. Differentiate between the terms "supervisor" and "foreman."
3. Which areas are likely to have the most and the least restrictions on supervisory authority?
4. In what respects does a typical supervisor play a dual role in business?

5. Cite evidence to indicate the relation between foremen and production.

6. Define judicial and educational discipline, and explain why one is more effective than the other.

7. On the basis of survey figures, does it seem advisable or inadvisable for supervisors and their superiors to meet regularly for coaching by the superior?

8. Explain the aims that supervisor training courses should have and the needs for the aims.

9. Discuss the supervisors' conflict as to goals.

10. What problems must a skilled leader overcome when using the role-playing method of training?

11. Does an effective supervisor give general or close supervision?

12. Of the various ideas presented in the chapter, which ones are of special interest to you?

13. What did the chapter contribute toward your future relations with (a) the men who supervise your work, (b) the employees whom you may supervise?

PROBLEMS AND PROJECTS

For All Students

1. Here are four typical problems in the supervision of employees. The problems can be used for discussion or for role playing:

    a. Assume that you, the supervisor, have done what you think is a good job in orienting a new employee. You have turned him over to an old employee for further guidance. The next day you check up on the new man and find him sitting down, doing nothing in the midst of work that should be done. You are sure that he is loafing. What is the first thing you would do or say?

    b. Assume that you have just explained the work to a new employee: the rate of pay, hours of work, nature of the job, etc. You ask whether he has any questions and his first question is, "The rate of pay on this job is ten cents an hour lower than it ought to be. How soon will I get the ten cents an hour more pay?" How would you answer him?

    c. After you have explained the job to a new employee who seems to be satisfied about the instructions, he says, "One thing I didn't mention to anyone is that I have to ride to and from work with my brother. He will get here about a quarter hour before starting time and leave about a quarter hour before quitting time. Will it be all right for me to start a quarter hour ahead of time and quit a quarter hour sooner than the other employees on the same job in the plant?"

    d. An old company employee has been transferred from another department to your department. When you start to explain the work to him, he says, "That's all right, young man. I've been around here for a good many years and I know all about this job." What would you say or do?

For Advanced Students

2. Make a study of the organizations and services available for the training of supervisors. Consider the American Management Association, Inc., New York; Society for Personnel Administration, 529 Fourteenth St. N.W., Washington, D.C.; Bureau of National Affairs, Inc., Washington, D.C.; British Association for Commercial and Industrial Education, London; and others.
3. Investigate available tests and other measures of supervisory ability. You might begin your study with Solomon L. Schwartz and Norman Gekoski, The Supervisory Inventory: A Forced-Choice Measure of Human Relations Attitude and Technique," *Journal of Applied Psychology,* August 1960.

For Men in Business

4. Assume that you now have no supervisory responsibilities but that management has told you that you are to be made the assistant head of the department. How would you prepare for it? In what ways would you try to change your behavior patterns?
5. Several companies publish booklets, pamphlets, and cards which are sold to manufacturing firms to distribute to their supervisors. Examples of titles are "Are You Too Busy to Train Your Men?" and "Do You Play Everything Close to Your Chest?" Collect some of these aids and evaluate them by discussing their effects with supervisors.

COLLATERAL READINGS

For All Students

Gellerman, Saul W., *Motivation and Productivity.* New York: American Management Association, Inc., 1963. Chapter 2 presents a summary and discussion of the Michigan studies.

Newman, Summer, and Warren, *The Process of Management.* Englewood Cliffs, N.J.: Prentice-Hall, Inc., 1967. Chapter 26 deals with giving instructions, planning, and reviewing personal performance, disciplining and rewarding, and other aspects of supervision.

For Advanced Students

"Behavioral Science—What's in It for Management?" *Business Management Record,* National Industrial Conference Board, Inc., June 1963, pp. 43–44.

Tannenbaum, Arnold S., ed., *Control in Organizations.* New York: McGraw-Hill Book Company, 1968. Deals with the process by which members determine or influence how things get done in an organization. Concerned with questions both of theory and of practice.

For Men in Business

Bittel, Lester R., *What Every Supervisor Should Know*. New York: McGraw-Hill Book Company, 1959. Deals with special techniques of managing the supervisory job and helping oneself to succeed.

Haynes, W. Warren, and Joseph L. Massie, *Management: Analysis, Concepts and Cases*. Englewood Cliffs, N.J.: Prentice-Hall, Inc., 1969. Chapter 23 treats aspects of production such as measurement of work, motion study, process analysis, workplace layout, and human factors of equipment design.

Personnel
Management

SITUATIONS YOU ARE LIKELY TO MEET

How would you meet each of these situations:
- a. *Before* you have read the chapter? What would you say to yourself or to the individual?
- b. *After* you have read the chapter? How have your answers changed?

1. One of your younger nephews who has had one year of a commercial school program tells you that he is planning to go into personnel work in industry because he likes people and wants to represent them to management so that management will be more fair in its dealings with employees. He asks for your reactions to his plan and for your advice.
   What comments will you make?

2. When you are traveling on a plane, you happen to talk with an older man, a stranger who is on his way to attend a convention for personnel men. He tells you that he is disappointed in regard to the advancement he has made in twenty years of experience as a personnel manager in a small company—he is doing essentially the same work in the same ways as in years past.
   What questions would you ask him?

One of the first things for the student of business to learn in this field is how to spell "personnel." Too many students irritate executives and teachers by spelling the title as "personal manager." ("Personal manager" applies to the personal business representative of a star of stage or screen, not to a corporation executive of the kind discussed here.) A personnel manager is an important executive whose functions are summarized in Table 14-1.

In some companies his title may be "director of industrial relations." This title is likely to be found in heavy industry and similar companies where labor unions loom large in management's thinking. In that case, his functions and training for them might be organized along the following lines:

Collective bargaining: multiemployer and industry-wide bargaining, union security, studies of collective bargaining in the industry and the company.

Management relations: executive training, managerial decision making, and the role of supervision.

Employee relations: job satisfaction, productivity, and morale.

Labor disputes and their settlement: strikes, mediation, arbitration, grievance procedures.

Labor economics: wages, employment, unemployment.

Labor law and legislation: regulation of internal union affairs, labor injunctions, restraints on featherbedding.

Employment management: employing regular and other workers such as the seriously handicapped, merit or efficiency ratings, testing.

Trade unionism: policies and practices of American unions, union procedures for settling jurisdictional disputes.

Social security: health insurance, workmen's compensation, and others.

The importance of the personnel director, whatever his title and specific functions may be, becomes evident when we recognize that a company's vitality and growth are determined by its manpower. A personnel

---

TABLE 14–1

THE PERSONNEL ADMINISTRATOR'S "MY DAY"

The American Society for Personnel Administration reported the results of a recent survey made in a midwestern city as to where and how the average personnel administrator spent his day. In theory, this is how his day should be spent:

60 percent in his department.
35 percent in the plant or other offices.
5 percent away from his work area.

Here is how the work day averaged out:

18 percent, hires, separations, transfers, etc.
11 percent, personnel department operations (reports, correspondence, records, etc.).
12 percent, union matters (formal or informal).
8 percent, employee counseling.
6 percent, employee activities (recreation, mutual benefit, social, etc.).
6 percent, training.
4 percent, matters pertaining to the Cafeteria, Plant Protection, Dispensary, etc.
4 percent, wage and salary administration.
3 percent, safety.
12 percent, forward planning on personnel programs (reading, research, conferring with executives, etc.).
11 percent, promoting and activating the personnel program (preparing material, meetings, selling supervision, etc.).
5 percent, outside committee work, civic participation, etc.

SOURCE: *Personnel Panorama* (Pacific Northwest Personnel Management Association), June 1951. Reprinted by permission of the American Society for Personnel Administration.

man's responsibilities are likely to include any human relations function from management development to organizing the company glee club.

In recent years, the personnel manager has, in a few instances, become a key executive in developing not only employee relations programs but also new social and community relations programs. The likelihood of his having these newer kinds of responsibilities depends upon many factors, such as top management's respect for the progressiveness of his leadership programs within the company and his training in the behavioral sciences. If he is given high level responsibilities in this new field, top management usually provides for his benefit one or more consultants who have specialized in the behavioral sciences. Chapter 2 deals with this area.

We shall treat in separate chapters some of the representative person-nel functions of interviewing, appraising employees (merit rating), and dealing with employee relations and with labor unions. This introductory chapter to the field will present some of the organization structural relations and typical human relations aspects of personnel management, particularly those aspects not usually treated in formal courses in personnel manage-ment.

The personnel executive does far more than hire new people and dis-charge incompetent employees. His functions are in the staff rather than the line. He thinks of himself as a colleague of both the management and the employees of the company. He is also an analyst of employee relations af-fairs: he studies the company's current labor turnover figures, promotions and transfers per hundred employees, and other data that enable him to inform and counsel management in regard to management's responsibilities for its manpower.

Of course the functions and objectives of the personnel manager vary with the man and the company. A few still think of their job as essentially paternalistic. Some think of it as specialization in the scientific techniques involved in testing applicants and rating employees. The more advanced men in the field think of themselves in a facilitating rather than an operat-ing role. A survey of the personnel men in a typical industrial area is likely to indicate that the personnel worker sees his primary purpose as one of im-proving the working relationships between employees and supervisors so that the supervisors can perform their responsibilities effectively. Their ob-jectives are those helpful in improving the work performances of the indi-vidual employee.

As a member of the managerial staff, the personnel director under-stands management's viewpoints and has perspectives that enable him to help others get work done. Ideally, he works with line executives to enable them to become creative leaders rather than operational supervisors only. He is a human relations catalyst for the line people. The present-day personnel manager, regardless of whether he is an untrained traditional employment man under the production superintendent or a vice-president in charge of industrial relations under the president, is still essentially a colleague of the line. He does not work *for* the line but *with* the line. His basic job is to help the line get work done.

In progressive managements, the personnel executive has a greater responsibility than that of facilitating production alone. His responsibility is often defined as "productivity plus."

The "plus" includes developing a real sense of affiliation with the company on the part of employees, providing a satisfying work atmosphere, establishing effective relationships in the organizational structure, and ar-ranging for a framework of personnel regulations and practices in which people understand what is expected. The personnel function is a permeating one that concentrates on the human values—the release of human values that tend to increase productivity.

The number of personnel officers who are full-fledged major executives in their companies is increasing. Unfortunately, there are also many companies that have "personnel directors" in name rather than in function. In these instances, the man in charge of "personnel administration" may be a member of the third, fourth, or fifth echelons of management. If he is a member of the lower echelons, the personnel man himself is likely to be someone grown old in company service whose performance in his better days was such as to justify "making a place" for him. Or he may be a promising young man who is being "brought along" until he can be given something to do that is considered more important.

Of course an effective personnel man, in practice, must be more than "purely advisory." Even though his authority is vested in his chief rather than in himself, he must accept some responsibility for carrying out his plans with line people. Basically, the status of the personnel man is dependent upon the way in which he perceives his functions.

Observations indicate that most personnel directors have the status they deserve in the managerial lineup. As one analyst stated: "This is true of every executive whether a personnel director or a line operating manager. He is accorded the status he deserves by reason of his ability to contribute to the progress of the business. If his contributions are small, his status is low. If his contributions are great, his position is treated with respect. Those personnel directors who attain higher status than others do so because of their personal qualifications. Status must be earned."[1]

"Frankly, Mr. Farrell, what I'm looking for in an efficiency expert is someone who'll leave the Personnel Department alone."

Source: by Evan D. Diamond, *Manage* (August 1957). Courtesy The National Management Association.

[1] McCoy C. Campbell, "Personnel Man in Key Spot So Long As 'People Make Profits,' " *Personnel Journal*, February 1957.

Relations with other executives

To be effective, the head of the personnel department must guard against accepting the tendency of those executives who want to rid themselves of what are really their responsibilities. This hazard becomes most evident when a medium-size or small company has not had a personnel department and labor troubles arise. Members of management are apt to say: "Let's hire a personnel director. Then he can solve all our labor troubles." Smart personnel men do not accept a job of this kind until they change management's philosophy about the place of the personnel department in the company's corporate life. Most personnel work of the personal contact variety is part of day-to-day supervision and is the responsibility of the operating departments. Both supervisor and personnel man must realize that principle.

Some executives, particularly heads of the departments of finance and accounting, may fail to appreciate fully the need for or importance of the personnel department. "It's just another intangible," they say. When these men note the budgets of the personnel department they are likely to wonder what use has been made of the money to increase profits.

What this kind of opinion signifies is that the personnel director has failed to give his critics a full appreciation of the department's objectives and programs. He should give them a part in attaining his objectives. People tend to accept ideas that they help to develop. For this reason, it is highly desirable to have the widest possible participation by all persons involved in a personnel program. Where that is not appropriate, either because the plan is already well established or because of the nature of the organization, the next best line of attack is to review periodically with members of management the various steps that were taken in the development of the program. Criticisms and suggestions can be invited. Regular reviews and appraisals are essential in having a personnel program accepted by staff members.

Relations between foremen and the personnel department

The chain of command in any company is frequently modified by the informal organization as explained in Chapters 7 and 10.

One of the problems that often occurs is that employees fail to follow the chain of command. Certain employees have a tendency to come directly to the personnel department without first seeing their foreman. This, in some cases, gives the foreman the feeling that he is being left out.

Actually, the typical foreman knows a great deal about his workers, and he resents the efforts of staff members who come between him and his employees. He frequently feels that management and staff members put tasks upon him and his workers without understanding the employees or the difficulties of the job. Many foremen feel that staff and management men understand so little about the employees and their problems that they hate to take time off to go to meetings or classes that deal with personnel problems. Such meetings, to them, are just a waste of company money and time.

Foremen think that the personnel people are too willing to accept as fact every complaint from a worker. This is especially likely to occur when members of the personnel staff are young college graduates who have not worked their way up from the shop.

Some foremen also believe that personnel men are too willing to sympathize with the employee. Personnel men must, at times, disagree with the supervisor. When a foreman fails to consider the feelings of the employees or makes excessive demands on them, the personnel worker is likely to point to his failures in maintaining happy relations.

If the personnel man succumbs to the natural tendency to take over an employee relations responsibility that should remain with the foremen, he finds it very difficult to help foremen and other members of the line through training, coaching, and coordinating. The line man just "washes his hands" of the situation. Instead, the personnel man must avoid coming between a foreman and his worker except when genuine cooperation can be achieved. If the personnel man has or takes authority and tries to correct the actions of a supervisor, he not only arouses resentment but also interferes with normal organization practices.

As one writer has stated:

> The relationship between staff and the line in *any* function may be improved if the staff man is guided by the following precepts:
>
> Help in every way you can in selecting, coaching, training, advising, and the like.
>
> Resist the temptation to take over any responsibility in the interest of expediting results. This takes infinite patience—but it will be rewarded in the end by a program that works more effectively. . . .

A typical example, which actually took place in a plant, points up work relationships that often occur:

Screw Machine Foreman to Personnel Manager: "Some of my men cannot reach their production quotas when the tolerances are close."

Personnel Manager: "Are you being fair about it—have you trained them as you should?—are the standards right?"

Foreman: "The standards are not right in every case but they are not 100% wrong. Some of the men shouldn't have been hired in the first place. They are not grade 'A' mechanics but they are drawing top rates. I haven't the time to wet nurse them."

Personnel Manager: "How did they get to the top of the range if they didn't deserve it?"

Foreman: "Through union pressure and seniority. They were raised before my results were being measured as they are now."

Personnel Manager: "According to the contract we can terminate anyone who consistently fails to earn his guaranteed rate. I'll check with Industrial Engineering and see that the tight standards are adjusted. Then if the fault lies entirely with the men, I'll transfer them to work they can do or I'll take some other action to relieve you of the loss."[2]

TYPICAL PERSONNEL PROBLEMS

Now let's look at some of the common situations that create problems the personnel manager must deal with in his work.

The "captive employees"

Almost every company has certain employees who cannot leave because they are "tied" to the company. Some are tied by inertia—it's easier to stay than to seek employment elsewhere.

Captives to "benefits." One large classification of captive employees is those who have worked for many years with a company and have acquired important "benefits," particularly seniority and pension rights. Under the provisions of union contracts or the company's benefit plan, they would have to sacrifice all these accruals if they left the company.

Captives to the community. Even though Americans are noted for their mobility, numerous individuals will remain with a company because the job enables them to enjoy old friendships, their relatives, and the community life to which they have become accustomed.

Captives of their special skills. The employee who has attained special skills that are useful only in the company where he acquired them finds it hard to find another that can use him. If he moves, he must start a new career at a lower salary and less job status.

Many captives of this kind hold positions whose salaries are not affected by competition from other employers. They realize that they have not gained increased incomes to the same extent as other workers. Their

[2]Donald H. Sunderlin, "Each Supervisor a Manager," *Personnel Administration*, January–February 1957, pp. 27, 28.

morale and efficiency are lowered. They feel defenseless. Many employees of educational and governmental institutions are likely to be members of this group. Some progressive personnel men make systematic surveys of the company's salary structure in order to discover these defenseless people.

Public utilities are likely to have many captive employees among their power plant operators. Theoretically, a power plant operator is free to leave one company and seek employment in another, but the market for his skills is limited. Very few vacancies of certain job classes in public utilities occur often enough to enable a worker to move. Turnover is limited. Anyone who takes a job with a public utility should ask himself: "Will ten years of employment in this company allow me to move with greater ease to another industry at a higher rate of pay or will I become another captive employee?" Few managements want any employees to become captive, but some "captivity" does occur. Progressive personnel men try to identify it and develop training programs which help to overcome the problem.

Alert managements do not want to have an atmosphere or work situation where employees can neither quit nor be fired. The employee who cannot take a job offer because of a bonus for length of service or a retirement benefit is not likely to be an energetic, enthusiastic employee—he may merely be frustrated by management's good intentions.

Privileged employees

Almost every large company has certain privileged employees. The research men, for example, do not abide by the same rules as the engineers. Research men like to have time to think. They wander around the company offices in a seemingly aimless manner. Some habitually come to work late and leave early.

In a publishing office, members of the editorial department are likely to come and go as they please. But the employees of the accounting department in the same publishing firm are expected to obey punctuality rules meticulously.

Of course the privileged individuals, whoever and wherever they are, tend to be a source of irritation to nonprivileged employees. Departmental frictions often arise from this kind of situation, and the personnel man tries to placate the resentful ones without disturbing the work habits of the members of privileged groups.

Many blue-collar workers look upon their white-collar fellow employees of the company as having certain privileges that they do not hope to attain. The desks and offices of white-collar employees are of better quality and higher cost than those of shop employees who do similar work. Furthermore, certain white-collar members of the organization, particularly salesmen, have the privilege of spending the company's money to entertain

customers and at the same time enjoy luxuries that are not available to shop
people.

Salary payment plans during illness are likely to be more flexible for
office than for shop workers. Even though the plan of payment during illness may be published as the same for all workers, the trend in actual practice is toward two sets of plans—one publicly proclaimed, the other
practiced. And the latter is usually more flexible, but especially for the
office workers.

For salaried and executive personnel, there is likely to be a base plan
beyond which managers may grant extra benefits, depending on years of
service, value, and rank. Executives are close to and friendly with the
company heads and directors. Naturally they often get especially considerate
treatment.

Most pay plans for absence from work are discretionary. An electronics
manufacturer, for instance, will frankly admit, in private, that he coddles
research personnel—good research men are hard for him to get and hold.
Many companies have three sets of rules—one for hourly workers, one for
salaried employees, and a third for executives. For hourly workers, the
plan usually prescribes specific benefits hammered out in union negotiations
and regarded as "rights" by workers.

Transferring employees

Every company finds it necessary to transfer employees at times. One
department has a surplus of help and another needs help. Most employees
involved in a transfer do not object if it is temporary. If it is to be permanent, many do object even though the pay may be as good or even better.
The wise personnel man senses that the true causes for objection are likely
to be in the social aspects involved in the change. Perhaps the new supervisor is less understanding or the workers are strange. Logical arguments
are of little avail. The loss of old friends and the need for new habits of
work loom too large in the mind of the worker to dislodge them by argument. Instead of trying to "sell" the new job to the worker, it is better to try
to relieve anxieties by letting the employee try out the new job for a few
days before making the transfer permanent. The personnel man therefore
makes the transition on a tentative basis and allows the employee to alleviate his anxieties by giving him some time to make the adjustment through
the gain of new friends and new job satisfactions.

Old employees versus young college graduates—
pay differentials

Much rivalry occurs between senior employees and the new men
recruited from colleges. Almost every company has a number of employees

who are approaching retirement age. When the company grows, an active recruiting drive may expand the work force by hiring many young men. The older men feel greatly threatened, especially when some of the young men advance rapidly to better positions. Naturally, bitterness and resentment often develop on the part of the older men. They feel that with their experience and seniority they should have received promotions that have gone to the younger men. In the case of supervisors, it is especially difficult for an older supervisor having many years of experience to accept the authority of a young executive who has had little experience.

Starting salary rates sharpen the conflict. Competition between firms for new men with certain kinds of training has caused many companies to pay very high starting salary rates. For older employees, general wage increases have not always kept pace with the higher salaries paid the beginners. Hence, a company often finds itself paying a higher salary to a new man than to one who has worked there for years, even though both are holding the same job.

The executive who supervises the old-timers and the newcomers is in a policy dilemma. If, on the one hand, he chooses to hire the bright young men at the high starting pay, he makes his older employees unhappy. The squeezing on pay differentials can make his department a hotbed of discontent and bring about an uncomfortably high turnover. On the other hand, if he does not hire any promising young men, he accepts the lesser talent that he can get at the old starting scales. Eventually, he may end up with a comparatively lethargic department that is staffed with mediocrities.

During an inflationary period starting salaries go up faster than the whole general range of salaries. In many cases, new employees, whether beginners or job hoppers, ask for and get salaries as high as, or higher than, employees who have had several years' experience with the company.

If the executive ignores the situation, efficiency drops and more people quit. Then he must replace those who quit with higher-paid new employees and train them. If he tries to solve the differential to keep his oldtimers happy, his direct labor costs for the department immediately jump so far that his budget is warped out of line with the forecasts for costs of the product.

Some salaried men take advantage of the situation by frequent job hopping. They know that the easiest way to increase take-home pay is to move to another company. Most salaried workers have less mobility—they prefer to remain in one company to build up their seniority rights and pension benefits. When the problem becomes too acute, the personnel manager, in conference with top management, usually sets up a course of action to be followed consistently. The policy chosen may include one or more of the following alternatives:

1. Hiring superior new employees at whatever rate must be paid. If

old employees are not willing to accept the situation, some will leave.

2. Setting a rigid salary range for the job. If the personnel department cannot find a well qualified person who will accept that range, hire somebody of less ability who will.

3. Giving no general increases, but increasing the "merit" raises to those people whom management particularly wants to keep. Some companies have switched their entire pay system from one of periodic increases to a pure merit system. They have eliminated the seniority idea in relation to value. No employee is worth more merely because he has been there a long time. Of course this means that the personnel man must be especially alert to recognize the superior employees who themselves will not request increases. To prevent the overlooking or neglect of competent employees management must systematically identify and reward them.

4. Telling the new employees to keep their higher salaries a secret. A few companies warn new employees to keep their salaries secret. One company goes so far as firing any employees who are caught discussing their salaries, but such a policy is antiquated and unrealistic.

5. Hiring "second-best" employees and training them. This, to some personnel managers, is better than trying to deal with morale of employees who feel that they are being treated unjustly. They set a rigid price for a job, then go to extra effort to fill it by locating someone who will take that salary rather than hiring a more qualified person who demands a higher price.

Managements are aware of hard feelings on the part of the older men, but most executives have assumed that the problem is of a temporary nature and that, in time, the differentials would be corrected. They have hoped that the effects of economic evolution would pull the wage structure back into line to take care of inequities. Unfortunately, this kind of evolution has not always occurred. Many managements have to live with some tensions and bitterness on the part of older employees until they are retired. Theoretically, the problem could be solved by raising the salaries of the older workers, but this would throw out of alignment too many other salary differentials. Also, inflationary pressures would be increased. Very few managements have been able to provide a completely satisfactory solution for the problem. If men are to be promoted on the basis of their merits and potentials for the future, then some younger men will continue to receive salaries above those of the "old guard." Of course each young man who is affected by this kind of conflict situation can accentuate or lessen the conflict by his manner toward the older men.

Some personnel men believe that when an employee resents the narrowing differentials between old and new employees, the best practical answer is to admit the squeeze and state frankly that management has decided that it cannot maintain the old differentials and still survive. The best policy for the employee is to keep faith in himself and his future—to earn by extra effort the highest raise he can achieve. Merit raises to those who make a superior contribution should, in time, correct some of the inequitable differences.

Personnel management (industrial relations) as a career

In terms of importance and scope, one of the fastest growing management jobs in recent years has been that of the industrial relations executive. A survey by *Industrial Relations News* indicated that the men in the personnel field are an educated group; nine out of ten respondents hold a college degree, and one out of three holds an advanced degree. Many are supplementing their education with further training, both inside and outside the company.

Of special interest to the college senior: only 15 percent of the men surveyed entered the industrial relations field directly from college. One-quarter of the respondents were in the production field before they moved into industrial relations. The remainder came from a variety of other fields.

The survey indicates a growing trend toward moving men into personnel functions from other positions inside the company. An almost unanimous majority of the respondents believe that top management is cooperating with them in the areas of access to top management—development programs and budget allocations.

Most of the respondents perceive their biggest problems as internal rather than external: the most pressing being employee relations, communications, and morale. The single problems viewed as most important in the future were perceived, in order of rank given, as communications, collective bargaining, executive and supervisory development, automation, and employee development.

The majority of respondents believe that the industrial relations function will continue to grow in importance and value. One executive expressed it this way: "In an economy which is just discovering manpower as a capital asset, and with the increasing maturity of labor leaders, industrial relations will become a field on a par with sales and production."[3]

Young men and women in college and in industry who aim for the

[3]Adapted from "The Industrial Relations Executive," *Industrial Relations News* (1957). See also *The Management Review*, American Management Association, Inc., July 1957.

op jobs in industry find graduate professional training helpful. Legal train-
ng is especially valuable in handling labor relations problems that involve
tate and federal laws.

Personnel work in the government services usually requires a degree
n one of the social sciences. College personnel work generally requires a
naster's or a doctorate, particularly when the job includes teaching on the
graduate level. In secondary schools, a member of the personnel depart-
nent is likely to teach as well as counsel, hence he must meet the require-
nents for teaching.

Personnel work cannot be learned from books alone. Knowledge acquired through experience in industry is as important as degrees.

One of the outstanding characteristics of the personnel man is his
uperior ability to remember faces, names of people, and facts in the history
of each. Anyone who says that he can remember faces of people but not
heir names should improve this phase of his mental life before he enters
he field. It is a "must" for effectiveness in personnel management. For-
unately, anyone who determines to improve this mental skill can do so
hrough everyday practice in college, at work, and in his social life. (See
page 525.)

An executive in this field must enjoy working with people of all types:
he pleasant, the not-so-pleasant, and the downright unpleasant. He should
have a personality that expresses friendliness and sincerity so that he will
become the respected friend of both company officers and employees.

What are the main satisfactions that accrue to the member of a per-
onnel department? The kind of answer given most often is similar to this
tatement by one personnel man: "A satisfaction that I have found through
ny work is a sort of compensation for my own personality shortcomings.
My tendency toward introversion has decreased as a result of my work.
The more I work with people, the more I have found a usefulness and
confidence in myself. This is certainly more of a benefit or reward than any
wage or security benefits that I receive. I now live more richly as well as
more effectively as a person."

QUESTIONS ON THE CHAPTER

1. How does the typical personnel man see his primary purpose in the organization? What is his basic job?

2. What percentage of a typical personnel manager's time is spent outside of
his department? What functions take up the largest percentages of an average workday of a personnel man?

3. Is a personnel administrator a colleague of the management or of the employees? The personnel function concentrates on what values?

4. What is meant by the "plus" when it is said that the responsibility of the personnel executive is "productivity plus."

5. In what ways are many employees captives of their special skills or of the work situation?

6. What methods should personnel men use to alleviate many of the problems connected with transferring employees?

7. What problems do some salaried workers try to cope with by job hopping?

8. According to an *Industrial Relations News* survey, what percentage of the men questioned entered the personnel field directly from college? What does this signify for the student who plans to enter personnel work?

9. List the five most important internal company problems of personnel men.

10. What is a source of learning about personnel work that is as important as books?

11. Of all the ideas presented in the chapter, which ones were of special interest to you?

12. What did the chapter contribute toward your future relations with (a) the men who supervise your work, (b) the employees whom you may supervise?

PROBLEMS AND PROJECTS

For All Students

1. Ask several friends for their opinions as to whether you, if you were in personnel work, would tend to lean toward management or employees in a conflict between the two. How might your bias be corrected or utilized by yourself?

2. Examine the magazines in your library and list those that have regular departments or frequent articles that treat industrial relations problems. Examples of such magazines are *Business Week* and *Dun's Review and Modern Industry*.

For Advanced Students

3. Personnel men are seldom chosen for top management jobs such as president. Many think of themselves as professional aides to management, not as integrated management men. How does this affect your planning for self-development?

4. Assume that you wish to remain in personnel work. Note the functions in the list at the beginning of the chapter. Study sources for getting training in the functions. Suggest books and journals that would be helpful.

For Men in Business

5. Of all the employees whom you know, designate the "captive employees."

What is the nature of their ties to the company? Do these employees appear to be especially happy in their work? If not, how might they improve their morale?

6. Describe some of the "privileged employees" whom you know. How does their presence in the company affect other employees? If you were a privileged employee in a company, how might you try to gain the goodwill of other employees?

COLLATERAL READINGS

For All Students

Personnel Practices in Factory and Office: Manufacturing, Personnel Policy Study No. 194, National Industrial Conference Board, 1964. Reports information obtained from almost 2,000 manufacturers.

Porter, Lyman W., *Personnel Management: A Review of the Recent Psychological Literature*, Institute of Industrial Relations, University of California, Berkeley, Calif., Reprint No. 278, 1966.

For Advanced Students

Schuster, Jay R., "A Diagnostic Model for Industrial Relations," *Personnel Administration*, July–August 1969. This model is designed not only to provide insight into current behavior but to suggest how the industrial relations role might move toward providing a more important service to an organization.

Thornton, George C., "Image of Industrial Psychology Among Personnel Administrators," *Journal of Applied Psychology*, October 1969. Reports results of a survey of impressions of industrial psychologists among a national sample of personnel administrators.

For Men in Business

Marcson, Simon, "Motivation and Productivity in Industry," *Behavioral Science Research in Industrial Relations*, Industrial Relations Counselors, Inc., New York, 1962, pp. 157–58.

The Society for Personnel Administration, 529 Fourteenth St., N.W., Washington, D.C. 20004, has published annual proceedings on various topics in the field of personnel administration, such as automation and personnel administration. Ask for latest list of SPA publications.

Personnel Management: The Personnel Man's Sensitivity to Employee Relations

SITUATIONS YOU ARE LIKELY TO MEET

How would you meet each of these situations:
   a. *Before* you have read the chapter? What would you say to yourself or to the individual?
   b. *After* you have read the chapter? How have your answers changed?

1. You happen to work under an executive who is data minded. He likes computers and records of a statistical nature, and he frequently talks about the fact that lots of statistics are available but never used. When he examines the list of dispensary visits made by each of your employees in the previous month, he finds that one man made eight visits. This figure to him means that employee will have a serious accident within a year. He wants you to tell the employee the facts and what they forecast statistically for him. What would you do or say?

2. The supervisor of a group tells you that he cannot understand his employees. They frequently gripe to him about relatively trivial matters; however, when he tells the griper that the problem complained about will not be changed for certain reasons but that if the employee wishes he will help him get another job elsewhere, the answer is: "Oh I wouldn't want to leave this job—I like it here. I just wanted to gripe about something!" The supervisor wonders why employees who like their job continue griping.

Suggest possible factors that may cause the employees to express their feelings of insecurity about their situation through their gripes.

The one outstanding personality characteristic of personnel managers is, or at least ought to be, their *susceptibility to stimulation by the behavior of people*: how they feel, think, and live emotionally as well as how they work. The personnel man's most important professional skills are those associated with his keen sensitivity to people as persons. He makes his special contributions to the company, its managers, and its employees through his "feel" as to the hidden meanings that underlie the overt actions of individual members of the organization. At the same time, he respects the individual regardless of his limitations or peculiarities.

He deals with real human beings in real situations. He not only accepts people as they are but he also accepts the plant or office situation as he finds it. He knows, for example, that the company's work environment and equipment will be gradually improved, but in the meantime he works with the people and the equipment that are there. He does not try to reform or fire every employee or executive whose thinking is antiquated nor does he insist that every machine and typewriter be perfect. He works with what and with whom he has, but he moves toward the development of the better potentials in people and their situations. He accentuates the positive. Weaknesses are not emphasized as weaknesses but as opportunities for positive action.

Typical situations that exemplify the personnel manager's sensitivity and positive emphasis

The effective personnel manager is positive minded. He looks for the strengths in people and the organization. He enables each executive to feel better about himself and his employees by calling to his attention the good qualities in his employees. Whenever possible, he brings to the attention of the head of the department any evidences of growth or accomplishment that one of his employees has demonstrated by taking evening courses, by leadership in the company's recreational program, by performance in community organizations,·or by work suggestions made that may benefit the company or the employees. This does not mean that he is blind to weaknesses in certain individuals such as the clock watcher, the malingerer, or the expense account padder. He notes them too and guards against their influence, but he is more interested in the good than the bad that he finds in the personnel.

When he notes that one of the executives, perhaps the production vice-president, is being adversely conditioned against the factory employees because he is being harassed by several ornery union officials, the personnel manager brings to the production executive's attention some of the more worthy union members.

If the plant manager is so deeply engrossed in paperwork and in carrying out his responsibilities that he is not becoming acquainted with the employees as persons, the personnel manager arranges for the executive to meet and become better acquainted with some of his own employees. He may, for example, arrange for the plant manager to greet and chat with each new employee.

When the personnel manager finds that unnecessary frictions exist between two groups such as those often found on the part of the engineering department versus the shop, he brings it to the attention of the heads of the two groups and helps them arrange situations where members of both groups can meet and work together—perhaps setting up a committee that deals with a problem common to the two classes of employees.

The sensitivity of the personnel man also sharpens his perception of the ways in which other people perceive their situations. When he assigns a new employee to a supervisor, he tries to place him with a supervisor whom the employee will respect. A new shop man's pride may be in his work, another's may be in his physical strength. The former will do his best work for a supervisor who is an expert in the work being performed. The latter will be happiest under a supervisor who is physically robust and somewhat gruff, the kind of man the new employee can brag about when he is chatting with his cronies at the local bar.

When a department head decides to assign an assistant to a specialist or expert worker for the first time in order that the specialist may be able to get more work done, the personnel man must think of how the older employee will look upon the new assistant. Will he view the assistant as a threat to him? Will he suspect that management is trying to take his job away from him? The personnel man must help to anticipate and prevent the development of such suspicions and anxieties before they arise.

When a foreman finds that an employee violates an important safety rule or policy, the foreman may be able to think only in terms of the penalty that is deserved. Members of management are less interested in punishment than in finding out why the problem arose and in preventing its recurrence. The foreman may perceive any leniency toward his errant employee as a threat to his foremanship prerogatives. It is the personnel man's function not merely to pass on to the foreman the decision made by management but to help the foreman reinterpret the situation.

The personnel man's function of interpretation is especially important in such executive-employee relations as are found in committee meetings. If a major executive attends a meeting, some committee members will avoid getting openly involved in the issues under discussion. They will maintain a pleasant facade and show superficial interest in the problem, but they will not express their true feelings. Sometimes the personnel man can tactfully overcome a member's detachment by enabling him, through friendly questioning, to express his true feelings without embarrassing anyone present.

His contributions through his sensitivity can be illustrated in the way that he deals with records of employee dispensary visits. Statistics about dispensary visits are kept in most companies, but their meanings are not usually published. To publish the statistical analyses or their interpretations tends to cause employees to take care of their own minor cuts and bruises. The statistics are valuable, however, as possible indicators of sources of likely future accidents. If the figures are handed to the foremen without instruction, some foremen are likely to go to an individual worker and say: "Look here. You made eight trips to the company dispensary last month. The statistics show that you are going to have a serious accident within a year!" Instead, the personnel manager tactfully encourages every foreman to look for specific training problems with any of his employees who are having minor injuries. He can study the problem employee's work habits and teach him how to do his work safely. Furthermore, the personnel man should know which foremen are apt to misuse the information and be able to help them to use it constructively.

Another example of the personnel man's sensitivity occurs, or should

"I think I'll give you to Mr. Willoughby. He's seemed a bit despondent lately."
Source: *The Wall Street Journal* (Sept. 17, 1957).

occur, when the management considers the advisability of remodeling the company's cafeteria. Should a special dining room be built for the supervisors? Should it be designed to have supervisors and employees eat together? The answer depends upon the "tone" of the plant. If mixing comes naturally, supervisors and employees should be able to eat together with pleasure for both and with benefit for the company. The personnel man's feel for the situation should be a guide to management in planning the dining facilities.

The personnel manager should be able to convince management when employees need help in making adjustments to impending changes, such as moving the offices from a metropolitan center to the suburbs. One concern, for example, laid careful plans for three years to abandon the city for the suburbs. The company's officials and engineers pored over blueprints and plans for layouts of offices and placement of desks and equipment but failed to explain to employees the benefits they would gain from the move. As a result, many decided that they did not want to live in the country. Other companies in the same city were able to hire some of the firm's best secretaries, accountants, and experienced workers. When moving day was over, 40 percent of the regular employees had decided to remain in the city. The personnel manager had given management ample warning and recommended a program of education, but management was too busy looking forward to fewer labor problems, lower taxes, and the delights of working in the country to give heed. Now the personnel manager is running expensive help wanted advertising in the metropolitan dailies in attempts to induce workers to move to the suburb.

Of course we might say that every man in a responsible job in business should have the kind of sensitivity and make the positive emphases mentioned in the above examples. True, but the personnel man has extra responsibilities in these human relationships. He is a specialist in human relations.

Noting the unvoiced grievances

Every personnel man deals constantly with grievances presented overtly by employees. Dealing with grievances, particularly in a unionized plant, may require a large share of the personnel manager's working time. Usually, rather definite procedures have been establishd for processing the formal grievances.

In addition to the formally presented grievances, the personnel man must have alert antennae for the unvoiced grievances. These are commonly expressed in fairly subtle forms: noncooperation, chip-on-the-shoulder attitudes, insubordination, loafing, poor quality of work, and absenteeism.

Investigators have pointed out the need for distinguishing between the manifest and the latent content of grievances. When, for example, the manner of a supervisor is so threatening that it cannot be consciously faced by the employee, he may give as the cause for dissatisfaction anything from low pay to the location of the parking space assigned to him in the company parking lot. One woman employee expressed the correct interpretation of her grievance when she stated: "The company building is definitely too crowded. The employees, myself included, become annoyed at the implication of the 'cheapness' of the office. There is a need for better working conditions, for many times I have become tired and annoyed at physical conditions as an outlet for other annoyances. Any inadequate working condition tends to lessen efficiency."

A company that is known to be losing money is likely to have a high percentage of dissatisfied employees—their insecurity has grievance-generating effects in regard to numerous aspects of the work situation. Such unvoiced grievances and their effects may not always be approached through direct questioning about them. Sometimes they have to be brought into the open through indirect discussion. Employees who work in a company that is losing money can be encouraged to enjoy their work for the time being. Employees who are happy in their jobs usually have relatively few grievances even though the future vitality of the company may be in doubt. The first requirement, however, for dealing with the unvoiced grievances is the sensitivity essential to their recognition. If they are recognized in their early stages, their causes can be dealt with before they snowball into big grievances.

"You'll find we're just one big family here—intrigues, jealousies, fights. . . ."

Source: by Dale McFeatters, *The Management Review* (October 1957). Courtesy American Management Association, Inc.

"Satisfiers" and "dissatisfiers"

Formerly, managements assumed that all that was necessary to keep workers productive and happy was to provide high wages, good working conditions, and few hours of work. When these ideas were implemented, neither happiness nor motivation resulted. Then managements added more benefits and extra pleasant working conditions. Generally, such policies have not been especially effective.

Frederick Herzberg and his colleagues of the Psychological Service of Pittsburgh conducted careful interviews using the critical incident technique with some two hundred engineers and accountants who worked in eleven different firms in the Pittsburgh area. The men were asked to recall a time when they felt especially good about their jobs. They were also asked to describe sequences of events that resulted in negative feelings about their jobs. In both kinds of questioning, they were asked to describe effects these incidents had on their attitudes and on their performance and whether these effects were of short or long duration.

The findings demonstrated that when these men felt good about their jobs, it was usually because something had happened that showed that they were doing their work especially well or that they were becoming more expert in their professions. Good feelings were related to the specific tasks the men performed, not to background factors such as money, working conditions, status, or security. On the other hand, when they felt bad it was usually some disturbance in these background factors that made them feel that they were being treated unfairly.

This led the researchers to draw a distinction between what they called satisfiers and dissatisfiers, or *motivators* and the *hygienic* factors. They considered as a motivator any influence that usually has an uplifting effect on attitudes or performance. Hygienic factors produce no improvement in productivity but serve to *prevent losses* of efficiency or morale. Hygienic factors are prerequisites for effective motivation, but they do not by themselves motivate the individual. They help to prevent dissatisfaction and make it possible for motivators to operate.

Pay, job security, status, and working conditions are hygienic factors. When they are unsatisfactory, they have adverse effects on the men's attitudes and on their effectiveness. However, managements should not expect high motivation to develop simply through paying men well or by providing fringe benefits or an attractive place to work, but *depriving the men* of these things is likely to cause their motivation to deteriorate rapidly.

Praise and pats on the back have a temporary effect. The lasting good feelings are caused by the motivators: being assigned to stimulating work, having considerable responsibility, being advanced to positions of increased importance, having freedom to exercise initiative, and having the privilege of handling problems in their own way.[1]

Herzberg also found that the mentally healthy person seeks happiness from the growth factors and acquires knowledge and skill right where he is, and he seeks the avoidance of dissatisfaction from the hygiene factors. In contrast, the mentally ill person is a hygiene seeker, even though these factors are largely beyond his control.[2]

A special survey of engineers showed that over 80 percent of the job factors that were related to their job satisfaction were achievement items such as job completion, solution of difficult problems, patents and inventions, and acceptance of challenge. Frustrating factors confirmed Herzberg's contention that hygienic or situational factors are dissatisfiers. Some of the dissatisfiers found were inept management, poor administration, routine and, to the worker, monotonous work, and internal politics.[3]

These and other studies indicate that morale cannot be attained by having the company do kindnesses for employees or by solving their problems for them. Morale is likely to be higher when employees do things for the company and feel that they as individuals are also growing. Both management and employees gain growth and competence when management treats employees as colleagues in their joint economic enterprise.

The morale survey is a device that helps managements to listen to learn the problems and the needs for motivation on the part of the employees.

EMPLOYEE ATTITUDE OR MORALE SURVEYS

The modern personnel man, however sensitive he may be personally to the feelings of others, realizes that he is not keeping in touch with all the feelings and emotional undertows in a large company. Also, he knows that his management needs an occasional comprehensive view of the morale situation in every department of the company. To give management such a picture, he convinces top management that a morale survey would be helpful.

[1]See Frederick Herzberg, Bernard Mausner, and Barbara Snyderman, *The Motivation to Work* (New York: John Wiley & Sons, Inc., 1959). See also M. Scott Myers, "Who Are Your Motivated Workers?" *Harvard Business Review*, January–February 1964.

[2]See Frederick Herzberg, "Basic Needs and Satisfactions of Individuals," *Behavioral Science Research in Industrial Relations*, Industrial Relations Counselors, Inc., New York, 1962, pp. 35–36.

[3]See survey by editors of *Machine Design* and by Eugene Raudsepp, "What's Behind Engineers' Attitudes toward Their Jobs," *Machine Design*, June 12, 1969.

To conduct a survey of this kind, questions are usually developed by committees of management and employees. Some companies also purchase standard questionnaire forms such as the one published by Science Research Associates, Chicago. The *SRA Employee Inventory* is a widely used employee attitude survey instrument. It has been used to survey over six hundred thousand employees. The inventory is distinctive in that the percentage of favorable attitudes among any employee group toward various aspects of their employment can be compared with national norms. In addition, SRA has developed norms that are specific to particular industries and particular occupational groups. Specific norms are available for the following industries: food, manufacturing, retailing, and utilities. Norms are also available for the following specific occupational groups: administrative, office, sales, technical, supervisory, skilled production, unskilled production, and nonproduction hourly. This enables management to identify more accurately the specific areas of strengths and weaknesses within the company and within departments of the company.

If properly administered, tabulated, and interpreted, these anonymous responses give a representative picture of what employees think about the areas covered by the survey questions. The survey responses present a comprehensive report of employee attitudes or morale. The survey is usually conducted for a company by an outside consultant such as an industrial relations consulting firm. In most cases, some technical knowhow is required. Furthermore, outsiders are better able to keep the operation on a strictly confidential basis.

Generally, the survey is conducted so that no information can be traced back to the person who answered the questionnaire. Employees must be assured that they can express criticisms without any possibility of being identified. Also, employees should be told why their answers are sought— that management is sincere in asking the questions, and what management intends to do with the tabulated answers.

When the Industrial Relations Section, California Institute of Technology, had completed a total of twenty-five surveys in eighteen different companies, covering over fifty thousand employees, the section formulated a number of conclusions based on all of its studies of employee opinion. One of these was that

> Morale is affected by length of service. Employees with less than a year of service have almost as high morale as employees with 25 years of service or more. The morale of employees declines with length of service, reaching its low point after 10 to 15 years of service. After this point, morale tends to increase.[4]

[4]Excerpt from *Annual Report 1953–1954*, Industrial Relations Section, California Institute of Technology, Project 5, "Surveys of Employee Opinion."

THE MOST WIDELY-USED EMPLOYEE INVENTORY

SRA Employee Inventory
FORM A

Make no marks on these pages!

1. The hours of work here are O.K. ....
2. Management does everything possible to prevent accidents in our work.........
3. Management is doing its best to give us good working conditions, ...
4. In my opinion, the pay here is lower than in other companies................
5. They should do a better job of handling pay matters here....................
6. I understand what the company benefit program provides for employees...................
7. The people I work with help each other out when someone falls behind or gets in a tight spot..
8. My boss is too interested in his own success to care about the needs of employees...........
9. My boss is always breathing down our necks; he watches us too closely ....
10. My boss gives us credit and praise for work well done.............................
11. Management here does everything it can to see that employees get a fair break on the job......
12. If I have a complaint to make, I feel free to talk to someone up-the-line ....

AGREE ? DISAGREE
AGREE ? DISAGREE
AGREE ? DISAGREE
AGREE ? DISAGREE
AGREE ? DISAGREE
AGREE ? DISAGREE

The SRA Employee Inventory uses easy-to-understand language. Since it requires only a few minutes to administer, it can be given during working hours with little disruption or loss of production time. The brief time required for answering the questions is equally important when the Inventory is given to employees on their own time. Because employees are asked not to sign their names, they are willing to answer frankly. Management can use the Employee Inventory to: (1) measure morale for a company as a whole; (2) compare morale between departments or plants in an organization; and (3) compare morale in a company with the average of others, particularly in the same industry.

By using the Employee Inventory to find out what employees really think, companies can pinpoint weak departments, increase the effectiveness of supervision, learn if communication is adequate, discover training needs, improve employee relations, build community goodwill, and cut employee turnover.

The SRA Employee Inventory was prepared by the Employee Attitude Research Group in the Industrial Relations Center, University of Chicago. This group has members from both the University and industry.

The SRA Employee Inventory is published by Science Research Associates, Inc., 259 East Erie St., Chicago, Ill. 60611; copyright by the Industrial Relations Center of the University of Chicago.

The findings are most important concerning what they reveal about factors that cause satisfaction and dissatisfaction of employees. In one survey of one thousand persons, conducted by Robert L. Kahn of the University of Michigan Survey Research Center, 82 percent said that, all things considered, they were satisfied with their jobs—yet only 28 percent thought that they had a "fairly good" or "very good" chance of getting ahead. Of the others, 6 percent said the opportunity was there if they wanted it, and 57 percent saw little or no chance of advancing.

The biggest cause of job dissatisfaction was inadequate salaries (27 percent), followed by work pressure (12 percent), and "the hours" (9 percent). Dissatisfaction with the boss was listed by 5 percent.

Despite limited job satisfaction among respondents, 80 percent of them said that they would continue to work, even if they didn't have to. Among the positive reasons given, 48 percent wanted "to keep occupied," 15 percent said it "keeps the individual healthy," and 14 percent said that their job was the best they had ever had. Among the negative reasons for continuing to work, 83 percent gave such replies as "I'd feel lost," "Would go crazy," "Would feel bored," "Would feel useless." About half of the respondents said they would do the same kind of work, 5 percent would prefer to be self-employed, and 20 percent would change to a position of more prestige.

If they didn't work, said 40 percent of the respondents, they'd miss social contacts more than anything else. Only 15 percent would miss the kind of work they do, 9 percent would miss the regular routine, 28 percent would miss nothing specific—and 1 percent "wouldn't miss a thing."[5]

A one-year attitude survey was conducted for a subsidiary of one of the major oil companies. Over eleven hundred employees, the majority of whom were either professional or supervisory personnel, were interviewed. The workers were asked to rate morale within their own groups high, average, or low and state what they felt was important to their "local" morale. Company policy stressed good employee relations, and the company was a leader in providing employee benefits. The study found most of the professional workers satisfied with the jobs in terms of type of work and salaries received.

During the study there was a change in top management, and company policy shifted from centralization to decentralization with authority being passed down during the entire year of the study. Results of the study indicated that in almost all sections with low morale the principal cause was faulty supervision. Good morale exists when management

> . . . avoids too close supervision of workers, delegates more authority and responsibility to employees, permits participation in deciding matters, and keeps workers fully informed about all matters pertinent to their unit, and their relationship with other units and the company.[6]

---

[5]See *Personnel*, American Management Association, Inc., January 1957, p. 326.

[6]Paul A. Brinker, "Morale among Professional Workers: A Case Study," *Personnel Journal*, January 1957, adapted from *Personnel Management Abstracts*, Spring 1957.

Putting morale survey results to work

Obviously, making an attitude or morale survey is only a first step in the improvement of communications within a company. Business concerns have been making surveys among their employees for several decades, but the literature concerning their follow-through is sketchy. Generally, managements agree that at least two uses can be made: one, the findings can be reported to the employees, and two, remedial actions can be taken to improve the situations that need it.

Some managements conduct meetings with supervisors and employees to clarify the reasons for negative findings. Shortcomings on the part of management are brought into open discussion and improvements in managerial practices and communications are developed. If such "feedback" sessions are conducted in a sincere and constructive spirit, later surveys of employee morale are likely to produce higher percentages of favorable reactions to conditions that were previously found to be "least liked" by the employees.

Some companies have found that morale surveys with feedback sessions have more beneficial and widespread effects than speeches by executives or formal educational conferences. The feedback sessions help employees develop a better-adjusted view of their work situation.

Differentiating between griping on a questionnaire and productivity

Any person experienced in making morale surveys and in dealing with employees knows that some employees will complain constantly about their jobs yet, despite good employment opportunities in other plants of the area, they do not leave. These gripers may actually be loyal and hardworking employees. Morale may be high even though discontent is frequently expressed.

Individual productivity, often defined as morale, is more significant than contentment in situations where employees can contribute through positive action as in exerting skill or effort.

Current personnel research indicates that there is little or no proven relationship between morale, job satisfaction, and productivity. Studies conducted by the University of Michigan's Survey Research Center show that increases in production can be obtained with *either* favorable or unfavorable changes in employee attitudes. As far as job satisfaction is concerned, the all-important factors seem to be group cohesiveness, team spirit, and permissive, democratic supervision.[7]

Morale is a diffused or variable influence. It is the sum total of so

[7] See Julius E. Eitington, "Bigness and Morale, A Look at the Record," *Personnel Administration*, January–February 1957.

many factors that it is difficult to measure. From the standpoint of personnel management, the important factor is productivity rather than contentment or the absence of griping.

Employees may remain with an employer and work hard for many reasons as indicated by this interview with an employee who had, on a morale survey questionnaire, criticized many aspects of his work situation:

Brazing department employee to interviewer: "What is my opinion of this company? Well, I feel indifferent toward the place. As you know, I have a wooden leg and not every place will hire people like me. I am glad to have this job but I think I do my share of work so I don't owe the company a thing. Bill, the owner, is a friendly man. He knows almost all his employees by their first name. I wish he would do something in our department to clean the place up. I bet it hasn't been painted in over 40 years. The lighting is bad here. With these dark glasses we wear, we can hardly see what we are doing. We should have some type of hoist to lift our barrels of finished parts with. They weigh about 250 pounds and some of them haven't cooled off when we have to roll them out of the way as we haven't much room here to store our finished work till they cool off. This place is warm during the cold months and too hot during the summer months. Our holding vise isn't too good and we tell our foreman about it but he just laughs. You know, he was, at one time, the plant superintendent but he got moved down to be our foreman because he was charging the workers so much a month to keep their jobs. That was one of the first improvements Bill made when he took over as owner—he demoted the plant "super" to foreman.

The reason why I stay here is that it is the only place in town where I can work with a wooden leg.

Survey findings should be interpreted by someone who knows the individuals involved. As one psychologist has pointed out, management, looking at survey results, may conclude, for example, that the insurance plan is the real cause of irritation. It may be, or it may be only something for the employees' anxiety to attach to. Then the company might spend money on changes only to find that the anxiety had now attached itself to something else. Information may not be what is wanted. The needs of the group may be in their feelings and emotions rather than in their factual knowledge. In the follow-up, the employees may be less concerned with what is done with the results than with the supervisor's reaction toward them. It might even be that they do not really want the annoyance removed; it provides a convenient excuse for their attitudes.

Giving meaning to work

The fact that the relationship between morale (depending upon how t is defined) and productivity is difficult to measure does not prove that morale is of no importance to management. Most executives feel better when they know that their employees are enthusiastic about their jobs and the company. To that end, they try to strengthen rather than ignore morale. One of the most effective procedures for improving morale is to explain, even glamorize, the product made by the company. Here are two examples —the first is reported by F. J. Neary, personnel administrator with Don Baxter, Inc., Glendale, California.

1. We believe the best way to make the employee's work interesting is to acquaint him thoroughly with the end uses of the products on which he is working. Our products, intravenous solutions and blood transfusion equipment, are "naturals" for this purpose because they have a long and well-known history of life-saving performance in hospitals and blood banks and on the battlefield.

Not every company has so dramatic an opportunity to show end-use of its products. Yet regardless of the type of product, there is much that can be done to show how it is used, how it compares with competition, and what customers think about it. A considerable proportion of space in all employee newspapers and magazines is now being devoted to this purpose. . . .

2. Morale exists when a man has pride in his company, and that pride can be fostered by effective communication. A sign that hangs in our Brooklyn plant reads: *Pfizer Terramycin Saves Human Lives.* The message is simple, but it is written in a language that cuts through the barriers erected in a man's mind by the humdrum events of a working day. That message reaches the worker, because it is true and because it is important. It lives proudly in some part of his consciousness, and he is a richer man for it.

John J. Hall, director of Industrial Relations, Brown and Sharpe Manufacturing Company, Providence, Rhode Island reported:

We have a showroom where our finished products are displayed, and we find that it is of value for the worker who normally sees only raw material or parts of finished products to visit this show area and see the finished products.[8]

[8] From Fred H. Joiner, "Making Employees' Work More Interesting," *Personnel*, American Management Association, Inc., January 1953.

Satisfaction with the job situation does not necessarily bring about productivity. An employee may be quite pleased to be a member of a company organization but have no strong desire to contribute to its production goals. To be stimulated by production goals, the employee needs to see those goals as worthy for him.

Most line executives are incapable of, or uninterested in, verbalizing the meanings and values inherent in the job. Executives who are engineers, in particular, are inarticulate in this respect. Hence, the personnel department must help provide the interpretation of the job to the workers. The effect on production of such interpretation was dramatically illustrated during World War II:

> Take the case of the atomic bomb plant at Oak Ridge, Tennessee. The workers there were above average. They had been meticulously screened before they were selected—they had been chosen for their outstanding Americanism after a thorough check-up by the F.B.I. You would expect these people to give their best effort to war production, not only because of their general background but because they knew that "Manhattan Project" was considered an AAA1 priority operation. *But they did not know what they were doing,* for of necessity it was the policy of "Manhattan Project" not to let its "left hand know what its right hand did."
>
> Taking the normal level of production as 100 per cent base, I am told on good authority that the first week after the A-Bomb fell on Hiroshima and they learned the full meaning of their efforts, production at Oak Ridge doubled! The week following when the second bomb fell on Nagasaki and they could begin to see that they could help bring the war to a quick close it went up to 300 per cent of the original level. *Here, dramatically, is demonstrated the stimulating effect of knowing what one is doing and why.*[9]

The personnel man should know how the supervisor feels about his employees

Strange as it may seem to the uninitiated in business, almost every supervisor has certain employees for whom he does not feel essentially responsible. True, he knows that he is technically responsible for each member of his group, but his knowledge is on the intellectual level. Emotionally, or inwardly as he is likely to define it, he does not feel responsible for

---

[9]"Worker Productivity, A Challenge to Management," a talk by Robert M. Creaghead, Employee Communication Specialist, Greenwich, Conn., before Industrial Marketers of Cleveland, Chapter of the National Industrial Advertisers Association, Inc., Hotel Carter, October 25, 1946.

certain individuals. Perhaps he "inherited" them when he took over the supervision of the department. Perhaps he thinks of them as marginal employees whom he wants to transfer or discharge as soon as he can find a justifiable reason or an opportunity to get rid of them gracefully.

One of the most common causes for this feeling of nonresponsibility is the practice of letting the employment man interview and select the applicants to fill job vacancies without granting the supervisor the privilege of deciding which applicants he prefers. Naturally the supervisor feels that the personnel department "picked the guy." The foreman had to take him. Modern personnel managers recognize this hazard in hiring and try to increase the supervisor's feelings of responsibility for the new employee by giving the supervisor some participation in selection.

A few companies even carry this need for active participation in the hiring process by requiring each middle management executive to find and hire his own management trainee.

Executives and supervisors need this experience of participation so much that the astute applicant who is being considered for a high level job in management refuses to accept an offer unless the president interviews him in a rigorous manner. A casual meeting and handshake with the president is not enough—the president must himself go through enough thorough interviewing with the applicant to enable him to reach a firm decision: "This is *the* man I want on *my* team." Failure to carry through in this manner has caused many a potentially good applicant to be relegated, after having been hired, to the fringe of management by the president.

An important part of the personnel man's job is that of recognizing those situations where an executive or supervisor does not feel fully responsible for certain subordinates. These feeling-filled situations are not openly stated or expressed verbally to the personnel man. He must sense them from emotionally tinged statements and incidental comments. And then, if possible, he must try to correct them or at least contribute to their correction.

As one personnel man stated: "There are always some employees whom the boss would be glad to see leave. He won't fire 'em, but he hopes they'll quit. It's up to the personnel man to know who these employees are and to be as constructive as he can with both the supervisor and the employee."

OBJECTIVE FINDINGS CONCERNING EMPLOYEE RELATIONS

The personnel man need not depend entirely upon his sensitivity to the feelings of individuals or to data obtained from a morale survey. He has many figures and other objective evidences of what is going on among the employees. He, for example, knows the data concerning absenteeism, tardiness, numbers of employees who quit, kinds of employees who quit, extent of moonlighting, and reactions to fringe benefits. In the remainder of this chapter, we shall briefly treat a few of these indicators.

The "personnel flow"

Employees who quit may offer the personnel man clues about influences that he should investigate. Few executives are so naive as to imagine that the employee's first statement as to why he is leaving affords a wholly reliable guide to the real reason behind the terminating employee's decision to quit. If the real reason for his quitting would appear to criticize some other person or policy of the company, he is not likely to express it. To do so might bring about subsequent recrimination. (See "Exit Interviews," Chapter 17, page 342.)

In spite of the difficulties in learning the true reasons for quitting, the personnel manager wants to know the age and ability levels of employees who quit and of those who remain. To be healthy an organization needs a balanced structure in regard to factors such as age, technical training, and desire to advance. If a company has a disproportionally light or heavy concentration in any one bracket that is essential for the company's vitality, the equilibrium of the organization becomes unbalanced. Too many executives and employees of the same ability classifications may quit or retire in the same years. The personnel of a company contracts and expands in an irregular manner. The turnover of employees and the composition of the organization must be watched constantly to spot and overcome imbalance. It is up to the personnel manager to note the "personnel flow," the types of men and women who come into and leave the organization.

Fringe benefits and their effect on cooperation

Modern industrial firms provide a wide variety of fringe benefits that range all the way from prenatal care to provision for burial expenses. These include legally required payments for social security, workmen's compensation; pension, insurance, and other agreed-upon payments; paid rest periods, lunch periods, vacations, holidays, sick leave, and allowance for other time not worked, profit-sharing payments, bonuses, and so on. The costs of these benefits run to about one-fourth of the total payroll. Some executives hope that employees will feel grateful for these benefits and put extra effort into their jobs to show their appreciation.

Experienced personnel men know that employees seldom act in the hoped-for manner. Employees rarely have any ego-involvement or participation in the granting of the benefits. Many managements decide to rant them because the competition is already giving them or the unions lemand them. Enlightened managements tend to grant these benefits as one phase of their colleagueship with the community, employees, and stockholders. All are interdependent. The company should—must as a matter of course—provide all the benefits it can for its workers, but enlightened managements do not expect to receive any special gratitude or any obvious spurt n productivity as the result of granting fringe benefits or other "gifts."

The ultimate success or failure of personnel management will hinge on how people are valued as individuals—not by the gifts given them but by the attainment of values through participation in common goals. Personnel management cannot in itself give the highest values to the human beings in a company. It can, however, help to set goals and make its own unique contributions by working with management and employees.

The old authoritarian business structure in which management has power to demand and the workers are under obligation to comply is being displaced. In that kind of structure the management set up policies and procedures for the organized human relationships. Voluntary cooperation was excluded, the climate was dictatorial, and the full needs of the human personality were likely to be overlooked. Now the human personality is being taken into account to a greater extent in the attainment of corporate goals. We are learning that the corporate goal can be achieved and yet foster individual worth, health, security, and participation within the corporate venture.

Sensitivity training: group method for executive training

The personnel manager does not think of himself as the only person who should be sensitive to employee relations. He needs the help of every person in the company, particularly the executives. Sensitivity training is a type of human relations group training which aims to teach people to look more closely at themselves in order better to understand their own feelings and prejudices and to be more sensitive to the ways people relate to each other. This knowledge is essential for employees who must successfully adapt to change of any form. Further, the individual should have self-knowledge in order to recognize those aspects of his behavior that are used as defenses against real or imagined threats to his personal status, especially during these periods of change. This type of program is still in its early stages of development.

Sensitivity training may be referred to as T-Group sessions where the T stands for training, as D-Groups (development groups), or other terms such as "Self-Awareness for Managers." It is a training situation used to help individuals become more aware of their emotional effects on others and improve their "helping relationships" with associates at work and in other situations. The training method does not primarily rely on lectures or discussions in the usual sense. Members of the group become participants who experience emotional frustrations, overcome group problems, achieve successes, and experience failures. The purposes of the sessions are not to solve company problems but to learn the psychological dynamics of effective group relationships as they apply to each member of the group. Positive values to be expected from sensitivity training are improvements in behavior, increase in listening capability and sensitivity to the communications of others, better understanding, contributions in group situations, and increase in tolerance and flexibility.[10]

Sensitivity training sessions have been conducted by the National Training Laboratories, American Management Association, Institute of Industrial Relations of the University of California at Los Angeles, and other organizations.

As one would expect, any new form of training which is so highly charged emotionally as sensitivity training is subject to considerable criticism and is in need of intensive research.[11]

Results of such studies indicating the changes that this type of training has incurred are still incomplete due to its newness. However, individual studies of groups have shown that in the end the trainees became more aware of the process of sensitization in interpersonal relations. Further, they became more aware of themselves and their role in these relations.

The effects on the executive trainees are enlightening in the application of their newly developed human relations know-how in their later work, as reported by themselves and their co-workers. This, in turn, may lead to better morale, higher productivity, and lower turnover among workers.

QUESTIONS ON THE CHAPTER

1. In what respects is an effective personnel manager positive minded?

2. What kinds of company conditions should an alert personnel man recognize as unvoiced grievances?

3. In making a morale survey, why do some companies use the questionnaire form from the Science Research Associates?

[10]See Mary Ann Coghill, "Sensitivity Training" (Ithaca, N. Y., New York State School of Industrial and Labor Relations, Key Issues Series—No. 1), p. 22.

[11]See Martin Lakin, "Some Ethical Issues in Sensitivity Training," *American Psychologist*, October 1969; Byron E. Calame, *The Wall Street Journal*, July 19, 1969; John P. Campbell and Marvin D. Dunnette, "Effectiveness of T-Group Experiences in Managerial Training and Development," *Psychological Bulletin 1968*, Vol. LXX, No. 2, 73–104; and Max Birnbaum, "Sense about Sensitivity Training," *Saturday Review*, November 15, 1969.

4. In which age group does the lowest morale usually occur? Describe other general findings from morale surveys.

5. Comment on the statement that expression of discontent is usually a sign of poor morale.

6. What important principle concerning workers and productivity was demonstrated in the Oak Ridge bomb plant during World War II?

7. Why are the age and ability levels of employees who quit and those who remain important to the personnel manager?

8. Discuss the relation between griping and productivity.

9. What is meant by the "personnel flow" of an organization?

10. What is the value of sensitivity training? In what ways does sensitivity training affect the work of executive trainees?

11. How can work be given meaning for the employees?

12. Of the ideas in the chapter, which ones are of special interest to you?

13. What did the chapter contribute toward your future relations with (a) the men who supervise you, (b) the employees whom you may supervise?

PROBLEMS AND PROJECTS

For All Students

1. Interview several students of an educational institution. Have them designate the positive and negative aspects of their situation. Are the points of friction inherent in the institution or in the persons themselves?

2. Interview several employees of a company. Ask them about the things that affect their morale. Using your notes of the interviews, phrase questions that might be used in a morale survey of all the employees.

For Advanced Students

3. Interview several personnel men of your area. Find out what professional journals each reads. Do they attend seminars or workshops on personnel problems? Do they attend local professional organization meetings?

4. Make a list of sources that describe organizations and services that deal with personnel management and industrial relations. Examine available journals and textbooks for sources in this field. Describe them.

For Men in Business

5. Describe the fringe benefits available in a company of your area. To what extent do employees know about or understand them? Interview several employees to find out the accuracy of their knowledge.

6. Some day your management may ask you whether you would like to become a member of a sensitivity training group. To help you decide, read

Carl R. Rogers, "The Group Comes of Age," *Psychology Today*, December 1969, and related articles listed in the collateral readings.

COLLATERAL READINGS

For All Students

Hepner, Harry W., *Psychology Applied to Life and Work* (4th ed.). Englewood Cliffs, N.J.: Prentice-Hall, Inc., 1966. Chapter 22 presents steps in making a morale survey, feedback sessions, limitations, and relations between morale and productivity.

Marrow, Alfred J., *Behind the Executive Mask: Greater Managerial Competence Through Deeper Self-Understanding*. New York: American Management Association, Inc., 1964. Description of typical three-week program for executives, written by senior consultant of AMA's Executive Action Course.

For Advanced Students

Dunnette, Marvin D., John P. Campbell, and Milton D. Hakel, "Factors Contributing to Job Satisfaction and Job Dissatisfaction in Six Occupational Groups," *Organizational Behavior and Human Performance*, Academic Press, Inc., May 1967. The authors review Herzberg's two-factor theory. They feel that both satisfaction and dissatisfaction can reside in job content or context or both and that the most important job dimensions are recognition and responsibility.

Schein, Edgar H., and Warren G. Bennis, *Personal and Organizational Change Through Group Methods: The Laboratory Approach*. New York: John Wiley & Sons, Inc. 1965. An analytic and practical textbook on T-Group methodology.

For Men in Business

Argyris, Chris. "A Brief Description of Laboratory Education" and "In Defense of Laboratory Education," *Training Directors Journal*, October 1963. These items report the positive portion of a debate on sensitivity training.

Klaw, Spencer, "Two Weeks in a T Group," *Fortune*, August 1961, pp. 114–17ff. Description of National Training Laboratories training sessions for middle managers.

Personnel Management: Relations with Unions

SITUATIONS YOU ARE LIKELY TO MEET

How would you meet each of these situations:
  a. *Before* you have read the chapter? What would
     you say to yourself or to the individual?
  b. *After* you have read the chapter? How have
     your answers changed?

1. Assume that you are interviewing applicants for jobs
   in a plant whose hourly paid employees belong to a
   union. One applicant is an ambitious young man who
   has obvious leadership ability. When you tell him
   that he will be expected to join the union, he says:
   "In that case I won't take a job here. I am not against
   unions, but I think of myself as a trainee for management. As soon as I join a union, management will
   tend to think of me as an average factory worker,
   not as a trainee."
   How would you answer him?

2. An activist among dissident groups identifies with
   minorities whether of race, religion, income, or some
   other characteristic. His solution for all management-
   union differences is to require legally that business
   and social clubs, particularly exclusive country clubs,
   admit labor union officials to membership. This kind
   of integration, he believes, will lead to harmony between labor and management.
   What points of view will you offer him for consideration, assuming that he is open-minded to points of
   view that do not agree with his?

The personnel manager is likely to have important dealings with the company's labor union, but he is seldom alone in making decisions that involve major company responsibilities to the union. The responsibilities are so serious that the several members on the highest management level, particularly the president, consider themselves responsible for union relations, especially during contract negotiations. The personnel department often represents the management in certain union relations, as in handling grievances, developing procedures for resolving controversial grievances, and helping to interpret the contract. In some companies these relations are so numerous and involved that a special "labor relations" or "industrial relations" division deals with them.

Of course our major interest in labor unions is much broader than the functions of the personnel department in dealing with them. Unions have such varied aspects that any attempt to describe them in a comprehensive manner would have to be a description of human behavior plus much politics, psychology, economics, and sociology.

In addition to these varied aspects, a powerful new factor has appeared in the kinds of changed human relationships as described in Chapter 2. As stated by Abbé Dion of Laval University, Quebec City, Canada:

> Labor relationships are part of the overall pattern of human relationships. It follows that the social and cultural factors which exist at any time have impacts on industrial relations. In spite of the coming of the affluent society, there has been a constant re-examination during the last twenty-five years of the values and institutions of our civilization. There has been a feeling of dissatisfaction arising from insecurity and loss of faith in the future. This has given rise to a sense of frustration amongst many intellectuals.

Abbé Dion pointed out that unions are suffering from a lack of loyalty to their organization by increasingly larger numbers of members. New members bring with them concepts of rejection of organization. They refuse any loyalty to the agency of which they are a part and will often use their job ituations to further their own aims, aims that may be completely foreign to he organization where they are employed.

In the unions and staff associations, the activists will concentrate on opposing their own organization. They will expect the union to solve every problem and, as it obviously cannot achieve this perfection, they will seek to reject it. . . .

While stressing the need for individuals to combine in their right to hold their own opinions with a certain loyalty to the organization of which they are a part, Abbé Dion emphasized the fact that the training of men and women in all aspects of personnel relations is of paramount importance. The need of the future, he concluded, is to develop mutual trust and to proceed with the task of building institutions which will work. We shall look in vain, he said, for appropriate models in the past. "We must work today as if we were men from the future."[1]

Any description of unionism is likely to arouse criticism or defense on the part of some readers, depending upon the psychological needs and identifications of the individual. Each reader is likely to be either an advocate or a critic of unionism even though he imagines that he is objective in his thinking. Thorough objectivity in this field is rare indeed. Management men find it especially difficult to overcome bias in regard to unionism. One reason for their difficulty is that an executive likes to think of himself as the leader of his employees. Unions and union activities often interpose themselves between the executive and his employees. Some union leaders try to drive a wedge between the employee and his company. They may even go beyond the point of telling him that the union is a good thing and far into the zone of trying to persuade him that his company is his natural enemy, never to be trusted or respected.

The psychological climate in companies whose employees are unionized may be peaceful and one of cooperation or it may be full of friction: bickering, arguments about trivialities, employees demanding rights rather than expressing a desire to do good work, arguing about what the contract calls for, or attempting to give the contract some new interpretation that will provide an advantage for some person or group of persons. Union leaders may be mature or they may be so disputatiously concerned about what they do not have to do and what management must do that a normal person would prefer to work elsewhere. Certainly, many supervisors of unionized employees must learn to take carping by union officers for granted—it's all a part of the day's work!

[1]See *Professional Public Service*, July 1969, pp. 2 and 17. Abbé Dion is also known as Gerard Dion, editor, *Industrial Relations*, a quarterly published by Les Presses De L'Université Laval, Quebec City, P. Q., Canada.

Managements realize that any union leader who is ambitious for advancement in union circles must measure his success by his ability to outdo what other union leaders achieve for their members. The aggressive tactics of union officers for more money and benefits are bound, in our type of economy, to contribute to wage inflation. Individual managements cannot long resist wage demands because long strikes can lead to business suicide. Usually, too, continued industry resistance brings government intervention and the public's verdict that it is better for wage costs to go up than for unemployment of strikers to go on indefinitely. Most leaders of organized labor are critical of advancing prices, but they also advocate cheap credit and bigger government spending, influences that create the market conditions in which industry can advance prices and finance higher labor costs.

In spite of the difficulties in maintaining peaceful relations with a union, many managements prefer to deal with a strong rather than a weak union. A strong union has the backing of most of the workers. Such a union can be of great assistance in smoothing out the frictions that take place during and after contract negotiations.

A strong union can help management in carrying down to the workers the actions agreed upon in the contract. New contracts usually result in agreements that displease some workers. The union leaders can explain and justify the decisions to the displeased members. Management expects the workers' representatives to explain the agreements made and to induce any unwilling members to cooperate. Unfortunately, individual workers or groups sometimes refuse to accept the agreements. When workers refuse to accept the joint decisions, management is naturally disappointed and critical of the individual offenders and of the whole union relationship. The management then hopes that the next elected union officers will be strong enough as leaders to control the members.

Why workers join unions

Relatively few workers join unions because of coercion. If they do join for that reason, they are not likely to continue as members. Actually, most join because the union provides a business service: greater security in the job, higher wages, better working conditions, protection against arbitrary or unfair treatment by management, and other services. The worker who belongs to a union feels more secure—nobody in management can push him around unfairly. He cannot lose his job as easily as he might if he were dependent only upon his status as an individual.

Most employees have need for a business service organization that increases their feelings of job security. Even though the nonunion employee has a job that he likes and does well, he knows that he may be discharged because of arbitrary action by a superior. If he is discharged or laid off, his financial resources may not carry him over comfortably to the next job. As a family man, he probably is buying a home, a car, and one or more electrical appliances on an installment basis. As long as his regular income continues he can meet the payments and at the same time support his family adequately. As soon as his income stops for even one month, he and his family are likely to suffer and many of his savings in the form of equities in purchases may disappear. His financial reserves are so limited that he feels he should seek the protection and services that a union can provide. He also knows that the employer is not a completely free agent in the market— he must run the business to please the customers. Customers' wishes and the survival of the company take precedence over his welfare as an employee.

Workers naturally try to overcome this feeling of economic insecurity. The measures they and their union take are not always an unreasonable attempt to get "something for nothing." Managements should put themselves in the place of the worker confronted with this insecurity and seek to enable him to attain the maximum of security. If this is not possible, management should at least give the worker an appreciation of why the need cannot be answered by explaining the company's limitations and economic problems. Once the worker feels that his needs are understood and management wants to meet them, the worker can participate with management in dealing with the company's problems as a colleague, not as someone who must accept whatever management is willing to give.[2]

To the worker of the large corporation, members of management appear to be remote privileged persons who sit in luxurious offices. The union leaders, in contrast, are men like himself who cater to him and treat him as an equal. This is especially likely to be the feeling of people engaged in mechanized work. These are the employees who are more disposed to become union members.

To the worker, the labor union is an instrument for enhancing his dignity as an individual. When a worker's dignity is ignored and his human qualities are not recognized, his resentment is likely to be expressed by increased loyalty to the union. His incidental complaints and grievances are manifested, often irrationally, through wildcat strikes, slowdowns, and other forms of hostility.

Most employees who belong to unions are loyal to their union officials. They are not greatly concerned about newspaper reports of embezzlement and misuse of union funds by union leaders. After all, the members are getting a service from an organization that represents them and their interests.

Publicity and findings of union atrocities that are revealed in congres-

[2]See Rensis Likert, "Motivation: The Core of Management," *Personnel Series*, No. 155, American Management Association, Inc., 1954.

sional and other hearings will not destroy overnight the faith of a union member whose leaders have accomplished something for him. He reviews his wage increases and his improved benefits and working conditions, and he believes—rightly or wrongly—that these improvements have been brought about by his union. He feels that if his union were to be destroyed or weakened at the top, he might once more be at the mercy of an arbitrary representative of management. His employer might be a kind person, or on the other hand, he might not be. To the worker, his union provides a set of effective brakes on management. He is not too confident about how well the business mechanism would operate if the brakes were removed.

Psychological characteristics of union leaders

The personnel man and other members of management who deal with union leaders tend, in time, to find that these men have certain typical characteristics. Of course these executives recognize that individual differences occur among labor union leaders as well as among executives and other occupational members. They do, however, become aware of patterns, or signs of behavioral patterns, in the makeup of union leaders. These patterns have not as yet been studied by social scientists to the same extent that behavior of business executives has been studied. The reason may be that union leaders are more defensive, less secure, and less confident about themselves. They therefore do not like to be analyzed even though the purpose of the analysis may be friendly. In contrast, the able, self-confident, secure executive does not, as a rule, care how much anyone studies him. This means that when we attempt to describe behavior patterns that characterize typical labor union leaders, we have to depend upon empirical judgment rather than statistically significant measurements.

However, a few systematic studies have been made of union leaders. Howard M. Bogard, for example, administered a battery of tests and biographical inventories to forty trainees of the International Ladies Garment Workers Union and to the same number of trainees for management of the Grace Line, a major international shipping and chemical company. The two groups differed markedly. The union trainees were found to be somewhat less intelligent and less aggressive than the management trainees. However, both groups tended to score above the general population in both of these traits. The ILGWU trainees appeared to manifest less social maturity, to be less responsible, and to reveal a long-standing propensity to overt conflict with authority figures. They appeared to reveal the strong social feelings encouraged by the union—to be aggressive, assertive, and impulsive. Their data also suggested a lack of emotional maturity. However, in most of the traits studied, the picture of the two groups was close to the ideal types sought by the particular union or management administrators. As usual in studies of this kind, the individual differences found within each group were often considerable.[3]

Another study of sixteen personality and other variables of union stewards and managers was made in regard to thirty-three tool-and-die shops. One of the few statistically significant findings was that shops with a low emotional tone tend to have union stewards who are overly sensitive and thin-skinned.[4]

Those who have had considerable experience in dealing with labor union leaders recognize that many of them are capable and ambitious, but they have never learned to feel at home in the presence of people in management or in the social groups frequented by executives. Many college students feel the same way, but the ambitious student typically identifies himself with management. He looks forward to becoming an executive and associating with executives as an equal. The union leader does not. He does not identify himself with management and therefore has difficulty in understanding or trying to understand business problems and how to deal with them constructively. He identifies with the employees, whom he views as unappreciated, neglected, or exploited. He feels frustrated in his desire for advancement because he senses he does not fit into the group that is likely to advance into management.

Another type of leader is the one who is rebelling against authority. The man who has rebelled violently against authority is rarely found in management. He is, however, frequently found among those union leaders who are in power in the early history of unionism in a company—the fighting stage of union-management relations. He is elected to office because he has the characteristics that a new and insecure union requires if it is to achieve the things its new members desire of it at the time of organization. When such a union leader first appears across the table from management, he causes a good deal of consternation among the management men. Such a man is likely to be resentful toward management and completely unwilling to bury the past in order to build a new relationship. Consequently the growth of peaceful industrial relations is checked so long as he is in power.

In the normal course of events, however, the union achieves some of its purposes, and with this achievement comes a measure of security. When this happens, there is likely to be a change in union leadership. Men who are motivated by rebellion to authority soon get tired of fighting for rights that have been recognized and granted by management. The fiery oratory of the aggressive rebel against authority is no longer appropriate. He does not

[3]See Howard M. Bogard, "Union and Management Trainees—A Comparative Study of Occupational and Personality Choice," *Journal of Applied Psychology*, February 1960.

[4]See Ross Stagner, "Personality Variables in Union-Management Relations," *Journal of Applied Psychology*, October 1962.

get much response from members who cannot be whipped into a frenzy. He moves on to another company where his zeal fits the kind of situation that calls for inflammatory leadership. Of course a few of these leaders may remain for some years after management has accepted the union.

Mayo's Classic Illustration. Elton Mayo, one of the greatest students of the influence of feelings and emotions in industrial relationships, described the resistance to his search for union support for extending facilities for adult education in Australia as follows:

> Usually the more moderate and responsible union members sat in the front rows; the back rows were the haunt of those who represented the irreconcilable extreme left. Before long it became evident that six men were the nucleus of all the most savage opposition. In the course of many years, I came to know these six men well. The extreme party changed its name many times . . . but whatever the change of name or doctrine, it was always the same six who led the opposition at union meetings or spoke from soap boxes in the public parks. The fact that I came to know them personally made no difference to their platform attitude to me or to the university; but on other occasions they would talk freely to me in private. This enabled me to place on record many observations, the general tenor of which may be summarized as follows:
>
> 1. These men had no friends except at the propagandist level. They seemed incapable of easy relationship with other people; on the contrary, the need to achieve such relationship was for them an emergency demanding energetic effort.
> 2. They had no capacity for conversation. In talk with me they alternated between self-history and oratory which reproduced the compelling topic—revolution and the destruction of society.
> 3. All action, like social relationship, was for them emergency action. Any idea of routine participation in collaborate effort, or of the "ordinary" in living, was conspicuously absent from their thinking. Everything, no matter how insignificant, was treated as crisis, and was undertaken with immense and unreasoned "drive."
> 4. They regarded the world as a hostile place. Every belief and action implied that society existed not to give but to deny them opportunity. Furthermore, they believed that hostility to be active, not merely inert; they regarded everyone, even their immediate associates, as potentially part of the enemy forces arrayed against them.
>
> In every instance the personal history was one of social privation—a childhood devoid of normal and happy association in

work and play with other children. This privation seemed to be the source of the inability to achieve "ordinary" human relationships, of the consequent conviction that the world was hostile, and of the reaction by attack upon the supposed enemy. One of the six drifted into the hands of a medical colleague with whom I was accustomed to work on problems of adaptation. Thus was established a clinical relation of confidence in his physician. He discovered that his medical adviser was not at all interested in his political theories but was very much interested in the intimate details of his personal history. He made a good recovery and discovered, to his astonishment, that his former political views had vanished. He had been a mechanic, unable to keep his job although a good workman. After recovery he took a clerical job and held it; his attitude was no longer revolutionary.[5]

Imberman's study of labor leaders

The purpose of Imberman's study was to facilitate labor relations by an analysis of the leaders' characteristics. Over a two-year period, he worked for a public relations firm having two large unions as clients. His work brought him into friendly contact with 249 labor leaders of forty-two unions.

He found that most of the labor leaders come from a laboring class family, do not have much schooling above grade school, and have found the union the most feasible means of attaining financial success and power. But the labor leader finds that neither he nor his family is accepted socially because polite society thinks of him as on the occupational level of the members of the union and as a dishonest power grabber. Even political office, which many of the successful union leaders seek, does not protect him from social rebuff. The resulting frustration breeds bitterness.

The bitterness over being unaccepted socially works itself out by: (1) feeling antagonism toward the employer, resulting in unreasonable union rulings and demands; (2) accepting bribes for favorable decisions. The bribe may not be in the form of immediate cash but in an "arrangement" whereby the company agrees to buy products in accordance with a special contract that benefits the labor leader's private business on the outside. Bribes are a common practice with certain types of union leaders only, and when a bribe is refused by them it may be because of the insulting manner in which it is offered.

Imberman also found that a high proportion of these leaders found some solace in the company of women who were "of better social graces

---

[5]Elton Mayo, *The Social Problems of an Industrial Civilization* (Boston: Graduate School of Business Administration, Division of Research, Harvard University, 1945), pp. 25–27.

and elegancies than the original wife, seeming to indicate that even here the drive for acceptance and higher social status may be operating."

Imberman concluded that the difficulties that exist between labor and management exist not so much over issues as over the fact that management as a group snubs or appears to snub the labor leader socially. He suggested that the remedy is for management people to accept the labor leader, make him an important member of the community, and have him join exclusive clubs. This, he thinks, would tend to cause the antagonism expressed across the bargaining table to dissipate itself.[6]

This recommended remedy, unfortunately, is not feasible. Any union executive who would hobnob with management would cause suspicion on the part of his own rank-and-file members. They would assume that he was taking the points of view of management and would not fight for the members' rights. Such a union leader would be in office until the next election only. Few labor leaders would care to adapt themselves to a new social environment that would lead to identification with management. The main contribution of Imberman's study is its implication that management men in all their relations with union leaders should be relaxed, respectful, and friendly toward them as individuals even though they may be embittered and unreasonable.

In many companies, the psychological patterns of the union leaders differ markedly from those of the majority of members. Management men note this and often ask the question: "Why do our friendly well-balanced employees usually vote into union office the most cussed candidate rather than the typical normal cooperative type of employee?" The answer becomes simple when we appreciate that most employees think of the union as a business service—the contentious officer is more likely to get higher wage rates and better working conditions than the easy-to-get-along-with union official. The union leader must watch the wage increases being secured in other plants and be sufficiently aggressive to make his members feel that he is achieving the best wage arrangements that can be obtained. Union leaders do, of course, find causes of grievances and correct them, but these are extra services between contract negotiations rather than the main service to the members.

Characteristics in the pattern of typical union leaders, as noted from contacts with them, are:

1. Little education
2. High intelligence
3. Laboring class family
4. Leadership ability

[6]A. A. Imberman, "Labor Leaders and Society," *Harvard Business Review*, January 1950, pp. 50–60.

5. Feeling of rejection by members of social classes who are on same income level as the union leader—management symbolizes a social rank unattainable by labor leaders

6. Usually functions in a situation that does not permit close associations with management as a colleague of management for fear of being accused of "selling out"

Member participation in union affairs

Leonard R. Sayles and George Strauss have reported findings from a series of unstructured interviews with union members. They found that the members' participation in day-to-day union activities contrasted sharply with their loyalty to the union in strikes. Also, even though members exhibit strong loyalty toward their union as an institution they frequently criticize the union's officials.

The interviews revealed that the typical member is convinced he needs his union for protection against arbitrary management action and for obtaining economic security. Members expressed their need for the union: "Without a union we would be lost; the company could really take advantage of us." Members will endure privations to belong to the union and to win strikes. The typical member will remain loyal during a strike even though he is subjected to tremendous pressures such as those from seeing his children hungry, lacking his wife's sympathy, and putting up with an openly hostile community.

At the same time that the union member demonstrates firm loyalty in regard to the union's economic functions, he is apathetic toward the union's internal activities. For example, attendance at regular meetings of large industrial unions averages 2 percent to 8 percent of the total membership. Attendance at meetings for a strike vote or contract negotiation averages from 40 percent to 80 percent.

Many workers do not seek or accept union offices. Reasons given are "All those meetings to go to," "No time with the family," "Always some guy after something he doesn't deserve," and so forth. An important conclusion was:

> For a small group, the union is a way of life; for the majority, it is but a method of representation, although a very important one. For the leaders, the union has become an end in itself; for the rank and file, it is but a means to an end, a way of gaining greater security on the job, *not* a great social movement.[7]

[7]Leonard R. Sayles and George Strauss, "What the Worker Really Thinks of His Union," *Harvard Business Review*, May–June 1953. See also book by same authors, *The Local Union: Its Place in the Industrial Plant* (New York: Harper & Brothers, 1953), pp. 3, 4.

Management's insistence on management rights

Managements of unionized plants accept the principle that the company should delegate certain duties to its employees and that it is the proper function of the union to secure for its members the performance of these obligations. Decisions that lie beyond these areas are the function of management, not the union. And when the union wants to invade management's areas, management becomes adamant. Management must have the flexibility necessary to run the business efficiently and to maintain the vitality of the company as an enterprise. The areas of management's discretion include such matters as the unlimited right to decide upon the number and location of plants, the products to be manufactured, the schedules of production, the hours to be worked, the methods of manufacture, the purchase of equipment, and financing. They include the right to select employees for promotion within the bargaining unit and to select individuals for promotion to supervisory positions or other jobs outside the bargaining unit. Management wants responsibility for enforcing rules and regulations, imposing discipline, assigning work, and enforcing work standards. Management wants the right to introduce more efficient tools and methods of manufacture and to adopt whatever technological advancements may be vital to growth.

Perhaps the most common subject of conflict in regard to union-management relations is the union's rigidity in that portion of the contract that governs adjustments in the work force to meet changes in production schedules and unplanned interruptions, usually referred to as seniority provisions.

Many unions prefer to insist that all layoffs and transfers be made on the basis of lowest seniority. Managements prefer a more flexible procedure because of the evils of "bumping." "Bumping" is a common expression for the procedure of an employee of greater seniority employed in one department forcing, during layoff periods, an employee of lesser seniority in another department to be laid off so that the former may have his job. In many cases, the "bumped" employee is more efficient and cooperative than the one who takes his place.

In principle the unions want to participate in certain kinds of protection of rights of the personnel only, not in production. Changes in personnel as caused by bumping and other marginal areas of control may have marked impact on production. When a management feels threatened in regard to what it believes to be its rights in regard to production, management becomes as resistant as the union.

Featherbedding

One of the most frequent encroachments by unions on management's areas of operation takes place in featherbedding. This term is supposed to have originated many years ago when the local representative for the men on the Rock Island Railroad complained about mattresses that had been placed in cabooses for the train crews' use. The mattresses were composed of corncobs, shucks, and cottonseed hulls. The trainmaster's answer to the complaint was, "What do you damned brakemen want—feather beds?"[8]

The story may be apocryphal, but the term "featherbedding" has come to stand for rules or practices that require the employment of unneeded workmen or the slowing up of work under a featherbed rule. A common definition is getting pay for work not done. It also applies to those union contracts that compel management to put extra men on a job where they are not needed in order to spread the available work. An example is the successful insistence of railroad workers' unions that diesel engines be run by three men when impartial observers agree that two can easily do the job. The third man is a leftover from coal-burning steam engine days when three men were necessary.

In some cases, featherbedding provisions have increased an employer's costs to such an extent that he could not increase wages.

Traditionally, featherbedding is associated with the printing, building, amusement, and railroad industries, all of which have been organized for many years by craft unions. In these industries it includes employing unnecessary personnel such as standby musicians, doing unnecessary work as in cutting off factory-threaded pipe ends and rethreading on the job, insisting on time-consuming work methods as in using hand tools instead of power tools, and compelling the employer to hire skilled men to perform unskilled labor.

The craft unions have been most successful in imposing such uneconomic regulations because their members usually provide a service of skill or they produce against a time deadline. The companies are therefore vulnerable to strike action and to union power. Restrictions and requirements of the featherbedding variety increase gradually year by year. Eventually they affect the competitive position of the industry and bring about decreased opportunity for employment of members of the craft. Printers have been forced out of work because of newspaper consolidations and the shift to competitive reproduction methods. No one knows how much decline has taken place in the railroad industry as an effect of featherbedding, but the demand that requires a company to give two railroad men twenty-four-hours' pay for one man's eight hours of work has taken place during an era when railroad jobs are only one-third of what they were in the preceding generation. One reason for the rise of the do-it-yourself movement among American consumers has been the arbitrary rulings of building craft unions.

Certainly featherbedding rules have not eliminated intermittent employment in the building and amusement industries or halted the secular

[8]See "They Call It Featherbedding," *Financial World*, September 25, 1957.

decline in railway employment. There is some evidence that they have aggravated the problems in these industries.[9]

Thus far, legislation to prevent featherbedding has not been especially effective. One hope for its gradual decline is that big unions are beginning to realize that they are an integral part of big business. They share some of the problems of management. As unions accumulate pension funds and other cash assets, they must invest in revenue-providing securities, including common stocks. The profits on their common stocks depend on good management and a high level of productivity. More and more union officers who are entrusted with investment responsibilities are finding it necessary to consider the costs of featherbedding and production restricted by the unions.

Collective bargaining—contract negotiations

The negotiation of the contract in collective bargaining calls for high degrees of skill in human relations on the part of both the representatives of the company and of the union. To some, it is a process of "haggling," comparable to the bargaining in an oriental bazaar. The best price offered by the dealer at the outset is not his best price at the end of the last bargaining session.

In modern collective bargaining between the larger unions and companies, the business agent of the national or international organization negotiates the contract. He works full time at this, negotiates day in and day out, and is usually of an alert aggressive character. Business agents of this caliber receive salaries that compare very favorably with or exceed the salaries of company executives.[10]

Negotiating is no longer for the man who comes off a machine to sit at a bargaining table once every few years. In big union negotiations as in the automotive industry, economic and other specialists back up the teams of both sides. Experts are hired as consultants.

In some cases the dealings between the company and the union are approached in a legalistic manner. More often, they become similar to the last days of a hot political campaign.

Pitfalls that an experienced company negotiator avoids are:

1. *Smugness.* Representatives of labor unions are typically quick to resent any implications of their social or other inadequacies.
2. *A show of undue concern.* If management is scared at the start, the opposition can capitalize their defensiveness.

[9]See Herbert R. Northrup, "Plain Facts About Featherbedding," *Personnel,* American Management Association, Inc., July–August 1958, pp. 54, 55.

[10]For further information, see *The Management Review,* American Management Association, Inc., January 1955, p. 61.

3. *Personality conflict at the bargaining table.* If two or more persons there hate each other before the sessions begin, the negotiations will tend to accentuate the hostility. One or both parties should withdraw tactfully by claiming that his presence is needed elsewhere.[11]

The negative aspects are, of course, less significant than the positive as summarized in the following recommendations:

Collective bargaining is not an isolated event to be treated like a David Harum horse trade. It is a way of life—a way of living with the employees upon whose services you rely and with the union of their choice . . . resign yourself to the idea that you will have nothing better than a cold war, with only the hope of intermittent peaceful coexistence, if your labor relations are not well managed.

And since dealing with unions is a continuing job for management, I'd like to make some suggestions that may be useful in establishing sound labor relations.

1. Earn a good reputation with your employees so that you may bring it with you to the bargaining table. . . . I am speaking of a reputation for firmness, a demonstrated willingness to fight for your rights, together with a reputation for open-mindedness, reasonableness, truthfulness, trustworthiness and a decent respect for your fellow man at every level. . . .
2. Your representatives should be able to take advantage of your good reputation without soiling it. Be sure that they understand human nature. Brilliant men who quickly step on the toes of anyone who steps on theirs are not necessarily helpful in the long run. . . .
3. Never let your bargaining team forget that the union bargaining team has its own internal political problems.[12]

Employees respect firm leadership

Unions are constantly arguing for and demanding more privileges. There is no end to what they ask for when they know that they have a management that thinks in defensive terms only. Conversely, they will respect firm management.

[11]See Andrew J. Dalton, Jr., "Learn How to Deal with Organized Workers," *The Office,* November 1956, pp. 140, 224–26.

[12]Walter Gordon Merritt, from an address before the National Industrial Conference Board. Reported in *Management Record,* August 1955. See also *The Management Review,* American Management Association, Inc., April 1955, p. 257.

This firmness does not imply that management may use the same verbal tactics that are used by a union. A union representative or editor of a union journal may call a company president various vile names. The president, however, may not retaliate in kind. If he were to use the same language, no matter how great the provocation, he would lose the respect of the employees. He is in the same position as the lady shopper who is reviled by a fishwife—the fishwife can use that kind of language and remain a fishwife but the lady cannot use the fishwife's language and remain a lady! Similarly, union leaders may use language and tactics that are "out-of-bounds" for management. This limitation does not, however, mean that management cannot be firm in holding to those principles in which management believes.

Positive approaches to union relations

Most managements of unionized plants try to develop and maintain constructive relations with their unions. They realize that labor peace in the sense of absolute freedom from conflict is not possible. They do try to keep the conflict within reasonable bounds. Thus far, their best hope for doing so lies in maintaining a balance of power between management and union. Theoretically, this calls for men of mature leadership on both sides. Practically, that cannot be expected. It is up to management therefore to achieve on its own part the highest level of participative leadership it is capable of bringing about. Certainly, dealings with labor problems require the same executive strength and competence as do all other aspects of managerial responsibility. There are no solutions of the "quick tricks" or "gimmick" variety.

The employer who is experienced in union relations tends to develop certain helpful policies and procedures such as the following:

He gives full recognition to the union collective bargaining status. He wants the union to know that he fully accepts the union as the spokesman and voice of the employees on matters of wages, hours, and working conditions.

He does not compete with the union for the loyalty of its employees. Employees can be loyal to both the employer and the union for certain relationships.

He works with rather than around the union in the field of employee communications. He does not try to outmaneuver the union in getting a message across to employees. He works out with the union an agreement on channels of communication.

When possible, he tries to anticipate conflicts between the company and the union. In a few corporations, union contracts have been settled by advance discussions. Bargainable conflicts were handled as they arose instead of waiting until the contract was about to expire.[13]

He recognizes that the union is a political organization and that at times union officials will do certain things simply because it is politically expedient for them.

The wise employer separates the areas of conflict from the many non-conflicting interests between management and labor. In some relationships such as contract negotiations, grievance procedures, and arbitration, the interests of the union and the company are frequently at cross-purposes. In others, there is little or no conflict of interests, as in dealing with production problems, office methods, and marketing. Certain union leaders may be fanatical about the union, but most employees are mature, reasonable people who want to participate in the company's growth. Management should concentrate on earning their goodwill.

QUESTIONS ON THE CHAPTER

1. Why is it often difficult for management men to view unions objectively?

2. In what ways may a strong union rather than a weak union be preferred by management?

3. List some of the reasons why workers join unions. What are the main functions of unions to the workers as they see them?

4. Describe the role of the union leader who is rebelling against authority.

5. In labor-management relations, what problem and remedy did Imberman suggest? What problem would his remedy involve for union leaders?

6. Who are the most ardent and the least ardent supporters of unions among the membership?

7. What is the implication of the statement that unions are *not* a great social movement?

8. What is the relation between the seniority provisions of union contracts and "bumping?"

9. Define the term "featherbedding." Give examples.

10. What positive aspects of collective bargaining are experienced company negotiators concerned with?

11. What is meant by management rights in employer-union relations?

12. Describe management's positive approaches to union relations.

13. Of all the ideas in the chapter, which ones were of special interest to you?

[13]See "Noncrisis Bargaining Trend Is Spreading," *Industrial Relations News*, July 27, 1963.

14. What did the chapter contribute toward future relations with (a) the men who supervise you, (b) the employees whom you may supervise?

PROBLEMS AND PROJECTS

For All Students

1. Review some of the available literature on unions. Try to evaluate each writer as to his bias or objectivity. Which statements in the text, in the light of other published information, would you modify?
2. Interview several persons who belong to unions. Ask each why he belongs, the amount of the dues and fees, the extent of his activity at meetings, the quality of the leadership, the union's problems with management, and so on.

For Advanced Students

3. Make a study of arbitration, state and federal mediators, and related topics. Study arbitrators' actions in conflict situations. Consider the fact that arbitrators leave the situation when it has been resolved.
4. Make a study of the kinds of economic data published by unions. Do the economists who are not in the trade union circles tend to pay much attention to the data put out by unions? To what extent is it likely to be biased or objective?

For Men in Business

5. Describe some of the union activities that you have experienced. Did the experiences increase or decrease your respect for the unions or unionism? Why?
6. When a foremanship is given to a union steward, how does the company gain or lose by the typical selection of a union leader? What are the possible effects on the union?
7. From your own experiences with unions or from published literature about unions, evaluate the extent that certain unions pursue policies that benefit unions rather than society as a whole. Which unions have a laudable sense of social responsibility? Do unions participate in community service organizations such as Red Cross?

COLLATERAL READINGS

For All Students

Labor and Management Face the Future, Personnel Series No. 172, American Management Association, Inc., 1957, is an example of the kinds of reports on labor problems that are available. Ask for this and other reports.

Miles, Raymond E., and J. B. Ritchie, "Leadership Attitudes Among Union Officials," *Industrial Relations*, October 1968.

For Advanced Students

Chalmers, W. Ellison, et. al., *Labor-Management Relations in Illini City: I, The Case Studies; II, Explorations in Comparative Analysis.* Champaign: Institute of Labor and Industrial Relations, University of Illinois, 1954. Especially helpful to the social scientist who is interested in research in labor and management relations.

Steiber, Jack, ed., *U.S. Industrial Relations: The Next Twenty Years.* East Lansing, Mich.: Michigan State University Press, 1958. Presents six forecasts by leaders. Evaluations, interpretations, and analyses are given. Evaluate the forecasts in the light of events since the forecasts were made.

For Men in Business

Goodfellow, Matthew, "Is Unionization Inevitable," *Automation*, March 1969. Any program to prevent unionization must start by recognizing that union success in organizing a given plant is not inevitable. Often it is management's negligence that results in unionization of plant employees.

Ross, Arthur M., "Distressed Grievance Procedures and Their Rehabilitation," *Labor Arbitration and Industrial Change*, Proceedings of the Sixteenth Annual Meeting of the National Academy of Arbitrators, ed. Mark L. Kahn, Bureau of National Affairs, Inc., 1963, Series I.

The Interview,
with Examples of
Good Interviewing

SITUATIONS YOU ARE LIKELY TO MEET

How would you meet each of these situations:
   a. *Before* you have read the chapter? What would
      you say to yourself or to the individual?
   b. *After* you have read the chapter? How have
      your answers changed?

1. A friend is reading a Sunday newspaper article about
   the meanings of various bodily movements and gestures. He reads that "scratching and rubbing the
   nose" indicate feelings of hostility and that the individual may be difficult to get along with.
   What would you say about the statement?
2. You apply for a job with a company for which you
   would like to work in order to develop your ability in
   a certain field. The interviewer says that the sales of
   the company are so good that he cannot give the
   time needed to train beginners—he can hire experienced men only.
   How would you answer him tactfully but effectively?
3. A businessman says that he believes in trusting people. Most people are fundamentally honest, he
   claims. As an example, he accepts a job applicant's
   statements about his pay rate on previous jobs with
   other companies.
   How would you react to his hiring policy?

The interview may be defined as a purposeful conversational exchange of ideas between two or more persons. It is, however, more than a social conversation; it is a conversation having a serious purpose. In business, its typical purposes are for hiring an employee, for obtaining information as in credit arrangements, for learning unconscious motives as in motivation research, for counseling the employee as in the post-appraisal or merit rating of an employee, and for discovering the reasons why an employee quits his job.

The interview is an important tool in the daily work of the personnel man and of the professional member in the fields of journalism, psychiatry, and diplomacy. Almost everyone conducts and participates in numerous varieties of interviews. In business and management, the interview is so essential to effective human relations that many of its frequent users realize that they do not conduct it as effectively as they would like. One of the characteristics of the good interviewer is humility. Many people who do interviewing erroneously imagine that they are competent interviewers.

They fail to appreciate that an interview may last only minutes or a few hours. And yet, the interviewer is trying to understand a lifetime of past years and to predict the potentials of a stranger for the years ahead. All of which means that the interviewer should approach his task with humility and a desire to improve constantly his knowledge, skill, and judgment.

THE HIRING INTERVIEW

The man who does the hiring in a company contributes to the strength or weakness of the organization. If he hires strong applicants, the organization will tend to be strong. Conversely, if he hires weak people, the organization will be weak.

The employment interviewer must do far more than estimate abilities of applicants. He must also do a lot of screening to keep out persons who are drifters, troublemakers, seriously maladjusted mentally, epileptics, sexual deviates, and others who would be liabilities rather than assets. He must also know what kinds of persons mesh with the personality of each supervisor and his employees.

In the hiring interview, the main purpose is to evaluate the applicant's potentials for the vacant job, but an additional purpose is to forecast his behavior in relations with the other people who are involved in the job. The interviewer must forecast how they will react to him as a person. For this reason, the interview may be called a test of acceptability in human relations. It provides a basis for judging not only job skills but also the two persons, the employer (or his representatives) and the applicant, and how well they will get along with each other.

The incompetent interviewer often fails to get correct information and to make sound estimates of abilities and social characteristics because he is too easily influenced by an impressive personal appearance and glibness in oral expression. More basic facts about the applicant go unobserved or are overlooked.

The halo error

The halo effect to which all interviewers are to some extent subject is the tendency to accept an overall impression, either favorable or unfavorable. If we like a person, that liking casts its light over all his qualities. If we dislike him, that shadow envelops all his traits. Friends are viewed as superior in many characteristics, and enemies as inferior to a greater extent than they deserve. The interviewee frequently does or says something that causes us to see every other fact about him in accordance with the one outstanding impression. If he has some unusual ability as in art, music, mathematics, even crossword puzzle solving, we tend to overestimate his intelligence and probable competence for activities that are unrelated to the special skill.

Usually the interviewer gets scanty information, and he naturally fills in the gaps from the halo effect. He tends to assume that the applicant who is neat in appearance will also do neat work and come to work on time. The applicant who is good-looking, well dressed, and glib-tongued is often overrated. The homely person is likely to be underestimated as to his abilities. Instead of letting the halo effect influence us, each factor should be interpreted in terms of its specific value for the job under consideration. The interviewer should keep in mind the old saying: "You can't judge a book by its cover." Actually, good employees vary in appearance, size, age, education, and racial background. Generalizations to many factors cannot be made safely from one.

The mechanic who is reserved in manner during the interview may or may not be nonaggressive in performing mechanical work in the factory. Indeed, many skilled craftsmen are not socially aggressive during the hiring interview. The main value of knowing one's natural tendency toward generalization is to stimulate us to do further questioning. Research studies of interviewing indicate that many people tend to judge from key words or actions, inferring, for instance, superior traits about those labeled as "warm" as compared with those labeled as "cold."

Personal bias

Almost every person has certain likes, dislikes, and preferences which he in his better moments recognizes as unjustified. No one can escape all prejudices. Any distinctive feature of a good or poor applicant is likely to carry over to later applicants. This applies to such features as having a mustache, wearing a bow tie, having red hair, wearing a pink shirt, or any personal characteristic.

Investigations indicate that college students as well as interviewers have some tendency to be influenced in their estimates by incidental physical factors of appearance, such as the wearing of glasses. Wearing glasses tends to cause students to rate the wearer as more intelligent and more industrious, but not more honest.[1] The applicant who fails to get a job because of a simple personal characteristic should not lose faith in human beings. Instead, he should recognize that we are all "human," and that the same feature that caused one employer to turn him down may be the very feature that causes another employer to hire him.

One variety of bias, usually more important than simple personal characteristics, is directed toward the applicant's previous experience. If he has worked for a certain competitor, that may be a definite plus or minus for him. On the positive side, many employers like to hire men who have worked on certain jobs in companies that are known for the excellent training they give their employees. Some forward-looking college seniors know this. They take their first jobs with companies that offer relatively low pay but give especially good training in order that they may later move to other firms at an extra high rate of pay because of their training.

Some interviewers prefer college graduates who have been out of college for several years. They have done enough floundering by that time to be willing to work. Besides they may have learned how to work. Of course if an applicant is a recent college graduate and the last one hired from his college was a success or a failure, the applicant is likely to be evaluated in terms of the predecessor.

Some interviewers believe that young single men succeed better than young married men on the assumption that the young married man is either

---

[1] G. R. Thornton, "Effects of Wearing Glasses upon Judgments of Traits," *Journal of Applied Psychology* (American Psychological Association, Inc.), June 1944, p. 207.

too greatly interested in his wife to study his job or overly anxious to buy his young wife gadgets that they can't afford.

Beliefs such as these are the results of a few dramatic instances. Many are without sound statistical basis.

Prejudices creep into interviews that are supposed to be so systematic as to overcome subjective influences. In one famous study, the research man made an analysis of the findings of twelve trained interviewers as to the cause of the downfall of two thousand vagrants who had applied for free lodging. The interviews were standardized, but different investigators obtained different results. One interviewer who believed in socialism reported that 39 percent of the vagrants were down and out because of industrial conditions, and 22 percent because of excessive use of alcohol. Another interviewer, an ardent opponent of alcohol, attributed but 7 percent of the failures to industrial and economic conditions and 62 percent to drink. Prejudices were even more significantly revealed when we note that, according to the socialist, the *vagrants themselves* gave as the cause of their downfall: industrial conditions, 60 percent; drink 11 percent. But according to the prohibitionist, the *vagrants themselves* blamed industrial conditions in 42.5 percent and drink in 34 percent of the cases. Obviously, each interviewer influenced the interviewees to give answers in line with his own biases.[2]

When employment procedures are biased or faulty, labor turnover

Requiring applicants for salesmen's jobs to bring the wife along for the interview has been burlesqued by the cartoonist of a London newspaper. Note the applicant who gets the job!
Reproduced by permission of the *Daily Express*, London, England.

[2]See S. A. Rice, "Contagious Bias in the Interview," *American Journal of Sociology*, Vol. 35, 1929, 420–23.

costs are increased. Estimates of these costs vary considerably. One researcher estimated that every time an executive says "Good-bye" to an employee who quits, the cost to the average company is $482. The costs for hiring and training a new salesman in one industry were estimated as $7,000–$8,000 and above $10,000 for engineers and scientists. These figures do not include the additional costs of lost production or sales.[3]

The illusion of previous experience. Most employment men tend to assume that the applicant who has had previous experience on a similar job is bound to be a better employee than another applicant who may have superior potentialities but lacks experience. When a secretary is desired, the interviewer usually chooses the applicant who claims secretarial experience in preference to the stenographer, who may actually be brighter and more competent.

Previous experience should be considered in relation to other pertinent factors, but it is not, of itself, a guarantee of ability to do good work. Experience in mediocrity can continue for years before an employee seeks another job. This is indicated by the many instances of interviewer overevaluation of ability on the part of applicants who are hired mainly because of previous experience and then prove to be low-level workers. Hiring done on the basis of previous experience is more likely to result in perpetuating inferior performance than in improving the caliber of the staff.

Insisting on a duplication of ourselves is often called "projection." The interviewer has a tendency to put his own value system into the rating situation, to assume that only a duplicate of the interviewer can be successful. He prefers applicants who match his own age, appearance, manner, voice, and background. The applicant who deviates from his patterns is labeled as undesirable. As one writer stated: "This error can cause more harm to an organization than almost any other error; it tends to produce a homogeneity which often leads to mediocrity."

There is, however, an old saying among personnel men: "Each interviewer has a tendency to choose persons who are either similar to or the opposite of himself." Certainly, an interviewer's selections are greatly influenced by his images of himself and by his own psychological needs (see Chapter 24).

Practices that improve the interview

Any person who wants to become a trained interviewer can do so by means of special college courses, special institute courses for interviewers, and books. The material presented here has been chosen to show the need

[3]Frederick J. Gaudet, "Manpower Wastage," *Mechanical Engineering*, July 1963.

for training, not to provide that training. Practices that improve interviewing are known and can be acquired by the intelligent practitioner.

The good interviewer has a plan in his mind, a basic framework for his thinking, before he talks to an applicant. He knows the kind of information he wants and the techniques he intends to use to obtain it. This framework is developed from systematic training in the social sciences, particularly psychology. He has a background for interpreting the information that he obtains. He is a pattern-minded interpreter of what he hears, sees, and knows. He looks for patterns in the educational and occupational history that indicate growth rather than a series of erratic changes in courses and jobs. Also, he develops his skill in stimulating an applicant to talk freely. He tends to follow practices such as the following:

1. He puts the applicant at ease. He himself has a relaxed, cheerful manner. If the applicant is obviously tense, the interviewer may give him time to pull himself together by picking up the application blank and saying: "Do you mind if I look at this so that I need not ask you questions that you have answered on the application form?" He reduces the tension by purposely asking a question that makes the applicant feel a bit better informed than the interviewer. The question may deal with some fact about the applicant's hometown, college attended, or previous employer.

2. He asks many open-end questions, especially in the early stages of the interview. Direct questions are avoided. Instead of saying, "Did you like college?" he may phrase his question in a less directive manner as, "Tell me about your college and the courses you took there." After the applicant has answered the inquiry, the interviewer can elicit further revealing responses by saying, "Tell me, how do you now feel about your college education?"

When open-end questions do not elicit all the information that appears to be pertinent, the interviewer asks questions of a specific nature, such as,

"I like your looks Gillis . . . you're hired!"

Source: by Homer Reprinted from *Commerce Magazine*, published by the Chicago Association of Commerce and Industry.

"In the last job you held, what did you do? Please describe a typical day's work."

3. The effective interviewer listens. He gives the impression that he is interested and unhurried. He pauses for at least a few seconds after the applicant has seemingly finished his answer before he asks any more questions. He gives the applicant a chance to talk further. When the applicant stops talking, the interviewer asks questions about the last statements made, but he tries to keep the conversation moving in the direction of more complete information. He may also ask questions that reveal the applicant's level of aspiration such as "What kind of job do you think you should have to give you chances to develop your abilities?" "Tell me some of the things you liked better about your last job than about the one before the last"; and "In what ways do you think that you improved your opportunities when you changed from the second last to the last job?"

4. The good interviewer avoids or asks few questions of the following kinds:

(a) Questions that can be answered yes or no.

(b) Questions that invariably elicit the same answer from all applicants. *Example*:"Do you usually come to work on time?"

(c) Embarrassing questions that compel the applicant to defend a statement or admit an error in an earlier statement.

(d) Leading questions, such as: "You finished high school, did you?" "Would you be willing to work in an office where most employees are much older than you are?" "Were you a stenographer or a secretary on your last job?" and, "Don't you agree that this is a good company to work for?"

5. The good interviewer carries on a conversation that enables the applicant to state his job preferences and to express his feelings. He does not dominate the interview but encourages the applicant to describe his preferences, abilities, and inabilities. This kind of two-way conversation with a purpose means that the interviewer's statements consume less than 50 percent of the interviewing time, preferably less than 25 percent.

6. A great deal of the information obtained is in the nature of clues rather than facts. Clues are in the form of gestures, voice inflections, and avoidance of certain topics.

Every alert interviewer notices the applicant's appearances and gestures. These behavioral signs may or may not be significant. If, for example, a young man wears a beard, does it indicate that he has deep-seated need to feel recognized as an individual? It may or it may not, but it certainly suggests that the known facts in his development should be reviewed in order to note whether that hypothesis is confirmed. At any rate, the interviewer has a right to wonder why he chose a sign of individuality such as the growing of a beard rather than the development in himself of some ability having intrinsic value.

Does the careless appearance of the woman who obviously "tosses on" her clothes signify that she has given up the hope of making herself attractive, does she suffer from an emotional problem that is too great for her to solve, or does it mean that she is so deeply interested in her professional work that her appearance is incidental to her? Only further review of her developmental history is likely to indicate the significance of the lack of normal grooming.

When a person folds his arms firmly and quickly, is he outwardly expressing his inner hostility to the interviewer as a person or to what the interviewer symbolizes?

When the applicant is asked a question and he passes his hand over his face or covers his eyes, is he trying to avoid giving the answer that he feels is correct? Or is he trying to give a better phrasing of the correct answer?

When the applicant leans forward toward the interviewer, does it mean that he is doing so spontaneously or is he doing it consciously in a studied manner to make a favorable impression?

What do such clues or hypotheses really mean? What is the context of the clues? Little research has been done to answer these questions. However, one noteworthy study of the validity of specific clues was made of interviews conducted for the purpose of distinguishing between successful foremen and workers of equal technical skill who had been judged incapable of successfully supervising others. The relatively few significant conditions that occurred more frequently among the capable men were:

Good attitude toward early associates.
More than twenty years' experience in the company.

In contrast, items found more frequently among those believed to be incapable of supervising others were:

Restless movements in the interview.
Repetition of one or more subjects in school.
Self-conscious manner in the interview.
Tense or strained facial expression in interview.
Low intensity of voice during interview.[4]

Interview information that is based only on "face validity," that is, rapport between interviewer and interviewee, should be verified. Relative levels of invalidity of interview data are related to pressures of social de-

[4]Carroll Leonard Shartle, "A Clinical Approach to Foremanship," *Personnel Journal*, Vol. 13, No. 3, 1934, 137. See also Ralph F. Berdie, "Psychological Processes in the Interview," *The Journal of Social Psychology*, Vol. 18, 1943, 28.

sirability and ego involvement. Purportedly factual data of importance should be checked.[5]

Several researchers of the Industrial Relations Center, University of Minnesota, made a study of the validity of work histories obtained by interview. The work histories that had been obtained by means of structured interviews with 325 individuals were checked with former employers. Of eleven work history items studied, only three items showed validity of more than 70 percent, and on four items, 40 percent or more of the interview information was *in*valid. The most valid information was reported for separation and hours, the least valid for pay items. The upgrading type of error occurred more often than the downgrading type. "Social desirability appeared to be an important influence in the distortions."[6] These and other influences indicate the need for verifying the information obtained by interview.

Some of the best studies of the significance of gestures and body movements have been done in the fields of psychotherapy research. In one series of research studies of selected gestures and body movements of psychiatric patients during intake interviews, certain autistic gestures were often interpreted as indicated by these examples:

a. Rubs or touches nose—attitude of contempt, disgust, negative feelings.
b. Scratching self—inhibition of aggression.
c. Finger-mouth contact—oral erotic needs and gratifications.
d. Rubs self—tension reduction.

Many psychotherapists note such gestures and body movements in their interviews with patients and think of them as nonverbal behavior that may have a signaling or communicative function. It must, however, be considered in terms of some larger conceptual framework of thinking on the part of the interviewer. An outstanding research study in this field was made by George F. Mahl.[7] His report presents an enlightening summary of characteristic gestures, acts, and body positions; inferred personality characteristics; and relevant clinical data concerning thirteen patients. An important benefit to the layman who reads such a report is that he learns

[5]David J. Weiss and Rene V. Dawis, "An Objective Evaluation of Factual Interview Data," *Journal of Applied Psychology*, December 1960.

[6]David J. Weiss, Rene V. Dawis, George W. England, and Lloyd H. Lofquist, "Validity of Work Histories Obtained by Interview," Minnesota Studies in Vocational Rehabilitaion: XII, Industrial Relations Center, University of Minnesota, 1961, pp. 1–2.

[7]George F. Mahl, "Gestures and Body Movements in Interviews," *Research in Psychotherapy*, Vol. III, 1968.

he should not attempt to utilize such nonverbal cues in his interviewing unless he first acquires adequate theoretical and clinical training.

Interviewers need the benefit of more research studies essential to improvement of interview validity. We know that *expressions of emotion are dictated by the culture* and clues to feelings vary with the cultural background of the individual. To us, the clenched fist indicates anger, but it has a friendly meaning to some people of the world.

When a Chinese fiction character sticks out his tongue it means surprise—not what the small American boy means by the same gesture.

However, expressions of emotion that depend upon involuntary action of the body mechanisms are likely to be interpreted alike in the East and in the West.

"Every one of his hairs stood on end." "A cold sweat broke forth," and "His face was red and he went creeping alone outside the village" are understood in any land.

The good interviewer asks for facts and records that improve his interpretations of clues whenever possible. Then he tries to note relationships between clues and verifiable facts. He asks himself, "What kind of pattern of growth or decline in ability is evident from the facts?"; "When and why did the applicant change the direction of his growth or decline?"; and "Does he have the kinds of potentials needed for the job?"

NONDIRECTIVE INTERVIEWING

This kind of employment interview stems from the nondirective counseling interview developed by Carl R. Rogers and his disciples.[8]

The nondirective technique is well known to psychotherapists but is not as yet widely used in industry. The interviewer says little but concentrates his efforts on encouraging the interviewee to tell his own story in his own words. The interviewer listens closely and analyzes the interviewee's words, gestures, expressions, and meanings, both as to content and as to implication. The nondirective interviewer tries to keep the applicant talking by giving his entire attention to the applicant, by not interrupting or changing the subject abruptly, by using few questions, and by allowing pauses in the conversation.

One goal of a job applicant is to find out as much as he can about the job and then to present himself in the most favorable light for the job. The nondirective interviewer tells the candidate only as much about the job as is necessary. Only after the applicant's history has been thoroughly

---

[8]Carl R. Rogers, *Counseling and Psychotherapy* (Boston: Houghton Mifflin, 1942).

covered is job information given. A typical indirect interview usually begins with a generalized questions such as, "Tell me, Mr. Blank, how did you happen to get interested in coming in here to see us?" This kind of question is so general that each person has a tendency to talk about the things and feelings important to him, such as a desire to get away from a certain supervisor, to work where transportation to and from the place of employment is easier, to have a chance to advance, and so on. If the applicant is merely shopping, that fact too is likely to be expressed.

The nondirective interview does require special training and preparation. It must be conducted with care. If the interviewer knows a great deal about an applicant beforehand, he can alert himself to listen for the things he needs to know.

Responses should be brief and should refer to the applicant's interests or feelings. It is often helpful to repeat the last few words of the applicant's statement, make a short comment, or ask a brief question, such as:

"Tell me more."

"That's interesting."

"What were the circumstances?"

"What happened then?"

"Exciting, wasn't it?"

". . . until 11:00 P.M.?"

"You say, 'It's not worth the effort'?"

"H-hm."[9]

Even though the nondirective interviewer appears to function in a completely unguided manner, he actually structures the interview to some extent. Furthermore, his final evaluation of the applicant is usually modified by findings from home visits and investigations of school and employer references.

Of course the interviewer must be a good listener and sincerely interested in what the other person is saying.

He keeps his own emotions out of the interview.

He does not question the factual accuracy, inaccuracy, "rightness" or "wrongness" of statements, but he looks beyond the surface of expression for what the interviewee does not or cannot tell, as well as what he tells.

[9]N. A. Moyer, "Non-Directive Employment Interviewing," *Personnel*, American Management Association, Inc., March 1948, and "Using the Non-Directive Interview," *Supervisory Management*, June 1957, pp. 28–29. Also *Personnel Management Abstracts*, Autumn Issue, Vol. III, 1957.

EXECUTIVE INTERVIEWS

The good executive delegates responsibilities but must also keep himself informed about the progress being made. To get correct information from subordinates, he must be able to talk with them in a manner that does not cause feelings of threat. If the subordinate feels threatened by his superior's questions, he will not give complete answers. Too often the executive says to himself: "Everybody covered himself, and I learned very little. I know it's always tough to talk to the boss, but I've got to know what the problems really are before I can help my men solve them." The skilled executive learns to use the permissive or nondirective type of interviewing technique to get all the facts necessary for his effective guidance of operations. He needs accurate information to do his decision making.

Robert L. Kahn and Charles F. Cannell, Survey Research Center, University of Michigan, have given some examples of the benefits to the executive of the indirect technique as applied to a vice-president's inquiry of the production manager as to why a good customer has not been getting deliveries on schedule:

Suppose, after the introductory statement by the vice president, the production manager replies by saying: "Well, I think the main problem is that new die-casting procedure of ours hasn't really shaken down yet. You know conversion from sand-molding to die-casting really calls for a lot of changes and adjustments all along the line."

What should the executive-interviewer do next in order to increase the respondent's intrinsic motivation to communicate? Below are three possible rejoinders by the executive, along with the subordinate's probable reaction to each.

1. *Interviewer*: Well, let's not blame all our problems on a technical change, Bill. Changes like that one have been made successfully in thousands of plants.

   Subordinate: (to himself) The boss won't believe the truth when he hears it. O.K., I'll give him the kind of story he's looking for. Better watch out, though. Sounds as if he's trying to pin this one on me.

Another possible rejoinder by the executive is less threatening but has its own problems:

2. *Interviewer*: Bill, I'm only surprised that you're not in more trouble in the manufacturing department. You've been doing a marvelous job down there. I think your approach to this conversion is just terrific, and I want you to know I appreciate it.

   Subordinate: (to himself) Gosh, if everything's going so doggone

---

HOW GOOD AN INTERVIEWER ARE YOU?

What are the rules for conducting a successful executive interview? Test yourself by answering the following true-or-false questions, then check the answer panel on page 348.

	True	*False*
1. Wording questions in advance interferes with the spontaneity needed for successful executive interviewing.	——	——
2. Thinking about what you should have said after an interview is over is probably a neurotic waste of time.	——	——
3. If you are doing a good job of supervision, you have no need for special information-getting techniques.	——	——
4. A subordinate will give only information that he thinks will please the boss.	——	——
5. A subordinate never gets much satisfaction out of being interviewed by the boss.	——	——
6. The best way for the boss to get good information from an employee is to talk to him outside the office.	——	——
7. An executive learns the most when the employee does not even realize that he is being interviewed.	——	——
8. The good interviewer listens well and avoids directing the conversation.	——	——
9. The interviewer learns most by sometimes putting the respondent on the defensive.	——	——
10. The best way to get information from an employee is to convince him that you are meeting on an equal basis—that you are both just employees of the same firm.	——	——

SOURCE: Robert L. Kahn and Charles F. Cannell, "Nobody Tells Me Anything!" *Dun's Review and Modern Industry*, November 1957, p 37. Copyright © 1957 by Dun & Bradstreet Publications Corporation.

great, what am I doing here? Things aren't as good as the boss seems to think. Does he really believe what he's saying, or is he stringing me along? Either way, he's making it awfully tough for me to tell him what some of the real problems are.

For a more constructive alternative, consider the following:

3. *Interviewer*: Well, I can understand those die-casting problems. Changing manufacturing procedure always causes some difficul-

ties. Can you fill me in a little more on the kind of troubles you're having?

Subordinate: (to himself) I guess he's not going to put me on the spot, anyway. He seems to have some idea how tough these conversions can be. Maybe I can even get some help.

How do these three alternative approaches by the executive-interviewer measure up in the light of our criteria for developing intrinsic motivation? The first approach is openly threatening. It subjects the subordinate to immediate pressure, strongly implying inadequate performance on his part. The second approach appears to be more satisfactory: It meets the superficial "human relations" requirements. But as a method of getting information it isn't likely to work. The subordinate will evaluate his burst of praise in one of two ways. If it is insincere, the boss is merely trying to make him feel good. If it is sincere, he must live up to the image of impossible perfection the boss has painted. Far from stimulating frank communication, the boss has only made it more difficult for the subordinate to confess to problems or inadequacies.

Contrast these two approaches with the last alternative. Here the executive makes no evaluative judgment, either good or bad. Instead, his statement implies that he can understand the subordinate's difficulties and that he is interested in learning more about the nature of the problem. His subordinate concludes that the boss is genuinely interested and can accept the existence of problems without looking for a scapegoat. Because the subordinate does not need to be defensive or prove himself, he can communicate more freely and accurately. As the vice president continues to develop this type of relationship, barriers are removed and positive motivation to communicate is increased.[10]

EXIT INTERVIEWS

Some personnel managers conduct an interview with each employee who leaves or wishes to leave the company. Purposes of exit interviews are to keep good employees from resigning, build better public relations with former employees, clear up petty misunderstandings, spot faulty administration or supervision, and discover and overcome morale problems. Even

[10]Robert L. Kahn and Charles F. Cannell, "Nobody Tells Me Anything!" *Dun's Review and Modern Industry*, November 1957, pp. 99–101. Copyright © 1957 by Dun & Bradstreet Publications Corporation. These two authors have written a very helpful volume: *The Dynamics of Interviewing* (New York: John Wiley & Sons, Inc., 1957). As in most communications processes, we have in the interview two people, each trying to influence the other and each actively accepting or rejecting influence attempts.

though they are one-sided because they reflect only the feelings of an employee when he is leaving a job, they still help to indicate the attitudes of many workers who are staying with the company.

One investigator made a study of 125 employees who resigned during one year from a research laboratory. It was found that 90 percent of the professional workers who were quitting already had other positions. Only 50 percent of the nonprofessional workers had another job waiting for them.

Both professionals and nonprofessionals were concerned about "Opportunities for advancement," but many more nonprofessionals expressed it as a cause for leaving. "Pay not commensurate with work" was listed as the second major cause for quitting by nonprofessionals. The professional men, on the other hand, were more concerned with the "Accomplishments of your work unit" and the "Importance of your work."

Neither group felt that their abilities were being utilized enough, but almost twice as many professionals felt this as others. They were also three times more critical of the supervision they received than the nonprofessional workers.[11]

"You can't quit! You're the only one who knows how to shut this thing off."
Source: by Porges. Courtesy *Today's Health.*

[11]See Robert D. Melcher, "Getting the Facts on Employee Resignations: An Exit Interview Program," *Personnel,* American Management Association, Inc., May 1955.

When a supervisor is asked, "Do your workers have enough to do?" the usual answer is, "Of course they have." Yet a study by University of Illinois researchers indicated that one of the reasons for quitting is that some employees do not have enough work to keep them busy. Out of 2,713 persons who quit their jobs, 415 answered a questionnaire that included questions about the climate in which they worked and reasons for quitting. Answers to questions about the work load indicated that 19 percent felt that the load was too heavy and 9 percent felt that it was too light. "It will be no surprise to most employers that 19 percent of his employees feel that the work load is too heavy, but it will be a surprise to many to learn that one out of 10 who quits feels that he is not kept busy enough."[12]

The exit interview is a very difficult interview for both the interviewer and the interviewee. An employee who quits is likely to be under some emotional stress. He is leaving old friends and has many uncertainties about the future even though he has been hired for another job. The causes for his decision to quit have been the result of several cumulative influences: resentment of the pay, treatment by supervisors, limited chances for advancement, and so on. As a result, the quitting employee does not always state the true reasons for his leaving—he still wants the old employer to speak favorably of him when a future prospective employer investigates his record.

Obviously, the exit interview must be conducted with considerable skill if it is to elicit valid and truly useful information. One of the most effective techniques for the purpose is the nondirective approach.

Two examples of the nondirective approach, as contrasted with the directive method, are shown below.

Traditional Directive Approach

I–1 Well, Mary, you're leaving today, I hear.

E–1 Yes, I am. My mother is sick and I have to take care of her.

I–2 I'm sorry to learn that. I hope she'll be better soon.

E–2 Thank you. I do, too.

I–3 But don't you think you could have given us a little more notice? I understand your mother has been ailing for some time. It's not as though she had been taken ill all of a sudden.

E–3 I would have liked to, but it just didn't work out that way.

I–4 Well, you know the company expects you to give adequate notice when you leave. I don't think you're acting properly at all.

[12]Robert D. Loken, "Why They Quit" (University of Illinois, Bureau of Business Management, 1951).

E–4   Well, I'm sorry, but I couldn't work it out any other way.

I–5   All right, then. Good-bye and good luck.

E–5   Good-bye and thank you.

Non-Directive Approach

I–1   Come right in, Mary. This is your last day with the company, I see.

E–1   That's right. This is my last day here.

I–2   I understand from your supervisor that your mother is ill. I'm certainly sorry to hear that.

E–2   Yes, she's not feeling too well and I sure have my hands full these days.

I–3   Of course, with your mother ill there must be many more burdens on your shoulders.

E–3   You don't know the half of it. With mother out sick now, I've got to take care of the whole household—shopping, washing, ironing, cleaning—just about everything. I'm worn out, what with working here in the office until five and all the things I have to do at home.

I–4   That certainly doesn't leave you much time for anything else.

E–4   I would have given you a couple of days' notice if I weren't needed so badly at home.

I–5   Yes, I can see that as things are you weren't able to give much advance notice.

E–5   No. And besides you don't need me, anyway.

I–6   Oh, really?

E–6   Yes. If you ask me, I don't think anybody cares whether I stay here or not.

I–7   You feel you are not going to be missed at all.

E–7   That's just it. In my department, the supervisor leaves everything up to the assistant supervisor. And she's a part of the gang. They eat lunch together and since they all live in the same part of town, all they ever talk about is their boy friends.

I–8   That sort of leaves you out of things.

E–8   Yes, just because I live in a different neighborhood, they don't seem to care about me at all. They never ask me to come along for lunch, so I have to eat alone.

I–9   Eating all by yourself isn't much fun.

E–9   I'll say. After mother gets better, I'm going to find a job where the girls aren't so standoffish. I want to work with a bunch of friendly girls and not like it is here.

Traditional Directive Approach

I–1   So Bill, you've resigned, I hear.

E–1   Yes, I got a better job closer to home.

I–2   Better than your job here? What kind of a job is it?

E–2   Well, for one thing, there's more money.

I–3   More money than you're getting with us?

E–3   I'll say. You don't pay the going rate here.

I–4   I don't know how you can say that. Didn't you know that in the last wage survey of all the firms in this area our pay scale compared favorably with all the others?

E–4   Is that so? Well, I've got a friend with the Dalton Company doing the same kind of work as I'm doing and he gets twenty-three cents an hour more.

Non-Directive Approach

I–1   Hello Bill, I hear you've resigned your job.

E–1   Yes, I've found a better job closer to home.

I–2   That's interesting. Can you tell me a little more about it?

E–2   There's not much to say about it except that you pay such low wages here and I think I can get more pay elsewhere.

I–3   You feel that the pay scale here is not as high as it should be.

E–3   You're darn right. I've been doing work that's usually done by the boys in Grade 6, but I was just paid my old Grade 7 rate.

I–4   If a person does Grade 6 work, he should get Grade 6 pay.

E–4   That's what I told the foreman, but he said he couldn't do anything about it at that time. I spoke to him again a few weeks later and he said he would take care of it, but I guess he never got around to it.

I–5   You think the foreman should have taken the time to adjust your job grade.

E–5   Oh, he takes care of those boys that belong to his car pool, but the others he doesn't care about.[13]

The superiority of the nondirective approach in certain interviewing situations is self-evident, but the technique requires training and practice.

[13]Erwin Schoenfeld, "The Non-Directive Exit Interview," *Personnel*, American Management Association, Inc., November–December 1957, pp. 49, 50.

Any management that plans to use it should enlist the aid of specialists to instruct its interviewers and conduct the necessary practice sessions. A firm of management consultants who specialize in the training of interviewers may be used. The psychology or management department of a nearby college or university would also, in many cases, be able to render helpful advisory assistance.

Interviewing college seniors

One company in a recent year screened some twelve hundred students at twenty-two colleges and hired six. This suggests that college students should become acquainted with the procedures used by employment interviewers.

Each recruiter conducts his private meeting with seniors in different ways, but in general there are two main approaches. Some like to get right down to business, while others prefer a "bull session" first and business afterward. The reactions of the seniors showed that 57 percent prefer the "bull-session"-business formula, and 33 percent favor the "brass tacks" approach.[14]

When the seniors of one college were asked to rate the relative importance of certain factors in influencing their final decisions, they listed "promotion possibilities" and the "nature of the firm" as their first two considerations. "Starting salary" was third, and "extra benefits" was a poor fourth.

One of the most striking findings from the study was the prospects' impressions of the role played by the company representative, the interviewer. In answer to the question, "Did the appearance and manner of the interviewers convey to you any immediate impressions of their firms?" 81 percent of the applicants said yes. A frequent kind of comment was, "The company was generalized by the interviewer."

One student felt that the recruiters were looking for stereotypes. "I took a look at the interviewer," he said, "and thought, 'Am I like him, or could I be like him? Could I fit into the mold?" In many cases, it was obvious to them that they couldn't or didn't care to "fit into the mold." In fairness to the regular interviewers, it must be recognized that company men are pulled from their regular departments to fill in during the recruiting drive. When these are drawn from the higher echelons, students are likely to gain good impressions. Those drawn from the lower ranks of superfluous staff men and long-service failures are not so likely to know enough about the overall operations of the company to interview effectively.[15] Of all ap-

[14]"Agencies' Baffling Personnel Problems," *Tide*, August 23, 1957, p. 33; and Stanley E. Smith, "What Companies Get the College Boys—And How Do They Do It?" *Sales Management*, June 7, 1957, pp. 38–40.

[15]See Robert N. McMurry, "What's Wrong with College Recruiting?" *American Business* (The Dartnell Corporation), September 1958.

plicants, 94 percent rated the interviewer's style of presentation as important.

QUESTIONS ON THE CHAPTER

1. What is an interview and what are its purposes in business?
2. Name the several kinds of interviews treated in the chapter.
3. Explain the halo error.
4. Describe the Rice study of vagrants and what it signifies for interviewing.
5. List practices that improve the hiring interview.
6. What are the values of nondirective interviews? Describe principles or rules for its effective use.
7. What are the purposes of the exit interview? Why is it difficult to use effectively?
8. Under what conditions in a nondirective interview should the interviewer talk or ask questions?
9. What are two approaches that recruiters use when interviewing college seniors and which do the students prefer?
10. Of the several ideas presented in the chapter, which ones were of special interest or value to you?
11. What did the chapter contribute toward your future relations with (a) the men who supervise you, (b) the employees whom you may supervise?

> *Score yourself on the interviewing test, page 341, by counting one point for each "true" response. The perfect score is zero. In the opinion of the authors, every one of these ten statements is, in fact, incorrect.*

PROBLEMS AND PROJECTS

For All Students

1. Answer the questions on page 341. "How Good an Interviewer Are You?" Explain reasons for your answers. Also make a list of your bias tendencies and ask several friends to modify your list.
2. Do some role playing as an interviewer who is hiring college students on completion of their studies. Have the other students observe your procedures and make suggestions.

For Advanced Students

3. Get acquainted with the wide range of published material on the interview. Look for different varieties and purposes of the interview. Try to identify some of the patterns of thinking used by certain interviewers.

4. Make a special study of the nondirective interview and do some role playing with it. Note the extent to which you slip into directive procedures. Also try to make records, immediately after the interview, of what happened.

For Men in Business

5. Describe an executive whom you know and his characteristics that should be considered when applicants are hired to work under his direct supervision. What kinds of employees does he like? What kinds "get under his skin"?

6. Ask several persons in business to tell you about some failures in their interviewing. What did the interviewer fail to discover that was learned later and might have been caught in the interview?

COLLATERAL READINGS

For All Students

Hepner, Harry W., *Psychology Applied to Life and Work* (4th ed.). Englewood Cliffs, N.J.: Prentice-Hall, Inc., 1966. Chapter 15 treats the hiring interview, and Chapter 16 deals with the use of tests in hiring.

Leavitt, Harold J., and Louis R. Pondy, eds., *Readings in Managerial Psychology.* Chicago: The University of Chicago Press, 1964, pp. 157–73.

For Advanced Students

Ekman, Paul, and Wallace V. Friesen, "Nonverbal Leakage and Clues to Deception," *Psychiatry*, February 1969. Describes some of the research being done in finding out the extent that nonverbal behavior may escape efforts to deceive. Many interviewers note body movements and facial expression to supplement the interviewee's words. Edwin A. Fleishman, ed., *Studies in Personnel and Industrial Psychology.* Homewood, Ill.: The Dorsey Press, Inc., 1961, Chapters 1–3.

For Men in Business

Balinsky, Benjamin and Ruth Burger, *The Executive Interview.* New York: Harper & Row, Publishers, 1959. Presents examples of techniques in interviewing. Sample dialogues illustrate numerous principles.

Gilmer, B. von Haller, ed., *Industrial Psychology.* New York: McGraw-Hill Book Company, 1961, Chapter 6.

Appraising the Employee-Merit Ratings and Job Performance Coaching

SITUATIONS YOU ARE LIKELY TO MEET

How would you meet each of these situations:
- a. *Before* you have read the chapter? What would you say to yourself or to the individual?
- b. *After* you have read the chapter? How have your answers changed?

1. Two of your ambitious young friends are discussing the kind of company they want to work for in order to gain advancement. A says: "One practice that I insist upon finding in the company is a system of rating each employee at regular intervals so that he will know his strengths and weaknesses and what to do about them. How can a man earn advancement when he does not know his good and not-so-good traits?"

   B says: "That's not for me. I believe that I have potentials that cannot be measured by any kind of merit-rating system. I do not believe that the qualities and potentials of human beings can be measured by any formalized appraisal system."

   What thoughts would you offer for their consideration?

2. Assume that as an employee of a certain company you are told that you should interview Mr. C, a top executive, who is looking for a capable young man to assist him in managing his department. You want the job. To improve your chances of making a good impression you ask one of his employees to tell you

what to expect when you meet him. The employee tells you: "Look him squarely in the eye when you talk with him. He keeps his eyes right on your eyes— I don't know why. He really does not do it to dominate people. He's easy to get along with."

How would you interpret the purpose of the eye-to-eye contact of the executive?

The typical executive usually knows each employee under his direction more accurately and comprehensively than the employee realizes. The executive, however, does not usually tell the employee what he knows. At the same time, almost every employee asks himself the question: "How am I doing? In what respects is my work good, in what respects is it poor?" Management, too, must seek answers to the same kinds of questions about the employee when decisions must be made regarding a request for an increase in pay, selecting an empolyee for promotion, and deciding whether a problem employee should be retained or discharged. Management also likes to know the strengths and weaknesses of the individual members of its personnel in order that training and selection programs may be organized to improve the strengths. These and other needs on the part of the individual and the company have stimulated many managements to develop some kind of employee appraisal system.

Early appraisal systems utilized a merit-rating form that dealt with various personality and other employee characteristics such as cooperativeness, dependability, emotional stability, ability to get along with others, and literally hundreds of other traits of people. The great majority of these forms used graphic rating or check-list techniques. See page 550 for an example. Most companies still use this kind of form; it has become accepted mainly for its administrative advantages.

In recent years, however, the earlier merit-rating plan in some companies has evolved into a variation called "Appraisals for Coaching Purposes." Both types of plans are currently in use and are treated in this chapter.

MERIT RATING FOR ADMINISTRATIVE PURPOSES

Rating is a term used to refer to the process of judging people and things. A *rating scale* is a standardized device for recording personal judgments. The use of a scale provides a method whereby judgments may be secured in a uniform manner and treated quantitatively. Personal estimates and subjective opinions can be dealt with in much the same way as test scores and other psychological measurements. However, a rating scale is *not* a test and a rating scale should never be referred to as a test. It is a subjective estimate used because tests to measure certain personal characteristics are not as yet available.

The term "rating" applies to areas of judgment that are not susceptible to the testing process. A rating is a personal judgment, but a test is or ought to be an objective measure. If a characteristic of a person such as intelligence can be tested, it should not be rated.

Merit rating should also be differentiated from job evaluation. Merit rating attempts to measure some trait or characteristic of the employee, whereas *job evaluation* measures the job and usually includes a description of the ideal personal characteristics of the kind of person who should be hired to fill the job. A merit rating estimates the characteristics of the specific person who is actually holding the job—not the ideal person, in the abstract, who theoretically might be found to fill the job.

Ratings do *not measure* "merit"—they *portray* the pattern of perceptions that someone has about the individual. They present what certain acquaintances *think* they know or are willing to say about the person. Obviously what executives think they know about an employee is very important. They will treat the employee as they perceive him.

Purposes of employee evaluations

A rating system has the purposes that we would expect, such as giving each employee some information about his accomplishments, abilities, limitations, and potentials. Employees like to know where they stand in the opinion of the supervisor, particularly in regard to complimentary characteristics. They seek reassurance about themselves.

From the standpoint of management, the primary objectives of most merit-rating programs are to improve job performance, select individuals for promotion, and determine wage increases. Of these, improving job performance is most often cited as a primary aim. Secondary objectives include guiding supervisors in systematic appraisal, bringing about better communications, facilitating transfers, and determining fitness for continued employment. In most companies, ratings are made annually or semiannually.

One of the indirect benefits of ratings of employees by executives is that detailed attention is given to the person on the job. Raters are forced to analyze their men in a more or less systematic manner. This process often brings into the open potentials that might otherwise be overlooked. A good man is likely to get lost in the shuffle unless each employee's qualities are reviewed periodically.

Many employees who fail to meet normal work standards need extra attention to develop properly. Most managements prefer to develop rather than dismiss the marginal employee. Dismissal hurts the employee and costs the company money to train the person who takes the place of the one dismissed. Ratings are especially helpful in finding promotable employees. One of the critical needs of management is to identify and select those employees who are capable of advancing to executive positions. Managements conduct unceasing search for management talent, talent that will improve upon and eventually replace the existing management.

In spite of the many arguments for and benefits of merit rating, a few managements refuse to use them. They believe that a personnel function of this kind should not be formalized. They dislike the idea of cataloging any person's qualities and limitations. People, they say, deserve to be accepted and treated as members of a team, not as machines whose features can be listed on a sheet of paper. Those who cannot be fully accepted should be dismissed in a respectful manner.

Most managements believe that the use of an appraisal system does not detract from the dignity of the individual. They remind the critics that anyone who attends school is rated throughout the years of his formal education.

Recent college graduates take to merit reviews quite easily. They are accustomed to having their work graded and their characteristics listed. They look upon such devices as means of getting tips that will be of value in their growth. Rising young men are usually confident of their records. Those who dread the reviews are usually men who suspect or know they are doing poorly.

Employee reactions to a merit-rating plan

Surveys of employee opinions of rating plans are made by many companies, but many of the findings are of questionable validity. When employees know that management is enthusiastic about merit rating, they are less likely to express their true attitudes. Some ingenuity in making such a survey is necessary.

One of the senior writer's graduate students[1] was a regular employee

---

[1] Gerald H. Shaw, now in personnel management and teaching.

in a local metal working plant where management was enthusiastic about their rating plan. The student arranged to interview the employees as a fellow worker, not as a consultant or a personnel man. This particular plant was one of several operated by a large corporation whose personnel men had developed and installed an elaborate employee merit-rating system known as the "Job Performance Record." Each foreman was instructed to maintain a "Red-Blue Book," a record of each employee's poor and good job performances. The records were used as the basis for making the merit ratings. The foreman was required to rate each employee on a standardized form once every six months. He was also instructed to conduct a post-appraisal interview concerning the rating with each employee. The plan had been in operation several years before Shaw's survey was made.

The employees who were interviewed for this survey were approached while on the job by this graduate student, a fellow worker to them, who stated, "I am taking a course at the University. We're studying Job Performance Records like the one this company uses. The books tell us a lot on what they're for and what they're supposed to do, but they don't tell us how the workers feel about them. My instructor wants me to ask a number of fellows in each department how they feel about it. So I was wondering. . . ." He proceeded to ask each fellow worker the following four questions:

1. "What do you think about the Job Performance Record?" If the interviewee did not seem to understand, he continued, "That is, do you think it's a good idea or a waste of time or what?" If the interviewee did not voice an opinion, he then asked, "Do you think it helps the company or the workers or what?"
2. "Has it benefited you or been helpful to you?"
3. "How does the company use your Job Performance Record or for what?"
4. (a) "Do you think you know where you stand with your foreman?" If the employee was puzzled, he was then asked, "That is, do you know how you're doing?" Toward the end of the survey, another question, a (b) part, was added: "Do you know where you stand because of the Job Performance Record?"

In order to promote free responses by the employees no answers were recorded in the employee's presence. The interviewer memorized the answers of each employee to the four questions and, after thanking him, proceeded to record the answers in a place removed from his presence. This procedure was followed after each interview.

The total number of men working on the first and second shifts in this company under study was 271. Of these, 105 randomly selected employees were interviewed. All employees were either semiskilled or skilled machinists.

Of the 82 employees who indicated they knew where they stood or how they were doing, 47 were asked the question: (b) "Because of the Job Performance Record?"

Answer	Percent
Yes	60
No	36
No reply	4

The employee's attitude toward the Job Performance Record in terms of the entire interview given each was:

Answers indicated	Percent
Approval	44
Disapproval	15
Mixed	30
Neutral	10

Table 18–1 presents the findings, but the percentages of the responses to some of the questions should be examined for their significance. Example: Answers to question 2, "Has the Job Performance Record benefited you or helped you?" indicated that 63 percent of the employees interviewed felt that it had not. Yet a great many of them in answer to other questions said that they felt that it helped them to know how they were doing or that it would be used for promotions or references, and so on. They did not seem to perceive the Job Performance Record as being beneficial to them. This suggested that management had not made them aware that they were benefiting from the plan.

Another interesting finding occurred with question 4, "Do you know where you stand or how you're doing?" Approximately 78 percent said they did, but many of these same employees did not feel that it was because of the Job Performance Record. The reasons given were many, but the most frequently stated was that they had been given too few or no interviews by their foreman or that many of the entries made by the foreman were given unjustly so that such a record had little meaning.

The interviewer made other observations at the time which might be mentioned:

1. There is considerable variation in the way each foreman uses the Job Performance Record. Some foremen give only the minimum number of interviews (one every six months). Their employees do not seem to be as appreciative or interested in the program as the employees under a foreman who spends more time keeping

the records and discussing them with the workers. His employees are more aware that they benefit from it.

TABLE 18–1

FACTORY EMPLOYEES' OPINIONS OF THE EMPLOYER'S RATING PLAN

QUESTION 1. "What do you think about the Job Performance Record?"

QUESTION 2. "Has it benefited or helped you?"

Answers indicated:	Percent	Answer	Percent
Approval	46	Yes	29
Disapproval	18	No	63
Mixed	17	No reply	8
Neutral	19		

QUESTION 3. "How or what does the company use these records for?"
(more than one answer permitted)

Answers	Percent	Answers	Percent
Promotions: for filling vacancies	44	Incentive: gives the employees something to work for or to stimulate increased production	16
Tell how you're doing: a good or poor job	36		
Discharges or layoffs: those with the poorest records may be discharged or laid off first	25	References: record for future employer	13
Don't know:	23	Not used: they do not affect promotions, discharges, etc.	6
		Transfers: provide record of performance for new foreman	3

QUESTION 4. "Do you know where you stand with foreman or how you're doing?"

Answer	Percent
Yes	78
No	17
No reply	5

2. Those employees who show the most disapproval have usually been with the company many years. In most cases they have progressed little in their jobs. Newcomers, in contrast, tend to think it is a good idea and are interested in it.

3. Almost all the employees show a lack of knowledge about its application, uses, etc. A great many of them would like to know more about it.

4. Many employees feel that the only items the company is really interested in are production and absenteeism. Others feel that they are on jobs that do not permit much chance for their development or for the use of the Job Performance Record.

5. All employees were familiar with the foreman's "Red-Blue Book," the one in which he noted facts about each employee's work record. These facts were used by the foreman in determining his ratings and in conducting the interviews with his workers.

Of course the results of a survey such as this would vary with the specific company, but it does give emphasis to certain universal findings for management:

1. The management that installs an employee appraisal system must spend much time and effort in educating employees about the purposes and benefits of the plan.

2. Foremen need a great deal of training in order to have the plan used as management wishes.

3. Any survey for the evaluation of employees' opinions of an employee appraisal system should be made by persons in whom the employees have enough confidence to give their honest answers.

Experience indicates that the employees' reactions to and values of a rating program vary with the type of plan, its purposes, the way it is explained, and how it is used or misused.

When foremen conduct the post-rating interview

Most foremen find it difficult to discuss an employee's rating or appraisal with him. It is embarrassing to tell a subordinate to his face that he lacks personality or a sense of humor. The foreman realizes that when a man is informed that he lacks "vision" or a "dynamic personality," he is likely to feel baffled rather than enlightened.

When one foreman was told that he should conduct postappraisal interviews with his employees, he answered: "I'll be darned if I'll do that. I'll take the time to sit down and rate each one of my men, but I won't discuss the ratings with the man. When I tried to do the reviews last year, it took me several months to get back to normal with each man." Many foremen feel that it is useless to talk to a man about his personality and shortcomings unless it is possible to give each deserving employee a raise in pay right after the interview. As one foreman stated: "If he does not deserve a raise in pay, you can't convince him without a long argument." Some foremen feel silly when they sit down and try to talk to a worker as though the interview were a special occasion. They believe that if the worker deserves coaching, he should have it given to him as soon as the need arises— not once or twice a year on a special occasion.

The list of excuses given by foremen for procrastination in conducting a postappraisal interview are many:

The employee who is counseled may react badly, he may argue, he may be upset emotionally, he may be made to feel insecure, or he may become conceited about his own importance.

Some employees will tell others the complimentary content of the merit-rating interview and thus provoke jealousy on the part of fellow workers.

Foremen and lower-level executives are not sufficiently skillful to counsel their subordinates.

These objections are justified. Few supervisors know how to cope with an employee's resistance when it is shown by tense silence, obviously emotionalized but with resentment repressed rather than expressed openly. Nor do they like to deal with counterarguments.

The personal relationship between a supervisor and a subordinate is similar to that between two good friends—neither mentions to the other certain touchy subjects. Most foremen do not know how to conduct an effective interview of this kind. Some companies find it easier to spend money necessary to hire specialists such as psychologists and consultants to do it for the foremen. And yet few hired specialists are in so strong a position for counseling as the man's own boss.

The hired specialists, in time, discover that an employee's behavior will not be changed until he is involved in action—in the performance of a real task whose outcome will be significant to him. The most meaningful action plan to an employee is one set up under the guidance or direction of a senior who is responsible for the work being performed.

Why personality trait rating plans are of limited value

The one type of merit rating found most deficient even though it is still widely used is the kind that rates traits such as personality, initiative, honesty, and so on. Experience of executives who have used this kind of rating device shows rather definitely that it is impractical to try to measure a man's character and personality traits on a numerical scale.

Trait rating has a number of serious shortcomings. There is little or no scientific basis for deciding that certain personality traits are essential for good performance on a given job. The traits chosen for rating are selected by "common sense" reasoning, not by statistical validation. Extended experience in life situations often controverts the common sense variety of reasoning. Common sense, for example, may cause one to assume that a top executive needs a high degree of tact and skill in public relations. Much evidence to the contrary is available. Some of the most successful corporation presidents are low in this trait.

The best evidence available concerning the weaknesses of trait rating was developed by a committee of executives, researchers, and consultants in a four-year research program for the General Electric Company. The main conclusion from the research in regard to this question was the following:

> *You cannot base your development activity on "personality traits."*
>
> We have no idea what "personality traits" are needed to make a good manager. Men of widely divergent personalities are successful managers. Therefore, we are wrong when we appraise people and select people on the basis of "traits" which we cannot define or measure.
>
> Furthermore, if we did establish a "prototype" ideal manager, saying "We want only managers of this personality pattern," we would be in danger of pressing toward uniformity and conformity which are not only undesirable but dangerous.
>
> We must, therefore, focus on the *work* that a man does, and do all of our appraising, development, selection on the basis of observed work methods and performance.[2]

The main positive conclusion from the failure of systems of ratings that purport to measure personality traits is that employee appraisals should stress work performance.

APPRAISALS FOR COACHING PURPOSES

Merit-rating systems that involve the use of an elaborate printed scale for evaluating personality do not encourage the "judge" to examine the

---

[2]Moorhead Wright, "Development of Men," in Papers from the 38th Annual Meeting, American Association of Advertising Agencies, New York.

factors that are most important to the employer—getting the work done. After all, if management finds that the employee is not getting his work done, the employee needs coaching about the work and his procedures rather than an evaluation of his personality traits. Generally, merit-rating plans of the trait variety have been used mostly by personnel workers. Appraisal plans for coaching purposes are used mainly by executives above the average supervisory level.

EXECUTIVE APPRAISALS

(Reaction to a conference discussion of executive rating)

I listed all his qualities,
I measured them both fore and aft—
His prayers and his frivolities,
His immaturities, his craft.

I put them down upon a form
Replete with every latest symbol,
Reduced the angles to a norm
And hid a pea beneath each thimble;

Then plied the statistician's art,
His concepts, ratios and weightings.
But he spoke warmly from the heart,
"A fig for all your pompous ratings

"A twinkle in my father's eye,
A moon in May, a moment's passion,
A woman's pain—and there was I,
A unique creature in my fashion.

"All your psychologist's analysis
Tells nothing of my dreams last night.
It's just an infantile paralysis,
A play-pen. Learn to stand upright,

"To know me, use me, man to man,
To judge me wholly. In your eyes
I'll soon discover if you can,
For all your knowledge, still be wise."

—Anon.

Source: *The Management Review* (American Management Association, Inc.), December, 1952, p. 776.

The trend toward the use of formal appraisal systems for coaching purposes has increased. Executives do some informal coaching of their subordinates every day. The main value of a formal appraisal system is that the executive is encouraged to think more systematically about each subordinate and to review with him all those factors that might enable him to do a better job.

Several investigators of appraisal systems have pointed out the difficulties in trying to be judicial in appraising people and advocated the use of a plan that gauges "management by objectives" rather than by judgment of the personal worth of a subordinate.[3] Certain large companies such as General Mills and General Electric are experimenting with different methods that implement this concept.

The first stage in the procedure used in this new approach is a simple statement, conversational, of employee work responsibilities rather than a formal job description. From this the boss and the subordinate establish the subordinate's "targets" or short-term (about six months) performance goals. At the conclusion of the six-month period, the subordinate makes *his own* appraisal of what he has accomplished relative to the target that he had set. The boss and subordinate then hold an "interview" to discuss the record, evaluate the weaknesses and strengths in what has been done, and set new targets for the next six months. In this procedure the subordinate is an *active* figure in the system, and the major difference between this approach and the conventional trait-rating technique is that it "shifts the emphasis from *appraisal* to *analysis*." There is also a shift of emphasis from the past to *performance in relation to work goals* in the future, and this serves a more constructive end than judicial evaluations of the person. The personality of the subordinate is not a central issue, but the prospects for self-development through work are greatly enhanced.[4]

Coaching by the executive provides a meaningful method for letting a subordinate know where he stands in the company and for discussing specific ways in which he can become more effective in his job.

Many executives who believe in coaching would like to improve their skill in doing it. Psychologists who have done research in counseling techniques have found that when trainees for counseling make a conscious effort to "maintain eye-to-eye contact" with the person to be counseled, the interviews are especially fruitful. This does not mean that the counselor should try to dominate the counselee through "eye power"; it is more than merely

---

[3] See Alva F. Kindall and James Gatza, "Positive Program for Performance Appraisal," *Harvard Business Review*, November–December, 1963; and Richard S. Reichmann, "Letters," *Harvard Business Review*, March–April 1964.

[4] See Douglas McGregor, "An Uneasy Look at Performance Appraisal," *Harvard Business Review*, May–June 1957. See also *Personnel Management Abstracts*, Summer Issue 1957.

looking a man in the eye when talking with him. Instead, the counselor should maintain consistent visual contact regardless of which party is speaking.

In the research studies, one of the most important benefits from maintaining eye contact is that it helps the counselor to listen. One counselor explained the benefit by saying that previously he had spent "too much time thinking about what I should say instead of simply listening to the other person."

Coaching in the performance review requires concentrated listening and observing in order that the counselor may sense feelings in addition to other reactions that are being expressed by the subordinate. The executive who wishes to improve his skill in coaching as well as in other forms of effectiveness in personal contacts should practice maintaining intelligent eye contacts whenever appropriate.[5]

In an appraisal review session for coaching purposes the boss and the subordinate conduct a comprehensive give-and-take discussion of the subordinate's performance on the job, relations with fellow workers, standing with his superiors, and all strengths and weaknesses in regard to the work. The session ends with a summary of what the junior manager or subordinate can do to improve his performance. Great skill is needed by the executive who conducts a soul-searching discussion of the subordinate's performance and how he can improve it. Yet the practice is spreading as more top management men see it as a help in coaching junior executives. Before this interview takes place, the boss usually talks with and gets suggestions from other executives to improve his appraisal and recommendations.

The committee or group approach to appraisal review systems is gaining. The typical executive does not want to be the only person to evaluate a man. In the committee approach, the group consists of personnel specialists and senior executives, including the man's immediate supervisor. They hold an appraising session, essentially constructive in spirit. Later, the immediate supervisor sits down with his subordinate and presents the group's findings and suggestions. The two men then discuss ways in which improvements can be made in the performance. The committee approach eliminates tendencies toward personal prejudice. It also takes a great load off the supervisor. Instead of saying "I think . . . ," he can say, "We believe. . . ."

What goes on in a coaching interview varies with the individuals involved. The typical executive usually starts the interview with a review of the subordinate's strong points.

[5]See Mortimer R. Feinberg, "Performance Review: The Awful Truth," *Business Management*, May 1969, CCM Professional Magazines, 22 West Putnam Ave., Greenwich, Conn. Description of "eye contact" technique taken from a supplement to the *Journal of Counseling Psychology*.

Then he gradually moves into areas where the ratee could stand improvement. The executive will, if he is skilled, let the subordinate do most of the talking, let him tell what is wrong with himself. The executive adds comments of approval or disapproval, or makes recommendations.

Skilled interviewers use the "turnback." When the ratee asks a question, the rater turns the question back to the ratee before he tries to give an answer.

Here are four examples of turnback:

1. Ratee: *But how does my rating stack up with the other employees in the department?*
   Rater: *How do you feel you compare with the others?*
2. Ratee: *But I try hard all the time. What can I do to improve?*
   Rater: *What do you think you might do to improve?*
3. Ratee: *Have I been doing any better lately? Do you think my work is improving?*
   Rater: *Do you feel you have been improving?*
4. Ratee: *I would like some time to get to be a secretary. How should I go about it?*
   Rater: *Do you have any ideas as to what you might do?*

When the person rated responds with strong feeling, the interviewer does not give a logical explanation. Instead, he encourages the ratee to talk out his feelings and thereby clarify his thinking so that he can develop his own solution. If pent-up feelings have been released, he might become more receptive to a logical explanation.

These permissive techniques do not mean that an employee should not become aware of his weaknesses and needed improvements. On the contrary, the processes of making him aware are achieved by different techniques. The permissive procedure of the kind that uses the turnback is designed to enable the ratee to discover and to accept the criticism rather than hear it given but refuse its acceptance.

Some executives can or at least think they can do effective coaching. When they do, the executive and his subordinate try to agree on what areas of performance are poor and what the subordinate will do to bring about improvement. At the next appraisal, or perhaps sooner, they will meet to see how the improvement program is progressing.

Recommendations for effective postappraisal interviews

Experience of management men and researchers indicates that the effectiveness of interviews can be increased by means of the following procedures:

1. Do not tell a man how or in what respects he should change himself. Instead, ask him questions about his work responsibilities, his objectives, and his methods of work. Use a job-centered rather than a man-centered approach.

2. Interviews should not begin with a review of what is wrong with a man or his work. Let him suggest the first topics for discussion so that he may feel that his interests are being recognized. Always preserve a man's dignity.

3. Stress the team approach. Discuss the relationships with other members of the company and procedures for getting work done by bringing those people into the program who are or should be participants.

4. Some executives and others who do postappraisal interviews find that going through an interview themselves with their own chiefs helps them improve their interviews with others. To be effective with others, it is necessary to be relaxed and self-confident. The man who has experienced an appraisal interview himself usually improves his manner with his subordinates.

5. The coaching type of interview should not involve a review of the advisee's present salary or promises of reward for the future. The focus of discussion is the employee's job, not his pay. This procedure is the opposite of that used in merit ratings for administrative purposes. In many merit-rating programs, salary is discussed. Some companies use merit ratings in deciding whether to grant or withhold raises. In many companies the rating system has this meaning for the employees. When all appraisals are made in the same month of the year, the appraisal date becomes the time when every employee expects a raise. Hence, some managements conduct their appraisal of each employee about two months prior to the anniversary date of his employment. This spreads the administrative task throughout the year and prevents the expectation of an increase being given to most employees at the same time.

Even though a merit-rating system is well planned, it often raises extra difficulties as in the case of the worker who must be discharged. Too often, a poor employee is given a raise in the hope that the raise will improve his work. Quality and output in work frequently do not agree with the salary increases given an employee under a so-called merit-rating plan.

6. When an employee raises the question of pay during the coaching interview, the coach should point out that that subject must be treated in another type of interview. An appointment for the purpose can be made. During the coaching interview, the coach should stress satisfactions from the work in the "professional" sense. Doctors, teachers, and other professional workers are likely to continue to improve their work and abilities even though financial rewards do not follow immediately. Rewards are by-products of good work. As in the professions, most intelligent workers

in business improve their abilities because they increase their respect for themselves, not for money alone.

7. To be effective as a coach or counselor, the executive must be held in high esteem by the subordinate. If the subordinate merely acts in a respectful manner because the superior holds a higher rank, the coaching benefits will be negligible.

8. Executives who do systematic coaching as in postappraisal interviews realize that much skill is essential. This kind of interview cannot attain its full benefits when the executive acts in his usual authoritarian manner. If he is to learn to respect the special contributions that can be made through permissive techniques, he may have to develop a new kind of respect for himself as a skilled counselor, diagnostician, and teacher. The executive coach can get self-appraisal values out of the interview, too. He does this when he asks, "What can I do to help you make your job go better?" He reports that few hesitate to tell him frankly.

9. Use "playback." Ask him to state his ideas as to the conclusions and plans that were developed during the interview. If he wants to make promises that he cannot or is not likely to fulfill by the time of the next coaching session, it is necessary to help him set goals that are attainable.

Subordinates respond to what they think managers expect of them. Livingston has reported that in the granting of loans by over five-hundred branch managers, larger credit losses resulted when their lending authority was curtailed. "They appeared to do what they believed they were expected to do, and their supervisors' expectations became self-fulfilling prophesies. If a manager believes a subordinate will perform poorly, it is virtually impossible for him to mask his expectations, because the message usually is communicated unintentionally without conscious action on his part. Indeed, a manager often communicates most when he believes he is communicating least. Unfortunately and frequently, actions and feelings are generated by what subordinates think has been communicated to them rather than what their manager thinks he's told them. Too often instructions which the communicator thought he had given clearly are found to have been misunderstood. A typical example is that of the supervisor who receives a letter of commendation from his superior which is interpreted as criticism—the subordinate's emotional set was so intensely negative toward the superior that the message was completely misinterpreted. In this kind of incident, the superior has had low expectations of the subordinate's performance. All of which means that it's not so much what we think we say or write but what meanings the recipients give to the words."[6]

[6]See J. Sterling Livingston, "Pygmalion in Management," *Harvard Business Review*, July–August 1969, pp. 81–89.

Summary

Any rating or appraisal system is of little practical benefit if the results are buried in company files and employees never find out how their performance is measuring up against management's expectations. The communication of evaluations after they are made is, however, a more difficult process than is generally recognized. Currently, merit rating without emphasis on postappraisal is most commonly used for administrative purposes: to allocate wage and salary increases and to determine fitness for promotion and transfer. The appraisal procedure so used remains one of contributing to judgment rather than to stimulation of the employee.

Thus far, the focus of attention in merit rating has been on evaluation of the individual, but progressive managements are learning how to communicate the appraisals to the employee in terms of job performance coaching.

Companies vary in their use of appraisal systems. Some companies make appraisal reviews for clerical employees and executives but not for engineers and research staff members. Some have a program for getting the ratings but give interviews about them only to employees who ask for them.

In a few concerns, the junior executive not only sees the appraisal on himself but also helps to write it. In one branch of our armed services, officers are appraised but the officer sees the report only when it is bad.

Many executives do not write out any appraisal but conduct an interview in which the individual being appraised is asked how he himself thinks he is doing. The employee, in some cases, makes a written appraisal of himself in advance of the interview as the basis for the discussion. People who are given such a wide-open opportunity might be expected to overrate themselves. Actually, the majority underrate their own performance and usually mention, besides flaws in themselves and their work that the boss sees, others that have not occurred to him. This method of interviewing gives the superior ample opportunity to point out to the man where he is doing a better job than he himself imagines. The executive also gets helpful suggestions for himself when he asks: "What can I do to help you do your job better?" Employees frequently give frank and helpful suggestions to the executive who is so mature that employees know he can take them without resentment. Fortunately, the percentage of mature executives in America is on the increase. The novice who enters business today is likely to be surprised and pleased by the number of executives who are open-minded about themselves as well as sincerely interested in helping the man with growth potential get ahead.

QUESTIONS ON THE CHAPTER

1. Why should the term "test" not be applied to a rating scale?
2. Differentiate between merit rating and job evaluation.
3. What are the primary objectives of rating systems from the standpoint of management?
4. Do employees feel that it is more effective to have their own superiors do the counseling interviews, or hired specialists?
5. Describe the Gerald H. Shaw study of factory employees' reactions to an employee rating plan.
6. What was the main conclusion in the General Electric Company study concerning the weaknesses of trait rating?
7. Why is it difficult for foremen to conduct a postrating interview?
8. What is the main value for the executive of an appraisal system used for coaching purposes?
9. Differentiate between the trait-rating technique and the newer appraisal method.
10. Why is a group approach to appraisal review systems more effective than an individual approach?
11. Why do skilled interviewers use the turnback when talking with ratees?
12. What should be the focus of the postappraisal interview for job performance coaching in contrast to merit-rating interviews for administrative purposes?
13. How should "playback" be used for an effective postappraisal interview?
14. How should the question of pay be handled during a coaching interview?
15. Of all the ideas presented in the chapter, which ones were of interest or value to you?
16. What did the chapter contribute toward your future relations with (a) the men who supervise you, (b) the employees whom you may supervise?

PROBLEMS AND PROJECTS

For All Students
1. To appreciate the difficulties in conducting the postappraisal interview, rate a friend on a rating form. Try to conduct an appropriate postappraisal interview. Let some observers evaluate your skills and suggest improvements.

2. Have several persons rate themselves. Have acquaintances rate them on the same traits. How do the two kinds of ratings differ? On what kinds of traits do individuals seem to overrate or underrate themselves?

For Advanced Students

3. Examine several rating scales for traits such as initiative and personality. Classify the traits as to whether they are objective or refer to reactions to persons. Which kind seems to be the more useful in evaluating an employee?

4. Write anecdotal descriptions of a person, descriptions that seem to be characteristic of the individual. Show your descriptions to someone who knows the individual. Are your anecdotes truly descriptive in their opinion?

For Men in Business

5. Think of several executives whom you know. Describe the manner that is natural for each when he coaches a subordinate. Do you want the coach to adopt a special manner or to be natural in the counseling interview? Why?

6. Industrial Psychology, Inc., 515 Madison Ave., New York, N. Y. 10022, publishes a rating scale that has "bias" statements to show whether the rater is overly lenient and consistent in his estimates. National norms are available for the scale. Compare this type of scale with the one used in some company whose rating system you know.

COLLATERAL READINGS

For All Students

Fleishman, Edwin A., *Studies in Personnel and Industrial Psychology*. Homewood, Ill.: The Dorsey Press, Inc., 1961, Chapters 10–15.

Gellerman, Saul W., *Motivation and Productivity*. New York: American Management Association, Inc., 1963, Chapter 19.

Maier, N. R. F., *The Appraisal Interview*. New York: John Wiley & Sons, Inc., 1958. Discusses three kinds of appraisal interviews and offers valuable suggestions.

For Advanced Students

Dayal, Ishwar, "Some Issues in Performance Appraisal," *Personnel Administration*, January–February 1969. Mentions methods in use and points out some of the difficulties.

Karn, Harry W., and B. von Haller Gilmer, *Readings in Industrial and Business Psychology*. New York: McGraw-Hill Book Company, 1962, pp. 175–218.

For Men in Business

Personnel Practices in Factory and Office: Manufacturing, Studies in Personnel

Policy No. 194. New York, National Industrial Conference Board, 1964. Presents data regarding extent of use of merit-rating programs in industry as well as valuable information about other personnel practices.

Zander, Alvin F., ed., *Performance Appraisals' Effects on Employees and Their Performance*. Ann Arbor, Mich.: The Foundation for Research on Human Behavior, 1963.

Office Management

SITUATIONS YOU ARE LIKELY TO MEET

How would you meet each of these situations:
- a. *Before* you have read the chapter? What would you say to yourself or to the individual?
- b. *After* you have read the chapter? How have your answers changed?

1. A certain recruiter for a management training program tells almost every college senior whom he interviews that he can arrange for him to work in an office manager's department where he can become acquainted with the company's clerical operations. Eventually he could learn how to write office memoranda to direct employees what to do and how to do it.

   If you were offered such an opportunity, what would you say?

2. The recruiter also tells you that his company is developing a program designed to help urban disadvantaged citizens take training to learn certain office skills. As part of the preparation to work with the underprivileged of a ghetto area, the management wants the trainees to learn how to supervise the economically deprived who are performing simple, unskilled tasks—as in stockroom operations.

   Assuming that you do want to work with underprivileged groups, how will you react to the preparatory requirement of supervising a number of stockroom workers for twelve months before you can be assigned to a job that will enable you to learn about the company's operations on a higher ability level?

Most students of business and young people who plan to enter the business world think in terms of an office job. This is in line with the trend in the distribution changes of our working population. Back in 1945, there were 21.6 million blue-collar workers and only 17.5 million in white-collar jobs, but in 1955–56, white-collar workers in the United States displaced production workers as the biggest single group in the working population. Some firms such as insurance companies and banks have 90 percent to 100 percent of their employees in the office work classification.

As a result, the number of people in office management has increased greatly even though some office managers do not function under that exact title. Many firms are so small that they do not need the full-time services of an office manager—his duties may be performed under the title of vice-president, secretary, auditor, chief clerk, personnel manager, or something else. In spite of the importance of the job, many who earn their living as office managers dislike the title. They associate it with the old "chief clerk" concept and the "green eyeshade." They prefer to be called "director of administration," "auditor," "assistant to the president," or some title of recognized prestige. Every office must provide itself with the functions of the office manager. Even though he may not do detailed office methods study work or have major executive responsibilities, the company management must observe, carry out, and provide for efficient ways of filing, billing, and checking of records. Someone must be responsible for taking care of all the numerous operations performed in an office. The office manager, whatever his title, is in charge of clerical and related services.

Office management responsibilities that must be performed in every company are the following:

1. Planning and supervising office services such as filing, typing, and stenographic services
2. Preparing and submitting reports to management and governmental bureaus
3. Hiring office workers
4. Training office workers

5. Promoting and transferring office workers
6. Controlling office costs, budgeting office expenses
7. Purchasing adequate office equipment
8. Developing efficient supervision in the office
9. Carrying out the personnel policies of the company as they affect the office staff

Many of these functions involve personnel management. If the company has an organized personnel program, some of these responsibilities will be shared with the personnel manager or carried out in cooperation with him.

Obviously, a system of records, reports, controls, and forecasts must be directed by an office executive in order that the business may be transacted in an orderly manner. The office manager's job involves two types of responsibilities. As a *line manager*, he hires and discharges, gets production out, and worries about the thousands of details necessary to keep the office going. He is also a *staff man* whose reports and forecasts affect, directly or indirectly, the decisions of top management. His office is both an operations and an information center.

In many companies, the office manager is likely to be an important contact man to the community. He, to many people, represents the company because he is the executive whom many people call on when they apply for a job, want to sell a product, or get a donation for a local charity. His personality contributes to and, in some cases, represents the company's personality.

The "red tape" mind

"Red tape" is usually defined as the excessive making of records in operating a business—too much paper. It means making extra copies of letters and reports and storing them where they may be available in future years. It includes the unnecessary use of date stamps and the initialing of papers and reports by every member of the organization who might have a direct or a remote interest in the content. It may even bog down a business because of its costs.

Fundamentally, red tape is a state of mind, a kind of mentality that insists on self-protection rather than an emphasis on constructive action. The alert office manager must fight it in himself and in others.

Much of it develops from special or one-time needs. A vice-president, for example, asks for a special report on the date when the warehouse windows were washed and the amount of washing detergent used. The clerk who writes the report asks him whether he would like to have monthly and quarterly reports on the subject and the typical vice-president says yes. The reports continue to be prepared and sent to the executive for years, in many cases long after they have any usefulness for anyone. It is too easy for clerical workers and executives to continue making records simply because "We've always done it that way."

One cause for red tape is the new executive. He usually wants to in-

Most executives feel that they have so much paper work to do that they are working in a "blizzard of papers." As a result, the larger companies have adopted computers to handle many of their messages more quickly than is possible with the usual dictated-and-mailed letter.

In the above photograph we see the electronic heart of the Ford Motor Company's worldwide message center, located in Dearborn, Michigan. Switching computers process message and data transmissions within the company's private teletype network and some inter-connected commercial wire terminals. In addition to its private-line network of 119 stations, Ford uses 146 commercial TWX and Telex stations to connect low-volume locations to the Dearborn Message Center.

Although on the average day the center receives 11,000 messages and transmits another 16,000, the switching processors virtually eliminate delays and message "traffic jams." Even during peak periods, the center can send an average-length message from Dearborn to the West Coast in less than two minutes.

Messages are sent and received from both inside (parts depots, assembly, manufacturing and parts plants, domestic and foreign divisional offices) and outside (customers, suppliers, news media, governments) the company.

Source: Ford News Department.

form himself about every aspect of his job. He asks for special reports. He may even have consultants come in to tell him about accounting controls that are needed. Soon a flood of facts washes over his desk and leaves him gasping for air. But the reports keep coming. Eventually he must decide whether he should become an absorber of information or an active, effective executive. Some corporation presidents are expected to read and understand hundreds of reports every month, many dealing with trivialities. A review and housecleaning of all reports is necessary more than once a year. Even though the making of hundreds of reports may be eliminated in a large company during an annual housecleaning, the overload may be evident six months later. Daily supervision is essential. One man, usually the office manager, should have authority for records control.

The office memorandum

The office memorandum is universally used as a medium of communication. When used intelligently, it serves its purposes well, but it may also hinder true communication by management. As one management leader has stated:

> Recently I was discussing with an executive a number of things that should have been done several months before, some of which had now developed into crises. In great agitation he called for his general manager and asked for an explanation. The general manager went to his own office and quickly returned with a handful of memoranda.
>
> These memoranda, addressed to various members of the organization, contained instructions to take care of the items in question. Almost smugly the general manager put the memoranda on the chief executive's desk with an expression suggesting. "There, I have taken care of them." His attitude seemed to be that the writing of a memorandum had disposed of the matter.
>
> That is the great danger of memoranda. There is some kind of feeling that when you have dictated instructions to somebody the job is done. Unfortunately people do not always do what they are instructed to do in memoranda, and frequently they are not able to without further clarification and assistance.
>
> There is another aspect to memoranda that is a rather interesting commentary on human nature. We are inclined to speak much more harshly and dictatorially in a memorandum than face to face.
>
> It is virtually impossible to cover all aspects of a problem in a memorandum. Almost invariably the memorandum is written to the

wrong person, and others affected are not adequately informed. The result is friction, misunderstanding, and, many times, hard feelings.[1]

Typewritten reports to executives

Every college graduate who enters business is likely to find it necessary to write reports for executives. Executives are deluged by letters, reports, and other typed and printed materials that bear on their work.

Unfortunately for them, it is probable that more than half of that time spent in reading is wasted because the material the executive is required to read is of little value to him in carrying out his executive responsibilities. He realizes this and therefore skims and skips as a means toward getting his work done.

This means that a key problem in office communication is getting executives to read things. In one company, for example, the research department sends a detailed monthly report of work done to its members. The director tested the report's readership by sandwiching a fake report, decidedly offbeat, in the volume. It was meant to be quite funny, but he got not a single comment about it.

In another firm a rather complicated letter on a company matter was sent to some forty members of the company's management men. In it was buried the statement, "If you have read this, wire collect and we'll send you five dollars." Fewer than half a dozen readers cashed in.

These incidents mean that anyone who wants to communicate with busy executives should put forth extra effort to make reports inviting and readable.

The first page of most multipage reports is given over to "background material." This usually is well known to the reader. To save the reader's time, the purposes of the reports should be itemized.

In the body of the report, long paragraphs should be broken into keyed paragraphs of a few lines. Important paragraphs should be indented and underscored. Sections and paragraphs should be numbered for easy reference. Headings should be numbered in order. Underscoring should be used for a few key ideas only.

A report that is well written invites reading. To invite reading, solid pages of typed material can be broken into paragraphs of different lengths of lines. Pages should have a varied rather than a monotonous appearance.

At the end, a brief summary of points covered and recommendations for the action should be stated. Executives like concise reports that recommend action.

In writing, it is important to realize that management men are not

[1]Lawrence A. Appley, "Management Enemy Number One," *Management News*, American Management Association, Inc., May 1957.

interested in what someone thinks. They want to read what the writer knows. Executives also like reports that present both sides of a problem rather than a one-sided statement of a preconceived theory or opinion. Extravagant statements unsupported by facts and designed to "prove" a preconceived idea are anathema.

If the report quotes published authorities or sources of data, it should be documented by means of footnotes. Exhibits of tables, copies of questionnaires, and similar supporting material should be placed in an appendix or in a separate binder.

Few college students have developed their potentials for writing attractive, meaty reports. They still present term reports in pages of solid typewritten material. Worst of all, too many have not acquired the habit of reading and correcting every page before it is submitted. At least the misspelled words might be corrected!

Typical grievances of office workers

When one office manager was asked to state his biggest problem, he answered: "I'd say my biggest problem is to get people to work together.

"Didn't they teach you to make decisions at business school, Hobart?"

Source: by Joseph Serrano, *The Management Review* (*July* 1956). Courtesy American Management Association, Inc.

The girls seem to squabble a lot over trivial things. You can get them to work individually all right, but for some reason they don't want to work together. They get ideas that one girl is getting a bit more pay or recognition and then they get miffed. There isn't as much trouble with the men in this respect."

The alert office supervisor recognizes that, regardless of the seriousness of an employee's grievance, the way the employee feels about the grievance should dictate the amount of consideration he must give to it. If he gives an employee the brush-off or makes light of a grievance, he may intensify other dissatisfactions.

He cannot express indifference, but neither can he remove all the causes for grievance. There will always be, in most companies, certain salary differences that some employees will consider unfair.

There will always be some human relations situations that certain employees will construe as favoritism.

Temperatures in the office cannot be adjusted to the satisfaction of everyone.

Office surroundings are likely to be drab to a few employees.

And somebody will always want to take his vacation at the same time that somebody else wants to take his.

The most common grievance is the pay. The office manager is constantly besieged by employees who believe that they are underpaid. Surprisingly, however, a survey of turnover among office workers in twenty-five companies in the Philadelphia area showed that of the 1,186 employees who had left the employing company, only 129 had succumbed to the lure of higher salaries.[2]

One office worker summed up the problem of grievances as follows:

> During the past four summers I have been employed by Office Temporaries Incorporated, a New York firm that supplies temporary office help to New York business firms. While in their employ, I worked for three days to three months in the offices of approximately fifteen different companies.
>
> One of the very first and, I feel, the most basic lesson I learned from these experiences is that *every* office has problems. I have yet to work in an office in which everyone was in perfect harmony. There was always at least one employee with a complaint, a petty jealousy, or some frustration. If all employees could understand this basic fact, most offices would operate more pleasantly. I learned, through observation, to weigh in proper perspective the various advantages and disadvantages encountered in any working situation.

[2]See *Office Executive* (National Office Management Association), July 1957, p. 38.

The office neurotic

For supervisors in American offices, neuroticism among female workers is likely to be an especially difficult problem. Dr. Sylvia A. Sorkin in an address before a national conference of the National Office Management Association gave results of a questionnaire sent to office managers. Approximately nine hundred responded. She told the conference delegates that from a listing of nine common office management "headaches" mentioned in the survey, the problem of dealing with neurotic female workers was rated second only in importance to the problem of securing well-trained clerical workers.

Although a third of the executives who gave their opinions said that securing trained help was their biggest problem, nearly a quarter of them ranked the neurotic female as their most difficult problem. Neurotic male workers, on the other hand, got top billing as a problem by only 3 percent of the executives.[3]

The neurotic (see Chapter 25) is found in the factory and in the classroom as well as in the office. Somehow he seems to stand out more in the office than in the factory. Perhaps it is because most office workers can talk with their associates more easily in the office than in a typical noisy factory. At any rate, the office neurotic is a prominent member of most offices. He appears in many styles.

He (she) may be the chronic griper who interprets every incident as a threat to himself. He is unhappy with the world because he is unhappy about himself. He sees evil or danger in every happening. He is not sufficiently mature to view his work situation, the company, or his fellow employees in objective manner. He (she) may be a hypochondriac who constantly talks about his health. His desk drawers have bottles and boxes of medicines and pills. The weather outside and the air in the office are so unhealthy that he has numerous colds, ailments, and oncoming ills. He can't do his work because he doesn't feel well. Another headache and so on and on.

He (she) may be a projectionist, one who ascribes to others or the external world repressed mental processes which are not recognized as being of personal origin. A common example is the office worker who borrows money from a friend, fails to pay it back, and then subconsciously discovers that he really need not pay it because the person who loaned it to him is too despicable to deserve repayment! Some women employees also accuse the boss of immoral conduct because of their own repressed impulsions toward him.

The *office wolf* is not usually classified as a neurotic but he is a similar

[3]Condensed from a release from the National Office Management Association, 1954.

nuisance. If he is not too aggressive, the girls in the office may enjoy his threats—at least he relieves the monotony! If he is a persistent threat, he disturbs the work atmosphere and must be transferred to an all-male group or put into his proper place by an executive who calls him into his office and bluntly lays down the customs expected in a productive work environment. Of course the executive may also have to tell certain girls in the office that their attire seems chosen "to bring out the beast in the male" and that they must reduce their efforts to show off their physical charms.

Generally, the office neurotic utilizes his maladjustments to gain certain personal ends, to obtain answers to psychological needs such as recognition and attention. Sometimes the behavior also indicates that the office neurotic is trying to get other employees to do his work for him. Most normal employees recognize this subterfuge and simply say: "Sorry Mabel, I haven't time to do your work too. You just go ahead and do as I do when I have a headache—work harder and the headache will disappear."

Office customs and cliques

Each office has its own customs about matters such as attire, coffee breaks, extra time off from work without loss of pay, participation in the grapevine, and amount of work to be done. The employees may have one title for the supervisor when speaking in his presence and another, less conventional but more humorous, when not in his presence.

As in all groups, cliques develop. Here are comments from three office supervisors:

1. Most of the workers under my supervision are women: I have relatively little trouble because they get to know each other intimately and eat and take coffee breaks together. This causes some problems because they stick together against me when they want something. Also, if they get into any of their silly women's fights, they stab each other at their weak points. This isn't good and is hard to control. However, they usually work together pretty well but sometimes fight over who is doing more work or trying to take authority.
2. I really have quite a bit of trouble with the thirty girls who work on the bookkeeping machines in our bank. They don't want to do any more work than they have to. They want to get done so they can leave as near three o'clock as possible. If they're held up by the check sorters, they get all upset. And if a check has been misfiled and is out of order, they are ready to quit. The working quarters aren't as good as they could be, but with the space we have the layout is as good as possible. They all have new ma-

chines and all the latest equipment. Only about half of them come to me if they have a problem. The rest just complain to other girls and spend their time griping in the rest room. I guess the low rate of pay has a lot to do with it, but I assumed that they understood the pay situation when they took the job.

3. There's a clique going on right now that's really a headache. It's that switchboard. It's the smallest work area in the office but it gives me the most trouble. Mrs. McF. works it full time, and she gets two coffee breaks and lunch time like everyone else. The girls have their own groups that they like to go out with, and since there are two shifts going out at different times we have trouble getting girls to take over for Mrs. McF. Two girls, Edith and Laura, have been assigned to take over for her, but when one of them is out or wants a different lunch hour, things get all balled up. We've tried all sorts of plans to smooth out the problem without success. One of the causes for the problem is the fact that the girls are so anxious to be with their own clique members during lunch that they refuse to take over for Mrs. McF.

Office managers take these customs and cliques as a normal part of business life. People work together as human beings, not as mechanical robots. The function of the office manager is not that of trying to make perfect persons out of typical people. He simply does his best to direct the efforts of the typical employees and to encourage the development of the potentially superior few. He prefers that work get done in a reasonably pleasant atmosphere. Of course, if the work relations become a means for the office politician to gain his ends, management is anxious to correct the influence of undesirable cliques.

Office politics

This term is applied to the intrigues, spying, and talebearing of individuals or cliques who seek illicitly to gain privilege, control, or advancement for themselves. Every management must be alert to this kind of chicanery. It may appear in hostility toward certain employees, partiality by a supervisor, or inequitable salary schedules. Sometimes the office manager becomes a target of the individuals or factions that seek to control him. They may spread rumors about his personal life or seek to undermine his authority. If he merely goes to lunch with a certain clerk or drives to and from work with him, the office politicians will spread the rumor that his companion is the fair-haired boy of the boss.

Differences in pay often furnish grist for the mill of the office politician. Many office workers know the pay rates of their associates. No

WHAT SHOULD YOU DO?

Advice on how to succeed in office politics is virtually taboo. The personnel officer never explains the political setup when he gives you the orientation spiel. You will find no guidance in the employee's manual. You may get clandestine tips from your associates, but they are so inextricably entangled themselves that their counsel hardly can be unbiased.

There just is no mentor who can say, "Play your office politics according to my simple rules, and you are bound to succeed."

Yet there are some useful warnings that can steer you away from common errors and thus indirectly help you become a successful, even if unwilling, office politician.

According to experienced hands who are willing to talk, these five admonitions are sound in principle:

Don't let politics get you down. Angry frustration simply makes you look querulous and ineffective. Try to detect the political realities around you, and then accept them as you do the climate. You are not required to condone the climate, but you must live with it.

Don't blame politics for all your troubles. Politics has a bad name because it frequently is a scapegoat. Every bungler, misfit and incompetent is quick to excuse his shortcomings by blaming "politics." Remember that in most organizations politics is less a hostile cabal than the normal mode of getting things done. All your troubles may boil down to just one basic difficulty—your failure to catch on to the local rules of the game.

Don't be an angler or a fixer. This may look profitable. For the long haul, though, it isn't. Angle players and fixers usually are suspected of making their gains by back stabbing and hence are thought untrustworthy. You can't afford such a reputation, especially if you don't deserve it.

Don't lose sight of the ball. Good workmanship and good politics have the same objective: success of the business. Any maneuvers directed at other goals are dirty politics, likely to hurt the business and you, too.

Don't buy a raw deal. A few organizations have no politics but dirty politics. In such a situation, if you are sure you are appraising it fairly, you face a practical and ethical decision. You can refuse to play and go under. Or you can bow to the ground rules, get into the game and play rough. Since neither alternative is satisfactory, your best answer to a messy political setup is to get out.

Source: "How to Play Office Politics," *Changing Times*, The Kiplinger Magazine, December 1955, p. 18.

sensible management today assumes that salaries of employees below the supervisory level are kept confidential. When a department head tells a new employee that she should keep her rate of pay confidential, it usually remains confidential until her first lunch hour.

Sometimes a new employee is an innocent victim of office politics. If, for example, a girl is discharged for incompetence but is well liked by the other girls, the girls may decide that no one should be allowed to take her place. They may ostracize the replacement.

Similarly, when one employee is given a promotion over another who is better liked by the employees, they may carry on intrigues against the chosen person. Bitterness over situations such as these may start office politics going—it may even rankle in the minds of individual employees for years.

Of course factional groups can be broken by means of transfers, but the main solution for the control of office politics is that of keeping in touch with the attitudes of the employees and applying the principles of good supervision. When workers are treated fairly as individuals by impartial, competent supervisors, they are less likely to engage in office politics to a pernicious extent. But it must be admitted that some politically inclined workers are likely to appear in even those offices having excellent supervision.

"Clerical bandits"

Even though the typical office manager does not often mention it, one of his major responsibilities is working with the accounting department and management to prevent thefts, embezzlement, and fraud. Office employees are constantly handling the company's or the customer's money, the company's merchandise and equipment. It is easy for them to appropriate postage stamps, help themselves to expensive articles in the stockrooms, filch from the petty cash box, manipulate payrolls, or share in profits from inflated expense accounts. The dishonesty may be on the small change level or in the form of a complex scheme of embezzlement. The employees involved may be cashiers, salesmen, janitors, or even executives. Some just "borrow" from the company in order to clear financial emergencies or to overcome gambling losses.

In many companies it is fairly easy for clerks and salesmen who receive payments from customers to pocket some of the company money. False receipts can be given to customers. Eventually, some of these shortages are detected when customers complain of not having their previous payments credited on their accounts.

Many stockroom and shipping clerks handle thousands of dollars worth of company goods. A case often cited is that of a large television maintenance and repair firm that went bankrupt because its employees individually were doing better business than the employer. These employees just helped themselves to spare parts and materials which they either sold to dealers or used in their own television businesses.

Research studies of office supervisors

The study cited most often is the initial project in a long-range research program in human relations in group organization conducted by the Survey Research Center, Institute for Social Research, University of Michigan. The setting for the study was the home office of the Prudential Insurance Company. The persons studied were clerical workers and their supervisors.

The members of the clerical staff were divided into sections or work groups of ten to twenty-five people. The researchers evaluated the productivity of the various sections and chose for analysis twelve high-producing and twelve low-producing sections.

As one would expect, statistically significant relationships between the productivity and the supervision of the work groups were found to be very complex. The investigators were unable to find evidence for some of the usual assumptions about the nature of effective supervision such as the effects on production of different attitudes of employees. Certain findings, however, as reported by the investigators at the time followed consistent patterns:

> The supervisors of the high producing sections seem to think and act differently with respect to their supervisory functions than do the supervisors of the low producing sections. They regard supervision as the most important part of their work and spend most of their time on it. Their method of supervision appears to be one of setting up certain general conditions for their employees and then permitting their employees to work out the details of when and how the work will be handled. They do not seem to feel the need to get into the production process at every point to check on how things are going, to make changes, to reassign the work and, in other ways, to keep a close check on operations. Their attitudes toward the employees are consistent with this approach. They appear to look at the employees as people not essentially different from themselves, people capable of taking some responsibility, people with many different interests and needs.
>
> Most of the differences found between high and low work groups appear to be related to the differing nature of the supervision of these groups. This is revealed to a limited extent from the analysis of the nonsupervisory employee interviews, but primarily from the interviews with the supervisors themselves. Some of the most important findings indicate that the heads of the high-producing sections are significantly more likely:

(1) to receive general rather than close supervision from their supervisors.

(2) to like the amount of authority and responsibility they have in their jobs.

(3) to spend more time in supervision.

(4) to give general rather than close supervision to their employees.

(5) to be employee-oriented rather than production-oriented[4]

One outstanding finding was the greater degree of pride in their work group revealed among employees in the higher-producing sections. A second finding indicated that, in one department of the company, the higher producers were more critical of certain aspects of company policy, such as the rating system and the placement system. Interestingly, too, the employees in the low-productivity sections participated more in company recreational and athletic programs.

The introduction of automation in the office

The office manager's responsibilities for providing management with the basic data of the business mean that he must familiarize himself with the modern equipment and changes wrought by automation. The new concepts of integration of data that involve factory and office operations are as revolutionary as the invention of factory machinery. They require changes in the organizational structure of the company and the office staff, in the scope of decision making, and in business operations.

The increased use of automation means that every person who intends to become an executive should read about its benefits and limitations. He should, at least, be acquainted with the name of the science that is basic to its origin. That science is cybernetics.

Cybernetics is the scientific study of those methods of control and communication that are common to living organisms and machines, especially as applied to the analysis of operations of machines such as digital and other computers, the so-called "brain machines." Cybernetics is derived from a Greek work meaning "steersman."

We have read about guided missiles that automatically make adjustments for variations in the speed of the projectile, wind direction, wind resistance, temperature, and, most important of all, *select* the target that is to be hit! These feats would be impossible without cybernetic devices.

[4]Daniel Katz, Nathan Maccoby, and Nancy C. Morse, *Productivity, Supervision and Morale in an Office Situation*, Part I (Ann Arbor: Research Center, Institute for Social Research, University of Michigan, 1950).

Cybernetics as a science is likely to have a greater effect on our lives during the next thirty years than will the physics that may eventually give us ample and cheap atomic energy. Thus far, cybernetics has had its most prominent applications to the development of computing machines that reel off in four hours a seven-day job of preparing a payroll or do a three-week production-planning chore in twenty minutes. Everyone who reads newspapers and magazines has learned of machines that can multiply forty-two or more nineteen-digit numbers per second. Computations such as these, useful as they may be for office work, inventory control, production, and marketing, have a significance far greater than computational only. When a computing machine capable of making lightning calculations is teamed up with a feedback system that monitors an automatic process, the potentials for future production and our living standards become vast indeed. They bring about a new kind of automation in industry.

Automation in industry means automatic handling of materials and parts as they go through the production process. To some extent, automation has been used in industry for many years. The current development of this trend, however, which makes use of feedback or self-correcting controls, is a new kind of technology for production.

The electronic devices that are coming into modern offices gather and process data much faster than ever before and almost instantly present it in forms suitable for interpretation. As a result, the number of hands and feet required to run an office today may be approximately the same as several decades ago, but a different type of hands and feet is likely to be needed.

The trend is in "the direction of increased specialization and mechanization of white collar work." On the secretarial level, the demand for executive secretaries, secretaries, and stenographer secretaries is increasing, but the number of senior stenographers is decreasing. This indicates that the number of dictating machine operators is going up because "millions of words once aimed at a waiting lass are now first being funneled through a machine."

In accounting work the trend toward mechanization and specialization is also evident. The number of accountants remains nearly stable, but the accounting clerical staff is increasing in order to handle the growing number of tax returns and other records required by law. There are fewer bookkeepers but more accounting clerks, statistical clerks, and statistical typists.[5]

These changes mean that the office manager and his colleagues must acquire special knowledge and judgment to gain the potential benefits in the use of automation for obtaining, recording, and interpreting data, but

[5]See Melvin J. Goldberg, "Today's Silent Office Revolution," *Dun's Review*, April 1960. Surveys made by Commerce and Industry Association of New York.

their biggest problems will not be technical. The most difficult problems will be the selecting and training of people who will provide the benefits on a practicable level. When automation is installed in an office, management must expect more grievances about unfair work assignments, noise, the condition of machines, and fatigue. Even though such grievances usually have a more deep-seated origin, they are projected against the mechanical device because it is a tangible symbol against which the employee can direct his dissatisfaction. The office manager should help employees to become more conscious of what they can do with the machine than with what the machine does to them.

QUESTIONS ON THE CHAPTER

1. Why do some "office managers" dislike the title?
2. Why is it said that an office manager is both a line manager and a staff man?
3. Comment on two major reasons why red tape develops.
4. In what ways may written reports be made inviting and readable?
5. What is the most common problem that the office manager must cope with?
6. Explain some of the behavior patterns characteristic of office neurotics.
7. Why is the presence of cliques considered a normal part of business life?
8. What methods in dealing with employees did the supervisors of the high-producing section employ in the Survey Research Center study?
9. What is one of the office manager's biggest problems involving dishonesty among employees?
10. Define the term *cybernetics*.
11. Define the term *automation*.
12. Why must management expect grievances from workers when automation is introduced into an office? How can some of the grievances be prevented?
13. Of all the ideas presented in the chapter, which ones are of special interest to you?
14. What did the chapter contribute toward your future relations with (a) office managers, (b) office employees whom you may supervise?

PROBLEMS AND PROJECTS

For All Students

1. One of the criticisms made by some office managers is that college graduates do not learn, while in college, how to write a good business letter or a

technical report. Discuss the criticism and the facilities available to you for overcoming this kind of criticism before you enter business.

2. One of the significant findings from studies of the factors influencing the productivity of office workers is the pride of the high-producing worker in his work group. Pride in the group, or lack of it, is often evident in college groups. Discuss factors that seem to bring it about in college groups with which you are acquainted.

For Advanced Students

3. Examine some of the available books and business journal articles on office management. To what extent and in what ways does each stress the human relations aspects rather than procedures or equipment?

4. Interview several office managers of your area. Ask each to cite some of the human relations problems he has experienced. What are his policies in the supervision of office employees? How does he try to raise the importance of his own job in the estimation of top management?

For Men in Business

5. Describe the functions and status of the office manager in a company where you have worked. What are his relations with other executives? What are his influences on the supervisors in regard to their relations with the employees whom they supervise?

6. One of the big human relations problems in some offices is the office or Christmas party. Describe some of the parties you have attended. Suggest some rules or policies you would follow in planning a Christmas party for the office employees.

COLLATERAL READINGS

For All Students

Haynes, W. Warren, and Joseph L. Massie, *Management: Analysis, Concepts and Cases.* Englewood Cliffs, N.J.; Prentice-Hall, Inc., 1969. Chapter 25 deals with information systems and routinization, computer systems, and operational information systems.

Hoos, Ida Russakoff, "When the Computer Takes Over the Office," *Harvard Business Review,* July–August, 1960. Discusses the view that all classes of jobs, from office clerk to vice-president, are affected, quantitatively and qualitatively.

For Advanced Students

Katz, Daniel, et al., *Productivity, Supervision and Morale in an Office Situation.* Ann Arbor: University of Michigan, Institute for Social Research, 1950. A leading study, still a classic, on the subjects listed in the title.

Simon, H. A., "The Shape of Automation." New York: Harper and Row, Publishers, 1965; Harper Paperback, 1966. A highly regarded treatise on automation and its implications.

For Men in Business

Keelan, C. I., "How the Office Manager Can Improve His Status," *The Office*, March 1959. Recommends that office managers produce fewer reports and discover how to operate office functions at lower cost.

Niles, Henry E., et. al., *The Office Supervisor: His Relations to Persons and to Work*. New York: John Wiley & Sons, Inc., 1959. Emphases are given to major management developments and to relationships between group and individual values.

Women as Office Employees and as Participants in Business

SITUATIONS YOU ARE LIKELY TO MEET

How would you meet each of these situations:
- a. *Before* you have read the chapter? What would you say to yourself or to the individual?
- b. *After* you have read the chapter? How have your answers changed?

1. An interviewer who is seeking young men for management training tells you that each trainee is given the choice of supervising female office employees for two years or supervising male factory workers for the same length of time. Which would you choose? Why?

2. Assume that you are still uncommitted as to the choice of a mate. You happen, however, to be interested in two young women as possibilities for marriage. Both are of the maverick variety. One is an "independent" in her relations to the company. The other is a "meat-eater," one who will prod her husband in regard to his advancement. Insofar as these factors are concerned, which one will you probably prefer? Why?

3. Assume that you are supervising the work of several men. The men and their wives attend company social affairs where the wife of one of your men reminds you on every possible occasion of the superior qualities of her husband, hoping that you will help bring about a promotion for him. What will you say to her the next time she reminds you of her husband's fine qualities?

The need for skill in supervising women who are employees in business has increased rapidly in recent decades. Anyone who successfully supervises women employees must do more than ask the women what they want—he must use insight and ingenuity of the kind that develops from extensive experience.

Psychological characteristics of women

Investigations of psychological sex differences show that the individual differences within one sex so enormously outweigh the differences between the sexes in *intellectual* and *semiintellectual* traits that such sex differences in practical affairs may be disregarded. When men and women show equal ability in an aptitude test, it is because they are equally gifted, not because women are less talented than men and have to work harder to get equal results.

In *nonintellectual* traits, the sex differences are more pronounced. Women exceed men in interest in persons rather than in things, in emotionality, impulsiveness, religiousness, sympathy, vanity, and shyness. Men exceed women in traits such as pugnacity, humor, and independence.

Several studies of conversations of men and of women suggest that women are more likely than men to talk about clothes, about what to do in social situations, and about the opposite sex; men are more likely to talk about sports, business, and things having money value.

Almost every woman, of course, is keenly interested in her personal appearance. The salesman who barges in on a woman at home when her hair is in curlers and her face lacks makeup is likely to find her irritable. If she can get her glamour on, she is more likely to be in a receptive mood. She feels better when she knows that she looks all right. The responsiveness of women to offers of information about improvement of personal appearance has been demonstrated again and again by publishers and advertisers.

A woman is deeply interested in people. She wants to be liked, admired, respected. Generally, she lives for others: the members of her family, friends, and those with whom she identifies herself. Because the goodwill of others is so important to her, she needs more encouragement than men. She responds to praise and admiration.

Her sense of humor differs from a man's. She does not care for practical jokes nor does she like to be kidded or teased. Contests do not challenge her, especially when the contest involves women whom she knows. And yet she will consider other women personal rivals for the admiration of those people who are important to her, particularly the boyfriend or husband.

Women identify with other women whom they admire. One reason for the use of advertising that depicts beautiful women is that those who see the illustration wish hopefully that they will look like the model.

No man can understand women fully, but some of their ways of behaving can be recognized for their importance in supervision. A woman, in some circumstances, as in opening a window, will ask a man to help her in order to stimulate interest in her. Under other conditions, as in moving a typewriter to another desk or in carrying a heavy bag of groceries into the house, she may not ask her for help—a man ought to see that she needs help and offer it without being asked!

Whenever we deal with a specific woman, at work or elsewhere, she resents comparisons of herself with other women. The supervisor, for example, should never say to a woman employee: "Do it the way Betty Jane does it." A woman knows that she is inferior and superior to other women in certain respects, but far more important to her is her intuitive knowledge that to compare one woman with another, as in comparing one wine with another wine or one mountain with another mountain, is to miss the essence of both.

The woman who is learning a new job such as operating a machine will hesitate to ask for help even though she needs it. She does not like to admit ignorance. As a learner, she feels insecure, anxious, and friendless. If she must compare her bumbling efforts as a learner with those of a skilled worker, she will feel unduly discouraged and quit. Quit rates of beginners in machine operation are high. Some training directors follow the policy of training women only in groups of learners so that each woman will compare her output with that of other learners, not with experienced operators.

Women feel less secure than men in regard to their work abilities. They have less knowledge of the business as a whole. Hence, they learn and follow rules. If rules are not available to guide them, they will look for symbols of status to guide them. In hiring and evaluating people, they are more likely than men to depend upon academic degrees and other symbols as indications of ability. Men, on the other hand, are more likely to evaluate ability regardless of degrees or symbols of status.

Women are especially observant regarding details of appearance. If, for example, the supervisor wears the same shirt or tie to the office two successive days, the women employees will notice it. The men, as a rule, will have no recollection as to what the boss wore yesterday. Also, in television commercials, the housewife usually pays more attention to the dress worn by the demonstrator of the refrigerator advertised than to the refrigerator itself. They even note whether the demonstrator is wearing a wedding ring. When a television station used a commercial showing a baby being bathed by a mother who was not wearing a wedding ring, the station received numerous letters of protest.

Women are supposed to be less business minded than men in regard to such details of business as getting their fare ready in a taxi before the destination is reached. The typical woman seldom has the fare ready. She will not start to fumble in her purse for the money until after the destination has been reached.

Women will take low-paying jobs in a city center because the place of work is convenient for side activities such as shopping. Industrial concerns on the outskirts of a city often have to pay higher salaries to hold women employees than firms near the city center. Some companies that have moved out of congested metropolitan centers into the suburbs have had much difficulty in getting women to come to the new office even though the working conditions, once the worker is there, are excellent.

The emotionality of women

Few situations in business disturb a man as much as a woman who weeps, especially when the situation is one that either arouses his sympathy or disagrees with his point of view. And when a woman cries simply because she finds that a friend bought a hat like hers for a dollar less, a man can't understand "why a woman should carry on so." Most men wish that women were less emotional. Actually, their emotional sprees probably have a great deal of the therapeutic value.

Dr. Wilson T. Sowder, U. S. Public Health Service, has stated that women escape the consequences of woe and worry in our complex civilization "by being more vocal about these conditions through tears or, occasionally, hysterics." Men shun feminine actions, but women outlive men. Their emotionality seems to contribute toward survival. And as one writer has stated "Nothing succeeds like survival."[1]

Women deal with many of life's catastrophes by means of good crying spells, but men tend to let the emotional back pressure accumulate. Women are more susceptible to troubles of an emotional sort, but three

[1]See Sidney Feldman, "Physiology of Women in Business," *The Office*, November 1956, p. 103.

times as many men as women commit suicide. However, many more women than men make an unsuccessful attempt to commit suicide!

Of course men as well as women suffer emotional upsets, but men have been taught to show only certain kinds of emotion, while women have been taught to show other kinds. The fact that men swear at a recalcitrant golf ball may be just as emotional as a woman's crying when her roast burns to charcoal.

Women who work

Women not only work to a greater extent than in previous generations, but a sizable portion of the gain is from older and married women. The increase in the number of married women who work is not caused solely by the middle-aged matrons returning to the labor force. Many working women are mothers of dependent children. Nor are most of the working women widows who must work. The percentage of wives in the labor force has been rising. In 1950, less than one in five wives of husband-wife families brought home a paycheck. Twenty years later this had risen to one out of three. Total family incomes are decidedly higher when the wife works. It is the income from the wife's work that enables many families to lift themselves into a higher standard of living.

A high percentage of women work for a while after getting married and then retire to start their families. As soon as it is practical, many of them return to take their place in the working world. This additional income adds to the disposable-income status of the family. They can buy more clothes and grooming aids, as well as contribute to paying the mortgage on the home, meeting installments on the new car, and paying for the children's education.

The woman who works increases the sales not only of semiluxuries but also of certain necessities. She is likely to shop for "convenience foods" and thereby helps to stimulate the food industries to improve their product and process research. New convenience items have gained sales much faster than standard products. By spending two dollars on convenience foods, a housewife can save herself four hours of work. Of course she can earn more than that in the four hours saved.

Individual women work for many different reasons. Some enjoy work. Many have to work to maintain the family. As one stated: "I have to work to support myself and the children because my husband is so lazy that he wouldn't put his hand out to keep from falling out of bed!" Anyone who knows the personal and family life of women employees will find numerous examples of heroism on the part of women in their effort to keep the family together.

The reasons for and importance of working can be surmised to some extent from the reasons for leaving a job. One survey of reasons for termination of employment of 498 single girls and 499 married women indicated that about 16 percent of the single girls were discharged for incompetence. Less than 4 percent of the married women had to be discharged for the same reason. Generally, single girls seem to be a somewhat uncertain bet until they have been on the job several years. Like the men, they are frequently tempted by higher money, more opportunity, and more congenial work. Married women, on the other hand, seldom seem to leave for these reasons, though they are much more likely to give up work on account of family obligations.[2]

Employer considerations in hiring women

Employers do not expect most women to be seeking a career in the job. The quest for a mate is primary. When a single woman takes a job, one of her first thoughts in looking over the place is the number and kinds of males eligible for marriage. Young girls who seek short-term jobs want regular hours, little overtime, and no other conditions that might hinder their leading a normal social life.

Generally, women have less physical strength than males and less interest in gaining advancement or earning more responsibility, but they do have certain abilities such as greater manual dexterity and usually more tolerance of routine. As a rule, women employees have better morale than male employees.

Physically, most women are chunkier than men. The trunk is relatively longer than that of the typical male, but the arms and legs are shorter. She cannot reach far or often without strain. Hence, her work

"I can take 70 words a minute, if you can spell that fast."
Source: Modern Office Procedures.

[2]See *Office Executive*, National Office Management Association, July 1957, p. 38. See also *Personnel*, American Management Association, Inc., September–October 1957, p. 4.

equipment should be designed for about 10 percent less reach than for male use. However, a woman's arms and muscles are structured so that she can fasten a dress that buttons down the back—a man imagines that he is breaking his arm when he tries to reach an itchy spot on his back.

Women tire easily when they must perform a rotary action as required in turning knobs or dials. Machines with foot pedals should be built so that little pressure is required to operate or control the machine. Seating for female workers requires special consideration.

Women tend to tire more quickly than do men when the job requires physical stamina. Their lungs are not as well adapted as those of the male to eliminate waste products by means of oxygen supplied through the lungs.

Generally, the influence of physiological and structural differences varies with the culture and with the attitude toward the work.

Women who work differ from males in that their absence record is worse at *all* ages, and the difference is even greater after age forty-five than before. Their absence frequency rate, already somewhat higher than males under forty-five, does drop with advancing years, but the severity rate (duration of absence) goes up so much faster than the males' that their overall disability rate (frequency rate $\times$ severity rate) is actually higher after forty-five whereas the males' is lower. Physicians' diagnoses, however, indicate that so-called female disorders are *not* what makes the rate so high. Attitude toward the job and responsibilities in the home are more significant as causal factors.[3]

The experience of some companies indicates that the problems of excessive female absenteeism can be dealt with effectively by intelligent management. A number of companies have found that the women in jobs that afford them little recognition are the ones most likely to be absent and that when women are upgraded or given more recognition as workers, they are more regular in attendance.

Supervising women employees

Managements often have difficulty in persuading a man to take over the supervision of an all-female or largely female work group. Some men feel that they do not want to cope with all the special difficulties.

Women as employees have somewhat different attitudes toward their work than do men. Women tend to be less interested than men in the work itself. They place more emphasis on "human relations" in supervision, as contrasted with the "work" orientation of most men. When men are offered a transfer to another job, they usually ask questions about the work, the rate

[3]See Hilda R. Kahne, Claire F. Ryder, Leonid S. Snegireff, and Grace Wyshak, "Don't Take Older Workers for Granted," *Harvard Business Review*, November–December 1957, p. 92.

of pay, and the chances for advancement. Women want to know about the friendliness of the new group.

Women want to know how to get along with the boss. When one woman, for example, resigned from her job, she was asked to break in her successor. She started by showing the new girl the files, how to handle routine work, and where the supplies were kept. Before she had gone very far, the newcomer interrupted her: "I can learn the systems without much trouble, I think, but you can help me most by telling me about the boss. What is he like? What jobs are most important to him? What upsets him most easily? Does he have moods? What puts him into a good mood? When is the best time to ask him questions?"

Most women employees want the supervisor to show his friendliness by pleasant greetings and conversation, but they do not desire close friendship. They prefer to maintain a slight social distinction between the supervisor and themselves. They define the supervisor's human relations skills in terms of impartiality, respect, and courtesy.

Women as employees deeply resent favoritism. The supervisor must be extra careful to avoid giving the impression that he has any "pets" in making his assignments of work. He cannot even smile more cordially or use a more friendly tone of voice in greeting one woman employee than another. If he wants to talk to one of three women employees, he must also recognize the presence of the other two. He should at least show that he knows they are there!

Women like to be with other women. Office executives whose desks happen to be located where they can see the entrances to the men's and women's washrooms are amused to see so many women workers go to the washroom by twos and threes. Women are gregarious but they are poor team workers. Note the differences in athletic interests of the team variety. Girls have almost no team interests such as those of boys' team sports.

Women are especially aware of the moods of those with whom they work. They take comments and simple questions as personal matters. As one supervisor stated: "Ask a man where he got a new suit and he'll name the store; ask a woman the same about a new dress and she'll likely respond, 'Do you like it?' "

Women as executives

The rarity of women as executives or as holders of the higher salaried jobs is indicated by the fact that only one-half of one percent of employed women, compared with 12 percent of men, attain this level. When male executives are asked for the reasons, their answer is usually that women are a poor investment for training—by the time they are trained they get married and leave. To a woman, her family, not her job, is her first responsibility and interest. Men cannot talk to women or associate with them in the same ways that men can with men. Keeping the sex urge under control requires rigid adherence to established custom.

Women have difficulty in making tough decisions, especially when the decisions involve people whom they like. Most important of all, very few women are willing to study and work as hard for advancement as are ambitious men.

The ambitious man has an upward career orientation. He has a long-range point of view toward job rewards and satisfactions. He is willing to make sacrifices of time, money, and energy to earn future rewards. He will tolerate poor supervision and unpleasant working conditions on a job because the experience gained there leads to another higher objective. He identifies himself with top management men and is willing to earn their approval. The typical female worker, even though she may like her job, usually has a different image of herself, different goals for her ambitions. Even though she has high intelligence, vocational training, and some ambition, she still sees her greatest career as one of getting married, taking care of a home, and rearing children.

The ambitious-to-succeed-in-business type of woman senses the differences in attitudes toward women and men executives. Most men who work under the supervision of a woman, particularly older men, have difficulty in tolerating her. They get enough of that kind of supervision at home! And they resent the kidding of other men in regard to having a woman supervisor. Men are quite willing to employ women in the office and in certain kinds of factory jobs, but they do not want to accept women as their equals in directing a business. To be successful as an executive, a woman must be better than a man. To accomplish this, some women adopt male personality characteristics, but these are disliked by both women and men. The woman who wants to advance in business must not act too much like a man or too much like a woman. As one woman stated: "The woman who wants to advance in business must look like a girl, think like a man, act like a lady, and work like a horse."

In many instances a woman's greatest difficulty, if she advances, is not in overcoming the prejudices of men but of women. They are apt to rationalize her success by attributing it to the unscrupulous use of sex.

Women have achieved recognition in certain fields. One is personnel work in department stores, hospitals, banks, and insurance offices. The fact that the New York Personnel Club membership of several hundred is exclusively female, indicates their achievements in this area of business. The positions of members range all the way from interviewer to industrial relations director and officer of the company. Job titles they hold are job analyst, training director, company communications editor, and assistant manager of compensation and benefits programs. Their functions include hiring, testing, employee relations, training, counseling, handling welfare programs, writing employee magazines, preparing cases for arbitration, exit interviewing and handling grievances.

Few women are in the top personnel jobs in heavy industry or in collective bargaining positions.

Women are especially fitted for work where extreme patience is required, where individual personnel problems arise, and where details are extremely important. As one man puts it, "She doesn't lose patience when the details would drive a man crazy."

Executives' wives

Many managements realize that the wife often plays a controlling influence in a man's upward movement in a company. When a junior executive is being considered for advancement to a senior job, the wife's possible influence may be reviewed. In a few cases, she may be invited to a social affair for the purpose of giving her a "once-over" evaluation. This kind of special examination is, however, exceptional. It usually is not necessary. If her husband has been in the company for several years, she has probably met his associates and superiors on numerous social occasions. Her major characteristics are likely to be well known long before her husband's abilities, qualities, and limitations are considered in relation to a higher executive opening. Certainly, wives are not subjected to any rigid corporate pattern to which they are expected to hold in regard to conduct or personality.

If her antennae for social situations are sensitive, the wife has learned that she can help or hinder her husband's chances in many ways. On the negative side, she has learned certain "don'ts" such as

1. Do not visit him at the job. Do not drop in on him just to pass the time of day or to tell him that one of the children has a cold.
2. Do not gossip with the wives of other employees about what is going on in the company. Avoid hearing or passing on information about company policies with which you disagree. This applies particularly to conversations at bridge parties of wives where most of the gossip deals with real or imaginary scandals of executives, who is going to be promoted or demoted, and exaggerated reports on salary increases of lucky employees.
3. Do not "high-hat" any other employee's wife, no matter how low her husband's position in the organizational hierarchy. Be a congenial mixer with wives of low, middle, and high position employees. If they like you, they will also tend to like your husband.
4. Do not expect your husband's secretary to defer to you or perform errands for you. Be friendly but not suspicious of her. Limit most

of your contacts with her to necessary telephone conversations.

5. Do not tell your husband how to run his job or the company. You should take a sincere interest in your husband's job and company but not a meddling one. Do not tell him whom to hire, fire, or promote. When a wife tries to call the shots at home, others will soon learn it, and management will consider the husband less likely to succeed as a responsible executive. (As one humorist said: "The woman who insists on wearing the pants frequently finds that some other woman is wearing the mink!")

6. Do not complain to other members of the company about your husband's job. Above all, never tell the president that your husband is not appreciated and that he could handle a much better job if the company management were less stupid. And do not complain to your husband about his lack of promotion.

One study of today's executive wife found that the malleable conformist who is willing to do or be most anything to please husband and company is becoming scarcer. The study identified two maverick types: the "independent" wife who does not care what the company thinks of her and resists corporate intrusions into her family's affairs—her husband's interests are not necessarily her own. The second type is what one executive calls the "meat-eater." She is a dominant personality who is likely to drive her husband to work harder than the employer drives him. Some executives like to promote the husband of this type, others fear the possibility that she may become too aggressive.[4]

To obtain suggestions on the positive side, John A. Patton, Chicago management engineer, decided to ask the women themselves. He polled 230 wives of executives. His findings indicated that for all the talk about the allegedly domineering attitude of women of the United States, the wives he polled took an essentially traditional view of themselves and their influence on their husbands.

The women did not think that office politicking was the best way to help their husbands. Instead, a clear majority said they could be most helpful by sending their man on his way in the morning in a good mood, feeling that he was tops so far as his family was concerned.

In the light of his survey, Patton listed these five ways in which a wife can best advance her husband's career:

1. Supplement his abilities by encouraging him and supporting him morally.

[4]See Steven M. Lovelady, "A Mind of Her Own: Today's Executive Wife Can Shun Conformity and Get Away with It," *The Wall Street Journal*, December 5, 1968, p. 1.

2. Be his sounding board. Be genuinely interested in letting him un-
   burden himself.
3. Act as a publicity agent, though a wise, discreet, and modest one,
   for the man of the house.
4. Be friendly, but not intimate, with other wives in the corporation.
   Be gracious both to peers and subordinates.
5. Realize that the rewards of higher income and prestige demand
   the sacrifice of certain other privileges. A strictly nine-to-five job
   usually means a strictly nine-to-five income.

When Patton asked the 230 wives whether they considered *money* or
standing in the community more important, 90 percent said they would
prefer their husbands to take a job with more prestige and a lower salary
rather than sacrifice social standing to money.

Most wives of executives do not resent the amount of extra time the
husband's business consumes or do they resent the intrusions of business
entertaining. Most executives' wives seem well satisfied with their lot. When
asked how they felt about the term "business widow," most of the wives
were philosophical. Some of the answers Patton received were "No differently than about golf widows"; "It's the price you pay for your husband's
success"; and "If you want the advantages of being an executive's wife, you
have to go along with the disadvantages—and there is no other way to
look at it."[5]

Wives of executives also realize that American business requires executives to change their location at short notice. An advancement or a
transfer often means severing pleasant social connections, taking children
out of school, selling one's home and buying another. Pulling up roots and
moving is to some a painful procedure, especially to women. This means
that wives of ambitious men have to learn how to look with hope for new
satisfactions in a new home, a strange community, and with new neighbors.
Some company personnel departments are careful to explain this job requirement to the ambitious men on hiring so that the man may either refuse
the job or try to educate his wife about her need for adaptation to company
transfer requirements. Many Army and Navy men usually make these adjustments with pleasure.

Employees' wives

Companies that wish to do a comprehensive job of communications
include the employee's family members, particularly the wife, in their program. The majority of wives have a vital interest in their husband's job, its

[5]See Malcolm S. Forbes, "Fact and Comment." Reprinted by permission of
Forbes, September 1, 1957, p. 12.

HOW TO DEAL WITH THE MAN

As every woman knows, the way to a man's heart is through his ego. It's also the way to prime him for success. Nothing will put so much steam into your husband's ambition as his faith in himself; and no one can bolster that faith as well as you can.

So build him up: praise and encourage him. Show that you're proud of him, and teach the kids to show their pride, too. Give him credit, when you possibly can—for his good looks, good taste, wit. When he falters, remind him of past successes and spur him on.

But—and as a woman you know this by instinct—while you boost him, also guide him. As unobstrusively as you can, help him to improve himself. Perhaps an evening a week at school would strengthen his technical background, or would help him speak better before large groups.

Above all, help him to set a goal. Are you both chiefly interested in money, prestige, security, power, job satisfaction, early retirement? Choose your priorities. Talk over your aims together. Help find direction for his ambition and you find it for your marriage, too.

Be certain, though, that you do not dominate him or push him beyond his capacities. He must be able to make decisions on his own. And there's no point in setting a goal that he cannot possibly attain.

Source: "Help Your Husband Get Ahead," *Changing Times*, The Kiplinger Magazine, November 1957, p. 41.

social status, and the dependability as well as the amount of the income. Her main interest is in the steadiness of the income.

Investigations indicate that when the company sends literature to the home such as an employee publication, a letter, or an annual report, the wife's interest in the company is increased. She must depend on the company and friends rather than the husband for information. Most husbands do not tell their wives very much about their jobs or the company. The wife would like to know more. Usually, a wife wants to feel that the company is interested in giving her understandable information. After all, the union communicates with her by sending her information and asking for her goodwill. She'd like to hear the company's story as well as the union's. Most wives are against strikes of any kind at any time and therefore have a tendency to advocate agreements that will prevent a strike.

Most wives of industrial workers are ambitious for their husbands in regard to getting more money, but they are not especially concerned about advancement opportunities in the company. They do not visualize their husbands as future executives. They want a steady income more than prestige.

Of course actions that are helpful to her count greatly. One company that had been active in communicating with the home had a business slump.

"It's a fringe benefit that goes along with being a wife."
Source: by Lepper. Courtesy *Banking* (December 1957).

To help the employees, the company set up an employment bureau to get other jobs for laid-off employees. One wife said that the first job they got for her husband went sour, but they took the trouble to get him another. She was deeply appreciative.

Some managements aim at the personal touch: a potted plant for the employee's wife when she enters a hospital or a gold brooch for her when her husband receives the twenty-five-year service watch. One company gives a party for workers and their wives when a plant passes the one million mark in man-hours without a lost-time accident.

Programs for workers' wives are especially important for those families who are transferred to new locations. They give attention to housing problems, loneliness experienced by the wives in the new community, and the school facilities for children. The stage is set for making new friends and getting oriented in the new community. Tours are arranged to points of interest. Old employees welcome the newcomers.

QUESTIONS ON THE CHAPTER

1. In what ways do men and women differ in nonintellectual traits?
2. What does it mean when it is said that a woman lives for others, and what is the importance of realizing this?
3. Why is a new woman employee often trained in a group with other learners?

4. Why are the weeping sprees of women therapeutically valuable?
5. In what percentage of American husband-wife families does the wife work?
6. Compare the percentage of male and female executives.
7. What types of work are women especially fitted for?
8. List three ways that a wife can hinder her husband's chances for success on the job. How do wives contribute to success?
9. Which factor do wives rate as more important—money or standing in the community?
10. What methods should a woman use to reach her husband's heart and also prime him for success?
11. Give suggestions for the supervision of women workers.
12. Of all the ideas presented in the chapter, which ones are of value or interest to you?
13. What did the chapter contribute to your future relations with (a) women executives, (b) women employees whom you may supervise?

PROBLEMS AND PROJECTS

For All Students

1. Interview a woman who has worked about a year and another who has worked for about twenty years. Ask them to describe their problems with supervisors and fellow workers. What studies on your part might deal with the problems they present?
2. Summarize some of the articles in current journals that treat problems of women who work. Does the material modify or amplify contents of this chapter?

For Advanced Students

3. Study available published material concerning courses or meetings for executives' wives. List the suggestions made for the wives. Show the list to a college girl. How does she react to the suggestions?
4. Interview several mothers who are working about their special problems. Study the literature on the measured effects on children of the mother's working. Compare the popular assumptions about the effects with scientifically made studies.

For Men in Business

5. Interview several women employees where you work regarding their suggestions as to what management might do to enable them to do better work in better spirit. Are any of the top secretaries working in an "isolated island" social situation?

6. To what extent are the career-minded women employees of your company encouraged to develop their career potentials? Can any of the secretaries become executives?

COLLATERAL READINGS

For All Students

Heal, Edith, *The Young Executive's Wife*. New York: Dodd, Mead & Co., 1958. How the young executive's wife can learn to enrich her own life by being an affirmative force in her husband's career.

How American Women See Feminine Types, A Series of Portraits by Social Research, Inc., for Public Relations Board, Inc., Copyright 1961 by the Public Relations Board, Inc., 75 E. Wacker Drive, Chicago.

For Advanced Students

Srole, Leo, et al., *Mental Health in the Metropolis: The Midtown Manhattan Study*. New York: McGraw-Hill Book Company, 1962.

Stessin, Lawrence, "Managing Your Manpower," *Dun's Review and Modern Industry*, October 1959. Discusses a survey of several thousand office secretaries.

For Men in Business

Newcomb, Robert, and Marg Sammons, "Easy Life for the Office Worker," *Advertising Age*, May 30, 1960. Presents a summary of a survey of office workers of two thousand American and Canadian industries made by The National Office Management Association.

Slote, Clair Trieb, "Women Executives: Fact and Fancy," *Dun's Review and Modern Industry*, December 1958. Discusses possible effects on the character of management of having an increasing number of women executives in industry.

INTERPERSONAL RELATIONS OF TYPICAL DEPARTMENTS

PART **IV**

Human Relations
in Accounting

CHAPTER

21

How would you meet each of these situations:

    a. *Before* you have read the chapter? What would you say to yourself or to the individual?

    b. *After* you have read the chapter? How have your answers changed?

1. Two friends, Mr. A and Mr. B, are arguing about the benefits of learning the business operations of a company by working in the accounting department for several years. Mr. A says: "Accounting is the nerve center of a business. That is where the data are for managing intelligently." Mr. B disagrees as to the benefits of learning about managerial techniques in the accounting department—too much dependence on logic and not enough learning about getting things done through people.

What would you say to Mr. A and to Mr. B?

2. You happen to hear comments by two top-level executives in regard to the extent that some of their subordinate executives react to the budgets for the costs of operations under their supervision. One executive says: "Last year I asked each man to express his opinion about the budget for his department. None said much of anything about it. Now most of those same men are griping because they say the budget figures were unfairly determined." The other executive says: "My men gripe too, only they are worse gripers than yours—I had each man sign his budget figures

when they were agreed upon but now they gripe anyway. What's wrong?"

Can you offer any helpful suggestions to the two executives?

Many students and businessmen think of accounting as an impersonal part of business. The student who takes an accounting course is likely to have so much trouble in learning the logic and the mechanics that he fails to appreciate its interpersonal relationships. Actually, if he enriches his perspective by means of the human relations approach, the logic and the mechanics often become more understandable and stimulating.

Accounting is the nerve center of a business. The department members collect, sort, classify, record, analyze, and distribute the data essential to directing the business intelligently. Many of the data are necessary for the *control* of operations: to keep score on the number of units produced in the factory, to determine the costs of producing them, to check the number sold and the costs of selling them, as well as to obtain numerous other data to tell management whether things are going as desired.

The term "control" can be defined as a system or procedure that provides standards of comparison and means of verification or a check on operations. A typical example might be that of a company that manufactures five product lines. The president may organize the company into five semi-autonomous divisions, each charged with a specific share of the total invested capital. Each division is held accountable for earning a stipulated return on that investment. The accounting department sets up a system of internal records and reports which enable the president to see regularly how each division is meeting or failing to meet the designated standards or objectives.

The control process involves three ingredients: the *goal*, which states what is to be done; the *procedure*, which specifies (1) how and when something is to be done, (2) who is to do it, and (3) what makes up satisfactory performance; and finally, the *checkup*, which indicates how well the job was carried out.

Obviously, many people feel resentful toward being controlled and judged. They think of the accounting reports as "report cards" to management. Supervisors, for example, feel that the reports put pressure on them and the employees. The figures do not, for example, show when standards were not met because of factors beyond the responsibility of the supervisors or the employees. The accounting controls usually cause supervisors to believe that they are constantly being goaded into greater efficiency. This kind of reaction is, of course, one result of inadequate communication.

In a sense, accounting is or should be a tool of *communication*. It collects and organizes facts and communicates to management the financially significant facts of the business. The accountant is far more than a calculating machine. He not only records and reports data but also communicates with others about the data that are necessary for conducting the business. In his informative relations with others, he:

(1) communicates to management the data necessary for decision-making.

(2) communicates by means of internal reports with other people inside the company, particularly department heads.

(3) communicates with many employees about the necessary instructions for making records and gathering data.

(4) communicates with people outside the company, usually in the form of financial reports to stockholders.[1]

The accountant's first responsibility is to do accurate recording and reporting. A correlative responsibility is to convey understanding. When he writes a report, for example, he should write in terms of the person who is supposed to read and understand it. Major points must be properly highlighted. Even the bias of the recipient should be recognized.

When he gives instructions to employees outside of the accounting department, extra difficulties arise. Most employees know nothing about accounting and care less. They may even be antagonistic to accountants' requests. A natural reason for the antagonism on the part of some employees is that they have been required to make and send to the accounting department certain records that require a lot of bother and extra labor on the part of the employee. The records go to the accounting department where the employee suspects that they really are put to little or no use. No one in the typical accounting department has ever made an effort to explain to him the need for or the uses of the records. As a result, some employees who record figures for the benefit of the accounting department consider the figures unimportant. This lack of respect for the need for certain data may

---

[1] See George R. White, "Accounting Is a Communications Tool," *National Association of Cost Accountants Bulletin*, September 1956.

affect the accuracy of the reports the accountant will compile. The human-relations-minded accountant will follow up his requests to employees in other departments to make sure that they appreciate the importance and uses of the records that they are asked to provide. He shows the employees that their reports are put to good use. He may also ask them to suggest suitable procedures for getting the information from them.

Accountants are technical men

Generally, accountants have been technically trained in the handling of figures rather than in the human relations skills involved in the figures. The personnel in the accounting areas are likely to be more intensively educated than their colleagues in sales or manufacturing. As one consultant stated, the relatively concentrated training of accounting people, coupled with the technical demands of the job, raise these questions:

> "Does the well-trained accountant use his personal ability as efficiently as he uses his technical ability? Does he tend to rest his case primarily on the facts and figures? Is he careful to convey a personal message when he is communicating his conclusions? Does he lead the horse to water and try to make him drink—when he should first make him thirsty?"

> The problem is one faced by all trained specialists. It is no small task for these men to learn to think in different ways than they have previously. It is not simple to shift from a tightly analytical approach to a broader outlook. It is quite difficult to change from dealing with tangible, quantitative, and specific matters to broad, vague, and intangible ones.

> I would like to urge industrial accountants to make the most of their technical training, but also to master it. In reports, remember that you are communicating to another person and that the extent to which you get through is in many ways directly proportionate to the keenness with which you appraise the receptivity of your listener.[2]

The accountant who senses the importance of human relations will have many opportunities to apply his insight into the way people feel about his activities. Let us assume, for example, that the management sets up a suggestion system for cost reduction. The plan is to be designed to have each employee receive a definite percentage of the savings that accrue from his suggestion. The logically minded accountant may argue that a 25 percent share of typical gross saving on a suggestion that reduces production costs

---

[2]James W. Rohrer, "To Technical Competence, Add the Human Touch," Letters to the Editor, *N.A.C.A. Bulletin*, September 1956.

$1,000 is just exactly the same as a 50 percent share of a net reduction (after deduction for costs of extra equipment) of $500. Actually, the typical employee would, however, prefer 50 percent of $500 to 25 percent of $1,000! To the employee, the division seems more fair even though the number of dollars he receives is exactly the same. To the logically minded accountant this kind of reasoning does not make sense—to the person-centered accountant it does.

Compliance with the mechanics of accounting tends to modify the thinking of nonaccounting employees

The accounting department may have need for so much data from so many employees outside the department that the mechanics of figure gathering tend to divert the employees' thinking from the productive and the creative aspects of business to the purely routine and mathematical. When a foreman, for example, is required to fill in ten copies of each of several forms every working day, plus numerous other periodic reports, he gradually learns to think in terms of the mechanics rather than the spirit of the business. Consider also the salesman who must spend hours each evening and weekend in writing up reports for the home office. His attention is directed away from his own functions to the performance of clerical work.

Peter F. Drucker has described this influence on executives and others, in part, as follows: "The things he is asked about or required to do for control purposes, come to appear to him as reflections of what the company wants of him, become to him the essence of his job; while resenting them, he tends to put effort into these things rather than into his own job. Eventually, his boss, too, is misdirected, if not hypnotized, by the procedure."[3]

The industrial accountant as a "go-giver"

In addition to his usual property and legal control functions, the industrial accountant has certain management service functions.[4] These services assist management in formulating policies, planning long-range and short-term programs of business activities, and controlling operations. The services include reports that provide a picture of current business operations plus those required for decision making. When the reports deal with the setting of budgets or standards and the making of forecasts, the accountant can think of his function in either of two ways:

[3]Peter F. Drucker, *The Practice of Management* (New York: Harper & Brothers, 1954), p. 134.
[4]See David R. Anderson, "The Industrial Accountant as a ' Go-Giver,' " *N.A.C.A. Bulletin*, June 1955.

1. He can set the standards entirely independently of the operating men who are responsible for meeting the standards. He can set up checks and balances that provide the control, or
2. He and the management can follow the policy that the operating executives should determine the standards for their own activities. The accountant, in this case, supplies information, and makes reviews and evaluations of the standards.

Typically, accountants tend to lean to the side of thinking of control as a matter of mechanical checks and balances. Those who have this tendency may try to "sell" their ideas to management and the operating employees, but they hold to the idea of control as a force that is imposed upon the members of the operating organization. This kind of auditing often results in an implied or even a direct evaluation of the competence of executives and other employees in meeting the standards. This means that the accountant becomes in essence the authority who rates the performances of the operating executives in all major areas of the business. No accountant is adequately equipped to assume such broad responsibilities even though he may carry the title of controller and be a member of the board of directors.

Since the industrial accountant is not equipped to control operations by mechanical checks and balances, he can meet the needs of the situation by putting the emphasis of his thinking on cooperative effort. He should learn all he can about the operating men's problems and establish a basis for working with them toward common objectives.

Audits

In most large companies, a control section or accountant examines and verifies the records of each one of the managerial units of the company. The results of the audit go to the president or executive vice-president. He then requests each manager or department head to come to his office where he is in many cases "put on the carpet" on the basis of the audit of his operations. The effects of this procedure are likely to be just what one would expect. The control section is referred to by numerous disdainful terms, and the members of the control group are looked upon as stooges. One of the most common criticisms of auditors, for example, is that they seldom read or understand contracts with the labor unions. As a result, the managerial head of a production unit may be criticized unfairly. The department heads after such a session then run their units to make a good showing on the control-section audits. Instead of trying to reduce costs and make profits in the most practicable manner, the goal becomes one of operating in terms of the factors that happen to be measured by the audit.

Fortunately, some managements recognize this hazard and require the auditors to make their reports directly to the head of the managerial unit studied. Here the stimulation becomes one of self-administered control rather than control by a distant authority whose evaluation is dependent upon the figures obtained in an audit.

In some companies, a Cost Control Council is organized to meet at regular intervals to review cost figures and search for means to keep them down. The accounting department's cost forms are carefully studied. If any members of the council such as supervisors do not know how to read the forms, accountants are invited to attend the sessions to explain the figures.

Such a procedure trains the members to cut down delays due to mechanical failures, to reduce training time by giving more personal attention to learners, and to encourage employees to perform economically. The effects are better control of work flow, superior quality, less absenteeism, and closer communication between all departments from designing to shipping.

Audits by independent accountants

The primary purposes of audits by professional outside firms are to ascertain the earnings and financial condition of an enterprise and to obtain certification of such condition by a disinterested and competent authority. An independent audit may be of value or necessary for these and other reasons:

1. To establish credit with or to obtain a loan from a bank—it gives the banker a complete picture of the financial essentials of a business.
2. To protect the stockholders. Theoretically, every stockholder has a right to inspect the accounts of the corporation, but the audit report usually does this for him.
3. To supply information for obtaining indemnity bonds on employees. Bonding companies want periodical audits made in order that any financial discrepancies caused by bonded employees may be discovered as soon as possible.
4. To detect technical errors in books of accounts. Clerical errors may occur in footings, in postings, and in failure to record some transactions. These aspects of independent auditing have become doubly important as a result of computerization. (Any customer who gets repeated bills for a charge he has paid will attest to the need for improved computer operation.)
5. To sell or buy a business. An audit discloses the financial condi-

tion and earning record of a business, thus enabling prospective buyer and seller to do their bargaining in terms of facts and without undue delays.

In addition, certified public accountants are able to help clients by checking their awareness of legal requirements, forecasting cash requirements, and providing data for presenting appeals to tax bureaus and boards of tax appeals. When desired by the client, the independent public accountant can make studies of departments and subsidiaries to evaluate their operations as to whether operating units are functioning properly.

Obviously, reports of such functional units are likely to reveal the effectiveness and the shortcomings of executives and other members of the operating groups. In years past, both internal and independent auditors were viewed with trepidation by some members for fear the audit might produce only criticisms. In recent years, the more usual reaction to auditors has been the assumption that their study will be helpful to the company, to the executives, and to the other employees. All are interested in improving operations, not in finding reasons for criticizing certain individuals.

Budgets

Most well-managed companies use a budget system that consists of estimates of the financial needs of each department. Usually, budgets are accounting techniques that are designed to control costs for a given period in the future. Overall estimates are made of the future needs of the business, the funds available, and the amounts to be spent by the various managerial units. Estimates of expenditures are set up for certain purposes: materials, equipment, maintenance, direct labor, and administrative expenses. Each managerial unit operates or attempts to operate within the framework of predicted expenditures. The budget has so much importance in some companies that virtually every member of the organization feels its impact.

Budgets are frequently used as a basis for rewarding and penalizing the members of the organization, particularly executives and supervisors. Failure to meet the budget in many plants may invite a reprimand or may result in a lower estimate of ability. Success in meeting it brings rewards or at least smiles from management.

Budgets affect people so directly that special consideration should be given to their human relationships.

In some companies, department heads set up an excessively tight budget. Some executives have a fetish for making up a budget lower than any other department of the company and then trying to have expenses run far below estimated expenditures. Since cutting costs frequently means holding the line on wages and salaries, ill feeling is often created between the employee deserving a raise and his immediate boss, whose hands are tied by the budget.

Budgets have a very common influence on the morale of employees who deserve increases in pay. Raises and promotions are supposedly given on the basis of merit. The immediate boss or supervisor initiates the request for an increase, but the recommendation must be approved by a department head or other member of management who is budget conscious. He protects his budget figures by means of rules and procedures. A great deal of red tape must be unraveled before a raise is approved.

Chris Argyris[5] made investigations of the impact of budgets upon front-line supervisors. This was a field study of three small plants, each with less than fifteen hundred employees. The plants manufactured both "custom made" products and products "for stock." All three were unionized, and the work covered the full range from highly skilled to nonskilled workers.

Argyris pointed out that some negative reactions to budgets are perhaps inevitable:

(1) Budgets are, first of all, evaluation instruments. Because they tend to set goals against which to measure people, they naturally are complained about.

(2) Budgets are one of the few evaluation processes that are always in writing and therefore concrete. Thus, some of the supervisors tend to use budgets as "whipping posts" in order to release their feelings about many other (often totally unrelated) problems.

(3) Budgets are thought of as pressure devices. As such they produce the same kind of unfavorable reactions as do other kinds of pressure regardless of origin . . . the effects of management pressure upon supervisors is not necessarily limited to budgets. For example, a company "saddled" with a domineering executive but which has no budget may well be affected by the same factors as those reported.

Argyris found that one of the most common of the factory supervisors' assumptions about budgets is that they can be used as a pressure device to increase production efficiency. The need for pressure is based on the assumption that most workers are inherently lazy. Many employees also believe that top management thinks the workers do not have enough motivation of their own to do the best possible job. Such feelings, even if never openly expressed to the employees, filter through to them in very subtle

[5]Chris Argyris, "Human Problems with Budgets," *Harvard Business Review*, January–February 1953.

ways. Once they sense that feelings of this kind exist in top management, they may become very resentful.

The pressure, while increasing efficiency, may also release forces that pull in the opposite direction. Employees try to keep production at the new level and to prevent it from rising again. Tensions begin to mount. People become uneasy and suspicious. They increase the informal pressure to keep production at the new level.[6] The employee can release some of his tensions by joining a group against management. The supervisor cannot because he at least partially identifies himself with management. Certainly, he would not help his chances for advancement by joining an antimanagement group.

Of course, relatively few supervisors get ulcers or experience a nervous breakdown because of pressure from budgets. Managements must, however, use intelligent approaches to the problem of pressure. One of the approaches invariably recommended is to gain acceptance by having supervisors participate in the making of the budgets that affect them. Controllers usually emphasize the need for participation of all key people in instituting any changes in budgets, plus the willingness on the controllers' own part to revise their budgets whenever experience indicates it is necessary. Argyris's observations indicated, however, that some controllers find it easier to follow the form than the spirit of participation:

> The typical controller's insistence on others' participation sounded good to us when we first heard it in our interviews. But after a few minutes of discussion it began to look as if the word "participation" had a rather strange meaning for the controller. One thing in particular happened in *every* interview which led us to believe that we were not thinking of the same thing. After the controller had told us that he insisted on participation, he would then continue by describing his difficulty in getting the supervisors to speak freely. For example:
>
> "We bring them in, we tell them that we want their frank opinion, but most of them just sit there and nod their heads. We know they're not coming out with exactly how they feel. I guess budgets scare them; some of them don't have too much education. . . . Then we request the line supervisor to sign the new budget, so he can't tell us he didn't accept it. We've found a signature helps an awful lot. If anything goes wrong, they can't come to us, as they often do, and complain. We just show them their signature and remind them they were shown exactly what the budget was made up of. . . ."
>
> Such statements seem to indicate that only pseudo-participation is desired by the controller. True participation means that the people

---

[6]See Kurt Lewin, "Group Decision and Social Change," in Theodore Newcomb and Eugene L. Hartley, eds., *Readings in Social Psychology* (New York: Henry Holt and Co., 1947), especially p. 342.

can be spontaneous and free in their discussion. Participation, in the real sense of the word, also involves a group decision which leads the group to accept or reject something new. Of course, organizations need to have their supervisors accept the new goals, not reject them; however, if the supervisors do not really accept the new changes but only say they do, then trouble is inevitable. Such halfhearted acceptance makes it necessary for the person who initiated the budget or induced the change, not only to request signatures of the "acceptors" so that they cannot later on deny they "accepted," but to be always on the lookout and apply pressure constantly upon the "acceptors" (through informal talks, meetings, and "educational discussions of accounting").

In other words, if top-management executives are going to use participation, then they should use it in the real sense of the word. Any dilution of the real thing "will taste funny," and people will not like it.[7]

Of course budget installations should not be made to appear as edicts of accounting department experts or as dragnets for substandard performance. Budgets should be looked upon as aids in achieving objectives. Lack of understanding of these objectives can lead to suspicion of the budget— even to its rejection. Top management should therefore state the objectives in a manner that causes employees to desire a budget that is reasonable and challenging.

Generally, one reason for hostility toward existing budgets is the typical accountant's tendency in reporting budgeted performance to show, and even to emphasize disproportionately, what is wrong, without considering why variances occurred. The budget reporter should note first where actual performance has been significantly better than estimates and then mention what has fallen short of expectations. Analysis of the latter should be cautious because the origin of shortcomings may be in factors not evident to the financial analyst.

Department heads, for example, should not be held accountable for machine downtime, unavoidable reruns, and faulty material unless normal allowances for these are made in the departmental budgets. Also, if budgets are based on standards of maximum possible efficiency at full production, it is likely that actual costs can never approximate budgeted goals.

As a teacher of accounting has stated:

Because of the complexities of budget preparation, especially at first, perhaps the best policy is to make the program frankly experimental. By doing so, management is saying, "Here is a plan based on the best judgment of all of us and on certain available past-perform-

7Argyris, "Human Problems with Budgets," p. 108.

ance data. Let's try it out and use it for what it is worth. After this first tryout, we shall be in a position to have more insight when we prepare our next budget." Such an approach puts operating department heads on their mettle. If the experiment is even partly successful, it will be because junior echelons of the management team have helped to make it so. And, in the right kind of business enterprise, foremen and other leaders should welcome the opportunity to take a greater part in management through further development of the budget as a useful means of planning and controlling business operations.[8]

A controller may control so rigidly that management cannot discover its competent men

Most executives should, of course, know how to interpret financial records. All find it helpful to be aware of the effects of accounting controls on the spirit of the organization. The controller's primary function is to gather and interpret data that will assist other executives in the determination of sound policies and their successful execution. In some cases controllership is performed by the financial vice-president; more often it is the chief accountant who is responsible for this function.

Anyone who notes the influence of the controller in a number of companies is likely to find that some managements follow so rigid a policy of accounting controls that top management has difficulty in discovering its competent self-initiating employees. Advocates of rigid executive controls insist they are guarding against broad delegation of authority to employees who do not have the capacity to exercise it efficiently.

Some accountants think that it is more important to set up controls that will assure behavior than to find out which individuals are men of initiative.

Management men who are more interested in discovering their men of initiative than in having the benefits of obedience may resent the rigidities imposed by the controller type of mind. The senior vice-president of a large corporation, for example, voiced his objection to the tight mechanical controls set up by the company's controller by defining a controller as "an accountant who thinks slowly!"[9] Such an executive would say that it is usually more important for a supervisor to find out which one of his employees is capable of exercising initiative and good judgment than to control the actions of all the employees in accordance with the policies laid down by the supervisor himself.

[8]See Colin Park, "Giving Budgeting Appeal for the Foreman," *N.A.C.A. Bulletin*, October 1951.

[9]This kind of humorous definition of an occupational member is found in many groups and mature members do not resent it—they accept it as humor. Consider the many definitions of statisticians you have heard.

The term "controller" in itself implies a firmness that calls for obedient rather than creative thinking.

Obviously, different philosophies of management are followed by different managements. Some have developed the practice of very rigid controls; others have set up controls in a manner that still allows ample breathing and working space for the men of initiative. This suggests that the student of accounting, or perhaps better, the practicing accountant, should note whether the internal controls set up by the accounting department or controller tend to inhibit or release the creative potentials of the people in the organization.

Typically, the technically minded accountant is trained in the importance of standard procedures and good business practice. A system, once it has been set up, should be obeyed. It is perfectly natural for him to check the work records of others. However, we should also bear in mind that not all rigidities are discretionary. A lot of record keeping must also be attributed to the nature of the business, not to the zeal of the controller.

Usually, the personnel man and the other alert members of an organization recognize this kind of influence in the company. When, for example, an applicant applies for a job, the human-relations-minded interviewer tries to estimate the extent to which the applicant would fit into the company's rigidities. Consultants who make incisive observations in many different companies note that employees who like a rigidly controlled working environment tend to find that kind of employment. Employees who like the opposite work situation tend also, in time, to find it. The student who is aware of company and individual personality similarities and conflicts should, when choosing an employer, consider the influence exerted by the accountants—would he be happier in a rigidly controlled working situation or in another company where controls are more flexible? To make his decision, he should discuss with the prospective employer the kinds of controls that are made on operations by the accounting department.

Cost controls should be checked to find out their actual rather than their imagined effects on costs

One of the stories often told to illustrate the effects of absurd rigidities in controls is that of the "railroad washroom doors." According to the story, the new president of a railroad was surprised to find that some twenty thousand dollars was being spent each year to replace the damaged outer doors of washrooms in small stations on the line. Upon investigation, he learned that the doors had been damaged and had been replaced in accordance with the company's accounting rules. Doors to washrooms were kept locked except just before and after trains were at the depot. Quite frequently a traveler who had come to wait for a train would request the key and thoughtlessly not return it before boarding the train. Station agents were allowed to spend only twenty-five cents a year to buy new keys for the washrooms. The station agent reasoned that if he sent through a requisition for a new key, it would be six weeks before his request was approved. Furthermore he also had to file a detailed explanation. If, however, he should break open or otherwise damage the door, he could purchase a new door because according to the controller this was a capital improvement, whereas a new key was an "expense item." The simple practice of breaking the door was followed by all the station agents and was costing the railroad a considerable sum of money a year! If the controller had allowed the station agent to buy a new twenty-five-cent key whenever one was needed, this unnecessary expenditure could have been saved—and the dignity of the agent preserved.

Retrenchment periods—cost-cutting drives

When profit margins are being pinched, managements know why. The usual causes for the pinch—higher labor and material costs plus sharpened competition—are evident. To bring profit margins back to normal often necessitates the cutting of costs.

This kind of situation is so common in American business that the sophisticated old-timers look upon a retrenchment period as the expected phase of a familiar cycle. When business is good, no one worries very much about extra expenses and minor added costs. When profit margins dip, the cost-cutting programs multiply. The drive usually starts in the manufacturing operations and then moves into the offices where expense accounts, telephone bills, paperwork, and added personnel are coldly scrutinized. Departments are often merged to reduce supervisory costs.

The effects on the morale of many employees is, of course, terrific. To most employees, the terms "economy program," "cost reduction," and "retrenchment" are frightening, particularly to recently hired employees. They fear that their jobs will be the first to be eliminated. Older employees, too, particularly those who feel insecure about their positions, begin to fear the possibility of dismissal. This fear has special portent for the old employee who suspects that the boss thinks of him as being out of date in his methods. Perhaps, he thinks, he's only deadwood in the organization to his superiors?

Doubts and worries accumulate during these periods, and managements wonder how the unnecessary fears may be prevented. Should management tell the employees that expenses have to be reduced? Or should the economy program be put into effect quietly and unobtrusively?

Progressive managements know that there is no alternative—employees *must* be told. They must be told because expenses cannot be reduced without the cooperation of the people down the line. But they need not be scared if the accounting department is human-relations minded and works with management and men to show where costs are out of line or might be reduced.

Transal Engineering Corporation, a relatively small producer of electronic equipment and radio gear, found one way. With ten separate assembly lines for different products, relatively long runs, and a simple assembly task, management improved the profit rate from 4 percent or less to 12 percent by means of daily cost reports to the ten foremen. Each day each foreman was given a statement telling in dollars and cents whether his operation was in the red or black, whether it was on schedule the previous day, and what his current standing was on his contract. These daily statements replaced previously used month-end reports that usually came too late for action. Under the old system, by the time a foreman realized something was wrong the damage was already done.

In a larger company with a more complex production setup, this daily type of control is next to impossible. Such companies turn instead to standard costing and the targeting of specific savings goals for divisions and departments.

Regardless of whether the company is large or small, when employees are told about the need for the economy drive and their participation is sought in a sincere spirit, the drive does not arouse unnecessary fears. A favorable human-relations climate is basic to make the program effective.

One company president launched an expense-reduction drive with a memorandum to all department heads stating that the economies must be realized "without hurting any of our people."

This phrase got around via the grapevine, and was probably more responsible for the success of the program than any other factor. Some jobs were eliminated, as was inevitable, but other jobs were found—some of them much better—for those affected. The organization was tightened up and made much more efficient because of the cooperation of the whole working force.

The cooperation was insured in advance by the simple phrase— "without hurting any of our people."[10]

Property control and auditing functions of the accountant

One important function of the accountant and auditor is to keep an accurate check on the property and assets of the company, not only for the

[10]"Keeping Morale UP and Costs DOWN," *Modern Management,* March 11, 1957. Copyright © 1957 by The Bureau of National Affairs, Inc., Washington 7, D.C.

use of management but also for the protection of the stockholders who own the business.

The fact that some large and small losses are sustained by companies and are allowed to continue undiscovered over long periods of years brings blushes to the faces of the accountants who are expected to devise proper systems of control. Accountants are supposed to prevent dishonesty losses and to make an early discovery in the event of any serious breakdown in operational procedure.

Two things are essential in preventing dishonesty losses and assuring early discovery when they do occur:

1. A good system of internal control. Poor internal controls are an invitation to the dishonest employee.
2. Continual vigilance. The success of the system of internal controls depends entirely on the human beings responsible for its administration.

    The system may break down through an officer or employee allowing someone else to reconcile his bank accounts for him; through his failure to maintain proper control over customers' accounts; or through relinquishing any part of his assigned duties (no matter how small) to another employee who volunteers to perform them. Large scale embezzlers are generally the most willing and hardest workers in an organization and often when a loss is discovered the management or executive officer is surprised to find the scope of the defaulter's activities. . . .

    Employees may be divided into two groups. There is the larger group which is thoroughly honest and trustworthy. They are morally honest and just could not be dishonest under any circumstances. We do not have to worry about them. On the other hand, there is a second group of employees—I'm glad to say in the minority—who consider themselves honest and actually do not think they will ever be dishonest. But, let them have domestic trouble, sickness or become involved in gambling or women, and then expose them to a loose system of internal audit and to a good system which has sprung a leak, and they have an open invitation to steal, or, as they feel, "borrow," their employers' funds. In my opinion, management is largely responsible for the casualties in this second group. It is necessary to protect these employees from themselves by keeping temptation out of their way. Practically all large dishonesty losses are caused by persons who were never found guilty of prior dishonest acts. Occasionally we have repeaters, but these are very much the exception rather than the rule.

All officers and employees should be required to take a vacation. A successful embezzler cannot afford to take a vacation or even get sick. For that matter, he cannot afford to die. Beware of the person who voluntarily assumes to take care of part of another employee's duties or operations.[11]

Typically, embezzlers are trusted employees. It is believed that they steal more than all the nation's professional criminals.

The typical embezzler usually has no previous police record. He earns enough to live comfortably. The employer usually has a high regard for his work. He is usually considered a desirable employee with a secure future. Sometimes he is even looked upon as a pillar of society. To his friends he is quite normal mentally. Actually, inside his head he is fighting battles with himself. The origin of the conflicts is not so much in the opportunity to steal as in his early childhood history. His thievery may be a maladjusted attempt to gain the affection of others. When caught, he usually feels better because the element of self-punishment is mixed in with his crooked motives.

Some thieves of company property have a vengeful motive, like the employee who justified helping himself by saying he was underpaid. Hotel patrons steal towels partly because they feel they are overcharged.

When the accountant sets up safeguards to prevent defalcations or thievery, he does not remove the embezzler's motives. That is a psychiatric function, but the accountant can help detect these badly motivated individuals as soon as possible and help place them in positions where their conflicts do not damage themselves, the employer, or their friends. Sometimes he may even be able to get them to seek psychiatric treatment. Certainly the usually designated motives of "high living, slow horses, and fast women" only tell us where the money went. Removing the opportunities to gamble does not change the urge to gamble. Only psychiatric treatment can do that.

When you study or practice accounting

Accounting to many students and employees in business is viewed as a mechanical, mathematically precise operation only. Actually, it is the center of a communications system for management and employees. All the accountant's figures and reports involve people. This means that when you study or practice accounting, you should do more than record figures accurately—you should also think of them as a means of conveying understanding.

[11]George A. Conner, "Management's Responsibility for Dishonesty Losses," *The Office*, November 1952, pp. 69, 140, 157.

"Methods may be different from the old days, Perkins, but we still check expense accounts in the same old way." Source: by Charles D. Saxon. Reprinted from *Sales Management*.

This kind of attitude should make the subject and the people in accounting more interesting to you. Bear in mind, that accountants are intelligent. Most are receptive in regard to the effects of their work on others. They want to do their work in ways that develop goodwill toward them as well as toward other members of the business team.

QUESTIONS ON THE CHAPTER

1. Name several ways that enable an accounting department to be a tool of communication.
2. Why and how should an industrial accountant become a "go-giver" instead of a "go-getter"?
3. What is the value of having auditors report directly to the head of the managerial unit they are studying?
4. According to Chris Argyris's field study, what is the most common negative reaction to budgets by factory supervisors, and what effect may this have on the employees?
5. In what ways do supervisors ease the pressure applied to them by top management and how do these differ from the employees' reactions to the same pressure?

6. Explain the functions of a controller. Name some of the ways in which he can help or hinder the effectiveness and spirit of management and employees.

7. What principle of cost controls is suggested by the story of the "railroad washroom doors"?

8. What action should management take toward employees to prevent unnecessary doubts and fears from accumulating during a retrenchment period?

9. Discuss ways to prevent dishonesty losses in a company. Should the main objective in the prevention be catching the thieves or giving honest employees more emotional security? How do you personally look upon the purposes of the cash register where you buy merchandise?

10. Cite from your own experience any instance of thievery from a business concern. Could a better accounting system have prevented that kind of theft?

11. Now that you have read about ways in which accounting may dominate the spirit in a company, would you prefer to work in a company that has many or few accounting controls? Explain your reasons for your choice.

PROBLEMS AND PROJECTS

For All Students

1. The student who has majored in accounting may find his first jobs dull and routine. His supervisors may know little theoretical accounting. How can the well-trained young accountant make his first jobs challenging and enjoyable?

2. Examine recent issues of the *Harvard Business Review*. Read articles that deal with accounting. To what extent do they treat human relations?

For Advanced Students

3. Make a study of human organizational accounting. See D. C. Miller and W. H. Form, *Industrial Society: The Sociology of Work Organizations*, New York: Harper & Row, Publishers, 1964, as an example of a resource.

4. Some persons think that accountants are likely to be introverted and impersonal. Study the question. Start your study with Stanley J. Segal, "The Role of Personality Factors in Vocational Choice," *The American Psychologist*, August 1955.

For Men in Business

5. Make a study of economy programs that have been made stimulating to the employees. For suggestions, read E. Lee Tallman, "Top Management and Cost Reduction," *The Management Review*, American Management Association, Inc., October 1957.

6. Describe some of the human relations problems of members of accounting

departments of companies with which you are well acquainted. To what extent does the content of this chapter treat or fail to treat the problems observed?

COLLATERAL READINGS

For All Students

Massie, Joseph L., *Essentials of Management*, Englewood Cliffs, N.J.: Prentice-Hall, Inc., 1964. Chapter 9 treats managerial accounting, particularly budgeting, responsibility accounting, and trends in management accounting.

Morell, R. W., *Management: Ends and Means*. San Francisco: Chandler Publishing Co., 1969. Chapter 4 emphasizes the ends and means approaches to management rather than traditional functionalism.

For Advanced Students

Brummet, R. Lee, William C. Pyle, and Eric G. Flamholtz, "Human Resource Accounting in Industry," *Personnel Administration*, July–August 1969. Describes a human resources accounting system designed to measure investments in employees.

Likert, Rensis, and David G. Bowers, "Organizational Theory and Human Resources Accounting," *American Psychologist*, June 1969. Presents additional information related to human resources accounting.

For Men in Business

Haynes, W. Warren, and Joseph L. Massie, *Management: Analysis, Concepts and Cases*. Englewood Cliffs, N.J.: Prentice-Hall, Inc., 1969. Chapters 15–18 deal with basic cost concepts, distinctions between financial accounting and managerial decision making.

Newman, Summer, and Warren, *The Process of Management*, Englewood Cliffs, N.J.: Prentice-Hall, Inc., 1967. Chapters 27–29 discuss basic elements in controlling, securing flexibility, and responses of people to controls.

Human Relations in Finance

SITUATIONS YOU ARE LIKELY TO MEET

How would you meet each of these situations:

    a. *Before* you have read the chapter? What would you say to yourself or to the individual?

    b. *After* you have read the chapter? How have your answers changed?

1. An enthusiastic factory worker tells you that the morale of his fellow workers is excellent—every employee works hard to bring about quality production and to reduce costs. He says: "A company that has cooperation of that kind is bound to make money." You, however, happen to know that the company has not been making an adequate return on its operations. How would you explain the situation to the employee so as not to dampen his enthusiasm and yet help him understand why the company is not making money in spite of excellent employee cooperation?

2. One of your friends tells you that the next time he applies for a job it will be with a company that has a lot of cash in the bank—he is tired of working in his present company where management seldom has enough money in reserve to pay for the things that should be done, such as buying needed production equipment that would reduce costs.

    What comments would you offer for his consideration?

Finance can be defined as an application of accounting, business economics, business law, and statistical inference, plus experience and human relations, to the acquiring, managing, and allocating of business funds. Money is so basic a resource of a business firm that the head of the firm usually retains control or close supervision of its finances. He may be an owner or chief executive officer. In some corporations major responsibility for financial policies is vested in a committee of the board of directors. In most corporations a treasurer or a financial vice-president functions as a center of financial matters.

The financial executive of a company provides information currently essential for guidance of the administrative officers in many of their functions. In this way the finance officer participates in determining policies in wage and other union negotiations, and in such decisions as whether to meet competitors' prices. The prospective effect on the company's earnings of new services or products or product changes is an important concern of the chief finance officer. He is also vitally concerned with stockholder relations and to a considerable extent with public relations since he is the authority on questions relating to any aspect of the company's finances in which the public is interested.

The chief financial officer has work relations with almost all executives of the company. When the board of directors and the chief executive officer are considering any program for expansion such as the building of a new plant or the purchase of a costly machine, the inevitable question is, "Do we have (or will we have) the money to pay for it?" When the production manager, research director, or sales manager wish to set up expansion programs, the counsel of the chief finance executive is essential. He must have money available whenever it is needed. His responsibilities usually involve the development of contacts with sources of money such as banks and other financial institutions. The effective financial officer sounds out bankers long before the company actually needs money. He finds out which ones are willing to participate in serving the company's financial needs. When he is ready to borrow money, he knows which banks are favorably disposed toward making the loan. Before making the final approach for a substantial amount, he has informed the bank's officers of his company's financial status and the plans for the use of the money. A well-formulated plan for the use and repayment of the loan is basic to the getting of a loan or raising capital.

One important finance function that affects the job security of employees is obtaining working capital for the company. The finance officer must decide whether the company's working capital will be obtained through borrowing, through retaining profits, or through selling securities in the stock market. He must be acquainted with the profit possibilities and the risk factors in the business.

The finance officer has major responsibilities in regard to the financial health of the company, and he must guide the management in its use of the company's funds. He must help to keep the members of financial circles, the public, and the employees properly informed in regard to the company's financial status and needs. Much of his work is informative and educational.

Need for educating employees in regard to the employer's finances

We can appreciate the need for informative services when we review the opinions and attitudes of employees toward the finances of employers. Employees are likely to have warped opinions about wealth and how it is acquired. Many individuals are likely to be defensively envious toward persons of wealth rather than objective about the economic benefits of saving. This attitude toward wealth is very old as indicated by one of Socrates' statements made more than two thousand years ago, approximately 354 B.C.

> "When I was a boy, wealth was regarded as a thing so secure as well as admirable that almost everyone affected to own more property than he actually possessed. . . . Now a man has to be ready to defend himself against being rich as if it were the worst of crimes. For it has become far more dangerous to be suspected of being well off than to be detected in crime."

Worker bitterness toward company and profits is frequently found today. Surveys of employees' opinions have brought up statements such as the following:

> "This company has lots of dough! They could pay us more wages out of their big profits if they wanted to."
> "Let business pay all the taxes. They can stand it better than we can."
> "Wage increases don't need to raise prices to the customers."

"All profits ought to go to the workers. The stockholders are all rich people who have too much money now."

" 'Capitalism' means that my employment is insecure and that my opportunity for advancement or self-employment is reduced."

" 'Capitalism' means that the world's wealth is unfairly distributed."

"Profits are idle dollars in the bank."

"All profits go to stockholders."

"Profits are something in the nature of a gift to the owners, something obtained without work."

"Most stockholders are rich men, and chief among them are the officers of the company."

The errors in some of these opinions are indicated by surveys of stock ownership in America. Of all adults, about one in seven owns some stock. The number of shareholders in the United States is greater than the number of factory workers. Most shareholders need their dividends. They are not persons of great wealth. In United States Steel, for example, the owners of the business outnumber the employees by a considerable margin. No one person holds as much as three-tenths of one percent of the outstanding stock. A survey showed that more than half of the shareowners had incomes that were less than the average wage the company was paying to its steel-workers.[1] Similar findings have been obtained from analyses of stockholders of many of our largest corporations.

Companies that have tried to teach workers the economic facts of life find the task very difficult.[2] The management of a large manufacturing company, for example, planned and conducted a campaign of economic education among its workers to explain the benefits of profits, the need for adequate returns for investors, and the values of our system of free enterprise. The campaign failed to make any change in the workers' attitudes. As a result, the company officials concluded that the workers were shortsighted and stubborn.

This particular management did not realize that the employees were as interested as management in what affects the security of their jobs. The problem had not been presented to the employees as one that was related to the workers' bread and butter. Logical reasoning and economic abstractions about the need for a more adequate return on the investment of somebody who, in the opinion of the employees, had a good deal more money than they did, aroused no interest on their part. Instead of recognizing the

[1]Roger M. Blough, *Learning to Multiply and Divide* (United States Steel Corporation, 71 Broadway, New York, 1957).

[2]For a more complete treatment of false ideas about profits and efforts of companies to give employees economic facts, see *Telling Employees about Business Operations: Profits*, Policyholders Service Bureau, Metropolitan Life Insurance Company, New York.

contribution of stockholders to the employees, the effect was to cause the workers to think that people who had enough money to invest in the corporation were avidly arguing for even more.

Very few employees think of the need for adequate financing, yet the problem, illustrated in the Thompson Products' story of the "The Solid Gold Turret Lathe" is a very serious one to management.

The story starts back in 1942 when the company bought a lathe for $12,000. Under federal tax laws, the company was permitted to depreciate the cost of the lathe over a 14-year period. So, last year, when the lathe became obsolete, there was $12,000 to buy a new one, plus $1,000, which was the resale value of the old one.

But the replacement cost in 1956 was $35,000 for a lathe that would perform the same functions as the old model, or $67,000 for a new one with attachments to meet today's more exacting needs.

The company had only $13,000 to do a $67,000 job. The difference of $54,000 had to come out of profits, and in order to get that amount in 1956 the company had to earn a profit of more than $112,500 before taxes, because $54,000 was all there was left after taxes. The corporate profit tax is 52%.

And to earn that amount of profit, the company had to sell more than $1,250,000 worth of products to replace one lathe which originally cost just $12,000!

Sounds like a lot of profit—$112,500. BUT: The stockholders got none of it. The government took more than half of it. The rest went to replace a machine so three Thompson people—one per shift—could continue working.

Sounds fantastic? Sure. But it's true. It's fantastic *because* it is true! This tale of the million-dollar lathe was part of Thompson Products' annual report to its stockholders which gives details on how much money the company took in and what happened to it.

Only a relatively small amount of profit a company makes is paid to stockholders in dividends. A large portion must be retained and plowed back into the company to finance expansion and replacement costs so the company can continue operating and employees can continue working.[3]

Annual financial reports

The key medium of the typical employee educational program when sponsored by a financial officer is likely to be the annual report. The extent to which these annual reports are read by employees of a typical industrial

[3]"To Members of the Thompson Organization," annual report of Thompson Products, Inc. (Cleveland, Ohio, March 5, 1957).

company is indicated by the answers to four questions used as part of an employee morale survey:

1. A 24-page copy of the company's "Annual Report for the Past Year" presented to employees for the first time the financial facts, balance sheets, dividends paid, average weekly earnings, etc. Did you see a copy of the report?

	Men	Women
Yes	87%	73%
No	12	20
Not sure	1	7

2. If you saw a copy of the report, about how much of it did you read?

	Percentage of Men Who Saw Report	Percentage of Women Who Saw Report
a. All of it	60%	16%
b. Most or about ¾ of it	17	14
c. About half	12	16
d. About one-fourth	3	8
e. Glanced at a few pages	8	42
f. None	1	5

3. If you gave a copy of the report to any other members of your family or friends to read, about how many persons read parts of the report?

	Men	Women	Total
a. No one	20%	22%	21%
b. One or two persons	52	47	50
c. Three to five persons	17	9	13
d. Six to nine persons	3	0	1
e. Ten or more persons	2	0	1

The response to this question indicated that for every employee who saw the report there were 1.3 other people who saw it.

4. After seeing the report, what is your impression about the division of the income of the company in the last five years?

	Men	Women
a. The payments to *stockholders*, in comparison with payments to or for the benefit of employees, went up and payments to the employees went down (wrong answer)	3%	4%

	Men	Women
b. The payments to *employees* went up and those to stockholders went down (correct answer)	64	20
c. Don't remember	33	77

One of the basic ways in which reports may be improved is in their tone or spirit. Too many reports still have a protestation-of-virtue tone. Information is usually presented in a manner that is decidedly favorable to management's interests. A low-paid manual worker, for example, is not likely to be impressed by a chart that shows that the compensation paid to executives is only a tiny slice of the sales dollar pie while the portion that went to labor is represented by the biggest piece of all. The employee thinks in terms of the relative number of individuals involved and the average per capita income of the persons represented by the two cuts of the pie.

Some reports present figures to show that if executives worked for nothing and their salaries were divided equally among all the other employees, the increase for each employee would amount to only a few cents per week. The employees know that the salaries of executives on an individual basis are much higher than the wages of the worker. Why try to kid the worker? Why not simply state that good executives, like good workers, cost money?

Some reports present the stockholder's financial investment in the company as one of benevolence—he puts his money into the company in order to give employees good jobs at a high rate of pay! To the typical employee, the stockholder's risks are meaningless. The stockholder to the typical employee is a rich person who doesn't have to work while the worker is investing all his "capital"—his skill and energy—in the business.

The evolution of accounting and financial reporting has been influenced by the needs of those whose interests are affected—the proprietor of the business, the creditors, the stockholders, the investing public, the tax gatherer, the regulatory agency. In many companies, labor is recognized as having a legitimate interest in the overall results of business operations, and it has become a new addition to the list. As a result new accounting and reporting methods are being devised to serve this purpose.

The writing of financial statements for employees, as well as for stockholders or anyone else, is a very difficult task. One of the main difficulties is the commonly held belief that all corporate income is in liquid form, that it is all available for distribution to the employees and stockholders, and that it is annually distributed by the management. To most people, corporate income and corporate cash are the same. To them, all the corporate income can be distributed without impairing the business. Actually, income may be in the form of land, plant, machinery, patent licenses, or contractual benefits as well as money. The distribution of all income would in most cases require the liquidation of assets necessary to the continued operation of the business.

Most people do not understand the nature or dynamics of business. Many persons, college educated as well as not, imagine that business organizations are deliberately designed to extract unfair profits from the public and the employees. To them, corporations constitute a system of power which will be exploited for selfish benefit only. Those corporations that are owned by absentees, they feel, bleed the communities where they manufacture or sell goods. Presumably, the only cause of unemployment is greed.

Financially alert men try to overcome these and other false notions. They realize that a corporation is the legal name for a group of persons who own certain facilities or tools of production and exchange that are used in a business. Improved tools enable man to change raw materials into products that contribute to better living. Such tools can come only from the savings of individuals who exchange some of their income, in the form of stock purchase, for eventual hope of getting some pay—dividends—for the loan.

Few people realize that the public interest is served through the mutuality of interests of manager, stockholder, worker, and customer of the business. All depend for their livelihoods upon the manner in which a company serves the public.

Stockholders' meetings

During recent years many companies have stepped up their efforts to lure stockholders to annual meetings. As a result, former poorly attended annual meetings are now attended by hundreds, even thousands of stockholders.

A cross-country survey showed that annual meetings are planned to be both entertaining and informative. Some companies arrange plant tours and provide attractive product displays. Management-shareowner discussions are becoming increasingly frank. In a few cases management hospitality has even become lavish. The reason for the attempt to increase attendance is the growing awareness that dissatisfied stockholders can make life rather uncomfortable for a complacent management.

When earnings drop, some shareholders place all blame indiscriminately on management. A marked downturn in profit margins causes the top executive in some companies to wince at the thought of the heat of stockholder wrath that he is likely to feel at the next annual meeting. Naturally management circles are anxious to keep stockholders off their backs. Small wonder that annual meetings are being planned more and more to please the shareholders. The good will that may be engendered toward management may be more important than the displays and plant tours organized to sell stockholders on company products. The development of respect for the competence of the management often dominates the program. The stockholder who has personally met or seen the top management in action is more likely to invest additional money in the company, especially when he has been impressed by the forthrightness and competence of the executives who conducted the meeting.

Many of the individuals at stockholder turnouts are likely to be employee-stockholders. In the case of one oil company, half the stockholders are employees, and they are allowed time off their jobs to attend the annual meeting.

A question often asked is, "What role does the annual meeting play in attracting—and keeping—investment dollars?"

The answer is difficult to ascertain. Finance officers, however, know that when the company needs additional financing, most of the new money will have to come from present stockholders. They will have to risk more dollars.

Success in getting new investor dollars is governed, to a large extent, by how well the investing public knows the company. Most finance officers therefore prefer to see the number of stockholders grow rather than shrink.

Each meeting has its share of "professional kibitzers"—men and women who own as little as one share in a large number of companies. These individuals make it a practice to attend every possible annual affair. The question period offers the kibitzers and the serious intelligent shareholders an opportunity to ask for information which otherwise might remain shut up in executive briefcases. Today's annual meetings in many companies are a step in the direction of shareholder democracy.

The best and most incisive questions are often those of the security analysts who attend annual meetings. For example, Merrill Lynch, Pierce, Fenner & Smith has fourteen specialists and ten assistants who make it their business to attend four hundred or more annual meetings a year. They ask questions and jot down notes. It is generally believed that the professional security analysts and counselors influence as much as 75 percent of all stock purchases and sales. They are equivalent, in a sense, to the dealers and distributors of a company's consumer product. Their sphere of operation is finance. Their analysis usually determines whether a company's stock is described as a "dog," a "blue chip," or something between.

Top management and financial men who preside at these meetings know that they may face tough and informed questioning. They come as thoroughly prepared as a British cabinet minister who must face questioning in Parliament. The presiding executive must prime himself so well with facts and figures that he can answer many who intend to ask questions before they have time to take the floor. More and more annual meeting audiences are showing a reluctance to allow themselves to be sidetracked.

The evidence indicates that annual meetings can be a valuable institution, one that an alert management does not ignore. If the meetings have not yet become the socially useful forum that they are capable of being, it is as much the fault of the stockholder as of management. As one writer stated: "It is not enough for stockholders simply to flock to annual meetings to prove that they are not acting like sheep. In the last resort, the annual meeting, and stockholder participation in general, can be no better than stockholders make them."

The need for the continued wooing of stockholders is indicated by the forecast of financially astute men who believe that if we are to find the private funds necessary for our anticipated economic expansion there must, down the years, be forty to fifty million stockholders in this country.[4] Keith Funston, former president of the New York Stock Exchange, stated that "everybody's capitalism" would provide the funds: "The spread of corporate ownership among additional millions of people willing to undertake the risks of stock investments—in return for the rewards, is not only a measure of the country's economic vitality. It is an indication that the goals of the future, which will require enormous quantities of risk capital, can be achieved." Certainly the healthiest condition for a capitalist economy to seek is one in which an increasingly greater number of people share in its fruits by becoming capitalists.

The term *capitalism* is still disturbing to some people. As a result, some spokesmen for business have dropped that word and taken up *free enterprise* instead. Of late the more fashionable terms in the executive suites are *people's capitalism* or *everybody's capitalism*.

Profit sharing

Some managements try to improve the employee's understanding of the business through profit sharing. Profit sharing is an agreement between the employer and the employees under which the profits allocated to the workers rise or fall in proportion to the increase or decrease in the profits realized by the employer. Plans of this kind are very old in the history of business. They were used in England as early as the thirteenth century. The earliest recorded plan in the United States began in 1784 in Albert Gallatin's glassworks at New Geneva, Pennsylvania. Hundreds of companies now have a profit-sharing plan of some kind. The numbers fluctuate over the years in accordance with influences such as the business cycle, long-term trends in stock prices, and inflationary tendencies.

A few plans were started by wealthy employers who wished to share

---

[4]Prediction made by Philip Reed, chairman, General Electric Company. See "Who Owns Industrial America?" *The Management Review*, American Management Association, Inc., September 1956, p. 748.

their success with the employees. Most plans, however, have come about as the result of the employer's belief that both the employer and the employee share responsibility for the success or failure of the business and that profit sharing would stimulate the employees to appreciate more fully the problems of management, especially when the employees imagine that the business is more profitable than it actually is.

Companies that adopt profit sharing usually hope that the plan will encourage employees to take the management viewpoint and develop a more helpful interest in management's problems. It is assumed that the employee will increase his efficiency because he will share in the rewards of greater productivity. Some plans, too, are designed to promote thrift among the employees and to help them provide for their retirement.

In general, profit sharing has not become the one simple hoped-for solution to employer-employee relations problems. One reason for the lack of complete success is that when profits shared are relatively stable over a number of years, the employees confuse them with or consider them a part of their regular wages. If the company suddenly finds that its profits are less than in the several preceding years, the typical employee feels that he has been given a cut in his wages.

And when a company makes more profits than usual, the employees tend to assume that the same or greater profits will be distributed in the years that follow. Profits are usually distributed at the end of the year, a time when employees have extra expenses for the holidays. Many do extra spending on the assumption that the profits distributed will be the same as before or greater. The disappointment of the overly optimistic employee can be imagined when he discovers that the profits to be shared in the current year are less than he had anticipated.

When the profits of the company do not allow the employer to distribute the expected amount of money to the individual employees, some question the honesty of the management. The integrity of the management is especially likely to be questioned when it is noticed that the president happened to buy a bigger house at the same time that the decreased profits were announced.

Many employees would rather have a definite wage than a basic wage plus an uncertain share in the profits. Furthermore, the profits to be shared in many companies are not especially exciting when the amount to be distributed to employees happens to be a relatively small share of the employee's annual wages.

Dissatisfaction over the amount received occurs more often with the good than with the poor employees. The reason is that when a profit-sharing plan is first inaugurated in a company, the good employee wants to work harder so that he may have more money at the end of the year. At the end of the year, however, the lazy employee by his side receives a check just as large as his own. As a result, he may decide during the following year to work as slowly and as carelessly as the poorest worker in his group. Thus, profit sharing under some conditions tends to bring the efficiency of the best workers down to the level of the poorest rather than to raise the productivity of the poorest up to that of the highest. Profit sharing benefits the undeserving as much as the deserving if it is on too broad a basis.

Actually, the making of profits in many firms is largely beyond the control of the wage earners of the factory and the office. Profits usually depend upon the managers' abilities to organize the whole scheme of production efficiently, to sell the product at a satisfactory profit, to purchase economically, and to find new products to take the place of those that have become obsolescent. The key executives such as the production manager, the sales manager, the purchasing agent, and the treasurer can see a direct relationship between their individual efforts and the profits made. They, rather than the wage earners, usually influence profits perceptibly. They can be stimulated by profit sharing more easily than can the workers.

The effects of money on the motivation of employees have pronounced limitations. This was pointed out in the answers to two questions asked of industrial psychologist Dr. Arthur Witkin when interviewed by an associate editor of *Dun's Review*.

> *Dr. Witkin, it is taken for granted in most corporations that certain tangible rewards motivate employees: money, for example. Did you find in your studies that the one leveling all-American employee incentive is money?*
>
> Psychologists have realized for quite a while that money is not necessarily a motivating factor, and our surveys pointed this up quite dramatically. Once an employee reaches a minimum level of compensation, other factors, such as job satisfaction, recognition, involvement and participation in decisions, become more important. For instance, if you take a group of executive trainees, relative increases in dollars seem far less important than on, say, the clerical level.
>
> *Does this also apply to compensation such as bonuses and profit-sharing?*
>
> From our surveys, we found that bonuses are vastly overrated as a technique for improving job satisfaction. At the executive level, when bonuses are just handed out because it is par for the course, management isn't getting much for its dollar.
>
> The same holds true for profit-sharing plans. One company had a very impressive plan, which produced different reactions depending on the level of the employee. The people in the upper echelon liked it because it was their way of saving, but those in middle management and on the supervisory level resented it because they felt they needed

the money now. If a bonus or profit-sharing plan is to have an effect on motivation, it must be tailor-made to fit the needs of the various groups.[5]

Employers who adopt a profit-sharing program for the workers on the lower levels of responsibility do so not to increase profits but to improve the psychological climate in the company and to express management's sense of colleagueship with the employees. If a management does decide to install a profit-sharing plan, the following recommendations are helpful:

1. Conduct a sound compensation program before the profit-sharing plan is adopted. Equitable base pay schedules should be in operation and well established before profit-sharing begins. If the pay structure is inequitable, a supplementary form of compensation such as profit sharing is more likely to accentuate the inequities than to correct them.

2. Provide a good psychological climate before setting up the plan. Management and workers must have confidence in each other, otherwise the sharing of profits is more likely to fail than to succeed. To succeed, a profit-sharing program must be consistent with the way the business has been managed in the past. Companies that succeed with profit sharing would, in most cases, also succeed without it.

3. Be willing to give employees the important facts about the business. Under profit sharing, management must be willing to share with employees many essential facts that otherwise might not be communicated to them. If certain kinds of financial information and sales records are withheld from the employees, they are apt to view the fluctuations in profits with suspicion, thus defeating the aims of the plan.

4. Have everyone share alike, percentagewise. Each employee expects to receive the same percentage of his annual wages as that of an employee in a different wage or salary bracket. The number of dollars received need not be the same, but the percentage must be. When the percentage varies with the wage or salary bracket, those in the lower brackets object to the differentials.

In general, the difficulties involved in the use of profit sharing are so serious that the adoption of this kind of plan should be approached with considerable previous investigation into the experiences of other companies, particularly those which have had plans and dropped them. Certainly,

[5]Report of interview with Arthur Witkin, "How Do You Motivate Employees?" *Dun's Review*, December 1968, p. 12.

when a management hesitates to adopt profit sharing after several employees request it, the employees should not immediately assume that all the members of top management are benighted tightwads who want to keep all the profits for themselves. Perhaps the management simply wants to be reasonably certain of the values of the plan for the employees as well as for the company before profit sharing is adopted.

Stock purchase plans for employees

Stock ownership by employees, rather than profit sharing, has been advocated by some executives. One argument for the stock purchase plan is the increased number of shareholders in our population. The popularity of stock purchase plans for employees is indicated by the fact that more than 150 companies listed on the New York Stock Exchange adopted a stock purchase plan for their employees during a recent ten-year period. Of all companies listed on the New York Stock Exchange, more than 50 percent have a stock purchase plan for their employees. This trend is in line with the belief that increased participation in the "people's capitalism" is beneficial to the public, the employees, and the employers.

When an employee owns stock, he is a financial partner in the business, though a small one. Advocates of the plan believe that it promotes loyalty to the employer, rewards the employee for faithful service, encourages thrift, and helps to educate the worker in regard to some of the basic principles in our economic life.

The extent of employees' ownership of stock in the companies where they work varies with the industry. Generally, stock ownership by employees is relatively greater in public utilities than in manufacturing or transportation companies. The percentage of employees who buy stock in the employing company when it is offered to them varies greatly—it may be as low as 1 percent and as high as 90 percent.

When employees who do buy are asked their reasons for purchasing, they are likely to answer in one or more of four categories: as a speculative venture, as a hedge against inflation, as a means of attracting the goodwill of management and thereby increasing the chance of promotion, and as a nest egg for old age.

Of course employers do not want to encourage their employees to speculate in stocks of their own or other companies. Employers know that those who buy in the expectation of making a quick profit are more likely to be interested in watching the stock market reports than in studying their jobs and trying to improve their work. Eventually, too, any paper profits made by the employee will rise and fall with the normal fluctuations in the prices of stocks. And whenever an employee's paper profits are lessened or even wiped out, he is apt to blame the employer for the loss and decrease interest in his work.

The older employers of today are likely to be especially conscious of the hazards in the owning of stocks by employees. They remember some of the tragic incidents that occurred after the crash of 1929. One railroad, for example, had sold stock to employees in 1925 at $115 a share. In 1932, the same stock sold for less than $9 a share! Even though the crash of 1929 may not be repeated, we do know that some severe fluctuations in stock prices are bound to occur from time to time.

The misgivings about the value of stock purchase plans become acute whenever the market price for the company's stock falls below the price paid by employees. When that occurs, some employees become disenchanted. Their morale suffers. To maintain morale and help employees overcome disenchantment about the company's financial progress, managements find it necessary to provide employees with educational programs that help them understand why some fluctuations in stock prices are an inevitable aspect of stock ownership. Special brochures and financial reports must be prepared and given the employees. Foremen must be trained to answer questions about the reasons for the price of the company's stock. Meetings must be held to give employees correct answers. Some managements have discovered that these difficulties and the costs of dealing with them are so great that the benefits of stock ownership are questionable.

In spite of the hazards and difficulties in operating a stock purchase plan for employees, the number of plans has increased in recent years. Stock ownership by employees fits into the American way of economic life. Our middle income class has increased to the extent where many people can afford to assume some minor risks in making investments. More and more people are buying stocks as indicated by the growing number of investment clubs and mutual funds which are now found in all sections of the country. Articles about finance and investments are constantly appearing in our mass publications because many people are interested in the possibility of buying new stocks or more of their presently owned stocks.

Many managements think of their stock purchase plans as educational services to the employees. The ownership of an employer's stock tends to encourage many an employee to direct some of his speculative tendencies into the study and proper evaluation of all stocks and the economic influences behind the prices. Managements are, of course, aware of the many unintelligent reasons for buying stocks and the hazards involved in their ownership, but they hope to set up their own company plans in ways that prevent disaster and, at the same time, increase good judgment in financial matters. Some companies do this by requiring regular savings, augmented with contributions from the company, and investing the funds in the stocks of several companies as well as in the equities of the employing company.

Most managements realize that they cannot hope to develop a stock ownership plan that will do everything that is desirable for the company and the employees. They also realize that the adoption of a stock ownership plan will not increase production or lower costs for every class of employee. Instead, they seek to plan and conduct a program that develops a more favorable psychological climate in which management and employees can share responsibilities and work together to mutual understanding and economic advantage. This is the main purpose of a well-designed stock ownership plan in many of our most intelligently managed companies. Another purpose may be as an incentive plan for salesmen.

Various meanings of money

Money itself has many unique meanings, and the people who have or deal in money also have special terms applied to them. "Wall Street's half-affectionate, half-mocking term for the average stockholder is 'Aunt Jane.' " "The old lady of Broad and Wall" is the term used by the common stock dealers when they refer disparagingly to the quiet, orderly corner occupied by the bond traders on the floor of the New York Stock Exchange.

Of course money has the important meaning of purchasing power to everyone. In addition, it also has many deeper meanings of a subconscious nature.

One of the most common meanings is *power* as exemplified by the expression "The Almighty Dollar." Many employees who resent employer wealth think of money as a form of control, a kind of control that they feel they cannot combat.

Money has had an *unclean* connotation for centuries. We often hear expressions such as "filthy lucre" and "the love of money is the root of all evil." The question as to whether a certain person's money is "tainted" also implies that the money itself rather than the means of its getting may be evil.

To some people, money stands for *security*. People who have suffered from financial difficulties during childhood are likely to become painfully thrifty in later years and remain parsimonious even though they have acquired ample income for their needs. Our best savers in this country, as a group, are the foreign-born poor who have suffered poverty in the country of their birth and still feel insecure in the adopted country. Money in the bank spells security.

To the young person who has just become fully self-supporting, the first paychecks signify *adulthood*. Some of these "new adults" spend money foolishly by buying items that they do not need, probably representing escape from parental restraint. They are one of several varieties of the easily recognized "compulsive spender," the person who has a strong compulsion to spend money.

Another variety of the compulsive spender is the extravagant buyer whose income, however large or small, is frittered away through the purchase of unnecessarily high-priced items. This kind of customer rationalizes his purchase of expensive clothing by claiming that the label from "Snob

Shoppe" will help him get a better job or associate with the "right people." Such extravagance may really have its roots in an unappreciated desire for companionship, a feeling that no one really cares for him. This kind of motivation may also cause the individual to lavish costly gifts on friends. The adolescent boy who buys an expensive wristwatch for a new girl friend is an example.

Both reckless spending and unnecessary hoarding often have their roots in disappointment and discouragement. The miser is likely to be a lonely person who does not know how to gain satisfying companionships and then takes recourse in the security and superiority that money symbolizes.

Young couples who bicker over money matters imagine that the lack of sufficient money for their needs is the crux of their marital difficulties. One writer has given a more significant explanation:

> Many young couples will tell you, "Our fights are mostly over money. If we weren't broke all the time, we'd get along fine together." This is putting the cart before the horse. Those who get along reasonably well in other respects, may still have differences over managing their money, but they tend to work out these disagreements without deep or persistent bitterness. Certainly a large proportion of marital troubles do focus on finances, but their roots often lie in entirely different situations. Disputes over spending or saving frequently provoke quarrels whose real cause may be resentment at a husband because he never hangs up his clothes or because he paid too much attention to that pretty girl at the party last week. If a man is annoyed at his wife because she sleeps late and leaves him to get his own breakfast, or because she has invited her sister to come for a long visit, a discussion over whether they can afford to go to the movies this week can flare into a nasty quarrel.
>
> It is easier to accept the fact that you are angry at your husband or your wife for being stingy or careless with money than to admit to being disappointed in him or in her for a reason harder to put into words.
>
> Nancy and Don Bryant, a highly competitive couple, each used money as a way of getting the best of the other. When she bought a blouse or a bedspread she didn't need, Nancy would say, "If I don't spend what we have, it's a sure thing Don will."
>
> Don, in his turn, took the stand, "If I let my wife get away with wasting money, we'd never have a cent. She's got to learn who's boss. Best way to teach her is to keep the cash right in my own hands."[6]

[6]Edith G. Neisser, *The Many Faces of Money* (Human Relations Aids, 104 E. 25th Street, New York, N.Y., 1958).

If you study or work in finance

The various meanings of money indicate how easy it is for anyone to react too strongly away from or toward money as a possession and finance as a subject of study or as a function of business. Objective thinking in regard to all aspects of finance is greatly needed. The more you study or work in finance, the more you will find that adequate knowledge of the subject becomes beneficial to you as a citizen, as an employee, and as an executive.

Regardless of the phase of business that you enter, you can add zest to your work when you appreciate the function of money in our economy and its meanings to you as a person. If you will increase your acquaintance with the people who are active in finance, you will find that most do not think of it as a symbol of power but as an instrument of service to mankind. Many are also keenly conscious of the human relations aspects of finance and are trying to inform employees and the public about it. Much remains to be done. Perhaps your study will stimulate you to see the human relations aspects of finance in our new social order as a challenging interest in your business career.

The objectives and responsibilities of modern leaders in finance have changed markedly as stated by a leading scholar in the field of entrepreneurial history:

> That business institutions should be concerned with money-making need not be elaborated. But it is important to notice, especially over the past two or three decades, how considerably American corporations have modified any rule of financial maximization that may have existed, so that corporate longevity, community relations, or public responsibilities might be taken into account. Especially significant has been the trend over an even longer period in the United States toward a reduction in the sovereignty of the stockholder.[7]

QUESTIONS ON THE CHAPTER

1. Describe the chief financial executive's work relations with other members of management.

2. In what ways do the surveys of stock ownership in America invalidate the opinions of many workers toward company profits?

3. In the morale survey concerning one company's Annual Report, what per-

---

[7]See Arthur H. Cole, *Business Enterprise in Its Social Setting* (Cambridge, Mass.: Harvard University Press, 1959), p. 15.

centage of the employees who saw the report read all of it? Half of it? None of it?

4. Describe several common errors made in the presentation of financial reports.

5. Explain a method of preparing financial reports so that they are understandable both on the level of the employee or general public and on the professional level of the investment men or security analysts.

6. State reasons for management's attempts to increase attendance at stockholders' meetings.

7. List several reasons why it is a difficult task to try to educate people to buy common stocks wisely.

8. Why should the student of finance also develop his insight into human relations especially in respect to buying stock?

9. Describe some of the deeper meanings that money may have for various people.

10. Is an adequate knowledge of finance of importance solely to the prospective financier? Explain your answer.

11. Of all the ideas presented in the chapter, which one is of most interest or value to you?

PROBLEMS AND PROJECTS

For All Students

1. Visit several brokers' offices in your community. Note the information that is available. Look particularly for booklets that warn the unwary about unethical salesmen or companies that exploit rather than serve investors.

2. Assume that you will have to borrow money to finance your education. Do you have a well-formulated plan for how you will use the money, repay it, and give evidence of good character in deserving the loan?

For Advanced Students

3. Make a study of the "psychology of the stock market." You might start by interviewing several knowledgeable brokers of a local firm.

4. The most dramatic conflicts in the financial world are the corporate raids in a proxy battle. Study such raids. Begin by reading James P. Selvage, *The Management Review*, American Management Association, Inc., December 1957.

For Men in Business

5. Collect several financial reports to stockholders. How could they be im-

proved for reading by employees? Interview several employees who own stocks in any company. What do they read in the reports?

6. Look through several business journals for reports of meetings for stockholders. Consult the *Industrial Arts Index* for current articles. What kinds of stockholders attend the meetings and what do they contribute?

COLLATERAL READINGS

For All Students

Forbes, Financial World, Barron's, The Wall Street Journal, and other financial magazines are available in many business libraries. They offer many articles on human relations aspects of finance.

"Shareowners and Employees: Who's Ahead?" *The Exchange,* December 1963.

For Advanced Students

Martindell, Jackson, *The Appraisal of Management for Executives and Investors.* New York: Harper & Row, Publishers, 1962. Treats management in relation to investment but also acknowledges that management does not deal with human and material resources alone—it deals also with problems of morals, ethics, and ideals because ends are determined by values.

Slovic, Paul, "Analyzing the Expert Judge: A Descriptive Study of a Stockbroker's Decision Processes," *Journal of Applied Psychology,* August 1969. Illustrates a technique for describing use of information by persons making complex judgments.

For Men in Business

Donaldson, Gordon, *Strategy for Financial Mobility.* Boston: Harvard Business School, 1967. Presents a strategy for redirecting funds flows as new and unexpected information changes the company's picture.

Wecksler, A. N., "A Case Study of The Lincoln Electric Company," *Mill & Factory,* April 1963.

Research
and the Development
of New Products

SITUATIONS YOU ARE LIKELY TO MEET

How would you meet each of these situations:
   a. *Before* you have read the chapter? What would you say to yourself or to the individual?
   b. *After* you have read the chapter? How have your answers changed?

1. Assume that you have been assigned to writing job descriptions of the only jobs in the research department of a company. These job specifications are to be used in hiring new men and in developing organization charts for each department. When you call on the members of the research department, you find that most of the best research men do not like to tell you about their functions in terms of a job-described slot—they want more freedom of action than the members of other departments.
   How would you try to gain their cooperation to obtain useful information about their work?
2. One of your friends recommends that you purchase stock in a new company that is being developed and managed by several able research men. Your friend says: "That stock *must* increase in value very rapidly because the men who head it are some of the best research men in the entire industry."
   What would you do or say to your friend?

Any person who works in or studies business is bound to become acquainted with modern research. Its spirit and benefits permeate all phases of business.

To the man in the street, research is often synonymous with progress. To the typical consumer, it means such things as more or better food, clothing, housing, health, life, and leisure. Also, these benefits are obtained with less physical effort than was needed in previous generations.

Research courses are found in almost every department of the large university. Research is defined and interpreted in many ways. The academic scientist sees it from the standpoint of exploring the unknown. He is looking for information for its own sake rather than for its use in the solution of a particular economic problem of immediate concern.

The tangible aspects of progress—new products and processes that produce a higher standard of living—very clearly derive from discoveries in pure science. Between pure research and the manufacture of new products, a wide middle ground is found. In this area, we have applied research, process development, and product development.

The term "research" is widely misused. A student, for example, goes to the library to investigate materials for writing a term report and blandly states: "I conducted a lot of research in order to write this report!" A more accurate statement would be "I did some reading on the subject in the library."

Many companies, too, kid themselves when they tag routine product testing as research. They should say that they have a product testing lab to provide certain limited services for the customers who use the company's products.

Pure research is generally carried out in an environment that allows the investigator freedom to follow the lead of his curiosity. In the words of Glen T. Seaborg of the University of California, the scientist in basic research is not concerned with "utilitarian goals, but a search for deeper understanding of the universe and the living and inorganic phenomena within it." In its initial purpose, basic research may be an essential prerequisite to applied research and product development. Some of the greatest technical advances of recent years have come from basic research projects

Ever notice how when products compete with each other,

they get better.

Write for our free booklet that tells how competition makes things better.

Brand Names Foundation, Inc. 292 Madison Avenue New York, N.Y. 10017

BRAND NAMES

that had no immediate practical objective. Examples are radar, transistors, neoprene, and nylon.[1]

[1]See "Basic Research More Practical Than You Think," an editorial that appeared in November and December 1957 issue of McGraw-Hill publications, (McGraw-Hill Publishing Company, Inc., 330 West 42nd St., New York 36).

Billions of dollars are spent annually for new plants and equipment as the result of research made in a previous decade, or even a year earlier. More than one-half of our jobholders in the United States are in industries that owe their birth to research laboratories. This means that industry is compelled to spend more and more for research each year.

THE BASIC LIFE CYCLE OF NEW PRODUCTS

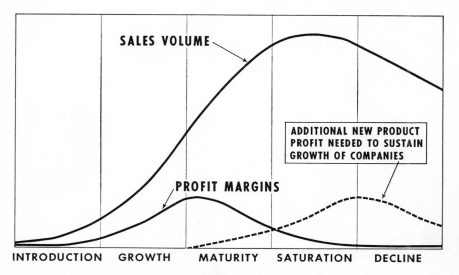

New products have a characteristic pattern to their sales volume and profit margin curves. The time scale varies by product and industry, but every product must expect to be pre-empted eventually by another product. And long before this occurs, production will catch up even with growing demand and the product degenerates into profitless price competition, as the typical profit margin curve shows.

This means that as a business strategy, a company must plan to run ahead of price competition by differentiating its products and introducing new products that can command better margins.

Business success is governed not only by what you do, but by what others do. Therefore, throughout history, the underlying secret of business success has been to be in the right business at the right time—and this strategy is expressed by the selection and development of company products. Over-all profit margins can be sustained only by a continuing flow of new products—not only to replace sales volume but also to bolster shrinking profit margins.

The company plans must begin with the product plans. To project sales, costs, capital, facility, and personnel needs without clear product plans is indeed a hollow activity. The growth plans of a company are at the core of management interests. New products are a major factor in the growth plans of companies today.

(Reproduced by permission from C. Wilson Randle, "Weighing the Success of New Product Ideas," *Industrial Marketing*, July 1957.)

Research is becoming an industry in itself. The percentage of a modern company's gross income allotted for research ranges from 2 percent to 10 percent or even more. The tremendous amount of effort that goes into intensive research is exemplified by the statement of a pharmaceutical manufacturer who described his company's experience in antibiotics in a recent year: "We screened approximately 40,000 substances for activity in this field. Out of that 40,000 we found about 200 which showed promise enough

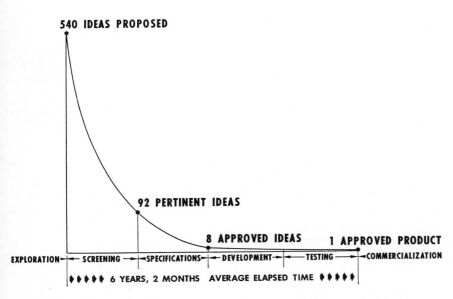

MORTALITY OF NEW PRODUCT IDEAS
20 Chemical Companies

Companies should seek literally those rare ideas that are both low-risk and high-payout. They can measure their effectiveness in product selection by examining the degree to which their projects cluster in the lower right-hand corner of the chart.

A characteristic of the new product selection game is the progressive rejection of ideas by stages. The chart above shows the survival rate curve for industrial chemical ideas. You might say, as in a poker game, you ante a lot of times before you develop a hand you're willing to play clear through to a final showdown.

As good a screening job as is represented here, we still see seven out of eight development projects—which run $150,000 to $500,000 or more each in this business—never reach the full commercial stage. This gives us a clue on what might be happening to some of our scientific manpower. A large share, by definition in commercial terms, is being wasted. Another characteristic of this game is that each stage is progressively more expensive; like in a poker game, each card drawn costs more than the one before it.

(Reproduced by permission from C. Wilson Randle, "Weighing the Success of New Product Ideas," *Industrial Marketing*, July 1957.)

to justify further study. Out of that 200 we had 30 that we actually manufactured for trial. Out of that 30, six wound up in the Department of Clinical Investigation. So you start with 40,000 and you wind up with six; this makes quite an interesting study in that particular field."[2]

Companies engaged primarily in producing products or services rather than research find it necessary to organize their research program systematically. Usually this requires the careful selection of people who are competent to do sound research.

TABLE 23–1

LEVEL OF EDUCATION
OF RESEARCH AND DEVELOPMENT EXECUTIVES

	Total %
Attended college, no degree	1.7
Bachelor's degree	25.7
Attended graduate school, no advanced degree	2.6
Master's degree	14.3
Ph.D. degree	53.0
A.M.P. certificate	2.6
	99.9

Comments: All attended college. Seven out of ten earned advanced degrees, and over half hold doctorates. The chief R&D executive of a large company is more likely to have a Ph.D. degree than his counterpart in a smaller company. Advanced degrees are important to aspirants of the chief R&D position in achieving consideration for the top job. However, managerial skill is the real key to the top R&D spot. The greatest hope of reaching the top R&D position with only a bachelor's degree is in the small companies.

Source: *Profile of a Chief Research and Development Executive*—A Survey of Chief Research and Development Executives in 232 of America's Largest Companies. Conducted by Heidrick and Struggles, Management Consulting Executive Selection. Copyright, 1968.

Personality characteristics of research men

If you were to visit a number of companies and ask executives about the personality characteristics of their research men, you might get comments such as the following:

1. "Good research men cannot be expected to conform to the behavior patterns typical of most other employees. The researchers

[2]Stated by Harry Loynd, former president of Parke, Davis & Co., as reported by William Bloeth, "Stock Movement," *New York World-Telegram and Sun*, January 26, 1959.

are likely to be seclusive thinkers, deeply engrossed in their problems, somewhat unconcerned about problems that bother most executives, poor coordinators of their own work, and likely to go off on any tangent that interests them."

2. "The feelings of research men are easily hurt. Many are pronounced introverts. The introverted person, who wants to keep to himself and to avoid social contacts, finds that laboratory work offers an opportunity to do so. He can bury himself in the lab and then build a shell around himself so that he can easily avoid social affairs, meeting people, and other situations unpleasant to him. A good research employee can lose all awareness of the people around him because he buries himself in his work. Although this form of adjustment may give us great scientists, many of them are not able to communicate their ideas to someone else. They have so little facility of expression that their good ideas fail to be modified by other thinkers and, as a result, they often fail to accomplish as much as they might."

3. "In our company's research lab a person at one desk will notice that his colleague at the next desk is going about something in a completely wrong manner but will not say anything to him. Oftentimes management finds that a research chemist or other type of lab worker hates to be questioned about his work. He feels that any questioning or checking proves that his boss doesn't trust him and won't give him a chance to prove what he is worth. In our research laboratories we have men and women who refuse to speak to their colleagues because of a difference of opinion that occurred years ago."

Admittedly, some unusual personalities are found in laboratories, but we should realize that research men and women exhibit all the individual differences found in any group. They are not personality freaks. In regard to a few traits, however, there is sufficient similarity to warrant generalization. In matters of judgment, most of them are careful and precise. They accept nothing on hearsay—every theory or claim must be tested and tested rigorously before it is accepted. They are intellectually curious. They respond to the challenges presented by the unknown. They are scientists and they realize that a science is only as sound as its research. They enjoy their work and often disregard hours of the working day as they respond to challenge. Many are unorthodox in their working habits. They are not awed by management because they are guided by the criteria of science—not the criteria of men.

They themselves can apply the appropriate criteria to their work and they take inner pleasure from achievement that stands the examination of sound scientific testing. Many have an air of assurance because of undeniable accomplishment. Each achievement leads to new search into the unknown. They have individual and group pride because they often know that they are spearheading some phase of technical progress of the nation and the age.

Great scientists have "respect for the power and beauty, not just the utility, of unrestricted human thought." Poincaré expressed the idea when he wrote, "The scientist does not study nature because it is useful; he studies it because he delights in it, and he delights in it because it is beautiful."[3]

Some persons think that creativity is one aspect of cleverness or great learning. Experience indicates, however, that many men who are very clever never originate anything. The true originator is usually a trained and alert observer. His chief asset is the ability to recognize analogies and appreciate the significance of apparently accidental happenings. Curiosity, alert observation, and the ability to recognize the importance of a finding are necessary qualities of a researcher.[4]

Organizing the personnel for effective research

About two-thirds of the total personnel in a typical research organization are nontechnical: stenographers, mechanics, operators, laboratory assistants, clerks, and so on. Two-thirds of those classed as technical personnel are usually engaged in development and engineering work, work that requires a great deal of planning and organization. This leaves only about 10 percent of the total personnel who are actually engaged in truly creative research.

To gain the benefits of what these men can do, managements have found it necessary to implement their talents and those of their associates by means of special organizations. "Research is people" as has often been stated, but the fruits of the labors of research people can be reduced or increased by means of the organization and environment where they work. Integration of their efforts through teamwork and good leadership by management is essential to their success.

In many companies, the research function began with a testing lab and in time was gradually elevated to a subdivision reporting directly to the president. As a result, it is still very much in the process of evolution in many companies.

[3]See J. H. Hildebrand, "Motivation of the Top Level Students Who Enter the Research Field," *Research Is People* (New York: New York University Press for the Industrial Research Institute, Inc., 1956), p. 19.

[4]See M. R. Feinberg, "Fourteen Suggestions for Managing Scientific Creativity," *Research Management*, March 1968; and J. Sumerfield, *The Creative Mind and Method* (New York: Russell & Russell, 1964).

Research men realize that they need direction as well as stimulation. Without the proper supervision, many a researcher will waste his potentials through unproductive efforts such as the following:

1. Working on a problem that interests him instead of the problem that has been assigned to him. An effective researcher will pursue the main problem without allowing his personal interests to side-track him.
2. Working in a sullen manner because the work of others is not coordinated with his efforts in the exact way he wants. The productive researcher is a member of a team, and he adapts his efforts to those of the team program.
3. Failing to maintain his own morale and that of subordinates and associates when difficulties arise.

Professional recognition is very important to the able research man. This may be granted by the company by means of a title such as "senior research associate," but this has more significance within than without the company where he works. He wants something more substantial than a title—he wants to be recognized as an outstanding scientist by those persons whose opinions he respects.

Some managements have found it necessary to give a certain amount of freedom to the research man who likes to work on projects that interest him personally. They let him experiment during working hours with pet projects of his own. A few companies give the research man free rein, but most put a limit on the time to be spent in this way. About 10 percent of working time is the maximum usually allowed by research administrators. This privilege keeps researchers happy and stimulates their creative ability.

Organizational structures and communication

Scientists, who think and talk among themselves primarily in a mathematical language, often have difficulty in putting their ideas on paper in ways that laymen can understand. When ideas are passed through many echelons of management, they lose so much in the interpretation that management is unable to see their implications. Also, when separated from other sections of the plant, researchers themselves can fail to appreciate what a discovery means in terms of a company's sales needs and capabilities.

The communications problem in research has prompted a great deal of analysis of organizational structure. Experts in management believe that research is likely to be more effective and researchers less disgruntled when they are organized on a project basis around their particular talents rather than on the typical functional basis usually found in the sales and production departments. Generally, an organization of some sort has to be built around the most able research men. This is better than trying to fit each man in some way into a job-described slot.

Research is problem solving, technical achievement by professionally trained men. Hence, relatively few levels of organizational structure are necessary even in large research staffs. The research worker should be close to his supervisor to prevent ideas generated "at the bench" from being lost or misinterpreted on their way to the top. Instead of increasing the number of levels of supervision, the number of subdepartments or laboratories may be increased.

When a research department is small, say fifteen people or less, all members of the staff can have enough personal contact with each other to understand each member's projects and problems. When the department has hundreds of employees, the group leader or head of the specific project functions as a director to the members of his small group.

Experience with research workers indicates that practices such as the following are dangerous: a strictly enforced chain of command or communications, strict office hours, requirement of frequent formal progress reports, strict scheduling or restriction of researcher attendance at seminars and meetings. When the personnel turnover is as high or higher than that of the regular work force this discovery should be a warning signal to the management.

Managements have found that a researcher can go stale if he continues year after year in the same narrow fields. He can become too satisfied with the way things are done. He loses his curiosity. Sometimes he can be rehabilitated by shifting him to another area of research where his powers of observation can be used afresh.

The research director

The research director is the focal point of the research problem. He must be able to act as a liaison between research and management as well as supervise research. He must understand and be understood by both sides.

One principle is clear; research cannot be integrated into a company simply by putting a scientist on the board of directors. In most companies where research has succeeded, however, a scientist is on the board. The research director should be a competent scientist, a qualified administrator, informed of company policies, and firmly grounded in economics and industrial technology. He should have a keen appreciation of the qualities of each individual researcher and sufficient flexibility to adapt his department organization so as to make best use of their unique talents.

Past practice has been to take technical men who are believed to have potentials for administration and make them directors of research departments. Most of those chosen are untrained in administration and have to learn from experience. Some become effective administrators, others never do. Sometimes a "business manager" is appointed to aid the director. He relieves the technical director of some administrative details. In small scale operations, this is not practical because of the expense.

The research director is likely to be a scientist because one of his principal tasks is the design of experiments. A carefully and creatively conceived design is the crux in research. Well planned, it can save money and time as well as increase the chances of success. An effective director must be a person who can ask the right questions, foresee the implications of the study, and stimulate others to develop new approaches to old problems.

Directors trained in science often fail to realize that human relations problems cannot be solved in the same way as problems in physics or chemistry. As a result, some of these directors fail as administrators.

If an administrator is appointed from the sales department on the assumption that he knows how to handle people and can direct research toward solution of the company's sales problems, little basic research is done. Instead of directing research to meet future needs, he is likely to have the department work only on the service needs of customers. A customer's complaints become more important than the search for new products that will enable the company to survive against competition five years later.

If the director has been trained by the controller, only beautiful reports are likely to be produced. If he has come from the production department, the research department will be busy on equipment and layouts.

It is easy to understand why scientists near the top of the research-administration ladder invariably insist that their own scientific backgrounds are the most appropriate for their jobs. They perceive the needs of the job in terms of their own experience. They assume that anyone else could not understand the technical aspects of the situation. In actual practice, any director who has earned his position on the basis of scientific merit usually gains the respect of research workers. If his shortcomings as an administrator are corrected by means of an assistant who can handle people, the research department can produce good results.

Attitudes of management men toward research

Most forward-looking members of top management appreciate the importance of research as a competitive weapon in the company's future, but we must not assume that all management men are enthusiastic about research. Only a few are antagonistic toward research, but many are impatient. We can understand the reason for such impatience when we realize that a high percentage of management men reach the top through produc-

More than in most occupations, the edu[cation] of a scientist is continuous and intens[e]. Today's methods may be obsolete tomor[row] . . . and long-accepted theories may be [dis]proved. It is one task of research to assem[ble] evaluate and share new knowledge.

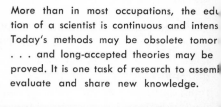

Modern research is generally a well-organized teamwork job . . . and cooperation is the key to success. Confronted by a problem, nobody in this laboratory hesitates to draw on the experience of a fellow worker.

Sometimes, of course, the problem is m[ore] than a little complex, and that is the time [for] putting heads together, perhaps with [a] learned book for reference. Usually th[ere] are several ways to approach a difficult [un]dertaking . . . but only one choice may be b[est].

There is fascination, even for men familiar with them, in every laboratory experiment . . . especially when a microscope is being used.

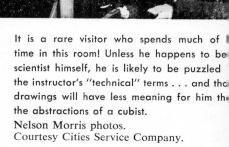

It is a rare visitor who spends much of [his] time in this room! Unless he happens to be [a] scientist himself, he is likely to be puzzled [by] the instructor's "technical" terms . . . and th[e] drawings will have less meaning for him th[an] the abstractions of a cubist.

Nelson Morris photos.
Courtesy Cities Service Company.

THE CREATIVE COORDINATOR IN THE DESIGN OF NEW PRODUCTS

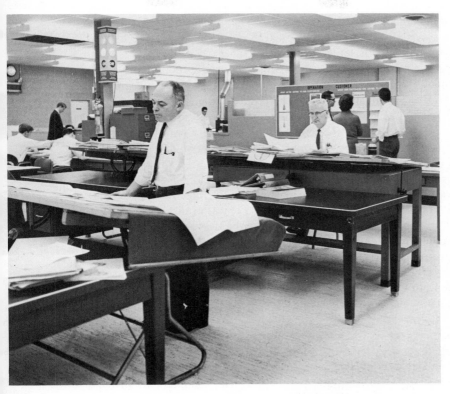

These engineers are reviewing an array of recommendations and comments before they improve the design of a new product.

The design of new products and the redesign of old products involves a wide variety of persons: the sales people who report what their customers like and do not like, the field researchers who interview prospective customers, and the company executives who believe that their ideas should be used in the new design. Usually, a management committee also states their wishes for the new product. Opportunities abound in all these fields for men who train themselves for the various aspects of design.

All the efforts of the design engineers must be coordinated by a man who knows not only the facts involved but is creative in the follow-through regarding the use of the facts and recommendations.

The follow-through man is not design engineer, but he is skilled in collecting ideas and in guiding others in the effective application of the ideas. That is why some companies call him their "Creative Coordinator in the Design of New Products."

Source: The Ex-Cell-O Corporation.

tion and sales. The production and sales executives need answers quickly. Results in these fields are attainable more quickly than in research. The immediacy of management's need for a new product to meet the competition of the moment is inconceivable to the research man who is developing new concepts for space travel or some equally great dream for the future. Management's urging toward specific dates in attaining cost reduction and product development elicits disdain and some pity from the research man. The two do not think or act according to the same time scale.

Management and research men often talk on different levels. One company president expressed the problem in a typical manner when he said "I ask for a yes or no answer and I get back a forty-page report that I cannot understand."

The research man realizes that he is misunderstood. He wants to be helpful and sensible, but he is often inarticulate, unable to communicate with members of management. Here is where a research director skilled in human relations can often integrate the thinking of the researchers with the needs of the company. He can help plan a committee control in which members of management from sales, production, and finance work more happily and effectively with research. The wise research director knows that he needs the counsel of men in production and sales—without it research may lead the company into fields where sales and production are not as yet ready to operate profitably.

Case histories of manufacturing companies that have been directed by a research man who was not intelligently guided by colleagues from the production and sales departments show that this situation can be disastrous. In one case, for example, a new president, called in to save an ailing company, found that under the administration of a research man the company's costs were excessively high and delivery dates on major contracts were running three to four years late.[5] Management as well as research men benefit from an integration of the company's needs through mutual respect on the part of all members of management. As Robert S. Ingersoll, president of Borg-Warner Corporation, indicated:

> Executives who think and speak of their research people as long hairs and ivory tower dwellers, are actually locking themselves in a tower and tossing away the key.
>
> Many executives tend to insulate themselves from those strange people and projects "over at the lab," and thereby lose out.
>
> Research is costly business and badly handled it will bleed away precious cash, time, and talent. Management should lay out clearly

[5]See "Putting Arma Back on Its Feet," *Business Week*, February 1, 1958, p. 84.

what it wants longterm. With this well established it mustn't hesitate to ride herd on its researchers.

What's more, it pays to keep researchers constantly rubbing shoulders with the production, sales, engineering, and management people.[6]

Management men have to learn how to guide research into productive channels through the use of the company's financial resources. One of management's fundamental roles is decision making. Management must perform its role in deciding what to research even though it cannot decide the date when the research is to be completed. Sound planning is a first requirement for success in industrial research. Planning is a top management responsibility.

One investigator who has studied the needs for and benefits of planning research reported that when a company analyzed the results of project work for a five-year period, it found that close to 35 percent of research and development time had been spent on projects that had proved useless to the company and this uselessness *could have been anticipated before the project was undertaken.*[7]

Naturally, management men would like to feel certain that the money spent for research is well spent. Some top-level executives realize that they are not sufficiently trained technically to evaluate what goes on in the research laboratories. They do realize that success in research usually requires a disregard for time and ordinary accounting of costs. Research men are dedicated in their effort to persist beyond hope. They pursue the chosen objective patiently, persistently. These virtues, however, do not guarantee results.

Social involvement

Until recently managements assumed that if corporate research was directed toward the discovery of new products, the improvement of old products, or giving better services to the customer, management had fulfilled its responsibilities. Now managements are increasingly putting special emphases on activities that are likely to answer social needs. Examples are

---

[6]"Executives Told to Rid Themselves of Ivory Tower Research Notion," *Business Week*, May 18, 1957, p. 107. This question from *Business Week* is a paraphrase summary of Mr. Ingersoll's talk before the National Industrial Research Conference, Chicago, April 24, 1957.

[7]See Robert K. Stolz, "Planning—Key to Research Success," *Harvard Business Review*, May–June 1957.

Several years ago a leading manufacturer of fireplace equipment hired designers to develop a prefabricated fireplace that could be completely factory-built, eliminate the need for costly masonry, and blend with any style of home architecture or room decoration.

Naturally, the first step was to get some indication of the market potential. Assuming that the product would be sold primarily to home builders, the market research men showed the product to the building trade at several trade conventions. The reactions were so favorable that further market studies were not deemed necessary and the fireplace was put into production. A complete marketing and promotional plan was developed, and distributors and dealers were appointed to concentrate on builder sales.

Unfortunately, the expected sales volume failed to materialize. The market research men had jumped to their conclusions too quickly. They had failed to uncover the fact that few builders would accept the new product until there was a recognizable consumer demand for it. As a result, the original enthusiasm for the product faded quickly when it was actually placed on the market. The manufacturer then had to completely revise his entire marketing approach, which entailed a substantial loss in both time and money.

Sooner or later, almost every large manufacturer goes through this kind of learning experience. That is one reason why preparation for marketing research requires good training plus astute insight into what the market research data really signify for the manufacturer.

Source: Vega Industries, Inc., Syracuse, New York.

solving urban housing and transit problems, training and finding jobs for the disadvantaged, and improving medical care.

Some managements do not think that such areas are merely altruistic. Instead, they believe that society's needs are so great that profits can be earned as a result of their economic as well as their social benefit.[8]

The *climate* for research is especially important for its growth. If the

[8]For examples, see "Westinghouse, in Self-Improvement Drive, Seeks 15% Return; Is Deep in 'Social Work,'" *The Wall Street Journal*, December 5, 1968, p. 36.

climate and objectives are inadequate, a research program does not contribute to the vitality of an organization. If, however, management's philosophy promotes the application of science and technology to current problems, the employees in the research department will know it and will produce all that it is humanly possible for them to accomplish.

This suggests that the student of human relations who expects to deal effectively with research workers should learn about the objectives and principles that guide them. If he can appreciate their objectives as well as their characteristics as individuals, he will merit their goodwill and gain their personal cooperation.

QUESTIONS ON THE CHAPTER

1. Differentiate between *pure research* and two commonly misused meanings of the term *research*.

2. What are some noticeable traits that can be attributed to many research men?

3. What percentage of the total personnel in a typical research organization are actually engaged in creative research?

4. Comment on the statement that many a researcher will waste his potentials through unproductive efforts.

5. Why is it important for adequate communications to be established by research directors in their departments?

6. Describe some of the qualities required of a competent research director.

7. Give arguments for and against having a scientist in the position of research director.

8. What does the statement "Success appears to diminish creativity" mean?

9. What are some of the problems of members of management who deal with research men?

10. Of all the ideas presented in the chapter, which ones had special interest for you?

11. How did the chapter contribute to your relations with (a) your future supervisors, (b) employees whom you may supervise?

PROBLEMS AND PROJECTS

1. As a student, if you are sincere and intelligent in your approach, you can have access to and interview many executives. You can call on the head of a research laboratory or a member of management who deals with researchers and introduce yourself with a statement such as "I am a student in———

and am taking a course in ———. I'd like to learn more about human relations problems involved in dealing with research workers. Would you kindly tell me about some of yours?" You may wish to utilize this procedure.

(a) What limitations can you recognize in this approach?

(b) What courtesies are expected by management from the student?

2. A survey of 252 companies made by the American Management Association revealed that the responsibility for the creation of new products rests with marketing management in 43 percent, with general management in 41 percent, and with directors of research and development or engineering in only 11 percent of the surveyed concerns. Some companies use product-planning committees. The best sources for new product ideas are the company's salesmen. Next are the research and engineering staffs, followed by suggestions from customers.

(a) Examine current journals of marketing to find articles that explain ways in which marketing departments function in new product planning.

(b) Look in the tables of contents of journals directed to marketing executives and salesmen for articles that state how managements stimulate salesmen to bring new product ideas to the attention of management.

3. Utilize the facilities of your library to make a study of the importance of research in our growth as a nation.

COLLATERAL READINGS

For All Students

George, Claude S., Jr., *Management in Industry*. Englewood Cliffs, N.J.: Prentice-Hall, Inc., 1964. Deals primarily with the principles and procedures employed in the effective operation of a business enterprise. Chapter 7 deals with research and product development.

Steiner, Gary A., (ed.), *The Creative Organization*. Chicago: The University of Chicago Press, 1965. The views of sixteen eminent persons whose varying experiences and points of view were directed to several aspects of the topic.

For Advanced Students

O'Donnell, Cyril, et al., *The Strategy of Corporate Research, A Symposium*. San Francisco: Chandler, 1967, see pp. 190ff.

Pelz, Donald C., and Frank M. Andrews, *Scientists in Organization: Productive Climates for Research and Development*. New York: John Wiley & Sons, Inc., 1966. The authors investigated the relationship between organizational environment and creativity for a group of scientists and engineers in a variety of research and development settings: a university, two industrial firms, and five government laboratories.

For Men in Business

Brown, Rex V., *Research and the Credibility of Estimates: An Appraisal Tool for for Executives and Researchers.* Boston: Harvard Business School, 1969. To assess the accuracy of past and future findings, this book develops a general purpose methodolgy, accessible to nontechnical executives and researchers alike.

Lothrop, Warren C., *Management Uses of Research and Development.* New York: Harper & Row, Publishers, 1964. Primarily addressed to the businessman who is concerned with the place of technology in a consumer-oriented industry.

IMPROVING
YOUR RELATIONS
WITH INDIVIDUALS

PART **V**

TomoRRow

Motivation—Increasing Your Sensitivity to the Individual Needs

SITUATIONS YOU ARE LIKELY TO MEET

How would you meet each of these situations:
   a. *Before* you have read the chapter? What would you say to yourself or to the individual?
   b. *After* you have read the chapter? How have your answers changed?

1. A supervisor of factory workers tells you that men work for money, *money only*. The nontangible reward of participation, self-fulfillment, social recognition, and similar satisfactions are totally useless—"Give 'em money," he says, "and you will get the best possible production from the employees."
What comments would you offer?

2. An ambitious young man who has been working in a certain company for three years is depressed in regard to his lack of advancement. He tells you that he has given management six reports that describe ideas that, if used, would improve the company's profits. The reports have been acknowledged, but no member of management has bothered to discuss any of his ideas very thoroughly with him.
What helpful suggestions can you offer him?

3. A new employee happens to be working in a group of men, several of whom are constantly criticizing the company. They also point to themselves as examples of what a young man can expect when he reaches their age. The young man is getting discouraged and is thinking of getting a job in some other company.
What would you say to the young man?

One of the most difficult lessons to learn about people is that they often react quite differently from what might logically be expected. To the obtuse observer, their behavior is unexpected, even senseless. A supervisor, for example, does a favor for an employee who becomes angry and berates the supervisor. The supervisor who is unaware of the employee's psychological needs in nonplussed. The more insightful person, however, realizes that people do not always act logically. Quite often they react psychologically, in accordance with their deep-seated needs.

We learn to become aware of the influence of needs when we deal with a person with whom we cannot discuss certain subjects. We discover that with regard to those topics, he will react in accordance with an unconscious motive. We do not, as a rule, know the exact nature or origin of the drive, but we recognize its influence as shown in his conversation or when it appears again and again as a dominating influence in his daily behavior. Every individual's life has certain patterns of behavior that indicate the motivating influence of continuing deep-seated needs on his part. The observer who studies and works with people is constantly improving his awareness of such motivations as expressed by the individuals whom he observes.

Most college students become acquainted with some aspects of motivation by their studies in literature. They read the biographies of famous men. An example is that of William Cullen Bryant (1794–1878), whose father was so strong a physical giant that he could "take a barrel of cider and lift it into a cart over the wheel." To toughen his son and make him manly, he dunked him in a cold spring each morning. To please his father, the son became a lawyer, but he spent more time writing poems than doing legal briefs. His poems "Thanatopsis" and "To a Waterfowl" show the tender side of his nature, which the dunking in ice water could not eradicate. After the father's death, William quit law entirely and became a quarrelsome editor who fought for the underdog. Journalism enabled him to fight the kind of tyranny that reminded him of his father's domination and cruelties. At heart, Bryant was a feminine sentimentalist. His father's "hardening" made him hate hard things, but fortunately it did not destroy his creativity. Instead, it caused him to have needs that he released through literary potentials.

Other examples in literature and art of how needs develop and their later influence in adult life can be perceived when we study the behavior pattern of a child who is physically weak, sickly, or deformed such as Henri de Toulouse-Lautrec (1864–1901). At the age of fourteen, he had an accident that broke both his weak legs. The legs did not mend well. Walking was a torment. His short stumpy legs and appearance made him an ugly cripple who was repulsive to most people. He was rejected by others but hungry for acceptance. He found acceptance in the cafés and brothels where he could practice his art making posters of café scenes and disreputable women. He used color and design to portray the life and the people whom he knew in the places where he was accepted. His art reflected his deep emotional needs.

The intelligent student of literature, philosophy, and the other humanities wants to know more than what the writer or speaker said—he also wants to know the early influences and the resultant needs that motivated him to choose and express the specific ideas that he chose and expressed.

Every man's points of view are colored by his inner needs. We can easily note the influence of needs on a person's thinking when we study people in stress situations as in war. A former prisoner of war described the outward changes in behavior of prisoners as their hardships changed. He wrote the following letter to Dr. Ernest Dichter, head of the Institute for Motivational Research, in regard to his concept of four basic drives in human motivation:

> "When we were starving and freezing (one bowl of watery soup per day over a month), we talked and dreamed only of food; when rations were increased to the point where hunger pangs were less severe, we talked about women; when the food situation improved still more, we became concerned for our safety; and when, on the two occasions we were privileged to eat all we wanted (Christmas 1944 and May 1945), we got ambitious and philosophical and began to talk about our stations in life and those to which we aspired."[1]

Dr. Abraham H. Maslow, professor of psychology, Brandeis University, is the author of several books and many researches in the field of motivation. He developed the frequently mentioned theory of the hierarchy of needs. Given the assumption that a satisfied need does not motivate, man

[1]Letter from Forrest W. Howell, Jacksonville, Florida, published in *Memo from Dr. Dichter and Staff* (Institute for Motivational Research, Inc., Croton-on-Hudson, New York), May 1956.

is seen as satisfying in ascending order the needs of hunger in an extended sense, safety, social affection, esteem, and finally self-actualization or self-fulfillment.[2] He also believes that some forms of motivation go beyond the satisfying of basic needs toward a recognition of the better nature of man. In time, emphases on physical needs will give way to self-actualization, to stress on dignity as a person. Money will become less important as men seek higher psychic incomes for themselves.

Numerous approaches to the "why" in the lives of people whom we see every day have been made by psychologists. They have developed special concepts such as "motive," "drive," and "need." The terms apply to predisposing influences in behavior of a psychogenic nature. Currently, the term "need" is receiving considerable emphasis in certain behavioral researches.[3]

The inner or unconscious needs of the individual are fundamental to understanding what he does and why. These are given much study by the psychologist, but the business man is more concerned with the manner of expression than the origin or the exact nature of the underlying influence. A good example is the need for personal recognition, which may be expressed either in selfish behavior that has a ruinous influence on an organization or, on the other hand, in outstanding work. Even though our main interest is in the outward expression rather than the origin of the drive, we can understand and, at times, direct the manifest behavior more intelligently if we can sense the motivating influences, the needs, that give the behavior impetus and continuity.

Even though he is not a trained psychologist, every socially alert person daily recognizes the special needs of friends. A supervisor, for example, receives a suggestion from a new employee. The suggestion, let us assume, has very little or no practical value. The socially alert supervisor does not immediately express his frank opinion of its value because he notes that the employee has a deep-seated need for recognition. He therefore expresses appreciation for the presentation of the suggestion and promises to have its value investigated. Furthermore, the supervisor realizes that complete lack of interest in the first idea submitted by an employee will cause him to submit few or no ideas in the future. The hope of eventually getting a few good ideas causes the supervisor to welcome the many poor ones, particularly from the employee who has a need for recognition.

Another example of insight into an employee's needs often occurs in the typical salaried worker's request for a pay increase. This request may represent a desire for recognition rather than an exigency for relieving fi-

[2]See Henry P. Knowles and Borje O. Saxberg, "Human Relations and the Nature of Man," *Harvard Business Review*, March–April 1967, pp. 20f.

[3]See Harold M. F. Rush, "The Language of Motivation," *The Conference Board Record*, January 1966.

nancial pressure. An excellent study of this kind of want as applied to industrial research scientists has been reported, in part, as follows:

> It is often said that people work mainly to get paid, and that the prospect of getting a raise is the main spur to hard work. Similarly, it is widely accepted that employees drag their feet if they think they are being paid under the prevailing rates. Salary is also generally regarded as an important status symbol. . . .
>
> In order to find out what industrial research scientists think about pay and other incentives the authors recently conducted a survey among two representative groups. Group A consisted of 102 non-supervisory scientists and technicians selected by random sampling techniques at a large research and development organization. Group B was made up of 70 research and development scientists enrolled in graduate evening courses in industrial engineering and physical sciences at Stevens Institute of Technology. Since the scientists in this group were employed by a variety of industrial concerns, they may be considered a heterogeneous sample.
>
> Asked how they felt about their current salaries, 74.5 per cent of Group A and 49.9 per cent of Group B expressed the opinion that these were lower than they should be. . . .
>
> . . . it must be remembered that complaints about salary are often symptoms of other dissatisfactions.
>
> How would these scientists feel about their jobs if their salaries were raised? In response to this question, 53.5 per cent of those in Group A and 64.5 per cent of those in Group B said that they would feel they were being adequately rewarded for the work they were doing. Yet, only a handful (6.6 per cent and 1.6 per cent respectively) admitted that they needed the money to relieve financial pressures so that they could give more attention to their work; and only about 15 per cent of the respondents in both groups felt they would perform their work with more enthusiasm.[4]

Every individual, regardless of whether he has had much or little formal education, has some inner needs. The need may give rise to demands for more pay or some other expression such as criticism of educated persons. Certainly, many a college student who has worked in factories during summer vacations has met a certain type of foreman who has had little formal education. The lack has made him both proud and resentful—

[4]George A. Peters and Max Lees, "Better Incentives for Scientific Personnel," *Personnel*, American Management Association, Inc., January–February 1958, pp. 59, 60.

proud because he has achieved a good position despite his lack of formal education and resentful because in the company where he works special recognition is given to "college men." A foreman of this kind is apt to divide industrial employees into two groups: the "practical" and the "theoretical" men. Whenever he deals with a college-educated man such as an engineer, he enjoys finding evidence of the theoretical man's stupidity. Such a foreman may treat members of management with great respect, but he likes to bawl out subordinates, particularly "dumb college men."

If the college man is aware of the influence of such a foreman's needs, he is not disturbed by the bawlings-out. Instead, he accepts them as of incidental note with a comment to himself such as "Aw, the boss just has to bawl me out occasionally—it makes him feel better!" The smart college man recognizes the probable origin of the foreman's behavior, overlooks it, and concentrates on learning worthwhile matters from the foreman's practical experience.

We must not assume that sensitivity to individual needs is limited to educated persons. On the contrary, many industrial workers are quite sensitive to the psychological needs of their fellow workers. A. Zaleznik has described an instance that occurred in a machine shop where he studied the workers. The occasion was a birthday party in the shop for an employee named Larry.

> One incident in relation to Larry's birthday party that we thought revealed a great deal about the group's sensitivity toward its members was described by Hal. Not only did the group sing "Happy Birthday" to Larry, but they also sang to Nick. It was not Nick's birthday, but the group, as we were told about the incident, sang to him as a joke. This is a matter of interpretation, and we do not have proof, but we believe the group had, intuitively, a serious intention behind their recognition of Nick. He was a sensitive person who seemed to need support and reassurance. He made cleanliness almost a fetish, and the men respected his feelings by keeping clean the soldering area if they had occasion to work there. He seemed also to be more bothered by assignments outside the machine shop than any other worker. We believe that the birthday song to Nick, even though done in jest, was nonetheless to support Nick and to reassure him that he had standing in the group.[5]

Each researcher uses a classification of needs that he finds appropriate for the specific project that he investigates.[6] The terminology in regard to

---

[5]A. Zaleznik, *Worker Satisfaction and Development* (Boston: Harvard Business School, Division of Research, 1956), p. 48.

[6]One of the oft-quoted lists of needs as developed by a psychologist is that of H. A. Murray, *Explorations in Personality* (New York: Oxford University Press,

the designation and definitions of needs is unstandardized. A reading of the current literature on the subject would, however, probably cause the reader to accept the list used in this chapter.[7]

Need for achievement

We can define this as the need to do useful work well. It is a salient influence characteristic of those who need little supervision. Their desire for accomplishment is a stronger motivation than any stimulation the supervisor can provide. Individuals who function in terms of this drive would not "bluff" to get a job in which they would not do well.

As everyone knows, some employees have a strong drive for success in their work; others are satisfied when they make a living. Those who want to feel that they are successes have high levels of aspiration for themselves. This drive is especially prominent in the evaluations made by the typical employment interviewer who interviews college seniors. He wants to find out whether the senior has a drive to get ahead or merely to hold a job. Too, some want to get ahead but have a stronger drive to avoid failure.[8] Most employers who seek future executives try to avoid hiring the seniors who are satisfied to become the passable performers. They look for those who aspire to the highest vocational levels that they might possibly attain. Generally, college men have stronger achievement needs, to dominate, to be aggressive, and to be autonomously self-directing, than college women. The college women have stronger needs to defer to others, to have close affiliations with others, to introspect regarding their personality, to help others, and to be dependent on others.[9]

Of course these differences in achievement needs between men and women often cause frictions in the marital state. The typical wife who is married to a man of high achievement needs cannot understand why he should neglect her and the children in order to give full attention to his job. She may feel neglected, treated unfairly. Her needs differ so decidedly from his.

1938). See also Calvin S. Hall and Gardner Lindzey, *Theories in Personality* (New York: John Wiley & Sons, Inc., 1957), Chap. 5.

[7]The fact that specialists do not agree in the labels that are applied to needs does not prevent researchers from obtaining valuable data. Chris Argyris, for example, was able to obtain high predictive validity scores from an apparently inconsistent list. See his *Diagnosing Human Relations in Organizations, A Case Study of a Hospital* (Research Project, Division of Labor and Management Center, Yale University, 1956), p. 32.

[8]See David C. McClelland, "Measuring Motivation in Phantasy: the Achievement Motive," in David C. McClelland, ed., *Studies in Motivation* (New York: Appleton-Century-Crofts, 1955), pp. 401–13. McClelland is one of the leading investigators in this field of motivation.

[9]See A. L. Edwards, *Manual of the Edwards Personal Preference Schedule* (New York: The Psychological Corporation, 1953).

If she accepts the situation but does nothing to lift her career or intellectual achievements, she may, in time, feel that her husband has risen to a high level but she has remained on a low level. This feeling on her part is likely to develop special needs which she may satisfy by positive or by negative value activities. Her special needs may cause her to become keenly devoted to children or friends. These are positive value tendencies. Of course she might instead acquire negative value adjustments such as neurosis and faultfinding toward those who appear to be on a higher career level.

Also, to satisfy this need, some women try to make themselves *indispensable* to others. The woman who makes this kind of adjustment wants others to be dependent upon her. Many college students have the kind of home situation where the father is a vocational success and the mother feels she has been left behind in the race. Hence, the mother tries to make herself indispensable to her children—she supervises and fusses over them to a degree that causes the children to rebel. Typical expressions on their part are "Oh, mother, I do wish you'd stop worrying about me and just let me alone."

Young men of high achievement needs are likely to have certain intense emotional problems not experienced by the low achievers. The *volunteer problem solver* in business is typically a high achievement-need person. He spends weeks or even months struggling with a company problem and, in the flush of success, submits his solution to a superior in a written report. He then waits. And waits some more. He is expecting something. His daydreams at this point would reveal that he expects anything from a friendly telephone call on up to a new office with a bigger title on the door!

ARNETT

"I'm glad to see that your sales equal your blood pressure."

Source: Arnett, caption by D. Phillips, *Tide* (July 30, 1955).

One writer suggested that the most acceptable approach for an ambitious employee to use when answers start popping into his head is usually the opposite of what he is naturally inclined to do. Instead of providing the answers on a volunteer basis, he should think in terms of questions that may stimulate management to give him a boss-requested assignment.

When the person of strong achievement needs finds himself in a work situation where he cannot make progress he feels frustrated. Tensions develop. It is the frustration of wanting promotion and perceiving no possibility of getting it that often contributes to the nervous tension of certain employees.

Occupational frustrations build up in him as a result of his gradually recognizing that his vocational progress is not reaching the level set in his earlier aspirations. Some develop an urgency that causes them to change jobs. Several investigators have concluded, as the result of analyses of life histories, that at age forty or thereabouts a certain stocktaking of progress with respect to goals is likely to take place. An upsurge of new effort occurs when the results of this evaluation are not satisfactory.[10]

Achievement needs do not usually decline steadily with increased age. Instead, there is a likelihood that frustrations tend to accentuate the need for achievement at certain ages as compared with the earlier years. We also know that some people who have achieved success are thereby stimulated by that success toward continued striving. For those persons, achievement needs may not decline at all with age; the drive toward more successes becomes increasingly stronger. A recent investigation, for example, indicated that a group of older "high achievers" of average age fifty-six reported greater willingness to move their homes and accept various other inconveniences, if this move meant greater opportunity, than younger men of average age thirty-six, who had also achieved success. Older as well as younger men need outlets for satisfying strong achievement needs.[11]

Of course many persons seek satisfaction for their achievement needs through status symbols: a respected title, a distinctively furnished office, a home in a high-income area, or ownership of a car that elicits social recognition. Many achievers are motivated by an urge to acquire status symbols. (See Chapter 6.) To some persons, however, status symbols are of little value. The lonely single girl who lives by herself in an apartment may, for example, decline an offer of a better job that includes a prestige title because she has a stronger need to work with old friends who are congenial.

[10]Sidney L. Pressey and Raymond G. Kuhlen, *Psychological Development Through the Life Span* (New York: Harper & Brothers, 1957), pp. 290–92.

[11]See L. Reissman. "Levels of Aspiration and Social Class," *American Sociological Review*, June 1953, pp. 233–42.

Achievement motivation can be developed

Most American businessmen who have had experience in selecting and training citizens of underdeveloped countries and needy individuals in depressed areas of this country have found that some people have a strong drive to get ahead and some do not. Those executives who have tried to develop drive on the part of individuals have reported little success in their well-meant efforts.

Recent experiments in this and other countries, cited by David C. McClelland, professor of psychology and chairman of the Department of Social Relations, Harvard University, indicate that where motivation is weak, it can be made stronger on the part of some individuals. Money incentives will stimulate some to work harder, but the individual who has a strong drive to achieve will work hard anyway as long as it is possible for him to achieve. McClelland has pointed out that such a person is interested in money rewards or profits primarily because of the feedback they give him as to how well he is doing. Money is not the incentive to effort but rather the measure of his success.

Many politicians, social workers, leaders of dissident groups, and others imagine that improving the environment by increasing the opportunities to make money will be sufficient to solve the economic problems of the poor. Programs are organized to help those who are in need. As McClelland has said: "These programs take for granted that it is enough to increase the opportunities available to the people in need of help. But often this is not enough. It is necessary to move in and increase the aspirations for achievement that the local leaders possess." His experiments confirm the feasibility of achievement motivational training.[12]

For one series of experiments, an area of India was chosen. The community was Kakinada, Bay of Bengal area. Work was done through the Small Industries Extension Training (SIET) located in Hyperabad and initially financed in part by the Ford Foundation. The purpose of the experiment was to find out whether it is possible to push a community into an economic "take-off" by training a number of its business leaders in achievement motivation. Most of the fifty-two men who took the training were heads of small businesses—bicycle shops, retail stores, and small foundries, but the four groups of twelve to fifteen men each also included lawyers and bankers.

Training methods included the setting of specific goals by the individual with periodic evaluations of progress; having the individual learn

---

[12]See David C. McClelland, *Harvard Business Review*, November–December, 1965, pp. 6f., *Forbes*, June 1, 1969, pp. 53–57, and David C. McClelland and David G. Winter, *Motivating Economic Achievement* (New York: The Free Press, 1969).

to think, talk, act, and perceive others like a person who has achievement, motivations; using the language and thinking of achievement so that it colored his thinking and mental life; modifying the self-image; developing new assumptions about what is feasible and important; and trying to feel emotionally supported as a member of a special group.

Results: In the case of the Kakinada experiment, six to ten months after training, two-thirds of the men had become unusually active in business in some observable way, whereas only one-third of these men had been unusually active in similar ways two years prior to taking the course.

In Bombay, a similar experiment was conducted in 1963 with thirty-two salaried men of large companies. In 1965, two years later, two-thirds of the men had become unusually active as compared with 20 percent to 30 percent who were quite active before the course.

McClelland thinks that under favorable conditions the drive to achieve can be improved in short intensive courses lasting ten days to two weeks. Long-term expensive educational programs that take months or years are not necessary for the purposes of achievement motivation.

The Human Resources Development Corporation, Cambridge, Massachusetts, has been organized to supply on a regular basis the kind of motivation training with which McClelland and his associates experimented in the United States, India, Mexico, Africa, and other areas.

Aggression needs

Almost every student has experienced the need for aggression. He has expressed some of his antagonisms toward unpleasant educational institution frustrations by criticism of a teacher's marking methods or even by derogatory comments about the college's food service. A wise administrator learns to differentiate between objective comments and griping. Generally, griping is only partially justified, but it frequently makes the griper feel better because it satisfies some of his aggression needs.

The aggression drive, in its simplest form, expresses itself in destructive thoughts. When the individual fails to grow up emotionally, the drive continues to express itself in acts of faultfinding, selfishness, procrastination, jealousy, and hostility. The aggression drive is a force that makes us want to hit out when we are frustrated or angry or hurt. It helps us defend ourselves against attack. However, when it is coordinated and balanced with a constructive purpose, the aggression drive can lead to or become transformed into a constructive drive. It will conquer obstacles that stand in the way of reaching a difficult but worthwhile goal. A constructive drive makes us want to build rather than tear down, to create rather than destroy. In infancy, the constructive drive is self-centered and pleasure seeking. Its primary aim is self-preservation as exemplified by the baby's efforts to obtain food, warmth, and affection from those around him. These things are essential to the baby's survival. In later stages, the earlier self-centered drives normally become constructive—they are expressed in thoughts and actions that are kind and creative. That is why we do not admire the adult who functions mainly in terms of aggression. We recognize that he has not as yet attained the maturity of control and direction of his aggression tendencies.

Sometimes the individual turns his aggressive drives against himself in self-punishment or, in extreme cases, suicide. In industry, this is seen most often in the form of accidental injury. Of course, many accidents are not a form of self-punishment, but close study of accidents has shown that the people involved often "forgot" or disregarded safety precautions in a manner that is difficult to understand on a conscious or logical basis. Unconsciously these individuals created a situation in which they could be and were injured.

Many of our aggressive drives go around our conscious guard to find expression in activities that we perceive as commendable. An example is the supremely honest man who must give his frank opinion to his friends on everything that they say or do. He not only believes that honesty is the best policy in all cases but practices it even though it sometimes harms those whom he likes. These are the self-righteous persons whom we avoid because they go out of their way to find fault in order to make themselves feel better.

An example of unconscious hostility is the not-too-well-disguised joke aimed at other people. We can temper aggressive feelings by humor that is enjoyed at the expense of the other person. True humor is enjoyed by all the persons involved in the joke. Humor, however, is one of the more subtle ways in which we can express our aggressions. We should all examine the forms of our humor and the people against whom it is directed.

The need for outlets of aggression tendencies is frequently exemplified in the history of nations. The demagogue has had great influence in the evolution of world affairs. He can always find some people who seek a new or better outlet for their hostilities. Scapegoats are universal in the history of nations. These destructive aggressors do not follow ordinary codes of ethical conduct—they have a deep-seated need to be cruel to even those people who treat them kindly and justly.

Every large business organization has one or more scapegoats or whipping boys—individuals who rightly or wrongly are targets for blame, even abuse. The individual chosen for the satisfaction of this need is likely to be a ruthless power-seeking person who recognizes that he is hated but is not emotionally disturbed by the brickbats tossed against him behind his back. Top management men are not ordinarily disturbed by the employees' hatred toward the scapegoat member of their group—they know that many employees have unconscious needs for such an outlet. Subconsciously, too, perhaps some feel that if one member of management is the unofficial whipping boy, the other members are likely to miss some of the mud balls that might legitimately be thrown at them!

The new employee who is unaware of the ways in which needs for aggression are expressed is likely to misunderstand the fellow employee who advises him to "tell the boss off." Many a novice has caused trouble for himself by listening to the fellow employee who advised him to loaf on the job and to resist the boss. This kind of unsophisticated youth believes the pseudo "big shot" when he describes how he put the boss into his place! Of course when the youth and the bad counselor are in the presence of the boss, the newcomer discovers that the loud talker is actually meek as a lamb.

Ideally, no one should have destructive aggressive tendencies. Practically, all people have them to some extent, but most people keep them repressed. When repressed, they are likely to appear in disguised forms, most commonly in psychosomatic or other functional disorders.

When tensions are strong enough and suppressed, they are a factor in headache, stomachache, ulcers, and other ailments. This is especially likely to occur with people who are under constant pressure but cannot speak out for some reason. Bank officers and public officials who have to be "nice" to everybody occupy this kind of situation. If a person in this kind of situation "blows up" occasionally, he should be forgiven.

Some children are reared in this controlled manner. The child from infancy on is taught not to show his anger openly. He is not allowed to quarrel with brothers and sisters, to express jealousy, or to say, "I don't like you!" He is taught that it is wrong even to *think* these things. In adult-

"Subconsciously you hate your grandmother, but you transfer this hostility to the troops by overseasoning the chow!"

Source: by Art Gates. Reproduced by special permission of King Features Syndicate.

hood, this kind of upbringing in regard to the firm control of aggressive feelings becomes an unconscious part of his psychic life. Consciously, he may not feel angry. He may not even realize that he denies his angry feelings. When, on occasion, he is provoked to anger, he unconsciously feels guilty about his feelings of hostility which he dare not express. On the job, he may be easy to get along with—he never picks a fight, he never questions his supervisor's commands, and he does not argue when he is passed over for a promotion that he believes that he deserves. Even though this kind of person gets along quietly with everyone, he seldom develops close friendships. He usually has no deep interests outside the job. Eventually, however, the pent-up angry feelings take their toll. He has no safety valves through argument or an absorbing interest. He becomes an asthmatic, ulcer, migraine, or some other variety of patient whose ailment cannot be cured by medicines.

Frustration arouses energy. If this energy cannot be expressed by prompt satisfying means of expression, it is nonetheless discharged somehow. If you are reprimanded but cannot talk back, you may later yell at someone for a minor misdeed. You may berate a waitress or yell at other drivers of cars you pass on the way home. Of course, if you are married, you can take out your irritation on the wife or the children!

Momentary and short-lived flareups of this kind are common to all of us. When, however, the aggression evokes feelings that are out of all proportion to the situation, we say that hostility is expressed. It is a common and important problem in industry, for unlike anger it tends to linger on. For example, we may find the man who dislikes everyone, supervisors and co-workers alike, because he feels that they are "out to get him" or are "constantly picking on him." He is the person who does everything with a chip on his shoulder. Such expressions of hostility are found not only on the employee level but among management men, too. For instance, there are days when everyone tries to avoid the boss because rumor has it that he is "on the warpath."

We can often find ourselves being hostile to someone for no apparent reason. By stopping and thinking for a moment we may see that perhaps we are transferring frustrations from other experiences into hostility toward others. Thus by looking for the causes of hostility in ourselves and in those around us, we will be taking a constructive step toward more satisfactory relations with others.

Need for security

The term security applies to the individual's seeking for certainty, stability, and predictability in life. Commonly, it is applied to the desire for economic security as in the preference for having a steady income and a pension in old age. Emotional insecurity is deeper than economic insecurity.

It often arises in broken-home situations where the child's world, particularly his relations with parents, are undependable. In adulthood, such a person tries to protect himself and his position. He likes routine, regular schedules, and obedience to precedent. The term also applies to stability in social relationships as exemplified by the person who avoids the making of new friends but clings tenaciously to a few old friends.

Employees who feel insecure are likely to have extra tensions which, in some cases, are relieved by criticizing the company. Older employees who resent their lack of progress often express themselves caustically toward management. Managements know this and try to have new and young employees work with employees who are not soured on the company. This is one of the factors involved in the first assignment of a capable new employee: are his associates old employees who feel defeated or are they well-adjusted men who enjoy the challenge in their jobs?

The "touchy" employee is a problem commonly encountered by almost every supervisor. This kind of employee is overly sensitive to any comments about his work, however well meant or constructive. The touchy employee magnifies or misinterprets incidental remarks that he hears even though not directed to him nor applicable to his situation.

Of course such a person is exceedingly insecure. He needs constant reassurance and approval. Some supervisors try to assure the individual of his value to the organization at every opportunity. They ask his advice about the work and praise him in the presence of more well-adjusted friends who "go along" with the ego-building praise.

Every alert supervisor does some of this kind of catering to the insecure person in his group. When, however, the task proves to be endless because the need is never satisfied or resolved, the supervisor gives up the

"Here's Mr. Apgar, Ed—set your watch for 7:32."

Source: by Jeff Keate. Reproduced by permission of The McNaught Syndicate, Inc.

attempt to satisfy the insecure person's needs and concentrates on the work rather than the person who does the work. Some of these supervisors become cynical about the values of human-relations skills—their answer is likely to be: "Aw, I fed so-and-so compliments every day for years but he never changed. I got tired of wet-nursing him along. From now on he's got to get his ego built somewhere else."

One answer to the discouraged supervisor might be to the effect: "Sure, you have to keep it up, maybe all your life. Your job in supervision is not to cure people of their peculiarities but to get along with them, day in and day out, as they are—not as they ought to be."

The need to overcome guilt feelings and projection

The process of ascribing to another person or institution the burden of our own repressions is commonly referred to as *projection*. The person who perceives in other people the traits and motives that he cannot admit in himself is probably using the mechanism of projection.

The personnel man must occasionally deal with pathetic cases that involve projection. One employee, for example, whipped his tiny baby because it cried. The employee's wife complained to the personnel man and asked his help. He found that the man had had sexual relations with the girl before marriage, and when she became pregnant, he thought he was the father. After marriage, he discovered that other men also had had intimate relations with his wife. The husband developed hatred of the baby but wanted to continue the marriage. Such impulsions are difficult for an employer to tolerate. A solution in this case was found by placing the baby for adoption through a social agency.

The student who has the barrier of failure in an examination often projects the cause to the unfairness of the teacher. The husband who slips in his marital relations may satisfy his feelings of guilt by accusing others of infidelity. The man who fails in business does not, as a rule, blame himself but imputes his losses to the "powerful forces of Wall Street," unfair competitors, or governmental interference. An executive may project his failures to factors other than himself. If the balance sheet figures are unsatisfactory, he can blame his employees, competitors, or government interference; or he can calmly analyze the situation for the causes of failure and then busy himself on an improved plan of procedure for the next fiscal period. "Passing the buck" satisfies the "passer" but does not bring objective results. The production foreman who falls down on his schedule may have sound reasons for so doing, but it is to be expected that he will suggest that the blame should be placed on some other executive.

To avoid such excuses, forceful leaders often develop the habit of asking their subordinates to perform certain jobs and of implying, when the orders are given, that excuses are not going to be considered. This method has decided benefits because it causes the subordinate executives to spend their mental effort in working out schemes for the accomplishment of the desired end rather than in seeking excuses of the projectionist's kind. The executive who insists upon results, the results he wants, may develop the reputation of being hard boiled, but his methods are sounder psychologically than those of the other man who accepts the excuses of poorly adjusted employees. Any organization that is made up of a large number of people who find it easy to excuse poor work on their part is a weak organization.

Our everyday human relations in business do not enable us to know how an individual's feelings of guilt arise. That kind of probing is in the province of the trained psychotherapist. We can, however, see the outward manifestations, as exemplified by the persons who wash their hands many times a day because they are afraid of contamination by dirt. Dirt symbolizes some factor in their guilt. Some wear gloves to overcome the fear. Compulsive habits of tidiness and accuracy often have their origins in guilt feelings. Compulsive spenders, habitual gamblers, and givers of extravagant gifts are likely to be motivated by an underlying feeling of guilt or some other inadequacy.

Similar but less important compulsions are counting the number of steps in every stairway, counting the cracks in the sidewalk, counting the letters in street signs, and putting dots inside all the "o's" on a printed page. Some count their change numerous times every day.

Need for recognition, acceptance

It is evening. A husband and wife are sitting in the living room. He is tired from the day's work. She takes a cigarette and insists that he walk across the room to light it for her even though a lighter is within her reach. Obviously she has strong needs for recognition and acceptance.

Each one of us has feelings of inadequacy, hunger for acceptance by others, and a desire for recognition. In our yearnings, we make demands on others, buy products, and go to certain places that appease our unconscious needs. Sometimes these inner strivings cause us to change friends, change neighborhoods, and change churches. We can see these strivings at work in the youth who must use profanity, drink to excess, or join a tough military outfit to prove that he is man!

The young college man who joins a business organization wants to feel that he is accepted not only by his fellow workers but also by the executives. If he has a strong need for acceptance by those of higher status, he is apt to try to become "chummy" with executives before he has earned their friendship. He may, for example, meet an executive a few times, note that his friends address him by a certain nickname, and then imagine that he, too, has acquired the privilege of addressing the executive by his nickname. Of course the older man resents it because such familiarity must be earned—not assumed by the beginner. The smart young man keeps on addressing the boss as "Mr." even though the boss addresses the young man by nickname.

Defensiveness

The most common description of the defensive person is, "He has a chip on his shoulder." This pattern is self-protective. The person who has difficulty in admitting to others or himself some inadequacy in his personality may try to guard it from scrutiny by others. He develops some modes of behavior that shield or appear to shield him. These protective forms of behavior are called *defense mechanisms*. He uses them to protect himself from anxieties, and his associates soon learn to avoid any mention of those inadequacies for which he adjusts by defensive behavior. They know that any mention of his defect, real or imagined, is likely to result in exaggerated behavior or withdrawal from the social situation.

Painful and unpleasant topics of importance to us are likely to bring out defense mechanisms, such as anger over a situation in which we have played an unintelligent part.

"Never talk to Oliver Gaskell about his son!" one of the new executives of the pottery plant was warned. "If you want to get along with the old man, don't mention Junior unless he brings it up first."

Why should Gaskell, Sr. become angry when someone discusses the son? Does he, perhaps, realize that he is responsible for wrecking his son's life, forcing him away from medicine into a career the son finds distasteful and in which he cannot be successful? Or does he secretly think of his son as a weakling, a failure? In either case, is he not trying to close his mind to a painful idea? When someone mentions his son, he uses anger as a defense.

The one situation in business where defensiveness is most often evident is in the ways certain employees react to criticism of their work. When the supervisor points out an error, the nondefensive person accepts it objectively. In contrast, the defensive employee tightens up and refuses to admit the error, however small. He may even refuse to admit the error when it is clearly evident that he made it and offers farfetched explanations instead.

The defensive person asserts his innocence even when not accused, as exemplified by one executive who said of his secretary: "She is so defensive that if you told her it was raining outside, she'd say it wasn't her fault."

A common example of defensiveness in social situations is the very dignified gentleman who seems to wear an armor plating of dignity as a protection against criticism and social inadequacy. As one humorist said: "Don't mistake dignity. Lots of times it enables a man who says nothin', does nothin', and knows nothin' to command a lot of respect!"

Everyone is certain to meet this type of dignity. It is protective. The individual avoids risks of social failure by means of a manner that causes others to treat him with the kind of respect his manner demands. In business, his associates sense his sensitiveness. They defer to him when in his presence, but they avoid his presence whenever possible. He is a lonely person and can be "reached" only when he is in circumstances where he feels secure from criticism. In previous generations, many of these dignified gentlemen held executive jobs. Today, if circumstances place them in executive positions, they are likely to be poor leaders. Modern business requires the ability to give and take criticism without excessive defensiveness.

Coping mechanisms

Even though much of an individual's behavior is an attempt to satisfy his needs, we must not imagine that he is the helpless victim of his need drives. He has many coping mechanisms. *Coping mechanisms* are related to the defense mechanisms. The defense mechanisms indicate how the individual adjusts to conditions that arouse his anxieties. The coping mechanisms indicate how he utilizes positively both his potentialities and his defense mechanisms in his life and work situations. From this standpoint, each person exhibits two varieties of behavior: one variety develops from needs to which he adjusts inadequately as in defense mechanisms, the other is an expression of the ways in which he channels his tensions and need outlets into the means of making a living, living with others, and living with himself. The human relations specialist sees examples every day of individuals who exhibit markedly disturbed personality patterns, inability to live with themselves, but they function effectively in work and certain other situations. They have good coping mechanisms.

Our major question about the individual's characteristic behavior should not be, "How normal or abnormal is he?" but rather "Are his coping mechanisms enabling him to function effectively in certain situations under certain conditions?" If the answer is yes, we want to note the favorable situations and conditions. In everyday practice, almost every intelligent executive does this. He knows that certain defensive or other inadequately adjusted persons do very good work and live happily when conditions are favorable to their needs.

Also, we need to realize that the employee's needs may change as he undergoes new experiences such as "shock" arising from a tragic experience. The earlier need drives may be modified by later needs even though the earlier patterns tend to remain in modified form.

The important objective for the human relations leader in business is to produce a satisfactory balance between the employee's needs and the full range of satisfactions that may be gained from his work. Management must keep the needs of employees in perspective with the needs of the company; both are evolving in accordance with their established patterns.

The supervisor who knows the dominant needs of his individual employees can often find ways to define work assignments in terms of their needs. The insightful supervisor can add to his work instructions statements about the need satisfactions that will accrue to the successful worker. A capable foreman will often explain to an emotionally insecure employee that accomplishment of a difficult assignment will make the employee's status so secure that he will be recognized by management as an especially valuable employee.

One basic conclusion from the study of the worker's needs is that we are not sufficiently utilizing his need to be needed, to make a contribution, to feel that he is a worthy participant in a great enterprise. He does not want to be used merely as a means to an end but as a partner in the attainment of worthwhile ends.

QUESTIONS ON THE CHAPTER

1. What is the significance in the example of the alert executive who reacts to a useless suggestion submitted by one of his employees?

2. Comment on the assumption that sensitivity to individual needs is limited to educated persons.

3. Differentiate between the need for achievement in college men and in college women. Can achievement motivation be developed?

4. How may an ambitious employee cope with his desire for advancement through problem solving?

5. How does increasing age affect achievement needs?

6. What is the difference between the aggression drive and the constructive drive?

7. Give the several definitions of the need for security.

8. Why does a person tend to use the mechanism of projection?

9. Describe the characteristics of the man with "a chip on his shoulder."

10. In what way are coping mechanisms related to defense mechanisms?

11. Which important worker's need should be taken into consideration more often by business executives?

12. Of all the ideas presented in the chapter, which one had most value for you?

13. How did the chapter contribute to your future relations with (a) your supervisors, (b) employees whom you may supervise?

PROBLEMS AND PROJECTS

For All Students

1. Examine several magazines that publish human interest cartoons. Clip some that amuse you. Can you recognize any relationships between your own psychological needs and the ideas or characters in the cartoons? How might this insight be of value to you when you supervise others?

2. Give an example of an embarrassing situation that you brought about because of your failure to sense some other person's unspoken needs.

For Advanced Students

3. Make a study of problems involved in developing standard labels of needs. See footnote 7 in the early part of this chapter regarding Chris Argyris's ability to obtain high predictive validity scores from an apparently inconsistent list of needs.

4. Of course much behavior takes place as the result of joint effects or interactions of several motives. This fusion has been recognized for years. See H. A. Murray, et al., *Explorations in Personality.* New York: Oxford University Press, 1938. However, little research on fusions has been reported. Why?

For Men in Business

5. Discuss the influence of psychological needs in customers. To see an example, visit a hearing-aid sales office. There you can note customers whose need for personal attention seems to be greater than their need for an instrument to overcome loss of hearing. Can you cite similar examples in other businesses?

6. Describe some examples of effects of needs in the employment of workers, particularly as to the kind of job for which the person applies.

COLLATERAL READINGS

For All Students

Herzberg, Frederick, "One More Time: How Do You Motivate Employees?" *Harvard Business Review,* January–February 1968. Discusses modern motivation theory for the layman.

Newman, Summer, and Warren, *The Process of Management.* Englewood Cliffs,

N.J.: Prentice-Hall, Inc., 1967. Chapter 9 discusses psychological needs that are satisfied through work.

For Advanced Students

Gellerman, Saul W., "Management by Motivation." New York: American Management Association, Inc., 1968. An excellent synopsis of motivational theories.

Lesieur, Fred G., "The Scanlon Plan Has Proved Itself," *Harvard Business Review*, September–October 1969, pp. 109–18. Scanlon Plan results are summarized with discussion.

For Men in Business

Hundal, P. S., "Knowledge of Performance as an Incentive in Repetitive Industrial Work," *Journal of Applied Psychology*, June 1969, pp. 224–26. Knowledge of results is a motivating factor even in repetitive industrial work where the pay rate is low.

Sorcher, Melvin, "Motivation on the Assembly Line," *Personnel Administration*, May–June 1969. Describes effect of a program in a manufacturing group to change employee perceptions of their roles and to improve employee performance.

Problem Employees Whom You May Meet in Business

SITUATIONS YOU ARE LIKELY TO MEET

How would you meet each of these situations:
- a. *Before* you have read the chapter? What would you say to yourself?
- b. *After* you have read the chapter? How have your answers changed?

1. In previous situations described on the opening pages of chapters, the answers you were asked to give applied to some other person. Now let's see how well you talk to yourself about your own problems and answers.

   Assume that you are working for an executive who has lots of ability and you are learning a great deal from him. However, you find that he is also opinionated and sarcastic. His negative qualities are "getting on your nerves." Regretfully, you are thinking of asking for a transfer to a more congenial executive's department.

   Okay, give yourself a "talking to" before and after reading the chapter.

2. Assume that you come from a broken home. As a child you keenly felt the lack of a father in your home, and when you had to adapt yourself to a stepfather, your emotional reaction was severe and belligerent. Later, as you heard others talking about the difficulties of boys who come from broken homes, you found it easy to excuse your failures (due mostly to laziness), and you realized that you had learned to excuse your failures to yourself.

Well, maybe you did not come from a broken home but you have learned to excuse yourself for some real or imagined deficiency in your early environment.

Talk to yourself on this subject, if you have the courage.

Then read the chapter. Note the additional topics that deserve attention.

How does your "self-talking to" or self-review change after reading the chapter?

Very probably, some of your interest in studying human relations stems from your difficulties in dealing with problem persons. Each one of us meets some people who are maladjusted, neurotic, suspicious, unkind, sarcastic, opinionated, or destructive. As employees they not only lower morale and retard production but also add to our burdens. Sometimes we react to them by ignoring them, sometimes by trying to change or improve them. In the end, we may conclude that since we cannot ignore or change them, our best policy is to strengthen ourselves so that we can endure them without too much emotional strain on our part.

Dealing with difficult people can strengthen you

Each one of us has need for the ability to objectify and understand problem persons in order that we may treat them intelligently and rise above being hurt by their orneriness. The qualities we develop in ourselves are more important than the few modifications we can help bring about in others. You should not look upon most difficult people as persons whom you should "cure" or change. Instead, look upon them as opportunities for strengthening yourself. Each difficult person has certain inherent rights to become and be what he is—why should you assume that every one should do or be what you choose for him? This does not mean that you should ignore the difficult person. Perhaps you can understand him, work with him, and thereby enable yourself and him to grow to a higher level of maturity.

492

One of the most helpful points of view for us to acquire is that problem people are not wholly bad. Even the most cussed have some good characteristics. They are cussed only in "spots." They have the same psychological needs as the well adjusted, but they use inappropriate behavior to satisfy their needs.

Vocational self-sabotage

Anyone who does vocational counseling of adults is certain to meet individuals who have high intelligence, pleasing personalities, seemingly good habits, and many good character qualities; but who always manage somehow to fail in their vocations. In contrast with them, other individuals of less intelligence, more irritating personalities, and poorer personal habits manage to succeed, regardless of their opportunities. Both types are difficult to explain as long as we use quantitative approaches only. When, however, we think in terms of unconscious motives, we get plausible explanations. We discover that many of the men who always manage to fail are really expressing an unconscious urge toward self-sabotage in their vocation.

Failure enables the maladjusted person to accomplish aims that are more important to him than success. Such aims have been revealed by Friend and Haggard in the systematic investigation of two classes of unemployed adults: those *high* and those *low* on eight basic criterion items of occupational adjustment. One of the striking differences between the two groups was described, in part, in their findings.

Topping the many sharp contrasts in personality, the stronger tendency of the *Lows* to defeat themselves and spoil their job chances stands out as an indicator of adjustment at work. It is often evidenced by excessive drinking, quarreling, and illness. The *Lows* seem to marry the wrong person and to have families so large that they experience difficulty in supporting them. Correlational and other special analyses of the extent of the tendency toward self-sabotage link it with the extent of the following attitudes: parental rejection, antagonism toward the father, resentments both of dependence and domination of families, rigidity, buried fear of failure, and self-attack, unrealistic thinking about jobs, ambivalence, and reliance on pull. . . . Although the relationships suggested are not necessarily causal ones, these factors do seem to serve as devices through which the maladjusted individual accomplishes an aim. They seem to be ways of settling early parental scores; or of handling the guilt which demands constant failure; or of protecting himself against fears of being unable to cope with work. . . . This extreme type of "vicious-circle" behavior seems related to the well-known proclivity of those seriously disturbed emotionally (the *Lows*) to make things generally hard for themselves —a trait which is slight in the *Highs*.[1]

Whatever the explanations that may eventually be found most appropriate for the understanding of capable adults who manage to fail, the fact is that they do manage to fail in spite of apparently excellent outward reasons for success. The only helpful psychological explanation, thus far, is that they themselves are unconsciously sabotaging their own efforts in order to attain aims more important to themselves.

The person who, for example, has a strong drive to dominate or control others may try to do so by being a tactful executive or he may be merely abusive and sarcastic. Both positive and negative value kinds of behavior may originate from the same kind of basic need. Criminals have the same inner needs as good citizens, but the criminals satisfy their drives through behavior that is dangerous to society. They have not learned the art of satisfying their own needs through service to others.

When we deal with problem people we should observe the characteristic ways they use in dealing with life's situations. We may, for example, note that a person expresses egotistical behavior. Most people say that he "*is* conceited." Instead, we should say to ourselves that he "*uses* conceit" as his characteristic way of dealing with others.

The people who use poor techniques in dealing with life's situations are everywhere. We cannot escape them. They are found in the primitive societies of Africa and Australia as well as in America. Many savages as well as civilized persons fail to gain happiness and serenity. The faultless, guiltless persons of the world cannot be found in the sunny, palm-treed islands of the South Pacific any more easily than in our own cultures.[2] Perfection in humanity cannot be found by going to some new environment. Instead, we have to find examples of fine ways of dealing with life's situations among the persons wherever we are.

After all, most people try to live what they think is the good life. Most employees are anxious to please, to do a good day's work, even though a small percentage, estimated as 10 percent by one executive, may loom too large in our thinking. This executive stated his observations, in part, as follows:

> People are the same everywhere I have been. I have found employees in all parts of the country equally competent and willing to

[1]Jeannette G. Friend and Ernest A. Haggard, "Work Adjustment in Relation to Family Background," *Applied Psychology Monographs*, No. 16 (Stanford, Calif.: Stanford University Press, 1948), pp. 58–59.

[2]Fereidoun Estandiary, "Is It the Mysterious—or Neurotic—East?" *The New York Times Magazine*, March 24, 1957.

turn out a good day's work, but wherever I have gone I found my "Ten percenters." My experience has proved that regardless of what you do for your employees about 10% will never be satisfied. . . .

Regardless of how good the conditions or how good the wages these "Ten percenters" can never be satisfied. Maybe this is exaggerated a little but these are the only people I can't seem to please or become friendly with. I don't hold any grudge against these people— I feel sorry for them. Complaining and being dissatisfied is their petcock and method of emotional relief. Other people get the same by being loyal, happy and complimentary. The way I get around this situation and the reason why I don't have ulcers is I overlook their shortages. My deepest concern is for the other 90%.

There is no use worrying about getting rid of this 10% because you will get another 10 just as bad. You will always have them—it just seems to be the law of averages. You will find them in all departments and in all walks of life. Some employers have been condemning the whole 100% because of the "Ten percenters." In visiting plants around the country I have noticed everyone is always ready to complain about their 10% group but fail to give credit that is due the other fine 90%.[3]

Some problem persons make important contributions

In business, it would be easier to deal only with well-adjusted mature individuals, but we have to recognize that some very great contributors are maladjusted and immature. Many problem persons have certain strong traits that offset some of their bad ones. In one of our leading corporations, there is an unofficial company policy "never to stop hiring a screwball" if the man shows a quick mind, a knack for ideas, and ambition.[4]

Findings from the extreme stress conditions of war vindicate this policy. Of all those who have broken down in action under stress, the contributions of those who have done so in wartime have been given special study. The investigations indicate that, as a group, the psychological patients of our recent wars served as long and as well as the average soldier. Before the breakdown took place, official evidence indicates that in a very large proportion of cases, the man did credit to himself and his unit. Statistically, the proportion of men with neuroses who received decorations for

---

[3]William S. Sadler, Jr., "Human Evaluation and Business Profits," *Mechanical Bulletin 578* (American Newspaper Publishers Association), July 3, 1956, pp. 47–49.

[4]See *Business Week*, August 2, 1959, p. 57.

valour showed little difference from the proportion of other soldiers who received decorations. Indeed, there is considerable evidence to indicate that some measure of mental peculiarity may endow a man with extra spirit, conscientiousness, and additional grit.[5]

Executives who direct engineers and research workers know that a preconceived pattern of personality adjustment does not hold for all occupational groups. They know, for example, that the compulsive-looking, tense, rigid, introverted person, not infrequently found among expert research men and engineers, might erroneously be considered as maladjusted. Clinicians realize that such a picture often contributes to successful functioning in engineering and research.

Psychiatrists recognize that most persons in business have their peculiarities as individuals. Emotional problems that are handicaps in one job may or may not be handicaps in another job. As one practitioner in the field of the problem person in industry has stated:

> . . . it is widely accepted today that a "healthy family background"—whatever that is—is the Golden Key to productivity, happiness, and success in most (if not, in fact, *all*) occupations and activities. Yet there is mounting evidence that *it is not at all necessary to have a "healthy family background" to perform successfully in business and industry today.* Indeed, there is considerable evidence that many people are outstanding in their jobs or professions precisely *because* they come from psychologically unhealthy homes. . . .

There is, of course, a considerable body of sociological literature

"Two years ago they'd of fired me for goofing off. Now they promote me for 'creative thinking'."
Source: by Angelo. Courtesy *Sales Management* (January 3, 1958).

[5]See several authors in Emanuel Miller, ed., *The Neuroses in War* (New York: The Macmillan Company, 1940).

demonstrating that city slums, generally regarded as a breeding-ground of poor home environments, produce more than their share of delinquents. But the same literature also reveals, upon closer inspection, that city slums have provided certain individuals with powerful motivation to "make something of themselves," and that many men and women from the slums have risen to the top in their business, or professions.

In the same way, from families which are clearly not ideal, we may get both delinquents and top executives. . . .

Of course, it should be acknowledged that not everyone who has an emotional problem or a psychiatric syndrome is a desirable person occupationally. Further, it should be emphasized that, although emotional disturbances may be assets, they are not assets in every type of job; frequently they are assets in only one or a very few jobs. In other words, emotional disabilities may sometimes be outright handicaps because of the individual himself, because of the job he is in, or even because of the emotional disabilities of his superior.

Purely for financial reasons—but not ignoring the humanitarian and morale factors—we must raise the question of what can be done with such people. Facing this issue involves many factors, including timing of action. For instance, one company sent eight superintendents to us at Stevens' Laboratory of Psychological Studies; all were chemists or chemical engineers. Their question to us was: "Are any of these men salvageable?" It turned out that two of the men were "salvageable." Among the others were two men over 60 who had been considered unsatisfactory for more than 15 years.[6]

Generally, psychological disability is not synonymous with occupational disability.[7]

Enlightened managements realize that it is management's task to discover the maladjusted individuals, to correct any work conditions that contribute to maladjustments, and to decrease the harmful influences of psychoneurotics who inoculate large groups of otherwise efficient workers. The main channel for providing favorable influences is through selecting and guiding the supervisors and foremen. To many employees, they are "the company." They can, at times, reduce or accentuate the individual employee's anxieties and fears.

---

[6]Frederick J. Gaudet, "The Problem Employee: Some Points of Confusion," *The Personnel Function: A Progress Report*, Management Report No. 24, Personnel Division, American Management Association, Inc., New York, 1958. Reprinted with special permission of the AMA.

[7]As an example, see Kenneth Rexroth, "Robinson Crusoe," *Saturday Review*, November 9, 1968, p. 18.

The neurotics in industry[8]

The neurotics (also called psychoneurotics) are emotionally immature individuals. A neurotic is likely to be a nuisance to himself, to others, or to both. The kind that is a nuisance to himself is the more common. He fixates the attention upon himself and has emotional reactions out of proportion to his difficulties. Frequently his symptoms are a direct appeal for sympathy and attention. Or he may be setting up an excellent alibi for possible failure in a given situation. His lowered efficiency and emotional distortions affect other employees around him. The morale and working efficiency of the whole group may seriously be lowered by the continued presence of just one neurotic.

The neurotic who is a nuisance to others is likely to be arrogant, demanding, or just plain cussed. He has trouble getting along with his associates: he gets angry easily, is irritable, hostile, and faultfinding.

The alert management notes that emotional upsets appear in greater numbers in specific departments than in others. This may be due to a maladjusted supervisor who keeps his subordinates emotionally upset. The foreman may have a disrupting effect by exerting excessive or constant pressure on the employees. He may criticize too much. He may praise certain employees and ignore others. He may lean over them at work and tell them how to do work that they know well. He may find fault with incidental details. He may insist that everything must be done his way even though the employee knows a better way. Studies have shown that poor supervisors take their sickness rates with them when they move from one part of an organization to another.

Interestingly, too, neurotic employees tend to gravitate toward other neurotics. They seem to feel that they are among persons of their own kind. Neurotics attract neurotics in industry as well as in marriage. When management spots such a situation, the maladjusted persons are not promptly fired because the typical neurotic does good work or, at least, has learned how to give the impression that he is doing good work. As an employee, he tends to punish himself. He feels that he is not doing his job well. He needs constant reassurance that his work is passable. He may be especially agreeable toward others, but he has personal problems that are overwhelming, problems that his well-adjusted associates usually ignore.

Neurotics differ from psychotics. Psychotics must or should be hospitalized. They cannot hold jobs. Neurotics seldom receive hospital treatment. They can and do hold jobs. Many, but not all, psychotics are out of touch with reality. Neurotics live in touch with time and place, but do not enjoy it. As one humorist expressed this difference: "A psychotic thinks

---

[8]For a related description of neurotics in business, see pages 378–379.

that 2 and 2 make 5. A neurotic knows that 2 and 2 make 4 but he is unhappy about it!"

Contrary to general belief, many neurotic workers are valuable workers, likely to be among the most conscientious members of the company's workers. Many neurotics when working individually give as good an occupational performance as non-neurotics. Certain jobs lend themselves to a person who is excessively suspicious as long as he has good control over his judgment. Many neurotics are submissive people who will do extra hours of work because they are afraid to say no. Others are extreme perfectionists who turn out accurate reliable work at the price of tremendous internal discomfort if it is not perfect.[9]

The complainers

Any executive who keeps in touch with the feelings of his employees is likely to find that he has some gripers in his department. One of the most common variety is the employee who constantly complains that he works too hard. He imagines that he is doing more than he should. If job descriptions have been written for each job, he will use the description of duties as evidence of the claim that he is asked to do tasks that he should not be expected to perform. If the job description has the statement, "Performs other related duties as assigned," this part of the description is overlooked by the complainer.

To the executive who looks upon complaints as symptoms, the claim that the employee works too hard usually means that the executive has failed to give the employee ego-involvement in the work. The employee who identifies with his superiors and the company tends to see his tasks in terms of his own ego needs. He has few complaints even when invited to express them.

Investigators who have studied complaints of employees have found that the complaints may be classified into three major groups:

1. Those which can be clearly seen and agreed upon, such as a broken tool. Sensory experience can define them.
2. Experiences or conditions which cannot be clearly seen and agreed upon, such as, "The room is too hot."
3. Complaints in which sensory experiences play a small role but hopes and fears are involved. Conditions complained about are expressions of the sentiments of the person, such as complaints about wages, supervision, or advancement. Complaints of this

[9]See S. L. Warner, "Spotting the Neurotic and Helping the Maladjusted," *Personnel Journal*, September 1957.

third group are the most disturbing. These are likely to be symptoms of some deeper or symbolic need rather than justifiable complaints about objective matters that are easily verified.[10]

We should also view some complaints as tension releasers. Perhaps, for some individuals, gripes are just another variety of goose pimples or allergies! As one physician has well stated:

> Many of us react to being chilled with goose pimples. Some persons react to emotional tension in the same manner. Around the bottom of each hair on the body is a tiny muscle, and it is this muscle that our nerves activate under certain conditions of stress and strain. Actually "goose pimples" can be as much a tension outlet as hysterical crying or over-eating.
>
> Another way to relieve tension would be to regrow our prehensile tail. It has been shown that monkeys do not suffer from mental ailments or strokes because wiggling their tails seems to relieve them of pent-up emotional disturbances. In surveying the emotionally disturbed in mental hospitals, it has been reported that persons with asthma or hay fever are rarely found to be patients in these institutions. The belief is that certain allergic symptoms may be the method whereby some "normal" people blow off steam.[11]

A common reason for the dissatisfaction voiced by a disgruntled employee is likely to be his pay, but it is not usually the basic motivating factor. Insufficient salary is repeatedly used as a pet peeve, but this claim often turns out to be a means of release from some troublesome but submerged and unidentified irritation. The lack of money is a real problem with many people and it does cause worries, but it also symbolizes or covers up the seat of many a complainer's troubles. Frequently, other factors are involved in the frustrations that the lack of money symbolizes. (See page 442.)

Many complaints about wages are not cured by wage increases. Too many executives take for granted the idea that everyone wants more money and that if employees are given more money, they will be happy. Desire for more pay may really mean that the employee believes that his foreman does not give sufficient recognition for years of service or that a certain rate of pay symbolizes answers to status needs.

[10]See F. J. Roethlisberger and W. J. Dickson, *Management and the Worker* (Cambridge: Harvard University Press, 1939), pp. 255–69.

[11]Edward R. Pinckney, M.D., "From a Doctor's Notebook," *Blue Print for Health*, Fall 1958. Dr. Pinckney is director of the Comprehensive Medical Clinic, Northwestern University Medical School.

If the foreman does get a raise for the complainer, he will be treating symptoms rather than causes. Logic and fact will not satisfy the dissatisfied employee who is seeking emotional satisfactions. Logic merely disgruntles him more. The supervisor is more likely to be helpful by evaluating the worker's need for a feeling of worthwhileness. Perhaps he needs recognition as a person, new assignments that challenge him and that may lead to a higher rate of pay. Certainly, the supervisor should let the complainer air his grievance before he offers logical answers.

Well-adjusted happy people accept or improve difficult conditions. Unhappy inadequately adjusted persons are seldom satisfied with the job or life, but some of the tensions involved in their complaints can be redirected into useful satisfactions.

Complaints should be examined for their direct objective meaning, and any causes for complaints in groups 1 and 2 should be corrected when possible. Complaints that are in group 3 must often be approached with insight into their obscure meanings.

The ideological "expert"

Of all the problem persons in industry, one of the most baffling is the employee who has developed some elaborate scheme for interpreting the world or some complex aspect of life. He usually has only a smattering of knowledge of a favorite field of study such as philosophy, economics, or political science, but he becomes convinced that his superficial explanations and remedies would, if accepted by others, solve the world's ills. He expends much time and effort in explaining to others his panaceas. Those who listen do so out of courtesy rather than interest.

He may, for example, have a line of reasoning that divides the world into two conflicting groups: (1) the employers or managers and (2) the workers. He can take any event in his work surroundings and translate it into the differences that he sees in the goals of managers and workers. Even the most altruistic action by the company is interpreted as an attempt to gain ends that benefit the managers at the expense of the workers.

Men of this kind are likely to be lonesome, isolated from their immediate social world. They have few satisfactory relations with their colleagues. Hence, they move from one job to the next, and each job is terminated by a crisis caused by misunderstanding on the part of those whom he perceives as exploiters or at best as stupid. Even though some member of management such as the personnel manager may appreciate the nature of the employee's unconscious motivations, he cannot redirect his drives into constructive channels. The self-styled "expert's" drives continue to be expressed through warped thinking. Eventually he may find himself dropping to the lowest levels of jobs or even placed in an institution where he can continue to "preach" until he reaches the end of his wasted life. Perhaps he never learned to like himself well enough to like other people.

The ideological expert should not be confused with the temperamental artist. He usually applies his energies to an ideal greater than himself, and he makes contributions that are beneficial rather than beyond man's needs.

The problem drinker

Many persons still think of the employee with a drinking problem as something of a moral degenerate. Some managements try to deal with him by giving him numerous "last chances" and eventually using discharge when admonitions fail.[12] Fortunately, however, new attitudes toward such employees are emerging, particularly among members of management. See "Some Developments, 1958 to 1964."

Many companies now look upon alcoholism as a form of illness. They think of alcoholics as sick rather than morally corrupt individuals. They

---

SOME DEVELOPMENTS, 1958 TO 1964

During the six years 1958–1964, there were a number of developments in the field of alcoholism. Chief among these was the greatly increased number of companies that are giving attention to the problems. Whereas no more than a dozen companies had well-established programs in this area six years ago, hundreds of companies have such programs today. Among these are 23 of the 100 largest companies on the FORTUNE list.

More doctors, including psychiatrists, now are treating alcoholics and more hospitals are providing beds for those needing fulltime, intensive care. Alcoholics Anonymous is reaching 100,000 new members. The Yale School of Alcohol Studies has moved to Rutgers University in New Jersey. Other universities, too, are conducting research in alcoholism and offering courses on the subject. Last summer, 553 students participated in the program of one of these schools—the University of Utah in Salt Lake City. And the National Council on Alcoholism, through Information Centers, now offers free assistance to alcoholics and their families in 70 communities across the United States.

Source: The National Industrial Conference Board, Inc., 845 Third Ave., New York, N.Y. 10022 publishes at irregular intervals an updated research report, *The Alcoholic Worker*, "Studies in Personnel Policy Series," No. 166. Ask for latest edition. These reports provide excellent information for members of management. The above panel is taken from 1964 edition.

[12]Some employers believe in giving the alcoholic absentee only one "last chance." See "Case of the Alcoholic Absentee" (Problems in Review), *Harvard Business Review*, September–October 1969.

believe that many can be cured and that the company can assist in the curing process. They believe that it is better policy to try to rehabilitate the problem drinker than to fire him. They think in terms of therapy rather than punishment. They have worked out specific personnel programs and procedures toward this end.

Of course these companies and organizations are not trying to help the employee who goes on an occasional binge but the worker whose job suffers from his drinking.

Psychiatrists who work in the clinics realize that they have no one cure for alcoholism. They seek to find the causes for the drinking. Causes are likely to be so deep-seated in the mental life that special training and clinical practice are necessary for giving helpful treatment. They cannot transfer their clinical techniques to personnel men of industry so that they can give treatment, but they can help educate supervisors in regard to the "covering up" aspect of the problem.

Anyone who has dealt with problem drinkers knows that friends often cover up for the drinker. When he is absent on a Monday morning, his wife reports him "sick with a cold." The fellow worker at the next desk or the next machine does his work for him on his bad days. The supervisor, who likes the drinker as a person, overlooks his absenteeism, especially if he is a good worker on good days. These loyalties all help to keep the alcoholic or incipient alcoholic from getting prompt remedial attention. The "cover-up" practice is the reason many managements imagine that they have "no alcohol problem." These pre-alcoholics are usually viewed as social drinkers by most members of management.

Managements of large companies have found it helpful to brief supervisory personnel on the signs to watch for, such as frequent absenteeism (usually beginning on Monday), irritability, and sloppy appearance. Supervisors are also warned that sheltering the problem drinker does him a disservice.

The problem drinker, when spotted, is usually given a friendly talk by his supervisor or by a member of the firm's counseling staff. They refer him to the plant's doctor, local clinics, or rehabilitation groups.[13] These programs are voluntary, but the worker who refuses help gives management little choice but to discipline him by short layoffs, or by eventual discharge.

Alcoholics classified

The staff at the Yale Center of Alcohol Studies estimated that 40 percent of alcoholics might be thought of as persons who have discovered

[13]"What to Say to an Alcoholic," *Management Review Magazine,* January 1964.

TABLE 25–1

A Profile of the Problem Drinker

Pre-alcoholic Symptoms	Early Stages	Alcoholism
1. Gross drinking behavior	5. Loss of control	12. Benders
2. Blackouts	6. Alibi system	13. Tremors-shakes
3. Gulping and sneaking drinks	7. Eye-openers	14. Protecting supply
4. Hangovers	8. Changing the pattern	15. Unreasonable resentments
	9. Antisocial behavior, solitary drinking	16. Nameless fears and anxieties
	10. Loss of friends, jobs	17. Collapse of alibi system (admission to self that drinking is beyond control)
	11. Medical aid	18. Surrender process

Source: *The Alcoholic Worker*, NICB report, "Studies in Personnel Policy," No. 166, p. 10.

the pampering effect of alcohol and embraced it as a "solution" to their problems. Another 40 percent might be classified as psychoneurotics and the remaining 20 percent as psychotics (those suffering definite mental illness).

Others say: "All alcoholics are crazy or close to it"; "Alcoholics suffer from some sort of allergy"; "Alcoholism is caused by a nutritional imbalance in the system"; and so forth. There is no end to theorizing about alcoholics. The truth seems to be that no one knows for sure *what* causes some people to become alcoholics. There is, however, wide agreement that there is not one cause but many.

The following things seem to be true in a majority of cases:

When sober, they are likeable individuals and good workers.
They are slow to seek help or to admit they need it.
They often have other problems which may be more basic than their drinking.
They can be helped, and it is better for all concerned to help them than to leave them to their own devices.[14]

Counseling problem employees

Everyone who works in business, whether he is a top executive or on some other level, takes some personal interest in each of his work associates.

[14]*The Alcoholic Worker*, NICB report, "Studies in Personnel Policy," No. 166, p. 11.

He usually knows each working associate by name and, to some extent, each one's personal problems. If he is an executive, he often lends money, helps find a doctor, or obtains legal advice for the benefit of the employee.

As an executive, he finds that this kind of close acquaintance with each employee, however well-meaning, also involves certain difficulties as indicated by this example:

> An employer learned that one of his young, unmarried women employees was pregnant. He talked it over with her, knowing she had no family nearby. She was frightened and helpless, feeling desperate.
>
> He arranged for her confinement and subsequent care of her child. When she was able to return to work, he rehired her.
>
> One month later she quit.
>
> This seemed to him like the rankest kind of ingratitude. Someone with greater understanding of psychology would see the outcome as inevitable. The girl felt a deep sense of guilt. She could not stand working in a place where her boss, and possibly others, knew her secret.[15]

The more experienced executive in human relations would not have handled this kind of situation himself. He would have recognized that if he wants the employee to be able to continue to work with her fellow employees and supervisors, she should be able to do so without the usual feeling of guilt. Astute executives who learn about acute problems of an embarrassing kind usually arrange for someone to help the person with minimum dangers of embarrassment. When they deal with embarrassing situations, they operate behind the scenes.

Most executives follow the policy: "Stay out of private lives." An employee's private life is *his* private life. The employee's life away from the plant is his own. The only occasions when attempts to regulate his life are justified occur when an employee says or does something outside the company that injures the company's business or reputation.

The good supervisor is a good listener

Many employees, particularly those in repetitive and routine work, tend to become preoccupied with personal problems. If the supervisor can get the employee to talk about his problems and the supervisor listens, this may be sufficient in itself to relieve him of many of his symptoms. The employee perceives his difficulties in better perspective and he decides how he himself will deal with his problems more objectively and constructively.

The supervisor need not, and in most cases should not, give very much

---

[15]John Perry, "Human Relations in Small Industry," Small Business Administration, Washington, D.C.

advice. Nor should he try to solve the employee's problem for him. He should be supportive in his attitude toward the employee and his problem. He should listen with an understanding ear but encourage the employee to develop his own solution or action plan.

As someone has said: "A good listener is not only popular every-where, but after a while he knows something."

Psychologists have found the *nondirective* interview especially helpful in dealing with individuals who have difficult problems.

In the nondirective technique, the counselor allows and encourages the individual to talk freely about those things that worry him. The counse-lor does not have a set of questions to which he wants answers. He does not try to get the individual to see things the same way the counselor sees them. His objective is to get the person to talk as freely as possible about the things that matter to him.

This technique is more difficult for the counselor than most super-visors appreciate. The person with a problem feels some embarrassment in telling another person about feelings that are often considered wrong. Nondirective counselors must be systematically trained in the interviewing technique before they can function properly.[16]

Diagnosis of psychoneurosis should remain in the hands of the expert psychiatrist. Supervisors should be trained concerning symptoms, but they should not try to become practicing psychiatrists. A little knowledge of psychiatry can be a dangerous thing.

Signs that alert the supervisor to the employee's need for special treat-ment are the following: if he is frequently absent from work, if he is ir-ritable, if he is prone to accidents, if he becomes angry or excitable, if he has widely fluctuating moods, if his work pace varies greatly, or if he cannot get along with other people.

The psychiatrist must make his diagnosis in terms of the individual's family background, education, health, training, social relationship, and general history, past and present. His interpretation depends upon what he can learn about the individual. If he has accurate background informa-tion about the patient, he can better interpret and weigh the various com-binations of factors that must be considered in the treatment. Supervisors and personnel men can furnish much helpful information to the psychiatrist to aid him in his diagnosis.

Managements that decide they need a counseling program usually de-velop one of two general categories of counseling programs. (1) They use presently employed personnel who have demonstrated their qualifications for counseling, or they hire a trained counselor and place him under the

[16]Methods in dealing with problems of individual adjustment can be found in Carl Rogers, *Counseling and Psychotherapy* (Boston: Houghton Mifflin Co. 1942).

general supervision of the personnel manager. This kind of counselor is more likely to be a friendly listener who saves time of busy executives than a therapist.[17] (2) They utilize an outsider, a professional counselor, who does not come under any jurisdiction of the company. He is employed on a fee basis as a consultant. Most companies do not attempt to provide a counseling service. They simply refer the troubled employee to a consultant. The consultant does not, in most cases, cure the problem person, but his counsel often enables management to reach an intelligent decision as to what action, if any, will be taken in regard to the problem employee.

For your further consideration

The presence of problem people in business should accentuate your interest in human relations. Difficulties in dealing with them should stimulate you as a student to study the social sciences as thoroughly as you can. You should not, however, imagine that taking a few courses in abnormal psychology or a related subject will enable you to be a therapist. The treatment of the maladjusted and mentally ill requires years of special training. Experienced psychiatrists will, for example, tell you that the proper treatment of the mentally ill requires a medical degree plus several years of clinical experience under supervision.

Even though you do not wish to become a professional psychotherapist, you can improve your insight into the needs and problems of problem persons. You can increase your helpfulness to the therapists. You can also become a more intelligent friend to those who need special understanding. And in the process you too will attain a higher level of maturity that will strengthen you as well as those who are problems to themselves.

QUESTIONS ON THE CHAPTER

1. Why should an untrained individual not attempt to "cure" a problem person?
2. Can the same basic need lead to both positive and negative value kinds of behavior? Give an example.
3. Who are the "ten percenters," and should they be eliminated?
4. Why is a healthy family background not the only Golden Key to success in all occupations and activities?
5. In what ways is the neurotic employee a problem to those around him?
6. Differentiate between the neurotic and the psychotic in industry.

[17]See Robert B. Morton, "Straight from the Shoulder—Leveling with Others on the Job," *Personnel Magazine*, November–December 1966.

7. Describe the most disturbing of the three major groups of complaints.

8. Why is it undesirable to "cover up" for a problem drinker in a company?

9. What are some early signs of alcoholism that management should watch for?

10. Explain the interview technique most applicable in dealing with persons who have problems.

11. When a management decides to have a counseling program, what two forms is it likely to take?

12. Of all the ideas presented in the chapter, which ones are of most interest to you?

13. How did the chapter contribute to your future relations with (a) your supervisors, (b) employees whom you may supervise?

PROBLEMS AND PROJECTS

For All Students

1. Describe the characteristic behavior of several problem persons whom you know. To what extent does the content of this and the preceding chapter add or fail to add light on each described person's behavior?

2. Describe some variety of behavior on your own part that has been a problem to others. Suggest possible causal or related factors. Can you suggest ways in which you might redirect your behavior into positive channels?

For Advanced Students

3. Make a study of mental health clinics and published materials on mental hygiene. Describe publications of the National Association for Mental Health, Inc., 10 Columbus Circle, New York, N.Y., and other organizations that can furnish objective information.

4. Interview several men in business in regard to specific problem employees with whom they have dealt. Write descriptions of each person's behavior as reported to you. Then investigate the literature for light on the problem persons.

For Men in Business

5. Perhaps you have heard the statement: "The bartender is the poor man's psychiatrist." What counseling facilities, better than those of the typical bartender, are available in your community or nearby?

6. Assume that the constant use of profanity is a problem in certain departments of your company. Some employees seem to try to outdo their associates in offensiveness. Tell how you would introduce the subject at a foremen's meeting in order to bring about improvement.

COLLATERAL READINGS

For All Students

A. A.: An *A. A. Publication*, The Alcoholic Foundation, Inc., P.O. Box 459, Grand Central Annex, New York, N.Y. 10017.

Hepner, Harry Walker, *Psychology Applied to Life and Work*. Englewood Cliffs, N.J.: Prentice-Hall, Inc., 1966, Part II. Presents an easily understood description of adjustments of problem persons in business and elsewhere.

For Advanced Students

Rogers, Carl R., *Counseling and Psychotherapy*. Boston: Houghton Mifflin Company, 1942. A classic in the field. Counseling is presented as a process that can be learned, tested, and refined.

Shaffer, Laurance Frederic, and Edward Joseph Shoben, Jr., *The Psychology of Adjustment*. Boston: Houghton Mifflin Company, 1956. Presents a comprehensive scholarly treatment of adjustment and adjustment patterns.

For Men in Business

Milt, Harry, *How to Deal with Mental Problems*, National Association for Mental Health, 10 Columbus Circle, New York, N.Y., 1962, p. 9.

Troubled People on the Job, American Psychiatric Association, Committee on Occupational Psychiatry, Washington, D.C., 1959. Distributed by Mental Health Materials Center, 104 East 25th St., New York, N.Y. Designed to help the supervisor deal with the problem employee. Offers pointers on recognizing symptoms of mental illness and tells where he can get professional aid.

YOU AND YOUR ADVANCEMENT IN BUSINESS

PART VI

Developing
Your Social Skills
in Business

SITUATIONS YOU ARE LIKELY TO MEET

How would you meet each of these situations:
   a. *Before* you have read the chapter? What would
      you say to yourself or to the individual?
   b. *After* you have read the chapter? How have
      your answers changed?

1. Assume that when you are transferred to a new department in the company where you work, the department head says: "Well, young fellow, I suppose
   you've been sent here to take my job away from me?"
   How can you answer him in a way that will develop goodwill on his part toward you and enable
   you at the same time to learn from him?
2. When you come into the new department, you note
   that the employees josh each other and have nicknames for everyone. Accordingly, you address an old
   employee by his nickname and he then says to you:
   "To you, I am Mr. ———."
   What do you say now?
3. The job you have, let us assume, requires you to meet
   and talk with visitors. Some of the visitors remain
   with you and talk longer than necessary, especially
   when you have work waiting to be done. You realize
   that you cannot be discourteous to your visitors.
   How can you expedite their departure and at the
   same time keep them happy?

Many a student can make a high grade in a course on human relations, but he is unable to carry on a conversation with the janitor—the janitor prefers to talk to more interesting people! The academic student, the science scholar, the introverted research man, even the alert extroverted administrator, may have need to improve their social skills. Certainly, book learning must be supplemented with daily intelligent practice in dealing with people if we want to make our relations effective to all concerned. Human relations skills can be sharpened especially when we ourselves determine to do the sharpening.[1]

A nationally known consultant in personnel management phrased well the inadequacy that many of us feel in regard to social skills:

> We hear a lot about "working with people" and "social skills" and their importance in business today. There are many niceties in dealing with people that come naturally to some people and are acquired "the hard way" by most of us. These small "social lubricants" contribute a great deal to the smoothness and pleasure with which a day's work can be accomplished. I envy those people to whom these little niceties of human communication come easily for I am rather impersonal and logical.[2]

Social skills are essential to the ability of each person who is expected to lead a work group and get willing cooperation from the workers. His skills in human relations are likely to be as necessary as his technical knowledge about the job itself. Social skills are, however, more difficult to impart than technical skills. No one can be taught how to handle an employee's grievance or to inspire men merely by being told how to do it.

[1]Robert L. Katz, "Human Relations Skills Can Be Sharpened," *Harvard Business Review*, July–August 1956. The author, a professor of business administration at Dartmouth College, reports his findings of a survey of several company training programs in human relations. He concluded that despite the many shortcomings in such training programs, human relations skills can be improved.

[2]Ned Hay, "Editor to the Reader," *Personnel Journal*, October 1956, p. 163.

Even though executives recognize the difficulty in teaching social skills, they attend the many seminars and workshops in better management currently conducted throughout the country. The programs range in length from a day to a year. Many of the programs include sessions in human relations. Generally, courses in human relations are attended not so much as a result of definitely proven effectiveness as the hope that some benefits will accrue.

The need for sensitivity training

Training in sensitivity to social situations may take either of two directions: increased insight into one's own motivations or greater understanding of the other person's characteristics. The first objective is by far the more difficult. Only a few business groups have made systematic attempts to achieve it. The process is slow, time consuming, and the benefits are often difficult to measure. And yet some persons can never become effective in their human relations—the barriers to their development in this field of action are so deep-seated within themselves that they cannot function effectively in social situations. Examples are the extremely rigid personality, the introvert, and the defensive person. They need much courage to gain insight into their motivations and to overcome the inhibiting influences within themselves. Most others as well as those mentioned find it easier to try to change the other person than to change themselves. Thomas G. Spates has stated:

> From my own study of the work of the social scientists, clinical psychologists and psychiatrists, and from my own experiences, the conclusion is overwhelmingly clear that the most important field for future action for all of those who direct the work of others is to know and understand themselves and their impact upon those whose work they direct. That is the latest major development in the evolution of personnel administration.
>
> That new and important item, so far as I have been able to find out, has not yet been put on the agenda of a management meeting. I've tried to get it there, but in vain. A few months ago I made the recommendation to an audience composed almost entirely of personnel specialists. Within an hour they were asked to record on a questionnaire what, as a result of their participation in this particular meeting, they would like to see on the agenda for next year's meeting. Not a single one recommended that next year's meeting include even preliminary discussion of knowing and understanding themselves and their impact upon others. I wonder how you would account for the difficulty of getting this important phase of administration on the

agenda. My explanation is this: consciously or unconsciously we realize that knowing and understanding ourselves as others see us calls for more courage and more perseverance than any project we have yet undertaken.[3]

Even though we do not have the courage to understand ourselves as others see us, we can increase our sensitivity to the ways other people feel.

The socially sensitive person recognizes the *mental set* of each person whom he meets. As commonly used, the term *set* is applied to a relatively restricted temporary attitude or to momentary states of readiness.[4]

A good example of the need for recognizing mental set occurs when we try to teach the older worker. To begin with, the instructor should try to sense whether his pupil has any resistance to learning because his self-esteem makes it difficult for him to admit to himself that the instructor has superior skill. Perhaps the worker is proud of having learned to perform skillfully an operation by hand and resents learning how to operate a machine that displaces his skill. Older men are proud of their abilities in performing the line of work they know and regard a transfer to some other work as unfair disregard of their skills. Also, many an older man is conscious of his long years of experience and rebels against being returned to the rank of novice, particularly when he must take instruction from a younger person.

Young people as well as older employees must be treated in accordance with their mental set. The smart mother who has dinner prepared and announces it to her two small boys may find that they are wearing space helmets and are just about ready to take a flight to the moon! She doesn't say: "Come on kids, forget that stuff—dinner's ready!" Instead she says, "The moon? How wonderful! Tell me about it while you're eating dinner. You could go after dinner, couldn't you?"

Likewise the alert supervisor who wants a certain employee to do a task but finds him talking with several other employees does not say: "Come on, Joe. Do this job." Instead, he realizes that the employee has a certain mental set in his conversation. The supervisor breaks it respectfully by explaining to the several men: "Say, fellows, I've got to get a job done quickly and need Joe's help. Do you men mind if he breaks off with you now so he can help me? Come on, Joe, let's get going."

[3]Thomas G. Spates, professor emeritus of Personnel Administration, Yale University, "Crisis and Promise in Collective Bargaining and Interpersonal Relations," address delivered in January 1958 at the University of Michigan (Bureau of Industrial Relations, University of Michigan, Ann Arbor, Michigan).

[4]The word *stereotype* is applied to an intense and rigid attitude. The word *prejudice* applies to an attitude still more rigid and intense and one generally based on false information. The term *opinion* is generally used to describe an attitude that is or has been expressed and that is based more on objective conditions than a stereotype or prejudice. *Set* is a temporary mental state that favors the selection of certain stimuli or facilitates a particular type of response.

Obligations should be felt but not mentioned

People in business have so many mutually shared experiences that individuals are constantly doing favors for each other. A supervisor, for example, helps an employee get a pay raise, allows him to leave work early to take care of a personal matter, or arranges to get him a discount on the price of an appliance for the home. The one who has granted or arranged the favor may be conscious of his kindness to the employee, but he should not mention it to him. Ideally, he should not even be so conscious of it that the employee can sense his consciousness!

The supervisor who does favors for employees cannot, if he is sensitive to the feelings of his employees, remind the employees that they are obligated to "put out" for him because of the favors. Nor can he grant favors in order to get back more than he gives. If he gives favors in a calculating manner, to make employees feel obligated, they will sense it and convince themselves that the obligation really does not exist. The usual reaction of the obligated employee is, "I don't owe him a thing."

Social skills must be adapted to the relations between the individuals

The typical college student who takes a summer job with an outdoor construction gang may hear the men cuss each other out in rather caustic terms. They call each other nasty names but remain friends. The student naturally tends to assume that he can apply the same terms to the men without objection on their part. To his surprise, he is usually given a first-class verbal lacing by the first man toward whom he expresses friendliness in the same phrasing used by the members of the gang to each other. To them, he is a newcomer, an outsider on a different level from themselves. Later, when he has proved himself and become an accepted member of the group, he is privileged to treat the men in the same manner in which they treat each other.

Anyone in a supervisory position must be especially sensitive to differences in degree of acceptance by members of the group. Even though his employees use sarcasm freely with each other, he is not privileged to use sarcasm with them. Sarcasm from someone at the men's own level is quite a different matter from sarcasm from a supervisor.

Corporation presidents become acutely aware of these differences in status levels when talking with subordinates.

Sensitivity to the feelings of others is one of the commonest perplexities of presidents and other members of management. When they make decisions and inform subordinates of the decision, they soon become "concerned about hurting people," "hesitancy to hurt others," and "personal loyalties." This is one of the greatest handicaps in making decisions in a

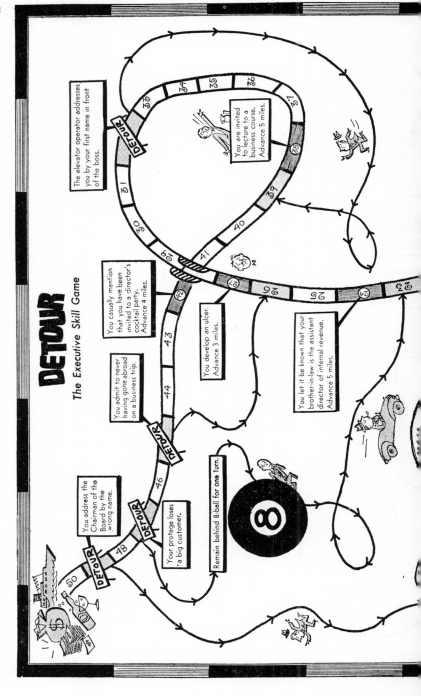

DETOUR

The Executive Skill Game

The elevator operator addresses you by your first name in front of the boss.

You are invited to lecture to a business course. Advance 5 miles.

You casually mention that you have been invited to a director's cocktail party. Advance 4 miles.

You admit to never having gone abroad on a business trip.

You develop an ulcer. Advance 3 miles.

You let it be known that your brother-in-law is the assistant director of internal revenue. Advance 5 miles.

You address the Chairman of the Board by the wrong name.

Your protege loses a big customer.

Remain behind 8-ball for one turn.

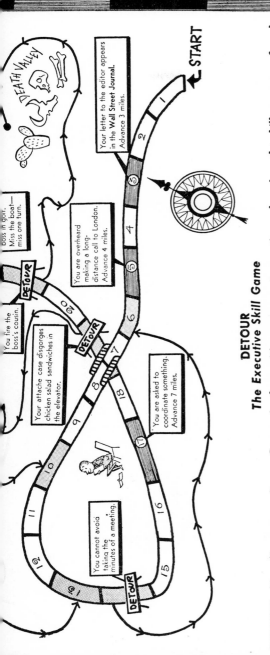

DETOUR
The Executive Skill Game

DETOUR, THE EXECUTIVE SKILL GAME, is the exciting new way to practice and analyze the skills necessary for advancement in management. A few pleasant and profitable minutes spent with this game will enable the aspiring executive to test his ability to get ahead in business today.

Rules

1. Any number can play; for most realistic results, loaded dice should be used.

2. Players move in turn, each advancing the number of miles indicated by their throw of the dice.

3. Any player landing on a town moves ahead the number of miles indicated on the sign.

4. Any player landing on a Detour square loses status to the end of the detour road.

Source: *The Management Review* (December 1957). Courtesy American Management Association, Inc.

logical manner—their question is likely to be not "What is the logical decision?" but "How will those affected by the decision react to or take the decision?"

Of course sensitivity to people is largely a matter of feeling developed through many years of experience with people. Many a student of the social sciences fails to appreciate this principle. He imagines that the ability to classify the behavior patterns such as compensation, projection, identification, and others is all that he needs to learn. To the mature specialist, such labels are merely incidental to becoming acquainted with the dynamics in human behavior.

The cataloging of a person's peculiarities, when told to the other person, usually arouses antagonisms. We do not like tags. The fact that an especially loquacious person uses talkativeness as a form of defense does not mean that you should tell him so. You should avoid mention of the label but increase your efforts to make his defensiveness unnecessary when he is with you.

Selling as a means of learning social skills

Many a retiring or socially inadequate college student has been advised: "Get a selling job—it will help you learn how to get along with people." Certainly some salesmen are highly alert to the little cues that indicate the prospect's unvoiced antagonisms, feelings, and questions. One salesman, for example, notes the position of the prospect's hands: If the hands are open, he is supposed to be receptive; if closed, antagonistic. This salesman believed in the value of his system of observation but no one, so far as known, has ever made a scientific study of the validity of his method. Perhaps it would stand up under scientific analysis, perhaps not. Generally, when scientists have investigated the validity of such systems of analyzing people as used by salesmen, they have found that the system, *per se,* proved to be only slightly better than chance in its objective soundness. However, they also found that when a salesman used a system, any system in which he believed, he became a better salesman than he had been. This indicates that the use of a system for analyzing people gives the salesman more confidence in himself and he does a better selling job! It's the self-confidence, not the system, that counts.

Generally, experience indicates that the typical observer of people concentrates on details such as clothing and bodily features. Observation of a person's clothing will suggest whether the person is neat in his appearance, but the neatness may apply to appearance only, not to every activity. Some stenographers are well groomed but turn out poorly typed letters. If, however, the supervisor is impressed by her personal neatness, he is likely to be more patient in teaching her how to produce acceptably typed letters.

Most of us observe the other person's eyes on first meeting. The fact that they are shifty does not mean that the person is evasive or dishonest, but he may be more submissive than the average person. If his gaze is direct and piercing, he is likely to be above average in aggressiveness. To keen observers, the mouth, especially when the person is in sleep or in repose, is especially indicative of the individual's degree of happiness.

Observing and understanding is a continuing process. Few reliable conclusions can be made on a first meeting. Most good judges of people want to observe and be with the person on a number of occasions so that they may add to and modify first impressions.

The student of human relations should, of course, realize that cues or clues such as those mentioned are often learned in a mechanical manner only. Students have a tendency to note one bit of behavior that in some cases is significant and conclude that the individual observed has the specific trait or problem that is, in some cases, related to the cue. The person trained in human relations seldom jumps to conclusions so quickly—he wants to see a pattern. Any one cue must fit into a larger pattern before it is accepted as significant.[5]

Listening is a social skill

Most persons assume that socially skilled persons do a lot of talking and that they dominate conversations. On the contrary, they are more likely to be good listeners than loquacious talkers. They not only listen in order to learn the other person's points of view but they also listen "between the lines" in search of the meaning that is not necessarily put into spoken words.

The good listener pays attention to nonverbal communication: facial expressions, gestures, tone of voice. He knows that these add meaning to the spoken words. He asks himself, "Why does the talker purposely emphasize certain phases of the subject? Why does he avoid other phases?"

According to surveys reported by Ralph Nichols, Department of Rhetoric, University of Minnesota, the average industrial executive spends at least 70 percent of all his working moments in verbal communication. His communication activities are divided as follows: 9 percent of this time is devoted to *writing*, 16 percent to *reading*, 30 percent to *talking*, and 45 percent to *listening*.

While the executive is listening, he can study the visitor and his state of mind.

Seminar discussions led by Nichols revealed that executives in attend-

[5]See Marvin D. Dunnette and Wayne K. Kirschner, "Psychological Test Differences between Industrial Salesmen and Retail Salesmen," *Journal of Applied Psychology*, April 1960.

ance did not consider listening to be a passive affair. As one put it, "You don't just sit there and say nothing. That is not enough. It requires real effort to concentrate carefully on what the speaker is saying, to miss no point he is making, to put in just the right question at the right time, and to give proper voice inflection to these queries. And you must do all these things while another part of your mind is busy studying the visitor and deciding what you are going to say after he has finished speaking. That's listening!"

Another executive put it this way,

> It takes a lot more out of you to *listen* well for an hour than it does to *talk* well for an hour. This is particularly the case should the visitor's attitude be antagonistic, or when you find yourself altogether opposed to the ideas he is presenting. Such situations call for the exercise of real effort in repressing your natural desire to argue with the visitor.[6]

Researches concerning the art of listening have shown the importance of attitude while listening: a facial expression that denotes interest, physical relaxation on the part of the listener, meeting the eye of the speaker squarely but without antagonism, and careful avoidance of any movement or mannerism that would distract the visitor's attention from his own recital.

BRAILLE BY HEART

Could I not see, were wholly blind,
  I still could trace
  Upon your face
The telltale imprints of your mind.
  —Merhl Norton Doren
    Ogdensburg, N. Y.

The questions asked by the listener should be brief and slipped into the visitor's recital without interrupting his train of thought. These may be along the lines of "How?" and "Why?" They lead the speaker to discuss phases of the problem he has failed to cover and encourage him to think. They may even make it possible for him to work out his own solution to the problem that occasioned the interview.

Listening as well as talking is an art. Sometimes it is even effective in dealing with a hostile person. One corporation president has described his technique in controversies:

---

[6]Alfred M. Cooper, "The Executive Art of Good Listening," *The Office Economist*, September–October 1958. Copyright © 1958 Art Metal Construction Company, Jamestown, N. Y. Also Ralph G. Nichols, "Listening Is a 10-Part Skill," *Nation's Business*, July 1957, p. 58.

The next time you find yourself confronted with a serious difference of opinion, try "sitting out" the controversy. Just sit and listen to all the arguments of the group or an individual. If you can become an active and absorbing listener, you may sometimes be able to dissolve the whole problem or dispute without saying a word!

Here is how it works for me: The proponent for some opposing view enters my office and proceeds to advance his views. I simply listen intently to everything he has to say. He continues to expound on his story until he expects me to introduce a counterargument, but I say nothing. Then I suppose he feels tempted to mention my side of the case or at least to refer to it in some way. And so he ventures into my viewpoint and finds himself talking about the things which I now do not have to mention. He believes he is doing a fine job—and so he is—until he finally concludes that there are perhaps two sides to the controversy after all. On a number of occasions I have seen situations completely solved, believe it or not, in just this way. I simply allowed the other fellow an opportunity to talk himself out of his own erroneous position.

We cannot always tell the other fellow what our story is—he will not believe us. But when he comes to that same realization by way of his own route and reasoning, he informs himself. In that respect an intelligent listener is actually a communicator, isn't he? Since it is natural for men to want to talk, I find that listening is one of the most valuable executive techniques I can use.[7]

In addition to the open hostility in controversy, hostility often occurs in the form of "unvoiced threat." An easy place to note unvoiced threats is an office where two women have been working together for years. A new girl, younger, better dressed, having more education and greater appeal to men, is hired to work with the two older women. The new girl is likely to be a terrifying threat to the two older women, and they usually make life miserable for the newcomer unless management defines the new girl's status in a manner that removes the threat. The supervisor can also eliminate the threat feeling by having the women participate in the hiring of the new girl. If the two older women are made to feel that they helped select the new girl and that they are responsible for her, they are apt to "mother" and protect as well as advise her.

Another situation where threat is obvious occurs when management places a young well-trained specialist in a department headed by a less-trained executive. The department head usually says to himself, "Is this

[7]Robert C. Hood, president, Ansul Chemical Co., in an address before the California Personnel Management Association. Reported in *The Management Review*, American Management Association, Inc., May 1956, p. 405.

new guy really here because he has been selected to take over my job?" Again, management can remove the feeling of threat by defining the man's status and by increasing the department head's feeling of security by conferring with him about the best way to utilize the specialist.

Threat is expressed in many forms. One of its most common forms of expression is shown by a change in the conversational pattern.[8] As an example, the typical college girl's social affair reveals threat when a new girl appears to have special appeal to any girl's boyfriend. Everyone present may be "awfully" friendly—so friendly that the threat is veiled but obvious to the alert observer.

Consciousness of threat can be developed by keen observation and by listening for "between the lines" meanings.

Situational allergies often reveal repressed dislikes. An example is a sneezing fit brought on by having to look at other people's travel Kodachromes or at their home movies. Certain individuals who hate to attend committee meetings blow their nose repeatedly even though the room is free of drafts. The person who develops a coughing spell and must leave the room may not want to be there even though he feels obligated to be present. The astute host either makes it easy for him to be excused or gets him to participate in the discussion to the extent that his attention is directed to the main topic and away from his affective reaction to the situation.

Helping others to save face

When the situation is embarrassing to the other fellow, making it easy for him to "save face" is an old axiom of the socially skilled person. The

"Listen Dear—the Boss insists on coming for dinner. Hide the TV set, park the car in the next street, don't serve anything fancy, wear something old. . . ." Source: by Hank Baeb, Courtesy *The Office* (July 1956).

[8]See William H. Pemberton, "Talk Patterns of People in Crisis," *Personnel Administration*, March–April 1969.

supervisor who discovers that an employee has made a mistake can treat the error objectively but still allow the employee to feel that he is not disgraced. This applies also to the employee who has prevaricated in order to make himself appear more important. Unless a lie is a legal offense, the liar should, in most cases, be allowed to save face. After all, many untruths are really just phases of gossip; if all gossips were to be jailed, we would have more jails than residences.

In business, many executives are skilled in enabling employees to save face. Supervisors who have responsibility for checking an employee's work can check openly, but a great deal of checking is also done casually. The executive who has an extrasensitive stenographer need not check her typing —he can instead check his dictation!

The production manager of a plant, for example, knew that union members were restricting production. He proved to the head of the labor union that the men were not producing as much as the same kind of equipment was producing in competitors' plants. To enable the union leader to save face, the production manager offered to attach an inexpensive facilitating device to each machine to help the men produce more. The device itself had little value, but it gave the union head a reason for asking the men to raise their production instead of restricting it to abnormally low levels. The new mechanical device allowed the men to save face.

The supervisor who has the knack of making men feel honorable in his presence and gives them ego-involvement in their work will often find that his men are willing to help him in an emergency. Moreover they will also help him to save face by compensating for any lack of technical knowledge on his part with their productive shop know-how. An awful lot of everyday human relations in business consists of saving face and is practiced by employees for the benefit of executives as well as by executives for the benefit of employees.

Remembering names and faces

Each one of us has need for a good memory, especially memory for names and faces. It is an art that adds more charm to the personality than many other skills.

WORDS TO THE WISE

Here is a "thought-provoker." In human relations the
—five most important words are "I am proud of you."
—four most important words are "What is your opinion?"
—three most important words are "If you please."
—two most important words are "Thank you."
—smallest word is "I."

From *Mill & Factory*. Reprinted in *The Management Review*, American Management Association, Inc., May 1955, p. 320. Original author unknown.

Many people think that the ability to remember names and faces is some kind of inborn gift. Actually anyone who wishes to do so can acquire the habit. The main factor in its learning is to determine to remember names and faces. Certain persons such as the personnel man need this ability. They practice it until they master the ability. Here are several simple rules which, if practiced, are bound to produce marked improvement:

1. Be sure that you get the name correctly. If in doubt, ask the person how he spells it even though it is a simple name such as "Brown" or "Smith."
2. Use the stranger's name several times during the first conversation.
3. Associate some pertinent facts about the person with the name—his occupation, color of eyes, way he shakes hands, manner of speaking, and so on.
4. While still with him, look away from him and visualize him.
5. After he has left you, visualize him again and repeat his name to yourself and the pertinent facts you noted.
6. At the end of the day, visualize all the faces and say all the names of the persons whom you met that day.
7. Practice constantly, again and again.
8. Take pride in your ability to remember names and faces. Utilize the ability whenever you can.

Accurate and frequent observations are essential. Avoid generalities such as "a fat lady of about thirty" or "a gray-haired old man." Be specific. Add details.

Add associations such as "The fat lady of thirty who talked so much about the fine qualities of her husband that I wondered whether she fears that she may lose him" and "The gray-haired old man who bragged about the important job he had years ago with the XYZ Corporation."

The ability to remember names also involves our emotions at the time when we wish to use the name. No doubt you have had the unpleasant experience of being unable to recall the name of an old acquaintance when you wanted to introduce him to someone. This inability is accentuated when you are more concerned about the impression you are making than about enabling both persons to have a pleasant experience. To avoid such embarrassing situations, concentrate, in advance of the introductions, on the ways in which you can help the two strangers have a pleasant meeting. Transfer your self-centered thoughts into thinking about the pleasures that the two may gain through mutual acquaintance.

Skill in ending the interview

One of the most frequently mentioned questions asked by young executives who are called upon by customers, applicants, and friends is, "How do you get rid of the guy, tactfully, who stays with you too long?" Most of these visitors have a normal business reason for calling. They must be treated respectfully. Typically, too, the visitor often keeps on talking long after the business transaction has been completed.

The old-timers in management learn the art of easing these overstayers out of the office in a manner that maintains cordial relations between host and guest. They do it simply by telling a story or humorous incident. When both are laughing, the host stands up and the guest rises without realizing that he has risen. The host moves to the door and continues talking in a manner that keeps their conversation mutually interesting. Usually, the guest leaves in a good mood.

Some executives and personnel men have this problem so frequently that they train their secretaries and other staff members to speed the visitor's departure by reminding him of his overlapping appointments.

Keeping the secrets in business

People who work in the business world soon learn that certain topics are "off limits" for discussion with outsiders. Other topics may be discussed only with certain members of the organization, and some should never be mentioned to anyone within or without the company. Every employee has an unwritten assignment to learn what may and what may not be discussed. The employees, of course, discuss certain topics through the grapevine rather than openly. These are topics that interest the employees: scraps of information about the likelihood of layoffs, reasons for failure to get an order, and personal matters such as scandalous conduct, real or imagined, on the part of members of the organization.

The most important secrets are not those of the grapevine variety but facts that provide a competitive advantage: technical discoveries that improve the product, marketing plans for the next year, and financial data which, if known to a competitor, would enable him to underbid the company in presenting his bid for a contract.

Executives soon learn which employees are too gabby in the rest rooms, at social affairs, or with members of the family. Those employees are not entrusted with information that must be kept under cover until the stipulated release date. Mimeograph machine operators, secretaries, research men, and accountants are always under some observation in order that loose talkers, informers, and talebearers may be spotted. Most smart employees learn to avoid the giving of "classified information" when asked for it by a simple statement such as "I have no special knowledge about that part of the business" or "Mr. Blank heads up that work—he can tell you more about it than I can."

Sometimes managements must code secret information, record the name of every person who handles it, and set aside certain offices as "off limits" to everyone except to designated personnel. Security measures similar to those used by governments are at times necessary in business.

Speak of your company and work associates
with pride

Even though certain company matters should not be discussed with outsiders, the employee who likes his company should speak well of it to others. If he does not like his job or the company, he should do what the college student does who does not like his college—transfer to another institution as soon as possible. Only the inadequately adjusted person remains with a college or a company that he does not respect.

One of the characteristics of the well-adjusted person is that he habitually speaks well of the institutions to which he belongs: his family, community, and the company that employs him. This does not mean that he is blind to their shortcomings. But he respects his colleagues and the institutions to which he and they belong. He speaks well of them whenever the opportunity arises. After all, some admirable persons belong to each institution.

It is, of course, easy to parrot the gripes of those employees whose unconscious needs for aggression are expressed against the employer. But when they do, they merely make some people unhappy. Criticism against the institution to which one belongs decreases the stranger's respect for the griper rather than the institution toward which the faultfinding is directed. We can see examples of this in college. Every college student is likely to be asked during vacation by someone in his hometown: "Well, Bill, how do you like your college?" If the student answers: "Aw, heck, the place stinks!" the listener is likely to say, "That's too bad." What he probably thinks, however, is "Maybe it's Bill, not the college, that stinks."

The employee who takes an objective, sincere pride in his company and its products is more likely to develop himself and contribute to the company's success than the chronic faultfinder.

The titles used in conversation

In a few companies, the president makes a fetish of having everyone use first names and nicknames in conversations in the office and plant. This is disliked by many employees who prefer to recognize the greater responsibility and status of major executives by referring to them as "Mr." In some firms, almost everyone is addressed as "Mr." regardless of his job status.

Generally, secretaries and young men use the "Mr." even though the supervisors use first names and nicknames in addressing the secretary or the young man. The practice is similar to that of the college classroom where few students would ever think of addressing the teacher as "Bud," "Bill," or "Hank" even though the teacher addresses students by their first names.

Incidentally, many American college students do not know the differ-

How's Your Etiquette?

You know, of course, which fork to use when, and how to make introductions without stumbling, but are you up on the intricacies that make the rules of etiquette as fascinating as they are maddening? To find out, test yourself with these 22 questions. [See answers, page 556]

	true	false
1. When walking or sitting with two women, the man should place himself between them.	—	—
2. A man should offer his arm when walking with a woman at night but not in the daytime.	—	—
3. An engaged man may give his financée a fur stole but not a fur coat.	—	—
4. A bride's linen is always marked with her initials as an unmarried girl.	—	—
5. At weddings it is proper for each bridesmaid to be escorted down the aisle by an usher.	—	—
6. A recent death in the family automatically rules out a church wedding.	—	—
7. It is proper to telegraph either formal or informal invitations.	—	—
8. Typewriting personal letters, even long ones, is not in good taste.	—	—
9. A married woman never, never signs a letter with "Mrs."	—	—
10. Letters to teen-aged boys are addressed: "Master John Jones."	—	—
11. Butter plates are always used at a luncheon, never at a formal dinner.	—	—
12. Napkins are folded flat and laid on the plates at a formal dinner.	—	—
13. A hostess is served before any guest.	—	—
14. A guest may ask for anything that is not served.	—	—
15. At the start of a meal, shake out your napkin and lay it on your lap.	—	—
16. It is good manners to leave a portion of food uneaten on your plate.	—	—
17. You may properly use your knife or a crust of bread as a food pusher.	—	—
18. Never use bread to sop up gravy or sauce.	—	—
19. Head lettuce may be cut only with a fork.	—	—
20. A woman never takes off her gloves to shake hands.	—	—
21. The host at a cocktail party should be prepared to serve almost any drink.	—	—
22. The christening gift from a godparent is always something in silver.	—	—

Source: *Changing Times*, The Kiplinger Magazine, January 1958.

ence between the titles "doctor" and "professor." The doctorate is a title conferred on anyone who has completed a specific program of graduate study. It has no professional status other than that. The title of "professor," in contrast, has professional status. It indicates professional achievement. The full professorship is attained in the larger institutions only after years of professional work. To become a full professor, the teacher, who may or may not have a doctorate, must start as an instructor and advance to the assistant professorship, the associate professorship, and finally to the full professorship. The last-mentioned level is normally accorded to those few men whose colleagues meet in a formal meeting and vote as to whether he, in comparison with other teachers of the subject, is one of outstanding ability among his colleagues in the nation. Generally, the younger faculty members can be addressed as "doctor" because they have not as yet risen to the full professorship. The older men of distinction are full professors and should be addressed as "professor."

These differentiations are fairly well standardized in the older and larger institutions of this country and in most European nations. In some universities, particularly the newer ones, the differentiations are not well standardized. One of America's leading universities, for example, is especially confusing to the student—every faculty member regardless of degrees or academic rank is customarily addressed as "Mr." The student in college or the employee in business should use as his guide the customary titles used by his superiors rather than the titles used by his colleagues—his colleagues may be out of line with the right practices.

Of course when a man is truly great, no title should be used. A title would have been superfluous for an Albert Schweitzer or a Winston Churchill! The same principle applies to the great scientist or teacher.

Social skills are learned through daily contacts

A student who realizes that he ought to improve his social skills is likely to learn rules or to assume that when he gets into business, he will develop the human-relations skills needed by the effective executive. If he postpones his practice that long, it may be too late. The way to learn how to get along with the boss and employees is to get along with people. To get along well with the boss is easy for the student who has learned to get along with his fellow students and work associates. The best laboratory for learning these skills is with members of the family, companions, salesclerks, policemen, janitors, waitresses, and others whom we meet every day.

QUESTIONS ON THE CHAPTER

1. What attempts are made to teach social skills?
2. What are two important phases of sensitivity training?

3. Differentiate between the terms *set* and *prejudice*.
4. Discuss sensitivity to cues in the behavior of the other person. A system of interpreting cues as used by a salesman may not be valid but it may, nonetheless, be effective. Why? When does a cue become significant?
5. Describe some of the practices essential to effective listening.
6. Discuss sensitivity to "unvoiced threats."
7. Give examples of the executive's way of "saving face" of an employee.
8. How is the communication time of an average industrial executive divided?
9. Define situational allergies.
10. Why is it beneficial for a supervisor to make his men feel honorable in his presence?
11. What are some of the factors involved in learning to remember names and faces?
12. Describe a method of easing overstayers out of an office.
13. Discuss the importance of keeping business secrets.
14. Why should an employee speak of his company and work associates with pride?
15. What is the best "laboratory" for learning how to get along with the boss and employees?
16. Of all the ideas presented in the chapter, which ones are of special value to to you?
17. How did the chapter contribute to your future relations with (a) the men who supervise you, (b) employees whom you may supervise?

PROBLEMS AND PROJECTS

For All Students

1. Describe a personal experience that indicated that your social skills were inadequate in the situation. What did you learn from it?
2. The skilled conversationalist tells his listeners when he changes topics by making a "switch comment" such as "Let me change the subject for a moment." Suggest additional switch comments that may be made to help the listeners.

For Advanced Students

3. Social skills are not taught as formal courses in many colleges or if given do not receive academic credit. Ask several faculty members for the reasons.
4. Assume that training in social skills should be given to trainees for management and supervision. Consult the available literature for descriptions of such programs, the methods, objectives, and so on.

For Men in Business

5. Interview several friends in regard to their failures in social skills in business. An example might be: A research specialist made a study of a problem and wrote a report on his findings. Later, he learned that his supervisor resented the writer's use of his own name on the report without mention of the supervisor's name.

6. Every person has some "blind spots" in his thinking, certain topics that he cannot discuss objectively. Usually, his associates recognize these blind spots and adjust their thinking to them. Think of the supervisors and executives under whom you have worked. Describe some of their blind spots and possible stages in their development.

COLLATERAL READINGS

For All Students

Hepner, Harry Walker, *Psychology Applied to Life and Work* (4th ed.). Englewood Cliffs, N.J.: Prentice-Hall, Inc., 1966. Chapter 9 offers suggestions for personality development.

Leavitt, Harold J., and Louis R. Pondy, eds., *Readings in Managerial Psychology*, Part II. Chicago: The University of Chicago Press, 1964.

For Advanced Students

Carson, Richard E., "Praise Reappraised," *Harvard Business Review*, September–October 1963.

Heider, Fritz, *The Psychology of Interpersonal Relations*. New York: John Wiley & Sons, Inc., 1958. The behavioral sciences are gaining in significance in our understanding of the interactions of people in the work situation.

For Men in Business

Luken, H. E., "A New Approach to Training in Leadership Skills," *Advanced Management*, July 1958. Report of an important pilot project that was conducted, known as "The Society," for the Advancement of Management Workshop in Leadership Skills. The staff members who conducted the workshop were members of the National Training Laboratories of Washington, D.C.

Pigors, Paul, "Of Giving Orders and Getting Results," *Personnel*, American Management Association, Inc., March–April 1960. Offers suggestions to first-line supervisors in the principles of effective order giving.

Your Own Advancement in Business

SITUATIONS YOU ARE LIKELY TO MEET

How would you meet each of these situations:
   a. *Before* you have read the chapter? What would you say to yourself or to the individual?
   b. *After* you have read the chapter? How have your answers changed?

1. A forty-year-old employee who has had fifteen years' experience but has made no significant job advancement says to you: "You're lucky to have a good education—you will advance more than I ever did. I always worked hard to please the boss. I've always done what I was asked to do, but I've never been considered for promotion. Your education will get promotions for you."
   What would you say to him?

2. The man under whose direction you work is an able man. You are learning a great deal from him. You admire him. This morning when you came to work he bawled you out for a serious mistake in judgment—at least, you felt that you had been bawled out and that you deserved it.
   What reaction would you express to him?

3. Even though you are not an old-timer as an employee, a teen-ager asks for your advice in regard to studying business as preparation for his career. He is interested in what business can mean in regard to its contribution to social advancement.
   What would you say to him?

Most young men who study business look forward to advancement. They expect to attain jobs on the department head level, or higher still, in top management. Some, of course, will become specialists rather than executives, but their jobs too will be on the department head level or possibly higher.

Any personnel man or management consultant who interviews applicants and employees learns to think of the abilities of men in terms of the individual's age when he begins to "level out" in his growth. (See chart on next page.) Many men who enter business level out fairly quickly after they leave school or college. They take various jobs that enable them to make a living, but all the jobs are on about the same difficulty and pay level. Many of the these men work as semiskilled mechanics, routine clerical workers, retail salesclerks, order-taking salesmen, bookkeepers, typists, and in similar low skill, low pay jobs. They grow very little in ability through the years. Some realize that they do not want to put forth the effort to lift themselves to a higher ability level and therefore join labor unions because the union will get them a few nickels more per hour.

Contrast these lower-level workers with the high-grade professional man who keeps on growing all his life (or until he reaches senility). The normal well-motivated physician, lawyer, engineer, or teacher, if his standards for himself are at all worthwhile, is constantly challenging himself to learn more, to increase his ability, to improve his judgment, and to handle more difficult responsibilities than he is handling in the current year. These growth men seek to know the latest technical information. They tackle problems more difficult than any they have tackled before. They associate with other growth men in their field. They think in terms of problems and methods of dealing with them—not in terms of nickels more per hour worked. Most of these men do not know exactly how much money they make nor do they care about their titles. They know that more money and titles come to them as by-products of their greater abilities. They do not, as a rule, seek money or status as an end in itself. They seek growth for themselves because true growth brings the many satisfactions of greater service that come to the person of inner maturity.

The mature men in business, particularly those on the executive levels, realize that they must function anonymously rather than in a spectacular manner. Crawford H. Greenwalt, former president of du Pont, stated that ". . . achievement in the executive field is much less spectacular than comparable success in many of the professions—the scientist, for example, who wins the Nobel Prize, the headline name who is elected governor, the skillful politician, the articulate college president. In fact, the more effective an executive, the more his own identity and personality blend into the background of his organization. Here is a queer paradox. The more able the man, the less he stands out, the greater his relative anonymity outside his immediate circle."[1]

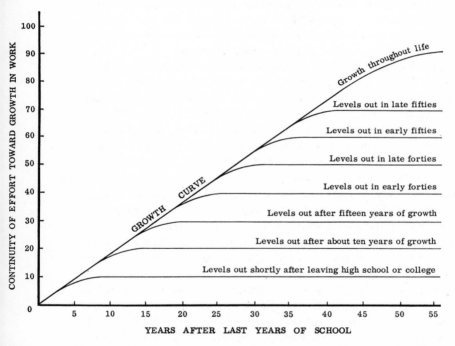

The true growth men of business and the professions continue their growth efforts throughout life. Others level out in their efforts to seek growth, many early in life. Those who drop out early hold the lower-level jobs.

Anyone who interviews an adult applicant tends to note the approximate stage in his life history when he leveled out in his developmental efforts. Also, the human relations specialist who interviews employees finds that many employees would like to continue to grow in their work, but they do not know how to go about it. They need and would like to have counsel and encouragement from their supervisors.

[1]Crawford H. Greenwalt, *The Uncommon Man* (New York: McGraw-Hill Book Company, 1959), p. 66.

Young men who note the by-product benefits of high income and social status that come to some of these growth men tend to see only the incidental signs of better income and higher status. They make the mistake of thinking of wealth and status as ends in themselves. As a result, they strain too hard, and when the wealth and status do come to many of these, they find the rewards empty and meaningless. The great religionists and philosophers of the past have known this for many centuries, but most young men have to rediscover this old truth for themselves.

The men who have not as yet learned the principle that inner growth usually precedes and gives rise to achievement are the overanxious, tense men who have caused observers to imagine that personal advancement in business invariably involves the development of ulcers. Occasionally a college man will even say to himself: "No ulcers for me—I'll settle for less and enjoy life instead." They choose a way of life even worse than one involving ulcers when they decide to vegetate rather than grow.

Most normal men must work in order to be happy. People need work almost as much as they need food; without it they're devoured by discontent. They become defensive and embittered when they cannot respect themselves because of their own lack of growth through work.

People who think they hate to work should recognize it as the thing they need in order to find contentment. The man who goes to work for years often discovers when he retires that working was one of his finest privileges. He wants to continue to work.

The housewife who groans over the chores of raising a family realizes later—after the children have left home—that those were among the happiest years of all. What a pity she didn't know it at the time!

The daily enjoyment of working is part of growing up. Unfortunately, many people never learn it, and so they never achieve the peace of mind and contentment that might be theirs.

Young men who apply for jobs are apt to say: "I'm looking for an opportunity" or "I am a financial man. I'd like to be considered for any spot you have in the treasurer's or controller's line." Or "I'm good with people. I can sell anything. If you have a sales opening or a public relations spot, I'd be a natural."

These men are misdirecting their thinking. They have not thought through the problems and responsibilities of the fields they are applying for. They are thinking of themselves more than of the contribution they can make to a future employer. They are thinking in terms of job vacancies, the kinds of jobs that are most plentiful on the lowest level of the chart on page 535.

Vacancies in business that are worthy of a growth man arise as a result of problems that have developed in the business.

Responsibility is often assumed as well as granted. The growth man is challenged by problems rather than by vacancies. Admittedly, desire for advancement can be overemphasized. Each job itself should be rewarding and satisfying, not just another step up the promotion ladder. When promotion is sought merely to satisfy ego needs, failure to attain it causes frustration. (See poem, "Ladder of Success.") It may also lead to the wrong kind of competitive spirit in which a man becomes ruthless in his desire to get ahead at the expense of his fellow workers.

Fortunately for the ambitious young man, most companies have a shortage rather than a surplus of promotable men. The annual growth pattern of American business means that we have a need for about 5 percent more able men each year. In addition, over 40 percent of all top management personnel are in the age bracket from fifty-five to sixty-five—their retirement is necessary within ten years. Death, disability, and turnover continue apace. The sum total of these demands makes the finding of an available supply of persons who are promotable to executive jobs difficult for many managements.

The effectiveness and growth of an organization depend upon the upward career orientation of its members. That is why many companies like to hire some college graduates each year. Of all college graduates hired

LADDER OF SUCCESS

When I was starting out, and
  young,
My foot was on the bottom rung,
And then, by standing on my
  toes
And straining hard, one step
  I rose.

So I was on my way. I lifted
My foot and thought myself
  quite gifted.
I bent my knee, I took a flier
And there I was, up one rung
  higher.

Sometimes the chap above me
  stepped
Upon my hands. I nearly wept,
But using muscles, mind, and
  will,
I kept on climbing, climbing still.

Now that I'm almost up the
  ladder
I should, no doubt, be feeling
  gladder.
It *is* quite fine, the view and
  such,
If just it didn't shake so much.

Source: by Richard Armour, *The Management Review* (October 1957). Courtesy American Management Association, Inc.

by business each year, approximately 35 percent will leave their jobs within three years. The major reasons for leaving are those attributed to salary and advancement considerations, but an almost equally important reason is the desire for more challenging work. College students are accustomed to meeting academic challenges in their college work, and they expect to be asked to solve equally numerous and complex problems, though of a different nature.

Some managements now realize that they have been giving their recently hired trainees from college too much breaking-in time. The trend, as described by one vice-president of industrial relations, is "Challenge the recruit, throw it at him fast and work him hard."[2]

Marks of the growth man

The growth man is easily recognized by executives and personnel men. He has a pattern of greater ability each year than the previous year. Whether in college or at work, he develops his abilities through regular reading of the journals in his field, purchase of technical books, membership in business or professional organizations, and attendance at some meetings where he can exchange ideas with men who are working in his field. He likes to associate with people who are more competent than he. When he seeks a new employer, he looks for a job in a growth company. He has a disdain for unemployment compensation and for jobs that pay income in the form of tips for service.

He is honest in his financial dealings. He seldom borrows money but when he does, he pays his debts. Nor does he help himself to an employer's property such as postage stamps or supplies. When he is an applicant for a job and is invited to visit an employer's premises at the employer's expense, he includes on his expense report only those costs that actually pertain to the trip. If he visits several employers on the same trip, he prorates the costs among them.

He can be entrusted with records of a confidential nature. As a student, he can work in a professor's office and not steal copies of exams. When he takes an examination, he need not be proctored because he depends entirely on his own knowledge to answer questions. He finds few courses dull because he is anxious to learn about every field. Even though some courses are difficult for him, he studies them in the hope that eventually he can master whatever they offer.

As an employee, he believes that plain old-fashioned hard work is still one of the most important ingredients for success in business. He has a desire to excel rather than get by. He rarely thinks about the number of

[2]See Charles W. Ufford of Warner & Swazey Company in "Making Employment Meaningful—College Students View Business and Vice Versa," *The Conference Board Record*, May 1968, p. 49.

hours he works. Instead, he thinks in terms of getting the job done. If it is necessary to work overtime or skip lunch, he does so without feeling heroic or imposed upon.

As a young employee, he takes advantage of opportunities to learn more about the company's equipment and methods. If he is a technical man who works for a manufacturing company where operating equipment must be repaired over weekends and holidays, he arranges to spend some time with the repairmen so that he can see the company's dismantled machines. He wants to know how the equipment really operates.

In his conversations, he uses reasonably good English. He would not be guilty of an error such as "He don't speak very good English!" In one survey that included a poll of forty thousand people, seven of every ten put good grammar and correct pronunciation first as characteristic of a well-educated person. Second on the list was the ability to meet people, and third was the ability to say what you mean. Only one of every twenty people polled considered the amount of money a person makes an indication of how well educated he is.[3]

One method of gaining recognition is that of the trade journal. The trade journals are interested in shop talk, and any systems or ideas that have been of value to men in their field will be of interest to their readers.

Talent scouts, usually called executive recruiting consultants, note such articles and their authors. These recruiting or professional search firms differ from employment agencies in regard to the source of their fee—the employment agencies collect their fee from the man who gets a job through their services, but a recruiter receives his fee from the employer. The employer requests the recruiter to find the kind of man who has the qualifications desired for an important position and pays a fee of five thousand dollars or more for the service. Recruiters do not as a rule seek applications from men who are unemployed or wish to change jobs. Instead, they note the outstanding men of certain fields and usually recommend those who are happy and effective in their work. This means that they notice men who write for trade and technical publications, make speeches at conventions, or offer unique management ideas. Men in the limelight are likely to end up in recruiters' files.[4]

Advancement through a company or through a "function"

Some ambitious men identify with a company. They study the company and try to move upward through the various supervisory and managerial levels. If they find it necessary or expedient to move from one

---

[3]See *Changing Times*, The Kiplinger Magazine, September 1956, p. 18.
[4]See Leonard A. Stevens, "The Great Executive Talent Hunt," *Think Magazine*, November 1961.

company to another, they still think in terms of advancing in the company where they are employed.

Certain others, fewer in number, identify with a specific field of business such as accounting, production, finance, or some other function. The functions in which they excel may be technical research, operational analysis, coordinating, evaluating, promoting, interpreting, or teaching. As functional specialists, they are not likely to be especially loyal to any company that employs them nor are they emotionally disturbed if they happen to be laid off or discharged. They are like scientists—loyal to the science rather than the company or institution that employs them.

Two types of men are active at the executive level in American industry: (1) the "company" man and (2) the "profession" man. The first is essentially job directed, security oriented. The emphasis in his thinking is not on analyzing but on achievement, action, accomplishment.

The second is function oriented. He is analytical in his approach to a problem. Many of these men become consultants to business. Some do become executives in companies, but they are likely to move to other companies where they can practice their chosen specialization in a new setting.

Of those who seek to gain advancement through a company, a special variety consists of those individuals who become known as a "second man." They always remain in staff jobs or as assistants to higher executives. They are like the nice girl who is often a bridesmaid but never a bride.

Many of these second men are very intelligent and have had excellent formal training in our graduate schools of business. Because of their extra formal training they can easily get well-paying staff jobs. However, they tend to remain on the staff or assistant level simply because they have learned how to deal with business problems on paper but they have not learned how to handle the actual responsibilities in engineering, production, sales, finance, or any other field. They are excellent statistical analysts and report writers but untested performers on the firing line. They also fail to develop strong ties of full colleagueship with other action-minded executives.

In the course of time, a few of these educated second men recognize their predicament and wish that they had passed up the plush staff job in order to earn their spurs on a line job, but they cannot afford to quit a well-paying staff job to go down the scale to a lower-paying line job. They usually remain where they are, as assistants to executives while men from the line move past them into jobs of greater actual responsibility. Fortunately for them, some of these second men are sufficiently intelligent and mature to continue to grow as professional specialists rather than general executives. Because of their strong intellectual rather than action interests, they lead a very satisfying work life as second men.

Pathways to advancement are not well defined

Young people who wish to advance in the professions can follow a definite educational program that will lead to admission to the profession.

Unfortunately for the recent graduate, the pathways to advancement in business are not as clearly marked as the grades and semesters in grammar school, high school, and college. In school, the pupil moves from one grade or year to the next higher stage. The levels or stages in business are not definite and have no timetable. Working hard on the job does not always assure promotion. This fact has been illustrated by the old example of the employee who had served loyally for many years and was disgruntled when he was not given a salary increase. He decided to needle the boss about it by reminding him: "I have had twenty years of experience here; that's worth a raise, isn't it?" "No," replied the boss, "you have had one year's experience twenty times."

Of course many employers allow employees to expect promotion as the result of mere length of service. They continue to give increases in pay without much regard to improvement in the quality of the job performed. Relatively few employers have definite salary standards nor do they communicate to the employee evidence of his progress or lack of it.

In some crafts, it is possible to take certain steps necessary for progress from one level to another. Young people enter an apprenticeship program which they must complete before they can be accepted as journeymen. The crafts are limited largely to the shop. To advance in the business fields studied in college, the ambitious young man must move out of the craft level if he wants to move up the promotional ladder.

Many factory jobs are blind-alley jobs which do not lead to anything better without training. To advance, the young man who finds himself in a craft job in a factory must take more technical training for engineering or for business. If he has extra ability in human relations, however, he may be able to move on to the upper levels of management through supervisory functions.

The benefits of an "adviser"

One of the best pieces of advice to the ambitious young employee is, "Work for an executive who likes you." This should not be confused with the "drag" idea. Drag is usually applied to the situation where family or financial connections cause an older executive to feel obligated to help a young person advance. He feels that to please someone else he should open doors and smooth the way for the young man even though he has little real liking for him or respect for his potentials. He may even resent the obligation. Many sons of men whose fathers hold important positions recognize the possible resentment and decide to retain their own self-respect by working in companies where the management has no obligatory feelings of responsibility toward them.

When a young man finds that an executive likes him, the executive rarely says: "You are the kind of young fellow whom I admire. I'll help you to advance." The astute executive does not want to do so much for his assistant that he becomes his "crutch." He does want to be a guide and stimulator, but no commitments are made or assumed. Instead, the alert young man becomes aware of the executive's tendency to give him special or difficult assignments. As part of an assignment, the older man gives advice, praise, and reprimands. The smart young man is pleased when he finds that a top management man is sufficiently interested in him to bawl him out! If no one takes the trouble to put him on the carpet for an obvious failure, that should be more discouraging than a first-rate reprimand.

The typical growth man tries to associate himself with a boss who is a good teacher. A good teacher is hard and demanding, but if the pupil admires him both benefit from the relationship, particularly the pupil. He learns to recognize his strengths and weaknesses. He soon reaches out for more responsibility. He learns to delegate some of his work to others. He improves his communications skills. He grows intellectually as well as professionally.

The young man can, however, "select" an adviser. His work is bound to have some direct and indirect relationships with able members of management. The young man can ask him a definite question he can answer, in his field, and one that applies to work rather than himself as a person. A genuine interest in work and a desire to learn always impresses an older man. Without being aware of it, the older man acquires a protégé, but the young man should never think of himself as a protégé. (As a student, you can develop this kind of relationship while you are in college—with one of the professors.)

Dangers of over-identification with management

As Diogenes stated: "A man should live with his superiors as he does with his fire; not too near, lest he burn; nor too far off, lest he freeze."

The ambitious junior executive may identify so fully with management that he forgets his team responsibilities. This is especially likely to happen if the junior knows that he has developed the goodwill and admiration of a top-level senior. The junior no longer feels obligated to maintain cordial relations with colleagues on his own level. After all, he knows the boss likes him—why should he bother about the fellows on his level? So he thinks, but this kind of thinking has its hazards as stated by one executive who was asked to write his evaluation of a promising junior executive:

Junior Executive "Y" has always identified himself with management. He thinks of himself as a member of middle management and as eventually becoming a member of higher management. In general, this is a good tendency. The tendency, however, has also caused him to acquire a handicapping characteristic—he has identified himself so decidedly with management that he has not developed the knack of gaining the spontaneous good will of the colleagues on his own level. I do not think that any one could point to any serious deficiency or defect in his business behavior but many of the men on his own and on lower levels of supervision seem to have a lukewarm attitude toward him. They sense that he is not one of them. If, for example, he is late in coming to a meeting, some of the others will assume that he feels he does not have to be on time even though they are expected to be on time.

"Y" is intelligent and adaptable. If he were to make up his mind that he should get the good will of his colleagues as well as members of management, he could do it.

Keep the boss informed

A good rule for all men is, "Do not let the boss be surprised." If he is taken by surprise about anything that happens in his department or is about to happen, he is jolted. He expects his people to keep him fully informed about any happenings that involve his responsibilities. To the executive few things embarrass him as much as reports from outsiders of important events that happen in his area, especially when the "news" is indicative of failure on the part of some member of his department.

The head of a department or division needs to know at all times what is going on in his area of responsibility, and he also wants to know what progress is being made with specific plans, projects, or programs. If he knows which plans are going well, he can concentrate on other matters that need extra attention.

In modern managements, a great all-controlling leader is seldom found. However, the top executive must be consulted, and subordinates are expected to carry out his policies. The subordinates want to perform as expected, but at times that subordinate must make a decision without knowing whether his decision would be approved by his superior. The superior may be absent or preoccupied with a critical issue. The subordinate therefore worries as to whether he should postpone action or take action and later appear to be guilty of insubordination. This means that he should confer with other members of the team who can advise him and give him support in case the superior is later displeased with the subordinate's action.

Keep your superior informed, but use discrimination. Do not waste his time with trivialities. Bear in mind, too, that whenever your boss asks for your opinion, he wants your opinion, not necessarily an agreement with his own.

Be a member of the team

One of the best comments on the part of management in regard to a subordinate is, "He is one of us. He is on the team. We can depend upon him."

The good team member demonstrates his team spirit most frequently by the way he presents new ideas. He follows the lines of organization. He knows that suggestions should be approved by lower levels of authority before the upper levels will give them much consideration.

Presenting important suggestions to management requires special skills. The originator has a tendency to overestimate rewards and to underestimate costs and difficulties. An extreme overstatement can produce a loss of confidence so great that the suggested idea is never considered. Overstatement, rather than *wrong* statement, may be disastrous.

The suggester's personal role is important. The right man should be chosen to push the idea. Sometimes a smart suggester realizes that he is not the man who can sell or execute his idea. He therefore makes a "gift" of it to the person who can develop and present it most effectively.

The employee who regards his immediate superior with a suspicion that he is throwing cold water on his efforts and trying to keep him down is wasting his time and may build up an antagonism that will destroy the boss's confidence in him. One of the major criteria in evaluating a subordinate's loyalty and cooperation is the way he presents suggestions. If it is obvious that the subordinate's first thought is to assist the superior in promoting the interests of the firm rather than his own, he thinks of the subordinate as a member of the team. Besides, the boss knows that if an idea is important, he himself must sell it to several persons higher up and lower down in the hierarchy of operational direction. The boss must be sure the idea is sound before he will want to sell it to other members of management.

Selling an idea to management

Employees on almost all job levels of a company have asked the question, "How can I sell an idea to management?—management ought to make certain changes, but I do not know how to convince them of the need." Members of middle management, too, ask the question even though they have daily working contacts with the men to whom they refer. Getting acceptance of an idea from top management is no more difficult than getting an idea across to a parent, spouse, or neighbor. In each case, we have to consider the personalities of the individuals, their psychological needs, and their work interests. This kind of person-to-person persuasion is dependent upon our social skills as discussed in Chapter 26. To gain acceptance by management of a plan of action, certain factors should be considered:

1. Instead of trying to *sell* something to management, as though the seller and management had opposing interests, assume that both have common business objectives. Both are members of the same team regardless of differences in rank. The first requirement is to overcome any tendency to think of yourself as an outsider who must battle an entrenched management. Such thinking tends to bring out latent difficulties in communication. Bear in mind that management and men are not ordinarily on two sides of a fence.

2. Present your plan with the expectation of bringing about exchange of ideas rather than an immediate acceptance of the plan. The act of persuasion has the double aspect of having two minds consider an idea. Important plans often require discussion and lengthy consideration. Without deliberation, management is likely to do too many things in the half-cocked manner.

3. Communication to be easy must be frequent rather than spaced by long intervals of silence. People must deal with each other so often that each party to a question feels that he knows how the other individual is likely to conduct himself in the future. An idea that comes from a person unknown to us is likely to be weighed more carefully than the same idea from a person whom we know and respect.

4. Present your plan in oral as well as in written form. A salesman could not hope to make many sales by means of written reports only. If he uses printed material in his interview, he depends mainly upon his oral presentation—the printed material has the secondary function of backing up the oral presentation. Visual materials should not be handed out until the oral presentation has been completed.

   An oral presentation is better if it can be developed step-by-step, without the detours that interruptions often bring. On the other hand, questions asking for clarification often help to strengthen interest. They give the opportunity for additional stress on points that may be bothering the approving authority and tend to prevent his closing his mind to later refinements on a crucial point. Accept questions as you go along. If you find that this breaks the thread of your presentation, you can always suggest that you go completely through the rest of it and then go back for questions. Many of the most likely questions will be answered by later material in your presentation.

5. Consider the climate in which the idea is offered. A management

that is aggressive and determined to be the leader in its industry is more likely to be receptive than one that is "hanging on" until the head of the firm dies or retires. The best way to learn whether the climate is warm or cold is to raise the problem that the plan will solve before presenting your solution. If management's interest in the problem can be aroused, you may be able to get their blessing in the search for a solution.

The first supervisory job

Executives are developed from men and women who have demonstrated ability as supervisors. An employee's first important chance for advancement comes the day he is placed in charge of a small group of fellow workers. The young man who proves that he can supervise twenty people may expect a chance to show what he can do with a hundred and possibly, in time, a thousand. If he can prove that he has what it takes to handle even a small group of people, he is in direct line for the bigger executive jobs. Supervisors do not automatically slide into executive jobs, but they do have extra opportunities to demonstrate their growth potentials.

The supervisor must win people's respect. If he is too genial (a common defect in new supervisors), he should tighten up. He must learn how to be firm, play fair with everybody, and keep his word. Fraternization with a select few is bound to bring about criticism of favoritism. The new supervisor must find ways to avoid this criticism even though some of his old friends may accuse him of going snobbish now that he has become a "little boss."

The transition from worker to supervisor is often one of the most difficult for the young employee. He must make certain adjustments in the way he thinks and works. He must renounce his earlier habit of doing all the work himself—he must turn it over to others and take on the specific functions of supervising. He must learn to see his role as one of getting others to perform their responsibilities rather than of doing the work for them. At the same time, he must be able to learn from the fellows who sweep the floors, operate the machines, do the clerical tasks, sell the products, and collect the bills as well as from his colleagues in management. He can learn from the machine operator with a sixth grade education and from the foreman who is a member of the old school. They all have a great deal to teach him. And he must show them that they can depend upon him.

One of the greatest needs of major executives is for subordinates upon whom they can place absolute reliance, knowing that responsibilities given to those individuals will be properly handled. Such people are identified quickly. When the executive must be away from the job, he wants to have the comfort of complete assurance that there are people on the jobs under his supervision and that they will carry on normally. This is a basic quality that managers look for in people they hope to promote.

Most companies do not have a systematic method for training their oncoming generation of executives. They do, however, have a selection plan of the "progressive hurdles" type. Under this procedure, a growth man is

---

TABLE 27–1

WHAT FACTORS INFLUENCE THE JOB SELECTIONS OF YOUNG ENGINEERS AND SCIENTISTS?

In a McGraw-Hill survey, 2,596 recently-hired engineers and scientists employed in 57 companies listed the factors they had considered before accepting a position. The replies of the younger engineers and scientists—those with less than five years' experiences—have great significance.

Potential growth of the company was listed by more young engineers and scientists than any of the 42 other items on the list as a factor that influenced greatly their decision in accepting a position: challenging opportunity was second, the company's prestige and reputation ranked third, progressive research and development program was fourth, but starting salary ranked only seventh.

Factors Influencing Decision Greatly	Per Cent Listing Factor
Potential growth of company	55
Challenging opportunity	53
Company's prestige, reputation	44
Progressive research and development program	41
Geographic location	37
Permanent position	35
Starting salary	34
Educational facilities in vicinity	33
Regular salary increases	31
Chance to work on specific project, or in certain field	27
Company's facilities (laboratories, technical libraries, etc.)	25
Tuition for graduate study	25

Based on replies by recently-hired engineers and scientists with less than five years' experience to questionnaire distributed by McGraw-Hill Classified Advertising Division.

Source: "Is Industry Creating a New Breed of 'Bonus Babies'?" Classified Advertising Department, McGraw-Hill Publishing Company, July 1957.

given a number of assignments, or "hurdles," to overcome. If he makes good on the first test, he is advanced to more difficult ones. If not, management loses interest in his potentials for advancement to the top.

Another testing procedure is to pick prospective future managers for jobs that carry "assistant to" or "acting director" titles. Important committee assignments may be used as testing grounds. In these assignments, candidates are given ample chance to show their abilities. If they fail, little harm has been done. But most managers believe that a man must be held responsible for certain accomplishments during the test period. Otherwise there is no real test of his ability.

Ambitious men who are promoted to greater responsibilities often wonder why they are not given the title that usually goes with the new responsibilities. Failure to grant the title usually means that management wants to try out the promoted man before giving him the full title. Top management does not like to be put in the position of having to back out of a bad situation.

Some want the veneer but not the discipline of growth

If a survey were made of young men and each were asked whether he considered himself a growth man, most would answer in the affirmative. The answer would not have much meaning for some men. Many young men want the appearance and illusion of growth, but they do not care to discipline themselves enough to earn it.

One of America's leading manufacturing concerns prided itself on its comprehensive approach to selecting and training college graduates for executive work. Recently, however, the company's critical review of its experience shook this pride. This company had centered its recruiting activities in eastern colleges that made a special effort to attract a large number of young men from families distinguished for their wealth and social position. It had induced many of the most likely graduates to work for the company. Yet the review showed that most of these promising young men were not so promising after five years— that many of them would not rise to the top, or even close to the top. This selection program was almost doomed to failure from the start. For, if reaching the top in business requires an overriding commitment to work, these young men were not likely to fill the requirement. They came from upper socioeconomic groups. Long weekends and vacations were embedded in the family value structure. Most of them married girls from the same groups, and these wives were more interested in having their husbands home on week-ends than in having them fight for the presidency of the firm. Thus these men were willing to work—but not as they would have had to work in order to reach the top.

A major steel company, realizing these facts, scours midwestern state universities for its engineers and future production executives. The company's rationale is simple: The farm boy is accustomed to working till the job is done; if he has to begin at 5 or even 4 A.M., he will do so; and if he has to keep going until 10 P.M. or midnight, he will not feel abused.[5]

Obviously, an intelligent athlete would not expect the social status of his family or his own easygoing efforts to train him for competence in his chosen sport. He would take for granted the need for continuous effort regardless of social relationships or congenial hours for himself or his family. Industry and business require the same kind of devotion to daily performance for the attainment of superior competence and recognition. The qualities often considered in hiring the college graduate are indicated by the guide for company interviewers, pages 550–552.

Education in relation to advancement

Anyone who associates with college students has met the senior who has decided to continue his education by going to a graduate school. Graduate work, he claims, will increase his chances for advancement. In some cases, as in research, graduate work is essential. It is helpful in many fields. For action fields, however, such as production, marketing, and retailing, a decision to do graduate study may mean that the individual is either thinking of himself as a staff specialist or simply postponing the day when he must enter the hurly-burly world of business. By continuing as a student, he can let his personality remain as it is.

Of course, he should seek to do good work in his studies regardless of his underlying motives. Superior scholastic ability in college is related to success in later occupational life, but it is not the only factor so related.

Richard Husband, Dartmouth graduate, class of 1926, made a survey of the 368 members of his own graduating class and carefully compared their records in college with their standing in the world thirty years later. In the main, his findings indicated that an outstanding college record is certainly no bar to success in later life.

He found that activities afforded another significant clue: the more activities, the higher the later income. He concluded that companies would

[5]Eli Ginzberg, "Perspectives on Work Motivation," *Personnel*, American Management Association, Inc., July 1954, pp. 44, 45.

Rating scale for recording interview with applicant

Applicant's Name _____ Date _____

College or University _____

After a careful appraisal of the applicant you have just interviewed, consider each of the points listed below. Place a check-mark (✔) on the line above the comment which in your opinion best describes this applicant. Rate each applicant immediately after the interview. Do not check those items on which you have not had the opportunity to formulate an opinion.

(1) Consider his judgment. Does he appreciate the relative value of important and unimportant material? Is he diplomatic in what he says and does?

Seems to be inaccurate in judgment. Spends time on unimportant details.	Is somewhat undependable in judgment. Often wastes time on non-essentials. Says wrong thing frequently.	Uses good judgment on simple problems, but sometimes gets confused on more complex problems.	Is level-headed. Recognizes important material.	Is accurate and prompt in judgment. Spends time on important material. Says and does right thing at right time.

(2) Consider the possibilities of his becoming a leader. Has he a past record of successful leadership? Will he inspire confidence and respect?

Has been a follower. Lacks desire and ability to lead.	Wants to be a leader, but never has been. Lacks ability to inspire confidence and respect.	Was leader in minor affairs. Probably will not develop further leadership powers.	Has been leader in minor affairs. Will develop. Has knack of inspiring cooperation.	Has demonstrated leadership ability. Inspires respect and confidence.

(3) Consider his initiative. Does he impress you as having drive and force? Is he a "self-starter"?

Apparently has little initiative. Will need detailed instructions to carry out ideas.	Will be content to let others go ahead. Has ability, but no drive.	Will keep going at a satisfactory level if some one starts him. Needs prodding.	Apparently is very resourceful in carrying out other persons' ideas.	Is a "self-starter." Will attack own and others' problems with drive and enthusiasm.

(4) Does he appear to be well-informed in his major field? Can he talk intelligently about what he has been studying and doing?

Is unable to talk about his field of specialization. Does not display knowledge of his field.	Talks glibly about field, but does not appear to know very much about it.	Somewhat hesitant in talking about his field. Appears to have only average grasp of the material.	Does not talk about field easily, but gives impression of knowing it well.	Talks easily and intelligently about his field. Appears to know it thoroughly.

(5) Consider his ability to express himself. Are his statements clear and simple? Does he use good English?

Gets tangled up frequently. Has poor command of English.	Is hesitant in expression. Frequently uses poor English.	Is somewhat hesitant in expression, but uses good English.	Has fairly easy, informal expression, but occasionally makes a grammatical error.	Expresses self easily and accurately. Uses good English.

(6) Consider his ability to conduct himself appropriately in the interview. Is he receptive? Does he make valuable contributions?

Is not receptive. Makes no valuable contributions to the interview.	Doesn't react to questions well. Must be prodded into saying anything.	Listens fairly well, but makes only a few contributions to the interview.	Is receptive, but makes only average contribution to the interview.	Listens carefully and asks intelligent questions. Makes valuable contributions.

(7) How does his appearance impress you? Consider his facial expression, physique, carriage.

Physique and carriage are not impressive. Creates poor effect.	Physique and carriage are satisfactory, but bears some marked physical disfigurements.	Has fair physique and carriage. General appearance is not outstanding.	Has good physique and carriage. General effect is fairly good.	Is well-built. Carries self well. Creates a favorable lasting impression.

Source: Richard S. Uhrbrock, *Recruiting the College Graduate: A Guide for Company Interviewers*. Courtesy American Management Association, Inc.

Below are some statements which might be made concerning the applicant you have just interviewed. Consider each statement.

Place a check-mark (√) in front of the statements which describe the man most accurately.

Check not less than five and not more than ten of the statements.

Check only such statements as you yourself would make in describing the applicant you have just interviewed.

_____Does not know how to work.
_____Talks disrespectfully of former employers.
_____Would become dissatisfied readily.
_____In the long run could not stand the competition.
_____Is easily discouraged.
_____Lacks force or drive.
_____Suggests instability of emotional control.
_____Is shy, embarrassed, ill-at-ease.
_____Has reached his upper level of development.
_____Does not seem to know what he wants.

_____Is probably not a good teamworker.
_____Would have difficulty in finding common ground with workmen.
_____Tries to impress others too much.
_____Is slow to express own ideas during interview.
_____Is too much concerned with his appearance.
_____Prefers to be a follower rather than a leader.
_____Expects too rapid advancement.
_____Is a little slow to catch on.
_____Is too much interested in initial salary.

_____Is not so mature as the average for his age.

_____Does not impress one strongly one way or the other.

_____Gives impression of being opportunist.

_____Has had too much training for this job.

_____Will be a good prospect if permitted to work in his narrow range of interest and training.

_____Is not so good as some, but is acceptable.

_____Knows what he wants to do about as well as the average.

_____Would be good on specific assignments.

_____Is outspoken in his opinions.

_____Has not formed definite goals as yet, but will as he matures.

_____Is a plugger who will work his way up slowly, but surely.

_____Obviously is in need of coaching but it would be worthwhile.

_____Is not brilliant, but is able above the average.

_____Does not appear to be afraid of work.

_____Would probably cooperate well.

_____Is a better man than the average we have hired in past years.

_____Is a careful and systematic thinker.

_____Has a good foundation for further development.

_____Possesses considerable initiative.

_____Will get along well with associates.

_____Looks like a "live-wire."

_____Is self-confident, yet conservative, in his opinion of his own abilities.

_____Has an analytical mind.

_____Has a well-rounded personality.

_____Asks pertinent, intelligent questions.

_____Sets a definite goal for himself and works toward this end.

_____Gives impression of possessing ability to handle people.

_____Is a good prospect for executive development.

_____Compares favorably with the best men we have hired.

_____Is best prospect I have seen in some time.

_____Is outstanding in all respects.

Would you recommend this man for employment?   (Check one)

With no reservations.   ☐   With reservations as   Applicant rejected be-
Under no consideration.   ☐   listed below.   ☐   cause of obviously
                                                            poor health.   ☐

I would recommend him if ....
....
....

The applicant's most outstanding characteristics are: ....
....
....
....

The applicant's weakest points are: ....
....
....

....
                                       Signature of Interviewer.

be well advised to look for "the man in the top quarter of almost anything: . . . Actually, *it does not seem to make much difference in what field, or fields, he made his mark*. Together or singly, in sum, grades and extracurricular activity furnish an excellent predictor of later success."[6]

[6]Dr. Richard W. Husband, "What Do College Grades Predict?" *Fortune*, June 1957, p. 158.

Many able men of business did not go to college. Some learned more outside, on their own, than they would have if they had gotten a diploma. The diploma *per se* is not important. The test of a man is what he can do and what he is worth to his society. Where he acquired his training and his ability is incidental. Perhaps the best evidence of potential ability is proven past ability and the urge to improve oneself, to grow.

And finally

A man's search for growth may be directed toward material possessions and social status or toward growth as a person. If you seek inner maturity for yourself, you will be inspired by your work relations with people. You will discover that the basic patterns in human behavior as exhibited in business are remarkably stable through the ages in the history of man. And when you study business, you will also want to study the classics. You will want to learn about history, literature, and art as well as about business in order that you may integrate the past with the present and the future. Of course you will never learn all that you would like to know nor attain the full maturity that you desire, but you will enrich your living through the delightful never-ending quest.

QUESTIONS ON THE CHAPTER

1. Discuss the "leveling out" of men in regard to their occupational growth.
2. Explain Greenewalt's paradox about the anonymity of the effective executive.
3. Describe the personal benefits that come to the man who enjoys his work.
4. Describe the marks of the growth man.
5. Differentiate between the "company" man and the "profession" man in business.
6. What are some of the effects of favoritism on advancement?
7. Compare the effects of definite steps for advancement in education with the poorly defined pathways for advancement in business.
8. What method does a good team member use to demonstrate his team spirit?
9. How may an ambitious person gain the benefits of an adviser?
10. When a worker advances to the position of supervisor, how is his role changed?
11. How should an employee "sell" an idea to management?
12. Explain the "progressive hurdles" type of selection plan.
13. According to the McGraw-Hill survey, what were the two most important factors that young engineers considered before accepting a position? What ranked seventh?

14. Discuss education in relation to advancement.

15. Of all the ideas presented in the chapter, which ones are of special interest to you?

16. What did the chapter contribute to your future relations with (a) the men who supervise your work, (b) the employees whom you may supervise?

PROBLEMS AND PROJECTS

For All Students

1. If, as a student, you can still elect certain courses before graduating, discuss the possibilities with others. Give reasons for any decisions.

2. Have you established friendly relations with any members of the faculty or with business executives? A growth man does. If you have not as yet done this, describe how you plan to do so in a sincere manner.

For Advanced Students

3. Before you finally leave school, you should prepare a résumé of your job qualifications. List the main characteristics an employer would want to know. Discuss your first draft with others and prepare a final copy for future use.

4. Plan a direct mail campaign for getting a job. Write a letter of application to be sent with your résumé. Ask others to review and suggest improvements in your job-getting program.

For Men in Business

5. Look over the suggestions for advancement presented in this chapter. Which ones have you already fulfilled? Describe any specific plans you have for gaining advancement where you are now working. Discuss them with several friendly colleagues.

6. When Robert H. Finch, former secretary of Health, Education and Welfare, addressed the National Industrial Conference Board, 4th Annual Conference, New York, on "Management and Man in the Computer Age," he asked a basic question that you may try to answer:

> "If there were one question which, in the spirit of this conference, I could address to you for your advice today, it would be this:
>
> *How can we, in quantity and in depth, educate to produce the whole man—the individual skilled in techniques, yet sensitive to the lasting human values that measure the real worth of our civilization?"*

COLLATERAL READINGS

For All Students

Ford, Robert N., and Edgar F. Borgatta, "Use of the Work Components Study with New College-Level Employees," *Journal of Applied Psychology*, October 1969. Reports a study that suggests that it is not the "organization man" who is likely to be promoted but the man perceived to be highly competitive, intelligent, and responsible.

Thorndike, Robert L., and Elizabeth Hagen, *Ten Thousand Careers*. New York: John Wiley & Sons, Inc., 1959. A report on the findings of a study of seventeen thousand men who were given a battery of aptitude tests in 1943 and from whom educational and vocational histories were subsequently obtained.

For Advanced Students

Taylor, Erwin K., "The Unsolved Riddle of Executive Success," *Personnel*, American Management Association, Inc., March–April 1960. We still have a great deal to learn before we can pinpoint what makes a man a success in his particular field.

Uris, Auren, *The Executive Breakthrough*. Garden City, N.Y.: Doubleday & Company, Inc., 1967. Presents the stories of seventeen men and four women who made it to the upper regions of business success.

For Men in Business

"Educational Assistance Programs," *Journal of the American Society of Training Directors*. A large number of companies have set up plans whereby their employees may undertake further educational course work with some form of employer reimbursement. Look for latest article on the topic.

Guide to Intensive Courses and Seminars for Executives (Annual). American Management Association, 135 West 50th St., New York, N.Y., 10020, 59 pp., 75¢. Courses and seminars for executive and management development conducted regularly by educational institutions, associations, and consultants. Also list of universities sponsoring evening classes or periodic conferences.

1. False. It is preferable that the man stand or sit so that he can speak to both women without turning away from one.
2. True. But he may offer help, even in daylight, if the woman is aged or the way very rough.
3. True. A stole is adornment, but a coat is wearing apparel, and he can't appear to be supporting her—yet.
4. False. Nowadays trousseau linen is marked with the initials of the bride's given name, her maiden name and her husband's last name.
5. False. The processional would look as if there were several brides and bridegrooms.
6. False. A wedding during mourning should be smaller and quieter, but it may be in the church.
7. True. And just handing over a list of names and a form invitation to Western Union is convenient.
8. False. Typewritten personal letters are polite, but messages of congratulation or condolence must still be handwritten.
9. True. But she may put "Mrs." in parentheses or add her full married name in parentheses below the signature.
10. False. After the age of 12, boys are given no titles. When they finish high school, they get the "Mr."
11. True. Butter plates are for informal service only.
12. True. Fancy folds are in bad taste. And napkins at a formal dinner are never put beside the plate, as at a luncheon.
13. False. This custom is held in horror. The ranking feminine guest should always be served first—never the hostess, unless she is the only woman.
14. False. A guest should not ask for anything except possibly water—especially any item that has not already been offered.
15. False. Don't make like a headwaiter. Lay your dinner napkin, folded double, on your lap.
16. False. The practice is wasteful. If you eat properly, you won't have to prove you are not a glutton.
17. True. Bread is the preferred pusher, but a knife may be used if handled properly.
18. False. You may sop up gravy with a bit of bread if you use a fork to transport it to your mouth.
19. False. The old rule grew out of an effort to protect silver from salad dressing vinegar, but this solicitude for silver has gone out of style.
20. True. On the other hand, men must apologize if they keep on their gloves when shaking hands.
21. False. One or two kinds of drinks are sufficient. Avoid the bartender's professional-sounding "What'll you have?"
22. False. Gifts in silver are traditional, but nonsilver things may be just as appropriate.

Want to argue about any of these pronouncements? *Changing Times* bows before the authorities Emily Post and Amy Vanderbilt and the editors of other etiquette books, such as *Vogue* and *Esquire*.

SOURCE: *Changing Times,* The Kiplinger Magazine, January 1958.

Name Index

Subject Index